Handbook of Ethics of Islamic Economics and Finance

De Gruyter Studies in Islamic Economics, Finance and Business

Edited by
Abbas Mirakhor and Idris Samawi Hamid

Volume 5

Handbook of Ethics of Islamic Economics and Finance

Edited by
Abbas Mirakhor, Zamir Iqbal, Seyed Kazem Sadr

DE GRUYTER

ISBN 978-3-11-059042-5
e-ISBN (PDF) 978-3-11-059341-9
e-ISBN (EPUB) 978-3-11-059054-8
ISSN 2567-2533

Library of Congress Control Number: 2019956377

Bibliographic information published by the Deutsche Nationalbibliothek
The Deutsche Nationalbibliothek lists this publication in the Deutsche Nationalbibliografie; detailed bibliographic data are available on the Internet at http://dnb.dnb.de.

Cover image: nnnnae / iStock / Getty Images Plus
Typesetting: Integra Software Services Pvt. Ltd.
Printing and binding: CPI books GmbH, Leck

www.degruyter.com

Preface

In the Name of God – The All Merciful, The All-Compassionate

Islam created a major world civilization that spread from China to Europe and in which there was ample activity that today would be called economic activity. In Islamic languages the Latin word *oeconomicus* (itself derived from Greek) was identified, as it was in the in the Greek and Latin worlds, with running of the household and managing one's private affairs and called hence *tadbīr al-manzil* in Arabic. The contemporary word *iqtiṣād*, when used in classical Islamic languages, did not convey the modern meaning given to it as one sees in the famous book of al-Ghazzālī, *al-Iqtiṣād fī'l-iytiqād* which deals with theology and principles of faith. But many aspects of Islamic thought, practice and law have always dealt with what is now called economics. The Qur'ān and *Hadīth* are themselves full of injunctions that would now be said to be concerned with economic matters. In the Islamic context, laws governing economic activity were always in the context of the *Sharī'ah* and wed to Islamic ethics. It is not accidental that throughout most of Islamic history the bazaar has been also the arena in Islamic society where religious piety has been most strongly present and this fact remains true to this day in most Islamic urban environments. Devout Muslims have never forgotten that the Prophet himself was a merchant when God chose him as His messenger.

With the penetration of modernism into the Islamic world in modern times, gradually the attention of some Muslim scholars was turned to the task of creating "Islamic economics." Such men had good intentions but were for the most part unaware that Western economics developed in a secularized ambiance in which the mechanized world view of 17th and 18th century physics was dominant and in which spiritual and religious elements were considered to be merely subjective realities bereft of any objective reality. Without critically appraising the philosophical foundation of modern economics, early Muslim scholars, trying to develop an Islamic economic theory, concentrated their attention mostly on the question of *ribā'* and related issues. Some did write against the shortcomings and errors of both capitalism and Marxism but hardly anyone provided a cogent criticism of the very world view upon which modern economics, both capitalist and socialist, is based.

Fortunately a number of scholars of Islamic economics have appeared during the last few years who are fully aware of the truth that Islam is based on a world view

https://doi.org/10.1515/9783110593419-202

very different from that of modern economics, a world view in which economics is never divorced from ethics and Islamic Law, nor is it Islamic if it does not consider the reality of spiritual and non-material aspects of both nature and human beings. Such scholars have brought to light again the primary and not secondary importance of nature as nourisher of the human soul as well as body and the principle significance of charity, *karāmah*, *īthār* and yes truthfulness even if they be materially unprofitable for those Muslims who want to follow their religion fully.

The Muslim scholars whose works appear in this volume belong to this category. They hail from different areas of the Islamic world as well as of the West. Some have been educated in modern universities and others in traditional *madrasahs*. Some are young scholars and others of an older generation. Yet, they all share the concern for the centrality of ethics in Islamic economics and think about the issues of relevance in this subject from within the Islamic world view. This trait renders the present volume especially valuable for those seeking real Islamic responses to present day economic challenges.

Dr. Abbas Mirakhor, Prof. Seyed Kazem Sadr, and Dr. Zamir Iqbal, who have done so much already for the propagation of serious Islamic economics, on both the practical and theoretical level, are to be congratulated for producing this volume. I hope that this book will have wide dissemination especially in the Islamic world itself and that those who are in a position to implement Islamic economic teachings in an authentic manner will benefit from it.

wa'Llāhu a'lam
Seyyed Hossein Nasr
Washington, D.C.

Rabīʿ al-Awwal, 1444 AH
October, 2019 AD

Introduction

Since the financial crisis of 2007/2008, discussion on the ethics and finance has attracted attention in academic research as well as in public policy debates. This topic is being examined from different dimensions – finance for good society, responsible finance, ethical finance, and financial repression. The principal objective of this Handbook on Ethics of Islamic Economics and Finance is to provide a deeper understanding of the ethical underpinning of Islamic economics and finance.

The undertaking of this project was inspired by two factors. First, given the renewed interest in the study of ethics in economics and finance since the 2007/2008 financial crisis and rapid growth of Islamic finance, a need was felt to understand and develop the knowledge about the embedded ethics in the teaching of Islam and particularly the implication on Islamic economics and finance. Second, although extensive research has taken place in Islamic economics and finance in the last four decades, most of the mainstream research has not benefitted from the research on the topic in the languages of Islamic societies such as Arabic, Bahasa, Farsi, and Urdu. This project provided an opportunity to attract scholars from different parts of the World with diverse backgrounds and perspectives. Therefore, the reader will notice that the Handbook reflects a diversity of views on the subject of economic and business ethics in Islam across the intellectual spectrum of Muslim thought.

Before describing different parts of this Handbook and the contributions of the collaborators it might be instructive to pose some questions concerning the definition and characteristics of the ethical system in Islam. What is its goal and how do its rules and practices ensure welfare for individuals and society? Are the moral principles universal and invariable or do they change and adapt with the social changes of communities and progress in science and technology? Is the present generation accountable for the welfare of future generations? Where is the boundary between law and ethics and who guarantees their adoption and implementation?

Before these questions are entertained, it might be helpful to review briefly the evolution of thinking of Muslim scholars on ethics. Discussion on business ethics in Islam is not new but has been dealt extensively since the early history of Islam. Significant discussion and analysis of the positions of the Qur'an and the Sunnah on morality and ethics were provided by 4th Caliph Imam Ali in a compiled book, titled *Nahjul Balaghah*, and by his grandson, Imam Zayn al-'Abedin in his book, *Risalah al-Huquq* (Treatise on Rights) covering moral and ethical behavior towards others according to the Qur'an and Sunnah.[1] Another important early work on morality and ethics in

1 One of the sources of Imam Ali teachings on ethics that is extant and is an authentic reference for ethical studies is the letter that he wrote, as his last will and testament, to his elder son Imam Hasan. This letter and others that Ali wrote to his followers are reported by Kolaini in his Ar-Rasael book. The first written book on the subject in the second Hijri century belongs to Ismail ibn Mahran Sokuni who was one of the companions of Imam Ali ibn ar-Redha(as) who titled his book Attributes of Believers

https://doi.org/10.1515/9783110593419-203

Islam is by Abu Ali ibn Mohammad ibn Ya'qub Miskawayh (born 320 AH, died 421). His work is considered to have influenced the thinking of leading thinkers such as Al-Ghazali and Nasiruddin Tusi on this topic. Subsequently, the discussion mainly took place while developing principles underlying legal axioms. For example, scholars such as Al-Ghazālī (2005) dealt with ethics of earning and living as he dedicated one full chapter in his classical work Iḥyā' 'Ulūm al-Dīn (Revival of Islamic Sciences).

Definition and Essence of Ethics

Core of ethics is doing good and avoiding evil. Empowering the human will to behave well and refrain from doing harm to others is the foundation of ethics. For instance, helping a blind person to find his way is positive form of ethical behavior while restricting a child from an activity in the playground for his/her safety is negative form of ethical deeds. Taking up any initiative to enhance the wellbeing of the community and mitigating hardship born by its members is another example of an ethical act. Even taking care of one's health by exercising and abandoning consumption of narcotics is practicing ethics. Overall contributing to the creation of good and elimination of evil is the essence of ethics.

Some critics argue that the concepts and practice of good and evil are relative and depend on social and economic conditions of human communities as well as their belief systems. In a developed economy with full employment conditions, government intervention to boost aggregate demand would instead create inflation. However, in a developing economy suffering from high unemployment, government intervention to boost aggregate demand is an advisable policy provided the public debt is on sustainable path (i.e. fiscal space or primary fiscal balance is positive). The effectiveness of the same policy is dependent on the conditions of the economy. Financial assistance to the unemployed in a developed economy may not enhance work incentives while it could be effective in doing so in a developing economy. Therefore, the changes in the stages of economic growth and social and political regimes will dictate what is good or bad for the economy. Ethical ideals and measures, according to this view, are not absolute and fixed; they vary according to time and place.

The Greek philosophers maintained that human intellect is the basis of ethics. People judge goodness and badness of principles and practices by their own wisdom which is a common attribute of all human beings. Critics claimed that peoples' intellect is not invariable and so are their views and understanding. Disputes among groups, parties and nations are cited as examples. The philosopher and Islamic scholar Motahhari (1365/1986) disagrees that intellect is the basis of ethics. To him, ethics

---

and Depraved (Sadr, Hasan, 1375/1996,P.404,). According to S. R. Sadr, the best compilation prior to the fifth century is by the renowned scholar Ibn Miskawyeh (2014) called Purification of Ethic which is also called Virtues of Morality (Tahzibol Akhlaq). The great Naseeruddin Tusi has benefitted from this work in his invaluable book *Naseri* Ethics (Tusi,1397/2018).

is the power of controlling and ordering instincts. Medicine regulates different body organs, which is not an intellectual process. Neither is organizing human instincts a rational process. The basis of ethics is safety of spirit. Ethics means that people can control their habits by their will and raises the question whether there are general and absolute ethical principles or "musts" that all human beings cognate and accept? If there are such principles, how could their existence be rationalized and explained?

The discussion of ontology and epistemology of ethical norms is not complete unless the above questions are addressed. Philosophers classify knowledge into pure reason and practical reason. The former investigates ontology and causal relationship among the phenomena that exist independent of human beings while the latter deals with those phenomena that are made by men. The "ought", "must" or "necessity" concepts, which belong to phenomena that are made or created by human decisions, are facts and not abstract concepts. They are derived through logical judgments. When they are included in describing phenomena that are volitional, they are called "ought or necessity" copula. When they are applied in non-volitional descriptions they are "is" predicate. Clearly, all ethical statements fall in the "ought" category.[2]

To illustrate the logical derivation of ethical concepts from the external real facts, Hairi (1982) explains the process by presenting two logical deductions. The first deduction is a general apprehension related to pure reason as stated below:

Minor premise: Poverty-reducing policies are viable economic policies.
Major premise: All viable economic policies deserve adoption.
Consequence: Poverty-reducing policies deserve adoption.

In this deduction, the two premises and the conclusion are general and belong to pure reason, not the practical reason as far as the form and conditions of syllogism is concerned. To arrive at a specific deduction stemmed from this general deduction, we constitute the following deduction:

Minor premise: Investment promotion policies reduce poverty.
Major premise: All poverty-reducing policies deserve adoption.
Consequence: Investment policies deserve adoption.

The conclusion of this latter deduction, which is derived from the previous one, implies that governments should boost investment activities. As this conclusion stems from a general pure theoretical premise, it belongs to pure reason and is an intellectual inference. However, this special deduction has a practical consequence that falls under practical reason. Thus practical reason outcomes and events are logically derived from pure reason.

The concluded facts of the pure reason deductions and the concluded decisions of practical reason are both actual beings. The only difference between the conclusions

2 Hairi (1982)

of the deductions of practical reason and those of pure reason is that the actual being or occurrence of the conclusion of the practical reason is conditioned by the will of intelligent agents who entertain them. Ethical ought or must refer to the power and decision of persons. That means when people wish and decide to do something they make their decision happen, or in other words, bestow necessity of being to their decisions. As soon as the agents' will is determined, the agent makes that decision, and the decided event becomes a necessary being. Thus "ought" deeds are volitionally necessary beings whereas logical "is" facts are non-volitional necessary beings. The former phenomena belong to normative ethics, the latter to meta-ethics or pure reason.

To further clarify that ethical principles are logically derived and match with the real beings out of our mind, distinctions between the essence of these principles and that of means of achieving them should be discerned. The renowned philosopher and astute Qur'anic interpreter Mohammad Hosain Tabatabaei (1370/1991) states that the means and methods of achieving beauty or good varies by circumstances and that is the reason why people have differences in opinion. At varying circumstances alternative ways and measures could be used for reaching a target. It is natural that groups and divisions or majorities and minorities in communities evaluate diversely the usefulness and effectiveness of those measures. People's judgements are expected to vary with regard to means, tools and methods of achieving goodness and avoiding evil, but the essence and basis of ethics remains intact and invariable. For instance, economic stability is an optimal state of economy though the policies to attain it may be judged differently by economists.

Motahhari (1986) explains the invariable origin of ethics and what makes it universal and absolute. The essence and foundation of ethics is the human conscious. It is the vigor of conscious in humans that always coincides with truth and reality. People everywhere, due to their conscious, condemn injustice no matter who commits it. It is the power of conscious that rules everybody's right should be fulfilled and justice maintained. If beauty and ugliness were relative and variable, man's conscious must be unstable and judge these attributes differently depending on time and place.

Motahhari (1981) further elaborates the essence of conscious. He opines that human beings are gifted with an intrinsic source of magnificence that is the presence of Divine in them; they inattentively feel a state of dignity. While deliberating their wishes and deeds, humans recognize which specific action or attribute is in conformity with their dignity and conscious and which is not. They embrace the former as virtue and reject the latter as vice. Human beings are all endowed with this magnificent soul that gives all of them a common ethical taste. Humans are dissimilar with respect to their physical needs and material wants, but because their Divine souls are the same, their ethical attributes and preferences are similar, permanent and universal.

The Holy Qur'an (91:7–10) declares that Allah has imprinted in man what is good and evil. That is, people are cognizant of good and evil deeds and need not learn them from a teacher. In effect human conscious is inspired by the principles of ethics. In another verse of Qur'an (73:21) Allah states that "...We revealed to people good deeds and prayer". The Almighty did not command doing good things, rather revealed to man what is good (Motahhari1365/1986).

One of Prophet's companions asked the Prophet to explain Verse (5:2) which calls people to seek beneficence and avoid sin. Before responding to the question, Prophet asked him if he wants to learn about sin. His answer was positive. The Messenger affirmed that the evil is what your heart does not approve to do. He further commented that the Almighty has bestowed to man a heart which is joined with good and is alien to bad deeds (Motahhari, 1365/1986).

Tabatabaei (1370/1991, p. 317) remarks that men naturally and inherently admit and follow everything that is right and real. For example, fire makes heat. This effect which is associated with fire most of the time is a real phenomenon not imaginary; so people believe it as it is. Truth and righteousness is similarly a reality not a sheer idea in the mind. Tabatabaei explains that righteousness is an external reality that humans believe and practice. Naturally, people follow what they consider to be a real being. On the other hand, human perceptions and ideas are not necessarily true unless they correspond perfectly with outside reality. Consequently, the views of the majority in contrast to that of minorities, in democratic societies, are not always right, that is the majority rule is not objectively right and best for society. What is in fact right and true is that which has been inspired by Almighty in the heart and conscious of citizens.

Moreover in democratic societies, Tabatabaei (1370/1991, p. 329) adds, the rules are concerned mostly with secular affairs. They are adopted to prevent harm and interference among citizens. The goal is to gain happiness by maximizing consumption. On the other hand, Islamic rules and ethics are not confined to secular life. It is based on *Tawhid*, the Oneness of creator and the unity of the whole universe. The laws, morals and guidance that are revealed by the Qur'an and taught and implemented by the Messenger are based on the same worldview. Islam has warranted the implementation of laws and the practice of ethics not only by the state but also by believers themselves as it commands: "Enjoin good and prevent vice" (104:3). Evidently, compliance with rules depends on motivation and will of citizens; the consolidation of which depends on appropriate temperament and disposition regulated by the belief in *Tawhid*.

Islam perceives the life span of human beings as much longer than just the worldly life. The eternal life is the real immortal living. In this worldly life what is beneficial for mankind, in Islamic view, is acquiring divine wisdom which is reflected in *Tawhid*. This knowledge is attained and preserved only by moral munificence and purification of the soul from any evil habits. According to Islamic teachings, ethics will not become complete and perfect except when accompanied by a decent social life which will be based on the Almighty's obedience and just behavior toward other fellow beings. As said, Islam has prescribed laws of behavior on the basis of *Towhid* and has augmented the laws with rituals and morals to direct and moderate human behavior. It then has delegated the responsibility of implementation of the rules not only to the state but also to the members of society by commanding them to enjoin the good and discourage evil. In short, safeguarding and execution of rules is dependent on the will of nations. The guarding force of the will is ethics (Tabatabaie, 1991, p. 332). The latter is preserved by the belief in *Tawhid*. Belief in the accountability in the Hereafter will prevent people from being capricious.

Before leaving this part of the introduction, it should be emphasized that in Islam both individuals and society have authentic entities with rights and responsibilities; that each is bestowed rights to maintain and enhance the prosperity of their own generation and future ones. The fact that every generation is made accountable for the well-being and preservation of future generations is due to the specific and prominent rights that are prescribed for society in the Islamic property rights system and which must be safe guarded. Justice will be maintained when the rights of individuals, society and future generations are fulfilled. The goal of every Islamic community is submission to the will of and esteem to Almighty (Tabatabaei, 1370/1991, p. 329). This goal, if reached, will function as an internal monitor to guarantee the operation of Islamic rules and conduct of morals. Consequently, people will seek moderation in their social and economic life; they fulfill their physical needs and desires to the extent that it will not impede the rights of others or their own and those of others in worshiping Allah and complying with the rules prescribed by the Almighty. In contrast, Tabatabaei argues that the goal of modern societies is the best utilization of material resources. This life style will foster a sense-based living conforming to people's wishes and wants which may or not be congruent with what is right instinctually. Subsequently, many norms and codes of behavior that the religion has praised or condemned may not be adopted by citizens due to their "secular legal freedom" for disobedience. Many virtues and divine teachings may thus be abandoned. He cites one Qur'anic verse (34:9) which states Allah has missioned his Messenger with guidance and the right religion. He bestowed righteousness to people but most of them do not like it (78:43). Finally, the Qur'an insists that it is the duty of individuals to invite each other to righteousness (3:103).

Review of contributed papers

The papers that are compiled in this Handbook can be broadly classified into principles and applications of Islamic business ethics. Although all contributors have discussed morality and ethics from the view point of the Qur'an, the Messenger's teachings, and companions, still their focus, approach and emphasis are different. The first set of chapters provides a broader view of ethical dimensions at a system level dealing with the issues of Islamic economics and finance, spiritual roots, historical context, and environment crisis. The second set of chapters provide the building blocks of ethical framework and emphasizes the essence of ethics and foundation of morals in Islam. The third group discusses select issues from macro and micro economics focusing on markets, production, trust and specific business practices. Overall the volume presents the essence of the principles and practices of Islamic ethics and its specific features which distinguish its system of ethics from other systems.

In Chapter 1, "Ethics of Risk-Sharing Economics and Finance," Iqbal and Mirakhor, argue that the present form of capitalism and the overall society in which it is embedded need to regain a "moral sense." The question is asked how can finance become sacralized? Sacralized finance requires a paradigm that focuses on: concerns for others rather than on pure self-interest; morality and ethics; giving instead of taking; cooperation rather than competition; being instead of having; and sharing the risks and uncertainties of life rather transferring or shifting them to others. Based on Islam's strong foundation to promote social and economic justice, the chapter argues that risk-sharing system as advocated by Islam would lead to better human welfare when compared to conventional risk-transfer and risk-shifting financial system. This is due to several important characteristics, such as ensuring economic and social justice in economic and financial transactions, financial stability, mutuality, commitment, and common good objectives. Risk sharing reduces or eliminates pro-cyclicality of finance. Also important is the fact that in the absence of a rentier class, risk-sharing finance improves income and wealth distribution through asset-based redistribution thus reducing inequality.

In Chapter 2, "Ethics in the Light of Maqasid Al-Shari'ah: A Case Study of Islamic Economics and Finance," Laldin provides a concise view of *Shari'ah* (Islamic Law) as a comprehensive concept that encompasses a set of welfare objectives which is manifested in ethical and moral values. It is a complete code of life that involves *al-ahkam al-i'tiqadiyyah* (belief), *ahkam al-'amaliyyah* (sanctions relating to conducts and worship), and *al-ahkam al-akhlaqiyyah* (moral and ethics). In fact, ethics (*akhlaq*) is considered the third building block in Islam after faith (*aqidah*) and law (*Shari'ah*). The key ethical principles underlying Islamic finance system such as promoting socio-economic justice, advocating fair and transparent financial practices, making one's work perfect, honesty and trust are built and inferred from Shari'ah sources that provide detailed commands of dos and don'ts on both legal and ethical level. Apart from the ethical principles which guide inner conducts, *Shari'ah* puts in place fundamental *Shari'ah* principles and mechanisms to effectively accomplish objectives of *Shari'ah* (*maqasid* al-Shari'ah). These involve firstly adherence to justice and promotion of ethical values in business and finance; secondly, safeguard of public interest in business and finance; thirdly, removal of hardship and prevention of unethical behaviours in business and finance. Compliance with these ensure preservation of three bottom line of sustainable development which are people, profit and planet that are in conformity with main five values Shari'ah urges to preserve.

In Chapter 3, "The Status of Economic Operations and Business Ethics in the Historical Mindset of Muslim Scholars," Yusefi maintains that Islam has formulated canonical requirements and ethical recommendations for its followers that, if observed, can lead to reducing trading expenditures, strengthening social capitals, and boosting business efficiency. However, a group of Muslim extremists believe working activities are in contrast with asceticism and reliance on the Almighty. This has made some orientalists who have the same perspective towards Islam as above to rebuke this religion. While the principal and dominant current in Islamic thinking has always expressed its opposition to the above mentioned issue during the past centuries, it has been able to brush aside the group. In the first section of the paper, the author expresses the importance of working in the Qur'anic doctrines, in the eyes of the Prophet Muhammad, and the great Islamic leaders, while in the second section the Sufi mentalities are dealt with as a diversion from the above mentioned path. The third section skims through the mentalities of some Muslim scholars as opposed to the Sufi extremists' ideas, and the fourth one explains the ethical and essential frameworks from religion standpoint towards business ethics and the status of working. And in the fifth section, the general framework of an economic operation is elaborated. Finally, the author concludes that the Qur'an, discourses and practical lifestyle of the Prophet and religious leaders have a large impact on the significance of working and effort.

In Chapter 4, "The Central Role of Spirituality & Ethics in Islamic Economics and Finance," Raquib, Qadir, and Channa present the Islamic worldview which establishes once and for all the fundamental truths about the nature of God; His Revelation; His creation, especially the human beings and the psychology of the human soul; knowledge; freedom; values and virtues; happiness. This constitutes the Islamic metaphysics or cosmology. In this context, they analyze the fundamental outlook of the late modern market-based society assuming that the economy of any society is a reflection of the moral-spiritual outlook of the society in question. The knowledge of the nature of God as understood through God's attributes, determines for Muslims, their systems of meaning, knowledge standards, value frameworks and ethical standards. The Islamic position on these fundamental concepts shape the Muslim ideas about change, development and progress. The terms freedom, happiness, consumption, development and progress, on the other hand, have altogether different connotations in the postmodern consumer culture, largely as a result of the ideas supplied by the conventional economic thought. These core values (understood widely in a modern or postmodern sense) challenge the basic elements of the Islamic worldview which has its own characteristic way of defining these ideas and value terms. The analysis and proposed solutions of contemporary problems encountering the Muslims – due to the global hegemony of the Western secular philosophy, mindset, culture and institutions – will be a plain mimicry of the secular models. Such faulty premises tend to lead Muslim academics, scholars and researchers in the areas of Islamic Economics, Banking and Finance to develop guidelines and models for their respective disciplines and industries that try to conform to the form and letter of the Shariah but since the spirit or the Islamic worldview is not understood and actualized, they not only fail to bring about the desired results or social changes but also serve to intensify the spiritual-ethical, socio-political and environmental degeneration.

In Chapter 5, "The Role of Spirituality and Morality in the Islamic Model of Economic Education and Training," Tavakoli raises the concern of segregating spiritual and moral teaching in teaching the discipline of economics. He claims that most types of economic education promote a "neoclassical model" of rational economic behavior, that leads to self-interest maximization. The promotion of a hedonistic logic of rational decision-making, however, might crowd out spirituality and morality such as important teachings of religions. Author asserts that the Islamic model of economic education and training is intended to improve spiritual/moral rationality in economic agents by the aid of some Islamic economic rules and policies. The Institution of *Zakah*, for instance, is intended to purify those who give this Islamic tax, whereas traditional taxes are obligatory and target no spiritual and moral goal. Attention to the Halal and tayyib (pure) income in the Islamic model of economic education and training is also a strategy for improving the logic of spiritual rationality in young people.

In Chapter 6, "Sustainable Human Development Ethics: A Quranic Perspective," Tag-el-Din presents the fundamental foundation of Islamic development ethics as it seems perceivable from the Noble Quran. It departs from a basic background on the new horizon of sustainable development with a view to derive relevant development ethics through reference to the Quran. More specifically, the generic concept of Religion, which arguably coincides with the doctrine of *Tawhid* (i.e. monotheism, or Oneness of God), is the primary source of inspiration in this chapter. Thus, in line with development economics where recommendable solutions and prescriptive polices come later after demonstrating the problematic characteristics of underdevelopment, the chapter prescribes *Tawhid*-oriented socioeconomic ethics after demonstrating the problematic counter socioeconomic ethics of its antonym (i.e. polytheism or *Shirk*). Tawhid-oriented development ethics, so derived, have proved particularly useful as the necessary socioeconomic 'vision' within the strategic framework that help instrumentalize Shariah objectives or *Maqasid Al Shariah*.

In Chapter 7, "Relationship Between Ethics and Economic Development from the Viewpoint of the Quran and Hadith," Hosseini attempts to provide answers for desirability of economic development from the viewpoint of Quran and Hadith. The results of his investigation reveal that from the point of view of the Qur'an, there are two types of development: One type refers to economic advancement based on moral and ethical teachings and which is considered praiseworthy and desirable. This type of development creates prosperity and welfare due to its inherent characteristics. Second type refers to development based on materialistic axioms and is considered by the Qur'an as undesirable. The first type of development to emerge and establish itself requires its own values and ethics defined by the totality of the system of Islam. If there is full coordination between the foundations of ethics and economic development, then divine ethics becomes the basis of economic growth and development. The second type of growth which the author calls *Takathuri* model is based on the doctrine of natural ethics and the belief that basic animal instincts govern and motivate human behavior. It results in the rule of "maximizing profit in production and utility in consumption." The *Kauthari* model, the first type on the other hand, is derived from divine ethics and values which govern human behavior and are discovered through the process of contemplation on the sacred narration and rational intellection and reasoning. The result is the emergence of the behavioral rule: "Maximum effort in production and moderation in consumption."

In Chapter 8, "The Environmental Crisis in the Islamic World – Pertinence of the Teachings of Traditional Islam," Nasr offers a provocative view claiming that to destroy environment is to veil Divine Presence. In the Noble Quran it is asserted that God encompasses all beings (*huwa 'alā kulli shay'in muḥīṭ*). Now, the term muḥīṭ also means 'environment' and it can, therefore, be said that God's Presence is ultimately the "environment" of His creation, more specifically the world of nature and of human beings. To destroy the natural environment, whose beauty and harmony are results of this Divine Presence, is to veil this Presence and disrupt the harmony and balance of nature, of human life and of their inter-relation. He claims that the key for Muslims confronting this crisis successfully, at least to the extent possible since some of the causes of the crisis are global and beyond the control of the Islamic world, is to return to the teachings of traditional Islam about nature and man's relation to it. Therefore, Islamic teachings can be used much more readily for this purpose than can religious teachings in secularized parts of the globe.

In Chapter 9, "Responsibility of Muslims versus Environment," Farahanifard and Farahanifard discuss the issue of environment as it has always been considered by the divine religions, and in case of Islam, it has also special instructions, respectively. The primary principle of Islam is based on the fact that through education it can make human being preserve his living place, and these methods in practice have certainly been effective. On the other hand, those who make the path of people polluted or bring about some barriers for them are reproached. The authors maintain that Islam takes into account the overall aspects of human beings, environment, and the universe in a balanced and coordinated relationship on the divine path and creates an interrelation among them. The crisis of environment is the outcome of the distance made between human being and its creation and religious teachings on the one hand and uncontrolled use of environmental resources that stem from the accelerating development of secularism. Religions have made strict emphasis on preservation of environment but Islam has further encouraged and obliged Muslims to achieve this purpose. The Islamic state, too, by means of the instruments at hand, can provide the performance guarantee for the principles and requirements of Shariah.

In Chapter 10, "Business Ethics," Reza'ei Davani provides a link between business ethics and economic system in Islam and advocates that in an Islamic Economy, economics is intrinsically tied to ethics and, therefore, financial markets also serve non-pecuniary functions. These functions include improving the livelihood of the needy, upholding individual rights, and curbing excessive risks associated with transactions. By aligning private investment decisions with the public good, an Islamic Economy creates a more efficient, ethical, and sustainable economy.

In Chapter 11, "Ethical Model of Business Ethics: Qur'an's View," Karimi presents ethical framework for business based on the injunction of Qur'an with the objective to institutionalize ethical values in the business environment in order to help society achieve desired elevated and perfected state. In Islam's view, he argues, ethics of business is part of the overall economic and social system and its effectiveness depends on coordination with other parts of the system. For example, its framework is balanced as it involves coordination between consideration of the spiritual and life in the Hereafter, on the one hand, and the material and worldly life, on the other. Further he states that the fundamental axis of ethical concepts in the Qur'an is the belief in the One Creator and the life in the Hereafter. Ignoring these two axioms, either explicitly or implicitly, causes retardation of growth and spiritual elevation of human beings as well as destruction of individual incentives to do good deeds. The ultimate objective of the Islamic model of business ethics is to institutionalize ethical values compliance with which allows humans to attain to the state of human perfection and drawing near to their Creator. It is on this basis that the positive and negative principles and components of ethics find meaning and in terms of compliance with the positive and avoidance of negative principles. The most important institution in this model is work within the context of it being an act of worship.

In Chapter 12, "Spiritual Excellence (*Iḥsān*) for Professionals: A Ḥadīth-Based Perspective," Qadir, Raquib, Ahmed discusses the critical role of *Sunnah*--the practice and the character of the Prophet (pbuh) who is considered the perfect embodiment of *Qur'ānic* morality and the guide towards the correct understanding of the *Qur'ān*, reached us through traditions (*Ḥadīths*) that have reported the sayings, actions, and tacit approvals accorded by the Prophet (peace be upon him). Islamic scholars agree that an appropriate understanding of *Qur'ānic* ethics can only be obtained in the light of the Sunnah by combining *Qur'ān* and the *Ḥadīth*. This chapter provides a survey of the *Ḥadīth* literature to highlight overarching themes in Islamic ethics. In particular, it focuses on the Islamic concept of excellence (*Iḥsān*) and describe the various manifestations of this virtue of *Iḥsān* by highlighting the seven salient characteristics of the people of *Iḥsān*. It also discusses how the adoption of *Iḥsān* could add to the modern ethical discourse and facilitate human development, wellbeing, and happiness at the level of individuals and community while also helping in earning God's favor and good pleasure.

In Chapter 13, "Human and Role of Ethics in His Interactions in *Makarim-ul-Akhlaq* Prayer by Ali bin Hussain (PBUH)," Habibian claims that humanity of mankind is related to his spiritual and celestial aspects that are associated and blended with material and physical constraints. He also reviews in brief such important principles as dignity, justice, fairness and freedom – that must be paid due attention vis-à-vis human behavior – with an ethical approach to show that ethics and these principles interchangeably affect one another. The paper continues with extracting and elaborating ethical recommendations from Makarimul-Akhlaq Prayer of Sahifeh Sajjadieh attributed to the fourth Imam of Shia Muslims, Hazrat Ali bin Hussain (Zeyn al-Abedin) and shows their impact on human life in business environment. He elucidates that human perfection primarily depends upon recognition of his mission and accomplishment of this mission in the restricted and transient material world. Further, all capacities and issues related to humanities must be at the service of man to recognize his mission and accomplish it. Therefore, the issue of man and the role of ethics in business environment must be also reviewed in this connection. The author classifies human dignity as 1- Inherent God-given dignity, and 2- Acquired dignity. All people possess God-given dignity and natural prestige. Acquired dignity is attained by employing talents and positive forces inside human beings and by efforts and endeavors toward human perfection and doing pious acts. Religiousness, piety, patience, gentleness, cheerfulness, bridling the tongue, virtue, forgiveness, lack of jealousy, forbearance, thankfulness and trust are among the criteria of dignity. Attaching less significance to materiality, seeking justice, generosity, good morals, happy end, minimizing discord with others, good deed and creed, tolerance, increased sustenance, satisfaction of God, and greatness before others are some of the aftereffects of dignity. To attain dignity one must attach greater significance to persistence in his acts, trust in God, God's satisfaction, doing good in material world as provisions for the Hereafter, and no complaint of God before the people in all his deeds and creeds.

In Chapter 14, "Shaheed Sadr's Perspective on Property Rights in Islam," Nourahmadi presents an important topic of property rights in Islam especially as understood by a renowned scholar. Ownership structure is the most important component of an economic system. On the one hand, it is based on the moral and legal principles governing the society and, on the other hand, it affects economic performance and distribution of income and wealth in the society. Since ancient times, when a fair society or an ideal society has been the subject of discussion by various thinkers, fair ownership structure has been at the heart of the discourse. Author explains Shaheed Sadr's views on the ownership structure in an Islamic economy with emphasis on its ethical dimensions. The most important moral factor in the ownership structure of Islamic economy is its fairness, which is based on the concept of the *Khilafah* (vice regency/trusteeship/agency) and it has important implications for all aspects of the economic system, including production, distribution, consumption, exchange, and government's role. Explaining the consequences of the fair ownership structure based on the views of Shaheed Sadr on distribution, exchange and production in order to achieve economic justice in the Islamic economic system is the key contribution of this chapter.

In Chapter 15, "Significance of "Trust" and Capital Formation in Islamic Finance," Fisher highlights that "trust" is an essential virtue and set of behaviors that supports our survival and continued evolution. Trust is not something that can be gifted – it must be mutually accepted as a social connection and, while research suggests trust may be instantaneous, generally it must be earned over time. Ethics become embedded in each individual based upon cultural upbringing and socialization, which influence each person's interpretation of Integrity for self and others. Islamic capital markets and Islamic banking can be understood as ethical finance that strikes a middle ground for commerce and financial transactions between opposing goals of maximum profit-making and social justice. Authors demonstrate how "trust" could play a significant role in development of Islamic capital markets in today's era of finance dominated by program trading in nano-seconds, mobile banking, financial engineering of debt securities and credit default swaps.

In Chapter 16, "Principle of Human Dignity: The Criteria for Ethical Assessment of Business Relations in Islamic Economy," Mohammadi Monfared and Tavassoli attempt to identify a criterion for understanding appropriateness of voluntary actions relating to work and business activities in Islamic economics. While it is possible, the authors argue, to rely solely on criteria of such determination provided by religious rules, intellect too can be utilized to make such determination. That is, intellect too can determine the ethical appropriateness of voluntary actions based on their beneficial or detrimental effects on human welfare, with the help of teachings of the revelation. In the view of the authors, actualization of dignity or ignominy in human behavior within the realm of work and business activities can be employed as a criterion or indicator for understanding the ethical appropriateness of behavior; that is, if such conducts are compatible with human dignity, they are righteous, else they are considered unrighteous. Accordingly, two aspects of any conduct are of significance in the determination of ethical appropriateness of work as well as economic and business behavior: 1) actualization or non-actualization of human dignity, based on the resulting benefits (or damage) of work and business conduct accrued to human welfare, constitutes the benchmark or indicator of appropriateness of behavior; and 2) whether the agent's intention is focused on the actualization of human dignity. Given these considerations, it can be claimed that behaviors such as hoarding and charging interest "*Riba*" are considered reprehensible and deserve the title of unethical conducts because they contradict personal and social human dignity and affect them adversely. Moreover, the ethical principles derived provide criteria for resolving the ethical challenges and conflicts facing work and business activities.

In chapter 17 "Domains of Probity ("Sidaqat") in Islamic Markets" Rajaee and Kazemi Najafabadi, argue that Probity in markets can be achieved by a number of methods and measures. They include type, quality, quantity and price of commodity as well as type of transaction, invoicing/payment and delivery times, parties to the transaction and the governing rules and regulations of the market. Probity not only builds confidence and establishes security and assurance, but renders the capacity to produce information in excess of what is required by the market and is effective in pricing. As a result, the information asymmetry in the market is systematically reduced and the Islamic market will benefit from Probity.

In Chapter 18, "An Index of Islamic Market Probity ("*Sidaqat*")," Raja'ee and Kazemi Najafabadi propose a "Probity Index" to measure the extent of probity prevailing in the market. This index can be used in all markets as an indicator of transactions. Implementation of this index, supplemented by other Islamic indices of market transactions, demonstrates the prevailing conditions of the market and evaluates its compliance with the desirable market characteristics from an Islamic point of view. The current research is an attempt to assess the application of the proposed Probity Index in the dairy market of the city of Mashhad, IR of Iran using interviews, questionnaires and available previous research and documentation on the basis of each of the above-mentioned indicators, obtained through "interview," "questionnaire," and "reviewing the available documents." Therefore, proper enculturation as well as the design and implementation of appropriate policies for the modernization and industrialization of breeding farms would lead to significant increase in the Probity Index of the dairy market.

In Chapter 19, "Fair wages in Islam," Pasebani looks at the place of fair wages in other religious societies and argues the necessity of investigating the relationship of justice and fair wages. In this context, he also considers the view of Islam related to work and investigates various dimensions of fair wages through institutional analysis levels. He maintains there is no doubt that paying fair wages prevents class conflicts in society by creating stable relationships among employees and employers while reducing poverty. This relationship is obtained when there is true motivation to pay fair wages. They will be determined by contract stipulation, commensurate with the level of general wages prevailing in the market, proportionate to the effort exerted, sufficient to meet the needs of the worker, and equivalent to the marginal product of labor. To implement such a system, its components must be institutionalized (as formal or informal institutions) and reflect in the management system of the society. Actualization of this ethical set up will lead to a more productive economy.

In Chapter 20, "Ethics and the Acknowledged Right of the Destitute in the Quran and Hadith," Baqeri Tudeshki attempts in his paper to analyze the status of "*Haqq al-Ma'lum, The acknowledged right*" from the point of view of the Qur'an, Riwayat, and that of jurisprudents and exegetists. He attempts to demonstrate that it is another obligatory duty. According to the author, two verses of the Quran and a number of Riwayat point to existence of an "acknowledged right" in the wealth of the believers. The status of this right seems to be different than that of Khums, Zakat and resources of Islamic government that provide support for the livelihood of the poor. Exclusively, the Qur'an establishes an obligatory "acknowledged right" in the wealth of the Abrar (the righteous) and believers to the support of the deprived and mendicants. Finally, the author concludes that "acknowledged right" can be sanctioned and enforced only by ethics.

In Chapter 21, "Influence of Piety (Taqwa) on Ethical Decision-makings in Business: Integration of Religious and Scientific Views," Jafari, Pirmaleki, and Kazemi Najafabadi analyze how a devout individual (inwardly religious) is one who considers every moment of life as an occasion for Divine trial, and thus, possesses a high degree of moral sensitivity. Having distanced himself from sins and reprehensible deeds, as well as having fulfilled obligatory and recommended duties, the pious individual is granted, by the Almighty, a standard or measure of distinguishing between the right and wrong (capability of making ethical judgment) and attenuated the sources of inclination towards unethical behavior. Empirical research shows that inward religiosity (piety) improves ethical decision-making in business (awareness, judgment, intention, and ethical behavior), both directly and indirectly, through strengthening idealism, enhancing the feeling of guilt caused by unethical behavior, as well as weakening of Machiavellian morality (ethics?). Most empirical research have shown that internalized religiosity exerts positive and meaningful influence, being stronger among the consumers than the senior executives and specialists, and weaker among the narcissists, the rich, the mischievous, and those with active ethical challenges.

In Chapter 22, "The Role of Religious and Ethical Teachings in Designing Social Welfare Function," Kia Al-Hosseini maintains that the economic welfare of a society is based on the judgement of policy makers. It follows that value judgments play an important role in judging whether a society's economic welfare is better or worse as a result of implementation of a given economic policy. In the classical theory of welfare, such judgments regarding welfare improvement is based on material wellbeing. However, with the passage of time, other dimensions of human life such as justice and freedom as standards of welfare enters the literature of welfare and are included as indicators of the measurement of wellbeing in the social welfare function by scholars such as John Rawls and Amartya Sen. In the teachings of Islam, however, while accepting the three conventional principles, i.e., comparability, anonymity, and symmetry other principles of other-worldly spiritual and altruism orientations are considered to be influential in designing social welfare function and demonstrates that a Muslim with these orientations will have a higher level of welfare and satisfaction.

In Chapter 23, "Towards an Integrative Framework for Understanding Producer Behavior in Islamic Economics Framework," Ahmed-Shaikh models producer behavior and finds marginal analysis for commercial undertaking by firms in the Islamic framework is similar to firms in conventional system. The explicit difference comes in the type of goods produced and the modes of financing used. The more significant and implicit difference comes in moral approach whereby an entrepreneur imbued with the spirit of ethos and philosophy of Islam avoids hoarding, anti-competitive behaviour, price manipulation, cheating, fraud, injustice and social harm in the form of negative externalities. The entrepreneur in the Islamic framework is conscious of the fact that all surplus investable endowments are a trust from Allah. The entrepreneur uses part of the surplus investable endowments in Zakāt, Sadqā (voluntary charity) and establishing Waqf (endowment).

In Chapter 24, "The Ethics of Consumption in Islam," Ezzati argues that Islam as a way of an ethical life that provides felicity in the Hereafter without harming life in the material world, has permitted its followers to enjoy the blessings of both lives. This is the comprehensive nature of Islam, in that it focuses on the life in this world and in the world to come. On this basis, religious teachings create an incentive for humans to exercise their free will to behave ethically. Religion has created an incentive structure based on a system of reward and punishment afterlife to motivate ethical behavior.

The incentive structure is so designed that believing individuals gain utility by complying with the teachings in their behavior voluntarily.

In Chapter 25, “Ethical Dimensions of Money in Islamic Economic System,” Tavassoli and Mohammadi Monfared raise the concern that the main source of economic crises is the incoherence of behavior of hapless governments and people in societies in relation to a phenomenon called “money.” Using historical, explanatory and analytical methods, the research tries to throw light on how usurious capitalists and hapless governments have abused money, in whatever form it existed, to their maximum advantage. With the advent of banks in the economy, these institutions too utilized various extortive contracts to enhance inequality of wealth distribution as the usurious capitalists have done and like governments have made wealth distribution much worse through their power of money creation. The authors concentrate on the relationship between ethics, economics and Islamic economy. Then they turn to various ethical dimensions of the relationship between money and *Riba*, money and government in different monetary systems, as well as money and banks are covered in some detail. They demonstrate that most of the economic challenges we are facing have their roots in the unethical behavior of society and government towards the phenomenon of money.

In Chapter 26, “Hoarding of Goods, Money and Financial Assets,” Sadr addresses unethical market behavior in his article. He argues that hoarding, warehousing, saving, investment and speculation are practices that share some features in common and are observed in the markets under various conditions. He attempts to define and explain these concepts clearly in order to identify distinguishing characteristics of each of these activities. The criteria for their differences are presented and the market condition under which these practices harm or improve the welfare of market participants is described. The chapter concludes that hoarding is a short-run market imperfection phenomenon when some necessary goods and commodities are stocked and made scarce in the market to force their prices to artificially rise. It is different from a monopoly condition which is a long-run market imperfection. Hoarding is also distinguishable from warehousing which is a valuable marketing practice. The latter makes the goods available at the time they are in demand whereas the former makes them unavailable and creates disutility for the consumers. Saving is also differentiable from hoarding. The former is practiced when a portion of households’ income or wealth is deposited in a financial institution to be pooled with savings of others and be invested in profitable ventures later. Although necessary goods are most often the subject of hoarding, the practice is not limited to them. Shari’ah prohibits withdrawal from the market of any commodity, good and asset, real or financial that is exchanged in the market. The Chapter relates Islamic rules governing market behavior that both enhance investment and savings and condemn hoarding and speculation.

In Chapter 27, “Ethics and Economics of Islamic Government,” Rezaee Davani explains the ethical aspects of Islamic government. This paper reports the results of its search in sacred texts and traditions of religious divines relating to these ruling systems in Islam. The results are presented in fewer than six headings: access to power, objectives, selection of personnel, decision making, collection of revenues and allocation of Bayt al-Maal (treasury of the Islamic government). Alongside the Qur'an and traditions of the Prophet (sawa), the paper also looks at the letters 'Ali, to his governors relating to the administration of territories under their care, represent important documents relating to public finance in Islam. In this letter fundamental missions of a religious government have been discussed in detail. They include domestic and foreign security, tax collection, economic development of the country, and attending to the livelihood of the people. Several valuable points are mentioned in these letters which are still considered as practical guidelines for the Muslim scholars.

In Chapter 28, "Principles of Defining Public Domain in Islam in Contrast to the Neoclassical and Communitarian viewpoints," Lashkari discusses how the scopes of government activities are defined on the basis of their respective ethical and philosophical viewpoints. By referring to the moral philosophy that is accepted in neoclassical, communitarian, and Islamic schools of thought, the current article attempts to define the public affair in those contexts. It also attempts to elucidate the mode of government intervention in the economy. While acknowledging the fundamental significance of individual expediency and the necessity of respecting it, the author commends that the Islamic ruler acquires the status of an authority that is responsible for protecting and safeguarding the "public expediency" and guarantees achieving felicity of the society. This attribute of Islamic state distinguishes it from liberal, socialist, and even communitarian states. Further, the paper argues that with the implementation of Islamic principles, not only the public domain emerges from the shadow of private sector and market, but it acquires such an importance that will prevail over the private domain. In the Islamic perspective, despite that the market is an institution with an extensive and important scope in the economic system; it can perform as an instrument for the realization of social expediency. However, it does not constitute the focal point of the economic system and does not define the values, ethical system and social expediency. As a result, the expected performance in view of neoclassical economists does not provide a fundamental measure for evaluating economic activities of the Islamic state, especially regarding decision- and policy-makings. The author illustrates through a table the attitude of different schools towards expediency and benefaction of individual and society. It also indicates their relation with distributive approach, as one of the most controversial duties of the state, the type of government, and the difference between the Islamic approaches with the rival schools.

References

Bayhaqi, Ahmad Bin Hosain, *As-Sonan al-Kobra,* Vol 10, Beirut, Dar al-Kotob al-Elmiah, (1424 L.H./2003).

Hairi Yazdi, Mehdi, *Practical Reason (KaveshhayeAqlAmali).* Tehran: Cultural Studies and Research Institute (1361/1982).

Ibn Miskawyeh, *The Rfinement of Character, (Tahdhaib Al-Akhlaaq)*, Translated by Constantine Zurayk, edited by Seyyed Hossein Nasr, USA, Kazi Publication (2014).

Motahhari, Morteza, Islam and Immortality, *Collection of Works*, Compiled by A.Sorush, Tehran, the Institute for Islamic Research and Education (1360/1981).

Motahhari, Morteza, *Islam and Dynamic Time Issues (Islam wa moqtaziat zaman),* Qum, Sadr Publication, (1365/1986).

Sadr, Hasan, *Tasees Ash-Shiah li Olum al-Islam*, Baghdad, Markaz An-Nashrwa al-Tiba'h al Eraqiah, (1375/1996).

Tabatabaei, Seyyed Mohammad Hosain, *Collection of Works (MajmooehRasael),* Compiled by Seyed Hadi Khosroshahi, Tehran, Daftar Nashr Islami (1370/1991).

Toosi, Naseeruddin, *Naseri Ethic (AkhlaaqNaseri),* edited by Mojtaba Minavi and Alireza Haidari, Tehran, Elmiah Islamiah Publication (1397/2018).

Contents

Zamir Iqbal and Abbas Mirakhor

Chapter 1: Ethics of Risk-Sharing Economics and Finance

The widening inequality, stagnant incomes, large unemployment, string of crippling economic and financial crises, huge growth of government and consumer debts, and a host of other ills consequent to the operation of present form of capitalism have seriously challenged faith in the system. In his recent book, Nobel Laurate, Joseph Sitglitz continues to show his concerns about the direction of capitalism, consequences of uncontrolled nature and the consequences especially the widening income inequality.[1]

The widely held perception of selfish, greedy, and harmful business has created a regime uncertainty where, as many argue, there is doubt if the system can be saved from itself or is even worth saving. There can be little doubt that the 2007/2008 financial crisis and its aftermath demonstrated a fundamentally massive moral failure that has, in turn, caused a moral panic that there is a systemic assault upon human dignity, trust, contracts and property, all of which constitute fundamental elements of the institutional structure of societies.[2] The question pertinent to the debate is whether it is the system that has morally failed or the people who operate in the system who have lost their moral and ethical moorings. Compelling arguments have been made that it is the system's moral failure when it creates incentive structures that unleash greed, selfishness and self-centeredness by removing legal and regulatory restraint on behavior of finance and business. In these circumstances, conditions are created for Gresham effect to allow bad ethics to drive good ethics out of the market.[3]

It is worth noting that Adam Smith, considered the father of Western economics, wrote his book *The Theory of Moral Sentiments* some decade and half before his other treatise *The Wealth of Nations*. An argument has been made that the proposition discernible from The Wealth of Nations regarding the workings of market capitalism must be placed within the institutional framework of *The Theory of Moral Sentiments*, which provides the mooring for them. The decoupling of the two books, in effect, cuts off economics and finance from the ethics of the system envisioned by Smith. This purging process to purify economics and finance in order to make them "value-free" began in earnest in the second half of the 20th century, leaving market capitalism with only one ethics: "*quid pro quo*."[4]

---

1 Stiglitz, Joseph (2019).

2 Iqbal and Mirakhor (2017).

3 Gresham's law is a monetary principle stating that "bad money drives out good".

4 See Mirakhor and Alaabed (2013).

https://doi.org/10.1515/9783110593419-001

Discussing the role of morals and ethics in economics and finance is not new but several developments as mentioned above can be attributed to a renewed interest in discussing the relevance of ethics to economics and finance.[5] Aragon (2014, 17) calls the phenomenon of ignoring the ethical dimension "moral muteness" and observes that some ethical issues "are transmuted into less morally charged terminology, for example, by referring to financial manipulation as 'income smoothing,' lying as 'cheap talk,' or theft as 'rent seeking'." He argues that vast research in financial economics on the economic consequences of imperfect information is actually dealing with ethical issues underneath expected behavior and, therefore, has ethical dimension embedded in the relevant theories. For example, two major concepts, moral hazard and adverse selection, are the foundation of several advance economic and financial theories such as agency costs theory and signaling theory. Furthermore, the development of means and mechanisms to reduce or mitigate costs associated with moral hazard and adverse selection has led to the development of a theoretical framework of institutional economics that focuses on the importance of formal and informal institutions. Therefore, treating these concepts in void of ethical dimensions would have serious implications on the development of economic and financial theories which would also be void of ethical aspects.

Both moral hazard and adverse selection issues are ethical issues but conventional economics tend to ignore the ethical dimension. The classic example of unethical behavior such as dishonesty and information asymmetries in economics is that of Akerlof's (1970) "lemons" model, in which information asymmetries would lead to market failure when agents are expected to be dishonest. The dual conditions for market failure (that is, information asymmetries and dishonesty) suggested by Akerlof's model reflect the key link between economic value and ethics. This necessitates deeper analysis of behavioral assumptions that have undeniable ethical implications.

Similarly, the actions of financial intermediaries and creditors can involve moral hazard if they involve excessive risk taking without providing full information to savers and lenders. Moral hazard arises when savers are not able to observe the risk-taking behavior of financial intermediaries while in fact the savers are at risk of losing their savings, should the worst case be realized. This was common in the 2007/2008 crisis known as the subprime crisis. If looked at in light of fiduciary responsibilities, excessive risk taking would be considered an ethics issue.

Whereas conventional economics remains value-neutral, ethics are embedded in the core principles of Islam and each rule prescribed has explicit or implicit ethical dimensions reflecting its adherence to core values and virtues.[6] Philosophical foundation underlying the development of legal rules as well as its objectives (*maqasid*)

5 Hoepnerab and Wilsona (2010) shows that the annual number of publications indexed by Factiva for the search words 'Bank' and 'Ethics' increased by 357.9% from 4,164 in the year 2000 to 19,069 in the year 2009. This indicates sudden increase in the topic in post financial crisis era.

6 See Naqvi (1981) and Naqvi (2003) for earlier discussion of ethics and Islamic economics.

are based on Islam's core values and virtues ensuring ethical outcome. Following of the rules will set the standards of an overall ethical behavior for individuals, firms, community, state, and the society. This defines a perimeter by sanctioning immoral and harmful activities with the objective to achieve overall welfare of the society as a whole. Perimeter defined by rules becomes the limits beyond which ethics would be compromised. As long as one is rule-compliant, there would not arise any question of any unethical behavior.

Ethics, morality, and justice are firmly embedded in the Islamic vision of how an economy and its finance are to operate. They are defined by a set of behavioral rules prescribed in *al-Qur'an* which include virtues such as respect for property rights, faithfulness to terms and conditions of contract, maintenance of trust, honesty, transparency, cooperation, reciprocity, and consultation, and a number of other institutional and behavioral rules. Participants internalize these rules before entering the market, which has rules governing its operations as well. Hence, what would be considered as moral, ethical values in contemporary parlance are endogenized within the economic and financial activities in Islam.[7]

Based on moral teaching aimed at promoting economic and social justice and to enhance solidarity among communities, internalization of rules and virtues of Islam determine all facets of an economy ranging from the rules of market conduct, production, consumption, distribution, and redistribution. In all these relations, emphasis is placed on the ethics of work and ethical treatment of workers and to maintain an ethical relationship between employee and employers, business and customers, business and stakeholders, and finally business and society at large including environment. Similarly to general business ethics, rules applicable to economic and financial transactions have specific ethical framework which has been discussed and debated for centuries. Two key features of Islamic economics and finance are the prohibition of interest in any form and deliberate creation of informational problems such as asymmetric information and moral hazard (*gharar*).[8] Each prohibition has its embedded system of values and virtues defining its ethical dimensions. For example, prohibition of interest is characterized with virtues of preservation of property rights and condemnation of economic and social exploitation. In case of prohibition of *gharar*, transaction can be declared null and void in considerations of fairness and justice as *gharar* in a transaction causes injustice and loss of property to one or both of the parties.[9]

---

7 Mirakhor and Alaabed (2013).

8 For example, any deliberate act to create information asymmetry to deceive a borrower, a buyer or any economic agent would be considered *gharar*. Its analogous case is the Akerlof's "lemon problem" where the used car seller designs an informational problem for the buyer in order to defraud the customer. However, this is a moral/ethical problem which is not referred to as such in the contemporary economic literature (including by Akerlof himself).

9 Kamali (2011) *Gharar* refers to elements of uncertainty in contracts that expose one or both of the contracting parties to risk. *Gharar* can also be caused by doubt or ignorance of one or both of the

Although the ethical dimensions of Islamic economics and finance are very deep,[10] in this chapter, we will focus on two key elements – core concept of justice and risk sharing aspect of financial transactions and their impact on Islamic economics and finance as a system.

1 Concept of Economic and Social Justice

One of the most serious evidence of moral weakness of capitalism is the emergence of highly skewed income and wealth inequality where the top 1% wealthiest individuals alone owned 33% of total wealth in 2017 compared to 28% in 1980. The bottom 50% of the population, on the other hand, owns almost no wealth over the entire period (less than 2%) and the bottom 75% saw its share oscillate around 10%.[11] Thomas Piketty in his *Le Capital au XXIe siècle* provides massive data going back two centuries to demonstrate that creation of inequality is an inherent characteristic of capitalism.[12] He shows that, with exception of few decades in which inequality's growth slowed, the general trend of inequality in the long run has been upward.

The concern with the twin problems of inequality and poverty dates back to the earliest recorded history as a dimension of justice which necessitates that we understand the concept of justice in Islam first. A just economy is part of a just, healthy, and moral society, which is the central objective of Islam. What underpins all the rules of behavior prescribed by Islam is its conception of justice, which maintains that all behavior, irrespective of its content and context, must, in its conception and commission, be based on just standards as defined by the Islamic Law (Shari'ah). Islam considers an economy, in which the behavior of its agents is so conceived, as an enterprising, purposeful, prosperous, and sharing economy in which all members of society receive their just rewards. Such an economy is envisioned as one in which economic disparities that lead to social segmentation and divisiveness are conspicuously absent.

Justice in Islam is a multifaceted concept, and several words or terms exist for each aspect. The most common word in use, which refers to the overall concept of justice, is *adl*. This word and its many synonyms imply the concepts of "right," as an equivalent of "fairness," "putting things in their right place," "equality," "equalizing," "balance," "temperance," and "moderation."

parties over the existence, quality, deliverability, or other material attributes of the subject matter of contract. The question whether risk taking in transactions amounts to *gharar* often depends on its scale and magnitude.

10 For an in depth analysis of ethics of Islamic economics and finance, see Iqbal and Mirakhor (2017).

11 World Inequality Database (2018).

12 Piketty (2013).

There is a consensus among scholars of Islamic economics that social justice is the most important objective of an Islamic economy and abstract models have been proposed based on the desiderata of justice and beneficence (العدل والإحسان). Even a cursory look at Islamic sources suggests a comprehensive conception of justice that permeates throughout individual and community life. Every dimension of individual behavior affecting the individual and social interactions is subject to some conception of justice. Each conception of justice, as applied in the Qur'an, refers to a specific dimension of individual and collective behavior. Associated with each conception is a term and a context. Based on the already available literature, conception of justice plays a major role in the formation of rules governing the allocation of resources, production, exchange, market, distribution and redistribution.

The components of economic justice in an Islamic society are (i) equality of liberty and opportunity for all members of society with respect to the utilization of natural resources; (ii) justice in exchange; and (iii) distributive justice – all accomplished within the framework of the Shari'ah.

In the Islamic conception, liberty means that others do not prevent a person from combining his creative labor with resources, which are designated by the Shari'ah for the use of the individual members of society. Opportunity, on the other hand, represents a favorable conjunction of circumstances, which gives the individual the chance to try it and success is dependent on the individual's efforts and abilities. This equality of opportunity must be secured deliberately by the collectivity. It not only denotes free and equal access to physical resources, but, generally, also extends to technology, education, and environmental resources. The basis for this equality of access to resources and equality of opportunity to use them is Islam's position that natural resources are provided for all members of society. Even if the opportunity to use these resources is not available to some, either naturally or due to some other circumstances, their original claims to resources remain intact and are not nullified. They must be remunerated for these claims, at some point in time, by the other members who happen to have "or get" greater opportunity to use them.

The concept of justice in exchange and economic transactions is that, by mixing their creative labor with resources, individuals create a claim of equity to the possession of the assets thus produced, by virtue of which they can participate in exchange. To allow exchange to take place on the basis of just standards, Islam places a great deal of emphasis on the market and its moral, just and – based on these two factors – efficient operation. To assure justice in exchange, the Shari'ah has provided a network of ethical and moral rules of behavior, which cover in minute detail the behavior of all participants in the market. It requires that these norms and rules be internalized and adhered to by all participants before they enter the market. A market that operates on the basis of these rules, which are intended to remove all factors inimical to justice in exchange, yields prices for factors and products that are considered "fair" and "just." Unlike the scholastic notion of "just price," which lacks an operational definition, the

Islamic concept refers to the price prevailing as a result of the interaction of economic forces operating in a market in which all rules of behavior specified by the Shari'ah are observed and adhered to by all participants. It is an *ex-post* concept, meaning that a just price has been paid and received.

The last component of Islamic economic justice, distributive justice, is the mechanism by which equal liberty and equity are reconciled without the least possible infringement. Insofar as the distribution of resources – the just and equal access to these resources, as well as equal opportunity in their use – is guaranteed, the claim to equity on the basis of reward and effort is just. The moral basis of property is the primacy given to equity and it is derived directly from human efforts and achievements.[13]

As we saw earlier, Islam recognizes claims based on equality of liberty and opportunity, which are reflected in the degree of access to resources, the degree and extent of the ability of persons to actualize their potential liberty and opportunity, and the right of prior ownership. The right that the less able have in the wealth of those who have greater ability and opportunity to produce greater wealth is redeemed through the various levies (*zakat, khums, sadaqa, nafaqa*, and so on), the payment of which is not beneficence but a contractual obligation that must be met. Islam also encourages beneficence over and above these obligatory dues, but these levies are in the nature of returning to others what rightfully belongs to them. Shirking from this obligation causes a misdistribution of wealth, which Islam considers as the major source of poverty.

To summarize, the central framework and operation of rules concerning economic and social life in Islam is justice. It ensures that justice is maintained in economic transactions as well as in social interaction such that the system as whole becomes embodiment of justice.

2 Ethics of Risk Sharing

Finance exists because of its ability to transform and manage risk and uncertainty. Humans live under conditions of uncertainty because the future is unknown. Faced with radical uncertainty and limited human cognitive capacity (Camerer et al., 2005; Kahneman, 2003), societies have three ways to manage risk: transfer it, shift it, or share it. Risk transfer is when, among two parties, one party completely transfers the associated risks to the other with the consent and acknowledgement of that party. However, in risk shifting, these risks are shifted to a third party or parties without their knowledge or consent, and they end up bearing all the risks and the associated adverse outcomes. A prime example could be the 2007/2008 global financial crisis: first, the

13 Askari, Iqbal, and Mirakhor (2015), Askari, Iqbal, and Mirakhor (2016), Mirakhor (1989).

risks were transferred through mortgage securitizations, and then, once the mortgage bubble busted, those risks were eventually shifted to the general taxpayers (without their knowledge or consent). More often than not, financial risk shifting occurs during the time of stress[14] when there is regime switching where individuals, corporations and governments switch their regime of risk management from risk transfer to risk shifting.[15] Finally, there is the regime of risk sharing in which the risk of contracts or transactions are shared among the participants. In the 1970s, Kenneth Arrow showed that when each economic agent is allocated the portion of risk of contracts or transactions commensurate with its capacity to bear it, there is optimal risk sharing.[16]

The idea of risk sharing goes back to the emergence of first agricultural and commercial human societies. Nor is it entirely foreign to conventional financial wisdom. Nobel Prize laureate Professor Robert Shiller, for example, is an advocate of risk-sharing instruments, arguing that risk sharing has much to contribute to the growth of economies and to social solidarity. As an instrument for social integration, risk sharing enhances human interaction and brings humanity closer to unity by requiring humans to share the risks of life with one another. Risk sharing also eases coordination and informational and collective action problems. Further, it allows parties to a transaction to maximize expected joint rewards, thereby promoting cooperation among all economic agents and facilitate collective action. This is further translated into close relationship between the real and financial sectors of the economy where risk is distributed through sharing contracts. The net effect of such fundamental linkage is greater stability of the financial system; crucially important in light of the recurring episodes of financial crises stemming from the phenomenon of decoupling of the real and financial sector, and the emergence of a paper economy.

Islam endorses risk sharing[17] as the preferred organizational structure for all economic activities, and in fact the most comprehensive application of risk sharing that goes beyond anything put forward by modern economic theories. Islam prohibits, and without any exceptions, explicit and implicit interest-based contracts of any kind and requires mandatory risk sharing with the poor, the deprived and the handicapped based on its principles of property rights. Moreover, even after these rights are redeemed, the remaining wealth is not to be accumulated, wealth is considered as the strength of the economy and means of support for the society.

The ideal Islamic finance points to a full-spectrum menu of instruments serving a financial sector imbedded in an Islamic economy in which the institutional

---

14 The current practice of Islamic finance seems to be an exception since "Islamic banks" appear to have adopted risk shifting as a risk-management tool even during normal times; see, Alaabed, Masih, and Mirakhor (2016).

15 Mirakhor, Krichene, and Shaukat (2012).

16 Arrow (1971); and Maghrebi, Mirakhor, and Iqbal (2016).

17 For in-depth discussion on risk-sharing aspect of Islamic economics and finance, see Askari, Iqbal, Krichene and Mirakhor (2012).

"scaffolding", i.e. rules of behavior and *virtues* as prescribed by Allah and operationalized and *internalized* by the Noble Messenger is fully operational.[18] The essential function of that spectrum would be spreading and allocating risk among market participants rather than allowing it to concentrate among the borrowing class. Islam proposes three sets of risk-sharing instruments:

i. risk-sharing instruments in the economic and financial transactions (*mu'amelat*);
ii. redistributive risk-sharing instruments (*zakat, sadaqat, qard-al-hasan,* etc.) through which the economically more able segments of society share the risks facing the less able segment of the population;[19] and
iii. the inheritance rules specified in the Qur'an through which the wealth of a person at the time of passing is distributed among present and future generations of inheritors.

Islamic finance encourages risk sharing in its many forms but generally discourages risk shifting or risk transfer, in particular interest-based debt financing. It is in part so designed to promote social solidarity by encouraging finance to play an integrating role between humankind (virtue of respecting unity of mankind). This form of finance would be inclusive of all members of society and all entities, especially the poor, in enjoying the benefits of economic growth, and to bring humankind closer together through the sharing of risk. Since risk sharing is the foundation and a basic activity in Islamic finance, it is governed by rules that, if and when observed, lead to lower transaction costs than in conventional finance. Risk sharing is a contractual or societal arrangement whereby the outcome of a random event is born collectively by a group of individuals or entities involved in a contract, or by individuals or entities in a community. In a company, all shareholders share in the risk inherent in the operations of the company. At the community level, a family or a nation shares in the risks affecting the wellbeing of the family or the nation.

Risk-sharing in economic and financial transactions is embedded with several virtues such as justice and is void of vices such as repression. Here we provide following select features of risk-sharing finance and argue that risk-sharing in economic and financial transactions when practiced with other virtues of Islamic ethics, would lead to an ethical and responsible financial system ensuring social and economic justice:

---

18 Iqbal and Mirakhor (2011), Chapra (2008). A "rule" is enforceable and sanctionable while a "virtue" is not. A "rule" becomes a "virtue" when it is internalized by the individual and operationalized in practice by that individual as he/she conducts his/her daily affairs. The Prophet (SAA) "operationalized" the rules in the society as the temporal head of state and then insisted that the members of the society "internalize" the rules before engaging in economic or social activities.

19 Mirakhor (2004) argues that the second set of instruments is used to redeem the rights of the less able in the income and wealth of the more able. These are not instruments of charity, altruism or beneficence. They are instruments of redemption of rights and repayment of obligations.

i. An interest-based pure debt contract is sub-optimal when compared with a risk sharing contract.
ii. A risk-sharing system would minimize financialization of economy and thus promote sustainable and equitable economic growth.
iii. Risk-sharing system is "antifragile" in the sense that shocks, when and if they occur, strengthen the system rather weaken it.
iv. Risk-sharing contracts and system safeguards against financial repression.
v. Risk-sharing transactions promote cooperation and solidarity among the economic agents and the members of the society.
vi. Risk-sharing contracts and system alleviate poverty, minimize the risk of emergence of large inequality, and increase employment, income and prosperity.

2.1 Sub-Optimality of Debt-contract Versus Risk-Sharing Contract

Interest based debt contracts are instruments of risk shifting, risk shedding, and risk transfer which are considered exploitative when compared to risk-sharing finance. Different rationales have been given about the prohibition of interest (*ribā*) but each reaching the same conclusion. Property rights rationale of prohibition argues that in interest-based debt contracts, the creditor acquires a property-rights claim on the debtor, equivalent to the principal plus interest and whatever collateral may be involved, without losing the property-rights claim to the money lent which violates the property rights principles of Islam (Mirakhor 1989). Other schools of thought argue that the prohibition of interest, is to prevent economic exploitation among the transaction parties which is contrary to the core values of economic and social justice (Chapra 2008, Kamali 2011). Since in Islam, money could only be a medium of exchange or measure of account rather than a commodity, paying rent for the use of money is not recognized unless money is converted to capital subject to a return. Therefore, money-lending without investment is forbidden as it involves exploitation and violates the spirit of social justice because it shifts all the risk from the financier to the borrowers and leads to imbalances in wealth and income distribution in society.

Furthermore, the reason for the prohibition of the contract of interest is the fact that opportunities for risk sharing are non-existence in this contract. It may be argued that the creditor does take risk – the risk of default. But it is not risk taking per se that makes a transaction permissible. A gambler takes risk as well but gambling is haram. Instead what seems to matter is opportunity for risk sharing. As Keynes emphasized in his writing, if interest rate did not exist, the financier would have to share in all the risks that the entrepreneur faces in producing, marketing and selling a product (see Mirakhor and Krichene, 2009). But by decoupling his future gains, by loaning money today for more money in the future, the financier transfers all risks to the entrepreneur.

In the context of risk sharing, two myths and realities are important to note. The first myth is that future payoffs on contingent claims have to be fixed because of risk and uncertainty as is the case of interest-based debt contract. Therefore, contracts need to be complete in such that debt is treated as less risky than equity. However, the reality is that contracts are incomplete because they cannot include all the information to ensure that the interests of both parties are served by the contract. An interest rate based debt contract is an "impossible contract," since under the standard axioms of economics (self-interest, scarcity, and rationality) the borrower has an incentive not to repay the loan. Debt contracts cannot include provisions of truth telling, speculative risk taking, malfeasance and other actions that affect the borrower's promise to repay. The problem of exchanging an amount of money now for a certain larger amount in the future is that the amount in the future is validated (underwritten) by a supposed stream of income which is radically uncertain (unknown unknowns). Making debt contract as possible or complete contract would have detrimental impact on society.

The second myth is that risk sharing contracts are costly and demand more information than debt based contracts. The reality is that risk sharing contracts are incentive-compatible contract because there is an incentive structure in place to elicit truth-telling, trust, cooperation, hard work, and efficiency in resource management; factors that could not be written into contracts and enforced. Hence, these contracts attenuate coordination problem and improve the efficiency of outcomes. Without this incentive structure, there are considerable transaction, monitoring and enforcement costs involved in designing and implementing contracts.

Given this background, the question is whether Islamic contracting (with risk sharing) is better suited to solving this contractual dilemma through its reliance on risk/reward sharing under conditions where interest-based debt financing is prohibited. In the presence of informational problems such as asymmetric information (where only one side of the contract, usually the agent, has information not available to the other parties) there is transaction cost as well as cost of monitoring the agent's activities and the project(s) to be taken into account. It could be plausibly argued that in Islamic contracts asymmetric information issues would be minimized. This assertion is supported by the strict rules governing contracts, exchange and trade. Such rules with the exercise of virtues such as justice, truthfulness, and trust by economic agents would reduce information asymmetry to a minimum. These include the need for written contracts that stipulate terms and conditions fully and transparently, the direct and unequivocal admonition that commitments to the terms and conditions of contracts must be faithfully carried out, and the strong emphasis on trust, cooperation and consultation. Ethics governing market behavior also create incentives – both positive and negative – to enforce honest, transparent and compliant behavior on the part of participants. Hence, risk-sharing contracts designed under Islamic rules would mitigate informational problems (Khan and Mirakhor 1987) and could be better structured than interest-based debt contracts with incentives to maximize both parties' expected joint rewards.

2.2 Preventing Financialization of Economy

By prohibiting renting of money and encouraging trade, financial instruments facilitate direct financing of real economy and therefore promotes allocation of resources to real sector. Although, debt obligations are created in the financial system, such obligations are results of the sale or lease of real assets through sale and lease-based modes of financing. The objective is to impose a fiscal discipline on individuals and firms to allocated financial resources to real sector according to their capacity to payback. Conditions stipulated by Islamic law such as (i) the asset which is being sold or leased must be real, and not fictitious or notional; (ii) the seller must own and possess the goods being sold or leased; (iii) the transaction must be a genuine trade transaction with full intention of giving and taking delivery; and (iv) the debt obligation as result of sale or lease contract cannot be sold or transferred to someone else and must be borne by the creditor himself, are put in place to encourage financing of real economy and to discourage uncontrolled expansion of debt.[20] These conditions ensure availability of financial resources for the real sector and thus expand employment and self-employment opportunities through the production of goods and services.

An interest-based financial system invariably creates a phenomenon known as "financialization" that results in a divergence between the real sector and the financial sector of the economy. In 1984, Nobel laureate in economics, James Tobin had warned that paper economy such as conventional system with its own ethics and morality was emerging where the object of finance was no longer intermediating funds for production of real output but creating a speculative environment of making money off paper trading; a "casino" capitalism.[21] In a short, concise and forceful article in Lloyds Bank Review, July, 1984, he warned that the risk-transfer debt system with new financial techniques and securitization would lead a productive economy to morph into a speculative economy; what he called "a paper economy." By this he meant that finance, which was supposed to intermediate between the surplus and deficit finance units in order to serve the real economy, was in the process of de-coupling from the real sector to have an independent life of its own in which most of its activities was trading in paper debt securities or trading in stocks which were already issued without creating additional and new capital stock. He argued that in these circumstances, the speculative paper economy would grow with finance outpacing the growth of the real economy. This process was later called "financialization."[22] His prediction saw its full validation before and during the 2007/2008 crisis. Even years after the crisis, Tobin's analysis has not lost its validity. In 2012, five years after the crisis, it was estimated

20 Kamali (2011).
21 Tobin (1984).
22 For a good discussion of financialization, see, Palley (2013).

that of the US$ 33 Trillion trade in the New York Stock Exchange, only 0.2 percent found its way into new capital formation, the rest constituted speculation in "paper trade."[23]

The conventional fractional banking system allows multiple amounts of money to be created out of a given amount of deposits received, facilitating and enhancing the process of debt creation. The development of complex financial derivatives has resulted in credit expansion outpacing the growth of the real sector of the economy. As layer upon layer of securitization decouples the connection between the financial and real sectors, an inverted credit pyramid is created to the extent that the liabilities of the economy becomes a large multiple of real assets needed to validate them (Mirakhor 2011). Additionally, such a system is characterized by mismatched maturity and values of asset and liability structure of balance sheet of banks. These institutions borrow short and lend long. When subjected to asset price shocks, the liability side of the balance sheet is very slow to adjust, while the asset side adjusts rapidly. Both mismatches create a potential for instability that can spread rapidly through contagion. The result can be an increase in the frequency, contagion, and severity of financial and economic crises (Askari et al. 2012).

Islamic finance advocating financing of real economy, promoting trade, asset-based financing, and risk-sharing would ensure that resources are allocated to real economic activities and decoupling between finance and economy is avoided.

2.3 Antifragility and Stability of the System

While, in our opinion, a risk-sharing financial system would be inherently stable, conventional finance – a debt-and-interest-based system – has proven to be unstable.[24] Minsky has dubbed the instability of conventional finance as "endogenous instability" because conventional finance experiences a three-phased cycle: relative calm, speculation and fictitious expansion, and then crisis and bankruptcy. Bankruptcy in conventional finance is not limited to the private sector as governments can also face bankruptcy. Again, recent historical analysis has demonstrated that all financial, banking and currency crises are, at their core, a crisis arising from debt.[25] In the recent past, the widespread bankruptcies of many developing countries have entailed debt cancellation or forgiveness. This is often because governments that borrowed at what were considered reasonable debt levels (normally as measured by debt/GDP) later found themselves in an unsustainable debt spiral as a result of increased debt-service

23 Boogle (2012).

24 For good discussion on antifragility of risk-sharing finance, see Rafi, Mirakhor, and Askari (2016).

25 Reinhart and Rogoff 2009.

obligations. Some countries even found themselves with debt levels many times larger than the original amount of borrowed principal.

Keynes was not the first to have noted the instability of risk transfer capitalism. However, he was the first to have so succinctly analyzed the causes as emerging from the financial sector. Minsky went much further in detailing how the risk- transfer finance creates inherent instability and fragility in a capitalist system. Debt-leverage drives the cyclical evolution of the economy as its firms move from being "robust units", as they have little or no debt, to become "hedge units," as they assume ever larger debt but still able to service their debt, to "Ponzi finance units," where these firms can no longer service their debt. At this point the system is rendered fragile and, ultimately, leads to crisis.[26]

An Islamic economic system has the potential of greater stability than its conventional counterpart. The main reason for this is the fact that when production is financed entirely by risk-return sharing or equity finance, in the case of rapid changes in the price, assets and liabilities both move in the same direction simultaneously – thus the financial structure adjusts in tandem on both sides of the ledger. A number of analytic models have investigated the adjustment process and have demonstrated the stability of Islamic finance in response to shocks as well as the growth implication of such a system in closed and open economy situations (Khan, 1987; Khan and Mirakhor 1987, Mirakhor, 1990).

A financial system based on risk sharing would be more stable than one based on risk transfer and on risk shifting. A main source of stability is the elimination of the interest-rate-based credit system, which has evidently created financial crises, distortions, unemployment, inflation, and unjust wealth redistribution (Mirakhor et al., 2012). In essence, risk sharing is a "contractual or societal arrangement whereby the outcome of a random event is borne collectively by a group of individuals or entities participating in an exchange contract, or by individuals or entities in a community" (Askari et al., 2011, pp. 70–71). Agents share benefits and costs in equitable proportions *a la* Arrow (1971) where efficient risk sharing means allocation of risk according to the ability of individual to bear it. In Islamic finance, there are different mechanisms for risk-sharing, including the muḍārabah and mushārakah financial instruments for equity partnership initiatives. There are also other redistributive institutions for risk-sharing such as obligatory levies of zakāh, and non-compulsory benevolent loans qarḍ ḥasan and charity ṣadaqah, and institutional endowment waqf. Finally, the inheritance levies constitute also a form of intergenerational redistribution of wealth and risks among the inheritors (Maghrebi & Mirakhor, 2015).

In addition to these problems, risk-transfer debt-economy faces other challenges. Its financial system is pro-cyclical and exacerbates the phases of the business cycle. It produces excess credit during the boom phase which, combined with leverage,

---

26 For detail of Minsky's thoughts see, Minsky (1982) and Minsky (1986).

create pressure on prices, strengthening inflation. In the down phase of the cycle, the system creates credit crunch and adds additional force to the downward movement of aggregate demand. Moreover, the system creates massive opportunities for mismatches in the balance sheet of its banking system which again serve to exacerbate cyclical phases. Finally, the risk-transfer financial system is riddled with moral hazards and other elements of principal-agent problem. Much of the moral hazard issues stem from the fact that the credit creation (central banks) and its allocation (private financial institutions, including banks) functions are separate. Central banks (monetary authorities) have a different objective function (price stability) than the private financial institutions (profits). This separation of creation and allocation of credit reduces the potency of monetary policy because the dissonance between the two objective functions make it difficult for the monetary authorities to achieve their aim since the financial institutions are at the core of the transmission mechanism of monetary policy. This has been the experience of nearly all countries in the post-crisis period where monetary easing aimed at inducing higher private investment has not been very successful. Adding to the strength of the moral hazard issue is the deposit guarantee the banking sector of these economies need to, ostensibly, protect the economy's payment system.

2.4 Safeguarding Against Financial Repression

It is clear that the nexus of fractional reserve banking – credit creation – debt creation – leverage – financial instability – financial crisis is the cause of financial instability and fragility. The evidence for this process is the massive debt build up in the world economy estimated to be US$ 50 Trillion larger than the period of run up to the 2007/2008 crisis. Recently, many books and articles (see for example, Adair Turner: Between Debt and the Devil, 2016) have appeared focusing on the dangers of "excessive debt" without realizing that the culprit is mispricing of financial resources attributable to the interest rate mechanism. If there is an eternal proposition of economics, it is that mispricing of any resource gives rise to disequilibrium and misallocation of that resource. Excess debt is a clear indication that financial resources are not priced to reflect their opportunity costs. By definition, opportunity cost of a resource is the price it could receive from its best alternative use. By this definition, the opportunity cost of financial resources is what these resources could earn in the real sector of the economy that is its rate of return in the production sector. According to the data-base Morningstar, global rate of return to the industrial sector averaged about 14 percent in 2014. Compare this with the negative interest rate prevailing in major economies. Is there then a surprise that there is "excess debt"?

Financial repression, the deviation of "administered" interest rate from the "market" interest rate, leads to market distortions thus discouraging saving, investment and economic growth. In the succeeding decades of fierce application of financial liberalization, a basic question never asked how and in what sense did the "market" rate of interest reflected the true opportunity cost of financial resources and whether indeed deviation between it and prevailing rates of interest truly measured the magnitude of financial repression. To the extent that neither the financial sector nor the governments are paying the true opportunity cost of financial resources, there is financial repression. In that sense, there is nothing new about "financial repression". It has existed and will continue to exist until and unless reforms force true "liberalization" of markets where prices all reflect opportunity costs.

Islamic finance addresses this mispricing and its consequent misallocation of financial resources through its requirement of materiality that financial resources must be used directly in production; a one-to-one correspondence between the financial sector and the real sector of the economy. This means that the rate of return to finance is determined by its productivity in the production sector rather than predetermined by policy or the monopoly power of rentiers. Islamic finance rules out maturity, value, and balance sheet asset-liability mismatches that create the dynamics of volatility. The result would be an antifragile and robust financial system by requiring risk sharing among participants in transactions each of which will have to have skin-in-the-game. Consequently, financial resources receive their true opportunity cost in a market-determined process where these resources are priced according to their most productive use. This process puts an end to financialization, financial repression and excessive reliance of financial activities on speculation.

2.5 Promoting Cooperation among Economic Agents

At the same time, it should be noted that there is an important moral dimension to Islamic risk sharing as it strengthens social solidarity by enhancing cooperation among all economic agents, which would also go some way in easing the coordination problem.[27] Moreover, when risk is spread by means of risk/reward-sharing contracts, closer coordination is forged between the real and financial sectors of the economy. Risk transfer by means of interest-based debt contracts, in contrast, weakens that linkage. Particularly when risk transfer is combined with high leverage, the growth of interest-based debt contracts and their pure financial derivatives – those with little or no connection to real assets – outpace the growth of the real sector, leaving the liabilities in the economy a large multiple of real assets needed to validate them.

Arguably, it can be claimed that through its rules (institutions) and ethics governing resource allocation, property rights, production, exchange, distribution and redistribution, financial transactions, and market behavior, the Islamic paradigm

27 For detail of these and other rules governing the economy see Mirakhor and Askari (2010: 158–70); and Mirakhor (2010: 8–19).

orients all economic relations toward risk-reward sharing. This can be said to be a logical consequence of insistence on the unity of mankind since through risk-sharing social solidarity is promoted through Islamic finance. “Massive risk can carry with it benefits far beyond that of reducing poverty and diminishing income inequality. The reduction of risk on risk on a greater scale would provide substantial impetus to human and economic progress,” (Shiller, 2003, p. 9). The most meaningful human progress is achieved when all distinctions the basis of race, color, income and wealth, and social-political status are obliterated to the point where humanity, in convergence with the Qur’anic declaration (Qur’an, 31:28), truly views itself as one and united. It can be argued that implementation of Islamic finance will promote maximum risk sharing, thus create the potential for enhanced social solidarity (Askari, Iqbal and Mirakhor, 2009).

2.6 Equitable Distribution and Enhancing Prosperity

Much has been said about damages of high income/wealth inequality to society. It erodes trust, creates barriers to social mobility for current and future generations, increases social resentment, undermines effective governance, creates a “winner-take-all” society, and breaks down social solidarity. The notion that financial stability is essential to economic growth, and the fact that the conventional financial system is inherently unstable, raises the question of whether the optimal mobilization of resources and financial stability are better achieved through risk sharing than through risk transfer and risk shifting. The central argument here is that if economic growth can be achieved only through the optimal allocation of resources, then risk sharing should be essential to the sharing of prosperity.

Risk sharing is shown as an effective method of expanding the opportunity and participation of agents in economic growth and development and sharing of the fruits of prosperity.[28] Two forms of redistribution, i.e. income-based versus asset-based have been debated in the literature with income-based redistribution dominating the conventional thinking. Bowles (2012) argues that there are distinct advantages to asset-based redistribution compared to income-based redistribution. The most important is former’s potential for combining equity and efficiency. Islamic finance provides a comprehensive approach to asset-based redistribution through risk sharing leading to achieving shared prosperity, while reducing inequality and poverty.

While risk sharing enables Islamic finance to promote economic justice and social participation, the asset backed equity-financing nature of Islamic finance is

28 For an in depth discussion of risk-sharing finance and equitable distribution and prosperity, see Iqbal, Omar, Manap, and Alawode (2018). See Mirakhor (2018) and Maghrebi and Mirakhor (2018).

conducive to financial system stability as discussed above. It is the risk-sharing and asset-backed nature of Islamic finance that allows for a participative securitization process that provides different segments of the society with fair opportunities to share economic prosperity. The allocation of risk commensurate to the idiosyncratic abilities to bear losses is arguably more conducive to a socially inclusive financial system. While systematic risk cannot be eliminated, it is collective risk taking and individual risk aversion that promote more efficient mobilization of resources, and more equitable sharing of economic risk and prosperity.

3 Conclusion

What is clear is that the present form of capitalism and the overall society in which it is embedded need to regain a "moral sense." The challenge is to awaken individual and collective consciousness to the moral compass inherent in "being human". Unfortunately, it is not only the willingness to ignore unethical finance and business practices that do enormous harm, it is also the fact that the present moral state of societies encourages distrust, fear and a cynical attitude, leading to widespread willingness to engage in unfair, harmful and even illegal behavior in the marketplace.

How can finance become sacralised? The answer lies in paradigm governing finance. Sacralized finance requires a paradigm that focuses on: concerns for others rather than on pure self-interest; morality and ethics; giving instead of taking; cooperation rather than competition; being instead of having; and sharing the risks and uncertainties of life rather transferring or shifting them to others. Finance is sacralised (sanctified) when all the elements of the paradigm are based on the rules prescribed by the Creator. Risk sharing Islamic finance meets these conditions.

There are strong arguments that risk-sharing finance such as Islamic finance would be better alternative to a risk-transfer or risk-shifting system because of several important characteristics, such as ensuring economic and social justice, financial stability, mutuality, commitment, and common good objectives. A risk-sharing contract mutually commits the participants to share resources, risks, and rewards. Because everyone has skin in the game, the governance structure will, most likely, be horizontal rather than vertical providing agility, flexibility and greater accountability in the management and operations of the venture subject of the contract. Moreover, all participants work to gain the most out of the operations of the contract since they all stand to gain from effective, efficient, and productive outcomes. Due to these characteristics, risk sharing resolves the issues of moral hazard associated with principal-agent problem since the parties to the contract are functioning as both. As well, in a risk-sharing system where financing is being provided by shareholders, there is no incentive to withdraw financing when there may be potential downturn as there would be in a risk-transfer system. Similarly, during upside, financing would be available commensurate with increased productive activities only, unlike the risk-transfer system which provides greater credit during the boom and withdraws credit during the bust phases of the business cycle.[29] Hence, risk sharing reduces or eliminates pro-cyclicality of finance. Also important is the fact that in the absence of a rentier class, risk-sharing finance improves income and wealth distribution thus reducing inequality.

Risk sharing also reduces or eliminates the coordination problem since in a risk-sharing contract savers and investors are both involved as owners. There is no rentier demanding a premium for providing financing. All parties involved work for the objective of greatest return to be shared by all. As mentioned earlier, risk sharing creates an opportunity for firms, at micro level, and the economy, at macro level, to experience X-efficiency and total factor productivity gains that increase output and growth. Another major source of output growth due to risk sharing is that the focus of contracts shifts from creditor-borrower to investor-entrepreneur relations and from credit rating/collateral to the viability/profitability of the project subject of contract. Consequently, large number of projects that in a risk-transfer financial system would be rationed out of the market due to lack of collateral or credit record would find funding in a risk-sharing system.

References

Arrow, Kenneth (1971), Essays in the theory of risk-bearing, Markham Publishing Company, Chicago, USA.

Akerlof, George A. 1970. "The Market for 'Lemons': Quality Uncertainty and the Market Mechanism." The Quarterly Journal of Economics 84: 488–500.

Alaabed, Alaa, Mansur Masih, and Abbas Mirakhor (2016) "Investigating risk shifting in Islamic banks in the dual banking system of OIC countries: An application of two-stage dynamic GMM" Risk Management, Vol. 18, No. 236.

Aragon, George A. 2014. Financial Ethics: A Positivist Analysis. New York: Oxford University Press.

Askari, Hossein, Zamir Iqbal, and Abbas Mirakhor (2009) *New Issues in Islamic Finance and Economics: Progress and Challenges*. Singapore: John Wiley & Sons.

Askari, Hossein, Zamir Iqbal, Noureddine Krichene, and Abbas Mirakhor (2012), *Risk Sharing in Finance: The Islamic Finance Alternative*. Singapore: John Wiley & Sons.

Askari, Hossein, Zamir Iqbal, and Abbas Mirakhor, (2015) *An Introduction to Islamic Economics*, John Wiley (Asia), Singapore.

Askari, Hossein, Zamir Iqbal, and Abbas Mirakhor, (2016), *Challenges in Economic and Financial Policy Formulation: An Islamic Perspective*, Palgrave, New York, USA.

Bogle, John C. (2012), The Clash of the Cultures: Investment vs. Speculation, John Wiley and Sons, New York, USA.

Bowles, S. (2012), The New Economics of Inequality and Redistribution. New York: Cambridge University Press.

29 See Stiglitz (1988).

Camerer, C., Loewenstein, G., & Prelec, D. (2005). Neuroeconomics: How neuroscience can inform economics. *Journal of Economic Literature*, *43*(1), 9–64.
Chapra, M. Umer (2008), "Ethics And Economics: An Islamic Perspective," Islamic Economic Studies Vol. 16 No. 1 & 2, Aug. 2008 & Jan. 2009.
Hoepner, Andreas G. F. and Wilson, John O. S., Social, Environmental, Ethical and Trust (SEET) Issues in Banking: An Overview (October 2, 2010). Research Handbook For Banking And Governance, J.R. Barth, C. Lin and C. Wihlborg, eds., Edward Elgar Publishing, Forthcoming. Available at SSRN: https://ssrn.com/abstract=1686240.
Iqbal, Zamir and Abbas Mirakhor (2011), An Introduction to Islamic Finance: Theory and Practice, 2nd ed., John Wiley and Sons (Asia), Singapore.
Iqbal, Zamir and Abbas Mirakhor (2017), Ethical Dimensions of Islamic Finance: Theory and Practice, Palgrave, New York, USA.
Iqbal, Zamir, Azmi Omar, Turkhan Ali Abdul Manap, and Abayomi A. Alawode (2018), Islamic Finance: A Catalyst for Shared Prosperity?" Islamic Development Bank, Jeddah, Kingdom of Saudi Arabia.
Kahneman, D. (2003). Maps of bounded rationality: Psychology for behavioral economics. *American Economic Review*, *93*(5), 1449–1475.
Kamali, Mohammad Hashim (2011), Ethics and Finance: Perspectives of the Sharīʿah and Its Higher Objectives (Maqāṣid), 8th Kuala Lumpur Islamic Finance Forum (KLIFF), 3–6 October 2011.
Keynes, John Maynard (1930) "A Treaties on Money". Macmillan, London.
Keynes, John Maynard (1936), *The General Theory of Employment, Interest, and Money* (London: Macmillan, St. Martin's Press, 1970).
Khan, Mohsin (1987) *Islamic Interest Free Banking: A Theoretical Analysis*, In Khan, M. and Mirakhor, eds., Theoretical Studies in Islamic Banking and Finance. Houston, TX: IRIS Books.
Khan, Mohsin and Abbas Mirakhor (1987), *Theoretical Studies in Islamic Banking and Finance*, IRIS Books, Houston, TX, USA.
Maghrebi, N., and Mirakhor, A. (2015). Risk Sharing and Shared Prosperity in Islamic Finance. *Islamic Economic Studies*, *23*(2), 85–115.
Maghrebi, Nabil, Abbas Mirakhor, and Zamir Iqbal (2016), Intermediate Islamic Finance, John Wiley (Asia), Singapore.
Maghrebi, Nabil and Abbas Mirakhor (2018), "Stability of Islamic Finance and Shared Prosperity," in Zamir Iqbal, Azmi Omar, Turkhan Ali Abdul Manap, and Abayomi A. Alawode (eds.), Islamic Finance: A Catalyst for Shared Prosperity?," Islamic Development Bank, Jeddah, Kingdom of Saudi Arabia. pp. 83–107.
Minsky, Hyman (1982). Can it Happen Again? Routledge, New York: USA.
Minsky, Hyman (1986). Stabilizing an Unstable Economy. Yale University Press, New Haven: USA.
Mirakhor, Abbas (1989) "General Characteristics of An Islamic Economic System" in Baqir Al-Hasani and Abbas Mirakhor (eds) *Essays on Iqtisad: The Islamic Approach to Economic Problems*. Nur Corp., MD, USA: 45–80.
Mirakhor, A., (1990), "Equilibrium in a Non-Interest Open Economy," IMF, published in Journal of King Abdulaziz University: Islamic Economics (1993), vol. 5, pp. 3–23.
Mirakhor, Abbas (2004), "Islamic Finance and Instrumentalization of Islamic Redistributive Institutions." Paper presented at Ibn Rushd Memorial Lecture, London, April.
Mirakhor, Abbas (2010). Whither Islamic Finance. Presented at the Securities Commission of Malaysia, March 2010.
Mirakhor, Abbas (2011). "Epistemology of Finance: Misreading Smith". Islamic Finance Review, vol.1, 9–15.
Mirakhor, Abbas (2018), "Understanding the Potential of Risk Sharing to Attain Shared Prosperity," in Zamir Iqbal, Azmi Omar, Turkhan Ali Abdul Manap, and Abayomi A. Alawode (eds.), Islamic

Finance: A Catalyst for Shared Prosperity?," Islamic Development Bank, Jeddah, Kingdom of Saudi Arabia. pp. 53–67.
Mirakhor, Abbas, and Alaa Alaabed. 2013. "The Credit Crisis: An Islamic Perspective." In Global Islamic Finance Report (GIFR) 2013. London, England: Edbiz Consulting Limited.
Mirakhor, Abbas and Hossein Askari (2010), *Islam and the Path to Human and Economic Development* (New York: Palgrave Macmillan).
Mirakhor, Abbas and Krichene, N., (2009), The Recent Crisis: Lessons for Islamic Finance. Islamic Financial Services Board. 2nd Public Lecture on Financial Policy and Stability. Kuala Lumpur: Malaysia.
Mirakhor, A., Krichene, N., and Shaukat, M. (2012). Unsustainability of the regime of interest-based debt financing. *ISRA International Journal of Islamic Finance*, *4*(2), 25–52.
Naqvi, Syed N.H., (1981), *Ethics and Economics: An Islamic Synthesis*, Leicester, U.K.: The Islamic Foundation.
Naqvi, S.N.H. 2003. *Perspectives on Morality and Human Well-Being.* Markfield, Leicester, UK: The Islamic Foundation.
Palley, T.J., (2007), "Financialization: What It Is and Why It Matters," Working Paper no. 252 (Annandale-on-Hudson, NY: The Levy Economics Institute).
Piketty, Thomas (2013), Le Capital au XXIe Siὲle. Paris: Éditions du Seul, 2013. Translated by Arthur Goldhammer as Capital in the Twenty-First Century. Cambridge, MA: The Belknap Press of Harvard University Press, 2014.
Rafi, Umar, Abbas Mirakhor, and Hossein Askari (2016), "Radical uncertainty, non-predictability, antifragility and risk-sharing Islamic finance," PSL Quarterly Review, vol. 69 n. 278 (December, 2016), 337–372.
Reinhart, C., and K. Rogoff (2009) *This Time is Different: Eight Centuries of Financial Folly.* Princeton University Press.
Shiller, Robert J. (2003) The New Financial Order: Risk in the 21st Century, Princeton University Press, Princeton, USA.
Stiglitz, Joseph E. (1988) "Why Financial Structure Matters". Journal of Economic Perspectives, Vol. 2, No. 4.
Stiglitz, Joseph E. (2019), "People, Power, and Profits: Progressive Capitalism for an Age of Discontent," W. W. Norton, New York, USA.
Tobin, J. (1984). On the efficiency of the financial system. Lloyds Bank Review, (153), 1–15.
Turner, Adair (2016), Between Debt and the Devil: Money, Credit, and Fixing Global Finance, Princeton University Press, Princeton, USA.
World Inequality Database (2018), World Inequality Report 2018, https://wir2018.wid.world/.

Mohamad Akram Laldin

Chapter 2: Ethics in the Light of *Maqasid Al-Shari'ah*: A Case Study of Islamic Economics and Finance

1 Introduction

Shari'ah is a complete code of life that encompasses *al-ahkam al-i'tiqadiyyah* or sanctions relating to belief, *ahkam al-'amaliyyah* or sanctions relating to conducts and worship, and *al-ahkam al-akhlaqiyyah* or sanctions relating to moral and ethics. In fact, ethics (*akhlaq*) is considered the third building block in Islam after faith (*aqidah*) and law (*Shari'ah*). Islam accords them a high value and consider them one of the objectives of legislation (Lahsasna, 2013).

Muslim scholars and economists unanimously agreed that the Islamic finance industry does not exists merely to capitalize the huge financial market rather it aims to achieve a greater and universally beneficial purposes through its various commandments, exhortations, prohibitions and doctrines. Al-Ghazali is widely acknowledged as the first to attempt to systematize thinking about the *maqāṣid* of the Shari'ah. In *al-Mustasfa* he classified the *maqāṣid* based on a hierarchy of priority into essentials *(ḍarūriyyāt)*, complementaries *(ḥājiyyāt)* and embellishments *(taḥsiniyyāt)*. He further stated that essentials *(ḍarūriyyāt)* involve preservation of five values namely faith or religion (*din*), life (*nafs*) lineage (*nasl*) intellect (*'aql*) property (*mal*) (Al-Khelaifi, 2004; Laldin, 2010).

The Shari'ah objective relating directly to Islamic finance obviously falls within the ambit of protection of wealth (*hifz al-mal*) (Al-Khelaifi, 2004; Laldin, 2010; Dusuki and Bouheraoua, 2011; Ahmed, 2011). However, the necessity of incorporating various aspects of sustainable development instruments into financing decision-making has always been envisaged in order to ensure the interconnectivity of the other rubrics in Islamic finance consideration. Recently, ethical and responsible financing and investment have been the central attention in business and finance. Several investment approaches such as responsible investment, socially responsible investing (SRI), impact investing, sustainable investment, ethical investment, green investment and value-based intermediary (VBI) have been developed to combine financing return and moral impact. More importantly, the use of green energy has become an integral

Note: The preparation of this chapter was assisted by Dr Fares Djafri (fares@isra.my), Dr Said Adekunle Mikail (saidmikail@isra.my) and Safiudin Ahmad Fuad (safiudin@isra.my) from International Shari'ah Research Academy for Islamic Finance, Malaysia.

https://doi.org/10.1515/9783110593419-002

part of the UN's Sustainable Development Goals (SDGs), which have been incorporated into the economic growth plans of many nations.

This writing discusses ethics in business and finance in the light of the objectives of Shari'ah (*maqasid as-Shari'ah*). The concept, components and categorisations of *maqasid* are also discussed in brief. It explains the key ethical principles underlying Islamic finance from Islamic perspectives. The Shari'ah mechanisms including the fundamental principles in dealings and human interaction to ensure wellbeing of every individuals are also discussed.

The last section discusses various sustainable development instruments such as socially responsible investing (SRI), principles of environmental, social and corporate governance (ESG), and value-based intermediation (VBI), with some examples on key roles each instrument plays in achieving sustainable development goals (SDGs) and relevancy from *maqasid* perspectives.

2 Overview of Ethics

2.1 Definition of Ethics

Linguistically, the word ethics is derived from the Greek term *ethos*, which means character (Haron, Musa & Shaarani, 2013). Technically, ethics is a branch of philosophy which studies human behaviour in differentiating good and bad. There are two approaches in achieving the answer, where philosophers (in theory) would raise questions on the nature of the issue and attempt to provide rational arguments in determining which is good and evil. On the contrary, theologians based on religions are provided the answers upfront by their scriptures and the scholars then attempt to justify them in practice (Ansary, Sairally, Habib & Furqani, 2017).

Ethics is synonymous to the Arabic word, *khuluq* (plural *akhlāq*). The word *khuluq* is mentioned in the Qur'ān specifically to show the very characteristic of the Prophet Muhammad:And indeed, you are of a great moral character. (Al-Qalam, 68:4)

The word *khuluq* can be defined as a state of the soul which determines human actions. This state is neither the soul nor the action, since the soul is innate while character is a state of the soul that causes the soul to perform its actions. Al-Farabī in relating the human soul to his action mentions that the condition of the soul whereby a man does good deeds are the virtues while those which he does evil and wrong are the vices (Omar, 2013). The soul is thus driven by the character in performing its action, in which *akhlāq* is synonymously used to showcase deeds which are good. In a broader sense, the Qur'ān also uses other terms to describe goodness such as *khayr* (goodness), *birr* (righteousness), *qisṭ* (equity), *'adl* (justice), *haqq* (truth), *ma'rūf* (known and approved), and *taqwā* (piety) (Fakhry, 1994).

2.2 Source and Origin of Islamic Ethics

In Islam, ethics find its roots – either implicitly or explicitly – in the primary sources of Islamic which are the Qur'ān and the sunnah. Even though neither of them provides a systematic ethical theory, Muslim scholars relied on them in formulating a framework by examining the fundamental ethical questions found within the verses of the Qur'ān and the teachings of the Prophet (Al-Dagistani, 2018). Many verses in the Qur'ān explains the multiple aspects of ethics and the explanations are found in different places throughout the 114 chapters in the Qur'ān. Even the Sharīʿah which is often referred to as a set of law, is first and foremost an encompassing ethos derived from the primary source (Sajoo, 2009). The Qur'ān mentions:

> Worship Allah and associate nothing with Him, and to parents do good, and to relatives, orphans, the needy, the near neighbour, the neighbour farther away, the companion at your side, the traveller, and those whom your right hands possess. Indeed, Allah does not like those who are self-deluding and boastful. (Al-Mā'idah, 5:36)

> The verse highlights two parts of Islamic ethics, namely the relation between a *mukallaf* (an accountable being) towards his creator and with his fellow mankind. As the servant of Allah, Muslims are ethically obligated to give their full commitment to serve Him and not to associate others to the virtues that is only fit for Allah. The verse also stresses on the importance of human interaction and humility, treating others in manners that is full of compassion as fellow human being. The Qur'an also highlights the responsibilities of those who are wealthy towards the poor: "And those within whose wealth is a known right. For the petitioner and the deprived." (Al-Maʿārij, 70:24–25)

Besides that, the Qur'ān provides some guidance in the form of prohibition which also shapes the Islamic ethical values in relation to life and justice within a society:

> O you who have believed, if there comes to you a disobedient one with information, investigate, lest you harm a people out of ignorance and become, over what you have done, regretful. (Al-Ḥujurāt, 49:6)

In translating these verses of ethical values comprising religious duties, social relations, moral reasoning, justice and human behaviour in a practical form, Prophet Muhammad becomes the main reference as he is the manifestation of the ethical principles put forth in the Qur'ān. As a human being living within the community, the Prophet set forth an example through his speech and behaviour which influences the Muslim community, forming a guideline to be followed throughout the generations of mankind. To this, the Qur'ān mentions:

> There has certainly been for you in the Messenger of Allah an excellent pattern for anyone whose hope is in Allah and the Last Day and [who] remembers Allah often. (Al-Ahzāb, 33:21)

In implementing the ethical values among mankind, numerous *ḥadīth* attributed to the Prophet can be seen where he emphasizes on just, integrity, accountability, righteousness and good deeds. This is evident based on a *ḥadīth* of the Prophet: "I was sent to perfect good character." (Al-Bukhārī, *ḥadīth* no. 207)

Among the teachings of Prophet emphasizing ethical values are:

> [Allah says:] "I am the opponent of three on the Day of Resurrection, and if I am someone's opponent I will defeat him: A man who makes promises in My Name, then proves treacherous; a man who sells a free man and consumes his price; and a man who hires a worker, makes use to him, then does not give him his wages." (Al-Bukhārī, *ḥadīth* no. 2227)

> "Kindness is not to be found in anything but that it adds to its beauty and it is not withdrawn from anything, but it makes it defective." (Muslim, *ḥadīth* no. 2594).

Furthermore, the Prophet (SAW) emphasized the rightful position of those with highest ethical value as mentioned in multiple *ḥadīth*:

> "Shall I tell you about the most beloved of you to me and the closest to my assembly on the Day of Resurrection?" They were silent, so he (pbuh) repeated himself two or three times. They said, "Yes, O Messenger of Allah." He said, "Those with the best character." (Ahmad, No. *ḥadīth* no. 6735)

These verses of the Qur'ān and *ḥadīth* forms a foundation on which Islamic ethics is built, guiding mankind to achieving the greatest level of moral and ethical life. Izutsu (2004) mentions how a large part of the Qur'ānic teaching focus on ethical values in daily life:

> In a certain sense, the Qur'ān as a whole is dominated by the very spirit of ḥilm (forbearing). The constant exhortation to kindness (iḥsān) in human relations, the emphasis laid on justice ('adl), the forbidding of wrongful violence (ẓulm), the bidding of abstinence and control of passions, the criticism of groundless pride and arrogance – all are concrete manifestations of this spirit of ḥilm.

2.3 Evolution of Islamic Ethics

The discussion on ethics in the Islamic world was largely sparked by the translation of writings by Greek philosophers in the 9th century. Among the influential works of the time includes among others, a compilation and translation by Hunayn Ibn Ishāq titled *Nawādir al-Falāsifah* (Anecdote of the Philosophers), the renown Muslim philosopher al-Kindī who compiled Socratic excerpts titled *Alfāz Suqrāt* and a work attributed to Pythagoras, Socrates, Plato, Aristotle, Alexander the Great, Hippocrates and Galen titled *Ṣiwān al-Hikmah* (The Closet of Wisdom) by Abū Sulaymān al-Sijistānī. Even though their ethical views are derived from Greek philosophy, they did not ignore the authority of the Qur'ān and Sunnah. In fact, scholars of the time use quotations from the Qur'ān and *ḥadīth* to support their claim (Fakhry, 1994).

Further progress in an effort to establish Islamic value of ethics as a new branch of knowledge, Muslim scholars then studied and published multiple books with the *Tahdhīb al-Akhlāq* by Miskawayh being the forefather of a structured Islamic ethics, detaching itself from other disciplines to become its own field of study. He was then followed by *Makārim al-Akhlāq* by Ibn Abī Dunyā, *Akhlāq Jalālī* by al-Dawwānī and others who based their writings on him (Mohd, 2013, p. 391). However, probably the most well-known writing on Islamic ethics comes from the magnum opus of al-Ghazālī titled *Iḥyā' 'Ulūm al-Dīn* (The revival of religious science). Al-Ghazālī aims at forming a religious ethics consisting of comprehensive theoretical knowledge that provides practical instruction to achieve spiritual purity, moral conduct and inevitably a state of true fulfilment and happiness. He has skilfully knit together philosophical reasoning, Aristotelian ethics, Qur'ānic fundamental, theological doctrines and Sufi teachings (Al-Dagistani, 2018), establishing a more comprehensive understanding on Islamic ethics.

2.4 Islamic Ethics and Other Traditions

> In terms of ethical value, Islam and the major religions in the world seems to confirm on most parts of the spectrum, with the belief in God being the centre of each religion and promotion of goodness and preventing evil. The Qur'ān mentions in reference to a part of the people of the book (the Christians and the Jews): "They believe in Allah and the Last Day, and enjoin right conduct and forbid indecency, and vie one with another in good works. These are of the righteous." (Al-Imrān, 3:114)

Furthermore, the message of righteousness and doing good that was brought by Islam are well-known even before the message by Prophet Muhammad was conveyed. This implies that the divine commands in the Qur'ān are reasoned, in line with the human ethical knowledge. This can be seen as the term *ma'rūf* which, although appears thirty-two times in the Qur'ān, was not given an explanation by classical commentators as it is taken for granted, probably as it is already well understood by the community. (Al-Attar, 2010).

However, Islamic ethical value does defer from others in a few major aspects. Oppose to the Greek philosophy, scholars such as al-Kindī views that the world was created in time, denouncing that the world is everlasting (Hourani, 2007). This is because the view of Greek philosophers is in contradiction with Islamic value whereby Allah as the creator holds the virtue of *qidam* (without beginning), and thus everything else in this world was created and comes after the Almighty.

In summary, there are five key axioms (see Table 2.1) that guide the ethical philosophy of Islam (Beekun, 2003) which encompasses religious identification.

These values guide the Muslims in leading a righteous life in this world, in hope of a better life in the hereafter.

Table 2.1: Axioms of Islamic Ethical Philosophy.

Axiom	Definition
Unity	It is the concept of *tawhīd* (oneness), whereby all aspects of a man's life including political, economic, social and religious are unified. It connects not only among the Muslim communities in submitting to Allah, but also among different communities in unity towards the universal character of the Islamic message. A Muslim will also maintain the same condition of piety and ethical regardless of being in a mosque or during business, for his fear and love towards Allah will guide him so. It is the vertical dimension of Islam.
Equilibrium	Also known as *ʿadl,* describes the overall harmony throughout the universe. It can also be seen as social harmony, striking a balance between two extreme sides as mentioned in the Qurʾān as *ummatan wasaṭan* (a just and moderate nation). A practice in daily life of a Muslim practicing the concept of *ʿadl* is by being just in doing business, fulfilling the measurement and weight for its price. This is the horizontal dimension of Islam.
Free will	It denotes a man's ability in making judgement and carrying out an action upon his own conviction, by carrying out its duty as Allah's vicegerent on earth. A Muslim practicing his free will is bound by his submission to Allah, thus holding firm to the axioms of unity and equilibrium. By applying his free will, man has a freedom to make good or break his contract. But as a Muslim, he will keep his promise so as not to go against the moral code laid out by Allah.
Responsibility	Refers to a man's accountability for his action. Any form of action is bound for a reaction. Thus, a Muslim that performs an unethical behaviour should be accountable for his action, not being able to shift the blame to other parties.
Benevolence	*Ihsān*. An act of kindness which benefits another without any obligation nor for any benefits. An act of benevolence can be done by reducing a debt owed by another, lifting him from his hardship and freeing him from his debt.

Source: Naqvi, 1981.

3 Maqasid al-Shari'ah: Concepts, Components and Classifications

3.1 Literal Meaning

The phrase Maqāṣid as-Shari'ah combines two words, Maqāṣid and al-Shari'ah. The first word is the plural form of Maqsad. The word 'Maqsad' in Arabic means intention, objective, aim, and ends. The word Shari'ah has been defined earlier. Thus, the literal translation of Maqāṣid as-Shari'ah is the objectives of Islamic law.

3.2 Technical Meaning

Ibn Ashur (2004, p. 165) defined Maqāṣid as-Shari'ah from two aspects – general and specific. The first (general) aspect of Maqāṣid is defined as "the purpose and wisdom behind the enactment of all or most of the Shari'ah rulings." The second (specific) definition is defined by Ibn Ashur as "the specific modes aimed by the lawgiver to achieve specific benefits or to preserve their prime interests in their daily activities so that their individual interests would not eliminate their general interests as a result of negligence or individual whims and desires."

The most comprehensive definitions as mentioned by Ayubi (1998, p. 37) is: "Maqāṣid as-Shari'ah is the meaning, wisdom and the related, sought in enactment - whether general or specific - to achieve the best interests of humankind."

Further Ibn Qayyim (1423) said: "The Shari'ah is based on wisdom and achieving peoples' welfare in this life and in the hereafter. The Shari'ah is all about justice, mercy, wisdom and serving the interest of all human beings. Thus, any ruling that replaces justice with injustice, mercy with its opposite, serving the interest to causing harm, or wisdom with nonsense, is a ruling that does not belong to the Shari'ah even if it is claimed to be so according to some interpretations."

3.3 Categorisation of Maqāṣid as-Shari'ah

Scholars have categorised Maqāṣid as-Shari'ah into three categories: The essentials (*Daruriyyat*), the needs/complementary (*Hajiyyat*) and the embellishments (*Tahsiniyyat*).

3.3.1 Essentials (*Daruriyyat*)

Ibn Ashur (2004) defined Daruriyyat as: "Things whose realization is essential for the community both collectively and individually, the social fabric of the community will not function properly if there is any defect in these things."

The essentials are the values on which the religion and worldly affairs of the people depend upon, in which their neglect will lead to total disruption and disorder and could lead to evil. These values must therefore be preserved and protected. All measures to safeguard them must be taken at different levels government, organisations and individually.

Daruriyyat can be further divided into the protection of the five fundamental values (al-Daruriyyat al-Khamsah), which are necessary to human life. These five values are:

1. Promotion and preservation of religion (*Din*)
2. Promotion and preservation of life (*Nafs*)
3. Promotion and preservation of dignity or lineage (*'Ird*)

4. Promotion and preservation of intellect (*'Aql*)
5. Promotion and preservation of property (*Mal*)

Imam Al Ghazali reported to have said: "Preventing the loss of these five fundamentals and protecting them can never be neglected in any religious community (*Millah*) or legal system that is meant for the good and well-being (Salah) of human beings, and this would be a consideration of a Maslaha that we know by necessity was intended by the Shari'ah, not on the basis of one single proof or particular rule, but on multiple proofs that are beyond enumeration."

3.3.2 The complementary Interests (*Hajiyyat*)

These are interests that supplement the five essential interests/values which, if neglected, will lead to hardship of the individual or community, but not to the total disruption of normal life.

Examples:
The dispensations or legal excuses (*Rukhsah*) granted by Shari'ah to eliminate hardship and difficulties in certain circumstances such as travelling and sickness:
- Travellers can combine and shorten their five daily prayers (*Jam' wa qasr*) and break their fast in Ramadan
- A sick person can pray in a sitting or sleeping position and break his fast in Ramadan

Examples of *al-Hajiyyat* in the area of *Muamalat*:
- The ban of profiteering/hoarding (*Ihtikar*) for example, or the sale of alcohol so as to prevent its consumption

Example in transactions include contracts that are deemed permissible under *Shari'ah* such as-*Salam* (Islamic forward sale) or *Ijarah* (lease) in consideration of the peoples' needs irrespective of the anomalies present in both transactions.

3.3.3 The Embellishments (*Tahsiniyyah*)

Embellishments (*al-Tahsiniyyah*) are interests which lead to the improvement of society and the attainment of desirable outcomes whether in customary matters or conduct of people.

Some examples of *Tahsiniyyah* include:
- Giving charity to those in need beyond the obligatory *zakat*
- In the aspect of customary matters and relations - a gentle demeanour, pleasant speech and manner, and fair dealings
- Using beautiful, comfortable things, eating delicious food and wearing fine cloths

A lack of al-*Tahsiniyyah* may not interrupt the normal life but might lead to a lack of comfort.

3.4 Maqāṣid Al-Shari'ah in Business Transactions

Unlike the conventional financial system, the philosophical foundation of the Islamic financial system goes beyond the economic and financial aspects of transactions. Rather, it places equal emphasis on the ethical, moral, social and religious dimensions in order to enhance equality and fairness for the good of society.

There are five dimensions within which *Maqāṣid as-Shari'ah* relates to achieving the preservation of wealth (Laldin, 2008). The dimensions are as follows:
1. Preservation of wealth through the protection of ownership
2. Preservation of wealth through acquisition and development
3. Preservation of wealth from damage through risk management and its harmful purposes
4. Preservation of wealth through its circulation
5. Preservation of wealth through its value protection

More elaboration will be under the Shari'ah mechanism for effective implementation of its objective in business and finance.

4 Ethical Principles Underlying Islamic Finance from Maqasid Perspective

Ethics (*Akhlaq*) is considered the third building block in Islam after faith (*Aqidah*) and law (*Shari'ah*). Islam accords them a high value and consider them one of the objectives of legislation. From an Islamic perspective, ethics and moral values are voluntarily and not compulsory upon conducting business except what is considered as an ethical part of the ethical system. In other words, to achieve success (*falah*) and ensure that a person is in the right path, he/she is obliged to promote the good and prevent the wrong doing whether in conducting his/her daily lives or in businesses (Lahsasna, 2013). This is because Allah is a witness to their acts and transactions:

> "And, [O Muhammad], you are not [engaged] in any matter or recite any of the Qur'ān and you [people] do not do any deed except that We are witness over you when you are involved in it. And not absent from your Lord is any [part] of an atom's weight within the earth or within the heaven or [anything] smaller than that or greater but that it is in a clear register" (Yunus, 10:61).

The key ethical principles underlying Islamic finance system are built and inferred from Shari'ah sources that provide detailed commands of dos and don'ts on both legal and ethical level. It represents the fundamental elements in the composition of the religion, and it has been addressed in Shari'ah to govern a person's behaviour in conducting any activities or transactions. Hence, Ethics in business and finance may take different forms such as (1) promoting socio-economic justice (2) advocating fair and transparent financial practices (3) benevolence (*Ihsan*) and making one's work perfect (4) honesty (5) and trust. All these forms are in line with the maqasid al-Shari'ah approach. This section discusses the above key ethical principles for business and finance.

4.1 Promoting Socio-Economic Justice (*al-'adālah*)

Upholding the principle of justice or *'adl* is a basic objective of the Shari'ah. *'Adl* literally means placing things in their right place where they belong. It is to establish a balance by way of fulfilling right and obligations and by eliminating excess and disparity in all sphere of life (Laldin, 2008). Imam al-Ghazali defines justice as to perform what is due by someone and to abstain from injustice (ISRA, 2015). Ibn Qayyim al-Jawziyyah mentioned that justice must be followed and upheld wherever it is found, within or outside the declared provisions of the law. it is the supreme goal and objective of Islam. Therefore, the concept of justice in Shari'ah is not confined to judicial aspects but it covers all area of life including individual justice, social justice and international justice. It is well established principle in Shari'ah and is fused in every aspects of life, including Islamic law, business and finance. This is obvious from the objectives and comprehensive approach that the Qur'ān has taken towards justice (Laldin, 2008). The Qur'ān says:

> We have already sent Our messengers with clear evidences and sent down with them the Scripture and the balance that the people may maintain [their affairs] in justice. (Al-Hadid 57:25)

Practically, The objective of justice (*al-'adl*) embraces in both individual transactions and social affairs. At the micro level, Islam demands any economic transactions should be done in an equal rights and opportunities and are not allowed to be enforced without mutual consent of two parties (*tarāḍi*). Likewise, any unfair dealings or unjustified actions that would lead to economic injustice or exploitation such as bribery (*rishwah*), fraud or deception (*ghish*), cheating (*tadlīs*), uncertainty and lack of clarity (*gharar*) or unjustified increase in wealth (*riba*) are condemned (Laldin and Furqani, 2013).

At macro level, the goal is to realize social justice. The Islamic financial system attempts to realize economic justice through wealth circulation, efficiency in resources utilization, fulfilling society's basic needs, elimination of poverty and improving human wellbeing. The main purpose of resource circulation (distribution) is to achieve justice, maximum efficiency and improvement of human wellbeing in general (Laldin and Furqani, 2013).

4.2 Fair and Transparent Financial Practices (*al-wuḍūḥ/ al-Shafafiyya*)

Fairness means equity and honesty between the transacting parties as well as efficiency in transactions. Fraud, deception and manipulation of any kind are therefore condemned. Islam's insistence on the mutual consent of the parties as a condition for the validity of any contract means that pressure, fraud, or misleading statements by any party render it invalid or voidable (Laldin and Furqani, 2013). Likewise, Islam disapproves all commercial practices which involve explicit or implicit harm and injustice to the contracting parties or to the public at large and which restrict the freedom of trade or stand in violation of the Qur'ānic injunctions or approved business conduct (Balala, 2011, p. 6).

Transparency means that all financial transactions must be conducted in such a manner that all the parties are clear about all important facts of the transactions necessary for the avoidance of disputes, clashes or damages to any party. It seeks to rid financial institution from misuse and squander, and to prevent dispute, arguments and grudges among the community and prevent one party gaining from another's loss (Laldin and Furqani, 2013). The Qur'ān has stressed that all agreements and contracts should be as transparent and clear as possible (Qur'ān, 2:282, 11:84, 17:35, 26:181–182, 55:9, 83: 1–3).

In Islamic finance, the example of transparency is evident in the contract of *mudarabah* and *musharakah*, in which both contracting parties are required to agree on the ration of profit to be shared between them. It has to be done in proportionate rather than the actual amount as both parties are required to share the profit and loss except in the case of *mudarabah* where the capital provider shall bear the loss. In this respect, even though transparent is required in business transaction, in some cases secrecy is allowed. This is evidence in certain aspects of *musharakah* financing. One of the criticisms against *musharakah* is that, by making the financier a partner in the business of the client, it may disclose the secrets of the business to the financier, and through him to other traders. However, the solution to this problem is very easy if we understand the objectives of *Shari'ah*. The client, while entering into the *musharakah* agreement, may put a condition that the financier will not interfere with the management affairs, and he will not disclose any information about the business to any person without prior permission of the client. Such agreements of maintaining secrecy are always honoured by prestigious institutions, especially those banks and financial institutions whose activities are based on confidentiality (Usmani, 2002, p. 29).

The other example that is relevant to this aspect of *maqasid* is the disclosure requirement in *mudarabah* transaction. It is a requirement of *mudarabah* contract that the original price and the mark up is disclose to the buyer as the failure to disclose such information will deem the contract to be invalid (AAOIFI, 2004). Therefore, the seller must ensure transparency in such transaction particularly in the pricing.

4.3 Benevolence (*Ihsan*) and Making One's Work Perfect

According to Imam al-Ghazali *Ihsan* is to perform above and beyond what is obligatory. In the context of transaction, *Ihsan* means to do what benefits the other party even though it is not obligatory (al-Ghazali: n.d., 2:79). Similarly, ISRA (2015) defines Ihsan as a voluntary kindness from each party to the other without any pre-arrangement. The Qurʾān says:

> "Allah enjoins justice (ʿadl) and kindness (iḥsān), and generosity to relatives, and forbids all that is shameful, evil and oppressive. He exhorts you so that you may be mindful" (Qurʾān, 16:90).

Moreover, it is defined also as to always seek continuous improvement in one's action. It includes the principle of *Itqan* (precision of action) which is mentioned by the Prophet Muhammad peace be upon him:

> "Verily Allah has prescribed ihsan (proficiency, perfection) in all things. So, if you kill then kill well; and if you slaughter, then slaughter well. Let each one of you sharpen his blade and let him spare suffering to the animal he slaughters" (Muslim, *ḥadīth* no. 17).

In addition, individuals should not only confine themselves to performing their duties, but should also strive to attain the degree of righteousness and perfection in their work by performing the duties assigned to them in the best manner possible. Several verses highlight the concept of *Itqan* and invites man to ascend the ladder of perfection. Allah, the Almighty, says: Allah commend justice, the doing of good (Qurʾān, 16:90); and do good; indeed, Allah loves the doers of good. (Qurʾān, 2:195). The Prophet, peace and blessing be upon him, says: "Allah like when someone performs his work to do it perfectly."[1]

> In this context, Islam encourages individuals to be excellent with any act, deed or work they perform, and called this *Ihsan* and *Itqan*. The word *Ihsan* described also in a long hadith narrated by Muslim when the Prophet Muhammad peace be upon him inquired by Jibril (Gabriel) to define *Ihsan*. He said:
>
> "It is to worship Allah as if you are seeing him; and although you do not see Him, He sees you" (Muslim, *ḥadīth* no. 60).

Osman-Gani et al. (2013) mentioned; "believing that one is always monitored by God (Ihsan) has a better impact than just performing ritual activities of religion" (p. 367). Therefore, the feeling of being watched by Allah might inspire employees to do their job in a perfect manner and motivate them to go above and beyond the call of duty. Similarly, Djafri and Noordin (2017) found that observance of Islamic values and principles

---

1 Narrated by Al bayhaqi in Shu'ab Al Iman, Ibn Askir and Abu Ya'la in his musnad (Book of narrated hadith).

such as *Ihsan* "excellence and perfection" and *Itqan* "precision of action" will lead to high level of organizational commitment and ultimately greater displays of organizational citizenship behavior at the workplace; which in turn will lead to influence the overall employee job performance greatly beyond expectation.

4.4 Truthfulness and Honesty (*al-siqd*)

Truthfulness and honesty are considered a noble character that should be acquired by any individual. Truthfulness means sincerity and honesty between the transacting parties as well as efficiency in transactions. Fraud, deception and manipulation of any kind are therefore strongly condemned. The Prophet (SAW) said:

> "You must be truthful. Verily, truthfulness leads to righteousness and righteousness leads to Paradise. A man continues to be truthful and encourages honesty until he is recorded with Allah as truthful. And beware of falsehood. Verily, falsehood leads to wickedness and wickedness leads to the Hellfire. A man continues tell lies and encourages falsehood until he is recorded with Allah as a liar." (Al-Bukhari, *ḥadīth* no. 5743).

According to Al-Ghazali, the virtue of honesty includes truthfulness in one's words, deeds, and intentions. Lahsasna (2013) mentioned that, adheres to these values, which include acting in good faith, fulfilling promise and standing by one's words, will lead to effectiveness in fulfilling the duties and responsibilities with a high degree of professionalism. Further, these values will lead to shifting the significance of the job from mere work and source of income to that of worship (*Ibadah).*

Being sincere entails that man does not subject himself to external influence or pressures but applies himself to his work as a religious commitment. As such, his professional duty and ordinary occupational turns into a form of worship (*Ibadah*), because one of the established Shari'ah fundamentals is that good intention turns a habit into worship (AAOIFI, 2008, p. 7). Likewise, Achour et al. (2014) stated that good performance of work is considered as an act of worship (*ibadah*) and have two critical criteria which set for the acceptance of job and deeds. The first pertains to the sincere intention of the doer, while the other one relates to the quality and perfection. This view of Islam toward job performance and tasks require Muslim employees to show a high commitment to their organization by respecting and setting of ethical values such as honesty, trustfulness, precision, and conscientiousness (Achour et al., 2014).

In the milieu of business, trustfulness and honesty refer to avoiding hypocrisy, fulfilling promise, being punctual, and giving fair advice to the clients. For instance, if an agent of takaful company knows that the takaful policy is of no interest to the client, fair advice should be given by showing the true features, without deception and wrong presentation of the product. Thus, Islam's insistence on the mutual consent of the parties as a condition for the validity of any contract means that pressure, fraud, or misleading statements by any party render it invalid or voidable (Laldin and Furqani, 2013).

4.5 Trust (*amanah*)

Trust (*amanah*) from Shari'ah perspective refers a trait/character that prevents a person from taking what is not rightful to him/her and enables him/her to discharge his obligation. It also refers to anything under the care of someone such as property, sanctity and privacy (Al Kafawi, n.d., 176,186). The scope of trust involves the act of obedience, the act of worship, safekeeping, confidence and protection.

Compliance with the Shari'ah mechanisms governing business and finance is *amanah* (trust) which *mukallaf* must observe in all his/her dealings. By extension, compliance of Islamic financial institutions with regulatory framework, guidelines on business conduct issued by relevant supervisory authority is *amanah*. It is part of *amanah* that IFIs ensure that all their products and services comply with the objective of protection of wealth and life in Shari'ah.

Ibn Jawzi stated that the word *amanah* in Qur'ān involves three meanings:

First meaning is obligations which are commands and teaching of the Qur'ān and Sunnah, the Qur'ān says: "O you who believe! Betray not Allah and His Messenger, nor betray knowingly your Amânât (things entrusted to you, and all the duties which Allah has ordained for you)" (Qur'ān 8:27). Second meaning is safekeeping which is due to other people. The Qur'ān says: "Verily! Allah commands that you should render back the trusts to those, to whom they are due..." (Qur'ān 4:58). Third meaning is trustworthiness, integrity and maintenance. The Qur'ān says: "O my father! Hire him! Verily, the best of men for you to hire is the strong, the trustworthy" (Qur'ān 28:26).

5 Shari'ah Mechanisms for Effective Implementation of its Objective in Business and Finance

Shari'ah plays essential role in life of all that exists. It is not overstated to say that Shari'ah is a divinely ordained blueprint for human conduct, a self-contained system, all comprehensive and all embracing (Bakar 2012 in Bakar and Engku Ali, 2012, 27).

Shari'ah technically are defined in different definitions. One of the comprehensive definitions is that of Mana' al-Qatan who defined Shari'ah as divine laws for His creatures concerning the belief, worship, ethics, transactions and code of life with all its various ramifications that govern their relationship with their creator and that govern their relationships in order for them to achieve *sa'adah* (happiness) in this life and hereafter (al-Qatan, M., 2001). Al-Zarqa (1998) defined it as the sum of commandments and divine laws relating to belief and conduct which adoption in Islam has been made compulsory to attain its welfare objectives in the community. Joseph Schacht described Shari'ah as the epitome of Islamic thought, the most typical manifestation of the Islamic way of life, the core and kernel of Islam itself (Dwyer, 1990).

From the above definitions, it can be concluded that, Shari'ah encompasses a set of divine laws concerning the belief, moral and conduct of human beings, deduced mainly from the Qur'ān and the Sunnah. In addition, the Shari'ah is more than just a set of laws in the modern sense because is an all-encompassing code of life. The definition of Al-Qatan and Al-Zarqa denote two important factors namely ethics and welfare objectives. They signify that Shari'ah encompasses a set of welfare objectives which are manifested in ethical and moral values. The ethical and moral values are in place to ensure welfare of human being.

Madkur (1996) identified five fundamentals Shari'ah principles underlying the Shari'ah rulings. They are adherence to justice, removal of hardship, less burden in Islamic legal rulings, gradual application of Shari'ah rulings and safeguard of public interest. The following discussion will focus on discussing fundamentals Shari'ah mechanisms for effective implementation of its objectives in business and finance.

5.1 Preservation of Wealth

Protection of wealth and property is one of the essential elements in *maqasid al-Shari'ah*. Islam gives an important status to wealth and has enacted rules and regulations to protect and preserve the wealth from violations and misuse. At the same time, Shari'ah offers guidelines to ensure that wealth accumulation is acquired through legitimate ways and mutual consent without violation of other rights. It is also obvious that, Shari'ah recognises property and wealth as an important aspect in life and illustrate the proper way and means that should be used to acquire wealth. Therefore, the preservation of wealth, includes acquiring it in a legitimate way and avoiding engaging in Shari'ah non-compliant activities, is vital to protect and preserve wealth. Lahsasna (2013) mentioned that there is a strong link between *maqasid* al-Shari'ah and Islamic finance, as both considered wealth and property as a subject matter of major concern. According to him, the common feature between *maqasid* Shari'ah and Islamic finance gives high credibility and recognition to Islamic finance, whereby the protection of the wealth will be the objective of Shari'ah, whereas Islamic finance will be the means to realize this objective". (p. 28).

5.2 Wealth Circulation in Society

Wealth circulation includes all the processes related to wealth creation, consumption and distribution. According to Laldin and Furqani (2013), the objective of wealth circulation is derived from the Qur'ānic explanation of the reason behind a rule regarding distribution: "[...] *so that wealth is not circulated among the rich in the society only*" (Qur'ān, 59:7). Islam intends that resources run smoothly throughout the economy in the pursuit of human well-being and intergenerational continuity. This perspective embarks from the concept that wealth is considered as a bounty from God and a trust (*amanah*) which He temporarily entrusts people with. As God's bounty, wealth itself reflects God's blessings on humanity (Qur'ān, 62:10) and it is therefore naturally good (Qur'ān, 2:215, 272–273). Working to acquire wealth is therefore not only legitimated but highly praised (Qur'ān, 4: 32); however, creating and augmenting wealth must be done using only the broad range of legitimate means (Qur'ān, 4:29). Since wealth is God's trust (*amanah*), it is to be spent in the right ends (Qur'ān, 3:92).

In addition, the objective of wealth circulation is underlined also in several *Hadiths* which call for the giving of zakat, the generous donation and spending for the sake of Allah and to refrain from hoarding and monopolizing the wealth. The Prophet has warned against keeping one's wealth without spending them wisely in the following *ḥadīth:*

> Narrated Abu Hurairah: Allah's Apostle said, "Whoever is made wealthy by Allah and does not pay the Zakat of his wealth, then on the Day of Resurrection his wealth will be made like a bald-headed poisonous male snake with two black spots over the eyes. The snake will encircle his neck and bite his cheeks and say, 'I am your wealth, I am your treasure.'" Then the Prophet recited the holy verses: "Let not those who withhold [...]" (to the end of the verse). (3.180). (Al-Bukhārī, *ḥadīth* no. 486)

Ibn Ashur (2004) indicates the legitimate circulation of the wealth among the largest number of people would surely and definitely bring prosperity and happiness to the whole society. Furthermore, it will protect the entire society against the crimes and greediness of few opportunists. This objective has been strengthened by several rulings and commands including those of contractual transfer of money, and other financial transactions such as *Mudarabah, Musharakah, Muzara'ah, Mugharasah,* and *Musaqah* etc (Laldin, 2008).

Besides that, commercial and financial activities are viewed positively as a mechanism to circulate the wealth and enable large sectors of the population to become part of the monetary cycle of wealth and to avoid the concentration of wealth in a few hands. Islam encourages wealth to be employed in productive activities. The funds should not be wasted, left idle (Qur'ān, 9:34) or managed unprofessionally (Qur'ān, 4:5). In fact, any funds which are not employed will be "penalized" through zakat, which will gradually reduce the volume of idle wealth and put it back into circulation. Zakat is an institutional mechanism that necessarily keeps wealth in continuous circulation (Laldin and Furqani, 2013).

Within this context, Islamic economic system as a general framework would ensure fair and equitable distribution of resources. Islamic finance in particular has come into existence in order to achieve the objective of Islamic law (*maqasid* al-Shari'ah), particularly the preservation of wealth (*hifz al-mal*). Islamic finance institutions, including Islamic banks, insurance (takaful) companies, mutual funds and other Islamic finance companies, play a key role in resources circulation in society and increasing human wellbeing. This would include all the chain from wealth creation, investment, until redistribution (Laldin and Furqani, 2013).

5.3 Adherence to Justice and Promotion of Ethical Values in Business and Finance

One of the important Shari'ah principle is adherence to justice and promotion of ethical values in dealing and daily transactions. This is because to achieve an ethical workplace environment, the relationship between Islamic banks and their customers must be guided by ethics enshrined in Shari'ah. As adherence to Islamic ethical conduct is an integral part of compliance with Shari'ah requirements.

The principle of justice refers to moderation and adherence to the truth (Abdul Mun'im, n.d., 2/483). The Qur'ānic injunction on justice is most succinctly captured in the statement: "Allah enjoins justice (*'adl*) and kindness (*iḥsān*) and generosity to relatives, and forbids all that is shameful, evil and oppressive..." (Qur'ān 16:90). This verse provides two fundamental ethical principles for human interactions and dealings namely justice and kindness. Justice means giving everyone their due rights. The concept applies to all human conduct and interactions, including the economic, social and environmental. Imam Al-Ghazali, defined *'Adl* as performing an obligation by someone in accordance with the nature of the transaction. He defined *Ihsan* as to perform above and beyond the obligation. In the context of transactions, *Iḥsan* means to do what benefits the other party even though it is not obligatory (al-Ghazali, n.d., 2:79). The two fundamental principles guide the relationship of the parties involved in all kinds of transactions including Islamic banking business.

These two terms and the message of the passage are the main principle of Shari'ah to guide conducts and contractual relationships in commercial transactions to ensure the spirit of Shari'ah is observed. It is noteworthy that *'adl* and *ihsan* can be applied in different contexts and at all categories of transactions. For instance, in sale contract, *'adl* on the part of seller (i.e. Islamic bank) is to sell lawful subject based on the agreed terms and conditions and in line with Shari'ah requirements and to take what is due to him/her. *'Adl* on the part of buyer (i.e. customer) is to give what is due to the seller/the bank and takes the possession of the subject purchase. Meanwhile, *Ihsan* is voluntary kindness from each party to the other without any pre-arrangement. On the part of the Islamic banker, its major manifestation is to act above and beyond what is due in terms of providing good quantity, transparency, socially and environmentally impactful services. On the part of the customer, it is to forego some portion of his/her rights.

Kindness can be seen as niceties Islamic banks offer to their customers to ensure stakeholders satisfaction including positive social and environmental impacts. However, there is difficulty in meeting up customer satisfaction and financial targets of the bank at all the times, therefore al-*wasatiyyah* (moderation) approach should be maintained from time to time.

Apart from the above two main values for dealings, Shari'ah enjoins certain values including among others trust, honesty, integrity, responsibility and openness.

5.4 Safeguard of Public Interest in Business and Finance

The principle of safeguarding public interest refers to the consideration of people's well-being in every aspect of life including commercial transactions. This principle is reflected in all Islamic legal rulings. The Shari'ah provides general principles to guide human interactions including financial and commercial transactions.

It is natural to have a set of ethical regulations in the society so that people don't unjustifiably tramp on other people's rights. Islam does not however wait till such ugly situation occurs before it puts in place these ethical values (Adebayo and Hasan, 2013, p. 65). All this is to ensure that public interest and social wellbeing are realized and preserved.

For instance, institution of *hisbah*, commonly known in modern day as ombudsman is established to safeguard of society from deviance, protect the faith and ensure welfare of people in both religious and worldly affairs. The Qur'ān says: "Let there arise from you a group calling to all that is good, enjoining what is right and forbidding what is wrong. It is these who are successful." (Qur'ān 3:104).

The role of the institution of *hisbah* encompasses monitoring the marketplace, craftmanship and manufacturing to ensure these sectors comply with Shari'ah tenets. With that, market behaviour embraces Islamic ethical values and strictly adheres to them in daily transactions. In the modern context, licensing and supervisory authorities today plays to a certain degree the role of *hisbah* along the institution of ombudsman.

5.5 Prohibition and Prevention of Unethical Behaviours in Business and Finance

Shari'ah has put in place some mechanisms to ensure its objectives are effectively implemented in dealings. In line with fundamental Shari'ah principle of elimination of harm, harm should be removed from business and finance activities. The principle of removal of hardship refers to the elimination of any conduct that causes difficulties and harm to body, life or property at present or that may lead to them in the future. The Shari'ah gives the highest priority to human well-being, the Qur'ān (17:27) testifies to this principle when it says: "Allah has not laid on you any hardship in your religion." As such, a number of unethical behaviours are prohibited including among others the practice of *riba, gharar,* deception, hoarding and monopoly. The next paragraphs discuss in brief these prohibitive items.

5.5.1 Prohibition of Riba

The Qur'ān and the Sunnah as the primary source of Shari'ah which aims at welfare and wellbeing of human being forbid dealing in *riba* (usury) due to its adverse impact on people, society and nation. The Qur'ān says: "Allah has permitted trade and forbidden *riba* (usury). (Qur'ān 2:275). This is due to injustice it causes to entire humanity. For that, Allah Has issued stern warning and admonition to those devour themselves in dealing in *riba* while saying: "And if you do not do it, then take a notice of war from Allah and His Messenger, but if you repent, you shall have your capital sums. Deal not unjustly (by asking more than your capital sums), and you shall not be dealt with unjustly (by receiving less than your capital sums)" (Qur'ān 2:279). *Riba* is of two types *riba* (usury) on credit which called *riba an-nasi'ah* and *riba* on trade (*riba al-fadl*).

Riba on credit refer to a fixed charge payable by borrower to the lender at the maturity day. The common form of this type of *riba* is bank interest. This is because main activities of banking are loans. Meanwhile, *riba* on trade/sale refers to exchange of *ribawi* items for an unequal countervalue or exchange of equal countervalues (*ribawi* items i.e. gold for gold) with a delay in delivery from one party (Laldin, 2008, p. 84). *Riba* is seen as one of the major deterrence of achieving the objectives of Shari'ah in business and financial activities from the past and present.

5.5.2 Prohibition of *gharar* (uncertainty)

One of the ethical values Shari'ah promotes is transparency in business and financial activities. As a means to prevent violation of the objective and minimise means to dispute and rancour in daily transactions, the Shari'ah prohibits all transactions that involve uncertainties. It is reported from Abu Hurairah that the Prophet (SAW) prohibited sale contract which involves elements of uncertainties. (Abu Daud, *ḥadīth* no. 3376; Muawatta' Malik *ḥadīth* no 1941; Musnad Ahmad *ḥadīth* no. 8884). In that regard, transaction should involve the following:

1. In sale contract, asset should be owned by the seller and known to transacting parties and capable of delivery;
2. Forward sales are not allowed except in the case of *salam* and *istina'*, this is because both satisfy certain condition prescribed in Shari'ah to avoid uncertainties;
3. Seller is required to fulfil either actual or constructive ownership requirement prior to sell the asset;
4. Price of the asset which forms the subject matter of exchanged contract must be fixed and known to transacting parties. As unfixed price or tied to uncertain events render the contract null and void.

Given the above discussion, it is a requirement that transacting parties should be transparent and free from uncertainties that may lead disputes and conflict which contravene the objective of Shari'ah for human to live in peace and harmony. Thus, the main purpose for this prohibition to protect the weak from being exploited by the strong and to prevent conflicts among the transacting parties.

5.5.3 Prohibition of Hoarding and Monopoly

Promotion and preservation of wealth is one of the essential values Shari'ah aims to protect as it is a must in every society. Shari'ah has also devised means for wealth circulation in order to achieve this underlying objective. In contrast, Shari'ah prohibits all forms of activities and conducts that inhibit actualization of this objective. Among several preventive measures Shari'ah put in place is the prohibition of hoarding. The Qur'ān says:

> "On the Day when that (Al-Kanz: money, gold and silver the zakat of which has not been paid) will be heated in the Fire of Hell and with it will be branded their foreheads, their flanks, and their backs, and it will be said unto them, this is the treasure which you hoarded for yourselves. Now taste of what you used to hoard". (Qur'ān 9:35).

In addition, Umar ibn Al Khattab reported that the Prophet said: "Whoever hoards food away from the Muslims, then Allah will afflict him with leprosy and poverty." (Ibn Majah no. 2155).

The above evidences affirm that Shari'ah disallows keeping wealth idle either by not investing it or by not paying *zakah* on it. It is disallowed because it contravenes the very objective of Shari'ah which is wealth development. In addition, it causes negative impact on society and leads to inflation, unemployment, nonproductivity, price hike, circulation of wealth among handful people. Unlike hoarding, wealth circulation helps increase economy activities and productivity as well as economy growth and development.

No doubt that hoarders inflict harm on society and humanity while Shari'ah strongly condemns all forms of harms at all levels, be individual, social, national. Shari'ah has devised some instruments to boost business and financial activities. Notably are *musharakah, mudarabah, mugharasah, musaqat, wakalah, ijarah* and others to ensure wealth development, wealth accumulation and circulation which in turn contributes to individual and social welfare and wellbeing.

Shari'ah also prohibits all forms of activities that deter the promotion and preservation of wealth. Among those unethical conduct that obstructs the circulation of wealth and healthy investment is monopoly. All forms of harmful monopoly are forbidden whether in goods, money or any other form. Several hadith have declared harmful monopoly unlawful and considered monopolist a sinner and invoked punishment on him/her from Allah. This is because it is an exercise that benefits a few at the expense of many. *Shari'ah* disallowed the accumulation of wealth in the hand of only handful people. The repercussions of such phenomenon include unemployment, inflation, nonproductivity, restriction of outputs onto the market, price hike and others.

6 Overview of Sustainable Development Instruments

6.1 Sustainable Development Instruments

One of the current trends in Islamic finance is ensuring sustainability of the industry and this is very much in line with the objective of Shari'ah and the ethical values propagated by Islam. Islamic finance has been criticised for being focusing more on the legal compliance aspect of the products and overlooking the philosophical foundation of Islamic economics which emphasizes on social justice, ethical finance and human well-being. In response to this concern, there are ongoing efforts and various initiatives that have been considered to reinforce ethics and social justice in Islamic finance. This section discusses various sustainable development instruments such as Sustainable and Responsible Investments (SRI), socially responsible investing, principles of environmental, social and corporate governance (ESG), value-based intermediation (VBI) with some examples on its role in achieving sustainable development goals (SDGs) and relevancy from *maqasid* and ethical perspectives.

6.1.1 Sustainable and Responsible Investments (SRI)

Sustainable and Responsible Investments (SRI) which originated from religious-based ethical background has developed into investments with values premised on humanism, environmentalism and/or socialism (Wilson, 2005). Initially known as 'ethical investments', it metamorphosed in nomenclature through 'socially responsible investments' and later into 'sustainable and responsible investments' to accommodate environmental concerns (Ansary et al 2017). In 1920s, the investments made by the Methodist Church of North America in the stock market was in exclusion of what was considered as "sin industries" such as gambling and alcohol companies (UK Social Investment Forum, 2003). The screening later encompassed other companies producing weapons, tobacco. Today, SRIs have included various positive screening and social and environmental factors take great prominence (Ansary et al 2017). In principle, sustainable, responsible and impact investing (SRI) is an investment discipline that avoids investments in controversial industries such as tobacco, gambling, alcohol, and arms companies, and seeking out for companies that engages in social justice, environmental sustainability and alternative green energy. It aligns with the rising convergence of Islamic finance with various streams of ethical finance such as Environmental, Social and corporate Governance (ESG), the United Nations Principles for Responsible Investment (UN-PRI) and Value-Based Intermediation (VBI) initiated by the Malaysian Central Bank. Altogether, these initiates aim to play an important role to the preservation of the environment and several socio-economic development issues. These considerations are in line with the objective of Shari'ah to bring benefit to mankind and prevent harm from them and are also part of broad ethical values propagated by Shari'ah.

6.1.2 Environmental, Social and Corporate Governance (ESG)

ESG, sometimes referred to responsible investment, is a consideration of environmental, social and governance factors alongside financial factors in the investment decision-making process. It refers to the three key factors – corporate governance and the environmental and social impact of a business' activities – when measuring the sustainability and ethical impact of an investment in a business or company. In other words, ESG is a generic term used in capital markets and commonly used by investors to evaluate the behaviour of companies, as well as determining their future financial performance. Ansary et al (2017) noted that ESG reflected a shift from an explicitly ethical basis for evaluating business activities to a pragmatic consideration of factors that affect a business's long-term profitability and sustainability.

It should also be noted that the term SRI tends to be associated with those for whom ethical concerns weigh heavier while ESG tends to be associated with those for whom profitability weighs heavier (Goud, 2015). All the relevant and Shari'ah compliant considerations in the ESG are part of the *maqasid al*-Shari'ah framework and in line with Islamic ethical consideration.

6.1.3 Value Based Intermediation (VBI)

In line with the international trend of incorporating other values other than just profit, the Central Bank of Malaysia developed a strategy paper on Value Based Intermediation (VBI) in 2018. It is an intermediation function that aims to deliver the intended outcomes of *Shari'ah* through practices, conducts and offerings that generate positive and sustainable impacts to the economy, community and environment, consistent with stakeholders' sustainable returns and long-term interests. It advances a rational of "not just *Shari'ah* compliance" to establish a culture that establishes the intended outcomes of *Shari'ah* (BNM, 2018).

According to BNM (2018, p. 6), VBI is defined as:

> an intermediation function that aims to deliver the intended outcomes of Shari'ah through practices, conduct and offerings that generate positive and sustainable impact to the economy, community and environment, consistent with the shareholders' sustainable returns and long-term interests.

This definition signifies that The VBI initiative aims in creating an enabling environment for Islamic banking institutions (IBIs) in Malaysia by focusing on sustainable impact to the economy, community and environment without compromising the financial returns to shareholders.

In his keynote address at the 15th Kuala Lumpur Islamic Finance (KLIFF) 2019, Tun Dr. Mahathir Bin Mohamad, Prime Minister of Malaysia, mentioned:

> The industry's move towards embracing VBI would further strengthen Malaysia's leadership position and advance the growth of Islamic finance towards generating positive, sustainable impact to the economy, community and environment.

It should be noted that VBI shares similarities with several well-established concepts such as Environmental, Social and Corporate Governance (ESG), Ethical Finance and Sustainable, Responsible, Impact Investing (SRI), specifically on the intended outcomes. However, the underlying reason for VBI is its reliance on Shari'ah in determining its underlying values, moral compass and priorities. VBI's launch was intended to position Islamic finance to become more prominent and leading agent of positive change for the financial system and operates within a network economy that is built upon shared values of integrity, inclusivity and sustainability (BNM, p. 14). VBI is another attempt to integrate Islamic finance with *maqasid al-Shari'ah* and the values propagated are also in line with ethical considerations in *Shari'ah.*

6.2 Ethics in the Context of Sustainable Development Instruments

It is worth noting that the preservation of environmental and socio-economic development issues has been the focus of renewed investor attention, as showed by growing interest in renewable and clean energy as well as socially responsible investment (SRI). For instance, the International Finance Facility for Immunisation Company (IFFIm) issued sukuk worth US$ 500 million for children's immunisation in the world's poorest countries through Gavi, the company of Vaccine Alliance. This landmark transaction is the first socially responsible sukuk with funds to be utilised for this purpose. Besides, it is directly aligned with the UN Sustainable Development Goal; which aims to end preventable deaths of new born and children under 5 years of age by 2030.

Malaysia, being the world's largest sukuk market, has established the enabling environment for Islamic socially responsible investing (SRI) and green finance. Over the years, the country has introduced several initiatives on sustainable finance to support the green agenda. This shown by the issuance of the first SRI sukuk, called *Sukuk Ihsan*, by Khazanah Nasional Berhad in 2015 under the SC's SRI sukuk Framework. The proceeds from sukuk issuance which is exclusively targeted institutional investors were channelled to Yayasan *AMIR*, a not-for-profit organisation to improve the accessibility of quality education in Malaysian government schools. It has reached over 65,000 students and 83 trust schools across 10 states in Malaysia. This shows that Islamic finance products such as sukuk Ihsan can be used positively as a means to provide funding for the wellbeing of mankind.

In addition, Bursa Malaysia has also championed the push towards SRI when it offers a sustainability-related index called FTSE4Good Bursa Malaysia, which "is designed to highlight companies that demonstrate a leading approach to addressing environmental, social and governance (ESG) risks" (FTSE Russell, 2016).

Several countries have also recently witnessed a remarkable development in renewable energy investments using SRI sukuk that has been introduced to facilitate and promote sustainable and responsible investing. Malaysia and Indonesia are among the first countries to issue this type of sukuk. In Malaysia, the first SRI sukuk, valued at RM 250 million, was issued to partly finance large-scale solar construction in Kudat, Sabah. Following that, Quantum Solar Park Malaysia Sdn Bhd launched the world's largest green SRI sukuk valued at RM1 billion to fund the construction of Southeast Asia's largest solar photovoltaic plant project in three regions: Kedah, Melaka and Terengganu. Indonesia has also recently issued USD 1.25 billion of green sovereign sukuk, whose revenues will be partly used to finance renewable energy projects. The increase in the adoption of green sukuk to finance renewable energy projects is attributable to the following factors: the increase in renewable energy projects, particularly solar energy projects, the low capital costs, and the fact that it is a Shari'ah-compliant instrument.

In a nutshell, sustainable development instruments such SRI, ESG and VBI can play a major role in addressing the threat faced by the environment and society and has the potential to achieve the SDGs. Interestingly, Islamic finance has a lot in common with impact investment and can play a major role in addressing the problem faced by the society and has the potential to bring additionality to the efforts of mobilizing resources for the sake of realizing the SDGs. In order to achieve this, there is a need to establish an enabling environment which includes strengthening the regulatory frameworks, develop instruments for liquidity management and standardization of contracts and *Shari'ah* rulings. The establishment of Islamic finance is not merely in offering financial products that are *Shari'ah* compliant, but also in the ability to offer innovative products that contribute to the broader notion of *Shari'ah* that requires our attention into the whole dimensions of human life and human wellbeing. Its establishment is purported to achieve various socio-economic justice as mandated by the objective of Shari'ah (*Maqasid al-Shari'ah*) which aims at realizing human wellbeing (*Maslahah*) and prevent harm and difficulties (*mafsadah* and *mashaqqah*) to the general public and complying to the ethical norms propagated by *Shari'ah*.

7 Conclusion

Shari'ah is a comprehensive concept that encompasses a set of welfare objectives which is manifested in ethical and moral values. It is a complete code of life that involves *al-ahkam al-i'tiqadiyyah* (belief), *ahkam al-'amaliyyah* (sanctions relating to conducts and worship), and *al-ahkam al-akhlaqiyyah* (moral and ethics). In fact, ethics (*akhlaq*) is considered the third building block in Islam after faith (*aqidah*) and law (*Shari'ah*).

The key ethical principles underlying Islamic finance system such as promoting socio-economic justice, advocating fair and transparent financial practices, making one's work perfect, honesty and trust are built and inferred from Shari'ah sources that provide detailed commands of dos and don'ts on both legal and ethical level. It represents the fundamental elements in the composition of the religion, and it has been addressed in Shari'ah to govern a person's behavior in conducting any activities or transactions. Therefore, the reputation of Islamic financial institutions is dependent on its development agenda and moral standing as it is on its financial acumen.

Apart from the ethical principles which guide inner conducts, *Shari'ah* puts in place fundamental *Shari'ah* principles and mechanisms to effectively accomplish objectives of *Shari'ah* (*maqasid* al-Shari'ah). These involve firstly adherence to justice and promotion of ethical values in business and finance; secondly, safeguard of public interest in business and finance; thirdly, removal of hardship and prevention of unethical behaviours in business and finance. Compliance with these ensure preservation of three bottom line of sustainable development which are people, profit and planet that are in conformity with main five values Shari'ah urges to preserve.

In addition, all the objective of the *Shari'ah* mentioned earlier are devised in order to prevent harm and bring benefits, not only to individuals, but also to the whole community. Nevertheless, in order to achieve the goals of this principles, several sub-principles and economic conventions must be followed, such as proper economic planning in investment and prioritizing the means and areas of investments and implementations. These principles will undoubtedly help in the achievement of the goals of diligence in work and lead to a successful and profitable business engagement, which in turn leads to individual and communal prosperity and happiness.

Besides that, *maqasid Shari'ah* is a comprehensive concept that explicates the objectives of the *Shari'ah* related to human life. Therefore, the *maqasid* discussion in the financial sphere should be extended to integrate various sustainable development instruments (i.e SRI, ESG and VBI) and provides a grand framework and direction of how financial transactions should be arranged in an Islamic economic system. Further, by pursuing sustainable development instruments such as SRI, ESG, VBI and *Shari'ah*-compliance hand-in-hand, the Islamic finance industry would benefit from a larger investor base and gain broader mainstream relevance. Finally, it is important to note that *maqasid al-Shari'ah* cannot be detached from the moral and ethical foundation of Islam which is embedded in the very meaning and definition of *Shari'ah*.

References

ʿAbd al-Munʿim, M.ʿA.R. (1999), *Muʿjam al-Muṣṭalaḥāt wa al-Alfāẓ al Fiqhiyyah*, Dār al Faḍīlah, Egypt.

Achour, M., Grine, F., Mohd Nor, M. R., & MohdYusoff, M. Y. Z. (2014). Measuring Religiosity and Its Effects on Personal Well-Being: A Case Study of Muslim Female Academicians in Malaysia. *J Relig Health*. Doi: 10.1007/s10943-014-9852-0.

Accounting and Auditing Organization for Islamic Financial Institutions (2008). *Code of Ethics for accountants and auditors of Islamic financial institutions*. State of Bahrain.

Accounting and Auditing Organization for Islamic Financial Institutions (2004). *Shari'ah Standards 1425-6H/2004-5*. State of Bahrain.

Adebayo and Hassan (2013). Ethical Principles of Islamic Financial Institutions, Journal of Economic Cooperation and Development, 34, 1, 63-90.

Ahmad, H. (2001), *Musnad al-Imām Ahmad bin Hanbal*, Mu'assasah al-Risālah, Beirut.

Ahmed, H. (2011), "Maqasid al-Shari'ah and Islamic financial products: a framework for assessment", *ISRA International Journal of Islamic Finance, Vol. 3 No. 1, pp. 149-160.*

Al-Attar, M. (2010), *Islamic Ethics, Divine Command Theory in Arabo-Islamic Thought*, Routledge, United Kingdom.

Al-Bukhārī, M. I. (1422h), *Ṣaḥīḥ al-Bukhari*, Dār Ṭauq al-Najah, Beirut.

Al-Bukhārī, M. I. (1997), *Ṣaḥīḥ al-Adab al-Mufrad*, Maktabah al-Dalīl, Saudi Arabia.

Al-Daghistani, R. (2018), "Ethics in Islam: An Overview of Theological, Philosophy and Mystical Approaches", ANNALES Series Historia et Sociologia, Vol. 28 No. 1, pp. 1 – 12, available at: https://www.academia.edu/37235267/Al-Daghistani_R._2018_._Ethics_in_Islam_An_Overview_of_Theological_Philosophical_and_Mystical_Approaches_.pdf

Al-Ghazālī, M.M. (n.d.), *Al-Mustaṣfā fī ʿIlm al-Uṣūl*, Dār Iḥyā' al-Turāth al-ʿArabī, Beirut.

Al-Ghazālī, M.M. (n.d.), *Iḥyā' ʿUlūm al-Dīn*, Dār al-Maʿrifah, Beirut.

Al-Jawzī, A.R. (1987). Nuzhat Al-Aʿyun Al Nawadhir Fi 'Ilm Al Wujūh wa Al Nadhāʿir, Muʿassasat Al Risālah, Beirut.

Al-Kafawi, A.ʿA. (1998), *Kitāb al-Kulliyyat*, Muʿassasat Al Risālah, Beirut.

Al-Khelaifi, R.M. (2004), "Al-Maqasid al-Shari'iyyah wa atsaruha fi fiqh al-mu'amalat al-maliyah", *Majallah al-Jami'ah al-Mulk Abdul Aziz: al-Iqtisad al-Islamy, Vol. 17 No. 1, pp. 3–49.*

Al-Qatan, M. (2001), *Tarikh Al Tashrī'Al-Islāmī*, Maktabah Wahbah, Cairo.

Al-Tirmidhī, M. I., (1975), *Sunan al-Tirmidhī*, Syarikah Maktabah wa Maṭbaʿah Musṭafā al-Bābī al-Halbī, Egypt.

Al-Zarqa, M. (1998), *Al-Madkhal al-Fiqhī al-ʿĀmm*, Dār al-Qalam, Damascus.

Ayubi, M.S. (1998). *Maqasid Shari'ah Al-Islamiyyah wa Alaaqatuhah Bi Al-Adillah As Shar'iyyah*, Dar Al Hirah, Riyadh.

Ansary, R., Sairally, S., Habib, F. & Furqani, H. (2017), *Islamic Finance and Sustainable and Responsible Investment (SRI): An Ethical Dimension*, International Shari'ah Research Academy for Islamic Finance (ISRA), Kuala Lumpur.

Bakar (2012) in Bakar and Engku Ali (ed). *Essential Reading in Islamic Finance*, Cert, Kuala Lumpur

Balala, M.-H. (2011), *Islamic Finance and Law: Theory and Practice in a Globalized World*. IB Tauris, London.

Beekun, R. I. (2003), *Islamic Business Ethics*, Goodword Books Pvt. Ltd, New Delhi.

Bank Negara Malaysia (2018). *Value-based Intermediation: Strengthening the Roles and Impact of Islamic Finance.*

Djafri, F., & Noordin, K. (2017). The impact of workplace spirituality on organizational commitment: A case study of Takaful agents in Malaysia. *Humanomics*, *33*(3), 384–396

Dusuki, A.W. and Bouheraoua, S. (2011). The framework of maqasid al-Shari'ah (the objectives of Shari'ah) and its implications for Islamic finance. *ISRA Research Paper No. 22, ISRA*, Kuala Lumpur.

Dwyer, D. H. (Ed.). (1990). *Law and Islam in the Middle East*. Greenwood Publishing Group.
Fakhry, M. (1994), *Ethical Theories in Islam*, E. J. Brill, New York.
FTSE Russell (2016). "FTSE4Good Bursa Malaysia Index", available at: http://www.ftse.com/products/downloads/FAQ-FTSE4Good-BursaMalaysia.pdf.
Goud, B. (2015). "Thomson Reuters – RFI Responsible Finance Report 2015: The Emerging Convergence of SRI, ESG and Islamic Finance", available at: https://www.zawya.com/saudi-arabia/en/ifg-publications/260815053724N/.
Haron, A., Musa, M. A. & Shaarani, A. Z. M. (2013), *Ethics in Islamic Finance*, IBFIM, Kuala Lumpur.
Hourani, G. F. (2007), *Reason & Tradition in Islamic Ethics*, Cambridge University Press, United Kingdom.
Ibn Ashur (2004) in Ibn Khawkhah, M.J., *Maqasid Al- Shari'ah Al Islamiyyah*, Wizarah Al Awqaf Wa As-Shu'un Al-Islamiyyah, Qatar.
Ibn Qayyim, J. (1423). *Ilaam Al-Muwaqqiʾīn ʾAn Rabb Al-ʾĀlamīn*, Dār Ibn Ḥazmi, Riyadh, vol.4/337.
Ibn Rushd, M.A., the grandson (1994), *Bidāyat al-Mujtahid wa Nihāyat al-Muqtaṣid*, Maktabah Ibn Taymiyyah, Cairo.
ISRA (2010), *ISRA Compendium for Islamic Financial Terms* Kuala Lumpur: International Research Academy for Islamic Finance.
Izutsu, T. (1964), *God and Man in The Qurʾān, Semantics of the Qurʾānic Weltanschauung*, Keio University, Japan.
Lahsasna, A. (2013). *Maqasid al-Shari'ah in Islamic finance*. Kuala Lumpur: IBFIM.
Laldin, M. A., & Furqani, H. (2013). Developing Islamic finance in the framework of maqasid al-Shari'ah: Understanding the ends (maqasid) and the means (wasa'il). *International Journal of Islamic and Middle Eastern Finance and Management, 6*(4), 278–289.
Laldin, M. A., Furqani, H. Riaz, A. Said, M. Azrak, T. (2015). *Debt from Shari'ah and Economic Perspectives: Concepts, Issues and Implications*. ISRA Research Paper No. 81, ISRA, Kuala Lumpur.
Laldin, M.A. (2008), *Fundamentals and Practices in Islamic Finance* (ISRA), Kuala Lumpur.
Laldin, M.A. (2010), "Understanding the concept of maslahah and its parameters when used in financial transactions", *ISRA International Journal of Islamic Finance, Vol. 2 No. 1, pp. 61–84.*
Madkur, M.S. (1996), Al Madkhal Li Al-Fiqh Al Islāmī, takhrikhuh, wa masadiruh wa Nadhariyyatuh Al ʾAmmah,Dār Al Kitāb Al Ḥadīth, Cairo.
Muhammad Abu Zahrah (1996). *Al-Milkīya wa Nazariyyah. al-'Aqd fi Al-Shari'ah al-Islamiyyah* Cairo: Dar al-Fikr.
Muhammad Taqi Usmani (2002). *An Introduction to Islamic Finance*. New York: Kluwer law International. Brill.
Muslim, H. (n. d.), *Ṣaḥīḥ Muslim*, Dar Ihyāʾ al-Turath al-ʿArabī, Beirut.
Naqvi, S. N. H. (1981), *Ethics and Economics, an Islamic Synthesis*, The Islamic Foundation, United Kingdom.
Omar, M. N. (2013), "Ethics in Islam: A Brief Survey", *The Social Sciences*, Vol. 8 No. 5, pp. 387 – 392, available at: https://www.researchgate.net/publication/308072115_Ethics_In_Islam_A_Brief_Survey.
Osman Gani, A. M., Hashim, J., & Ismail, Y. (2013). Establishing linkages between religiosity and spirituality on employee performance. *Employee Relations, 35(4), 360–376*. Doi: 10.1108/er-04-2012-0030
Sajoo, A. (2009), *Muslim Ethics, Emerging Vistas*, I. B. Tauris & Co Ltd, United Kingdom.
Wilson, R. (2005). "The Growth of Islamic Banking and Product Development among Islamic Retail Banks", in Jaffer, S. (Ed.), *Islamic Retail Banking and Finance: Global Challenges and Opportunities*. (18–28). London: Euromoney Books, pp. 18–28.

Mohammad Reza Yousefi Sheikh Robaat

Chapter 3: The Status of Economic Operations and Business Ethics in the Historical Mindset of Muslim Scholars

1 An Introduction to the Concept and Versatility of Topics on Business Ethics

The role of economic operation on the growing life of human being is something undeniable. The impact of this role in the world today is by far more than ever. The growing importance of business in the modern world illustrates the necessity of directing these activities in the correct path. Accordingly, there are a set of rules and regulations such as operational rules dedicated to activists and organizations in the field of business. Of course, in spite of the aforementioned rules and regulations, there are requirements over the professional ethics so that business could move towards human interests, the most important of which are ethical principles in business.

The purpose of business ethics is improving the quality of decision making and performances in the overall levels of an ethical and fair living.

Encouraging people to work and to have economic operations, Islam has formulated canonical requirements and ethical recommendations for its followers that, if observed, can lead to deducing trading expenditures, strengthening social capitals, and boosting business efficiency. However, a group of Muslim extremists believe working activities are in contrast with asceticism and reliance on the Almighty. This has made some orientalists who have the same perspective towards Islam as above to rebuke this religion. While the principal and dominant current in Islamic thinking has always expressed its opposition to the above mentioned issue during the past centuries, it has been able to brush aside the group.

This piece of writing is designed to have six sections. The first section expresses the importance of working in the Qur'anic doctrines, in the eyes of the Prophet Muhammad, and the great Islamic leaders, while in the second section the Sufi mentalities are dealt with as a diversion from the above mentioned path. The third section skims through the mentalities of some Muslim scholars as opposed to the Sufi extremists' ideas, and the fourth one explains the ethical and essential frameworks from religion standpoint towards business ethics and the status of working. And in the fifth section, the general framework of an economic operation is elaborated. Finally, in the sixth section the conclusion and the summary will be provided.

https://doi.org/10.1515/9783110593419-003

2 Emphasis on the Status of Working in Religious Mindset

God has bestowed a lot of gifts and virtues to human beings, but the prerequisite to utilize the God's grace is to work and to be active. Working is a social necessity, and based on working, the materialistic needs of human community will be resolved.

In the Qur'an, the Almighty has decreed us to develop lands as states "It is He the Lord that created you from the earth and decreed you to develop it".[1] Therefore, developing land is a divine task. Accordingly, it is not a need that causes working; rather, from divine perspective working is a mission for human being. As related, before Imam Sadegh someone said "I own a lot of properties and my family and I will be well off by the end of our lives. Thus, I have a feeling that I am no longer in need of working therefore I put aside my economic operation." His Excellency answered him that "Never leave your job, try working again so as to enhance your family welfare better than ever" (Muhammad bin alHassan Hor Aameli, Vasayelal Shiite, 12/6). In another relation it is stated that his Excellency deemed the idea to be satanic (Ibid). Related from Imam Ali states that "whether rich or poor, never leave out economic activities under any circumstances" (Muhammad bin alHassan Hor Aameli, Vasayelal Shiite).

The authentic historic documents reveal that the Prophet Muhammad used to be economically active before being assigned in prophesy. Therefore, he quoted the words of a lot of people in appreciating job and doing economic operations. His practical policy during the government in Medina was to pave the way for business and economic activities. Somebody by the name of Asbaat bin Salem quoted that "I went to visit Imam Sadegh. He asked me about Omar bin Moslem. I said that he was well, but he has left his business for some time to care more about his spiritual issues. The Imam replied that it was a devilish job. Doesn't he know that the Prophet did economic activities, too?" (Kolini, 1983, 75/5). Imam Sadegh not only encouraged other people but also he himself used to be engaged in business activities (Kolini, 1983, 75/5, p. 76).

Accordingly, one can conclude that human being will be included in the following remarks as stated by the religious leaders "Anyone who lives through economic activity will be able to swiftly dart across the Seraat bridge in no time" (Muhammad Reza Hakimi, Mohammad, and Ali, 1988, 5/295); "The paradise doors all will be open to him and whichever he desires to enter he is able to get in" (Muhammad Reza Hakimi, Mohammad, and Ali, 1988, 5/295, p. 296, 2); "The Lord will kindly take a look at him" (Muhammad Reza Hakimi, Mohammad, and Ali, 1988, 5/295, p. 3); "The only job to do is to clean some sins" (Muhammad Reza Hakimi, Mohammad, and Ali, 1988, 5/295, p. 7); "Anyone who makes a living through his own efforts will be accounted among other prophets" (Muhammad Reza Hakimi, Mohammad, and Ali, 1988, 5/295, p. 8);

1 هوالذی انشأکم من الارض واستعمرکم فیها (هود/61)

"He is just like activists on the Almighty path" (Muhammad Reza Hakimi, Mohammad, and Ali, 1988, 5/295, p. 297); and "The jobless human being's praying will not be met" (Mohammad Bin Al-Hassan Aameli, 12/15).

Following the Prophet, the lifestyle of Imams and religious leaders as the pattern of behavior for Muslim communities implies the importance of working in the lives of Muslims whereby any deviation is known to be staying away from the authentic religious canons. Imam Sajad Ali Ibn Al-Hussain believes that during the post Prophet Era some thoughts were promoted as a religion among people that had nothing to do with the original religion. Among the thoughts spread he mentioned sufism as an instance (Ali Ibn Easa Arili, 1981, 2/98).[2]

This writing will briefly illustrate a few instances of living practices by religious leaders and the significance of their jobs and efforts as follows.

Someone called Muhammad Bin Al-Monkader narrated that "Some day during the hot hours of the day in Medina I had to leave home to do something when I came across Imam Bagher Mohammad Bin Ali who was working hard in the hot air. He was rather a fat person. Surprisingly when I saw the situation I told myself Oh, Lord, someone among the senior fellows of Quraysh tribe was toiling for the worldly matters in high temperature. I approached him and saw that he was sweating hard. I asked him 'Oh, the son of the prophet, if you pass away right now, what would you have to tell the Lord? He replied, if I die right now, I will leave the world while worshiping God, because by working hard I have been gaining the subsistence of my family and I through which I will be able to save my reputation' (Kolini, 1983, 5/74–75)".

Similar to the above narration is related by Abdulali Mowla Aali Saam about Imam Sadegh, the son to Imam Bagher in which the response has been identical to that of his father (Kolini, Ibid, 74).

3 Working Viewed from the Standpoint of Some Sufi Groups

Regarding the aforementioned points, there was an inclination among a group of Muslims in which believing the other world was considered to be something in vain and the worldly joys and pleasures are not sustainable. With reference to some Qur'anic verses, they promoted seclusion while assuming that economic activities are in contrast with asceticism and reliance on the Lord.

Accordingly, there has always been a controversy between them and the Islamic legislators the result of which has been the gradual impairment of their controversy

2 و قد انتحلت طوايف من هذه الامه بعد مفارقها ائمه الدين و الشجره النبويه اخلاص الديانه و اخذوا انفسهم فى مخايل الرهبانيه و تغالوا فى المعلوم و وصفوا الاسلام با حسن صفاتهم ...

despite the fact that in our history it has always been available. This part of writing is about the account of the historical confrontation and how it happened.

Regarding the genesis of the above group, one can briefly state that the majority of Muslims were ascetic and abstinent under the influence of the character of the Prophet ever since the advent of Islam during which there weren't any specific classification. The Prophet would repeatedly underscored that the one who is after the afterlife eternity should go through this world for which asceticism together with giving up one's social tasks was always reprimanded by the Prophet. Later on, the growth of worldliness and its promotion among the public made some people change their course of life and avoided any encounter with them. In this era, they were called 'Zohad' (ascetic) or 'Obaad'. Of course, it was not that they deprived themselves of every virtue in life. They had a normal life, but they never lived like other person concerning worldly affairs, that is why they had a reputation accordingly. The group gradually diverted their path of doing their social responsibility.

During the second half of the 2nd century (first half of 9th century BC) some of the people in the group teamed up in a uniform and gradually put on wool clothes. This projected them to be avoiding the worldly living and materialistic joys. In Arabic the word wool is called 'Suf', that is why they were called 'Sufi' consequently. Ibn Al-Joze states that the word Sufi used to be applied before the lunar year 200 (ca. 815 BC) and they were called Sufis. During this time, Sufism was "the austerity of soul and the effort to change the vicious ethics to the beautiful ones including asceticism, patience, meekness, purity, truth, and the like that are preferred both in this world and the next world."

A group of them had an unconventional life specifically in the second half of the 2nd century lunar year (first half of the 9th century BC). Some of them were living away from the public in temples or deserts. Ibrahim Adham lived in a cave near Nishaboor city for 9 years and then 14 years in desert. Bashar Hafi didn't put on shoes so as not to be dependent on the public.

At any rate, what seems remarkable to notice is the impact of Sufi doctrines on the economic, social, and ethical aspects of a society. The following two instances are out of some Sufis' statements: "Sufi before the Almighty seems like a corpse against dead washers, something which is called poverty. Sufi should be time bound. That is, neither looking at the past nor thinking about the future". Mohammad Vasseh in the second century stated that "The person who has something to eat in the morning and knows nothing about dinner, and when having a dinner knows nothing about tomorrow is fortunate".

The growth of Sufism in the world of Islam stems from the two historical experience, after the demise of the Prophet Mohammad and the emergence of monasticism in Christianity.[3]

3 For further information, refer to *A Survey of Economic Mindset of Islamic Scholars*, Mohammad Reza Yusefi Sheikh Robaat, 2016. pp. 49–53.

The existence of such an attitude among Muslims made some non-Muslim people to consider Sufism and their particular approach towards asceticism, reliance on God, and belief in the other world, and the like to be main cause of the retardation of Muslims. Because when the idea of evading worldly affairs becomes deeply rooted and institutionalized in society, it will barricade growth and development. Accordingly, there are studies conducted by Muslims and non-Muslims over the level and extent of the impact of extreme beliefs by Sufis in the lives of Muslims which will be further investigated in itself. Generally speaking, there are two major attitudes in Sufism, namely particular look at the world and reliance on the Almighty, which naturally it affects the fields of working and business ethics.

Both the development of Sufism in the world of Islam and the threat of deviation from religious doctrines made a host of scholars in various periods to show their positions against them.

4 Importance and Necessity of Working from Islamic Scholars' Standpoints

4.1 Mohammad Bin Hassan Shaybani (750–804)

Mohammad Bin Hassan Shaybani was born in 750.[4] He took up the court judgement as his career. And in the year 804 BC when he was with Harun al-Rashid, the Abbasside caliph, he passed away in Rey city, Iran (Masoody, 2005, pp. 3/343).

Writing the book titled 'Al-Kasb' and with reference to the valid religious sources as well as the lifestyle of the Prophet disciples, Shaybani depicted that the religious logic does not advocate the Sufi doctrines. He mentioned the Sufi reasonings in any case and topics and then he began criticizing them. In his book Shaybani encourages his readers to work and endeavor in opposition to the Sufi doctrines of the time.

His methodology was that he first referred to the Qur'an, Sunna, and the Prophets' lifestyles, and then he explained the ideas and attitudes of the disciples and the associated[5] persons (Al-Jonaidel, 1986, 2/111).

At the very beginning he defined the concept of business, translated that into an economic activity, and made it synonymous with occupation. With reference to the Qur'an in which in Jum'ah Sura right after the Friday praying the people are invited

4 The birth and death dates are all stated in Gregorian Calendar.

5 The associates are those people who were not lucky enough to visit the Prophet in person. They received the relations from the disciples. Later on, there were a lot of controversy among the Islamic scholars concerning their circumstances.

to go to work,[6] then he mentioned some Hadiths such as "looking for an occupation is mandatory for every Muslim",[7] or "anyone who does not sleep for the purpose of earning a Halal property, his sins will be forgiven", and then he quoted that Sa'd the son to Maaz, the disciple to the Prophet Muhammad, someday he visited the prophet, they shook hands when the prophet noticed the severe harshness of Sa'd's hand, making him ask about the reason why it was harsh, for which Sa'd replied "To earn the living of my family I usually work in the palm tree farming using shovel and so on." At that time, the prophet kissed his hands and said "These are the hands that the Almighty likes them" (Al-Jonidal, Ibid, 2/112). Thereafter, Shaybani indicates the lifestyle of the prophets.

He states that his purpose to mention the above documents is of two reasons. First, human being is obliged to do the compulsory affairs. However, doing the obligations require physical competency and managing routine way of life. Thus, the necessity of occupation is just like ablution to praying. Second, he relies on the prophets' tradition. Since all of them made their living through economic activities, therefore, it is necessary for their followers to do the same (Shaybani, Bita, pp. 14–20).

Shaybani also believes that business has a hierarchy some of which are obligatory, some virtuous, and some others are permissible. The obligatory hierarchy includes working for maintaining one's life, working for the sake of settling dues and debts, governing one's family affairs in life adequately (spouse and children),[8] and working for the purpose of one's parents subsistence. One the other hand, the hierarchy of virtuous business involves working to provide further welfare for one's family and a better future for them. Of course, the last stage that Shaybani mentions is activity to increase further income and higher openings in one's life. At this stage, he wants to add to his own fortune. In his opinion this stage is neither forbidden nor obligatory nor virtuous, but something permissible and allowable (Shaybani, Bita, pp. 32–34).

Explaining the process of working, Shaybani answers a very important question that if someone provides his necessities in life whether it is a priority to have praying or go to work. There is an approach that pinpoints on activities on account that once the prophet Mohammad told Sa'd bin Abi Vaghas "Upon the time of death, is not it better to make your kids richer than the time when they are poor?" (Al-Awadi, 1984, 1/30).[9]

6 فاذا قضیت الصلاه فانتشروا فی الارض و ابتغوا من فضل الله» (جمعه/10)

7 طلب الکسب فریضه علی کل مسلم»

8 Adequately means the middle class lifestyle in a society.

9 انک ان تدع ورثتک اغنیاء خیر من تدعهم عاله یتکففون الناس

4.2 Yahya bin Omar (804–902)

Yahya bin Omar Kanani Andalusia was born in 213 Hegira in Qurtaba, Spain.[10] He began and continued his education in Egypt and Hejaz. He graduated in Kairouan[11] and began teaching over there. Yahya was the follower of the Maliki school of thought (madhhab). In that period, there was a controversy over the scholars of the both schools of Maliki and Hanafi in terms of their sovereignty.

During that period, Sufis would get together in one of the prominent mosques in Kairouan called Al-Sabt Mosque so as to read poems and the like and to encourage people toward asceticism and Sufism. As a result, Yahya bin Omar struggled against their way of thinking.

While rejecting the extreme Sufism and monasticism of Christianity, he believes that if Muslim communities could follow the Prophet's Sunnah and conduct his orders, the result would be their ethical behavior, and that whatever they are praying for would be bestowed by the Almighty, because the Lord has stated that "If the villages and cities could be faithful and pious the virtues of the heaven and earth would be unfold for them".[12] The Lord indicates in this verse that if people are practically faithful the Almighty will direct his virtues towards them. Therefore, observing the ethical principles of piety will have an impact on the materialistic life of human being and brings about their welfare.[13] (Yahya Bin Omar, 2002, 24)

4.3 Sheikh Sadough (918–991)

Sadough did not agree with the notions of a group of Sufis, too. Following the attitude of the alleged 'people of the house' (Ahlul Bayt), he believes that the individual who strives for the subsistence of his own and family living, he is identical to a 'mujahid' (the one who struggles) for the sake of Allah (Sadough, 1995, 361). He poses multiple reasons for the necessity of working. The first reason is relevant to human dignity. The needy human being should neglect his own dignity to earn his life expenditure. He should refer to various people here and there for that matter. This is not what associates with human dignity, even though he does not do the action and other people are touch by seeing his financial situation and take a merciful look at him, and even aid him with

10 The Spanish spelling is Córdoba.

11 (Arabic: القيروان *Al-Qairuwân)* It is a historical city in Tunisia which in 2008 was selected as the cultural capital of the Islamic world.

12 و لو ان اهل القرى آمنوا و اتقوا لفتحنا عليهم بركات من السماء و الارض (اعراف 96).
And in another verse God states و لو انهم اقاموا التوراه و الانجيل و ما انزل اليهم من ربهم لا كلوا من فوقهم و من تحت ارجلهم "(مائده/66)"

13 For further information, please refer to Mohammad Reza Yusefi Sheikh Robaat, Vahid Shabani, and Mina Sadaat Seyyed Asadullah, *Impact of Religious Investments (Ethics) on Economic Growth.*

some money. He will be degraded in the eyes of other people.Thus, Sadough emphasize on the necessity of working without reliance on others (Sadough, 1995, 363).

He tells that economic activity necessitates social presence; therefore, it adds to the further personal understanding of social issues. However, the important point is that he deems any economic activities to increase the status of family welfare to be something positive. Opposing the notion of Sufis, this idea implies that individuals can strive for higher welfare. This approach is in contrast with those notions that take working as something solely done at an adequate level (Sadough, 1995).

Despite the significance dedicated to working, occupation is valuable within a specific framework. In his opinion, Sadough believes that those jobs that lead to weakening the foundation of a family or is not compatible with the ethical principles and fundamental ideology of religion, or result in encroaching others' rights are all forbidden (Sadough, 1995, pp. 362–365, 390).

4.4 Seyyed Morteza (965–1045)

Seyyed Morteza allocated a portion of his writing to explaining the inaccuracy of Sufi notions. Since some Sufis assumed working and economic activities to be contrary to reliance on God, he tries to give a rational explanation on the concept of reliance on God and figure out that not only reliance has nothing to do with economic activity, but also those who regard these two concepts to be incompatible are in practice indulged with contradiction of behavior, and that sometimes pretending to have this notion is a manifestation of love of the world rather than staying away from that which is a means of earning money.

He thinks that human wisdom implies that to provide for his needs, human being should work and be active. Therefore, economic activities such as agriculture, business and so on are rationally accurate and there are so many times that working could be considered as something useful, the time when a person can work in favor of other people. Sometimes, it is mandatory when something damaging should be removed. Despite the rational approach, the Almighty God has invited human being to care about an occupation and an activity as in some verses in the Koran.[14] As such, Seyyed Morteza feels astonished to hear that some people take it as something forbidden in spite of rational and revealed reasoning on the necessity of having an economic activity; he does not assume their statements are in harmony with the principles of rationality and religion. (Seyyed Morteza, 2010, pp. 271–272)

He believes that those who religiously prohibit having a business are in fact revealing their own failure and incompetence. Perhaps some of them pave the way of their own income generation by proposing leaving business. Actually if they are true

14 Suras such as Jum'ah, verse 10; Nessah/29; Mayedeh/2; and the like.

in their words, they should not receive any public gifts such as edible things, and they should not chew any bites of food in their mouth before gulping, simply because this is in contrast with what they claim to be true. And then they try to explain the accurate concept of reliance on God whereby they assume reliance means an endeavor to obtain something based on rational and religious ways plus the fact that human being when losing something should not complain because it shows that he or she is relying on that matter, not relying on God that has bestowed everything to him or her (Seyyed Morteza, 2010, p. 272).

The interpretation of Seyyed Morteza's phrases such as "Perhaps, often true, they assume leaving an occupation as a means of their own income generation" (Seyyed Morteza, Ibid, p. 272) depicts that regardless of the incompatibility with rational and religious principles, the purpose of those groups who believe reliance is incompatible with occupation is that they want to fool the public while building up a spiritual popularity for themselves so as to spend their living through the public gifts.

4.5 Ibn Teymiyeh (1263–1328)

He mentions a relation by the Prophet Mohammad that "Asceticism in the world does not mean to make halal things prohibited or damage the properties, rather, asceticism comes when trust in God is above everything you own"[15] because the Almighty states "Neither regret for something lost, nor enjoy for the circumstances occurred".[16]

As a result, asceticism means that human being would be in a state of mind that if something is lost he or she is not sad about and if something is gained it does not bring happiness to him or her. Mankind should not forget about his or her position in the past upon achieving a better situation, nor lose his or her personality upon losing something. Thus, asceticism is a state of mind within which human being does not have a sensation to be dependent on or belong to the world.

On the other hand, he believes that a perfect example of asceticism is depicted by the Prophet, namely he did not turn down the food offered and he did not look for the food requested. It was true with his attire, too. He did not have any specific bias over clothing. When he witnessed that some of his disciples exceeded in their desires he just admonished them (Jonaydel, Ibid, pp. 272–274, as quoted by Al-Fatavi, 10/641).

Ibn Teymiyeh criticized those persons who in the name of asceticism neglected the rights of their spouses and children, believing that it is not something that the Almighty and the prophet and other prophets would agree because provision of family expenses is something mandatory and after some stages it is something voluntary;

15 "ليس الزهد فی الدنيا بتحريم الحلال و لا اضاعه المال و لكن الزهد هو ان تكون بما فی يد الله او ثق بما فی يدک" رواه الترمذی
16 Hadid Sura, verse 23.

therefore, how was it that these people would consider discarding mandatory or voluntary actions something religious? (Ibn Teymiyeh, 1970, 10/425–426)

4.6 Imam Mohammad Ghazali (1058–1111)

Ghazali in his book titled 'Ehya' (Revival) indicated that if someone was not able to work, unemployment as compared to employment is not at all in priority, even though he or she is well-off comprehensively. Everyone must have a job. Even if he or she could be financed by other people or else he himself or she herself would ask some people for financial aid, or that other individuals for any reasons would like to help him or her and keep his or her life adequately funded. Ghazali thinks that working and making money even under such a circumstance sounds better because working results in sustaining one's courtesy, chastity, and personality. Ghazali said "No person should ever imagine that he or she can work be means of others while I can dedicate my time to physical praying, for working is again beneficial."

Of course, in his opinion this kind of task is enough; however, if the person is seeking ethical sublimity he or she should look for the pious persons in the past. The methodology used by them was that whenever their worldly life reached to an adequate level then they devoted their time to spiritual affairs. Therefore, it is preferable to follow their suit (Ehya, 2/63).

Regarding the persons gaining income through halal means higher than the adequate level and willing to have a more consumer life than necessary, Ghazali states that living higher than the adequate level of welfare as long as it does not result in overconsumption is not a blunder in the canon law. Nevertheless, those who want to upgrade in their spirituality and have never assumed it from the standpoint of forbidden and mandatories, having a comfortable life is a barrier to that sublimity. The Muslim person should endeavor to invigorate his or her spirituality because strife for worldly affairs is generally not preferable. Of course, Ghazali has explained the points just made more intensively in his book titled "Al-Arbaeen Fi Osool Al-Deen" (الاربعين فی اصول الدين).

4.7 Khajeh Nasir Tusi (1201–1274)

In the eyes of Khajeh Nasir Tusi human being is a social creature instinctively, and the social system is based on cooperation and coordination between individuals. Therefore, there is a sort of give and take going on in society. The condition to use the services of other individuals is a reciprocal offer if service as valuable as they are. If that happens there has been a fair interaction development in social relation. This implies that individuals would be out of isolation, interacting with the society. But there are people who resort to seclusion for some reasons. This way they never offer any services to others, but since their vitality is bound to others' jobs, they enjoy the achievements of others, which per se it is a kind of cruelty and oppression, simply because without having an occupation and providing services to others they exploit others' services. Thus, those individuals who sometimes make their seclusion to have a religious color and conduct in the name of asceticism, and probably in temples, abbeys, monasteries, or crevices, live away from the public and avoid any services to the rest of the people, they are in fact oppressing the society. There is another group who call it reliance on God to have no endeavor and to exploit the achievements of other individuals. This kind of oppressing others is performed in the name of religion.

Since this group of people is not interacting with other ones, therefore they are not apparently committing mistakes or sins, thus their inappropriate features will not be disclosed. A group of simple-minded individuals position them as spirituals; of course, that is something wrong. Since they don't have any interaction with others, they never make any transparent error. It is not because they are ethically outstanding individuals.

Khajeh is of a believe that good features such as chastity doesn't arise from leaving social life in general, rather, it forms when human being is in interaction with other people and never exceed the limit. The imagination that these people have ethical accomplishments including fairness, justice, chastity, and so on, is absolutely a blunder. Because how can one make a comment on the fairness of a person who has no interaction with others? How is it possible to talk about the impartiality of a person who has no social relations with others? How can one claim that a person with no relationship with other people is a chaste individual? These kinds of personal traits could be realized when individuals interact with one another. Thus, those who prefer seclusion are not only in shortage of ethical accomplishments, quite contrary to what naïve people think they are, but also they have an incorrect understanding of asceticism and reliance on God and oppress those who take the toil to earn something in order to submit them (Khajeh Nasir, 1977, pp. 257–258).

5 Economic Framework from Religion Point of View

It is obvious that the lofty position of working is highlighted when the ethical frameworks is taken into account because Islam has always called human beings to behave ethically and by expanding their perspective to go through their restricted worldly lives toward the vast expanse of life after death, it has deeply rooted the ethical behavior profoundly. Accordingly, there is a profound inclination towards ethical behavior based on remembering God and the next world among religious people. In this insight, economic and commercial behaviors are included in the ethical framework.

Sadoogh believes even by assuming that a person's occupation is the one adverse to the ethical principles, a Muslim should constitute his or her own economic activities in accordance with spirituality and ethics. Therefore, he stated his ethical recommendations for an economic activist. He calls the attention to the ethical principles as "beauty of job".[17] In other words, a person should have a decent behavior upon an economic activity. To have a legitimate earning, a person should pay attention to the ethical aspects because in the eyes of a Muslim sustenance comes from God. Accordingly, Sadoogh believes the Muslim should avoid the following five things while having an economic activity. First, taking oath; second, lying; third, hiding the defects of the product or articles he is about to sell; fourth, admiring and appreciating the product upon selling; and fifth, finding fault with a product upon purchasing. (Sadoogh, 1995, p. 363)

In Sheikh Mofid's (1022–946 BC) opinion, who was the most outstanding student to Sheikh Sadoogh, the Almighty's purpose of creating human being has been to uplift his or her position to the highest point in worshiping God. And to do so, there are some affairs forbidden and some ones allowed (halal) for him or her (Mofid, 2009, 586). The overall things including business, industry, and other business that are allowed to be done by human beings are all means of achieving human desires and divine sustenance (Mofid, 2009, 587). In this regard, the foremost point is that mankind who wants to go through the religious path should be aware of the forbidden and allowed issues so as not to get into the forbidden trap. Thus, training and learning about the rules and regulations of dealing is vital for the Muslim so as not to fall into the trap of forbidden deals (Mofid, 2009, 591).

What matters most for human being is to be able to make his personal strife and take the main path of life into account. As a result, among the recommended actions (Mustahabb) is "beauty of job" or in other words, following ethical rules to make a living and do an economic activity. He mentioned a relation from the Prophet (pbuh) as quoted "Gabriel once had told him that no one leaves this world unless receiving his or her sustenance entirely, then addressing his disciples, the prophet states they should observe piety and commit their economic activities in a decent manner" (Mofid, Ibid, 586). Thereafter, while accepting the necessity of working and activity in life and not conflicting with asceticism and reliance on God, Mofid explains and recommends it within the framework of ethical standards.

Sheikh Tusi (997–1070 BC) approves the fact that anyone who is seeking an economic activity should learn about Sharia rules so as not to commit forbidden acts. He should recognize legitimate income gain, discriminate genuine from counterfeit contracts so as not to fall into the trap of usury or any other forbidden deals (Sheikh Tusi, *Al-Nahayah*, 371).

17 Ijmal Al-Talab (اجمال الطلب)

Sheikh Tusi refers to some forbidden contracts on products such as wine and pig that are religiously prohibited to use and trading them are also forbidden. In addition, dealing with forbidden services, including those occupations that are considered as games, are not allowed. (Sheikh Tusi, Ibid, 363). Another criterion pertains to the possibility that a product or service offered is not forbidden but due to the forbidden operations it becomes forbidden or results in a forbidden job, such as bribery, helping oppressor, or hiding defects of the product or service, that are all proofs of forbidden operations. (Sheikh Tusi, Ibid, pp. 365–364). Later jurists tried to make more accurate remarks on the rules of forbidden and allowed operations, but in that period of time Sheikh Tusi was ahead.

One of the important things to do is following ethical principles in trade. Regardless of the existence of privacies and mandatory things, Islam emphasizes observing ethics in transactions. Sheikh Tusi has pointed out to some of them. He recommends the following 5 principles in business. First, upon selling a product, human being should not appreciate it improperly and unrealistically by means of which he or she can sell it with a price higher than the real one. Second, upon purchasing a good as a buyer, he or she should not find fault with it so as to get a discount on the price. Third, as a seller he or she should not hide the defect of the good. Rather, the information should be accessed by the buyer. Fourth, the seller should not resort to taking oath for the purpose of selling good and meet the trust of the purchaser. Fifth, he or she should stay away from usury. He then underscores that cheating in transaction (playing trick in dealings) is forbidden in any case, be it when a good is sold or when a good is purchased. Included in the ethical principles is when the seller or buyer never distinguishes between individuals. For instance, there should not be any distinction between children or grownups,[18] those favoring bargaining and those who are not used to do so, bashful individuals who do not ask too much about the quality of goods and so on and those meticulous individuals who have various questions to ask. (Sheikh Tusi, Ibid, 372)

Another ethical principle that Sheikh Tusi deems necessary in transactions to be observed relates to decorating the good in a way that is over realistic. For example, if someone is selling fruit or similar thing that is a blend of good or bad features, he should not put the good articles before to be seen while hiding the bad ones from the customer, pretending everything is good enough; rather, it is fair to expose both good or bad articles mingled together before trying to sell them (Sheikh Tusi, Ibid, 373). In the above mentioned things, it is obvious that Sheikh Tusi agrees with the true way of presenting a good; therefore, in advertisement, too, the rule should be true introduction of goods. As such, all the cases pertaining to deceiving customer through hiding the defects, improper praising and appreciation, taking oath to attract the attention of

18 This is a symbol of asymmetrical information in addition to explanation of the difference between maturity and experience in life among partners of a deal.

the customer, decorating goods in various ways to show a good is worth more than it appears, hiding defects of goods, all have a direction towards deception of customers.

Another thing Sheikh Tusi points at is that there are times when a shopkeeper places some of his goods in front of the shop on a common pathway where people come and go. He raises this question that this act is confiscation in public, and if someone plans to confiscate a span of the place belonging to the public, it is religiously forbidden (SheikhTusi, Ibid, 423). Thus, the private sector is not entitled to violate public rights.

Mohaghegh Helli (dead ca 1278) had the idea that Islam has invited individuals to work and have an activity but at the same time, it has invited two types of framework. The first one are mandatory frameworks that the whole economic activists are obliged to work within that framework and that no one is able to ignore them. They are interpreted to be as the necessary conditions for economic activities. Mohaghegh Helli divides business activities into three categories of forbidden, disliked, and allowed, and whatever found essential is not entering into forbidden activities. He categorizes them into five group:

Group one: goods that are ritually unclean (Najis) and usually there is no specific use for them other than drinking or eating, such as alcoholic drinks and the overall unclean liquids or a pig, carrioin, etc. Therefore, production and trading them is not allowable.

Group two: activities that aim at forbidden purposes. For instance, idolatry is forbidden. Thus, those who are making idols are doing some forbidden jobs. In addition, those who are manufacturing gambling equipment or trade with them have committed forbidden activities. (Mohaghegh Helli, 1983, 263)

Group three: goods that have no benefits and don't fulfill any needs of human beings.

Group four: goods that are religiously forbidden in essence. Also, if they are changed into a profession they become forbidden, too, and no one is allowed to do economic activities. Professions such as the ones gaining income through gambling, rumoring round, and slandering others, fake advertisement for a person or special individuals or special goods, etc.

Group five: professions that are obligatory for human beings such as bathing, shrouding, burial of corpse, that are adequately obligatory. He then accounts some goods that the society needs but they are not viewed as an economic activity. For instance, the fact that nowadays people are needed to have some skills in shrouding and burial, or holding congregational praying, or judgement upon the time when an obligation is defined, and so on, are among the needs available in society. Now, if these kinds of jobs are done in small number, there would be no problems at all. But in big cities that doing the above mentioned jobs will take the daily time of the individual insofar as they hamper the economic activities and flow of life for the person, what should be done? He believes that the legitimate government is obliged to provide their living subsistence according to their competence and skills. (Mohagheh Helli, 1983, pp. 264–265)

In sum, it was found out that the Muslim's economic activity would be done within the framework of requirements.

Later, Mohaghegh Helli explains ethical recommendations in terms of business. In his opinion, a Muslim is ranked. At least, a human being dedicated to Islamic principles is the one who observes the requirements, trying to do the obligations and avoid forbidden things. This was dealt with in the previous paragraph on the required conditions for the economic activity of a Muslim. However, there is a category of Muslims who not only follow the religious requirements, but also try to observe the ethical advises that are not necessary but are effective on the ethical elevation of mankind and his perfection. (Mohaghegh Helli, 1983, 265)

Based on religious canon, Mohaghegh Helli takes it recommended to observe the affairs in an economic activity which are as follows:

1. Human being is good before he or she begins an economic activity, obtains the associated religious law information so as not to fall into the forbidden aspect.
2. Seller never makes a distinction between buyers, and he or she treats everyone fairly.
3. If doing transaction with someone, and the other party regrets the deal and requested to make it null and void, it is recommended for him or her to accept the case.
4. Upon purchasing something, utters the sentences on two fold martyrdom and cites Allahu Akbar, God is the greatest, so that upon transaction he would remember that he or she is a Muslim and the Muslim never commits treason other ones, and that he or she should remember that God is greater than any other things that he or she perceives, thus following the religious canon without letting routine worldly affairs to keep him or her engaged.
5. Once purchasing something he receives somehow lesser and when selling something he delivers a little more to the buyer. For instance, if he sells a kilo of lintel, he will weigh down somewhat more than a kilo to make sure the customer's rights are met, and upon purchasing the same amount, it should be a little lesser, again, so as to make sure there is no right of a person wasted. (Mohaghegh Helli, 1983, 274)

After indicating the recommended things, he deals with the disliked cases as well, those ones that anyone willing to have a lofty ethical life should observe in his economic activities where found decent:

1. He should not praise or appreciate the goods he plans to sell.
2. Upon purchasing a good, in order to reduce the price, he should not find faults with the goods.
3. Upon transaction he should not take an oath.
4. There are articles that if place in the shade or elsewhere makes their errors unnoticed. It is recommended that the seller avoid placing them in a place where their faulty parts are concealed so as not to be involved in hiding realities and distortion.

5. Human being should not receive interests unless when necessary and to some extent.
6. When promising the party to consider him for something, he would observe the promise.
7. From dawn to dust when it is the time of praying, he or she should not get involved in a business transaction.
8. He should not be the first one who enters the marketplace to begin his profession.
9. He should not make a deal with immoral people and wicked.
10. If having no familiarity with the scale or the profession, because someone's rights would waste, he won't do that.
11. After a transaction, and upon purchasing an article, it is not advisable to ask for further discount.
12. When two people are involved in a business transaction, it is indecent to get into their transactions (Mohaghegh Helli, 1983, pp. 274–275).

Paying attention to the points mentioned above will contribute to the ethicality of business, letting the marketplace to have normal activity, any extortion is obliterated, and meeting the rights of others upon transaction is considered. if the bazaar activists have the above principles in mind, the expenses of transaction will decline.

6 Conclusion

The Koran, discourses and practical lifestyle of the Prophet and religious leaders have a large impact on the significance of working.
1. Based on religious documents and Muslim scholars, the motivation of having a profession could be materialistic welfare, sustaining the dignity and courtesy of human being.
2. A branch of Muslim community think profession is at odds with asceticism and reliance on God, but upon conflicting with the dominant and strong flow of muslims, this idea was driven aside.
3. Despite the value of profession, in Islam any economic activity should be within the framework of ethical, legal, and efficient standards.

References

Al – Helli, Abolghasem (1983), Sharaye Al- Eslam, Dar Al – Hodi Le Tabaaa va Al – Nasher, Qum, Iran.
Alam Al- Hoda, Seyyed Morteza (2010), Al – Zakhirah, Massat Al – Nashr Al- Eslami, Qum, Iran.
Al–Ameli, Mohammad bin Hasan, Vasael Al- Shiah, Al- Maktabah Al – Eslamidh, Tehran, Iran.
Al-Awdhi, Siied Rafaat (1984), Men Al-Torath Al-Moslemin.

Al-Jonidal, Hamd (1986), Manahej Al-bahethin fi Al- Egtesad Al- Eslami, Sherkat Al- Abikan, Saudi Arabia.
Arbali, Ali (1962), Kashtol ghomah fi Maarefat al- Aemmah, Maktebat Banihashemi, Tabriz, Iran.
Ghazali Mohammad, Ehyay Al- olom Al din, Massat Al – Tarikh Al- Arabi& Dar Al- torath Al- Arabi, Lebenan.
Hakimi, Mohammad Reza & Ali & Mohammad (1988), Al – Hayat, Daftar Nashre Farhange Eslami, Tehran, Iran.
Harrani, Abn shubeh (1984), Tohaf Al-ogol, Massat Al – Nashr Al- Eslami, Qum, Iran.
Ibn Teymiyeh, Ahmad (1970), Al- Fatawa, Darolkotob al- jaded, Lebenan.
Kanani, Yahya bin Omar (2002), Ahkam Al-Soogh, Al- Tabat Al- Tunisia, Tunisia.
Kolaini, Mohammad (1986), Al-Kafi, Dar Al- Kotob Al –Eslmieh, Tehran, Iran.
Masoody, Ali (1984), Morooj Al-Zahab, Dar Al-Hejrah, Qum, Iran.
Mofid, Mohammad (2009), Al-Moqnaeh, Massat Al – Nashr Al- Eslami, Qum, Iran.
Sadough, Mohammad (1995), Al – Moqneh, Moassat Al –emam Al- Hadi, Iran- Qum.
Shaybani, Mohammad Bin Hassan (1986), Al – Ektesab fi Al- Rezgh Al- Halal, Dar Al- Kotob Al – Elmieh, Lebenan.
Tusi, Khajeh Nasir (1977), Akhlagh Naseri, Entesharat Kharazmi, Tehran, Iran.
Tusi, Mohammad, AL-Nahayeh, Moasseh Mohammadi, Qum, Iran.
Yousefi Sheikh Robat, Mohammad Reza& Vahid Shabani &Mina Syyed Asadollah (2013), Effecs of Religious Capital on Growth Economy, National's Seminar of Ethics & economy, Qum, Iran.
Yousefi Sheikh Robat, Mohammad Reza (1996), Koliyyat Egtesad Eslami, Nashre Khorram, Qum, Iran.
Yousefi Sheikh Robat, Mohammad Reza (2016), Tracing the Development of the Eonomic Thoughts of Muslim Thinkers, Samt, Tehran, Iran.

Amana Raquib, Junaid Qadir, and Bilal S. Channa

Chapter 4: The Central Role of Spirituality and Ethics in Islamic Economics and Finance

1 Introduction

The discourse on Islamic Economics and Finance often looks at the Islamic Sharia to seek practical and legal guidance for the establishment of economic and financial institutions. If we consider the Qur'an not merely as a book of law but as a book of spiritual-ethical guidance for all humanity, the focus in Islamic Economics and Finance would shift from a narrow focus on juristic (*fiqh*) rulings to the realization of the true spirit of the Qur'anic message. Helping individuals and communities develop higher spirituality (God consciousness or *taqwa*) and exemplary ethical behavior is the highest objective of the Islamic Sharia The discipline of Islamic law (*fiqh*) was developed to serve this higher end. It is in the discipline of the Maqasid (Objectives) of Sharia, that we find the overall rationale of the Islamic commands and prohibitions to be the spiritual-moral purification (*tazkiya*) of individuals and societies as a whole. Economic development and creation of wealth is a proximate objective that is supposed to contribute to the preservation of life and religion on the one hand and that must lead to the maximization of economic and social justice on the other. Even the attainment of an economically just society is not the final objective unless it is accompanied by piety, God-consciousness and cultivation of the traits of humility, compassion and cooperation to form a Godly and goodly society that sees all of creation as reflection of divine names and divine signs (Raysuni 2006; Qur'an: 2:177; 22:28–29; 2:183; 29:45). We have in our front the examples of Scandinavian countries that despite boasting optimum economic justice and citizen welfare, fare poorly on internal contentment and well-being which is visible form the high depression and suicide rates. Loneliness and mental health issues are often cited as reasons by the researchers.[1] The objective of preserving the religious, spiritual and moral integrity of human beings is the highest objective for which the objectives of intellect, wealth, family and lineage, economic and social justice serve as the essential prerequisites.

The pioneer Muslim intellectuals who proposed the new discipline of Islamic Economics such as Chapra (2008) and Siddiqui (2009) envisioned economic development along similar lines as conventional economics despite their emphasis on spiritual well-being, economic and social justice and stability as one of the key objectives (maqasid) of the Islamic Sharia. For instance, writers on the Maqasid al Sharia such as Chapra (2008: 29, 37) and Kamali (2006: 118) add research and development

1 https://www.bbc.com/news/world-europe-45308016

https://doi.org/10.1515/9783110593419-004

in technology and expanding technological base to the structure of the objectives, as a means of enhancing economic development. Chapra (2008: 2) states that, in past decades self-reported subjective wellbeing of people has in fact declined, despite economic development and strong rise in income; but while discussing technological development, he does not mention any different course of conduct or elaborate any objectives' (*maqāṣidic*) vision of technological development that does not create a similar paradox. Kamali (2003: 256–257) mentions economic development as well as protection of environment and constraining extravagant consumption as one of the objectives. These Muslim thinkers fail to see the problems inherent in contemporary models of technological progress and development. They miss out on the fact that excessive consumption leading to environmental destruction is built into the current cultural logic of technology, supported by the economic model, which represents and promotes a specific way of being and doing in the world (Raquib 2015). These earlier Muslim intellectuals and economists somehow were captivated by the utilitarian logic, so much so that they interpreted the Islamic maslaha (social good) and applied the maqasid as utility maximization, which was not much different from Utilitarianism as espoused by Jeremy Bentham and others (Setia 2016; Jha 2014). Of course the environmentalism had not been in as much vogue in the 1970's and 80's when these scholars began their writings on Islamic Economics, although the optimism in perpetual linear progress and growth had already dwindled as reflected in Marcuse's *One Dimensional Man* and the works of other critical theorists. Alternative technology movement and environmental awareness campaigns had already been taken up by Schumacher in his work *Small is Beautiful* and others. One would however expect their more recent writings to reflect a more critical assessment of some of the basic assumptions about individual and community development. Thankfully we have a new generation of Islamic economists who fill this much needed gap and propose a more holistic framework for economic development and discuss the dimensions of virtue and character building of individuals and communities that should then guide the physical development of the earth (See Mirakhor and Askari 2010; Iqbal and Mirakhor 2013; Iqbal and Mirakhor 2017).[2] Such a model does not lead to unidimensional

2 It is heartening to see that the recent generation of scholars of Islamic Economics and Finance have a more holistic approach toward the subject. Following conference represents the circular economy approach of this new generation of Muslim scholars.

https://www.hbku.edu.qa/en/call-papers-cis-qfc

CIS-QFC INTERNATIONAL CONFERENCE ON ISLAMIC FINANCE AND CIRCULAR ECONOMY Toward Inclusive Societies, Responsible Business, and Responsive Financial Strategies and Policies December 3–5, 2019 College of Islamic Studies, Hamad Bin Khalifa University Doha, Qatar.

Islamic finance has come a long way over the last four decades. During its current transformative decade, Islamic finance is facing the challenge of strategic sustainability and is in need of revisiting its operational paradigm; as landfills, ecological and environmental degradation, climate change and other factors stressing the planet are widely understood to be the by-products of the current linear approach of the world economy. While this approach of 'taking, making, using, disposing, and technicalistic progress but to the creation of a society in which individuals become cognizant of their capabilities and are able to maximize their potential- foremost being the spiritual potential to be actualized into virtue (*birr* and *taqwa*). Such a society would be far removed from sin, oppression and transgression (*ithm*, *'udwan* and *'tagha*).

"When humans are able to actualize these capabilities, it makes possible a life the Qur'an refers to as *Hayat Tayyibah*, the good life, a life free of anxiety, fear and regrets; a life full of awareness of the beauty of creation and Creator; a life of solidarity with other humans and the rest of creation; and a life lived in the full Grace of Allah (SWT). The final objective of such a society is to ensure the actualization of the capabilities of humans to progress along the path to perfection toward their Creator. This is the common objective of society as well as of individuals". (Iqbal and Mirakhor, 2017: 175).

This chapter will provide the fundamentals of the Qur'anic cosmology and the insights it brings for individuals immersed in the contemporary consumer culture.[3] Delineating the Islamic metaphysics is important because that is the basis of Islamic spirituality, morality and ethics. Once the underlying Islamic philosophy is understood, it will be easier to understand the ontological conception of the human soul (*nafs*). The right direction for the true flourishing of individuals and communities can only be set up once the true nature of human self is understood. Sections 2 and 3 of this chapter deal with Islamic metaphysics and ethics. In short, this chapter would serve to unpack the metaphysical, epistemological, ethical, psycho-social foundations of modern economics which require radical transformation in the light of Islamic normative principles derived from the Islamic metaphysics.

It is observed that the faculty, students and professionals of Economics, Accounting, Finance and Banking often lack a holistic perspective on Islamic ontology and ethics. That is why they fail to understand the pitfalls of a market society and the

---

wasting' the planet's resources is the dominant economic paradigm, the laws of ecology, like the water cycle, show us that nature does not ever waste. With this new perspective, over the last few years, a circular economic system is emerging; exploring ways, means, processes, and incentives to learn from nature and to minimize and ideally eliminate all types of waste. What are the prospects of a handshake between Islamic finance and this emerging new paradigm? Through studies and deliberations, the prospects for economics, finance, business, management, and other fields of humanities to learn from nature through the lens of Islamic values along with the multidimensional Sustainable Development Goals of the United Nations (UN SDGs), can be explored. This conference, organized by the Center for Islamic Economics and Finance of the College of Islamic Studies with the support of the Qatar Financial Centre, set out to probe and take stock of the existing knowledge and prospects for transforming economies to achieve and sustain multidimensional development bringing together original papers deliberating on Islamic finance and the circular economy

3 This emphasis is there in both the Quran and the Hadith. The Hadith perspective is elaborated in another chapter of this volume. See Qadir, Raquib and Ahmed, Spiritual Excellence (Iḥsān) for Professionals: A Ḥadīth-Based Perspective.

associated consumer culture. Here we define the market society as one where the logic of efficiency and utility informs all decisions at all levels and the only acceptable form of rationality is instrumental rationality.[4] They also do not fully appreciate the real import of Islamic teachings which is the character development of individuals and cultivation of virtues in a community. So when they become policy analysts or policy makers, the sole concern of most present-day Islamic Economics and Finance experts and policy analysts, despite their immense sincerity, is to only ensure the outward Shariah compliance of business and financial practices. One example is the business model of these Islamic banks which keep on offering incessant discounts and other services to facilitate shopping and encourage their clients toward mindless consumption of goods and services. Economists and Finance professionals need to realize that, in the current market society, the financial institutions actually play a decisive role in shaping individual characters and social preferences, norms and standards. They need to be informed, how the ultimate objective of all Muslim institutions in a Muslim community and even in predominantly non-Muslim communities, is to provide the right conditions for the nurturing and the purification of the human soul (*tazkiya*).

In order to develop a broader perspective on the prevalent crises in the contemporary world and how unthoughtful business models and practices, receiving investment via these financial institutions are wreaking havoc, it is important to have a deeper understanding of the functioning of late-modern market societies. We have tried to provide an in-depth analysis of these philosophical-social assumptions in Sections 4–8. Once they understand that the individual of Modern Economics is an individual defined by desires and self-interest, the logic of a market society is efficiency, and greed the highest virtue, the students and practitioners of Islamic Economics, Banking and Finance would understand the antagonism this worldview has with the Islamic worldview, that is, the basis of Islamic spirituality and ethics. However, it should also be noted that the absence of Islamic teachings – in spirit – within the Islamic Banking and Finance is, on occasions, not purely intentional nor attributable to the said professionals not understanding Islamic values but rather a constraint imposed by the conventional economic thought. The more traditional economic view of consumption has been that over consumption was based on human greed. However modern economists such as Douthwaite (1992), author of *The Growth Illusion*, bring a different assertion according to which the driving force behind consumerism is our economic system that requires increase of income and consumption each year for its flourishing. Such a system is antithetical to sustainable societies that are stable, hence do not constantly grow in terms of income and spending. Both Schor

4 A market economy is a tool; it's a valuable and effective tool for organizing productive activity. A market society is different. A market society is a place; it's a way of life where market relations and market incentives and market values come to dominate all aspects of life. And that's my worry. Q & A with Michael Sandel: From Market Economy to Market Society. https://www.thedailybeast.com/q-and-a-with-michael-sandel-from-market-economy-to-...

and Douthwaite are of the opinion that it is precisely our current economic system that precludes sustainability (Simon-Brown 2000). This is to say, that conventional economics thrives on consumerism and the other tactics it must employ to ensure its growth. Consequential then to this is that no system – even Islamic Banking and Finance – developed within the umbrella of this thought can ever completely nullify its characteristics (Also see Jha, 2013, p. 171).

Muslim students and professionals – fully aware of the underlying philosophy characterizing Islam and the late modern market society along with its ideational roots – will realize that the consumer culture does not cohere with Islamic ethics. Then onwards, through their research, policies and practices, they can try to implement the Shariah not only in its letter, but also the spirit of Islamic ethics in terms of character building of individuals and creation of strong, compassionate communities. Section 9 looks at the assumptions inherent in late modern market societies and the various psychological-social-environmental harms that have arisen as a consequence, as were shown in Sections 4–8, through the Islamic ontology of self and its subsequent ethical objectives, that were stated in Sections 2 and 3. Key Islamic concepts are used in this final section to provide a holistic perspective on the role of Islamic Economics and Finance.

2 The Qur'anic Worldview

A worldview should succeed as a doctrinal force that shapes the psychological, spiritual, intellectual and cultural lives of the people who adopt it. A clear and consistent worldview should therefore be both realistic and idealistic. It should be idealistic because human beings need an aspiration toward lofty goals that apparently defy actualization in order to move them higher up in the vicinity of those objectives. At the same time, principled action requires taking into consideration the real nature and behavior of the people and the context in which one sets out to live that worldview. A worldview that is far removed from the harshest aspects of reality creates little impact on either individuals or the society.

The narcissistic worldview that is prevalent in our ultra-consumerist societies, whether Muslim or otherwise, is merely a representation of the absence of a sound worldview that can stand up against oppression and tyranny, be it of the self, nature or other individuals, tribes, communities, societies, nationalities and races. The reason for the success of the Qur'anic worldview, in earlier periods, was due to its ability to inspire and foster the "realization and affirmation of the self in its various individual and communal ways. When people lived under the influence of the constructive Qur'anic worldview of the early days of Islam, their God-given spiritual nature responded with the values of justice, charity, brotherhood, and peace" (AbuSulayman 2013: 8). This resonates with the Qur'anic concept of reminder (*tazkīr*) which means that the Qur'anic message is a reminder for all humankind and anyone who wills to follow this worldview, will have their virtues kindled to the fullest. Allah declares in the Qur'an:

> "This [message] is no less than a reminder to all humankind – to every one of you who wills to walk a straight way" (81:27–28. Trans. Yusuf Ali).[5]
>
> Verily this is no less than a Message to (all) the Worlds. (With profit) to whoever among you wills to go straight. (81:27–28. Trans. Yusuf Ali).

The Islamic Worldview is thus not limited to merely the physical, socio-political, cultural and historical realms. The spiritual realm is not only included but also forms the bedrock for the examination of the physical and the mundane. This is unlike the dichotomy of the sacred and the profane that characterizes the modern Western scientific worldview which is by default restricted to only the world of senses and sensible experience. The eternal spiritual reality in the Islamic cosmology is the all-encompassing reality (*al-haqiqah*). The sensible or factual occurrence (*al-waqiyah*) represents only one aspect or level of reality whereas *al-haqiqah* encompasses all of reality (Attas 2001).

According to Attas (2001, 2–4),

> The Islamic vision of reality and truth, which is a metaphysical survey of the visible as well as the invisible worlds including the perspective of life as a whole, is not a worldview that is formed merely by the gathering together of various cultural objects, values and phenomena into artificial coherence. Nor is it one that is formed gradually through a historical and developmental process of philosophical speculation and scientific discovery, which must of necessity be left vague and open-ended for future change and alteration in line with paradigms that change in correspondence with changing circumstances [...] Islam is not a form of culture, and its system of thought projecting its vision of reality and truth and the system of value derived from it are not merely derived from cultural and philosophical elements aided by science, but one whose original source is Revelation, confirmed by religion, affirmed by intellectual and intuitive principles.

It is interesting to note that unlike the history of the secular West, Islam did not experience periods that can be termed classical, medieval, modern and postmodern. There was neither any renaissance nor an enlightenment to take the Muslim civilization from dark pits of ignorance to the shining light of knowledge and guidance. The Islamic worldview has an authenticity and finality about the ultimate reality and truth. It is therefore a complete perspective that encompasses all of existence.

The Islamic worldview establishes once and for all the fundamental truths about the nature of God; His Revelation; His creation, especially the human beings and the psychology of the human soul; knowledge; freedom; values and virtues; happiness. The knowledge of the nature of God as understood through God's attributes, determines for Muslims, their systems of meaning, knowledge standards and value frameworks. The Islamic position on these fundamental concepts shape the Muslim

5 https://quranyusufali.com/

ideas about change, development and progress, which are some of the key terms in the postmodern consumer culture of the West that has now engulfed the whole planet. Modernity and now postmodernity is challenging these basic elements of the Islamic worldview. All of this is important to be kept in mind in order to understand the contemporary dilemma that is faced by both the Muslim intellectuals and laypersons. If Islam is unjustifiably interpreted along the lines of the history of the secular West one will fail to appreciate the true essence of the Islamic metaphysics and its impact on Muslim history and civilization. Also, the analysis and proposed solutions of contemporary problems encountering the Muslims due to the global hegemony of the Western secular philosophy, mindset, culture and institutions, will be a plain mimicry of the secular models. Such faulty premises tend to lead Muslim academics, in areas as diverse as Banking and Finance on the one hand and biotechnology on the other hand, to be developing guidelines and models for their respective disciplines and industries that try to conform to the form and letter of the Sharia but since the spirit or the Islamic worldview is not understood properly, they not only fail to bring about the desired results or social changes but also serve to intensify the spiritual-ethical, socio-political and environmental degeneration (Nasr 1990, Nasr 2002, Pasquier 1992).

Islam as a religion is based on the transcendental truths but at the same time it affirms that the human existence is subject to both the physical and social limitations and the Islamic worldview is meant to be established and realized in the finite world bounded by limitations. In Islamic cosmology, God is the Lord ("*al-Rabb*") of both the transcendent and the mundane realms. This means He is the Lord, the Only Creator and true Owner of the creation. He is the only One who absolutely nourishes, maintains and Sustains this creation (Zarabozo 1999, 242). That is why He is also the God ("*Ilāh*") Who is to be submitted and surrendered to (which is what Islam means) in all matters of life and death, in the manner shown by His last prophet Mohammad. Allah as *Ilāh* is the ultimate object of adoration, devotion and worship. Allah is to be singled out for all acts of worship, external and internal, statements and actions. This worship which must be devoted solely to Allah covers everything that is pleasing and beloved to Allah, in all spheres of one's life, whether they be acts or statements, decisions or choices, likes and dislikes, priorities and ambitions. The person who considers Allah to be true *Ilāh* will have no other life goal than complete love and submission to Allah (Zarabozo 1999, 245).

3 Spiritual and Moral Excellence: Qur'anic Ideal for the Human Self and Society

The ideas of change, development and progress in the Islamic worldview derive their specific meanings from the Islamic metaphysics of *Tawhid* explained above, that affirms change only as successive actualization of inherent potentialities and that also through God's creative act, Who has the power to bring about changes in the permanent reality of beings (Qur'an 84:19). This leads to a very specific notion of change as one that brings about the fruition of a being to its self-realization. Just like a seed carries the potential to turn into a fruit-bearing plant so does human beings carry infinite possibilities for cultivating virtue and developing their essential nature which carries the divine substance (*ruh*) until they reach the highest possible level in this worldly, material realm. This is the *nafs* at rest or in peace with itself, its Creator and the social and the natural world, called the *nafs-al-mutmainnah*. This is a life time plan for virtue-oriented action because the certainty (*yaqīn*) only arrives with death (Qur'an 15:99). Human development and societal development acquire a unique characteristic in this framework, where, without denying or mitigating the outward aspects of human welfare and happiness, the true and genuine intention (*ikhlās*) behind an act determines the self-development of the individual performing the action. The external consequences are not the final measure. Instead the inward spiritual-ethical ascent towards God (*al- Ilāh*) accompanied by righteous outward deeds is what matters in this worldview. Since all internal and external changes are brought about by the creative will of Allah (*al-Rabb*) in the transcendental sphere of commands (*'ālam-al-amr*), the external actions and efforts for social change lead to internal change and an inner transformation or *tazkiyah* lead to positive consequences in the external world, both natural and social (Qur'an 13:11). That is why the Qur'an mostly juxtaposes faith (*īmān*) which is the inner dimension with pious deeds (*'amāl salehah*) that constitute the external dimension.

Within the Islamic worldview, the world (*al-dunya*) and the worldly life (*al- hayāt al-dunya*) are two distinct concepts (Attas 2001, 22–24). The world or nature carries high regard in virtue of being the creation of Allah. They world acts as signs of Allah, reflecting the various attributes and names of Allah in diverse natural and social environments. The world is thus sacred. The worldly life, on the other hand, in so far as it leads to the nearness of Allah and provides an opportunity for the cultivation of virtue is commended but if it leads human beings to becoming deviant and astray, away from virtue and love of Allah, it is called the deceiving object (*matā'a al-ghuroor*) (Qur'an 3:185). The worldly life is a sowing ground for human *tazkiyah* that is the inward development of character and virtues.[6] The progress for the human self would comprise in an upward ascent to Allah (SWT), culminating in the ultimate perfection of human soul in the afterlife (*al-akhirah*).

According to the Islamic worldview, the world or nature has already been created in the best mold and possible form (Qur'an 95:4; 87:2). The God-given nature (*fitrah*) cannot develop further. Instead there is a grave danger of the *fitrah* being corrupted by the worldly life and its deceptions. True development in the Islamic ontology, lies

6 See also, Qadir, Junaid., and Zaman, Asad. 2018. "The Ends of Development in Islam: Seven overlapping Concepts." *Journal of Islamic Banking and Finance*. 35(3).

in purifying the human soul and in preserving its primordial, innate goodness. This requires a lot of struggle (*mujāhadah*) but Allah has promised that whoever is prepared to struggle for Allah's sake will be shown the path leading to Allah (Qur'an 29:69). Development in the worldly life is to be decided at the scale of individuals who become successful in the hereafter. Change, development, and progress, all are defined and understood in terms of the *akhirah* or the final purpose and objective of the worldly life.

4 Progress and Development Ideals in the Contemporary World

When discussing the key notions of change, development and progress, one should be extra vigilant since these are worldview terms that have strong metaphysical bias and are culturally grounded. Change can occur in the exterior that is the outer world which includes the physical human selves as well as all kinds of changes in the landscapes and ways of living in the world that can be objectively witnessed. In the contemporary world this kind of a change is equated with development and henceforth progress of human individuals and the civilization as such. Tall towers and all sorts of construction miracles and medical advancements that have taken place with the help of sophisticated technology along with the advancement of technologies themselves, reflect development within the humanistic model of economic, technological and human, that is, civilizational development. In the contemporary late modern worldview, that calls itself secular, the external, material world is seen as divested of all sacredness. This makes it easy to use the physical world as a quantitative resource. Such a profane world is of necessity free of any telos or final purpose. The world as a resource then can be and should be used for materialistic ends. The world resources are therefore "changed" to bring about development (See Nasr 1990, Al-Attas 2001, and Chapra 2016, Jha 2013 Islamic Economics Pg 173, footnote number 13). Heidegger through his notion of *Gestell* had long ago warned us of the consequences of treating nature as a standing reserve (Godzinski 2005).

The question that arises here is, how in the absence of substantive final purposes one can determine the ends or goals to which the advancing technologies and growing economies should contribute? In the absence of long-term ethical ends derived from a specific metaphysical outlook, it becomes almost impossible to establish even the short term, proximal ends. If "materialism" is taken to be the metaphysics here, then an increase (change) in numbers and quantities, at all levels and in all senses, will be taken as "development" irrespective of any real and potential damages and threats it might have for the social and natural environment. Rather the concept secular implies a demeaning or desacralization of nature, both living and non-living, because it has now been divorced from the divine. The problem of preserving the environment and any concern for the decline in the quality of human life, becomes irrelevant in this system of thought. When nature is understood to be free of spiritual meaning and purpose, it becomes incomprehensible why one should be concerned about protecting pristine nature, its flora and fauna. The same turns out to be the fate of human beings. The simple "progressivism" holds that even when millions of lives are lost, in this atheistic, materialistic march of progress as in the Second World War, it only amounts to collateral damage in the long march of "human progress".

> The Second World War, a still more appalling tragedy, should have revealed to humanity the illusions and dangers of progessist and more or less atheistic ideologies which promise the achievement of happiness though purely profane, quantitative o materialistic means. But instead of discerning their illusory nature, and returning to more spiritual and traditional values, man speeded up the process of secularization. If the promises of happiness did not come true, then the ideologues of the system never drew the conclusion that they were false or groundless, but instead launched an assault on the last survivals of the old order and of traditional ideas, denouncing them as so many obstacles to the march of progress which must urgently be swept away. (Du Pasquier 2002, 3)

In contrast to the Islamic approach, the secular worldview of the late modern world looks at the world as if it has no inherent purpose. This relativizes all human values. The world is nothing but an ever-changing complex. In this context, it is considered the human task to shape and develop that change in a way that delivers objective and quantitative results in the most efficient manner. This efficiency acts as the logic of the late modern market society.

5 Objectives of Modern Economics

Economics, as a formal discipline, was one of the key developments of Enlightenment. When understanding the objectives of Economics, one must take into consideration the philosophical and social changes that directly led to the endorsement of the study of Economics. Post-Enlightenment Europe was one that was in the active search of creating principles that established the dichotomy between the Church and the State, and proclaimed the supremacy of an order free from any constraints which heretofore had been exercised to contain human ambitions. Human, and not the divine, came above all in this system which looked up to the rational-empirical way of knowing as the only mode of guidance.

It is verily here that we first witness our modern, overarching dependence on quantitative rather qualitative analysis. With techno-science making way through mathematics, and with the assumed value neutrality of numbers, the new principles, the new worldview to be established, was to be heavily dependent on numerical dominance. Over-simplification of how we experienced the world in numbers was at the helm of this development. This worldview catered for all that could be experienced and measured for that is what ascertained its' objectivity. On the contrary, the quantitative worldview, in principle, negated the presence of any axiological (value-based) worldview that had existed before, thus, stripping ethical and moral values away from the new order. Through this, not only was the divine separated from the social sphere but its negation took place in all forms: for the divine, ethics and values being immeasurable, were now all irrelevant (Jha 2013).

With this task accomplished, the characterization of an ideal human to be pursued for the society within this dynamic was needed to replace the ideal of the pre-Enlightenment time. This ideal human had to be someone who submitted to an objective view of phenomena that surrounded them. Moreover, the ideal human (the rational human) had to be in pursuit of something that was both unachievable, whilst it was still an objective closely classified within the empirical nature of the world so it was experience-able. The vague objective of happiness served the purpose. The objectives of modernity were eventually to be served by the market. The answer was the creation of the economic human being (homo economicus) whose sole objective was utility and who submitted his will to the "Free Market" where the market, through its manipulations, officially took over the role of the Church and the State (Poole 1996).

This discipline of Economics, then with its systemic presuppositions of rationality among others, was a tool that projected the same desires through enterprise and entrepreneurial work in the market with Economic wo/man's sole objective being the pursuit of the vague and subjective idea of happiness despite the otherwise claim to objectivity. No longer was business (craftsmanship) a mode to satisfy definite ends with certain specific means, to live a happy life, but was instead turned into a business (corporation) with its means and ends, both unbounded and un-submitting to any constraints. In the absence of metaphysical or communal ends, the pursuit of profit and capital served as both the means and the ends. Thus we see the emergence of corporation in its modern form. This corporation was void of an ethical framework relying only on a quantitative social and economic science to dictate its behavior.

No longer was the Economic wo/man a "human" either. The Economic wo/man, to retain their rationality, was conceived as someone abstracted from faith, culture, language, family and community. The Economic wo/man inspected everything through numbers, the sole mode of value-neutrality and objectivity, for taking decisions. The emergence of this behavior forces one to look at humans and human relationships, as mere assets and transactions of the market. Consequently, we see the emergence of utilitarianism among other frameworks to help the enterprise justify its methods of acquiring its means and setting up its ends. It is also here we see the inherent problems of the commercial or market society that was so far removed from the traditional civilizations.

What should be noted here is that the above discussion also highlights why the free market often struggled with establishing values or constraints to bar the capitalist greed it understood the market would otherwise manifest. Although, the free market offered a hitherto unparalleled freedom, it also largely understood that such freedom had to be constrained somewhere as it would lead to the development of demerit goods and “deadweight loss”. Utilitarianism and Kantianism, among other systems, were meant to develop in the market the consciousness it lacked after becoming perfectly rational and its participants’ identities abstracted of all values (Poole 1996 Chapter 1). However, it is also through this ironically, that the market itself turned into the biggest transgressor of rights that it so willfully promised to remove upon its conception. For instance, the exploitation of labor, and the historically famous abuse of Africans, corporations treating its employees as expendable and the development of monopolies that abused their market power serve as examples.

6 Behind the Economic Development Ideal: The Market Logic of Free, Self-Interested Individuals

> Freedom as it is understood in our day is a precious commodity [...] Any man who enjoys it in some limited way and aspires to possess it more fully is finally driven to admit that it eludes him to the extent that he pursues it. (Pasquier 2002, 27)

The free market necessitates three elements for its existence. It requires individuals who are driven by self-interested behavior governed by instrumental rationality – a mode of rationality that chooses the most efficient means for a desired end. This is followed by a legal framework of property rights and contracts, and social division of labor. These crucial presuppositions allow the free market to preserve its form and maintain its claim of being efficient and free for all. Freedom has a very limited meaning within the structure of the free market. Liberty and happiness are conjoined and both spring from the endless fulfillment of the individual’s desire. Freedom within this structure is guaranteed by such preconditions which make sure no single agent of the market is influential enough to create distortions for others which also means that no single producer or consumer can influence the general well-being of the economy and hence the society. The presupposition goes something like this; since the market is governed by the ideology of one’s pursuit of one’s desires, it should eventually create a web large enough to enable everyone to pursue their own interests – irrespective of the moral or ethical quality of the desire. Thus, more the number of desires, higher the general utility for the society, and greater the freedom and happiness for its members.

It is inappropriate to use the term community here since community necessitates thinking and action where the self-interest is not seen in isolation from and in contrast to the interest of other members in the community. The problem with this conception of freedom is that it not only ignores all other substantial ways of understanding and defining freedom, contrary to its claims of freeing up its denizens from all sorts of authorities, a huge number of other conditions have to be placed in the form of statutes and laws that are paramount in importance to its foundational principles. Since the governing principle is beyond the scope of good and evil and only looks at the procedural good that allows the fulfillment of any and every individual self-interest that is rationally motivated, many more laws and regulations ae indeed needed.[7] This is in contrast to a religious- ethical oriented community where altruistic actions originate naturally out of sheer care and love for the community members and nature in general. So, in the end, a free market society, based on the idea of freedom as property and commodity, end up enforcing laws in similitude to the religious and moral precepts, it promises to free its agents from.

To reach the level of self-interested behavior presupposed by the market, an individual must be alienated from all his/her previous marks of identity: faith, culture, language, land, tribe, etc. The legal framework in a religious or quasi-religious community is backed by a strong metaphysics in which the ethics is grounded. This spiritual and ethical backing is absent in the late modern market society. The market needs legal restrictions to exist, therefore some similitude of ethics or ethical illusions becomes a must. Adam Smith tried to implant the idea of "Virtue" as a cement to hold together the ethical fabric of the society (Poole,1996 15–16). The reason this solution proves to be hollow is that the idea of virtue emerges in an ethics-based community and is nourished by a conception of self and identity that is not exclusively equated with rational self-interest. Under these considerations, and others, it can be observed that the very existence of market requires a fundamental violation of human freedom by making the alienation of one's identity necessary, so limiting their choice and what they want from their lives. The assumption of virtue does not seem to work with the fundamental presuppositions that the market has about the human self and human ends. It is then the very profanity of these basic presuppositions of the market, and their deterministic way of molding human identity, entailing that any mold apart from the one that market puts you in is a violation of the efficiency of the system it strives to be, the free market undermines the freewill of its agents as well.

In addition to this, as mentioned before, the free market requires interdependence of individuals on one another as part of the social division that enables it to work efficiently. Due to these complex interdependent relationships, the expression of freedom for an individual in the market is then inherently associated with his/her duty to uphold this order; preserving the order is inevitably translated into consumption. Yet, consumption requires an individual to work more to have more money to consume more but it comes at the cost of their time and ultimately their freedom to do anything other than upholding the order of consumption s/he is bound to. It should be observed further that for one to preserve their place in the society, but more importantly within the hierarchy of the market, consumption always has to be done at

---

7 https://www.economist.com/briefing/2010/07/22/too-many-laws-too-many-prisoner

an increasing rate so as to preserve one's position that maybe in jeopardy from those climbing up the very social ladder, whilst one also entertains the desire of moving up the hierarchy. Since the market demands one to operate within the realms of instrumental rationality, it would be "irrational" to do and think otherwise. In retrospect, this is paradoxical to the very nature of freedom that the market otherwise promises. This paradox can only be resolved by accepting the article of faith that "freedom is tantamount to consumption".

The free market sets as its aim the accumulation of capital. Capitalists operate for sheer profit. The laws of the market demand from them that their expression of freedom required them to re-invest their profits back into their business – the accumulation of capital. This was done to maintain or increase their profit levels for the future which, much like the consumption for consumers, is connected to their place in the market and its overall hierarchy. This cycle is set to be endless in its architecture because capitalists will also be consumers, resulting in the pursuit of consumption for the sake of consumption, profit for the sake of profit, in order to be free. Here the commodity of freedom becomes the ultimate symbol of power while its pursuit eludes the agents of the market the more they pursued it. In this scheme private vices like self-love, greed, avarice, dissatisfaction and pride can be social virtues. Since the individual of a market society does not have substantive values or identity to provide any consistent meaning of happiness, the understanding of what would constitute happiness was so far vague. It could now be attached directly to profit, utility and satisfaction of individual desires – the attainment of which was the ultimate desire leading to the ultimate satisfaction – but ultimately with no end in sight. Consumption thus becomes an end-in-itself.

Additionally, the other more prominent freedoms that a "Free Market" promises its agents include freedom of competition, the freedom of movement of capital – capital here includes human capital i.e. physical and mental labor – and the freedom from the control of any religious, ethical, moral or governmental doctrine, the inconsistency of which becomes obvious upon inspection. The modern economic model, which idolizes the free market, is an example of the failure of the free market in its provision of conditions that maintain freedom of competition but also the freedom to maintain a natural, healthy, wholesome lifestyle (Leonard 2010).[8] We have observed the formation of large corporations across the globe, diversifying in multiple areas of production, simply too rich and influential for the smaller and medium scale firms to compete with. The lifestyle choices and options in the spheres of work, nutrition, health, education, housing, clothing, transportation, leisure and entertainment that are offered by these ultra-large corporations are enforced upon people simply because, given the structure of the market economy, offering alternative choices requires even

8 See also https://www.localfutures.org/wp-content/uploads/the_economics_of_happiness_discussion_guide.pdf

larger capital. This contributes to the idea of the limitation of an agent of the market in not being able to raise up the necessary capital to compete against such a large organization. Competition therefore has a cost and is not free. These irregularities in the freedom of competition can be vividly observed in all parts of the world, where small and medium scale businesses, are being forced to shut down struggling to compete against cheap subsidized produce of their larger counterparts. This translates on a global level as well where governments through subsidies to large-scale firms, equips them with means of generating foreign revenue. Consequently, this results in the destruction of domestic economies across the borders through international trade because the domestic suppliers of the importing country cannot compete. This disparity is not acknowledged and all forms of international trade are hailed as the prevalence of freedom.

In addition to this, the freedom of the movement of capital at many occasions appears to be impractical, especially, when the limitations of nature are taken into consideration. For instance, when one tries to transfer the economic commodity of "land" or natural resources from one place to the other. For instance, imaging moving the Atlantic Ocean where the Pacific is and vice versa. This, of course, has not stopped the disposition of the agents in the market from pursuing the idea of moving all other means of production that are easily transferable and trying to come up with ways of transforming those which cannot be transported. Thus, perhaps arguably giving birth to situations of modern-day human trafficking and sex labor only because there remains a demand in the market to be satisfied and so the capital and human resource must flow in that direction; doing so being rational.

7 Freedom and Happiness as Consumption

7.1 The Ideal of Happiness as Consumption

With all this established, one may question the reason behind the way the economic wo/man operates and behaves. It should be mentioned here that these developments took over a considerable period and at the core of these developments was one fact: the deprivation that the economic wo/man suffered in the pre-enlightenment era. To counter the material deprivation that people were exposed to, the market offered the idea of demand (consumption) as means for satisfaction of those desires that went mostly unnoticed before. The idea of consumption was connected to happiness, as can be inspected in the utilitarian system, where the economic wo/man was made a counter offer to live a materially enriched life which s/he had never been given a chance to live. It is this prospect of happiness through consumption that also drove the market to most of its evils. The economic wo/man chased the ideal of happiness and thus, wanted to consume endlessly. More consumption required more money, and more money required more enterprise which in return required more capital – both human and physical, i.e., machines.

This drive towards achieving the ultimate level of satisfaction, a vague idea of ultimate happiness drove the economic wo/man to do as the market dictated. All other sources of identity such as faith and family, that used to help the individual make decisions were no longer available. In the dichotomy of the private and the public sphere, the market was to be a self-governed entity in the public sphere, not falling under any foundational principles or ethics. The market desired capital, for it desired its growth, and so all steps taken forth were to satisfy this desire. A drive for becoming efficient was not only a presupposition but was a direct consequence of the market society itself. Demand for newer technology, longer hours of work, production and creation of more commodities and the creation of demand where it did not exist before, all are both the preconditions and effects of a market society. The market then was a person in its own capacity. The economic wo/man on the other hand that was forged, was now deprived of a different, significantly more crucial commodity, freedom of will: as market dictated his behavior. The ideal of happiness was a façade that did allow the economic wo/man to achieve a material well-being s/he could not have actualized before. However, the cost of this was allowing profanity to exist in society. Hence, the decadence of values, ethics, morality, relationships and everything that faith- based civilization had preserved. This slow but steady process of withering continued through modernism and is intensified in our post-modern globalized world.

7.2 Techno-scientific Progress and Financial Growth

> The trajectory of thought from the enlightenment era onwards can arguably be seen as an ever-increasing separation from the Divine. The physics of Galileo, Descartes, and Newton implied that with the new laws of motion, everything keeps moving by itself through rational, natural laws. Thus, with motion objectively extrinsic to and transferred between objects, God was no longer seen as necessary to animate the world. Descartes and others proposed that animals are machines too, that no inner anima, no spirit, is needed to animate them either. God was thus removed from the world of matter, becoming in a parable of the time, a watchmaker God, with creation becoming a discrete act existing almost independently of Divine agency. (Jha 2013, 173)

Modern science was practiced away from divinity and science was thus undertaken in search of what was profane and enabled the profane. Technological development, on the other hand aided science in being able to create what was profane. Science with its laws that now were projected upon nature, enabled the economic wo/man to see the world as what Heidegger calls the "standing reserve" (Heidegger 1977). Techno-science created new machines, pushed the limits of the boundaries that once caged humanity and at the same time allowed the economic wo/man to exercise their pursuit for profit, capital and consumption. Techno-science, void of the initial principles through which it was practiced by the Greeks up until the Muslims, was now a tool of the market to help it achieve its goals.

Technology, much like Economics, developed to serve late-modern market forces as a tool however, technology mutated itself into a view of world itself. Technology allowed the market to assert itself in both the public and the private life of an individual. Where previously private life was influenced by public life which remained under the market forces, through technology, the private life also reaffirmed and established the markets power. Being surrounded by mobile phones and all other gizmos in our current paradigms is no less than an epidemic. It is attributes and traits like these that enable the market to create demands for newer services and commodities.

Through the breakthroughs made by techno-science, the West and its worldview unlocked for its' citizens, an easy and cheap access to material well-being, its most prized goal – not taking the environmental loss, abuse of human rights, pillaging of continents through colonization, into consideration as its cost. On the same hand, this meant the everlasting idea of growth no longer could continue at the scale which science and technology had enabled. The West now searched for a new market but more important was the question of how to create one. It is here that a deliberate creation of the idea of development took place and hence the subsequent craze behind achieving economic growth. With the arrival of President Truman, the USA began a policy whereby it targeted different hemispheres of the world to adopt its world order – modern capitalism. In one of his speeches, Truman emphasized how the world could achieve the same living standards as those being experienced in the USA by adopting the developmental model of capitalism (Esteva 2010, 1–5). It is using this categorization not only was Truman able to position the USA as the leader of the modern world, as the USA already maintained a strong position on the socio-economic evolutionary scale but also persuaded the then devastated Europe to follow in its steps that desperately needed rescuing after World War 2. To become "developed", countries had to follow the capitalist framework and aim productivity, that is, economic growth. It was only through producing more, consuming more and producing further more to consume even more that such a goal could be achieved. With populace in the under-developed world made to feel inferior for their lifestyle and their anguish to be progressive and prosperous, at least materialistically, in trying to imitate the West, concessions were made in social, private, cultural, traditional and religious spheres to accommodate the new "divinity", i.e., the market. The market idealized the Western society with nations racing to achieve more and more economic growth, the decadence of culture and loss of morality in East occurred at an unprecedented rate. In the Islamic context, rites and practices were either abandoned or molded to accommodate economic growth and the ideals of the market. It is in this context that the Islamic Finance emerged as a field of study and as an industry.

Technology, when understood in a dynamic context, can be examined to have created many inventions. One of these inventions was Finance which is defined, as the art of managing money. To understand why Finance is recorded as a technology, one must understand the goal of the market. The market necessitates its growth which it does so through the manipulation of factors of production: land, labor, capital and enterprise. Finance, understood as a technology, was thus created to make sure that the power yielded by money could be used as impressively as it allowed itself to be. Finance manifested complex functions and formulas, harnessing the already complex web of rules that protected the markets, which corporations endorsed and used to grow further. One must first consider this context within which rules, that dictated the germination of Finance, were created.

7.3 Catastrophic Consequences of Misplaced Technological Development

The overconsumption that we witness in our global societies today, the shopaholism, and the unending cycle of production, consumption and waste accompanied by various mental disorders like narcissistic personality disorder (NPD) correlated with the low self-esteem caused by not possessing enough, reflect how people are now shackled to the chains of consumerism (Rosen, 2012, 17ɤ46). These are the results of the one dimensional or horizontal progress discussed in the previous section. With the advent of newer technologies, the commodities are projected to the individuals at an ever-increasing pace which lets them crave for more and more stuff. This possession of stuff becomes synonymous with self-projection via the same technological media, leading to narcissism, self-centeredness and alienation which lead on to depression and at times suicide.

In *iDisorder*, (Rosen, 2012) argues how our reliance on different mediums of technology is consequential to the development of special mental disorders. He argues how technology has led to the exaggeration of narcissistic traits, self-centeredness and overall love for one's self. He makes his case initially by arguing that majority of us remain fixated on our devices and the stimulation they provide; the younger the generation the greater the fixation. This habit allows us to be alienated from actual interaction in comparison to the virtual interaction as we value it more. The disconnection from real stimulus and the availability of technological substitutes in addition to the feeling of anonymity in the virtual world, as argued by the author, remain at the center of people developing an attachment towards the virtual playground: a world full of possibilities with a promise of ultimate self-expression; a representation of the ideal self. This in turn has the effect of development, or exaggeration, of the otherwise, normal narcissistic characteristics that eventually manifest narcissistic personality disorder (NPD). The manifestation of NPD is more evident in the youth due to the better integration of the younger generation with technology as compared to the older generations' reception of it. Disorder of this magnitude and others like it that are caused by technology and, especially, due to the invention of social media, give rise to social evils like narcissistic rage, anxiety, illusory superiority and inferiority, momentary pseudo-gratification, self-interest and the adoration of a false-self that is exhibited on the internet where people aim to accumulate social capital. This effect of narcissism is further aided by the TV shows and other forms of entertainment that emphasize on the development of a self-centered image of the audience where they are at the center of the world and everything is being offered to them.

8 The Nature of Modern Finance

The idea of unlimited economic growth necessitates Modern Finance. If the money, capital and profits earned by the capitalist, were not reinvested back into business, the capitalist, as mentioned earlier, would lose in the race of perfect competition: a necessary component of markets. Finance, with its management of money, allowed capitalists and corporations to assume a size bigger than one could ever imagine. For instance, statistics from World Bank show the GDP of Norway being 398.8 billion USD in 2017[9] whilst, data from SEC USA reveal Walmart to have earned revenues of approximately 500 billion USD.[10]

However, the way in which modern financial tools – created to sustain the economic growth model through financialization of economies – interacted with the world, they could only ensure growth up till a certain point: by taking the natural resources as a standing reserve, under the worldview of modern technology and market. Depletion of resources in a particular market meant the creation of more markets. Finance, allowed this through stocks, derivatives, bonds and securities that were a new source of revenue (market), often at the cost of people's life-long savings as seen in 2008 Financial Crisis. This was possible since the different intricacies, functions and, complicated models of Modern Finance allowed people to create more markets, markets for investment in property, loans, etc. One could question that these markets existed before, however, what should be noted here is the scale at which all these markets operated in the new Finance paradigm.[11] For instance, the 2008 financial crisis had led up to the creation of an artificial demand for property across the USA which, when examined under its current devastation almost 11 years after the crisis, could allow one to buy a townhouse in Detroit's suburbs at an extremely low

9 https://data.worldbank.org/country/norway

10 http://d18rn0p25nwr6d.cloudfront.net/CIK-0000104169/3460d423-ab69-4c7f-b7c0-ffebc209e2a7.pdf

11 See also; Tickell, Adam. 2000. "Dangerous Derivatives: Controlling and Creating Risks in International Money." *Geoforum* 31 (1): 87–99.

Crawford, Corinne. 2011. "The Repeal of the Glass-Steagall Act and the Current Financial Crisis." *Journal of Business & Economics Research* 9 (1): 127–34.

rate.[12] How did this happen? Cheap and easy loans were created through financial mechanisms which had been de-regulated by the US government to encourage business. Had it not been for Modern Finance, this tragedy could have been avoided.[13] But what can be easily missed out here is the fact that Modern Finance, as a tool, was created for the multiplication of one's money and its' management under the market system. It was then in the basic nature of Modern Finance to enable something like this. Since Modern Finance is not based on an axiological system of values, it works under the same value-neutrality assumption as the market. Hence, even if it could foresee the devastation, it would have not stopped the crisis for ethical reasons such as the loss for humanity that it resulted in, but purely for the purposes of preserving the market. That is because Modern Finance has been created as a tool to enable just that. It is entirely because of this that Modern Finance cannot be articulated without greed: the greed for more profits, more growth, more production and more consumption.

This can also be examined by inspecting the accounting principles which were a presupposition for Modern Finance. For instance, the monetary unit principle in accounting dictates that one can only record business transactions that are expressed in money (Weygandt et al. 2015, 9–10). This, then, in other words means that any loss that a business causes to an individual or environment, would be left unrecorded and more dangerously, un-regraded (Anielski 2007). This ascertains a Financial worldview whereby relationships, as mentioned before, are regarded as transactional and not transformational. There then is a complete disregard for the actual civilizational values that these financial instruments were meant to serve. Moreover, a person working in the financial sector would himself accredit these statements as truthful and yet disregard them as if they are insignificant stating that is how the world operates. A modern Finance expert would agree that reforms are needed in his job stating the long hours, the monotonous work that only benefits the big corporation that exploits the customers and yet, would interact with this very model and encourage others to do so by over-consumption and promoting the fashionable way of over-consumption. This inner struggle is often found in Muslims who have been raised with the ideals of Islamic ethics and morals. Islamic Finance was meant to be a response to this spiritual-ethical dilemma that is causing spiritual-ethical, societal and environmental harms.

---

12 https://www.urban.org/sites/default/files/publication/88656/detroit_path_forward_finalized.pdf, p. 30.
See also; Acharya, Viral, Thomas Philippon, Matthew Richardson, and Nouriel Roubini. 2009. "The Financial Crisis of 2007–2009: Causes and Remedies." *Financial Markets, Institutions & Instruments* 18 (2): 89–137.

13 See; LiPuma, Edward and Lee, Benjamin. 2005. "Financial derivatives and the rise of circulation." *Journal of Economy and Society*. 34 (3): 404–427.

Islamic Finance, however, fails fundamentally. It is not because of the intentions behind it but the under-estimation of markets' power to shape specific financial institutions, overwhelming the intentions of Islamic Finance. Some key characteristics that should be pointed out here are that Islamic Finance is, on principle, still shaped on the demand-supply laws of Economics that have created the modern markets. That is not to discredit the idea of the laws of demand and supply but rather to spot that IBF is fashioned out of the very ideas and principles – following the letter of Islamic law but not its spirit – that fashioned the very problematic view of the world that has us demanding for alternatives. It is interesting to note that within the Islamic worldview although demand ought to trigger supply, encouraging entrepreneurs to trade in the needed goods and services, with the current business models, it is the supply that triggers demand and encourages the consumers to unthinkingly consume ad infinitum (Raquib and Khan 2019). The revisionist Muslim scholars like Mufti Taqi Usmani fail to see this specific cultural/global context which is necessary to discuss if the traditional Islamic fiqh ideas and concepts are not to be applied without taking into consideration the current realities. (Ansari and Arshad, 2006: 64–69; 73–85, 120–127; 264–270; 281–82).

In that regard, with the incorporation of these principles, Islamic Finance has not emerged as a reformative system that could save the world from the existing crises. (See Asutay 2007; Javaid 2015; Javaid and Suri 2015; Javaid 2012). The commentators often regard Islamic Finance as following the letter of the law, a condition that holds on most grounds within the framework of Islamic Finance. However, what is largely ignored is the essence and the spirit of the Islamic law.[14]

9 Partial Muslim Solution or Holistic Islamic Solution?

The crux is that the psychological, social, political, environmental and financial crises in today's world that are attributed to the last vestiges of religion, are actually a reflection of the moral and spiritual subversion of human beings. Since that is not taken into consideration, the Islamic Banking and Finance (IBF), also being influenced by the modern ideas and ideals, stays oblivious to the postmodern nihilism inherent in the ideal of social progress through modern methods of Finance and industry. IBF thus tries to emulate the same foreign means and mechanisms which do not and cannot produce the spiritual reformation and transformation that is required to avert the financial crisis, human-induced massive poverty, environmental

14 https://www.academia.edu/35390608/Islamic_System_of_Production_and_Consumption_How_Schumacher_would_see_it

and accompanying social-political crises. Both the traditionalist and modernist Muslims have sought to revise the Islamic practices and institutions, that are of social-communal nature. Whether aware or unaware, their thinking and judgment have been influenced by the secular Western ethos of development and progress. The modernist Muslim intellectuals lack a complete understanding of both the Islamic and the late modern secular worldview whereas their traditional counterparts know the Islamic worldview but find themselves compelled to align it with the Western style progress. Globalization seems to be one factor but they are also awed by the technological and military advancement of the West. The traditional Muslim scholars, who are madrassa-educated, lack a holistic understanding of the philosophy behind technological progress and often take that to be value-neutral (Raquib 2016). The secular humanism desacralizes nature thereby letting the human will act upon it according to human needs and desires. As discussed earlier, in the absence of final purpose, desires are turned into needs ad infinitum. This underlying philosophy of humanism where human beings are the measure and yardstick, change is celebrated for the sake of change and is termed development. The Muslim traditionalists fail to realize that all development today is informed by this paradigm. This lack of understanding is reflected in the modern IBF industry. The centers of excellence that undertake research in Islamic Finance are mostly oblivious to these insights.

The Muslim students and practitioners of Islamic Economics and Finance must know that the disciplines of Economics and Finance need to be placed within the larger whole of Islamic knowledge (*al-'ilm*). It must be a fundamental requirement for them to know the general ethical-spiritual conception of goodness (*ihsān*), justice (*'adl*), right action (*adab*), right educational aims and objectives (*ta'dīb*) and also how these ideals might be concretized within the ambit of their disciplines of economics, finance and financial management. The knowledge of the essence of Islamic teachings will make them understand and realize that Islamic knowledge is not limited to jurisprudence, instead jurisprudence was and should still be a means to enact social justice, environmental harmony and beauty in the Muslim communities and world at large.

Right knowledge requires the effort to undertake the right actions in their respective fields, both in theoretical research and practice. This ensures justice not merely as unqualified equality but as the right balance within the spiritual-psychological selves of the individuals (via *tazkiyah*) and outside in their social and societal affairs (*mu'amalāt*). Right education, therefore is not technical know-how but a well-rounded understanding of the worldly affairs, along with ethical understanding and motivation for right conduct. The goal of *adab* or right education is the acquisition of virtue for the human soul. Since virtue is the discernment of the right conduct from the wrongful conduct, at both the personal and societal levels; ethics in Islam is intrinsically tied to knowledge – both of God and of the true nature of human self. This knowledge helps the human self to keep the appetitive and bodily desires under the governance of the spiritual intellect which is a prerequisite for *tazkiya*. The process of *tazkiya* results in the attainment of virtue and genuine happiness for the individual and justice, peace and harmony in the society and the environment.

Freedom or free will within the Islamic metaphysics is the choice to act according to one's true nature (*fitrah*), in accordance with the realization of truth (*al-haqq*). The true human nature seeks virtue. Hence it is injustice (*zulm*) to indulge one's self in evil. Thus injustice to the self and injustice to the society are two sides of the same coin. True happiness (*sa'ādah*) is also identified with the stability of the soul and not only with fleeting feelings and emotions that accompany psychological and biological pleasures. Happiness is both a psychological and an ethical-spiritual state of knowing and pleasing Allah (SWT). The worldly pleasures and joys, when needs and wants are fulfilled, bring a foretaste of permanent bliss in the hereafter and have their value in so far as these transient joys lead to permanent state of fulfillment and bliss (*nafs al-mutmainnah*). Amongst them, the highest worldly blessing is peace and tranquility of the heart (*qalb*) that is attained though the knowledge (*m'ārifah*) and love (*mahabbah*) of God. The knowledge leads to knowing one's proper place in the hierarchy of creation and hence assists one in developing the rightful relationship with the Creator and the creation (*adab*). All efforts and struggles to maintain that is aligned to the knowledge and mindfulness (*taqwa*) of God and is considered worship (*'ibādah*). The resulting balance within one's self, in the natural environment, family, society, economy and politics is justice. Happiness in the worldly life is not the final end, but it is the means via which one attains gratitude toward God and develops love for Him, which is the final end. The spiritual happiness experienced through closeness with God is the state of *nafs al-mutmainnah* where worldly wants are diminished and needs are satisfied through the bare minimum. At this stage, one sees a reflection of divine attributes in all physical and emotional pleasures of life.

The above exposition shows how virtue, justice, freedom and happiness, in the Islamic worldview, have entirely different meanings than their secular understanding. These values are intricately interconnected and form the pillars of the Islamic system (Qur'an 2:177). Unlike this, in the late modern secular understanding, the more one acquires freedom, the more increased one's wants become. Virtue consists in striving rationally to fulfill all wants. Happiness or pleasure is the *summum bonum* which is reached when all wants are fulfilled. Paradoxically this understanding has been challenged by the lived experience of the individuals hailing from the advanced industrialized nations. Increased pleasure leads to having increased desires and wants – since the satisfied wants are always less than the unsatisfied wants, the person never feels satisfied. We find increasing number of people reporting unhappiness in secular democracies[15].

---

15 https://www.localfutures.org/wp-content/uploads/the_economics_of_happiness_discussion_guide.pdf

10 Conclusion

The Islamic worldview is a set of fundamental values that do not change over time. There can be development in the schools of theology and jurisprudence but that does not mean a progressive worldview. Those changes reflect how different interpretations were attempted to preserve the values and keep the worldview intact in a changing world. Islam sees freedom and progress of individuals in freeing themselves from the entrapment of unending desires and wants so they can ascend vertically and work on their spirituality and relationship with God translating into higher character (*akhlāq*). On the social level, progress entails returning to the Islamic values and virtues and modes of conduct – i.e., to the Islamic way of life. Any apparent "development" in the material conditions or built environment can thus not be considered progress unless it contributes to the Islamic way of life. Development is the collective struggle to return to the straight path (*sirāt mustaqeem*).

According to al-Attas (2001, 39) the secular (un)civilization which is considered the model of development does not have God as a permanent point of reference. There is a continuous effort to make and remake the world and humanity. Without any final purpose, there is constant innovation, creation, manufacturing and dumping which cannot be called progress:

> The term progress refers to a *definite direction* that is aligned to a *final purpose* that is meant to be achieved in worldly life. If the direction sought is still vague, still coming-into-being as it were, and the purpose aligned to it is not final, then how can involvement in it truly mean progress? People who grope in the dark cannot be referred to as progressing, and they who say such people are progressing have merely uttered a lie against the true meaning and purpose of progress.

The purpose of economics in Islam is to facilitate the formation of homo Islamicus, a spiritual-moral being. Islamic finance, being a practicing tool, should have the same objective. Wealth creation is one of the five main objectives (*maqāsid*) of the Islamic Shariah. However, the ultimate objective of all wealth creation, and hence the disciplines of Economics and Finance, is to allow human beings to fulfill their basic physical, material necessities so as to allow for the spiritual-moral development of individuals and communities. The students, researchers and professionals related to the area of Islamic Economics and Finance should not lose sight of this fundamental religio-ethical principle.

References

AbuSulayman, A. 2013. *Abridged Edition of AbdulHamid AbuSulayman's Original The Quranic Worldview; A Springboard for Cultural Reform*. Herndon, VA: The International Institute of Islamic Thought.

Al-Attas, S.M.N. 2001. *Prolegomena to the Metaphysics of Islam*. Lahore: Sohail Academy.
Anielski, M. 2007. *The Economics of Happiness*. Gabriola Island: New Society Publishers.
Ansari, J. and Arshad S. Z. 2006. Business Ethics in Pakistan. 2006, Karachi: Royal Book Company.
Asutay, M. 2007. "Conceptualization of the Second Best Solution in Overcoming the Social Failure of Islamic Banking and Finance: Examining the Overpowering of *HomoIslamicus* by *HomoEconomicus*". *Journal of Economics and Management*. 15(2): 167–195.
Chapra, M. U., Khan, S., & Al Shaikh-Ali, A. (2008). The Islamic vision of development in the light of maqasid al-Shariah (Vol. 15). IIIT.
Chapra, M. U. (2016). The future of economics: An Islamic perspective (Vol. 21). Kube Publishing Ltd.
Douthwaite, R. 1992. *The Growth Illusion: How Economic Growth has Enriched the Few,*
Impoverished the Many, and Endangered the Planet UK: Bideford, Green Books.
Du Pasquier, R. (trans. by T. J. Winter). 2002. *Unveiling Islam*. Cambridge: The Islamic Texts Society. Originally published in1979.
Esteva, G. 2010. "Development" in *The Development Dictionary*, edited by Wolfgang Sachs. London: Zed Books.
Godzinski, R. J. (2005) "(En)Framing Heidegger's Philosophy of Technology". *Essays in Philosophy*. 6(1), Article 9.
Heidegger, M. 1977. *The question concerning technology, and other essays*. New York: Harper & Row.
Iqbal, Z. and Mirakhor, A. 2013. *Economic Development and Islamic Finance*. Washington: The World Bank.
Iqbal, Z. and Mirakhor, A. 2017. *Ethical Dimensions of Islamic Finance: Theory and Practice*. Switzerland: Palgrave Macmillan.
Jha, Y. 2013. "Examining the Meta-Principles of Modern Economics and their Implications for Islamic Banking and Finance". *Islamic Sciences*. 11(2); 169–184.
Jha, Y. 2014. "The Destructive Logic of Interest: The Fallacy of Perpetual Growth with a Discussion of Reformist Action by Islamic Banks". *Islam and Civilizational Renewal* 5(3), 409–29.
Javaid, O. and Suri, A. 2015. "Global Financial Capital vs. Islamic Concept of Wealth: The Question of Ideological Dominance". *Journal of Islamic Business and Management*. 5(2): 117–134.
Javaid, O. 2015. "The Original Socio-Cultural and Economic Context for Practicing Shirkat-ul-Aqd". *Int. J. Pluralism and Economics Education*. 6(4): 371–385.
Javaid, O. 2012. Revisiting the Islamic Conception of Economic Justice and Its Implication in Islamic Banking and Finance. Dissertation Submitted for qualifying the Degree of Master in Sciences. https://www.researchgate.net/publication/277329058_A_Comparison_of_Islamic_and_Capitalist_Conception_of_Economic_Justice. Accessed March 13, 2019.
Leonard, A. 2010. *The Story of Stuff*. NY: Free Press.
Marcuse,H. 1964/2002. *One dimensional* man. United Kingdom: Rouledge and Kegan Paul.
Mirakhor, A. and Askari, H. 2010. *Islam and the Path to Human and Economic Development*. NY: Palgrave Macmillan.
Nasr, S. H. (1990). Islam and the environmental crisis. Islamic Quarterly, 34(4), 217.
Nasr, S. H. (2002). Islam and the plight of modern man. Cambridge: Islamic Texts Society.
Poole, R. 1996. *Morality and Modernity*. London: Routledge.
Raquib, A. 2015. *Islamic Ethics of Technology; an objectives' approach*. Selangor: IBT/The Other Press.
Raquib, A. 2016. "Maqāṣid al-Shari'ah: A Traditional Source for Ensuring Design and Development of Modern Technology for Humanity's Benefit *in Islamic Perspectives on Science and Technology: Selected Conference Papers*,Kamali, M.H., Bakar, O., Batchelor, D.A.,F., Hashim, R. (Eds). Singapore, Springer.
Raquib, A. and Khan, I. 2019. "Entrepreneurship as an Agent for Social-Ethical Reform; an Islamic Perspective". *Islam and Civilizational Renewal*. 10 (1), 47–63.
Rosen, L. 2012. *iDisorder*. NY: Palgrave Macmillan.

Setia A. 2016. "Freeing *Maqāṣid* and *Maṣlaḥa* from Surreptitious Utilitarianism. *Islamic Sciences.* 14(2), 127–56.
Siddiqui, N. 2009. *Maqasid-e-Shariat.* Islamabad: Islamic Research Institute.
Simon-Brown, V. 2000 "Sustainable living – Strategies for breaking the cycle of work and spend", *International Journal of Sustainability in Higher Education*, 1(3), 290–297, https://doi.org/10.1108/1467630010378194.
Schumacher, E. F. 1973/2010. Small is Beautiful: A Study of Economics as if People Mattered. NY: HarperCollins.
Weygandt, J. J., Kieso, D. E. and Kimmel, P D. 2015. *Accounting Principles.* 12th ed. New York, NY: John Wiley & Sons, Inc.
Zarabozo, J. 1999. *Commentary on the Forty Hadith of Al-Nawawi.* Boulder, CO: Al Basheer.

Mohammad Javad Tavakoli

Chapter 5: The Role of Spirituality and Morality in the Islamic Model of Economic Education and Training

1 Introduction

Recent decades have witnessed an unusual attention to economic education for pre-college students. Traditionally, economists were engaged in their technical studies on the analysis of market mechanism with not enough attention to social factors that influence economic agents. They were mainly analyzing the effects of changes in prices on economic decisions of the so-called economic man. Such a man is known to have self-interested rational preferences. By considering preferences exogenous, economists typically have no plan for forming and changing desires. What they are expected to do is to manage price fluctuations by the aid of the invisible hand of the market or the visible hand of the government.

The project of economic education is a new plan for forming desires, tastes, preferences, on the one hand, and enhancing the knowledge of economic agents, on the other hand. This paper tries to evaluate this project from a particular viewpoint. The question is whether there is a place for spirituality in the traditional models of economic education for pre-college students? The main concern is to address the same question about Islam's plan for economic education. I hypothesize that spirituality is an important goal in an Islamic model of economic education.

2 The History of Economic Education in the West

Economic education has received attention in different religions, civilization and cultures. There is no clear record about economic education in the west before the renaissance. After it, however, we see great attention to economic education among families. It has been reported that French and British families tended to hire economic teachers for their children. Miss Edgeworth, a contemporary of David Ricardo, the famous economists of the 18th century, "states in her letters that political economy was so much the fashion that distinguished ladies before engaging a governance for their children inquired about her competence to teach political economy" (Gide & Rist, 1915, p. 119). At that time, abstract thoughts of Ricardo were presented in newspaper articles and popular tales such as *Conversations on Political Economy*, by Mrs. Marcet (1916), *Illustrations of Political Economy*, by Miss Martineau (9 vols., containing thirty stories, 1832–34)(Ibid).

https://doi.org/10.1515/9783110593419-005

A century later, the American Economic Association (AEA) was founded as a formal institution whose founders expressed their interests in economic education. "One explicit aim of the nascent society was to educate public opinion about economic questions and economic literature" (Hinshaw & Siegfried, 1991, p. 373). In 1891, Simon Patten, a future president of the association, published a paper named "The Educational Value of Political Economy", which deserves to be considered the seminal work in modern education. In this paper, Patten "argued that economics should place mathematics and physics for training in reasoning and that moral and political thought should be separated from instruction in economics" (Hinshaw & Siegfried, 1991, p. 373).

In the late 19th century, economics or political economy gradually changed to a separate discipline and found its way in the curriculum of famous colleges and universities. Attention to public economic education in the late 19th century is clearly manifested in a book by Fredric Clow (1899) named *Economic as a School Study*. In this book, Clow paid attention to the importance of economic education in high schools (Clow, 1899).

Under the influence of the first and second world wars and several economic crises, there was a lower attention to public economic education in the early 20th century. Nevertheless, the American Economic Association was active in organizing some scientific discussions on economic education. In the mid-20th century, AEA was the most influential association on economic education. It established "The Committee on Economic Education" in 1955 for improving economic education. In 1960, AEA formed the "National Task Force on Economic Education" as a subgroup intended to identify the minimum level of economic knowledge for ideal citizens. The group published a report on "Economic Education in the School" in the 1960s, which was an influential work for forming the structure of economic contents for educating in schools (Hinshaw & Siegfried, 1991).[1]

In 1969, "The Journal of Economic Education" started to publish papers on the new field of economic education. The journal and other publications in the field opened the way to the introduction of national standards for economic education by the so-called National Council on Economic Education in the USA. Even though such standards have been designed for American students, it had a decisive impact on designing economic education courses in other countries. Today, the American "National Council on Economic Education" is not only responsible for policymaking on economic education in the USA, but is also in charge of defining economic education programs all over the world. Therefore, the term "national" was omitted from the name of the council and its name was changed to the "Council on Economic

1 The National Task Force on Economic Education was also active in the production of a TV program on USA's economy, which was broadcasted from the national TV from 1962 to 1963 with about 1 million viewers (Toghyani & Payghami, 2016, p. 47).

Education". The Council is active in the determination of economic education models. It also acts as a supervisor on economic education programs (Toghyani & Payghami, 2016, pp. 46–50).

The first economic education model was introduced under the title of "A Framework for Teaching Basic concepts" by the National Council on Economic Education in 1977. The framework was revised in 1984 and with some modifications published as the "Voluntary National Content Standard in Economics" in 1997. The second edition of these standards was published in 2010. The standards refer to what students in each age level should know in order to improve their cognitive capacities, desires and behavioral routines in the future. These standards are the basis for specifying the content of books and other educational materials (Ibid, p. 50).

3 A Nation at Risk

In 1983, the National Commission on Excellence in Education issued a report about the quality of education in the USA, under the title of 'A Nation at Risk: The Imperative for Educational Reform'. Terrell Bell, the Secretary of Education in Ronald Reagan's administration started the investigation from 1981. The purpose of this investigation, as David Pierpont Gardner the chairman of The National Commission on Excellence in Education states, was "to help define the problems afflicting American education and to provide solutions" (Gardner, 1983). The report starts by warning against the risks of the low quality of economic education in the USA as follows:

> Our Nation is at risk. Our once unchallenged preeminence in commerce, industry, science, and technological innovation is being overtaken by competitors throughout the world. This report is concerned with only one of the many causes and dimensions of the problem, but it is the one that undergirds American prosperity, security, and civility. We report to the American people that while we can take justifiable pride in what our schools and colleges have historically accomplished and contributed to the United States and the well-being of its people, the educational foundations of our society are presently being eroded by a rising tide of mediocrity that threatens our very future as a Nation and a people. What was unimaginable a generation ago has begun to occur-others are matching and surpassing our educational attainments.–(Gardner, 1983, p. 9)

The report refers to the superiority of the industrial products of countries such as Japan and Germany over those of the USA due to their excellent educational system:

> The risk is not only that the Japanese make automobiles more efficiently than Americans and have government subsidies for development and export. It is not just that the South Koreans recently built the world's most efficient steel mill, or that American machine tools, once the pride of the world, are being displaced by German products. It is also that these developments signify a redistribution of trained capability throughout the globe. Knowledge, learning, information, and skilled intelligence are the new raw materials of international commerce and are today spreading

> throughout the world as vigorously as miracle drugs, synthetic fertilizers, and blue jeans did earlier. If only to keep and improve on the slim competitive edge we still retain in world markets, we must dedicate ourselves to the reform of our educational system for the benefit of all-old and young alike, affluent and poor, majority and minority. Learning is the indispensable investment required for success in the "information age" we are entering. (Gardner, 1983, p. 10)

According to this report, the concern "goes well beyond matters such as industry and commerce. It also includes the intellectual, moral, and spiritual strengths of our people". According to the report, "The people of the United States need to know that individuals in our society who do not possess the levels of skill, literacy, and training essential to this new era will be effectively disenfranchised, not simply from the material rewards that accompany competent performance, but also from the chance to participate fully in our national life". It was noticed that "A high level of shared education is essential to a free, democratic society and to the fostering of a common culture, especially in a country that prides itself on pluralism and individual freedom" (Gardner, 1983, p. 10).

After pinpointing the shortcomings of the American educational system, the report comes with some suggestion for solving the problem. It is proposed that there is a need for an educational reform that focuses on the goal of creating a learning society (Gardner, 1983, p. 14). It was conjectured that "formal schooling in youth is the essential foundation for learning throughout one's life. But without life-long learning, one's skills will become rapidly dated" (Gardner, 1983, p. 15).

The publication of this report had a decisive impact on theAmerican educational system. In 1980s, there was pressure on schools to improve their performance due to the proposed educational standards. In 1994, an act called "Goals 2000: Educate American Act" was approved. According to this act, all states were encouraged to introduce content standards for their educational system (Toghyani & Payghami, 2016, p. 53).

4 Content Standards in Economics Education

To provide a content standard for economic education in schools for the first time, Philip Saunders and June V. Gilliard published "A Framework for Teaching the Basic Economic Concepts" in 1977. Funded by the United States Department of Education, *The Voluntary National Content Standards in Economics*, which was revised several times from 2008 to 2010, contains concepts on Microeconomics, Macroeconomics and International Economics (Siegfried et al., 2010).

> The *Voluntary National Content Standards in Economics* provide a tool for educators, specifying what students, kindergarten through grade 12, should learn about basic economics and the economy as they go through school, so that they will be better-informed workers, consumers and producers, savers and investors, and most important, citizens (Siegfried et al., 2010, p. ix).

The proposed framework, shown in Tables 5.1–5.5, contains 20 basic economic concepts. "Each standard includes a set of benchmarks divided into achievement levels for grades 4, 8, and 12. The benchmarks "develop the economic reasoning behind the standard. In this way, the standards and benchmarks add up to more than a simple list of "things to know." As students observe the reasoning process used by economists and practice it themselves, they will acquire analytical skills they can apply to emerging economic issues unforeseen at the time these standards were written" (Siegfried et al., 2010, p. v).

Table 5.1: American Voluntary National Content Standards in Economics.

N.	Standards	Short description
1	Scarcity	Productive resources are limited. Therefore, people cannot have all the goods and services they want; as a result, they must choose some things and give up others.
2	Decision making	Effective decision making requires comparing the additional costs of alternatives with the additional benefits. Many choices involve doing a little more or a little less of something: few choices are "all or nothing" decisions.
3	Allocation	Different methods can be used to allocate goods and services. People acting individually or collectively must choose which methods to use to allocate different kinds of goods and services.
4	Incentives	People usually respond predictably to positive and negative incentives.
5	Trade	Voluntary exchange occurs only when all participating parties expect to gain. This is true for trade among individuals or organizations within a nation, and among individuals or organizations in different nations.
6	Specialization	When individuals, regions, and nations specialize in what they can produce at the lowest cost and then trade with others, both production and consumption increase.
7	Markets and prices	A market exists when buyers and sellers interact. This interaction determines market prices and thereby allocates scarce goods and services.
8	Role of prices	Prices send signals and provide incentives to buyers and sellers. When supply or demand changes, market prices adjust, affecting incentives.
9	Competition and market	Competition among sellers usually lowers costs and prices, and encourages producers to produce what consumers are willing and able to buy. Competition among buyers increases prices and allocates goods and services to those people who are willing and able to pay the most for them.
10	Institutions	Institutions evolve and are created to help individuals and groups accomplish their goals. Banks, labor unions, markets, corporations, legal systems, and not-for-profit organizations are examples of important institutions. A different kind of institution, clearly defined and enforced property rights, is essential to a market economy.

Table 5.1 (continued)

N.	Standards	Short description
11	Money and inflation	Money makes it easier to trade, borrow, save, invest, and compare the value of goods and services. The amount of money in the economy affects the overall price level. Inflation is an increase in the overall price level that reduces the value of money.
12	Interest rates	Interest rates, adjusted for inflation, rise and fall to balance the amount saved with the amount borrowed, which affects the allocation of scarce resources between present and future uses.
13	Income	Income for most people is determined by the market value of the productive resources they sell. What workers earn primarily depends on the market value of what they produce.
14	Entrepreneurship	Entrepreneurs take on the calculated risk of starting new businesses, either by embarking on new ventures similar to existing ones or by introducing new innovations. Entrepreneurial innovation is an important source of economic growth.
15	Economic growth	Investment in factories, machinery, new technology, and in the health, education, and training of people stimulates economic growth and can raise future standards of living.
16	Role of government and market failure	There is an economic role for government in a market economy whenever the benefits of a government policy outweigh its costs. Governments often provide for national defense, address environmental concerns, define and protect property rights, and attempt to make markets more competitive. Most government policies also have direct or indirect effects on peoples' incomes.
17	Government failure	Costs of government policies sometimes exceed benefits. This may occur because of incentives facing voters, government officials, and government employees, because of actions by special interest groups that can impose costs on the general public, or because social goals other than economic efficiency are being pursued.
18	Economic fluctuations	Fluctuations in a nation's overall levels of income, employment, and prices are determined by the interaction of spending and production decisions made by all households, firms, government agencies, and others in the economy. Recessions occur when overall levels of income and employment decline.
19	Unemployment and inflation	Unemployment imposes costs on individuals and the overall economy. Inflation, both expected and unexpected, also imposes costs on individuals and the overall economy. Unemployment increases during recessions and decreases during recoveries.
20	Fiscal and monetary policy	Federal government budgetary policy and the Federal Reserve System's monetary policy influence the overall levels of employment, output, and prices.

Source: Siegfried et al., 2010, pp. iii–iv.

The writing committees of these standards have clearly specified what students should know about each economic concept and how they should be able to use this knowledge at the completion of grades 4, 8, and 12.

Table 5.2: American Content Standards in Economics for Pre-College Students at the completion of grades 4, 8, and 12.

N.	Standards	Grades		
		0–4	4–8	8–12
1	Scarcity	✓	✓	✓
2	Decision making	✓	✓	✓
3	Allocation	✓	✓	✓
4	Incentives	✓	✓	✓
5	Trade	✓	✓	✓
6	Specialization	✓	✓	✓
7	Markets and prices	✓	✓	✓
8	Role of prices	✓	✓	✓
9	Competition and market	✓	✓	✓
10	Institutions	✓	✓	✓
11	Money and inflation	✓	✓	✓
12	Interest rates	–	✓	✓
13	Income	✓	✓	✓
14	Entrepreneurship	✓	✓	✓
15	Economic growth	✓	✓	✓
16	Role of government and market failure	✓	✓	✓
17	Government failure	–	✓	✓
18	Economic fluctuations	–	✓	✓
19	Unemployment and inflation	✓	✓	✓
20	Fiscal and monetary policy	–	–	✓

Source: Siegfried et al., 2010, pp. 2–48.

The committee also introduced the relevant benchmarks for each standard. As an example, Tables 5.3–5.5 show the relevant benchmarks for the standard of decision making:

Table 5.3: American Content standards in Economics; Benchmarks: Grade 4.

At the completion of Grade 4, students will know that:	At the completion of Grade 4, students will use this knowledge to:
1. Choices involve getting more of one thing by giving up something else.	1. Analyze how to divide their time on a Saturday afternoon when the possibilities are raking leavesto earn money, going to a movie with friends, and shopping at the mall with their aunt. Students will identify the possible uses of their time and explain how it could be an "all-or-nothing" decision or a decision to do a little more of one activity and a little less of another.
2. A cost is what you give up when you decide to do something. A benefit is what satisfies your wants.	2. List the costs (what you give up) and benefits of buying a pet.

Source: Siegfried et al., 2010, p. 6.

Table 5.4: American Content standards in Economics; Benchmarks: Grade 8.

At the completion of Grade 8, students will know the Grade 4 benchmarks for this standard, and also that:	At the completion of Grade 8, students will use this knowledge to:
1. To determine the best level of consumption of a product, people must compare the additional benefits with the additional costs of consuming a little more or a little less.	1. Solve the following problem: Your grandmother gives you $30 for your birthday and you are trying to decide how to spend it. You are considering buying t-shirts ($15 each), going to the movies ($10 per ticket), or taking some friends out for pizza ($7.50 per person). You do not have to spend all your money on one thing. You can use some money for one thing, and some for another. How would you spend your money to get the greatest satisfaction?
2. Marginal benefit is the change in total benefit resulting from an action. Marginal cost is the change in total cost resulting from an action.	2. Identify the marginal benefit of buying and consuming additional granola bars. Contrast this with the marginal cost of acquiring additional granola bars.
3. As long as the marginal benefit of an activity exceeds the marginal cost, people are better off doing more of it; if the marginal cost exceeds the marginal benefit, they are better off doing less of it.	3. Apply the concepts of marginal benefit and marginal cost to reducing pollution.
4. Many people have a tendency to be impatient, choosing immediate consumption over saving for the future.	4. Explain the benefits of having saved an allowance for an extended period.

Source: Siegfried et al., 2010, p. 6.

Table 5.5: American Content standards in Economics; Benchmarks: Grade 12.

At the completion of Grade 12, students will know the Grade 4 and Grade 8 benchmarks for this standard, and also that:	At the completion of Grade 12, students will use this knowledge to:
1. To produce the profit-maximizing level of output and hire the optimal number of workers, and other resources, producers must compare the marginal benefits and marginal costs of producing a littlemore with the marginal benefits and marginal costs of producing a littleless.	1. Decide how many workers to hire for a profit maximizing car wash by comparing the cost of hiring each additional worker to the additional revenues derived from hiring each additional worker.
2. To determine the optimal level of a public policy program, voters and government officials must compare the marginal benefits and marginal costs of providing a little more or a little less of the program's services.	2. Use the concepts of marginal cost and marginal benefit to evaluate proposals for making your school building more attractive; select the best proposal and defend your decision.
3. To compare marginal benefits with marginal costs that are realized at different times, benefits and costs must be adjusted to reflect their values at the time a decision is made about them. The adjustment reflects expected returns to investment compounded over time.	3. Discuss how a business might evaluate an investment decision that costs $10,000 today and returns $12,000 one year from now.
4. Costs that have already been incurred and benefits that have already been received are sunk and irrelevant for decisions about the future.	4. Explain why the fact that you lost your first ticket to an upcoming concert is irrelevant to whether you should purchase a replacement. Explain why some people would consider the cost of the lost ticket in deciding whether to purchase another ticket even if they had the money to do so.
5. People sometimes fail to treat gains and losses	5. Explain why some people might treat $100 found on the street differently than $100 that has been lost out of one's pocket.
6. Some decisions involve taking risks in that either the benefits or the costs could be uncertain. Risk taking carries a cost. When risk is present, the costs should be treated as higher than when risk is not present.	6. Explain why an investment that pays a guaranteed $1,000 a year, is more desirable for most people than an investment that pays $2,000 a year with a 50% chance and $0 with a 50% chance.
7. Risk can be reduced by diversification.	7. Explain why mutual funds have become a popular investment tool. Explain why it might make sense for someone who sells umbrellas to also sell suntan lotion.

Source: Siegfried et al., 2010, pp. 6–7.

5 The Ideal Economic Agent in the American Model of Economic Education

Even though it has been claimed that the "standards attempt to reflect consensus in the discipline," the Writing Committees declared that they used the "majority paradigm" in Economics: "The final standards reflect the view of a large majority of economists today in favor of a 'neoclassical model' of economic behavior". According to them,

> The Writing Committee's use of this paradigm does not connote a repudiation of alternatives. Rather, it reflects the assignment to produce a single, coherent set of standards to guide the teaching of economics in America's schools. Including strongly held minority views of economic processes and concepts would have confused and frustrated teachers and students who would then be left with the responsibility of sorting the qualifications and alternatives without a sufficient foundation to do so (Siegfried et al., 2010, p. vi).

In fact, the standards are "written for teachers to use to help students learn the crucial reasoning and decision-making skills" based on the "neoclassical model" of economic behavior" (Siegfried et al., 2010, p. ix). Such skills are expected to "serve them well all of their lives, in all of the many roles that they may play as responsible and effective participants in the American economic system" (ibid).

Looking at content standards, one could realize how the "neoclassical model" of economic behavior "is hidden behind them. Roughly speaking, the proposed educational model is intended to convince students that a free market economic system performs well in the economy and that it should be occasionally supplemented by governmental intervention due to market failures. In other words, it is implicitly argued that a free market economic system could satisfactorily allocate scarce resources to unlimited needs.

In the neoclassical model of Economic Education, a rational economic man is an ideal economic agent. He tries to maximize his utility or profit subject to budget constraints. Such an endeavor is supposed to satisfy social interests in a free market context due to the functioning of what Adam Smith calls the "invisible hand" of the market.

According to James Buchanan (1991), the above claim is grounded on three basic ontological foundations, namely individual autonomy, rationality of choice, and spontaneous market coordination (Buchanan, 1999, pp. 14, 22). Individual autonomy is "an idea that is generally understood to refer to the capacity to live one's life according to reasons and motives that are taken as one's own and not the product of manipulative or distorting external forces" (Chirstman, 2003). Here autonomy refers to methodological individualism according to which individuals are considered as the unit of analysis and not aggregate entities such as tribe, or family. Rationality is the logic of decision making by economic agents in the economy. A rational economic man is then considered to maximize his utility or profit subject to budget constraints. Finally, the spontaneous market coordination mechanism is a claim about the functioning of a free market economy. It is claimed that unintended social benefits result from self-interested actions of rational economic men. Adam Smith uses the metaphor of the Invisible Hand to address the capacity of a free market for ensuring social benefits.[2]

To justify their claim on the superiority of a free market system over other systems, neoclassical economists developed the Theory of Price or Microeconomics according to which market prices coordinate supply and demand and maximize social welfare. It is argued that in a free competitive market, output is maximized at the lowest possible price. As a result, both producers and consumers benefit from the functioning of the market so that both consumer and producer surplus is maximized. Such an economic system is a self-regulating system. If there was a deviation from the equilibrium price or quantity, market forces function to bring the economy back to the equilibrium. As a result, they claim that a free market system is the best way to allocate scarce resources to unlimited needs and desires.

6 Missing Spirituality and Morality in the Traditional Model of Economic Education

The traditional model of Economic Education for pre-college students aims to form the so-called economic men whose main goals are the maximization of self-interest (utility or profit maximization). Looking at the 20 basic concepts of the American economic education model, we see that the ideal economic agent is what we know in economics as the economic man or homo economicus. Absent among these concepts, are topics such as morality, ethics or spirituality.

The Content Standards convince students that the maximization of self-interest in a competitive market under the condition of scarcity not only provides "them the highest possible net benefits" (St.4: Incentives, G12, N.1), but also promotes "the national level of well-being" (St.9: Competition and Market Structure, G12, N.1):

- Responses to incentives are usually predictable because people normally pursue their self-interest or deviate from their self-interest in consistent ways (St.4: Incentives, G8, and N.1).

2 Based on methodological individualism, the individual element is an independent entity that has self-contained properties. It is followed by the idea that the individual is responsible for his/her own fate. Your success and failure depends on how hard you work. Holism says that individual element is inextricably tied to other individuals. Individuals are interdependent, and they are internally related. Holism regards individuals as reciprocally influencing each other. The child affects the family while being affected by it. Based on holism, the whole is more than simply the sum of the parts. Or the whole is different from the sum of individual constituents. This whole then affects the qualities of the constituents (Ratner, 2016).

- Acting as consumers, producers, workers, savers, investors, and citizens, people respond to incentives in order to allocate their scarce resources in ways that provide them the highest possible net benefits (St.4: Incentives, G12, N.1).
- People tend to respond to fair treatment with fair treatment, and to unfair treatment with retaliation, even when such reactions may not maximize their material wealth (St.4: Incentives, G12, and N.3).
- The pursuit of self-interest in competitive markets usually leads to choices and behavior that also promote the national level of well-being (St.9: Competition and Market Structure, G12, N.1).

Under the concept of decision making, students are explicitly advised to follow a marginalistic approach when they make a choice, which is consistent with a utilitarian approach:
- To determine the best level of consumption of a product, people must compare the additional benefits with the additional costs of consuming a little more or a little less (St.2: Decision Making, G8, N.1).
- Marginal benefit is the change in total benefit resulting from an action. Marginal cost is the change in total cost resulting from an action (St.2: Decision Making, G8, and N.2).
- As long as the marginal benefit of an activity exceeds the marginal cost, people are better off doing more of it; if the marginal cost exceeds the marginal benefit, they are better off doing less of it (St.2: Decision Making, G8, N.3).
- Many people have a tendency to be impatient, choosing immediate consumption over saving for the future (St.2: Decision Making, G8, and N.4).
- To produce the profit-maximizing level of output and hire the optimal number of workers, and other resources, producers must compare the marginal benefits and marginal costs of producing a little more with the marginal benefits and marginal costs of producing a little less (St.2: Decision Making, G12, N.1).
- To determine the optimal level of a public policy program, voters and government officials must compare the marginal benefits and marginal costs of providing a little more or a little less of the program's services (St.2: Decision Making, G12, N.2).

Costs and benefits are clearly defined as opportunity costs and benefits that are related to the consumption of goods and services:
- Economic wants are desires that can be satisfied by consuming a good (an object), a service (an action), or a leisure activity (Standard 1: Scarcity, G4, and N.2).
- Whenever a choice is made, something is givenup because resources are limited (Standard 1: Scarcity, G4, and N.4).
- Making good choices should involve trading off the expected value of one opportunity against theexpected value of its best alternative (Standard 1: Scarcity, G8, and N.2).

- The choices people make have both present and future consequences (Standard 1: Scarcity, G8, and N.3).
- The evaluation of choices and opportunity costs is subjective; such evaluations differ across individuals and societies (Standard 1: Scarcity, G8, and N.4).
- A cost is what you give up when you decide to do something. A benefit is what satisfies your wants (St.2: Decision Making, G4, and N.2).

The Marginalist Tradition is extended to cover temporal decisions. Students are then asked to compare marginal benefits with marginal costs over time by using the technique of discounting.

- To compare marginal benefits with marginal costs that are realized at different times, benefits and costs must be adjusted to reflect their values at the time a decision is made about them. The adjustment reflects expected returns to investment compounded over time (St.2: Decision Making, G12, and N.3).
- Costs that have already been incurred and benefits that have already been received are sunk and irrelevant for decisions about the future (St.2: Decision Making, G12, and N.4).
- People sometimes fail to treat gains and losses equally, placing extra emphasis on losses (St.2: Decision Making, G12, and N.5).

There has also been attention paid to risky decisions, which requires a comparison of expected marginal costs and benefits:

- Some decisions involve taking risks in that either the benefits or the costs could be uncertain. Risk taking carries a cost. When risk is present, the costs should be treated as higher than when risk is not present (St.2: Decision Making, G12, and N.6).
- Risk can be reduced by diversification (St.2: Decision Making, G12, and N.7).

It is again argued that the price mechanism yields the maximization of self-interest and social interest automatically with minor interventions by the government in the Economy:

- If a price is above the market clearing price, it will eventually fall, causing sellers to produce less and buyers to purchase more; if it is below the market clearing price, it will eventually rise, causing sellers to produce more and buyers to purchase less (St.7: Markets and Prices, G8, N.4).
- An increase in the price of a good or service encourages people to look for substitutes, causing the quantity demanded to decrease, and vice versa. This well-established relationship between price and quantity demanded, known as the law of demand, exists as long as other factors influencing demand do not change (St.8: Role of Prices, G8, N.1).
- An increase in the price of a good or service encourages producers to supply more, and vice versa. This relationship between price and quantity supplied is

normally true as long as other factors influencing costs of production and supply do not change (St.8: Role of Prices, G8, N.2).
- Competition among sellers results in lower costs and prices, higher product quality, and/or better customer service. When competition among sellers is limited, sellers have some control over the prices they set (St.9: Competition and Market Structure, G8, N.2).

The Content Standards, of course, admit the possibility of market failure. Due to market failure, "Governments often provide for national defense, address environmental concerns, define and protect property rights, and attempt to make markets more competitive". As a result, "There is an economic role for government in a market economy whenever the benefits of a government policy outweigh its costs" (Siegfried et al., 2010, p. 38).
- Markets do not allocate resources efficiently if: (1) property rights are not clearly defined or enforced; (2) externalities (spillover effects) affecting large numbers of people are associated with the production or consumption of a product; or (3) markets are not competitive (St.16: Role of Government and Market Failure, G12, N.1).

Nevertheless, there is also attention paid to the possibility of government failures, which happen when "costs of government policies [...] exceed benefits" (Siegfried et al., 2010, p. 41).
- A government policy to correct a market imperfection is not justified economically if the cost of implementing it exceeds its expected benefits. (St.17: Government Failure, G12, N.1).

All in all, the Content Standards admire the economic life style of a rational economic man who tries to maximize his self-interest by comparing the expected marginal benefits of consuming goods and services over time with the expected marginal costs.

7 Side Effects of the Traditional Economic Education Model

Some economists warned against the side effects of the formal model of economic education in colleges, arguments which could be also relevant to pre-college students. A substantial body of researches suggest that economics students are more selfish than other professionals, partly due to their particular model of education (Marwell & Ames, 1981; Carter & Irons, 1991; Frank, Gilovich, & Reg, 1993; Bauman & Rose, 2009).

In a study by Gerald Marwell and Ruth Ames (1981), students of economics were "much more likely to free-ride in experiments that called for private contributions to public goods" (Frank, Gilovich, & Reg, 1993, p. 160). John Carter and Michael Irons (1991) also measured the self-interestedness of economists by examining their behavior in the ultimatum bargaining game. In this study, "economics majors performed more in accordance with the predictions of the self-interest model than did non-majors" (Frank, Gilovich, & Reg, 1993, p. 161).

The results of the study by Frank et al. (1993), also showed that "the proportion of pure free riders among economists (that is, those who reported giving no money to any charity) was more than double that of any of the other six areas included in the survey" (Frank, Gilovich, & Reg, 1993, p. 162). Frank et al. (1993) found that "economists would be more inclined to construe the objective of the game in self-interested terms, and therefore more likely to refer exclusively to features of the game itself" (Frank, Gilovich, & Reg, 1993, pp. 166–167). They also found that the economists' higher defection rate is partly because they are more likely to expect their partners to defect. Frank et al. (1993) realized that "while expectations of partner performance play a strong role in predicting behavior, defection rates would remain significantly higher for economists than for non-economists even if both groups held identical expectations about partner performance" (Frank, Gilovich, & Reg, 1993, p. 167). They also found "evidence consistent with the view that differences in cooperativeness are caused in part by training in economics" (Frank, Gilovich, & Reg, 1993, p. 170).

Using administrative data on donations to social programs by students at the university of Washington, Bauman and Rose (2009) found that "economics majors are less likely to donate than other students and that there is an indoctrination effect for non-majors but not for majors" (Bauman & Rose, 2009, p. 1).

8 From Market and Government Failures to Humanity Failure (Economic Men at risk)

While the American model of economic education has correctly paid attention to the risks of the low quality of economic education in the USA, it found the solution in training some economic men in schools.

From a Qur'anic point of view, "verily Man is in loss, except such as have faith and do righteous deeds and (join together) in the mutual teaching of truth, and of patience and constancy" (Q 103, 2–3).[3] An economic man without faith and spirituality fails to perform well in the Economy. As soon as the Market and Government fail to function properly, the homo economicus also fails to perform well. It means that

3 Other translations: (1) Most surely man is in loss, except those who believe and do good, and enjoin on each other truth, and enjoin on each other patience. (2)By eventide, every man [is indeed] at a loss except for those who believe, perform honorable deeds, encourage truth, and recommend patience. ان الانسان لفي خسر الا الذين آمنوا و عملوا الصالحات و تواصوا بالحق و تواصوا بالصبر(عصر، 1–3).

the economic man is at risk and we face a failure of humanity, which roots in the spiritual and moral failure of human beings. It happens when they forget their origins and their connection to God. We read in the Qur'an: "And be not like those who forgot Allah, so He made them forget themselves" (Q 59, 19).[4]

It is tempting to argue that market and government failures mainly result from human failure. The market and government fail to function properly because economic agents are not perfectly rational.

9 Cultural Configuration of an Islamic Economy

To solve the humanity failure problem, Islam tries to incorporate morality and spirituality in the economy. By considering economic behavior as an act of worshiping God, Islam tends to integrate the economic and cultural realms. It also introduces some socioeconomic institutions for promoting spirituality in individuals. Among others, Islamic taxes, including *Khoms* and *Zakah*, are designed not only to perform as a tax for financing the government, but also to purify the taxpayers. Islam also promotes social norms such as *Halal* income, hard work, contentment and sacrifice. The internalization of such norms could help us to solve the humanity failure problem.

9.1 Economic Behavior as an Act of Worshiping God

One of the strategies of Islam for incorporating morality and spirituality in the Economy is to consider economic behavior as an act of worshiping God (*ibadah*). The prophet Mohammad (p.b.u.h) says: "Worshiping God has ten components; nine part of it is the seeking of halal earnings" (Majlesi, 1983, p. 9).[5] From an Islamic point of view, any activity would change to an act of worshiping God (*ibadah*), if the performer has the intention to satisfy God. Therefore, the concept of struggle in God's way, as shown in Figure 5.1, could intergrate different cultural, social, political and economic spheres of an ideal Islamic society.

In an Islamic culture, the seeking of *halal* earning looks like fighting for God. Imam Ali said: The person who troubles himself in seeking the halal earning, he looks like a fighter in the way of God (Ibn Abi Jomhor, 1985, p. 194).[6]

4 و لاتکونوا کالذین نسوا الله فانساهم انفسهم (حشر، 19).

5 پیامبر صلیاللهعلیهو آله : اَلْعِبادَةُعَشْرَةُأَجْزاءٍتِسْعَةُأَجْزاءٍفىطَلَبِالْحَلالِ(علامه مجلسي، ج 301، ص 9، ح 37).

6 قَالَعلي عليه السلام : الشَّاخِصُ فِي طَلَبِ الرِّزْقِ الْحَلَالِ كَالْمُجَاهِدِ فِي سَبِيلِ اللَّه(ابن ابي جمهور، 1405 ق، ج 3، ص 194)؛ قَالَ رسول الله (ص) الْكَادُّ عَلَى عِيَالِهِ مِنَ الْحَلَالِ كَالْمُجَاهِدِ فِي سَبِيلِ اللَّه(همان، ص 199).

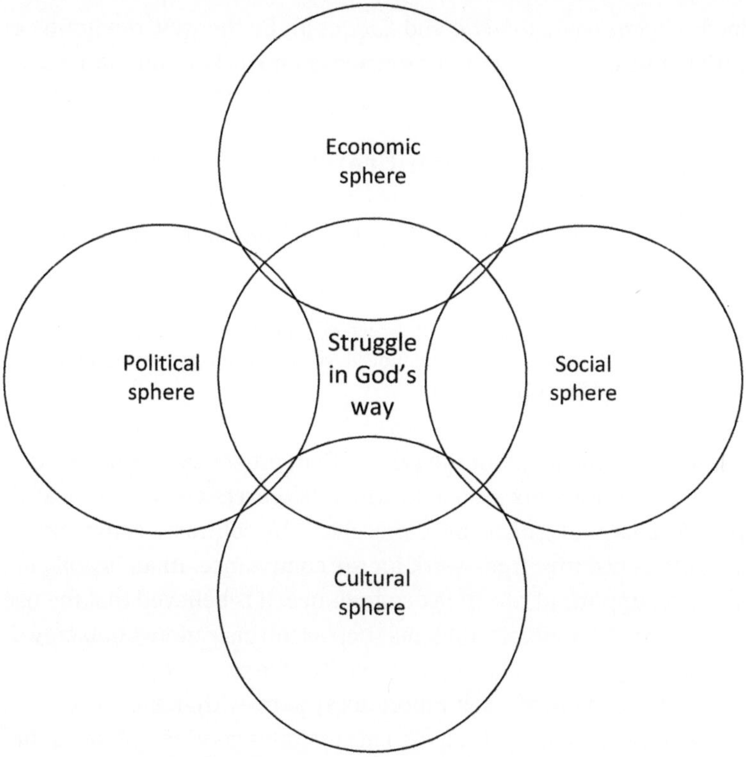

Figure 5.1: The Role of Struggle in God's Way in Integrating different Shperes of Human Society.

9.2 The Culture of *Halal* and *Tayyib* Product and Income

Islam is trying to develop a culture of *halal* and *tayyib* products and income. Halal (lawful) and tayyib (pure) products are goods and services that are pure and clean from any harm to individuals and society. Alcoholic drinks, for example, are not halal and *tayyib* products because they are harmful for the body and soul. From an Islamic point of view, harmful ways of earning income, such as earning income from usury, and gambling, are also prohibited.

9.3 Consistent Norms of Hard Work, Moderation and Sacrifice

In an Islamic economy, the norms of hard work, moderation and sacrifice are promoted in the matters of production, consumption and distribution, respectively. Muslims are asked to work hard, consume less and pay part of their income to the poor. The norm of moderation in consumption not only functions to control wasteful consumptions (*Israf* and *Tabzir*), but also enable individuals to devote their extra income to good deeds (*Infaq*: paying *Zakah* and *Sadaqah*). By the way, the norms of hard work, moderation and sacrifice guarantee efficiency and justice simultaneously.

9.4 Islamic Taxes and the Goal of Purification

One of the outstanding aspects of Islamic taxes such as *Khums* and *Zakah* (almsgiving)is that they are expected to purify taxpayers.

> Take, [O, Muhammad], from their wealth a charity by which you purify them and cause them increase, and invoke [Allah's blessings] upon them. Indeed, your invocations are reassurance for them. And Allah is Hearing and Knowing (Q 9, 103).

Muslims should pay *Khums* and *Zakah* for the sake of God, otherwise it is not acceptable. Islam introduces a voluntary tax system in which taxpayers are self-motivated. They calculate their *Khums* and *Zakah* by themselves. In contrast, conventional taxes mainly use a control-incentive framework for tax compliance. In an Islamic tax system, morality plays an important role in tax compliance. It is believed that the use of control and incentives might produce problems such as intrinsic motivation crowding out effect and weakening the moral training capacity of taxes.

It seems that Islam has expanded a self-report tax system, with flexible tax rates, to instill moral motives for tax compliance. It also necessitates good intentions in tax payment because such an institution is expected to purify people and train them.

10 Towards an Islamic Model of Economic Education (IMEE)

Muslim scholars rarely paid attention to the Islamic model of economic education. There are some references to the importance of issues such as morality in the Islamic economic system without attention to what we could derive as a model for policy making in the area of economic education. Nonetheless, there are many clues in the Qur'an and Hadith about economic education and training.

11 The Goals of Islamic Economic Education

Looking for an Islamic model of economic education, we mainly should pay attention to the ideal economic agent from an Islamic point of view as well as what we could call an Islamic Economic Life Style. The ideal economic agent from an Islamic perspective is clearly different from the so-called economic man or homo-economicus. The agent can be called a mature economic agent with spiritual rationality. One of the implications of admitting spiritual rationality in Islamic economics is the introduction of a particular economic life style, which goes beyond the neoclassical model of economic conduct.

11.1 An Islamic Economic Life Style

From an Islamic perspective, economic agents have imperfect rationality due to their problems in acquiring information, managing desires, and discovering the best means for satisfying desires. Religions, particularly Islam, help economic agents to recognize their real needs (*maslaha*), filter their desires and find the best ways for satisfying their needs. Islamic ideology, jurisprudence, and morality function to fix the problem of imperfect rationality.

Accordingly, a mature consumer is expected to follow Islamic legal and moral codes when she/he is consuming. Since a mature consumer believes in God and the life in the Hereafter, it is easy for him to regulate and modify his expenditure according to Islamic legal and moral rules. He then would follow the rule of moderate consumption, avoid wasteful expenditure, and restrict his consumption of luxuries. He also devotes some part of his income to others through obligatory and voluntary donations. In a Hadith from Imam *Sadeq*, the sixth Imam in Shia tradition, we read:

> Properties belong to God; they are just deposited in the hands of people. People are allowed to eat economically, drink economically, wear clothes economically, marry economically, drive economically and use the spare properties for helping the poor believers [...] (Majlesi, 1983, p. 225).[7]

From an Islamic perspective, producers have also imperfect rationality due to their irrational beliefs and desires. Islam is trying to fix the problem of imperfect rationality by encouraging producers to obey several jurisprudential and moral rules such as the rule of fair price and fair profit. By promoting the culture of *halal* and *tayyib* product, Islam wants to facilitate the efficient allocation of resources to needs. As a result, a mature Muslim producer will have a multi-objective production function in which different goals such as gaining profit, preserving the environment and giving priority to the production of necessities are guiding decisions.

From an Islamic perspective, the invisible hand of the Market and the visible hand of the Government could not guarantee the 'harmony of 'interests'. We need the invisible hand of morality under the guidance of religion as a mechanism for educating and purifying economic agents and modifying their economic decisions (Haneef, 1995, pp. 113–114).

7 الْمَالَ مَال اللَّهِ يَضَعُهُ عِنْدَالرَّجُلِ وَدَائِعَ،وَجَوَّزَلَهُمْ أَنْ يَأْكُلُوا قَصْداً، وَيَشْرَبُوا قَصْداً، وَيَلْبَسُوا قَصْداً، وَيَنْكِحُوا قَصْداً، يَرْكَبُوا قَصْداً، وَيَعُودُوا بِمَاسِوَى ذَلِكَ عَلَى فُقَرَاءِ الْمُؤْمِنِينَ، وَيَرْمُوابِه شَعَثَهُمْ، فَمَن فَعَل ذَلِكَ كَانَمَا يَأْكُلُ حَلَالًا، وَيَشْرَبُ حَلَالًا، وَيَرْكَبُ حَلَالًا، وَيَنْكِحُ حَلَالًا، وَمَنْ عَدَا ذَلِكَ كَانَ عَلَيْهِ حَرَاماً. ثُمَّ قَالَ لاتُسْرِفُوا إِنَّهُ لايُحِبُّ الْمُسْرِفِين (بحار الأنوار، ج1، ص: 225).

> Islamic economics is based on a paradigm which is not secularist and value neutral. It treats all human beings as vice-regents of God and brothers unto each other. All resources at the disposal of human beings are a trust and must be used for the well-being of all in conformity with the values provided by the *Shari'ah*. However, well-being in Islam is not a function of just material possessions and unlimited consumption. It is rather a function of the balanced satisfaction of both the material and the spiritual needs of the human personality. This can be done by actualizing the *maqasid al-Shari'ah* (goals of the *Shari'ah*) (Chapra M., 2000, p. 55).

Morality works as a filter for adjusting the choices by consumers and producers to the requirements of the social life.

> Before even entering the market place and being exposed to the price filter, consumers are expected to pass their claims through the moral filter. This will help filter out conspicuous consumption and all wasteful and unnecessary claims on resources. The price mechanisms can then take over and reduce the claims on resources even further to lead to the market equilibrium. The two filters can together make it possible to have optimum economy in the use of resources, which is necessary to satisfy the material as well as spiritual needs of all human beings, to reduce the concentration of wealth in few hands, and to raise savings, which are needed to promote greater investment and employment (Chapra M., 2014, p. 46)

11.2 Matured Economic Agents

Economic man is not an ideal economic agent in an Islamic society. He is not even considered an actual economic actor. Islamic economics recognizes the spiritual aspects of human beings besides their mundane dimensions. Accordingly, a mature economic agent is not trapped in a mundane game of self-interest maximization. Instead, he/she is looking for a virtuous life in this world and the world after. Prudence is then only one virtue besides other virtues such as justice, equality and fairness. By considering non-self-interested motives of economic agents into account, we could speak of a mature economic man in the light of Islamic teachings.

A mature economic agent is expected to solve the problems of imperfect rationality by acquiring appropriate information, managing desires, and discovering the best means for satisfying needs. She/he is then expected to have rational desires, beliefs and measures under the guidance of Islamic teachings. Having rational desires, the mature economic man has both self-interested and altruistic motives. In this way, we come to the so called spiritual rationality.

12 The Islamic Content Standards of Economic Education

As Islam considers humanity failure as the source of market and government failures in the economy, it is necessary to present new basic concepts or standards for economic training. Below the list of Islamic content standards of economic education are suggested in comparison with the “Voluntary National Content Standards in Economics” (see Tables 5.6 and 5.7).

Table 5.6: Islamic Content Standards in Economics versus Voluntary National Content Standards in Economics.

N.	Voluntary National Content Standards in Economics	Islamic content standards of economic education
1	Scarcity	Scarcity and misdistribution of income and wealth
2	Decision making	Mature decision making
3	Allocation	Allocation
4	Incentives	Incentives, intrinsic and extrinsic motives
5	Trade	Pure Trade
6	Specialization	Specialization and struggle for *halal* and *tayyib* Income
7	Markets and prices	Markets and prices
8	Role of prices	Role of prices and moral cleansing
9	Competition and market	Competition and cooperation
10	Institutions	Institutions
11	Money and inflation	Money, and inflation
12	Interest rates	Profit rates
13	Income	*Halal* and *tayyib* Income
14	Entrepreneurship	Entrepreneurship
15	Economic growth	Flourishing
16	Role of government and market failure	Role of government and market failure
17	Government failure	Role of morality and government failure
18	Economic fluctuations	Economic fluctuations
19	Unemployment and inflation	Unemployment and inflation
20	Fiscal and monetary policy	Fiscal, monetary and economic education policy

The proposed Islamic economic content standards have the following main characteristics:

1. There is a reference to market, government and human failures in the economy.
2. Human failure is considered the root of market and government failures.
3. Humanity failure happens because economic agents have imperfect rationality.
4. Economic agents have imperfect rationality due to their problems in acquiring information, managing desires, and discovering the best means for satisfying desires.
5. The internalization of morality and spirituality in economic agents is a solution to the imperfect rationality problem.

Table 5.7: Islamic Content Standards in Economics.

N.	Standards	Grades		
		0–4	4–8	8–12
1	Scarcity and misdistribution of income and wealth	✓	✓	✓
2	Mature decision making	✓	✓	✓
3	Allocation	✓	✓	✓
4	Incentives, intrinsic and extrinsic motives	✓	✓	✓
5	Pure Trade	✓	✓	✓
6	Specialization and struggle for ḥalal and tayyib Income	✓	✓	✓
7	Markets and prices	✓	✓	✓
8	Role of prices and moral cleansing	✓	✓	✓
9	Competition and cooperation	✓	✓	✓
10	Institutions	✓	✓	✓
11	Money, and inflation	–	✓	✓
12	Profit rates	–	✓	✓
13	*Halal* and *Tayyib* Income	✓	✓	✓
14	Entrepreneurship	✓	✓	✓
15	Flourishing	✓	✓	✓
16	Role of government and market failure	–	✓	✓
17	Role of morality and government failure	✓	✓	✓
18	Economic fluctuations	–	✓	✓
19	Unemployment and inflation	✓	✓	✓
20	Fiscal, monetary and economic education policy	–	–	✓

6. Morality and spirituality function to filter desires before they were subject to the market filter, so we could have spiritual rationality.
7. Institutions could function to internalize morality in economic agents.
8. As a socio-economic institution, *Zakah*, for instance, does not only perform as a tax, but also as a tool for purifying taxpayers.
9. Fiscal and monetary policies should be supplemented by moral policies.

13 Conclusion

Even though the economic system of Islam is primarily intended to coordinate the creation and distribution of income and wealth, it is also expected to perform as an education and training system. Islam considers the act of earning *halal* and *tayyib* (pure) income as an act of worshiping God. Some Islamic taxes such as *Zakah* (almsgiving) are designed to purify the taxpayers. It is then obligatory that they intend to please God by tax payment. Islam also tries to cultivate the culture of *halal* and t*ayyib* product and income in believers so that they have enough motive to perform according to the principle of justice.

Such a cultural view to the economy in Islam roots in the Islamic ontological outlook. Islam considers human beings to have imperfect rationality. According to the Qur'an, man surely is in loss, except those who believe in God and do good deeds. Being in danger of ignorance, human beings permanently need attention (*Zikr*). Hence all social systems should be in the service of notifying them and helping them to escape from the veil of ignorance. It means that we need to a model of economic education and training that help the economy to have the ideal matured economic agents with spiritual rationality.

Very recently economists have paid attention to the importance of economic education. They designed some models for economic education. In their model one could rarely see any reference to the important issue of spirituality in the economy. The so-called "Voluntary National Content Standards in Economics," promotes a mundane economic life style on the basis of a self-interest maximization paradigm (instrument rationality). Accordingly, students are informed that the invisible hand of the market perform properly to allocate scarce resources to needs. The government then plays a minor role in fixing market failures and supporting a market equilibrium.

From an Islamic point of view, just as markets and governments might fail to perform well, economic agents might also fail to perform correctly due to the problem of imperfect rationality. There is, then, a need to purify economic agents and cultivate spirituality and morality in them to have spiritual rationality. The proposed economic content standards in this paper take advantages of Islamic insights on the cultural configuration of the Economy such as considering economic behavior as an act of worshiping God, promoting the culture of *halal* and *tayyib* products, and introducing socio-economic institutions like *Zakah*.

References

Bauman, Y., & Rose, E. (2009). Why are economics students more selfish than the rest? *Working Paper*, 1–25.

Bauman, Y., & Rose, E. (2009, December 3). *Why are Economics Students More Selfish than the Rest?* Retrieved from Available at SSRN: https://ssrn.com/abstract=1518081.

Buchanan, J. (1999). *The Economics and the Ethics of Constitutional Order.* Ann Arbor: University of Michigan Press.

Carter, C., & Irons, M. (1991). Are Economists Different, and If So, Why? *Journal of Economzc Perspectzves*, *5*(2), 171–177.

Chapra, M. (2000). *The Future of Economics; An Islamic Perspective.* Leicester, UK: The Islamic Foundation.
Chapra, M. (2014). *Morality and Justice in Islamic Economics and Finance.* Cheltenham & Northampton: Edward Elgar Publishing.
Chirstman, J. (2003). *Autonomy in Moral and Political Philosophy*. Retrieved from Stanford Encyclopedia of Philosophy: www.plato.stanford.edu/entries/autonomy-moral.
Clow, F. (1899). *Economics as a School Study.* USA: Macmillan Company.
Frank, R., Gilovich, T., & Reg, D. (1993). Does Studying Economics Inhibit Cooperation? *The Journal of Economic Perspectives, 7*(2), 159–171.
Frey, B. (1997). *Not Just for the Money; An Economic Theory of Personal Motivation.* Edward Elgar.
Gardner, D. (1983). *A Nation at Risk: The Imperative for Educational Reform.* Washington D.C.: U.S. Department of Education.
Gide, C., & Rist, C. (1915). *A History of Economic Doctrines; From the Time of the Physiocrats to the Presnt Day.* Boston: D. C. Heath.
Haneef, M. (1995). *Contemporary Islamic Economic Thought: A Selected Comparative Analysis.* Ikraq: S.Abdul Majid & Co.
Haneef, M. (1995). *Contemporary Islamic Economic Thought: A Selected Comparative Analysis.* Ikraq: S. Abdul Majid & Co.
Heyman, J., & Ariely, D. (2004). Effort for Payment; A Tale of Two Markets. *Psychological Society, 15*(11), 787–793.
Hinshaw, C., & Siegfried, J. (1991). The Role of the American Economic Association in Economic Education: A Brife History. *The Journal of Economic Education, 22*(4), 373–381.
Ibn Abi Jomhor, M. (1985). *Avale Al-Lalie* (Vol. 3). Qom: Dar Sayed Al-shohada.
Majlesi, M. (1983). *Bahar Al-anvar* (Vol. 100). Bayrot: Dar Ehiae Al-torat Al-arabi.
Majlesi, M. (1983). *Bahar Al-anvar* (Vol. 1). Bayrot: Dar Ehiae Al-torat Al-arabi.
Marwell, G., & Ames, R. (1981). Economists Free Ride, Does Anyone Else? Experiments on the Provision of Public Goods,. *Journal of Public Economics, 15*(3), 295–310.
Siegfried, J., et al. (2010). *The Voluntary National Content Standards in Economics (2e ed.).* New York: Council for Economic Education.
Toghyani, M., & Payghami, A. (2016). *The Economic Education* (Vol. 1). Tehran: Imam Sadiq University Publication.

Seif I. Tag el-Din

Chapter 6: Sustainable Human Development Ethics: A Quranic Perspective

1 Introduction

God's revelation to Prophet Mohamed is portrayed in the Quran as aiming to usher people from darkness to light: "God is the Guardian of the believers leading them from darkness to light" (*Al Baqarah*, 43); which involves educating them and opening up their minds to wisdom and truthfulness: "God has granted a special favour onto the believers by sending them a prophet from themselves reciting His signs, sanctifying them, and teaching them the book and the wisdom whereas previously they had been in manifest misguidance" (*Al Imran*, 164). At least from the socioeconomic perspective, Mohamed's universal message to humankind comes down to the fundamental idea of "commanding on them the admissible (*ma'ruf*), prohibiting them from the inadmissible (*munkar*), disposing for them all that is benign (*Tayibat*), banning them from all that is malignant (*khaba'ith*)), and lifting from them the heavy bond and shackles that have been placed upon them" (Al *'Araf*, 157). In a nut shell, the last verse encapsulates the three core values of sustainable development: *self-sustenance, self-esteem and freedom*, through exhorting the provision of decent livelihood and emancipating humankind from senseless 'shackles' and 'bonds'.

The objective of this chapter is to suggest the fundamental foundation of Islamic development ethics as it seems perceivable from the Noble Quran. It departs from a basic background on the newly emerging horizon of sustainable development with a view to derive relevant development ethics through reference to the Quran. More specifically, the generic concept of Religion, which arguably coincides with the doctrine of *Tawhid* (i.e. monotheism, or Oneness of God), is the primary source of inspiration in this chapter.The chapter consists of five sections including this introduction. The second section below is meant to set the scene for introducing latest trends in the area of sustainable developments thereby providing the groundwork, respectively, for the third and fourth sections on *Tawhid*-oriented development ethics and the strategic socioeconomic inquiry. Finally, the fifth section sheds light briefly on the main findings of this chapter.

2 The New Approach to Sustainable Development

Over the last few decades a major change of emphasis has taken place in development economics from *developing national economies* to *developing people living within those economies* making it more of a humanitarian discipline than an abstract one.

https://doi.org/10.1515/9783110593419-006

In its earliest version, the state of the art in development economics focused primarily on GDP growth targets and industrialization policies in the bid to help undeveloped countries fulfil their prosperity goals and catch up with the more developed nations. Ironically, GDP targets and industrialization policies were fairly successful but at the cost of extreme income disparities, mass deprivation from basic health and education services and desperate poverty. Thanks to the wealth of useful lessons learned from the critical appraisal of earlier development experiences, the 1970s opened up a new horizon for economists to acknowledge the normative and multidisciplinary nature of human wellbeing, and hence amplify pure economic targets of sustainable development with cultural, social, ethical and spiritual values.[1] With this backdrop, the objective of this is chapter is to synthesize a theoretically consistent framework of socioeconomic ethics from the Quran that seem reasonably comparable if not integrable with the newly thriving humanist challenge of sustainable development.

However, the crucial factor that distinguishes the Quranic approach from the prevalent humanist approach is 'linking morality with belief in God'. This begs the key question: *how God-revealed ethics compare with the current humanist philosophy, and how an intermarriage is likely to arise between the two.* To say the least, there is concrete evidence from global survey reports that belief in God warrants worldwine support as an essential resquiste to morality.[2] This finding invokes the question *how could the socioeconomic ethics associated with belief in God usher a positive humanist insight into the pursuit of sustainable development?* The main snag with this question is that different perceptions about belief in God tend to prevail, not only among different religions but also within the same religion. This is further undermined by the traditional textbook viewpoint that, far from bolstering socioeconomic development, religious beliefs tend to embed counterproductive attitudes towards wealth creation if not to escalate sectarian strife and holy wars within the same national entity.

Therefore, given the objective of the chapter, the above question and related concerns with religiosity will have to be discussed by reference to the Quranic perception of belief in God. To set the stage for the needed discussion, a brief overview of the relevant literature is given below in terms of Dennis Goulet's development ethics, Richard Easterlin's economics of happiness and Amartyre Sen's *Capability to Function*, which have jointly commanded a major impact on the new humanist outlook to sustainable development over the last three decades. This mainstream humanist philosophty is often contrasted against the blossoming school of communitarianism which emphasizes the impact of communitarian values on people's personalities and rejects extreme individualism. Therefore, the idea is to show *what, how and where* the Qutranic perception of belief in God projects a unique ethical perspective within

1 See Susan N. Engel (2010) for a chronical review of development economics; and see Todaro (2011, pp. 17–24) for the socioeconomic anomalies created in the developing world through the pre-1970s development programs.

2 Pew Research center (2014).

the current discourse on sustainable human development. For brevity, the holy term Quran in the rest of this chapter will be referred to shortly by the letter Q so that for example the expression Q-perception means Quranic perception.

2.1 Late Developments in Human Development

Amongst the most vocal critics of development economics since its early beginnings were Dennis Goulet (1971), Amartya Sen (1980) and Richard Easterlin (1974). Goulet is credited for setting the ethical tone of the emerging human development trend. He was particularly instrumental in introducing *development ethics* as a special field of inquiry[3] "that examines the ethical and value questions related to development theory, planning and practice". The conventional treatment of human wellbeing in terms of utility generating commodities has been the primary target of Sen's criticism of welfare and development economics since the 1970s arguing that commodities are needed not for themselves but for the scope of *capabilities and functionings* they generate for human wellbeing. Sen defined capability as "a person's ability to do valuable acts or reach valuable states of being"[4] subject to a person's own free choice, whereas functionings represent actual outcomes of those capabilities. Thus, justice, equality and human rights from Sen's viewpoint should pertain not only to the distribution of the commodities themselves but more significantly to the distribution of capabilities created by those commodities in the way to enhance human wellbeing. Comparable findings about the true meaning of human wellbeing are embedded in Easterlin's survey analysis about the relationship between economic growth and happiness. The so-called *Easterlin Paradox* has originated in Easterlin's survey finding that people's happiness does not depend on the state of economic growth.

The above pioneering contributions appear to have made a lasting impact on the philosophy of human development; not the least, because they have triggered a new trend that has kept transforming the academic landscape of economic development. The international recognition of Goulet developments ethics, Sen's capability approach and Easterlin paradox is particularly manifest in the standard human development index, the annual publication of World Happiness Report and the universal recognition of the three core values of human development: *self-substance, self-esteem, and freedom.* While the main thrust of this trend has been to humanize sustainable economic development, it has equally well concerned itself with the recovery of individual liberties from the bondage of rigid dogma, authoritarian culture, oppressive political regimes and overbearing communitarian values. Nonetheless, the individualistic laissez-faire nature of this humanist philosophy has been

3 Des Gasper (2008), pp. 453–474.

4 Sen, Amartyre (1993), p. 30.

the object of strong criticism by the advocates of a newly emerging communitarianism, Amitai Etzioni (1998) and William A. Galston (1993) and others, who argue the case for restoring the necessary balance between individual liberties and community values endangered by excessive individualism. The title *responsive communitarianism* has thus been coined by this group of researchers as a stark warning against what they have perceived as a breakdown of the moral fabric of the modern society. To this cause, Etzioni established the Communitarian Network to study and promote communitarian approaches to social issues enhanced by the issuance of the quarterly journal *The Responsive Community*.

Incidentally, although the Q- perspective of human development has its own ethical character, it can be shown to fall at the centre of the current contention between liberalists and communitarianists. On one hand, the Quranic perspective can be shown to uphold the case for specific universal ethics and individual liberties in all human societies, yet on the other hand it acknowledges ethically sound communitarian values and upholds firm regulatory measures against excessive individualism. The criteria for setting the needed balance between these two ends will be shown in the Q- ethical perspective of human development.

3 The Q-ethical Perspective of Human Development

The ethical character of the Q-perspective is embedded squarely within the principle of monotheism or *Tawhid*, which means believing in One God, who is the Creator and Sustainer of the whole universe, as opposed to polytheism (*Shirk*). Notwithstanding the Q-recognition of different prophets who shouldered different messages of God to different communities throughout history, *Tawhid* alone can epitomize universally relevant socioeconomic ethics of world religions. Indeed, it is well affirmed in the Quran that belief in One God (*Tawhid*) is the common message revealed to all prophets: "Never did We send any messenger before you but to reveal to him that there is no deity except Me; so do worship Me" (Al Anbiyaa, 25).

In fact, the pivotal importance of *Tawhid* follows not only from the fact that it is the first pillar of Islam, but also from the fact it claimed 13 years out of the total 23 years which Prophet Mohamed had to spend as God's messenger. Thus, only 10 years were left for establishing the remaining 4 pillars of Islam (prayer, Zakah, fasting and pilgrimage) and setting up the detailed method and law, that governs Muslims' socioeconomic life i.e. the *Shariah*. Furthermore, the due emphasis on *Tawhid* does not contradict the fact that different prophets came with different God messages on the practical methods and laws (i.e. different systems of *Shariah*) to govern the socioeconomic affairs of their own communities: "To each of you, We have prescribed law and method; and had God willed, He could have made you all into one single nation (*ummah*)" (Al Ma'idah, 48).

The above Quranic verse raises another question about whether or not there have been common socioeconomic objectives shared by all the past different Shariah systems of different creeds. This key question will be addressed in next section, which will nonetheless fall back on the core ethical implications of *Tawhid*, or more generally the 'Religion' (*Al-Deen*) as expressly stated in the Quranic verse:

> The Religion He has chartered onto yourselves is the one He entrusted to Noah, and what We have revealed to you, and the one We entrusted to Ibrahim, Moses and Jesus, which is to establish Religion and never differ about it; what you are breaching is intolerable to the polytheists (*Mushriks*). (Al-Shura, verse 23)

Indeed, what was most intolerable with 'Religion' for *Mushriks* had not been the mere utterance of *Tawhid* phrase (*There no deity but God*) but the scrupulous moral discipline and socioeconomic justice attached with *Tawhid*. For example, lack of empathy towards the poor and needy is regarded in the Quran as typical of those who deny Religion: "Have you seen the one who denies Religion? It is him who rebuffs the orphan and does not urge food for the needy." (Al Ma'un, 1–3)

To bring this idea to sharp focus, *Tawhid-oriented* socioeconomic ethics have to be contrasted against their counter *Shirk*-driven ones. It is worth mentioning, however, that too little work has been done on this kind of inquiry. Apart from M. Choudhury's philosophical approach in relation to the epistemology of *Tawhid*, the received traditional approach has been devoted exclusively to theological debate (*'ilam al-kalam*) about the true and valid perception of *Tawhid* among rival schools of Islamic theology. Such theological concerns are well beyond the scope of this chapter though it is not unlikely for this inquiry to raise indirect issues in relation to theology. Yet in line with development economics which introduces solutions and policies after reflecting first on the problematic characteristics of underdevelopment, it is equaly reasonable here to introduce *Tawhid* development ethics after reflecting first on the counter development ethics *of its* antonym (i.e. *Shirk* or polytheism) as expressly portrayed in the Quran.

3.1 Counter Q-development Ethics

The contrast of *Tawhid* against its antonym of (*Shirk*) in the Quran seems more of a contrast between ethical and socioeconomic values than just a pure theological contention. In fact, the genesis of idol worshipping in the traditional practice of *shirk* is the arrorgance and self-gandiosity of Satan (*Ibless*) which is known to have been expelled from God's mercy. Thus, the Quran consistently links arrogance and self-grandiosity with denial of *Tawhid* – not only because *Tawhid*'s high moral ground is unattainable by arrogant people, but more crucially because *Tawhid* commands people to embrace this high moral ground and to stand accountable for it before God in the Hereafter. These key points explain why *Shirk* in the Quran is firmly linked with arrogant denial of accountability before God, and the tendency of the non-believing wealthy class (i.e. the prodigals or *mutrafin*)) to claim supremacy – no matter whether through economic power, racism, nationalism, tribalism, or otherwise – in the bid to enforce their own socioeconomic standards over the masses The following verses shed light on this fundamental idea:

- "When they [i.e. makers of *Shirk*] are told that there is no deity but God, they react arrogantly." (Al Saffat, 33)
- "Your God is One, but those who do not believe in the Day of Judgment have their hearts rebuff [this truth] arrogantly." (Al Nahl, 22)
- "When God alone is named, the hearts of those who disbelieve in the Hereafter react repulsively and when those other than Him are named they get filled with joy." (Al Zumar, 46)
- "Whenever We send a harbinger to a village, the prodigals would promptly say we disbelieve in what you have been sent with." (Sabaa, 24)
- "Whenever we sent a harbinger before you, the prodigals would say 'we have found our fathers on this track and we will follow their footsteps'." (Al Zukhruf, 24)
- "They were previously prodigals; and they used to insist on the grave sin (i.e. *Shirk*), and they used to say: how come if we were dead and transformed into dust and bones that we would be resurrected!" (Al Waqi'ah, 45–46, 476)
- "And they will say [i.e. the weak subordinates], Oh our Lord: we obeyed our masters and dignitaries and they led us astray" (Al Ahzab, 76).
- "Those deemed weak will say to those who were arrogant :'had it not been for you, we should have certainly been believers!'" (Sabaa, 31)
- "The day when We gather them all, We shall say to the *Mushriks* (i.e. the adherents of *Shirk*): 'Stick to your place, you and your [false] god-partners', so We separate them; and then their god-partners shall say: 'it was not us that you worshipped'." (Younis, 28)

The above verses portray a fairly consistent theme in the Quran where the two formative agents of *Shirk* in any community are brought to focus: (1) the wealthy masers who defy the prophets' message of *Tawhid* and claim supremacy over others – whether on racist, tribalist or simply economic grounds (2) the ignorant and poor followers who blindly obey their masters and pursue their track. Thus, the first six verses characterize *Shirk* masters as: arrogant, self-grandiose, prodigal and resistant to any interference with the prevailing socioeconomic order; while the last three verses describe the mass followers as ignorant, submissive with very low self-esteem.

This dual set-up was typical of ancient dynasties (mostly in Pharaonic Egypt) who enforced idol worshipping on their poor subjects while maintaining their own supremacy at the top of all gods. The Quran portrays this behavioral pattern most vividly through the story of Pharaoh, as for example in the warning given by Pharaoh's advisers against the threat that Moses made to Pharaoh's throne: "How come that you let Moses and his people abandon you and your gods?" (Al 'Araf, 127)

Or, even more strongly through Pharaoh's own proclamation that he stood at the top of all gods: "I am your supreme god!" (Al Nazi'at, 24)

The genesis of *Shirk* is, therefore, arrogance, self-grandiosity and indulgence into extravagant livelihood whereas physical idols emerged in the past centuries largely as pragmatic tools to enable powerful masters of *Shirk* command ever-lasting loyalty of ignorant and poor masses. At the same stroke, the cultural underpinnings of idol worshipping (i.e. black magic, mythology, superstitious beliefs etc.) relate primarily to the basic socioeconomic infrastructure that maintains the supremacy of the prodigal masters over their poor and ignorant followers. In particular, the last three verses show how deeply regretful the ignorant and poor masses would be in the Day of Judgment for blindly following false god-partners, which brings forth the pivotal Quranic idea that humans are individually responsible for utilizing their God-gifted mental endowments to independently, freely and prudently choose between the *Tawhid-oriented* ethical way of life and the counter *Shirk*-driven way of life. That is to choose for themselves between 'light' and 'darkness'

3.2 *Tawhid* Development Ethics

The above background drives home the idea that *Tawhid* is not merely a way of qualifying God with unit number but more profoundly about how the true perception of God's One-ness ensures sustainable ethics for human development. In direct contrast with *Shirk*-driven worldview which capitalizes on the power of wealth to claim ethical and socioeconomic supremacy over weak masses, the *Tawhid-oriented* worldview relies more on wealth diffusion, proper mass education and self-esteem assurance for all individual society members. There are at least five principles of *Tawhid-oriented* development ethics that follow directly from Q-sources:

(1) Principle of justice

The hallmark of God's message to all of the previous prophets has been to enable people establish justice on Earth among themselves: "We have sent Our messengers with clear signs and brought the Book and the Balance down with them so that people establish justice." (Al Hadid, 25)

'Book' and 'Balance' are generic terms referring, respectively, to: (1) books of *Shariah* systems revealed to different prophets, consisting of specific teachings, guidance, commandments and governing laws (2) and the balance which refers to the natural sense of justice (i.e. the *fitra*) that God has imbued on humans so they can make sound judgments about 'good' and 'bad' or 'right' and 'wrong'. As regards the association of different prophets with different *Sharia* systems, this merely reflects circumstantial differences between human communities at different times and different places – though it can be shown in the next section that there are commonly shared *Shariah* objectives among different religious creeds. Yet, what remains invariably the same across all human creeds is the core concept of 'balance' as highlighted through the following Quranic commandments:

- "Oh you who believe: stand up for justice as witnesses for God, even if it were against yourselves or parents or close relatives, however rich or poor it is God who cares for them." (Al Nisaa', 135)
- "It is not up to your wishes [you Muslims], or wishes of the People of the Book: whoever commits a sin shall be recompensed accordingly." (Al Nisaa, 123)
- "Never let repugnance of a people who once debarred you from the Holy Mosque lead you to turn offensive; and help one another in piety and benevolence and never help one another in sinfulness and aggression." (Al Mai'da, 2)

The first two verse are universal judicial criteria which guard human rights against all sorts of irrelevant considerations like social status, racial prejudice or vested interests, including Muslim /non-Muslim consideration. Yet, the last verse deserves special attention as it has been revealed after the conquest of Makkah which marked utter defeat of *Mushriks*, eventual termination of their long-standing sovereignty at Makkah and the victorious return of Prophet Mohamed to his original home and birthplace.

Ordinary leaders would normally like to glorify their victory through maximum suppression and humiliation of the defeated enemy, at least for the sake of rewarding their armies and boosting up their morale. However, the contrary is prescribed by the last verse. On one hand, it graciously permitted the conquered *Mushriks* to perform their own religious rituals at the Holy Mosque (i.e. the Ka'bah) freely and peacefully as usual. On the other hand, it prohibited the Prophet's Companions from transgressing the *Mushriks* on reprisal grounds, even though the *Mushriks* persecuted Muslims ruthlessly during the early period of the Prophet's message at Makkah. Admittedly, debarring Mushriks from the Holy Mosque could have been a justifiable option on two grounds: that they once did the same thing for the Prophet and his Companions; and that *Shirk* rituals were false from the viewpoint of *Tawhid*. Ceratainly, Mohamed (peace be upon him) was God's prorphet not an ambitious power-thirsty politician!

Although the above gracious offer to the *Mushriks* ended shortly afterwards due to their breach of the peace treaty with the Prophet and their plot to kill him, it nonetheless extols the moral value of forgiveness and tolerance from the position of power as well as giving concrete Quranic evidence for the provision of free religious practice in tandem with the other verse: "There is no compulsion in Religion." (Al Baqarah, 256)

The principle of justice should therefore underscore the fact that people are free to practice whatever religion they embrace so long as they practice it peacefully; and so long as people can rationally process the relevant knowledge and choose prudently what is good for themselves.

(2) Principle of human honor

This principle emphasizes equal worthiness of all humans regardless of color, ethnicity, social status or religious creed given that they have all originated from one and the same couple: Adam and Eve. The Quran asserts this principle and illuminates its socioeconomic consequences in various ways:

- "Verily we have honored the son of Adam" (Al Israa, 70)
- "And among his signs is the creation of heaven and the earth and the difference in your languages and colors." (Al Rum, 22)
- "Oh people, We have created you from male and female and made you into nations and tribes so as to make you know each other; verily your most honored for God are your most pious." (Al Hujurat, 23)
- "This is your community, a single community as it is, and I am your Lord, so worship me." (Al Anbiyaa, 92)

Thus, the Quran attaches 'honor' and self-steam as a fundamental human right uniformly to all of Adam's offspring, irrespective of language, ethnicity and color differences. The third verse explains God's wisdom in distributing humans among different tribal, social and national groups in terms of the encouragement for people to *know each other*. It is noteworthy, however, that the last italicized phrase is an English translation to the key Arabic word – *ta'arafu* – which is perhaps more precisely translated as *recognizing each other* since the linguistic sense of this Arabic term implies *recognizing* cross-cultural differences that characterize human groups (e.g. languages, habits and customs) rather than just *knowing* them.

It is therefore a moral duty on humans to view cultural difference as constructive recipes for sharing common humanist values and enhancing the socioeconomic quality of life in conformity with the popular slogan 'unity in diversity', more than a cause for supremacy claims among human ethnic groups. Endorsing the same ethical value, the last verse brings forth the complementary idea that humans are essentially one single unified community so long as they worship one God and strive with best effort to attain the high moral ground of *Tawhid*.

(3) Principle of trusteeship in wealth

As argued above, the power of wealth bears far reaching consequences on the ethical and socioeconomic order of human communities depending on whether it is being capitalized by 'prodigals' to claim socioeconomic supremacy over the masses, or properly diffused to ensure the three core values of development; *self-sustenance, self-esteem and freedom* among the masses. The *Tawhid*-oriented principle of 'trusteeship in wealth' contributes significantly to the latter as it defines wealth ownership as God's trust attached with moral duties on its holder towards the others rather one of absolute ownership. The importance of this principle cannot be exaggerated given the fact that denial of Religion has been identified in the Quran with disregard of moral duty towards the needy: (Have you seen the one who denies Religion? It is him who rebuffs the orphan and does not urge food for the needy). The following verses shed more light on different aspects of this principle:

- "Believe in God and His Messenger and spend out of that whereof He made you trustees." (Al Hadid, 7).
- "Give them from God's wealth that He has bestowed on you." (Al Nur, 33)
- "Do not give the irresponsible (*al-sufahaa*) your wealth that God has made as sustenance for you." (Al Nisaa', 33)
- "The Alms (Zakah) are for the poor, the needy, those who take alms out of their wealth to purify them." (Al Tawbah, 103)

The idea that wealth is God's trust on its holder with an attached moral duty towards others is clearly expressed by the first two verses. Furthermore, there is an explicit public duty – no matter how it may be defined and institutionalized politically and socially – to ensure that wealth holders expend it *responsibly* for both private and social purposes as clearly conveyed through the third verse above. This point, however, relates to the definition of *sufahaa* (i.e. the irresponsible wealth owners) in Islamic Jurisprudence which is beyond the scope of this paper. Yet, Shariah's major vehicle of wealth diffusion is the institution of mandatory alms (i.e. Zakah) as outlined in the fourth verse above. Zakah shares comparable structural features with the tax system in terms chargeable bases and rate structures but differs significantly from taxation as regards the utilization of collected proceedings. Unlike taxation system which leaves the utilization of tax proceeding at the disposal of government, the utilization of Zakah proceedings is earmarked in the Quran for eight primary categories (the poor, the needy, .. etc), which is the fundamental property that qualifies Zakah as a tool of sustainable wealth diffusion. On one hand, the fixed rate structure of Zakah makes it financially robust against any short or medium manipulations to which tax systems are normally prone. On the other hand, the earmarked spending of Zakah proceedings ensures its utilization in the relentless fight against poverty and need.

(4) Principle of collective integrity

This principle underscores moral commitment on society members to help one another in the way of promoting productive socioeconomic practices and deterring counterproductive ones; or alternatively, enjoin admissible order (*al-ma'ruf)* and prohibit inadmissible order (*al-munkar*) in conformity with the Quranic verses:

- "Help one another in piety and never help one another in sin and transgression." (Al-Ma'idah, 2)
- "There no good in much of their covert talks save for him who orders alms (*sadaqah*) or good practice (*ma'ruf*) or reconciliation between people." (Al Nisaa, 114)

- "You have been the best nation ever emerged to humankind [in terms of] enjoining admissible order (*ma'ruf*) and prohibiting inadmissible order (*munkar*)." (Al Imran, 110)
- "Those who follow the messenger, the unlettered Prophet, who orders them the admissible and prohibits them from the inadmissible." (Al 'Araf, 157)

Little reflection on the second verse above reduces the moral burden underlying the principle of collective integrity into three alternatives courses of action: (1) providing financial support for an urgent social cause (i.e. *sadaqah*) (2) Or catering expert knowledge for the promotion of some important socioeconomic practice (*ma'ruf* e.g. facilitating health, education etc.) (3) Or resolving some major tensions arising between social parties (*reconciliation between people*). This presentation raises an important question on how to interpret the idea of ordering the admissible and prohibiting the inadmissible, given the Prophet's hadith;" Whoever amongst you sees an inadmissible order (*munkar*), must correct it by hand; if he cannot, then by his word; and if he cannot, then by his heart, which the weakest belief"[5] as it has widely misunderstood by those who interpret the word "hand" to stand for the use physical force.

As a matter of fact, the word 'hand' can be used in Arabic to imply the use of physical force when military confrontation with enemies in implied[6] but in the normal circumstances it often implies the virtue of giving or helping. For example, in the *hadith* reported on the authority of the Prophet's wife Aisha *bint* Abu Bakr Al-Siddiq (may God be pleased with both that the Prophet described the fastest of his wives to follow him after his death as 'the one with the longest hand'.[7] Taking the word literally, the Prophet's wives compared the lengths of their hands to find out who was that fortunate wife. It turned out, however, that Zeinab *bint* Jahsh was the fastest to follow the Prophet after his death, and that the 'length of hand' was, in fact, a metaphoric measure of charitable giving whereupon Zeinab *bint* Jahsh scored the highest mark.[8]

There is hardly any supportive evidence in the Prophet's Sunnah for the interpretation of 'hand' as symbolic of physical force in the normal circumstances, whereas there is ample evidence to prove that the Prophet himself demonstrated how 'inadmissible order' (*munkar*) could be corrected 'by hand' in the sense of giving and helping. The story of poor wayfarers who travelled through Madinah pleading desperately for help reveals how the Prophet considered their abject state of poverty a typical case of 'inadmissible order'. The Prophet's immediate reaction was to express grave concerns with their humiliating state of poverty and passionately preached his companions to

5 Narrated in *Sahih Muslim* on the authority of Abu Sai'd Al-Khuari.

6 For example in the Quranic verse: "He is the one who kept off people's hand from you and your hands from them at the heart of Makkah"(Alfateh:).

7 Narrated in *Sahih Al-Bukhari* on the authority of Aisha bint Abi Bakr al-Siddiq.

8 ibid.

offer all necessary support to those wayfarers. While one Companions came forward with a heavy load of food provisions, thereby setting an outstanding example for the others, the Prophet made his widely quoted hadith: "whoever introduces a tradition of good practice (*Sunnah hasana*) will get its reward and the reward of those who practice it, without discounting their rewards and whoever introduces a tradition of bad practice will bear its sin and the sins of those who practice it without discounting their sins".[9]

Apparently, *Shariah* injunctions of "admissible order' (*ma'ruf*) against 'inadmissible order' (*munkar*) and the everlasting encouragement for people to promote good and productive practices (*Sunnah hasana*), are inextricably linked with the principle of collective integrity.

(5) Principle of self-esteem

Striking the right balance between 'communitarianism' (or collectivism) and individual human rights marks a deep ideological rift between liberalists and communitarians; while the tendency to overemphasize the constructive power of collectivism (*fiqh al-jama'ah*)) looms large within the contemporary Islamist thought. At any rate, constructive collectivism, no matter how defined, cannot be reconciled with maneuvering and exploiting low self-esteem individuals even if it were for a seemingly good collectivist cause. Indeed, the main reason why religiosity has often been linked with backwardness and blinkered behavior is the abuse of Religion by powerful preachers who possess the skill to secure unquestioning support of sincere low self-esteem followers through simple theological rehtoric.

The *Tawhid*-oriented principle of self-estemm is precisely meant to fortify Muslim beleivers against bandwagon behavior and blind following, through better education and trust in one's own independent jusgement. Individual accountability for one's own deeds and God-conscious responsibility are pivotal Quranic concepts that can be exemplified by the following verses:

- "And they will all come back to Him individually." (Maryam, 95)
- "Whatever [wrong] any human being commits rests upon himself alone and no bearer of burdens shall be made to bear another's burden." (Fatir, 18).
- "Do not pursue that of which you have no knowledge. Indeed, the hearing, the sight and the heart – about all of these one will be questioned." (Israa, 36)

This principle calls for better education of Muslim offspring in a manner that broadens their intellectual horizons; guards thm against blind following to others even if it were propagated in the name of Islam; enhances their cognitive competences for independent thinking; develops their creative capacities and imaginative talents; and eventually empowers them with valuable productive skills for positive engagements

9 Narrated in *Sahih Muslim*.

along the socioeconomic strategy of Shariah objectives (i.e. the *maqasid* as it is shortly introduced). A well principled God-conscious individual is the building block of a well principled Muslim society.

4 Approaching *Shariah* Socioeconomic Objectives

Finally, the question arises about whether or not there are common parameters characterizing different creeds of *Shariah* systems that God revealed to different prophets as it has been mentioned in Quran: "To each of you, We have prescribed law and method (i.e. *Shariah* system); and had God willed, He could have made you all into one single nation (*ummah*)." (Al Ma'idah, 48).

Early Muslim Scholars have, indeed, realized the fact that all past creeds *(milal,* the plural of *millah*), including Islamic *Shariah*, had recognized five fundamental objectives that ought to be sustained in relation to God's creation; namely: Religion, Self, Progeny, Mind and Wealth. That was effectively an alternative approach to understanding Islamic Shariah which laid down the foundation of a special field of inquiry that has become known as the Objectives of Shariah – or the *maqasid* of Al Shariah. Three major milestones are often associated with the disciplinary development of *Maqasid* between the fifth and eighth Hiri century: *'Al Burhan Fi Usul Al-Fiqh'* by Al Juwayni (died 487H), *Al- Mustasfa* by Al Ghazali (died 505H) and *'Al Muwafaqat'* widely acclaimed book of Al Shatibi's (died 790H), which assessed, assimilated and coalesced the earlier contributions of *maqasid* into a coherent discipline. Unlike the conventional sources of jurisprudence (*Usul al Fiqh*) which grapple literally with the linguistic interpretations of Shariah texts in the bid to settle persistent jurisprudential disagreements, the *maqasid* offers an alternative guidance by reference to generally accepted principles that epitomize the underlying wisdom of Shariah texts. Abdel 'aati (2007) brings forth the consensus among notable Muslim scholars (Al Ghazali, Al Amidy, Al Ensnowy, Al Qirafi, Al Soubki and others) that the above *maqasid* framework is recognizable in all human societies.[10] Bel'abbas (2014) accredited the publicity of *Al Muwafaqat* book of Al Shtibi in the Muslim world to the active role of prominent West Muslim Scholars (*Maghariba*) particularly the early founders of Ez-Zitouna University.

This source of guidance is believed to have contributed to the debate and deliberations among the first generation of Muslim scholars, even though it took five centuries after Hijrah for *maqasid* to be recognized as a supplementary source of jurisprudence. *Maqasid* has thus emerged as a special field of inquiry in Islamic jurisprudence to offer guidance on the basis of the logical rationale of Shariah texts whenever newly arising matters seem to instigate fresh jurisprudential reasoning. In the words of Ibn 'Ashur (died 1393 H), an eminent scholar of Ez-Zietouna: "Al Shatibi has, indeed, built

10 Abel'aati (2007), p. 166.

a towering pyramid of Islamic culture through this book, where he was able to oversee routes and ways capable of ensuring the immortality and infallibility of Religion; so rarely precedent was he that he left those who wish to embroil into the meanings of Shariah entirely dependent on him".[11] Ibn 'Ashur's book '*Maqasid Al Shariah Al Islamiyah*' is, yet, a remarkable milestone after more than six Hijri centuries from Al Shatibi's era. Departing from an insightful critical apparaisal of his predecessors (Al Juwayni, Al Qirafi and Al Shatibi), Ibn 'Ashur revived interest in *maqasid* and contextualized its findings within the modern world, thereby, inspiring not only Shariah jurists but equally well Muslim researchers in economic, sociological, and political fields.

Thus, the question how to ensure the relevance of Islamic heritage to our present day challenges seems to have gained momentum in the current litaterure whether morally and philosophically or jurisprudentially; Abdelrahman(1994), Al Raysouni (199), Abdel 'aati (2007), Al Qaradawi (2008) and many others. Here we are particularly concened with two basic issues in the received heritage of *maqasid*:

1. *First*, Al Shatibi's grouping of moral values within the set of perfections rather than necessities. This issue marks a crucial flaw in the conceptual buildup of *maqasid* as it has rightly noted by many researchers. Admittedly, Al Shatibi was well aware of the status of moral values in the Holy Quran and Prophet's traditions (e.g. the Prophet's well known hadith "I have been sent just for the completion of noble morals"[12]). Presumably, it was just part of the early orientation of *maqasid* towards visible jurist injunctions that overshadowed the status of morals.
2. *Second*, the lack in the received tradition of a standard criterion for ranking the five necessities (religion, self, progeny, mind and wealth); which can be clearly seen from the wide range of ranking criteria adopted by early scholars of *maqasid*. Abdel 'aati (2007) and Abdelhafiz (2016) explained various viewpoints whereby 'religion' itself has been ranked differently by notable scholars like Al Razi, Al Qirafi and Al Zamakhshari. Abdelhafiz (2016) has rightly emphasized the dire need for proper ranking of the five necessities if the *maqasid* has to play a constructive role in the modern life.

4.1 Ranking through the Strategic Socioeconomic Inquiry

Perhaps, the best approach to address the above two concerns is to ask the two question: (1) *what role do moral values play in human life, and* (2) *why should the ranking of the maqasid's five necessities matter at all*? At least from the socioeconomic perspective, the answer is simple: we need to identify *maqasid*-oriented moral values so as to accommodate them within a well-integrated ranking of the five necessities to

11 Cited in Al Mahati, Hamza, (2014).
12 Sahih Al Bukhari, within Al Adab Al Mufrad, 273.

manifest the strategic socioeconomic objectioves of a human society. It is noteworthy that the socioeconomic outlook to *maqasid* differs significantly from its traditional counterpart even though they both obey the same underlying structural framework of Al Shatibi's *Muwafaqat* which defines the five 'necessities' as the fundamental foundation wherefrom 'needs' and 'perfections' emerge.[13] Whereas the traditional jurisprudential appeal to *Maqasid* relates primarily to how it helps levelling out potential disagreements in the pursuit of valid *fatwa* at the inter-person level, the alternative socioeconomic appeal relates to the useful insight *maqasid* may offer in the statement of vision, setting of strategic goals, and formulation of policies. More formally, the five necessities: religion, self, progeny, mind and wealth, respectively, can be accommodated within the socioeconomic strategic framework as follows:

1. *Religion*: The vision that precipitates the necessary human development ethics, as in the above stated *Tawhid*- ethics, with the objective to govern the utilization of human and material resources in the pursuit of the socioeconomic goals.
2. *Self* (*nafs* i.e. human life): The central socioeconomic goal as it follows from various Quranic verses: e.g. (He devoted for your sake [humans] whatever is in the heavens and whatever is in the earth, all from him" (Al Jathiya: 13).
3. *Progeny*: The intergenerational goal which relates to the how future generations are brought up and enabled to shoulder major socioeconomic responsibilities in accordance to vision.
4. *Mind*: The necessary human resource that thinks, plans, organizes manages and engages in the technical production goods and services, depending on the amount and quality of education afforded to it.
5. *Wealth*: The necessary material resource that makes it possible to pursue the above goals in accordance with vision.

To instrumentalize the newly emerging culture of *maqasid* outlook and thereby address the sustainable developmental challenge in the Muslim world, Tag el-Din (2013, 2017) explains how *needs* and *perfections* may branch off dynamically from every constituent of the above *necessary* foundation. A three-stage development model has, thus, been introduced to see how the central goals (Self and Progeny) can be accommodated dynamically subject to the governing vision through proper utilization of resources (Mind and Wealth).

5 Conclusion

This chapter seeks to lay down the fundamental foundation of human development ethics as perceivable from the relevant Quranic verses at the back drop of the latest

13 See Tag el-Din,(2013), pp. 11–32.

trends in theory of sustainable development. Linking morality with 'belief in God' seems to have attained worldwide recognition in recent global surveys, thereby, begging the key question *how could the socioeconomic ethics associated with belief in God usher a positive humanist insight into the pursuit of sustainable development?* To answer this question, the chapter identifies 'belief in God' with the generic concept of Religion (*Al- Deen*) in the Quran, which incidentally coincides with the doctrine of *Tawhid* (i.e. monotheism, or Oneness of God). In line with development economics where recommendable solutions and prescriptive polices come after demonstrating the problematic characteristics of underdevelopment, the chapter prescribes *Tawhid*-oriented socioeconomic ethics after demonstrating the problematic counter socioeconomic ethics of its antonym (i.e. *polytheism or Shirk*). Thus, *Tawhid*-oriented development ethics have been formulated in terms of five main princilples: justice human honor, trusteeship in wealth, collective integrity and self-estemm. This has proved particularly useful within the strategic socioeconomic framework that helps resate Shariah objectives (i.e *maqasid Al Shariah*) in terms of vision, central goals and resources.

References

Abdel 'aati, Mohamed (2007) '*Al Maqasid Al Shariyah wa Aatharuha al Fiqhiyah*', Dar Al Hadith, Cairo.

Abdel Hafiz, Sali Gamal, (2016), *Tarteeb Al Maqasid Al Shar'iah,* alukah.net/ Sharia/0/105662.

Abdelrahman, Taha (1994) '*Tajdid Al Manhaj fi Al Turath*', Al Markaz Al Thqafi Al Arabi, Al Dar Al Baydaa', Berut.

Al Mahati, Hamza (2014), *Aqsam Al Maqasid ind Al Shatibi,* aluka.net/0/71903.

Al Raysouni, A (1995) '*Nathariyyat Al Maqasid 'ind Al Imam Al Shatibi*' Intenational, Institiute of Islamic Thought (IIIT), Series of university theses, Virginia, USA.

Al Qaradawi, Youef (2008), '*Dirasa fi Fiqh Al Maqasid*', Dar Al Shiruq, Berut.

Al- Shatibi, Ibn Ishaq, *Al Muwafaqat*, Dar Al Maktaba Al 'Alamiyya, Beirut, vol.1 & 2.

Al-Qaradawi, Yousef (1997) 'Economic Security in Islam'; translated by M. Iqbal Siddiqi, Kucha Chelan; New Delhi, India.

Amartyre, Sen (190) 'Equality of What?' Cambridge University Press, UK.

Awan Akhtar, A. (1983) 'Equality, Efficiency, and Property Ownership in the Islamic Economic System', University Press of America, Lanham, N.Y., London.

Bel'Abbas (2014) "*Ma sir Ihtimam Al Gharb Al Islami Bi Maqasid Al Shariyah*", Al Hijaz International Refereed Journal on Islamic & Arabic Studies

Chapra, M. U (2000) *The future of Economics,* The Islamic Foundation, Leicester, UK.

Chapra, M. U (1992) *Islam and the Economic Challenge*, The Islamic Foundation. F. and the International Institute of Economic Thought, USA.

Des Gasper (2008) Journal of Human Development, vol.9, issue 3, selected papers from the 2007 conference of the Human Development and Capability Association.

Choudhry, Massud Al Alam (2007) 'Absolute Reality in the Quran', New York, Palgrave, Macmillan.

Easterlin, Richard (1974) *Does Economic Growth Improve the Human Lot? Some Empirical Evidence*, in 'Nations & Households in Economic Growth' edited by Paul A. David & Melvin W. Reder; New York, Academic Press.

El- Ashker, Ahmed & Wilson, Rodney (2006) 'Islamic Economics: A Short History', Leiden, Brill
Engel, Susan N. (2010) *Development Economics from Classical to Critical Analysis, The International Studies Encyclopedia,* Vol. II, pp874– 892, West Sussex, Blackwell Publishing.
Etzoni, Amitai (1998) 'The Moral Dimension: Towards A New Economics', The Free Press, New York, London, Sydney, Toronto, Singapore.
Faridi, F. R. (1991) *Essays in Islamic Economics,* Nice –Printing Press, Genuine Publications and Media, New Delhi, India.
Farina Francesco and Hahn, Frank (1996). *Ethics, Rationality, and Economic Behaviour*, Stefan Vannucci, Clarendon Press, Oxford.
Galston, William. A. (1993) The Promise of Communitarianism, National Civic Review, Vol.82, issue 2, pp. 217–214.
Gorringe, Timothy (1999) 'Fair Shares, Ethics and the Global Economy', Thames and Hudson.
Goulet, Dennis (1971) 'The Cruel Choice: A New Concept in The Theory of Development' New York, Athenaeum.
Halim, Alan P. (1996) *Ethics and Economics.* Vol I and II. Cheltenham, UK, Brookfield, USA.
Hasan-uz-Zaman, M. (1981) 'The Economic Functions of the Early Islamic State', International Islamic Publishers, Karachi, Pakistan.
Huq, Ataullah (1993) 'Development and Distribution in Islam', Pelanduk Publications, Malaysia.
Iqbal, M. (1994) ed.: 'Distributive Justice and Need Fulfilment in an Islamic Economy', IIIE, IIU, Islamabad, Pakistan.
Islahi, Abdelazim (1988) 'Economic Concepts of Ibn Taymiyyah'; the Islamic Foundation, Leicester, K.
Islamic Economic and Research Bureau (1979), 'Thought on Islamic Economics'; University of Dacca, Bangladesh.
Isma'il, Syed Mohammad (1989) 'Capitalism, Socialism, and Islamic Economic Order', Oriental Publications, Pakistan.
Kahf, Munzir (1991) 'Lessons in Islamic Economics', IRTI, IDB.
Khan, M. Fahim, ed. (1995) 'Essays in Islamic Economics', the I.F., UK.
Mannan, M.A. (1970), 'Islamic Economics, Theory and Practice'. Sh. Mohammad Ashraf, Kashmir, Lahore, Pakistan.
Naqvi, Sayed Nawab (1981) 'Ethics and Economics; an Islamic Synthesis', The Islamic Foundation, Leicester, UK.
Naqvi, Sayed Nawab (1994) 'Islam Economics and Society', Kegan Paul International, London, New York.
Naqvi, Sayed Nawab (2003) 'Morality and Human Well-being' The Islamic Foundation, Leicester, UK.
Pew Resrach Centre (2014) *Worldwide, Many Believe in God as Essential to Morality*, Chapter 3, Vews on Religion & Morality, pewresearch.org golobal/ 2014/03/1.
Roy, Subroto (1989), 'Philosophy of Economics', Rutledge, London, New York.
Sahih Al Bukhari (undated), Darussalam Press for publication and distribution, Riyadh, Saudi Arabia.
Sahih Muslim (2010, 133H), 'Aamira Press, Dar Al Khilafa Al 'Aliyah, 1st edition.
Sen, Amartyre (1993), 'Capability & Wellbeing' in the Quality of Life (eds. Nussbaum, Martha & Sen, Amarture), Oxford, Calrendon Press, p. 30.
Shaghil, M. (1969) 'Islamic Economics', Patel Enterprises, New Delhi; India.
Tag el-Din, Seif I. (2007) 'Foundations of Islamic Economics' draft book at MIHE, the Islamic Foundation, UK, Leicester.
Tag el-Din, Seif (2013) 'Maqasid Foundations of Islamic Economics", UK, Edinburgh University Press.
Todaro, P. Michael & Stephen C. Smith (2011) 'Economic Development', 11th edition, Pearson.
Zarqa, M. Anas (2003) *Islamization of Economics: The Concept and Methodology*, Journal of Kind Abdelaziz University, Islamic Economics, no.1, 3–42.

Seyyed Reza Hosseini

Chapter 7: Relationship Between Ethics and Economic Development from the Viewpoint of the Qur'an and Hadith

1 Introduction

An objective, economic development has always attracted the attention of nations, schools of thought and societies. In recent centuries a model of economic development has emerged in the West that has been considered as desirable by many scholars and governments throughout the world due to it positive attributes such as scientific advancement, rapid technological progress and expansion of prosperity and well-being, such that it was adopted by governments as the principle tool of economic planning and policy. Concomitantly, however, this phenomenon was accompanied by major changes in the worldview and ethical values governing western societies, such as thirsting for worldly things, considering praiseworthy accumulation of wealth, and expansion of consumerism, that came into conflict with Islamic values, such as Zuhd (ascetism) and Qana'ah (austerity and being content with one possessed) in the world. Consequently, the desirability of the Western development model and how it could be accommodated within the ethics and the belief system of Islam has been subject of challenging debates. Facing this challenge, some Muslim scholars chose the path of secularism, some argued that this model results in growth and prosperity which will provide a basis for implementing ethical values and religious teachings, and still others considered that life in the environment characterized by continuous technological changes and the growth of new ways and means of consumerism is incompatible with spirituality and the Islamic way of life.

Mirakhor and Askari (2010) studied the evolution of the concept of economic development in the West from the beginning until now and considered this concept from the viewpoint of the Qur'an in their book titled *Islam and the Path to Human and Economic Development*. They conclude: "Islam's concept of development contains three interrelated dimensions of self-development, physical-material development, and societal development. The Creator has provided for humans the ways and means of achieving all the dimensions fully and comprehensively. The most crucial and central to Islam's concept of development is the progress humans make in developing the self. Without this, balanced and appropriate progress in the other two dimensions of development is not possible; any forward movement in them without self-development leads to harmful distortions. Compliance with the rules prescribed by the Law Giver prevents distortions. The rules constitute a network that regulates all dimensions of the human experience, individually and collectively, on this plane of existence. Rule-compliance promotes material growth through higher total factor

https://doi.org/10.1515/9783110593419-007

productivity (TFP)." This paper shares this conclusion. However, its focus is on the physical-material dimension of economic development and attempts to discover the interrelationship of this dimension with Islamic ethics from the viewpoint of the Qur'an and Hadith.

Study of the Qur'an and Hadith of Ahl Al-Bayt (as[1]) reveals that development of material means of life can be investigated through two different systems of thought and approach. One is founded on materialism and "Takathur" (literally, it means proliferation) which means to economic development based on accumulation of wealth by a few) and is therefore called "*Takathuri* model" of development. The other is development on the basis of monotheism and divine ethics. This model creates a broad-based prosperity for all and can be referred to here as "*Kauthari* model" of development. The word Kauthar means abundant. Therefore, the "Kauthari model of development" relies on values and ethics that promote development targeted at creating an abundant economy for all rather than for a few. Each of these visions and paths of development have their respective doctrinal, ethical and juridical principles, and lead to distinctive economic developments. Therefore, in discussing the compatibility of ethical principles with economic development, it must be made clear which of the two system is intended. In the Theo-centric perception and ethics, economic development is mandated but has its own distinctive methods and behavioral mechanisms which distinguish its path from that of secular system of development.

In other words, although some of the Islamic ethical values are considered incompatible with *Takathuri* model of development, they are not only compatible with Kauthari thinking on economic development, they also provide the foundation and the grounds for its actualization. In order to clarify this claim, this paper begins with investigating the doctrinal and ethical foundations of Western development and the resulting structure of the discipline of economics. The paper then investigates the degree of the desirability of economic advancement (Takathuri) as well as the fundamentals of perception and ethics of the desirable (Kauthari) economic development and some of its general approaches related to production, distribution and consumption behavior.

2 Natural Ethics (Utilitarianism) as the Foundation of the *Takathuri* Model of Development

The first and the most important characteristic of the Western economic development model which distinguishes it from desirable development from the viewpoint of Islam is its worldview and its ethical principles governing evaluation of good and bad human behavior which will be considered in this section.

1 Peace Be Upon Them.

The economic development in Western societies was triggered by the profound cultural, religious and social changes that occurred during the post-Renaissance centuries. The religious belief of the pre-Renaissance era was based on revelatory theology, which was gradually reformed and set aside from social affairs and was replaced by "Deism" (natural theology). The main characteristic of such thinking was its reliance on human intellect and reasoning and independence from divine teachings as well as denial of the Creator's involvement with the natural world after creation.[2]

The physiocrat economists were the first to implement deism in economics. "They considered the natural law as the best regulator of social relationships and believed that it is sufficient to understand the natural law in order to comply with them."[3] Before the last decades of the seventeenth century, ethical virtues and vices had their own distinct definition and criteria of determination of their role in human felicity or wretchedness in the ethical system of the European societies. However, with the publication of Bernard Mandeville's book: The *Fable of the Bees or Private Vices, Public Benefits*, the boundary between virtue and vice became blurred. According to Mandeville, wealth, fine arts and sciences are not due to human virtues, that is numerous natural that lead us to desire comfort, wellbeing, luxuries and all the worldly pleasures of life are all results of what he called vices and imperfections. According to Mandeville's particular belief, helping the poor, austerity and contentment in life and the like, despite appearing ethical and benevolent, will lead to recession and ultimately to evil. On the other hand, behavior that appear as unethical such as extravagance and prodigality in consumption and importation of luxuries will result in prosperity.[4] Adam Smith criticized Mandeville's opinion in his book *The Theory of Moral Sentiments* for calling the unobjectionable desires and tastes of human beings as vices. He wrote: "It is only self-interest (not as a defect but as virtue) that would, without the intention or knowledge of the individuals, naturally guide the society towards improvement, wellbeing and development."[5] Jeremy Bentham entered the debate with a more clear position that introduced goodness and happiness basically as synonym of the "usefulness," the "pleasure" or the "utility" that results from Consumption of goods and services.[6] Thomas Hobbes (1588–1679), a seventeenth century philosopher remarks: "Human intellect, in the final analysis, is a slave and servant of his passions. Therefore, its only duty is to search for ways and means that satisfy human desires passions."[7]

The most important issue that emerges from these views is that human basic (animal) drives constitute the criteria of ethicality of an action. Believing that human

2 See Barbour; 1362 SH; pp. 75 & 76.
3 Gide and Rist (Persian Translation); 1370 SH; Vol. 1; p. 2.
4 Dadgar; 1383 SH; p. 202.
5 Gide and Rist (Persian Translation); 1370 SH; Vol. 1; pp. 84 and 85.
6 Fitzpatrick; 1381 SH; p. 30.
7 Jones; No Date; Vol. 2; p. 490.

basic instincts and searching for personal benefits govern human societies, classical economists considered "self-interest" as the only motivator and the "natural law" governing human behavior that, under conditions of "free markets" would achieve individual and societal benefits. Based on this axiom, they then argued that the basic principle of human economic behavior is to "maximize utility, profit or income." Based on this axiom, they concluded that economic matters, like those of the sciences, are separable from ethics and normative values. Emergence of this view was the beginning of disengagement of humans from divine teachings and their bewilderment in the darkness of nature and led to the development of all secular sciences based on this point of view. Economic freedom meaning negation of state intervention as well as from religious mandates and ethical constraints, autonomous and mechanical equilibrium, free competition market mechanism separation of economics from high ethical and human values were the results of natural-ethics orientation. Scholars and thinkers who play a role in the structuring of such a science have no effective belief in religion nor the science they develop has any room for religious-oriented objectives derived from the sacred sources of religion. Reigns of such a science are in the hands of the rebelious whims of humans from which nothing results other than delusion and modern Jahilyyah (ignorance). In this context, the Qur'an (45:23–24) states:

أَفَرَأَيْتَ مَنِ اتَّخَذَ إِلَهَهُ هَوَاهُ وَأَضَلَّهُ اللَّهُ عَلَى عِلْمٍ وَخَتَمَ عَلَى سَمْعِهِ وَقَلْبِهِ وَجَعَلَ عَلَى بَصَرِهِ غِشَاوَةً فَمَنْ يَهْدِيهِ مِنْ بَعْدِ اللَّهِ أَفَلَا تَذَكَّرُونَ
(23) وَقَالُوا مَا هِيَ إِلَّا حَيَاتُنَا الدُّنْيَا نَمُوتُ وَنَحْيَا وَمَا يُهْلِكُنَا إِلَّا الدَّهْرُ وَمَا لَهُمْ بِذَلِكَ مِنْ عِلْمٍ إِنْ هُمْ إِلَّا يَظُنُّونَ (24).

> Have you seen the one who has taken his passion as his Lord? God has knowingly let him to go astray, and sealed off his hearing and his heart, and veiled his eyesight. Who besides God can guide him? Will you, then, not take heed? (23) They say: "Nothing exists except our worldly life! And here, we shall live and die. It is only fate/time which will destroy us." They have no knowledge about this. It is only their guesswork. (24) (Al-Jathia': 23 and 24)

It is therefore evident that the current economic development of the West is an offspring that came into existence with denial of the Creator's formative and legislative guidance and its role in regulating social relations and organization of life. The growth and evolvement of Western economies has been based on downgrading human beings from their supreme position of being Allah's agents (Khalifah state) on earth to the lower rank of animality and materiality. This model sanctifies some ethical vices, denies majestic human values and religious teachings, and turns human intellect into a servant of passions. Such kind of development will obviously not be approved by the value-based ethical system of Islam even if it is accompanied by high levels of economic prosperity. In this context, we note that a number of verses of the Qur'an describe the fate of peoples that achieved such material advancement that gained surprise and admiration of observers. However, these accomplishments did not last long and were destroyed because they were based on corrupt beliefs and ethics. The destructive process, once started, accelerated rapidly, according to the narration in the Qur'an, leaving the people in a state of despair and regret. The Qur'an explains:

فَلَمَّا نَسُوا مَا ذُكِّرُوا بِهِ فَتَحْنَا عَلَيْهِمْ أَبْوَابَ كُلِّ شَيْءٍ حَتَّى إِذَا فَرِحُوا بِمَا أُوتُوا أَخَذْنَاهُمْ بَغْتَةً فَإِذَا هُمْ مُبْلِسُونَ * فَقُطِعَ دَابِرُ الْقَوْمِ الَّذِينَ ظَلَمُوا وَالْحَمْدُ لِلَّهِ رَبِّ الْعَالَمِينَ (الانعام: 44 و 45)

> Then, when they forgot that whereof they had been reminded, We opened unto them the gates of all things till, even as they were rejoicing in that which they had been given, We seized them unawares, and lo! They were dumbfounded. So, of the people who did wrong the last remnant was cutoff. Praise be to Allah, Lord of the worlds! (Al-An'am, 6:44–45; see also Chapter 57:20).[8]

3 Divine Ethics as the Foundation of the *Kautheri* Model of Development

The ethical and value principles of *Kautheri* model of development have recognizable distinctions compared to those of *Takathuri* model of development. The ethical criteria governing the economic and other behaviors in Islamic thought originate from the belief and anthropological principles of Islam (like any other school of thought). In Islamic worldview (contrary to the materialist worldview of capitalism), Allah is not only the Creator of all beings, but the supreme Sustainer of the universe, human being as well as other creature. Therefore, Allah has not entrusted the fate of human beings to the traditions and laws of Nature. He has provided them with the gift of intelligence and has appointed prophets equipped with Books and the Scale to teach them the Straight Path as well as the just way of life in order that they find the path to felicity. Therefore, human felicity is in compliance with all the natural and legislative commands prescribed by Allah. This is confirmed by the Qur'an:

يُصْلِحْ لَكُمْ أَعْمَالَكُمْ وَيَغْفِرْ لَكُمْ ذُنُوبَكُمْ وَمَنْ يُطِعِ اللَّهَ وَرَسُولَهُ فَقَدْ فَازَ فَوْزًا عَظِيمًا (الاحزاب: 71)

> He will put your deeds into a right state for you, and forgive you your transgressions; and whoever obeys Allah and His Messenger, he indeed achieves a splendid triumph. (Al-Ahzab,33:71)

According to the vision of Islam, humans are creatures composed of corporeal body and incorporeal spirit, whose existence continues even after death of the body. They are the servants and agents (Khalifah) of Allah on the earth, and the Deen (the Way of life prescribed by Allah) provides the framework for their servitude and agency.

---

8 See also Al-Hadid: 20:
اعْلَمُوا أَنَّمَا الْحَيَاةُ الدُّنْيَا لَعِبٌ وَلَهْوٌ وَزِينَةٌ وَتَفَاخُرٌ بَيْنَكُمْ وَتَكَاثُرٌ فِي الْأَمْوَالِ وَالْأَوْلَادِ كَمَثَلِ غَيْثٍ أَعْجَبَ الْكُفَّارَ نَبَاتُهُ ثُمَّ يَهِيجُ فَتَرَاهُ مُصْفَرًّا ثُمَّ يَكُونُ حُطَامًا وَفِي الْآخِرَةِ عَذَابٌ شَدِيدٌ وَمَغْفِرَةٌ مِنَ اللَّهِ وَرِضْوَانٌ وَمَا الْحَيَاةُ الدُّنْيَا إِلَّا مَتَاعُ الْغُرُورِ (الحديد: 20)
Know that the worldly life is only a game, a temporary attraction, a means of boastfulness and competition among yourselves, as well as rivalry in wealth and children. It is like the rain which produces plants that are attractive to the uncredulous: then it withers away and you see it turning yellow; and soon it will be just bits of straw. In the Hereafter there will be both severe torment and forgiveness as well as approval on part of God. Worldly life means only the enjoyment of illusion.

Within this framework, the meaning of ethicality for a Muslim is organizing life to gain Allah's approval and implore satisfaction by complying with the rules and principle He has prescribed as well as following the tradition of infallible personages [the Messenger (sawa) and his AhlulBayt (as)]. "Justice, freedom and independence, as well as other instances of individual and collective perfections of human beings are limited and defined by the divine law and revelation for which rational as well as traditional narrative reasoning have been provided."[9]

Accordingly, as a guide toward a choice criterion, many Muslim economists do not consider appropriate the principle of "maximization of utility and profit" as a choice criterion for a Muslim since this principle is based on the criterion of desirability or otherwise of an action in terms of natural impulses and base passions.

To clarify economic behavior of a Muslim, Sayyid Kazem Sadr has proposed the principle of ultimate satisfaction, love and affection of Allah as the guiding principle for economic behavior of a Muslim.[10] He explains: "Consumers choose those goods and services that allow them to maximize Allah's satisfaction. This principle, which has been expressed clearly in the Qur'an, constitutes the ultimate goal of righteous servants of the Almighty. Only those who comply with this principle will achieve felicity in this life and in the Hereafter. In explaining the choices of this principle, it must be borne mind that according to Islam, the act of possession of different goods and services has been divided into four categories of *Wajib* (obligatory), *Mustahab* (recommended) *Makruh* (reprehensible) and *Haram* (forbidden). Exercising *Wajib* and *Mustahab* deeds will lead to Allah's satisfaction, while indulging in *Makruh* and *Haram* acts brings about Allah's displeasure and discontent. Naturally, every Muslim aspires to win Allah's satisfaction as well as felicity in the Hereafter based on his belief and understanding. Therefore, he will perform meritorious deeds and abstain from sinful activities."

Siddiqi reiterates:[11] "An individual who acquiesces to Islamic beliefs and goals must refrain from maximizing self-satisfaction and utility. For instance, consuming a *Haram* good or service may create a sense of contentment and utility for a consumer such that he is willing to spend money which has relatively less utility than the Haram good or service. However, a Muslim such satisfaction has no meaning since he knows that such consumption deprives him of the opportunity to achieve Islamic objectives."

Monzer Kahf argues:[12] "The idea of maximization has a serious and important place in Holy Qur'an and *Sunnah* (Tradition). Muslims have been invited to earn Hasanat (as the unit of divine reward) and they try to achieve maximum amount of Hasanat. According to the Qur'an and *Sunnah*, the Scale of Justice will be erected on

9 See Javadi Amoli; 1387 SH.
10 See Seyyed Kazem Sadr; 1387 SH; p. 194.
11 Ansari et al.; 1378 SH; p. 46.
12 Monzer Kahf; 2014; p. 155.

the Judgment Day. The Hasanat gained will be placed in one pan of the Scale and the transgressions committed will be placed in the other. The weightier the Hasanat pan, the better the position of the person in the Hereafter. Throughout their worldly life, Muslims are after acquiring Hasanat which are calculated, recorded and preserved by angels in their book of accounts…" Briefly then, a Muslim is a maximizer of those Hasanat that provide material pleasures (as well as rewards in the Hereafter). In other words, a Muslim is literally a true 'Maximizer.' However, the maximized entity is an Islamic activity and not an economic utility function."

In rejecting utilitarian ethics and introducing an Islamic substitute for it, Askari et al. state:[13]

> There is a stark divide between Islamic and conventional economics as to consumer behavior. Conventional economics makes assumptions in order to model consumer behavior, but it does not develop a model of how consumers actually behave or ought to behave. This is because conventional economics has no room for either realism or value judgments. It simply postulates that the pursuit of one's utility maximization is 'rational' and goes on to explain that, in fact, when each individual seeks to maximize his or her utility, this in turn maximizes the benefits of society as a whole. In contrast, Islamic economics begins with values and goals based on Shari'ah to shape ideal consumer behavior. It still has work to do in the area of formulating postulates that must be adhered to when analyzing behavior of a *rasheed* (mature) Muslim consumer. In essence, in an Islamic system, microeconomics can be modeled by changing human and firm behavior to comply with Islamic principles of justice, sharing, awarding factors of production their just reward, or by imposing a number of constraints to human and firm behavior that reflect Islamic requirements.

Various Qur'anic verses and Riwayaat (narrations) discuss in detail ethical virtues and vices as well as economic ethics that are praiseworthy or blameworthy by Allah. Praiseworthy economic characteristics or behavior include seeking Halal livelihood, independence from reliance on others for one's livelihood, work discipline, Zuhd (asceticism) and Qana'ah (being content), cooperation and coordination with others, Taqwa (piety), reliance on Allah, moderation, focus on the Hereafter, Shukr (gratitude), honesty, truthfulness, fairness, being brotherly, equality, altruism, and amiability. Blameworthy characteristics and behavior include indolence and laziness, beggary, voracity, rapacity, prodigality and profligacy, opulence, engaging in Riba-based transactions, materialism, Bokhl (niggardliness), Kanz (hoarding wealth) Ihtikar (hoarding consumer goods by producers or sellers).[14]

A general view of these ethical concepts reveals clear relationship between some of these praiseworthy or blameworthy characteristics, such as the affirmation of seeking Halal sustenance or rejection of indolence and laziness, on the one hand, and economic advancement, on the other. However, in case of some others, this relationship may not be as clear and may even appear incompatible with economic

13 Askari, Iqbal and Mirakhor; 2015.
14 See Reyshahri and Hosseini; 1386 SH; pp. 373–397 and 453–462.

progress, for example virtuousness of Zuhd (asceticism) and Qana'ah (contentment) and reprehensible characteristics of voracity and rapacity. Two important points must be noted in this regard. First, the correct connotation of such notions must be acknowledged, e.g. true Islamic asceticism does not mean abandoning work and labor. In fact, it requires workinh hard and not getting discouraged when experiencing challenges of life, on the one hand, and becoming boastful when experiencing life's pleasantries. Second, in evaluating compatibility of ethical values with economic values, it is crucial to bear in mind clear differences between the nature of the two models of economic development: Kauthari and Takathuri. *While some of these ethical values may appear as incompatible with Takathuri development, they are not only compatible with the Kauthari model of development but are the only means of achieving Kauthari growth and development.*

Among these values, "hard work" and "Qana'ah" (being content with what one has and being frugal) which hold greater capability in formulation the rule of "diligence in production and Qana'ah (frugal) in consumption" that governs the economic behavior of individual Muslims and plays a crucial role in economic growth. This rule is derived from the Qur'an and narrations from the Infallibles (as) which consider "little (personal) consumption and much assistance (to those in need)" ("قَلِيلَ الْمَئُونَةِ و كَثِيرَ الْمَعُونَةِ") among the characteristics that define a believer.[15] According to this rule, the faithful must work hard and spend as little as needed in order to have residual income in order to help those in need. Therefore, a believer must work hard to generate income not only to meet his own livelihood but also to have income leftover to help the needy such as the poor and the orphans. This rule not only guarantees economic growth but also enhances just distribution of income and wealth. It is clear that utilitarianism will not be the basis of economic activities since it is incompatible with the principle of "low consumption" and Qana'ah. Consequently, based on this rule, spirituality will not be sacrificed to materialism, thus, spiritual motivations will be actualized. According to this rule, economic activities of a believer must have the greatest social benefit. Therefore, he will avoid production of goods and service that lead to extravagance consumption and waste. Under any circumstances (such as natural monopoly or competition), he behaves in a way that satisfies greatest amount of the economic needs of others. For this purpose, he will avoid reducing the level of production or increasing the prices in order to gain more personal profits.

Within the framework of divine ethics, knowledge of economics is also different from secular economics. In the *Kautheri* model, knowledge is a divine gift that is constantly under the enlightened revelatory effusion of religious belief that, combined with human effort, assist individuals to achieve goals that are defined by the Deen (the way of life defined by Islam). In this context, the Qur'an declares:

15 See Al-Majlesi; 1403 LH; p. 310; H. 45; and, *Nahj Al-Balaqa*; Sermon 193.

... يَرْفَعِ اللَّهُ الَّذِينَ آمَنُوا مِنكُمْ وَالَّذِينَ أُوتُوا الْعِلْمَ دَرَجَاتٍ ... (المجادله: 11)

"Allah will raise those of you who believe, in rank, as well as the ones who are given knowledge. (Al-Mojadelah, 58: 11, in part)

Imam Ali (as) stated:[16]

وَ بِالْإِيمَانِ يُعْمَرُ الْعِلْمُ

"Science flourishes in the light of faith."

According to many narration, the pick of scientific flourishing of humanity with be achieved during the "Age of Appearance" [the time at which the twelfth Imam (as) of the progeny of the Messenger (sawa) will appear to all people of world], an Age in which the Oneness and Uniqueness of Allah swt will be manifest, and He and only He will be adored by all humanity".[17] Within this framework, religion-based understanding includes any form of practical knowledge, gained from and compatible with rational and revelatory sources, that provides the means necessary to meet human needs. Therefore, not only there will be no contradiction between science and the Deen (the Way of life prescribed by Islam) but, on the contrary, the two support each other mutually and synergistically to enhance the growth of both.

4 Prospects and Necessity of Kautheri Development in Contemporary Islamic Societies

The modern economic development is a phenomenon which has occurred in recent times especially during the 19th and 20th centuries. It has given rise to accumulation of wealth, rapid expansion of science and technology, and enhancement of welfare standards. The emergence of this phenomenon from the capitalistic systems of the West and its concurrent negative outcomes in the field of spirituality, culture and environment, and others which accompanied it has given rise to the serious question of whether, in general, such phenomenon is desirable. Muslim thinkers and scholars have responded differently to this question. Some of them have chosen the secular path in confrontation with this phenomenon. Some have proposed religious reforms for compatibility with the modern relationships. And still some others have taken refuge in reactionary asceticism.

Through contemplation on the verses of the Qur'an, it can be deduced that while *Takathuri* model of development is undesirable and destructive, from the viewpoint of

16 See Reyshahri; 1416 LH; p. 191; H. 1251.

17 Al-Majlesi; *op cit.*; Vol. 52; p. 336.

the Qur'an, *Kauthari* model is not only desirable but mandatory. According to the following verse of the Qur'an, every Muslim man and woman is mandated to exert their best effort in achieving the development and prosperity of the earth so as to actualize the results expected from *Kautheri* development:

... هُوَ أَنْشَأَكُمْ مِنَ الْأَرْضِ وَاسْتَعْمَرَكُمْ فِيهَا ... (هود: 61)

"He Has brought you forth from the earth and Has ordained that you develop it." (Hud, 11: 61; in part)

The Qur'an considers poverty as the illusory threat of Satan and his deception to drag human beings towards unrighteousness while the promise of Allah includes virtue, mercy and expansion of blessings.

الشَّيْطَانُ يَعِدُكُمُ الْفَقْرَ وَيَأْمُرُكُمْ بِالْفَحْشَاءِ وَاللَّهُ يَعِدُكُمْ مَغْفِرَةً مِنْهُ وَفَضْلًا وَاللَّهُ وَاسِعٌ عَلِيمٌ (البقره: 268)

Satan threatens you with poverty and orders you to abomination, while Allah promises you forgiveness from Himself with bounty. Allah is All-embracing, All-knowing! (Al-Baqara, 2: 268)

Allah's Messenger considered poverty as near to Kufr (unbelief)[18] and therefore, strongly advised the rulers of Islamic society not to do anything that would impoverish the people lest it leads to their loss of faith. He said:

كَادَ اَلْفَقْرُ أَنْ يَكُونَ كُفْراً

"Poverty is near to unbelief."

Moreover, based on the verses of the Qur'an and sacred narrations, property and wealth are considered as sources of strength for the Deen and worldly life of human beings. The Qur'an states:

وَلَا تُؤْتُوا السُّفَهَاءَ أَمْوَالَكُمُ الَّتِي جَعَلَ اللَّهُ لَكُمْ قِيَامًا ... (النساء: 5)

"And do not give the foolish your property which Allah Has granted you for your maintenance." (Al-Nisa', 4: 5; in part)

Imam al-Sadiq (as) referred to this sacred verse and told one of his followers:[19]

اِحْتَفِظْ بِمَالِكَ فَإِنَّهُ قِوَامُ دِينِكَ ثُمَّ قَرَأَ لاٰ تُؤْتُوا اَلسُّفَهٰاءَ أَمْوٰالَكُمُ اَلَّتِي جَعَلَ اَللّٰهُ لَكُمْ قِيٰاماً

"Safeguard your property because it is the support of your Deen" and then recited the Verse 5 of Chapter 4 of the Qur'an (above).

A number of narrations (Riwayaat) mention that the people of the days of the End of Time will consider excessive property and wealth as necessities. In a narration

18 Al-Koleini; 1389 LH; Vol. 2; p. 307; H. 4)
19 Al-Tousi; 1404 LH; p. 679; H. 1444; and, Al-Majlesi; Vol. 103; p. 92; H. 7.

from the Prophet (sawa) he has been quoted as saying: "When the End of Time nears, people have no choice but having dirhams and dinars so as to enable them establish their Dean and their life on earth"[20] and: "For my companions, poverty (voluntary) is a source of happiness, but for the faithful during days of End of Time, prosperity is felicity; (if you experience that time), be among the well-to-do if possible."[21]

In the letter to Muhammad bin Abu Bakr when the latter was appointed as the Governor of Egypt, Imam Ali (as) refers to a pious society as one in which, while enjoying the pleasures of life, including food, clothing, housing, means of communication and other desirable goods and services, the people also achieve the blessings of the world to come which result from living in this world with righteousness and justice."[22] There are many verses of the Qur'an that warn against accumulation of wealth and means of comfort from income gained through violation of rules prescribed by Allah and the dire destructive consequences of such behavior as interest-based transactions, accumulation of idle wealth, hoarding as well as extravagant, wasteful and profligate spending.

5 Ethical Attributes of Production in *Kautheri* Model of Development

Since any progress requires work and effort, the *Takathuri* model of development gives importance to work and production. However, what distinguishes the model of work and production different in the Takathuri framework are the following:

1. Based on its knowledge and ethical foundations, the objective in life is worldly pleasure and comfort. Since work involves causes pain and bother, it has disutility. It is necessary however in order to acquire the means of comfort and pleasure.
2. The fact that the belief in the concept of origin and end (including the concept of accountability humans) is either denied or has no influence in the way life proceeds, adoration of the Creator through work and production has no place in this model.[23]

Consequently, the rule governing the choice of quantity, quality and type of work and the resulting manufactured products would be enduring the least effort and expecting maximum returns in terms of comfort and pleasure. While compliance with this rule combined with greed and impatience may lead to high degree of progress in the

---

20 Al-Tabrani; 1404 LH; Vol. 20; p. 279; H. 660.
21 Al-Deilami Al-Hamedani; 1406 LH; Vol. 3; p. 158; H. 4427.
22 See Nahj Al-Balaqa: Letter 27.
23 See Javadi Amoli; 1389 SH; p. 15.

short run, because in this model there is no system of control and guidance to direct work and production toward objectives such as protecting the interests of the society and the environment, there is no automatic guarantee of the stability of progress and the protection of the society against potential damages of growth of production in this model.[24]

Within the framework of *Kautheri* development, however, in accordance with the ethical principle of "assiduousness in production and contentment in consumption," the production behavior will lead to achieving sustainable economic development. Some of the important indications of such behavior are as follows:

- While Allah has ordained that believers must stop all economic activities in order to participate in every Friday's collective ritual prayers, concurrently, He has ordained that they return to work immediately after the end of the prayers (Verses 9–10, Chapter 62) in order to earn their livelihood. Therefore, Islam considers prayers and work as one religious duty after another. From this Verse and as well as Verse 56: Chapter 51 of the Qur'an,[25] it can be deduced that the objective of the creation of man was not solely to engage in ritual acts such as prayers, fasting, pilgrimage, ... Indeed, the word "adoration" or "worship" of Allah has much broader meaning that includes work and economic production.[26] In this context, various Riwayaat (sacred narrations) proscribe indolence, laziness and idleness, while praising efforts to earn legitimate (Halal) livelihood, considering as equivalent of Jihad.[27]
- There are numerous sacred narrations that forbid selling of income-generating assets such as plantations and agricultural lands, considering as wasting of personal property unless the money earned from the transaction is again invested in a similar or even a more beneficial asset.[28] Moreover, providing capital for agriculture, trade and the like has also been encouraged. Imam al-Sadiq (as) stated that one does not leave anything as inheritance worse than idle cash. When asked what should then be done with that idle money, he replied that it must be invested

---

24 See Al-Baqara: 205

وَإِذَا تَوَلَّى سَعَى فِي الْأَرْضِ لِيُفْسِدَ فِيهَا وَيُهْلِكَ الْحَرْثَ وَالنَّسْلَ وَاللَّهُ لَا يُحِبُّ الْفَسَادَ (البقره: 205)

Whenever he holds the upper hand, he rushes around the earth ruining it. He destroys (people's) crops and breeding stock even though God does not like ruination.

25 See Al-Jum'a: 10

فَإِذَا قُضِيَتِ الصَّلَاةُ فَانْتَشِرُوا فِي الْأَرْضِ وَابْتَغُوا مِنْ فَضْلِ اللَّهِ وَاذْكُرُوا اللَّهَ كَثِيرًا لَعَلَّكُمْ تُفْلِحُونَ (الجمعه: 10)

Once prayer has been performed, then disperse throughout the land and seek God's bounty. Remember God frequently so that you may prosper.

26 See Al-Zariyat: 56

وَمَا خَلَقْتُ الْجِنَّ وَالْإِنْسَ إِلَّا لِيَعْبُدُونِ (الذاريات: 56)

And I have only created sprites (jinn) and men so they may worship Me.

27 See Hosseini and Reyshahri; 1386; pp. 131–136.

28 *ibid.* p. 367.

in orchards or real state. The Imam (as) himself invested in trade activities and directed his agent to reinvest the earned profits as capital.[29]

- While Islam emphasizes working to earn a decent livelihood for oneself and family, gaining economic ability to manage personal life and assisting others, it considers laboring and producing with such motives as examples of "Hasanaat" (acts of beneficence performed with the intention of pleasing Allah) deserving of divine rewards. In consequence, rather than maximizing their profits, the believers tend to increase their beneficial deeds and their Hasanaat in order to gain maximum level of satisfaction of Allah and His rewards. When work and production are accomplished on the basis of this principle, they will have a divine orientation. This means, first, that there will be a balance in allocation of time to work, rest and spiritual affairs. There will be compliance with the rules of Shari'ah in economic work (e.g. avoiding Haram revenues or unethical deeds), therefore, a healthy concern for social interests ensue. Second, work not only has no disutility but, in and of itself, has utility as ritual prayers or any other special act of adoration and worship of Allah (swt). Any work that is undertaken with the intention of achieving the approval and satisfaction of Allah, is an act of worship even if it has less reward and more bother for the doer than other work. Such work will also secure the doer's interests as well. conceived undesirable, but in the same way as prayers and other worships for the Almighty, they will be estimable *per se*. What turns work and production into a type of worship is their execution just for the sake of God's satisfaction, even if they have lower return and greater inconvenience for the individual. Nonetheless, the work which is aimed at satisfaction of the Almighty will definitely serve the individual's interests as well. The working hours, type of the labor, quality and quantity of products in *Kautheri* model are determined based this principle. A clear example of economic behavior that removes any doubt about the success of the Kauthari model of development is that of Imam Ali (as). The Imam (as) was one of the richest people of Medinah at the time and had gained his wealth through his own efforts and hard work. Emulation of such behavioral role model within the Islamic society will lead to its economic development and prosperity.[30]
- Based on Islamic values, employment and business are among the material agents of production and any achievement depends on human endeavors, as the Qur'an states:

وَأَنْ لَيْسَ لِلْإِنْسَانِ إِلَّا مَا سَعَى (النجم: 39)

"And that every human shall receive only that for which he makes an effort." (Al-Najm, 53: 39)

29 *Op. cit.*
30 See Hoseini; 1387 SH; pp. 20–65.

Along with work, there a number of spiritually productive agents such as Sadaqah, trustworthiness, marriage, good words, cleanliness and others which greatly enhance production efficiency.

6 Ethical Attributes of Income and Wealth Distribution in *Kauthari* Model of Development

Fair distribution of income and wealth is one of the most important economic issues and one of the most serious challenges of the contemporary capitalist model of development. As the name implies, the principle governing the capitalist system is protection of the concentration and accumulation of capital, defined. In contemporary capitalist economies, nearly all the wealth is concentrated in the hands of few capitalists. In socialist systems, all the wealth is in the hands of the government. Both systems are Takathuri, therefore, rejected by the Qur'an and Hadeeth (narrations from the sacred sources). A behavior which has been criticized strongly and it adverse consequences have been enumerated in the Qur'an and narrations from the Infallibles (as) is that of accumulation of and refusal to distribute wealth. The Qur'an promises severe chastisement to those who accumulate wealth and refuse to spend it in the Way of Allah:

... وَالَّذِينَ يَكْنِزُونَ الذَّهَبَ وَالْفِضَّةَ وَلَا يُنْفِقُونَهَا فِي سَبِيلِ اللَّهِ فَبَشِّرْهُمْ بِعَذَابٍ أَلِيمٍ (التوبه: 34)

> "Announce painful torment to those who hoard gold and silver and do not spend them in the Way of Allah." (Al-Tobah, 9: 34; in part)

A number of the verse of the Qur'an define the roots of such behavior as substitution of property and wealth for Allah under the illusory belief that wealth can be one's savior:

وَيْلٌ لِكُلِّ هُمَزَةٍ لُمَزَةٍ * الَّذِي جَمَعَ مَالًا وَعَدَّدَهُ * يَحْسَبُ أَنَّ مَالَهُ أَخْلَدَهُ (الهُمَزَة: 1-3)

> Woe unto every slanderer, defamer Who amasses wealth and arranged it (as precaution) thinking that his wealth will make him immortal" (Al-Homazah, 104: 1–3; see also, Verse 24: Chapter 18; and 9: 63)[31]

31 See also:
Al-Toba': 24
قُلْ إِنْ كَانَ آبَاؤُكُمْ وَأَبْنَاؤُكُمْ وَإِخْوَانُكُمْ وَأَزْوَاجُكُمْ وَعَشِيرَتُكُمْ وَأَمْوَالٌ اقْتَرَفْتُمُوهَا وَتِجَارَةٌ تَخْشَوْنَ كَسَادَهَا وَمَسَاكِنُ تَرْضَوْنَهَا أَحَبَّ إِلَيْكُمْ مِنَ اللَّهِ وَرَسُولِهِ وَجِهَادٍ فِي سَبِيلِهِ فَتَرَبَّصُوا حَتَّى يَأْتِيَ اللَّهُ بِأَمْرِهِ وَاللَّهُ لَا يَهْدِي الْقَوْمَ الْفَاسِقِينَ (التوبه: 24)
Say: If your fathers, your sons, your brethren, your spouses and your family ties, as well as the wealth you have acquired and the business you dread will fall off, plus the dwellings you are so fond of, are all dearer to you than God and His Messenger, or striving for His sake, then wait till God brings about His command to pass. God does not guide such transgressing people!

Humans engage in this kind of behavior even though the Qur'an states emphatically that what humans have is ultimately perishable while what is with Allah is permanent and undying:[32]

وَلَا تَشْتَرُوا بِعَهْدِ اللَّهِ ثَمَنًا قَلِيلًا إِنَّمَا عِنْدَ اللَّهِ هُوَ خَيْرٌ لَكُمْ إِنْ كُنْتُمْ تَعْلَمُونَ * مَا عِنْدَكُمْ يَنْفَدُ وَمَا عِنْدَ اللَّهِ بَاقٍ وَلَنَجْزِيَنَّ الَّذِينَ صَبَرُوا أَجْرَهُمْ بِأَحْسَنِ مَا كَانُوا يَعْمَلُونَ (النحل: 95 و 96)

> And purchase not a small gain at the price of Allah's covenant. Lo! that which Allah has is better for you, if you only knew. That which you have wastes away and that which is with Allah is everlasting. And verily, We Shall reward those who are steadfast a recompense in proportion to the best of what they used to do. (Al-Nahl, 16: 95 and 96; in parts)

One of the major causes of the emergence of lack of balance in the distribution of inequalities in the distribution of wealth and income is the disregard of just distribution of initial resource endowments and opportunities which belongs to the society as a whole. In the Takathuri model – which existed during the Age of Ignorance (before Islam) and, unfortunately, also during parts of Muslim history [from the time after the passing of the Messenger (sawa) to the present] – wealth circulates among the rich only. It is for this reason that such behavior is condemned by the Qur'an and commanded that wealth be spent in the Way of Allah so that it will not circulate among the wealthy:

... كَيْ لَا يَكُونَ دُولَةً بَيْنَ الْأَغْنِيَاءِ مِنْكُمْ ... (الحشر: 7)

> *"... so that it may not circulate merely between the rich among you ..." (Al-Hashr, 59: 7; in part)*

Within the framework of *Takathuri* model, distribution of the proceed from the sale of products among the agents of production, especially the wages of laborers, as well as distribution of the profit between the parties in exchange depends squarely on superior bargaining power among the participants in a transaction; the party with larger wealth has superior bargaining power thus take larger portion of the gains. This leads to imbalances in distribution of income and wealth. To stop this undesirable behavior was an important missions of the great messengers recounted in Chapter 11 of the Qur'an where Prophet Hud (as) tells his people:

Al-Kahf: 46
الْمَالُ وَالْبَنُونَ زِينَةُ الْحَيَاةِ الدُّنْيَا وَالْبَاقِيَاتُ الصَّالِحَاتُ خَيْرٌ عِنْدَ رَبِّكَ ثَوَابًا وَخَيْرٌ أَمَلًا (الكهف: 46)
Wealth and children are an attraction during worldly life. Yet honorable deeds that last forever are better as a recompense from your Lord and ever better to hope for.
Al-Monafequn: 9
يَا أَيُّهَا الَّذِينَ آمَنُوا لَا تُلْهِكُمْ أَمْوَالُكُمْ وَلَا أَوْلَادُكُمْ عَنْ ذِكْرِ اللَّهِ وَمَنْ يَفْعَلْ ذَلِكَ فَأُولَئِكَ هُمُ الْخَاسِرُونَ (المنافقون: 9)
O you who believe! Let neither your wealth nor your children distract you from the remembrance of God. Those who do so will be the losers.

32 See Javadi Amoli; 1389 SH.

وَيَا قَوْمِ أَوْفُوا الْمِكْيَالَ وَالْمِيزَانَ بِالْقِسْطِ وَلَا تَبْخَسُوا النَّاسَ أَشْيَاءَهُمْ وَلَا تَعْثَوْا فِي الْأَرْضِ مُفْسِدِينَ * بَقِيَّتُ اللَّهِ خَيْرٌ لَكُمْ إِنْ كُنْتُمْ مُؤْمِنِينَ ... (هود: 85 و 86)

And, O my people! Give full measure and full weight with with fairness, and do not undervalue the products of others. And do not do evil in the earth, causing corruption. That which Allah has left (for you) is better for you if you are believers. And I am not a keeper over you. (Hud, 11: 85 and 86; in part).

In its early days, the capitalistic development model did not believe in addressing the needs of the destitute by taxing the rich within the framework of redistribution of wealth and income. But when the increase in class inequality and the widening economic gap began to shake the foundations of capitalism, the programs to support vulnerable populations were put on the agenda.[33]

The *Kautheri* model of development places the fair distribution of income and wealth as well as establishment of various aspects of social justice at the top of its social objectives. The aim is to prevent accumulation of wealth and its wasteful consumption and to allow all to enjoy divine endowments and blessings and to provide the ground for their growth and excellence. Within the framework of this model, distributive justice is not only a social objective, but constitutes the most important ways and means of achieving these objectives. Income distribution within *Kautheri* model of development is based firmly on the foundations of law, ethics, and faith. The most important means of establishing balanced distribution of income is a system of rights composed of three categories:

- General rights of individuals. All members of the society have the right of equal access to the means, resources and wealth created for all. Based on the Principle of Permissibility[34] (*Ibaha*), every member of the society has the right to access these resources to (in combination with their own labor and effort) increase the society's prosperity and development.
- Rights based on individual work and effort. Individuals acquire full right of ownership of what results from expending their labor and efforts. Those who work harder and invest greater time and effort in production receive a greater share from the added value of the product. The following two verse of the Qur'an, in combination, relate to this category of rights:

... وَلَا تَبْخَسُوا النَّاسَ أَشْيَاءَهُمْ (الاعراف: 85)

"... do not undervalue things that belong to people..." (Al-A'raf, 7 : 85; in part) and:

وَأَنْ لَيْسَ لِلْإِنسَانِ إِلَّا مَا سَعَى (النجم: 39)

"And that every man shall receive only what he makes an effort for." (Al-Najm, 53: 39)

33 See Namazi; 1389 SH; pp. 115–125.

34 It refers to the principle and rule that it is permissible to enter into any and all transactions and contracts, provided there has been no express and unequivocal rule prohibiting it and declaring them illicit/illegal (*Haram*).

- Rights arising from needs. As mentioned earlier, Allah (swt) has created all resources on earth for the benefit of all humans and has allowed all human beings to combine their labor with these resources to produce goods and services through which they earn their own livelihood and add value to the society. At times however individuals are unable to exercise this right due to physical, mental, old age, and other disabilities that do not permit these individuals to access their share of these resources. Inability to exercise this right however does not negate this right, it remains intact and must be remitted by those who use these resources. Islam, therefore, has mandated a share for these individuals in the wealth of the rich as evidenced by the following Verse:

  وَفِي أَمْوَالِهِمْ حَقٌّ لِلسَّائِلِ وَالْمَحْرُومِ (الذَّارِيَات: 19)

  "In their (that is the rich) wealth there is a right for the destitute and the deprived" (Al-Zariyat, 51: 19).

  Imam al-Sadiq (as) stressed that Allah has mandated a right sufficient for the livelihood of the deprived in the wealth of the rich. Implementation of these rights will lead to just distribution of wealth and the achievement of the objectives of Islamic economics. Redeeming these three rights will prevent inordinate accumulation of wealth as has occurred in contemporary capitalist societies. While it is possible that there will be some differentiated inequality even after implementation of these rights, insistence on correct circulation of capital and wealth will prevent emergence of such inequalities.[35] Such policies not only assure that just distribution of income and wealth in the society but also growth and development of the economy.[36]

The most important attribute of regulating income and wealth distribution within the framework of *Kautheri* development seems to be the existence of people-oriented solutions provided by Islam such as Infaq (spending in the Way of Allah) charities, Sadaqah (expenditure specifically intended for the destitute and the deprived), alms (*Sadaqh'*), *Waqf* (endowments), and Nadhr (pledge). In capitalist societies much of such expenditures intended to help the poor are incentivized by government policies or are supported directly from the government budget that create a welfare state. However, at times, both sources of helping the poor become subject to instability caused by economic crises that threaten private contributions to poverty alleviation as well the financial stability of the welfare state.[37] In the earliest days of Islam, social mutual insurance, intense feelings of brotherhood and the spirit of self-sacrifice for

35 Mohammad Hassan Al-Horr Al-Ameli; *Vasayel Al-Shia*; Qum; A'l Al-Bayt (PBUT) L-Eh'ya Al-Torath; Vol. 9; pp. 45–52.

36 See Javadi Amoli; 1389; pp. 618–625.

37 Bonoli et al.; 2000; p. 243.

the interests of others created a miraculous growth and prosperity in the society. Throughout the history of Muslim civilization, much of investment needed for social capital, such as schools, hospitals, and other public goods and services were financed from the proceedings from private endowments. Even today, there is a strong source of belief-based and benevolence-based motivations among Muslims which, if properly mobilized, can lead to emergence of a successful model of development with justice.

7 Ethical Attributes of Consumption in *Kauthari* Model of Development

One of the basic differences between the *Kauthari* and *Takathuri* models of development is the consumption behavior. The consumption model in the *Takathuri* model, as was the case in its work and production model, is oriented toward profligate and demonstrative (or conspicuous) consumption. Based on the underlying conceptions and ethics of this model, consumption and its pleasures determine social identities of individuals and ultimate goal of human behavior. Therefore, incomes in their totality must be used to spend for immediate gratification of desires. Even the motivation to save is justified by future consumption. Behaviors that have been chastised in the Qur'an and in sacred narrations, such as Israf (profligacy), Tabdheer (squandering), Itraf (opulence), are manifest attributes of this model of Takathuri consumption. In some verses of the Qur'an and narrations, this type of consumption behavior has been prohibited and in others their harmful effects are enumerated.[38]

Another attribute of consumption within the framework of *Takathuri* model of development, which has its roots in the principle of "maximized utility and maximized benefit or revenue," is the extensive advertisement of consumer goods to promote increase in the consumption level of the audience. Any means that achieves this end is justified no matter how unethical--such as stimulating the most basic of animal instincts in humans as well as degradation highly valued feminine personality to the level of being an instrument of advertisement of corporate products--are among the essential requisite instruments of this model. The important point to bear in mind in this regard is that despite the possibility of limitless consumption for all the inhabitants of the society in the *Takathuri* model, the benefits from stimulation of consumer tastes are predominantly for the rich. This is because through profligate and opulent consumption the rich are able to demonstrate their social status to others, on the one hand, and, on the other, the manufacturing firms are mostly owned by the rich who benefit from increased consumption of other as their profits and incomes increase.

38 Reyshahri and Hosseini; pp. 235–245.

This is why Thorstein Veblen considers conspicuous consumption as a collective game with net losses where the losers are the majority of the members of the society.[39]

The values and ethics governing the consumption behavior within the framework of *Kauthari* model lead to moderation in consumption which, while satisfying rational needs of the individual's life, will focus deeply on the satisfaction of the spiritual needs of individuals as well the interests of the society. The most important ethical principle of consumption in this model of development are as follows:

- In religious texts, the subject of consumption as well as its dos and don'ts are discussed under the more comprehensive theme of *Infaq*.[40] For instance, Holy Qur'an states:

  وَالَّذِينَ إِذَا أَنْفَقُوا لَمْ يُسْرِفُوا وَلَمْ يَقْتُرُوا وَكَانَ بَيْنَ ذَٰلِكَ قَوَامًا (الفرقان: 67)

  "And they who when they spend, are neither extravagant nor parsimonious, and hold a just (balance) between those (extremes)." (Al-Forqan, 25: 67)

  Genrally, Infaq is understood to mean spending wealth and income which, in addition to shared social expenditure, includes consumption expenditure and investment. Therefore, rules governing Infaq covers consumption behavior as well. Philosophy of inclusion of consumption under the general Infaq is that wealth is a gift of Allah which is placed in the hands of humanity in trust and, therefore, must be spend within the framework prescribed by Allah (swt). On this basis, allocation of income to expenditures, in addition to personal consumption and saving, includes costs of social participation as well. If expenditures on any of the three categories were in accordance with moderation, and Shari'ah principles and criteria, they would have divine character and would be counted as expenditure in the Way of Allah.[41] The priority of expenditures is mentioned in the Hadith of the Messenger (sawa):[42]

  إِذَا كَانَ أَحَدُكُمْ فَقِيرًا فَلْيَبْدَأْ بِنَفْسِهِ فَإِنْ كَانَ فِيهَا فَضْلٌ فَعَلَى عِيَالِهِ فَإِنْ كَانَ فِيهَا فَضْلٌ فَعَلَى قَرَابَتِهِ أو عَلى ذِى رحِمِه فَان كانَ فضلاً فَهاهُنا و هاهُنا

  If anyone of you is poor, he must initially spend whatever he has on himself. If there is a residual, then spend it on his family. If there is (still) a residual spend it on the members of his extended family. Any remaining residual can be spend here and there (where need exists)

- Although most individuals may believe that increased consumption brings about greater welfare for human beings, such notions are against the teachings of

39 https://en.wikiquote.org/wiki/The_Theory_of_the_Leisure_Class

40 Infaq literally means spending and expenditure. It connotes spending to seek God's pleasure, whether to discharge a liability or voluntarily, on the poor, needy or to meet social needs. Infaq also covers one's expenditure to meet one's own personal needs and those of the family.

41 Hosseini2; 1388; p. 136.

42 Al-Nesa'ei; 1407 LH; Vol. 7; p. 304.

Islam. The Messenger of Allah (sawa) declared: "A smaller and sufficient amount is better than larger amount that would lead to human unawareness and heedlessness.[43] Real welfare and comfort of human beings do not lie in wasteful consumption, but in not having to rely on or become dependent on others for one's livelihood. If one is able to liberate oneself from the attachments of this world, one can live more comfortably rather than excessive spending in the desire to have all that one needs and wants.[44]

- Martyr Sayyid Mohammad Baqir al-Sadr argued that one of the foundation pillars of social justice in Islam is social balance, i.e. balanced distribution of means of consumption among the general public. In order to achieve this objective, Islam prohibits Israf (profligacy) and Itraf (opulence) of the rich, on the hand, and increases consumption of the lower classes through its mandate on Zakat and all forms of Sadaqaat, on the other.[45]
- In brief, the affirmative principle governing consumption of *Kauthari* model of development include: desirability of sufficient levels of consumption; comprehensive consideration of present and future needs of oneself and others; prudence in planning; balance in in income and expenditure, setting priorities in spending; balance and moderation; being satisfied with sufficient level of livelihood of ; ("النَّظَرُ إِلَى الأدنى مَعيشَةً"), "look at those who have lowest level of livelihood); low personal spending and providing as much as possible to help others, that is "modest consumption and ample benevolence", ("قَلِيلَ الْمَئُونَةِ و كَثِيرَ الْمَعُونَةِ") choosing high quality goods; Qana'ah (contentment) and Zuhd (asceticism); and, having a presentable appearance, as well as fulfilling financial obligations. The negative principles governing consumption include prohibition of profligacy, waste, squandering, opulence and demonstrative (conspicuous) consumption, niggardliness, consumption of prohibited goods and services, and rejection of imitating the consumption behavior of the unbelievers.[46]

Here, a question may arise that since the purpose of production is to provide means for consumption, would not restricting consumption constrain production and lead thereby to reduction of employment and income and ultimately to economic recession? Moreover, if consumption is to be limited to moderate levels, then why must we try to produce as much as possible? In other words, the question suggests that reducing consumption to moderate levels (Qana'ah) implies, first, that it is inconsistent with the command that maximum effort must be expended to produce and, second, command to Qana'ah (moderation in consumption) creates a binding constraint on

---

43 Reyshahri and Hosseini; op. cit.; p. 606.
44 Javadi Amoli; op. cit.; p. 635.
45 Al-Sadr; 1417 LH; p. 673.
46 Hosseini2; 1388 SH; pp. 19–22.

consumption which is essential in increasing production thus constraining economic development.

In responding to this question, we argue that this question, in the first place, arises from misunderstanding the rule of content of the principle of "maximum effort in production and Qana'ah in consumption" and, second, from confusion between micro- and macroeconomics. To clarify, it should be noted that the rule "Qana'ah (contentment) in consumption" applies to economic behaviors at the level of individuals, i.e. microeconomics. This rule, in combination with that of "maximum effort in production," means that individuals do their best to produce and earn maximum income possible which is neither to be hoarded nor spent irresponsibly on profligate consumption. On the contrary, all of the income is to be used carefully to provide one's own moderate living expenses, in the first place, with the residual spent on the costs of social participation and invested in providing meeting the future needs as well as in strengthening the economy. Therefore, the intention of the rule is not meant to withdraw from consumption the proceeds from production to create the paradox of increasing production in face of reduction in (personal)consumption. Consumption, in the context of the rule, means expenditure on personal needs, social consumption, and consumption on future provisions and the strengthening of the economy (through investment and capital formation). Looking at consumption in this broad sense makes it clear that the rule (of maximum effort at production and moderation in consumption) will not lead to slowdown in the economy but, on the contrary, it leads to its expansion. This is because capital formation, as is demonstrated in many economies, plays the most important role in economic development as is demonstrated in many economies. Moreover, sustainable development depends crucially on social justice. Actualization of both objectives of stable and sustainable development concurrent with social justice is only possible through adoption of the model discussed here.

To explain differently, contrary to the *Takathuri* model of development – which sees growth of overall consumption in the society as resulting from the opulent consumption of the rich and motivated by advertising aimed at creating external stimulation of base instincts – in the *Kauthari* model, overall consumption in the society is balanced, growing with a view toward increasing the level of consumption of the lower classes. Therefore, the cultural and promotional policies relating to consumer behavior must emphasize such values as contentment in consumption, keeping in view the conditions of those who have less resources than oneself, spending of surplus to help those in need and avoiding prodigality, opulence and conspicuous consumption. Additionally, care must be taken to prevent Takathuri advertising methods as they contradict the values of the *Kauthari* model. Finally, it must be noted that implementation of such behavioral model within the framework of natural ethics which considers human motivation a result of basic animal instinct is not possible. Most certainly in such a framework, Qana'ah (moderation in consumption and avoiding profligacy, opulence and wasteful expenditure) will mean reduction in production and recession. In the divine ethical framework, however, there is no alternative to the Kauthari model.

8 Summary and Conclusion

The purpose of this paper was to provide answers to the question: Given the characteristics and the requirements of the current model of economic development, is it a desirable model from the point of view of Islam? If so, is it compatible with the ethics and values advocated by Islam? The answer to this question was obtained by investigating related documentation in the Qur'an, Hadith, and the writings of scholars which can now be summarized as follows:

1. There are two different models of economic development: The *Takathuri* model, which is rejected and the *Kauthari* model which is approved and desirable from the Islamic point of view. Each of the models possesses its own ethical and legal attributes. The *Kauthari* model of development is not only approved, but, based on the fundamental teachings of Islam, individuals singly and collectively are mandated to implement it. the individuals and Islamic society are obligated to undertake its cause.
2. *Takathuri* model is based on the doctrine of natural ethics and the belief that basic animal instincts govern and motivate human behavior which results in the rule of "maximizing profit in production and utility in consumption." The *Kauthari* model, on the other hand, is derived from divine ethics and values which govern human behavior and are discovered through the process of contemplation on the sacred narration and rational intellection and reasoning. The result is the emergence of the behavioral rule: "Maximum effort in production and moderation in consumption."
3. The most important features of *Kautheri* production are:
   a. Reprehensibility of consumption of the capital base, the need to preserve it to be employed in productive activities, and meeting the need for current expenditures from income accrued to capital's productivity and not from the capital itself;
   b. Obligation of human beings towards development and prosperity of the land;
   c. Consideration of labor and effort as acts of adoration and worship;
   d. Reprehensibility of voluntary unemployment, laziness, indolence, hiring out oneself;
   e. Focus on the spiritual factors that enhance productivity and efficiency of work and labor;
   f. Lastly, the objective of Islam in work and production is not accumulation of wealth, but creating opportunity for utilizing gifts and endowments of Allah (swt) in developing one's excellence of character, helping those in need, placing resources and wealth on their rightfully productive path of utilization intended for them by their Creator.
4. The most important attributes of income and wealth distribution within the framework of the *Kauthari* model of development are:
   a. Rejection of circulation of wealth within a small group of the rich and necessity of comprehensive development in order to guarantee its sustainability for the present and successive generations;

   b. Respecting the rights of all members of the society to share equally, based on the principle of "Ibahah" (permissibility), the opportunity to access to public resources and endowments, and designing policies that ensure such equal access;
   c. Respecting the rights that derive from work and effort by ensuring that each participant in the process of production receive returns commensurate with the value their participation has added to production; Observin; and,
   d. Respecting the rights that are derived from the needs of individuals (i.e. the needs of those who, for reasons of mental, physical or other limitations are unable to participate in the process of production such as those who are mentally or physically impaired, the elderly, the orphans and the sick, or those, who, despite their best efforts, are unable to earn the true value of their work and labor).
5. The most important attributes of consumption behavior in the *Kauthari* model of development are:
   a. Desirability of proper utilization of resources and endowments gifted to humans by Allah (swt) as He has prescribed toward developing humans' excellence of character;
   b. Demonstrating gratitude to the Creator for all of His gifts and blessings;
   c. Rejection of the idea that one's identity id determined by one's consumption and possessions of things of this world. This means believing that one's real wellbeing and comfort do not lie in wasteful consumption, but in becoming needless and independent of reliance on others for one's livelihood and in reducing one's attachments to the things of this world;
   d. Condemnation of competition with others in conspicuous consumption;
   e. Emphasizing the necessity of balanced distribution of consumption opportunities among various social groups;
   f. Belief that resources and wealth are placed in the possession of humans as trust by their Creator and, hence, complying with His rules that are to govern consumption behavior including prohibition of tightfistedness or prodigality in consumption, and commitment to moderate living standards.

Finally, in the course of the discussion, most important characteristics of the Takathuri model of development was presented in order to differentiate this model and the *Kauthari* model. And, where necessary, we addressed issues relating to the compatibility of divine ethics and economic development.

References

Holy Qur'an; *translated by* T.B. Irving (Al-Haj Ta'lim Ali); Suhrawardi Research and Publication Center, Tehran-Iran; 2003.

Ansari, Mohammad Jafar; Dirbaz, Asgar; Karami, Mohammad Hossein; and Mohammad, Mehdi; *An Introduction to Foundations of Microeconomics: The Islamic Perspective*; First Ed.; Howza and University Research Institute; 1378 SH.

Askari, Hossein; Iqbal, Zamir; and Mirakhor, Abbas; *Introduction to Islamic Economics: Theory and Application*; John Wiley & Sons, Singapore; 2015.

Barbour, Ian Graeme; *Religion and Science*; First Ed.; translated by Baha'oddin Khoramshahi (1382 SH); University Publication Center; 1997.

Bonoli, Giuliano; George, Vic; and Taylor-Gooby, Peter; *European Welfare Futures: Towards a Theory of Retrenchment*; First Ed.; translated by Hormoz Homayoonpour (1380 SH); Tehran; Social Welfare Institute; 2000.

Dadgar, Yadollah; *History of Economic Thought*; Mofid University; First Ed; 1383 SH.

Derakhshan, Masoud; *Crisis Hits the Foundations of Capitalist System*; Vista.ir; 1390 SH; Downloaded on September 5, 2012.

Dugger, William M.; and Peach, James T.; *Economic Abundance: An Introduction*; First Ed.; translated by Seyyed Mohammad Reza Hosseini and Hanzaleh Soleimani (1392 SH); Islamic Parliament Research Center; 2009.

Fitzpatrick, Tony; *Welfare Theory: An Introduction (What is the Social Policy?)*; translated by Hormoz Homayoonpour; (1381 SH); Tehran; Social Welfare Institute; 2001.

Gide, Charles; and Rist, Charles; *A History of Economic Doctrines from the Time of Physiocrats to the Present Day*; translated by; Karim Sanjabi; Third Ed.; 1915.

Hosseini, Seyyed Reza; *Economic Behavior of Imam Ali (PBUH)*; Tehran, Kanoon Andishe Javan; Fifth Ed.; 1387 SH.

Javadi Amoli, Abdollah; *Message to "Akhalqona Bain Al-Nazariya' va Al-Soluk, Asbab va Moa'lejat; Congress in Bahrain*; Dated October 4, 2008; 1387 SH.

Javadi Amoli, Abdollah; *Archetypal Development*; Hamshahri Magazine; Sp. Vol. on Islamic-Iranian Development Model; 1389 SH.

Javadi Amoli, Abdollah; *Mafatih Al-Hayat*; Qum; Asra' Publication Center; First Edition; 1391 SH.

Jones, William Thomas; *Masters of Political Thought; Vol. 2 Machiavelli to Bentham*; translated by Ali Ramin (No Date); 1967.

Kahf, Monzer; *Theories And Institutions*; Published by Monzer Kahf FE; 2014.

Koleini, Abu Jafar Mohammad Bin Al-Yaqub; *Al-Kafi*; *edited/corrected by* Ali Akbar Al-Qaffari; 8 Vols.; Dar Al-Kitab Islamiye; Tehran; 1362 SH.

Majlesi, Mohammad Baqer; *Behar Al-Anwar*; 110 Vol. Tehran; Al-Maktabat Al-Islamiya; 1375 SH.

Mirakhor, Abbas; and Askari, Hossein; *Islam and the Path to Human and Economic Development*; Palgrave Macmillan; 2010.

Namazi, Hossein; *Economic Systems*; New Edition; Tehran, Inteshar Joint Stock Co.; First Ed.; 1389 SH.

Razi, Al-Sharif Abu Al-Hassan Mohammad; *Nahj Al-Balaqa*; translated by Seyyed Jafar Shahidi; Islamic Evolution Teaching Publications; Tehran; 1374 SH.

Reyshahri, Mohammad; *Mizan Al-Hekmat*; Qum, Dar Al-Hadith; Second Ed.; 1416 LH.

Reyshahri, Mohammad; and, Hosseini, Seyyed Reza; *Al-Tanmiya' Al-Eqtesadiya fi Al-Kitab va Al-Sonna'*; Qum, Dar Al-Hadith; Third Ed.; 1386 SH.

Sadr, Al-Seyyed Mohammad Baqer; *Eqtesadona*; First Edition; Maktab Al-E'lam Al-Islami; 1417 LH.

Sadr, Seyyed Kazem; *Economy of Early Islamic Era*; Shahid Beheshti University; Second Ed.; 1387 SH.

Seyyed Hossein Nasr

Chapter 8: The Environmental Crisis in the Islamic World – Pertinence of the Teachings of Traditional Islam

"All things hymn His (God's) praise" (The Quran)

1 Background

The environmental crisis is now fully upon us and no one with an open eye and mind could deny it seriously. From global warming and the greenhouse effect to the loss of species and the pollution of land, air and sea there are evident signs for everyone to see the problem. Yet, many neglect the roots of this crisis because if they were to accept the real causes, then it would mean that they would have to change their worldview and manner of living. That is why most people seek technological solutions drawn from modern technology itself and the view of the relation between man and nature upon which it is based, factors that are themselves the causes of the crisis in the first place. Moreover, this crisis is now global. The pollution of the waters of the Atlantic near big ports in America affects the fish in the waters of Iceland and the cutting down of the trees of the Amazon Basin affects the quality of air in Africa.

The environmental crisis did not, however, begin globally but locally in the West during the Industrial Revolution in such places as the Ruhr Valley in Germany, the middle part of England and Lowell, Massachusetts. Some have tried to draw a continuous line of cause and effect between goats eating the lower branches of trees in Syria two thousand years ago and the pollution of the Thames River in the 19th century. This view is, however, false. With the Industrial Revolution a major quantum jump took place in the negative impact of man's activities upon the natural environment. A traditional Afghan or Indian village was and to some extent still is in harmony with its natural surroundings and could continue its life in this manner for as far as one can project into the future, but the same cannot be said of a modern city such as New York, Cairo or Seoul. It is also essential to remember that the environmental crisis began locally and then became global when non-Western countries, which were dominated by the industrialized West economically, politically and/or militarily, sought to regain their independence and also to take advantage of the economic benefits of modernism by adopting Western norms and practices, especially Western technology.

As one would expect, awareness of the environmental crisis also began in the West. When I gave the Rockefeller Series Lectures in 1966 at the University of Chicago,

https://doi.org/10.1515/9783110593419-008

entitled "The Encounter of Man and Nature," which predicted what was then called the ecological crisis, at first the published form of my lectures met with great opposition especially by Christian theologians in Britain who, like many other Christian thinkers of the day, took pride that it was in the Christian West that modern science and technology had been born. They saw that fact as a proof of the superiority of Christianity over other religions, but soon the situation changed. It also needs to be added that most propagators of the environmental movement at that time did not think and act within the Christian tradition and would not consider themselves Christian thinkers. And yet, concern of Western Christian thinkers with the environmental crisis has grown from strength to strength since the 1980's.

One of the most important figures in the history of the rise of interest in the crisis was a Canadian political and intellectual leader named Maurice Strong. He had read my *Encounter of Man and Nature* (that was reprinted later as *Man and Nature*)[1] and arranged to see me. In 1971 he and a few of his collaborators organized the first Earth Day in Stockholm and he invited me personally to give a keynote address there. Delegations were invited from all over the world. The two major Communist countries, the Soviet Union and China, did not even accept that they had such problems and claimed that the crisis was the result of capitalism, but nevertheless they sent observers. My own country Iran sent a very large delegation chosen and led by the brother of the Shah, Prince Abdol-Reza, but I was not a member of the Iranian delegation and not bound by political directives of the Iranian government and so could speak without any political constraints. During my lecture I refuted the view that the environmental crisis was the problem of only capitalistic countries and said facetiously that there was no river that was "more Communist" than the Volga River that flows for a thousand kilometers in Russia before joining the Caspian Sea. Yet, it was so polluted that many fish like the sturgeon were spawned in the Volga Basin, but as soon as they grew in size swam south to the Iranian part of the Caspian Sea that was less polluted. That comment angered the Soviet delegates and many of them stood up in protest and walked out. The truth of the matter was revealed to the world after the fall of the Soviet Union.

Meanwhile, delegations from Islamic countries put all the blame and responsibility for the environmental crisis on the West and spoke as if Muslims themselves had no responsibility in this matter. Alas, since then the environmental crisis in the Islamic world has gone from bad to worse. When I first visited Lahore in Pakistan in 1958, the city was like one big garden. You saw green everywhere and the sky was blue. Look at it now. In Iran some national parks were established during the time of the Shah and the habitat of animals, many rare, was preserved. After the 1979 Iranian Revolution, however, it was said that this was a cruel act of the Shah against peasants who had been moved from the national park areas and settled elsewhere and they were allowed

1 Published soon thereafter as *Man and Nature*, (London: Allen & Urwin, 1976) and translated shortly after its publication in English into French and Italian and later into several other languages.

to return into the protected areas with the result that the habitat of many animals was destroyed, causing the extinction of some rare species. It was President Rafsanjani who realized the folly of this way of thinking; re-established the national parks and tried to make environmental concerns part of the program of the government, not that he had much success in preventing environmental degradation and pollution with the result that today Tehran is one of the most polluted cities in the world, not to speak of Mashhad, Ahvaz and other major Iranian cities similar to the fate of many other large cities in the rest of the Islamic world and in fact the world at large.

2 Islamic Teachings about the Environment

As I have always said, the key for Muslims confronting this crisis successfully, at least to the extent possible since some of the causes of the crisis are global and beyond the control of the Islamic world, is to return to the teachings of traditional Islam about nature and man's relation to it. This assertion is made in light of the fact that faith in Islam is still strong throughout the Islamic world. Therefore, Islamic teachings can be used much more readily for this purpose than can religious teachings in secularized parts of the globe. With this reality in mind, let us then summarize the traditional Islamic teachings concerning the natural world and men's and women's rights and responsibilities concerning God's creation.

In the Noble Quran it is asserted that God encompasses all beings (*huwa ʿalā kulli shay'in muḥīṭ*). Now, the term *muḥīṭ* also means 'environment' and it can, therefore, be said that God's Presence is ultimately the "environment" of His creation, more specifically of the world of nature and of human beings. To destroy the natural environment, whose beauty and harmony are results of this Divine Presence, is to veil this Presence and disrupt the harmony and balance of nature, of human life and of their inter-relation.

The Quran itself in the deepest sense addresses both man and nature and in certain verses calls upon and takes as witness elements of nature such as mountains, the sun and the moon and certain animals and reminds us of His Wisdom reflected in creatures both animate and inanimate. It refers to water as the indispensable substance for life and uses symbols drawn from the natural world such as the tree or the bee to teach us about the nature of the cosmic reality that surrounds us. In the Quran God's creation is shown to have a sacred quality. There is in fact no sacred scripture, except perhaps the Tao te-Ching, in which nature plays as central a role as it does in the Quran. On the basis of the Quran traditional Islamic thought even speaks of each living species having its own *Sharīʿah* or Divine Law.

The actions, sayings and teachings of the Prophet of Islam are also replete with environmental lessons and directives. It was he who created what today would be called a national park or protected area, from the south of Makkah to the north of

Madinah, where animals and plants were to be protected. Fortunately, the idea is being revived by environmentalists in Saudi Arabia today. He forbade the wasting of food, the polluting of water and the cutting down of fruit trees. He taught Muslims to live in harmony with nature and not to be at war with it. He emphasized the Quranic teaching that creatures have a direct nexus to God and pray to Him in their own fashion. It is this teaching that has been immortalized in Islamic literature, for example in the famous Persian poem of Jalāl al-Dīn Rūmī:

> If only existence had a tongue,
> So that it could lift the veil from Divine Mysteries.

The Prophet encouraged his followers to plant trees and ordered ʿAlī to plant many palm trees in Madinah (many of the palmeries originally planted by him are now being forced to die through the lack of water, so that the land on which they were planted can be sold at exorbitant prices). And it was the Prophet who said that it would be a blessed act in the Eyes of God if a person were to plant a tree on the day before the end of the world and the Day of Judgment. A hefty book could be written on the prophetic understanding of the philosophy of the natural environment and the relation of human beings to the rest of God's creation. If only contemporary Muslims were to heed the teachings of their Prophet on this crucial subject!

When it comes to the Islamic *Sharīʿah* or the Divine Law promulgated for all Muslims, it does not discuss the philosophy of the natural environment, but it does contain many laws and instructions on the practical level that are related to the environment directly from those concerning cleanliness, care of waste and treatment of animals and plants, to excess in the acquisition of material things, and numerous other matters including economic ones. The *Sharīʿah* emphasizes not only the rights of man but also his responsibilities in honoring the rights of other creatures especially animals including domesticated ones. Also, its moral teachings about avoiding greed, gluttony, aggression and similar vices have a direct bearing upon the environment.

It is in the teachings of Sufism, Islamic metaphysics, cosmology, philosophy and anthropology that the full exposition of the Islamic philosophy of the environment should be sought. The Islamic sapiential teachings speak about the correspondence between the cosmic Quran, the human microcosm and the macrocosm. They speak of the lessons to be learned from the "pages" of the cosmic book, the wisdom that can be gained from seeing the signs (*āyāt*) of God in the world of nature and to realize the importance of the reality of the harmony of creation and the inter-relatedness of all beings that are consequences of the oneness of the Author of the book of existence.

The Islamic sapiential tradition also emphasizes the love that persuades creation and issues from the Love of God for His creatures and of His creatures for Him. As the Quran says, "They love Him and He loves them." Muslim sages see this love as the moving force of the universe and agree with Dante when he speaks of "the love that moves the Sun and the other stars." In light of this view the famous Persian Sufi poet Saʿdī says,

> I am joyous with the world since the world is joyous with Him;
> I am the lover of the whole world since the whole world issues from Him.

This sapiential tradition can provide the categorical refutation of the secularized and materialistic view of nature that is a basic cause of the present environmental crisis, a view that had its birth in the West but has now spread globally.[2]

3 Manifestation of Islamic Environmental Teachings in Space and Time

It is also important to discuss how Islamic teachings about the environment and man's relation to it manifested themselves in Islamic history and culture. Perhaps it would be best to begin with the division of Islamic society into nomads and sedentary people whose interactions as the driving force of Islamic history were so profoundly analyzed by Ibn Khaldūn in his *Muqaddimah* ("Prologomena") to his universal history.[3] As he wrote, the nomads lived in the bosom of nature and were its protectors while sedentary people built towns and cities which were centers of both cultural refinement and decadence. The Mongols who were nomads decimated much of the sedentary centers of Central and Western Asia. While their invasion was a major social and civilizational catastrophe for the eastern regions of the Islamic world, from the point of view of the environment it had a "positive" effect. It reduced the population of areas such as Persia to probably about 50% of what it was before the 7th/13th century and destroyed much of the irrigation systems of many towns and cities, causing them to recede from their earlier boundaries towards foothills. The fact that Central and Western Asia have not had problems of over-population to the extent that one finds in South and East Asia is to a large extent due to the Mongol's destructive invasion in the 7th/13th century.

It needs to be added that even in traditional Islamic architecture and city planning in sedentary settings, the harmony between man and the natural environment was almost always kept in mind. On the basis of principles drawn from the Quran and *Ḥadīth*, Islamic architecture grew with full awareness of the necessity of preserving harmony and balance with the natural environment. The use of space, building materials, water, heat and cold, sunlight and shade, the wind, the creation of gardens and many other elements in Islamic architecture and city planning were based on the balance and harmony between man and nature, in contrast to today's cities, which are out of balance with nature and their very existence depends on the intrusion

2 See our *Religion and the Order of Nature* (New York: Oxford University Press, 1996).
3 F. Rosenthal, *The Muqaddimah: An Introduction to History* (Princeton: Princeton University Press, 1969).

into and destruction of the natural world. A traditional village in the mountains of Afghanistan or deserts of Persia or North Africa could in principle continue its life for eons without causing an imbalance with its natural surroundings. As for traditional cities, they did not cause pollution in their own air nor a thousand miles away as we see today. Even with the changed conditions of today, Muslims can learn much from their own traditions of architecture and urban design amidst the environmental crisis that they now face along with the rest of the world.

The practice of agriculture in the traditional Islamic world was also carried out in such a way that harmony with the environment was taken fully into account as we see likewise in other traditional societies. Soil that was rich from an agricultural point of view was not used for building towns on it but such soil was preserved for agriculture. A fine example of this principle is traditional Cairo which was built not completely adjacent to the Nile but some distance away from the edge of the river to preserve the land on the edge, which, because of the annual inundation of it by the Nile that resulted in the deposition of rich soil, was saved for agricultural purposes. We had to wait for modern times to see this rich soil, agriculturally speaking, being taken over by the sprawl of the city and becoming lost to food production. Also, the types of vegetation planted were chosen with environmental considerations in mind. Such consideration must not be seen only as making a virtue out of necessity, because goods could be transported to some extent from one region to another in the Islamic world and occasionally some fruits such as dates *were* transported and sold in regions some distance from where palm trees grew. There were in many cases choices to be made.

Closely related to this subject is the question of diet. On the basis of the science of the four natures (*ṭabāyiʿ*) (hot and cold; dry and moist) various cuisines were developed in the Islamic world that aimed to preserve the balance between the human body, food and the natural environment. This is a vast subject that cannot be treated to any extent here, but just to cite an example, much of North Indian cuisine has Persian origins and many North Indian dishes still bear Persian named but Indian food is hot while Persian food is not. This difference is due to the fact that most of Persia is hot and dry but India hot and moist, and so this addition of hot spices to Persian recipes was carried out in India to preserve the harmony and balance between the body and the natural environment.[4]

---

4 The *Qānūn* ("Canon") of Ibn Sīnā, the bible of Islamic medicine, as well as many other Islamic medical texts are replete with references to diet in relation to balance with the natural environment and the rhythms of nature especially the seasons.

4 Natural Environmental Teachings in Islamic Literature and Ethics

Lessons about the spiritual significance of nature and the bonds between man and nature beyond the material and utilitarian, bonds reflected in Quranic teachings, are also abundant in Islamic literature especially in poetry to the extent that some Western scholars have characterized such poetry as being naturalistic and even pantheistic. Such a characterization is, however, false. "Nature poetry" in Arabic, Persian and other Islamic languages is always based on the awareness of the reality of the transcendent nature of God while emphasizing the sacred nature of His creation and must not be equated with 19th century "nature poetry" of English Romantic poets although there are some similarities. Some English poets of this period in fact did have to some extent familiarity with poetry from the Islamic world, especially poems translated from Persian. Furthermore, this type of poetry in the Islamic world was not confined to the educated classes but percolated into all levels of society. Many of these poems are quoted in the daily life of ordinary Muslims to this day and have left a profound effect upon the attitude of traditional Muslims towards nature over the ages.

The spiritual and religious attitude towards the natural environment is integrated into traditional Islamic ethics although many Muslims are ignoring it today. Traditional Islamic ethics includes not only the human social order but also animals and plants and even running water, mountains, lakes and seas. It is of the utmost importance for Muslims to formulate their traditional environmental ethics in its totality in a contemporary language and then put it into practice and not only read or speak about it. Moreover, this ethics includes much more than not throwing garbage into the street or breaking branches of trees in the park near one's house about which some preachers speak today during their Friday sermons in various mosques although of course such matters are also of importance but are not the whole story.

5 The Islamic Sciences of Nature and Technology

We cannot conclude this essay without saying a few words about the traditional Islamic sciences of nature and technology although their full treatment in relation to the question of the natural environment would require a separate treatment.[5] Islamic science is one of the major scientific traditions in world history, one which

5 See our *An Introduction to Islamic Cosmological Doctrines* (Albany: State University of New York Press, 1993). See also S.H. Nasr and Muzaffar Iqbal, *Islam, Science, Muslims and Technology* (Kuala Lumpur: Islamic Book Trust, 2007).

not only exerted some influence upon medieval Chinese and Hindu sciences, but also, shorn of its cosmological and metaphysical dimensions, exercised a major influence upon later Western science. Where would the development of mathematics in Europe be without the translations of Arabic works on the science of numbers, geometry, algebra, trigonometry and other related subjects? To demonstrate this basic influence it is enough to just recall that numbers used in the West are still called Arabic numerals. Muslims made vast contributions not only to mathematics, but also to physics, astronomy, alchemy/chemistry, botany, zoology, medicine, pharmacology, cosmography and geography, along with many other fields. But all of these sciences, including the so-called exact sciences, were developed within a worldview that was based on the harmony between man and nature and the balance (*al-mīzān*) within each level of the cosmos as well as between the various levels of cosmic reality.[6]

Blinded by modern technology, many Muslims have forgotten the many forms of technology that the Muslims invented and used from the *qanāt* system for irrigation to metallurgy to weaving to technologies associated with architecture to windmills and many other technologies. What characterized these traditional technologies was balance with the order of nature and the natural environment and minimum intrusion into the natural order. It is not accidental that many environmentalists in the West today are proposing a return to the extent possible to traditional technologies. In the contemporary Islamic world one cannot expect realistically that people would stop using electricity but there are many forms of traditional technology that can be preserved or revived from architecture to agriculture to weaving of carpets and cloth. If Muslims were to follow this path, rather than emulating blindly whatever form of new technology comes their way from the West, they would face less crisis in their natural environment. I do not say no crisis at all because the environmental crisis has also many global causes that cannot be removed by local action. Yet, let us remember the truth of the prevalent saying of many serious environmentalists, "Think globally but act locally."[7]

According to a famous Chinese saying, "The journey of a thousand miles begins with a single step." When it comes to the environmental crisis in the Islamic world, that first step is to recognize and accept that the environment crisis *does exist* in the Islamic world and that it is not a problem only for the West or China. Once having

---

6 On Islamic science see our *Science and Civilization in Islam* (Chicago: ABC International, 2001); our *Islamic Science – An Illustrated Study* (London: World of Islam Festival, 1976); and A.Y. al-Hassan (et al.), *The Different Aspects of Islamic Culture*, Volume Four, *Science and Technology in Islam* (2 vols.), (Paris: UNESCO, 2002).

7 For a profound critique of modern science and technology see the works of Ivan Illich and E. F. Schumacher. Although these authors do not speak of the Islamic world specifically, their works possess much significance for those contemporary Muslims who are concerned seriously with the environmental crisis in Islamic countries and also globally.

developed this awareness fully, Muslims have to accomplish two crucial tasks: the first is to revive the knowledge and actions of traditional Islamic society concerning the environment; and the second is to know the modern world in depth so as not to repeat its errors and also to learn about positive actions taken by the Occident to confront this crisis. It is especially important for Muslims to be aware of the in-depth studies made in the West by well-meaning and knowledgeable environmentalists about the deeper causes of the crisis.

6 Conclusion

Let me conclude by posing the question, "Is there a solution?" If one looks at the situation from only the perspective of natural and human factors and extrapolates the present trends into the future on the basis of considering man and nature from only an "earthly" point of view, then indeed the situation is bleak and catastrophes awaiten us all. But from the Islamic point of view the future is in God's Hands and one must never lose hope. Resignation to environmental catastrophe is not an Islamically acceptable attitude and does not absolve us from our responsibilities towards God's creation as His *khalīfahs* on earth. We must do what we can to ameliorate the environmental situation to the extent of our possibilities and then and only then leave matters in resignation in God's Hands with complete *tawakkul* in Him and the full realization that we are not only *khalīfat Allāh* on earth, but also God's servants or *'abd Allāh*. Not performing our duties with the excuse that God will take care of His own creation and therefore abdicating our positions as His *khalīfahs* on earth is not Islamically speaking acceptable.

Deterministic futuristic extrapolations cut off the Hands of God from His creation and are not Islamic any more than is the attitude of doing nothing with the pretext that God's Will dominates all things. Muslims must resuscitate the traditional Islamic view of nature and man's relation to it.[8] Let us not forget the saying of the Prophet that I already mentioned, namely that it is a blessed act to plant a tree even if it were the day before the Day of Judgment, and the saying of 'Alī that we should live as if we were to die tomorrow but also as if we were to live a thousand years. And God knows best, *wa'Llāhu a'lam*.

---

8 On the issue of the Islamic view of this subject and the present day environmental crisis as it involves the Islamic world see also R.C. Foltz, F.M. Denny and A. Baharuddin, *Islam and Ecology* (Cambridge: Harvard University Press, 2003); R.C. Foltz, *Environmentalism in the Muslim World* (New York: Nova Science Publishers, 2005); and F. Khalid and J. O'Brien (eds.) *Islam and Ecology* (New York: Cassell, 1992). During the last few years the literature on Islam and the environment has grown in both the Islamic world itself and the West. *Islam and Ecology* has a good bibliography for up to 2003.

References

Foltz, R. C. (2005) *Environmentalism in the Muslim World* (New York: Nova Science Publishers).

Foltz, R. C., F.M. Denny and A. Baharuddin (2003) *Islam and Ecology* (Cambridge: Harvard University Press).

al-Hassan, A. Y. (et al.) (2002) *The Different Aspects of Islamic Culture*, Volume Four, *Science and Technology in Islam* (2 vols.), (Paris: UNESCO).

Khalid, F. and J. O'Brien (eds.) (1992) *Islam and Ecology* (New York: Cassell).

Nasr, S. H. (1976) *Islamic Science – An Illustrated Study* (London: World of Islam Festival).

Nasr, S. H. (1976) *Man and Nature*, (London: Allen & Urwin).

Nasr, S. H. (1993) *An Introduction to Islamic Cosmological Doctrines* (Albany: State University of New York Press).

Nasr, S. H. (1996) *Religion and the Order of Nature* (New York: Oxford University Press).

Nasr, S. H. (2001) *Science and Civilization in Islam* (Chicago: ABC International).

Nasr, S. H. and Muzaffar Iqbal (2007), *Islam, Science, Muslims and Technology* (Kuala Lumpur: Islamic Book Trust).

Rosenthal, F. (1969) *The Muqaddimah: An Introduction to History* (Princeton: Princeton University Press).

Saeed Farahanifard and Mohammad Ali Farahanifard

Chapter 9: Responsibility of Muslims versus Environment

1 Introduction

Ever since its creation, human being was scared of nature wholeheartedly; the danger posed by beast of prey, the risk of inclement weather, and the peril of wild environment. Nevertheless, the very nature has endowed him or her with the necessities of life including plant or animal food supply.

Later, by means of its own thinking and other tools, human being prepared himself against encountering dangers so that he reined natural causes and eventually exploiting them in his own favor. Through being unified and severe mutual efforts, human beings could convert forests into cultivated and arable lands, change the course of rivers, and build giant buildings and constructions such as pyramids in Egypt. However, these actions would stay restricted as much as human population was subject to the turbulence and upside downs stemmed from events, wars, contagious diseases, and or great natural disasters.

Along with scientific, technical, and medical advances, industrial revolution evolved the situation. Modern economy, because of the greedy insanity stemming from the notion of continuous economic growth, tried to explore techniques to utilize, as well as destroy ever more, natural resources. The economic man in this arena believed that he could perpetually make use of the reservoirs and resources the nature had bestowed to him.

Schumacher believed that this phenomenon was in close contact with philosophical evolutions of human attitude toward nature, if not religious, during the past three or four centuries. Modern man does not experience himself as a part of nature, rather, he deems himself as an external force whose mission is to dominate over nature. Even he talks about battling with nature; while he forgets the fact that even in case of his victory in the battle, he will find himself beside the loser.[1]

Nonetheless, there were some people, however few, who indicated this type of danger including Jean Restan's foreword in the book titled "Man or Nature", where he confessed that from now on human is going to figure out that to retain his or her own interests and benefits he or she should guard and watch for nature and at the same time harness his manner and behavior against nature.[2]

1 Ernest F. Schumacher, The little is beautiful, Tr. by A. Ramin (Tehran: Soroush, 1993).

2 Edward Bonfeau, Reconciliation of Man and Nature, Tr. By Salah al-Din Mahallati (Tehran: Center for Academic Publishing, 1996), 265.

https://doi.org/10.1515/9783110593419-009

The issue of environment has always been considered by the divine religions, and in case of Islam, it has also special instructions respectively.

Islam takes into account the overall aspects of human being, environment, and the universe in a balanced and coordinated relationship on the divine path and creates an interrelation among them. In the Koran's perspective, the Almighty is overshadowing humans and everything else so that mankind should be able to comprehend His presence everywhere. The position of man should be surrendering to God and justice to everything else. In addition to dealing with Islamic solutions to preservation, maintenance, and improvement of environment, this paper tries to point out to the responsibilities of Muslims accordingly.

2 Environment and Modern Civilization

Even though some environmental scientists use their own projection to assume that religion is the source of environment degradation and claim that by exploiting nature for human being and having a transient look against this world pave the way for degrading environment;[3] however, the truth is modern civilization by keeping human beings away from their essence and arousing human whims and desires plays a significant role in destroying environment.

Allameh Tabatabaei said that the nature of human being is urgently and out of choice is naturally civil, and in order for life not to be bitter and severe, he or she resorted to imposing and committing to rules and regulations so as security could prevail the world.[4] Therefore, human is instinctively prepared to assault and foray the defenseless nature. Nevertheless, in the past it was less likely to happen to him, and blocked the way towards the predominance of human beings through religious values and beliefs. Nonetheless, in modern civilization, the human's change of attitudes and central role of human being as well as the removal of materialistic and spiritual hurdles, environmental degradation took a different face and was accelerated. Shahid Motahhari denies the impact of machine force upon environmental pollution. Adversely, he believes that greed and craving create artificial consumption in various means so as to sell products that are less needed by human beings.[5]

On the other hand, Nasr believes that empirical science will damage environment due to lacking celectial principles. Therefore, he deems that supernatural approach and a shift of viewpoints toward nature and humanity are major solutions to get out of environmental problems. Some of the contemporary theologians have endeavored

3 M. Haddadi, "Religions and the environment", Religious News no.12, (2005).

4 Mohammad Hussein Tabatabaii, Al-Mizan fi Tafsir-alQur'an, vol.2 (Qum: Jameae Modarresin, 1417ah), 117.

5 Mortaza Motahhari, Philosophy of ethics (Tehran: Sadra, 1993), 237.

to propose a kind of environment theology the outcome of which would be formulating environmental ethics, not just a revival of religious perspective towards nature. Muslim scholars, too, following this pattern have tried their hands on environmental ethics rather than reviving the celestial science of nature. Nasr pursues the revival of celestial recognition through the legacy of the Islamic philosophy. In his opinion, after the official Christianity felt at risk against rationalism, it differentiated between natural and supernatural which per se is one of the profound root causes of current crises. Proceeding to this period, the Avicennian rationalism is superseded with Averroes Rationalism in which heavenly creatures are denied and desacralization from the universe was accelerated. Along with the element of faith, science was deprived of philosophical certainty. After two centuries of philosophical skepticality, the scientific revolution and new science birth came into being and desacralization came into its acme.[6]

Western civilization has considered terrestrial human something absolute ever since the emergence of renaissance humanism. While depriving human being of its central source, western humanism has endeavored to dedicate some absoluteness to such a decentered human being. This kind of man is merely terrestrial as defined in rationalism and humanism which brought about the seventeenth century science based on the authority and domination over nature: a human that supposes nature to be the enemy. Such as secular human that is not absolute has destroyed a vast number of jungles in the name of economic welfare without thinking about the consequences for a little while left over to the future generation of mankind or other creatures of the world. Islam never allows human being to venerate himself through contempt of God or His world of creation. Nothing is more detestable to Muslims than renaissance titanic art for which to have its dignity, it has created a human being who rebels against God.[7]

Furthermore, Schumacher stated something in this regard that modern man does not experiment himself as a part of nature, rather, he deems himself as an external force whose mission is domination over nature. He then stated something about battle with nature that he nevertheless forgets that even upon victory he will find himself beside the losers. In this mentality, he forgets his religious rites and values, and basically, he owes achieving such a dream goal to such an oblivion. Accordingly, Keynes states "time is not ripe enough to refer back to a portion of certain principles religion and ethical virtues (for instance, greed is mischief; usury is a sin; cupidity is detestable).[8]

---

6 A. Ghasemi, "Seyyed Hossein Nasr's Views on the Crisis of the Environment and its Solutions", Hikmat Moaaser no.3, (2011).

7 Hussain Nasr, Religion and the system of nature, Tr. By M. Ghafouri (Tehran: Hikmat, 2000), 225–226.

8 Ernest F. Schumacher, (1993), 23.

The human nature relationship involves three eras: dominance of nature over human; dominance of human over nature; human nature convergence and interaction era. In modern civilization, by dominance over nature and exploiting it, human has wreaked a lot of havoc on nature extremely. Carbon dioxide in the air emitting from fossil fuels, pouring factory wastes and various toxic substances into the seas and rivers, drowning of oil tankers and release of oil substances and other pollutants into the sea, atomic accidents, nuclear wars, chemical accidents, global warming, Ozon layer depletion, climate changes, acid rains, population explosion, forest degradation and rare flora and fauna destruction, all in all have turned into an environmental disaster that has endangered the future of the earth.[9]

The western civilization model that has an economic look at and evaluate the entire living and non-living things on the earth, even human beings, is the main cause of environmental pollutions. When the main purpose of production is forgotten and is not used for meeting the personal and social needs, when consumption is meant to be not only for survival but for more consumption, when innovation and technology are turned into the ever more exploitation of natural resources, when all these factors are for obtaining profit ever more, then no one can expect something more than annihilation and devastation; it is unfortunate that this story has spread all around the world after the industrial revolution more intensively.[10] Industrial nations are the biggest contaminators. Environmental threats are border crossing and affects the health of all the nations and states. Neither in developed countries nor in those developing ones are the development patterns defined along with preserving environment, and today mankind should definitely think about a green global movement toward saving the earth planet. Environmental commitments have not become something compulsory and publicly inclusive yet. Environmental degradation is the effect of social inequalities and abuse of environment.[11]

3 Erroneous Religious Beliefs and Environment

Mackibben stated that "For several centuries some ancient religions perceived the world nature as a guaranteed virtue which is merely a background and behind a scene for the various relations that humans and gods make with each other". In his opinion, the project of using religious texts and rites about environment should continue so as

9 M. Firuzi, The right on the environment (Tehran: Publishing House for Jihad Daneshgahi, 2005), 19.
10 F. Simbar, "Environmental degradation and its consequences for developing countries", Syasi Eghtesadi Journal, no.203–204.
11 H. Movassaghi, "Environmental rights: past, present and future", Journal for Vokala-e-Dadgostari Association, no.16, (2009).

the theory and practice could be used together.[12] One the challenges ahead of religions is how to confront environmental crises. Some believe that detaching religion from the secular life could be one of the major reasons for this problem. On the other hand, some scientists including Arnold Twinby and Lynn White believe in the negative role of Abrahamic religions in such a crisis. This is while these religions introduce man as the successor of God on the earth, they attribute some responsibilities for him toward nature.[13]

In their opinion, the most significant challenges include the following:

a. Conquest

Due to the ideas of religious followers the Almighty created this world at the disposal of man and as an agent for him, and made it obedient to mankind so as he can make an easy use of it. Some biologists believe that this idea still existing in Muslims' and Christians' beliefs is one of the factors for environment degradation. They think that man can treat the nature however he wishes to do so due to the dominance he is bestowed by God over nature. White Junior deems the environmental crisis is rooted in the domination awarded to man by the bible. This humanitarian pride has let this religious right to take control of nature and misuse it.[14]

In Islam, man is the successor of God on the earth and the attribution of succession is complemented with his servitude. In the position of God's successor, he is in charge of the worldwide coordination, and in his position of servitude, he is preserving the trust he accepted; therefore, whenever conquest is accumulated with the successorship of man for God, environmental degradation will not occur. Nevertheless, the man who will not accept servitude of God and is not following his rules will take nature as his enemy and for further comfort he will stimulate it.

In a part of his speech that Haught studies the issue of religion and environment with a distinct perspective, he replies to this deficiency that "The meaning of conquest is not dominance; rather, the purpose is the role of human being as the successor of God against the non-humane nature. This means that since God is the savior of life, the holy book indirectly directs us to imitate God in this regard."[15]

In response to this problem, Nasr also states that "When the Koran says that nature is conquered by man (Sura Hajj (22), Verse 65) this does not mean the normal defeating of nature, not that much claimed by a great number of modernized Muslims who are thirsty of that power that modern science is supplied for man; rather, it means overcoming those things that human is allowed to apply, just provided that it should

12 B. McKeiben, "The role of religion in saving the environment", Syahat-e- Gharb No. 17 ,131–132.
13 M. Haddadi, "Religions and the environment", Religious News no.12, (2005).
14 John F. Haught, Science and Religion, Tr. By Batul Najafi (Qum: Ketab Taha, 2003 (originally in 1982)), 304.
15 Ibid, 305.

match divine laws, and certainly since he is the successor of God on the earth, he has an authority that eventually belongs to God. That is why nothing in nature is more dangerous than exerting power in a position of successorship in human community by which he will no longer accept servitude to God and obedience to His law."[16]

As a result, all these evidences show that environment degradation is not only the result of the virtue of conquest over nature given to human being by God, but also due to deviating from religious values and the prophets' recommendations to their disciples respectively.

b. Silence

Some scholars express their objections against religious communities from this stand point of view that these communities are keeping their silence against this crisis. The classic texts on religious customs own little contexts on deforestations, soil erosion, wasting water supplies, air and soil pollution, global warming, etc. in addition, some religious teachers still neglect the growing human population, something that remarkably worsens all the above-mentioned threats. Russel Train, 1990, believes that:

> Religion and theology are well-known for the fact that they pay no heed to the prudence of the natural world. Traditionally churches and synagogues and mosques have paid little attention to the major environmental issues. He who has been over thirty years of leading an environmental movement believes it is amazing that religion and theology have been so indifferent toward the crisis to this extent.[17]

In response to this problem one can say that normally judging the impact of religious education on some topics such as environment comes from the study and observation of Christian actions. Although Christian tradition as one of the Abrahamic religions has endorsed the importance and spiritual value of nature, the entanglement of Christianity in secularism and refraining from worldly affairs and putting it aside, resulting from the battle between Christianity and humanism, rationalism, and secularism during five centuries before Renaissance, has paved the way for the notion of secularism. However, the fact that nothing is heard from Islam is because the West has dedicated its research over Islam to two groups of radical reformists (Wahhabism and Salafism) and Modernists (Syed Ahmad Khan, in India, Abduh, in Egypt, and Taqizadeh, in Iran) – the two rivals that during the past few decades have differences in many issues; but recently they have reconciled the blind adoption of new technology and complete ignorance to the traditional Islamic comments about science.[18]

Studying religious perspectives in general, and those of Islam in particular, about the nature and environment is an obvious evident to reject this claim.

---

16 Hussain Nasr, Religion and the system of nature (2000), 222–223.

17 John F. Haught, Science and Religion, (2003), 300.

18 Hussain Nasr, Ibid, 227–230.

c. Temporariness of the world

Some people, too, assume that the environmental crisis is because the religions are considered to be hereafter centered, and that the ultimate goal of human being is the other world.

> An essential principle in the environmental ethics is that the earth is assumed to be the real house of our own; nevertheless, religion cannot accept this world to be ours [...] Religion tells us that we are merely pilgrims or passengers on the earth. How can this unsecular perspective claim that we should take ecology as something serious? Cosmopolitanism that religion talks about is not able to produce enough ethical energy to contribute to the ecology movement.[19]

On the other hand, the prophetic religiousness of a lot of religious persons has allowed them to think that this world is prone to annihilation whereby it is not worth saving it.[20]

With reference to the rich religious literature, especially that of Islam, and investigating the attitude of religion towards this world will solve the problem, that is, a remote and dull sensation towards this world that causes lack of endeavor to preserve and take care of it. In the eyes of religion, though the ultimate goal is another world and the attempt of divine religions has been to prepare their disciples to make a long time for their afterlife, this does not at all mean to neglect and refrain from the world; rather, they presume the world to be just like a farm for the afterlife in which the felicity of that world goes through this world. Anyone who ruins his or her farm and does not pay any heed to that will have nothing to harvest for the afterlife.

In Imam Ali's words, the world is introduced as a commercial firm and a place of worship for God's followers, and those who reproach the world are rebuked.[21]

Likewise, Allameh Shahid Motahhari believes that love of the world is something intrinsic,[22] and it is quoted that he referred to Ali's words that love of the world is analogous to the love of a human mother.[23]

What religious teachings try to negate them are worldliness and ignorance toward the ultimate goal.

It is obvious that worldly people attend to the world to gain further profit and to enjoy it more. They are a typical set of people who voraciously make the use of the finite resources and ruin them so as to deal with their luxury world.

The Koran, too, regards this concept wrong that believers should not utilize the virtues of the world (E'raf, (7), 32).

---

19 John F. Haught, Ibid, 303.

20 Ibid, 304.

21 Al-Sharif Abolhasan Mohammad Razi, Nahj al-Balaghah, Sobhi Salah (Qum: Al-Bohoth al-Islamiyah Center, 1997), 384, wisdom131.

22 Mortaza Motahhari, Seiri Dar Nahjol Balagha (Tehran: Sadra, 1987), 264–265.

23 *Mohmmadi Rayshahri, Mizan Al-Hikmah, 2nd review, vol.2 (Qum: Dar al-Hadith, 1416 A.H), 890, Hadith 5741.*

Any effort toward the worldly affairs is encouraged to be accompanied by efforts toward the afterlife, while isolating from the world is deprecated (Ghasas Sura, (27), verse 77).

Imam Ali calls those who never leave the afterlife for the world and vice versa as the best people.[24]

In sum, the investigation of the suspicions posed as well as the study of various perspectives about environment including the schools and religions, or non-religious philosophical theories, and a historic and analytic approach toward the genesis of crisis will lead us to the fact that the established crisis is generally stems from deviation of man from religious beliefs, and that the solution to the environmental crisis is merely out of healing the spiritual disease of modern man and retrieving the spiritual universe. By strengthening the social faith, the altruistic motivations along with respect toward flora and fauna will be growing among them, hence, the rules and regulations related to environment will be guaranteed through the religious support.

4 Human and Nature Position in Islam

A survey over the Koran verses and relations stated by pure Imams represents the real position of natural phenomena from the brilliant religion of Islam perspective, and the study of the solutions that Shari'ah has proposed to control human beings for the purpose of preservation of divine trust will strengthen the belief inside our mind that within the core nucleus of religion there is an environmental concern existing.

1. The generous God that is the manifestation of beauty and liveliness praises the whole universe beautifully (Prostrate (32), 7)
2. Whatever God has bestowed in nature for utilization of human being has indicated as Tayyebat (Virtues) so that such a virtue is introduced in the shadow of Human dignity. (Asra (17), 70)
3. Whatever existing in this universe, including birds, animals, mountains, seas, and so on, is introduced by The Almighty to have common sense and commending, and stars and trees are also introduced as His shadow face stating that mankind is unable to figure that their eulogy (Al-rahman (55):6; Ra'd (13):13; Osarah (17):14; and the first verse of the Sura Hadid (57), Hashr (59), Saff (61), Jumah (62), and Taqabon (64)).

This point is reminded in various relations for instance in Tafsir Almzan in a relation by Imam Sadegh "The Prophet (pbuh) prohibited to brand animals, and as for

24 Alaa al-din Hendi, Kanz al-O'mmal fi sunan al-qwal va al-af'al, vol.3 (Maktabe al-turath al-Islami, 1397 AH), 732, Hadith 8604.

people slapping them in their face, he stated that quadruped animals worship God as well."[25]

As a result, one can claim that the foundation and basis of the existing universe is on love and cognition, therefore the amount of comprehension and common sense of living beings is different in proportion to their inner capacity.

4. The Almighty God has frequently sworn in natural manifests in the holy Koran (First verses of Shams, Zoha, and Teen Suras), and it is clear that the items sworn in is of importance and validity for God, and in similar cases the Almighty has taken oath in his own glory, the prophet, the Mecca city, etc. the importance of which is well-known for everyone, in addition to the fact that the items that are sworn in by God for their proof including judgement day and the like are all of significance and worthiness.
5. The creator of the universe has introduced nature as the symbol and sign of self-recognition and understanding His glory as well as the changeable seasons(Al-e Omran 190, Nour 44) and the new life of the nature after the winter death to infer resurrection (E'raf (7), 57); while inviting human beings to ponder upon the creation of the heaven and earth, He has named those who learn from these signs as wise and intellectual people (Roum (30), 19).

   Muslim scholars and intellectuals, too, have in turn expressed their valuable opinions in terms of the importance of environment among other points. Shahid Motahhari believed that environment impacts the human morals in spite of affecting their body and materialistic features, just like the case in which people who live in mountains have different behaviors from those who live in desert areas.[26] therefore, polluting or destroying environment not only deprives man from having a healthy environment for life, but also affects their moods.

Imam Khomeini, too, emphasized the necessity of the correct use of natural resources and utilizing the rivers for land reclamation for the purpose of self-sufficiency, assuming agriculture to be the top of all affairs, believing that being thankful for God is not met otherwise.[27] He deems the environmental issues as the things that religious scholars should reflect upon their new issues.[28] In Ayatollah Khamenei's opinion, the most comprehensive perspective and the most accurate way of interacting with nature and environment is explained by Islam. God has created the cosmos and the whole phenomena beautifully, balanced and solid so that we should revise

25 Mohammad Hussain Tabatabai, Al-Mizan fi Tafsir al-Qur'an, vol.13, 166, underneath the verse 44 Osarah Sura.

26 *Murtaza Motahari, Man in the Qur'an: An Introduction to the Islamic Worldview, vol4 (Tehran: Sadra, 1994), 37.*

27 Ruh-Allah Moussavi Khomeini, Sahifeh Nour (Tehran: Institute for publishing of Imam Khomeini's works, 2000), vol.11, 402 and vol.17, 130.

28 Ibid, vol.21, 177.

our relationship with them, and should not make them ruined and polluted with improper seizures so as to make society faced with disaster and catastrophe. The Islam stance toward nature and environment including living and nonliving beings is something emotional, ethical, spiritual and guiding, and enjoying natural virtues is based on the principles of humbleness, justice, balance, and constructiveness. The ultimate goal of Islam is that all the generations enjoy divine virtues and build up a healthy society far from social class discrimination and talented for growth and flourishing, and it has provided the religious requirements to keep the balance in utilizing natural virtues by preventing from extravagance and bound not to tease other people.[29]

5 The Status of Government in Destruction and Improvements of Environment

With the environment endangered, the most basic right of human being that is right of living will be in jeopardy. Thus, any government should organize the social life in a way that it guarantees the maintenance of the fundamental and natural basis of life. Accordingly, the responsibility for future generations is primarily directed toward government so as to pursue this task in the national and international level.[30] The ever-growing development of knowledge and technology which entailed environmental issues, environment has become a supranational issue and a subject for international rights. Passing through the first and second human rights and the attention to the right for collective and further attention to the integration of various human rights, the right of a healthy environment was considered as the background for enjoying other rights.[31] The existing 300 international documents in terms of environmental rights as one of the four-fold rights of collective represent the special status of environmental rights in the international arena.[32]

The initiation of the meetings on environmental rights happened in Rio de Janeiro in 1992, in which by emphasis on the approvals in Stockholm meetings, new solutions were predicted for 21st century and thereafter holding these kinds of meetings and signing treaties continued. The outcome of the meetings, in addition to approving agreements and numerous regulations, was the establishment of UNEP organization in 1972 succeeding Stockholm meetings which provided a plan concerning the

29 Ali Husseini Khamenei, *Statements, "a message on the occasion of Environmental Rights of Iran", (Tehran: Office of Publishing, 2003), 19.*

30 M. Firuzi, The right on the environment (2005), 97.

31 Ibid, 25 and 51.

32 R. Ghasemzadeh, "Assessing dimensions of the environmental rights with emphasis on environmental pollution prevention", Allameh Quarterly.

structure and finance of the field of environment. The worldwide control over environment is delegated to UNEP which is known as Earth-watch program. Sustainable development commission was also established after Rio Summit in 1992 along with sustainable development to keep environment.[33]

Recently the establishment of the international environmental court within the framework of a new environmental organization or another structure in which a pile of multilateral environmental agreements is amassed is proposed. This court may have a significant role in expansion and enhancement of international rights for environment including the cooperation between the building blocks and their connection with other regulations of international rights.[34]

Certainly, the international environmental rights are faced with great challenges such as changing the recommended principles into something binding as well as the optimal principles into the existing ones. However, the conflicting interests of states is the deterring force against attention toward environmental indices. Implementation of collective rights mentioned in third-generation human rights possess problems due to lack of a comprehensive and coordinated definition, unclear quality implementation and guarantee for that, lack of definition for human rights framework.[35]

In the economic system of Islam, government has a lofty position. It has enormous authorities but in turn, it bears a heavy load of task. The most authority of government in terms of the subject matter is that a number of natural resources are in its possession or under its supervision. Therefore, the Islamic government can precondition the compatible use of environment for delegation of the resources to the private sector, while in its efforts to enhance the status of environment. Directing toward the right way of consumption pattern and solemn prevention of misuse and extravagance in micro and macro levels is an earnest axis in accurate management of environmental resources and refraining from environmental pollution because the greatest threat existing is from the cancerous consumerism which devastates the body of nature rapidly.

The government behavior and state officials along with correct policy making and gaining the public trust is another aspect emphasized because as long as people don't witness any coordination between the behavior of state officials and their policies, they won't trust so that the best solutions will also not be effective.

---

33 H. Bahrami Ahmadi, "Political-legal policy of the Islamic Republic of Iran in protecting the environment", Danesh-e-Syasi 5th year, no.1 (2009).

34 H. Najandimanesh, "The necessity of establishing the International Court of Justice", Political Economic Information no.247–248 (2008).

35 H. Movassaghi, "Environmental rights: past, present and future" (2009).

6 Strategies and Must-have of Maintenance and Enhancement of Environment

The orientation of Islam concerning the creation of man is that it should be God-like for which the overall necessary backgrounds including wisdom and instinct as an internal prophet accompanied by prophets together with the life manual is supplied and for instance it is recommended that he should decently look after the trust left for him as a tool in line with his perfection.

Whenever human beings pay heed and implement these kinds of trainings and follow the path of servitude and divine succession and the trust left by God to them, and act according to the guidance provided, the enormous environmental problems that we are facing with will vanish. For example, when human beings meet the rights of one another, and keep a balanced way of using natural virtues, and leave aside the extravagance, greed, abuse, and waste, as a result he will find the existing world as a paradise. Nevertheless, in addition to the fact that orientation of divine religions is having human being reach the top of perfection and humanism, to prevent from unrealism there are solutions seen in the context of religion so that the communities at any level of faith in God and agency to implement the commands and religious guidelines could have a fairly healthy environment and prevent the imposition of wrongdoing human beings.

The divine trainings in this regard are usually of two faces. Some of the trainings are meant to sustain the minimum necessities as the required obligations and even there are mechanisms to guarantee their implementation. Another category is designed as ethical guidelines in order to movement toward an ideal and optimal society of the Almighty.

A. Required Obligations

Some of the required obligations that make use of the relations and verses as well as religious jurisprudence are:

1. **Refrain from Oppression**
   According to the rule of justice, we should refrain from oppression and aggression against other people in other behavior in terms of environment (including existing or future generations). There is no doubt that any action that results in the pollution of the environment is an evident of oppression.
2. **Refrain from causing harm or abuse of public properties**
   Some people and enterprises are likely to devastate environment by maximizing their profit. Polluting air, seas and rivers, activities affecting ozone layer are among the evidences of devastating environment, proceeded by other outcomes such as shortage of human life, outbreak of diseases especially skin diseases, disappearance of some flora and fauna. And based on the rule of damage free principle, anti-abuse principle, and causation principle, the cause of these outcomes is

sinful and from the perspective of situational judgement, too, it is considered as a guarantor.

3. **Refrain from Extravagance**
   Although the evidences of extravagance are few, and includes excessive use of natural resources, devastating environment, pollution of water, and other evidences of pollution that reduces the enjoyment of these resources are as examples of extravagance and is religiously prohibited.
4. **Refrain from corruption on the earth**
   The Almighty God, while emphasizing the fact that the existence is created by prudence, prohibits corruption in numerous cases and states: "Do not do any corruption on the earth after doing good things" (E'raf, 56)
   Also, the evidence of corrupt people on the earth are those people who devastate it and annihilate the farms and generations:
   و اذا تولی سعی فی الارض لیفسد فیها ویهلک الحرث و النسل و اللّه لا یحب الفساد (Bagharah (2), 205)

   All those people who destroy the possibility of using the earth in different forms, or by polluting the air, extravagant use of resources, etc. pave the way of devastation of future generations are included in this verse.

   In another verse in the Koran, the almighty reproaches those who try to devastate the manifestation of the God's beauty and try to spoil the glorious system of creation by pollution, and deems the deficiencies and problems on the earth stemmed from the actions of corrupt men (Roum, (30), 41).

   The strong tone of voice exerted in these verses against corrupt and devastators indicates the severe attention that God has to keep environment as a human perfection and growth plate. The main purpose of creation of this universe has been human being and that he should not have any imperfection in his way toward sublimity.

B. Encouraging guidelines (Ethical)

As discussed at the introduction of this paper, the primary principle of Islam is based on the fact that through education it can make human being preserve his living place, and these methods in practice have certainly been effective. Thus, there are a lot of verses and relations with this attitude some of which are indicated as follows:

1. God has introduced human being as His successor and trustee (Bagharah (2): 30) and has provided him with the means of succession through educating him His good names(Bagharah (2):31), in addition he is required to develop the thing entrusted to him that is the earth and its outlook and keep it from any harm or loss(Hood (119): 61)
2. There are numerous relations regarding the emphasis of religion on sanitation (including personal, household, and environment) and even they are known as the signs of faith. Furthermore, God has juxtaposed His worshiping with

sanitation. Ablution and bathing that are recommended to Muslim are because of sanitation.[36] When attending mosque, it is recommended that Muslim put on their best clothes. Also, in a relation by Imam Sadegh pbuh it is stated that:

Life without three things is not pleasant for human being: clean air, abundant water, and cultivated land.[37]

It is evident that the above cases are evidences a healthy environment and as a result a pleasant life.

3. There are a great number of relations that emphasize preservation of roads, waters, and other public places, and any damage to these treasures is prohibited, and those who try to do so are praised so that in a relation by the holy prophet anyone who removes something that bothers by-passers on the Muslim paths, God will record the reward of reading 400 verses of the Koran for him or her.[38]

On the other hand, those who make the path of people polluted or bring about some barriers for them, are reproached. The Prophet of Islam stated that:

There are three group of people who are cursed by God: a- those who in public places, shades, and travelers' boarding places make pollution. B- those who confiscate public water sources. C- those who make a hurdle for others and block their passage.[39]

In another relation, Imam Sadegh quotes from his ancestor about the Prophet that:

The Prophet prohibits urination near the drinking water well, stream, or under a fruit tree.[40]

These all prove the emphasis of religion on hygiene of living place and its preservation from any pollution, even in some cases these kinds of actions brings liability. Imam Sadegh for instance stated that:

"anyone who builds a water gutter, or dig a hole or well on the path of a Muslim, or hammer a nail in a place or fasten an animal in a place where someone would be hurt by hitting to them, he is responsible for that.

4. There are numerous relations in which Muslim are encouraged to plant trees, farm lands, or other activities that are effective in the freshness and greenery of the environment. For instance, in a relation by the Prophet:

   Any Muslim who plants a sapling or cultivate a farmland, out of which a human being, a bird, or an animal could enjoy, his or her actions score letter will be filled out with the alms reward.

---

36 *Mohammad Bagher Majlisi, Bahar Al-anwar, (Al-Wafa Institute, 1403 AH), vol.63, 364; vol.78, 2.*
37 Ibid, vol.75, 234.
38 Mirza Hussein Nouri, Mustadrak Al-Vasael (Qum: Al-Albeit Institute, 1408 AH), vol.12, 385.
39 Mohammad ibn Hasan Horr Aameli, Vasael-al-shia (Qum: Ahl-al-bait Institute, 1409AH), vol.1, 325.
40 Ibid.

In addition, he stated that:

Anyone who plants a fruit tree, God will reward him/her in proportion to the fruits grown.

Imam Sadegh considers farming and agriculture as the most favorite actions and said that the entire prophets were farmers excluding Edris who was a tailor.

5. Institutionalizing the culture of foresightedness and exiting from self-sightedness cocoon are seen in various relations and jurisprudent trainings. Relations that encourage human beings to develop the earth, those that encourage inheritance and think about the future of children and those that encourage alms and give-aways are among them. Naturally, this kind of culture comes along with tactfulness for the future of environment.
6. In a relation from the holy prophet encouragement for foresightedness is well designed. His highness stated that:

   Whenever you were holding the sapling of date tree in hand and the resurrection occurred, if you were able to plant it up until the resurrection time, do plant it. Development of land is optimal for human being though no one may not be able to enjoy it.

7 Wrap up and Conclusion

The crisis of environment is the outcome of the distance made between human being and its creation and religious teachings on the one hand and uncontrolled use of environmental resources that are stemmed from the accelerating development of secularism. Religions especially Islam has made strict emphasis on preservation of environment and has encouraged and obliged Muslims to achieve this purpose. The Islamic state, too, by means of the instruments at hand, can provide the performance guarantee for the principles and requirements of Shari'ah. In sum, one can categorize the solutions to face with the environmental crisis as follows:

1. Revising attitudes and insights through culture making and educating the correct religious teachings
2. Revising ethical values: such an ethical principle should come from divine resources and suprahuman sources so as to be able to consider the overall mankind and heaven expediencies. In addition to recommending justice and piety and mediocracy, Islam has bound consumption to prohibit extravagance, outbreak, violation, and earn wealth invalidly.
3. Revising behavior through jurisprudent must-have: hygienic jurisprudent solutions which have great effects on preserving environment and its care.
4. Legal solutions: the principle of no damage, extravagance and abuse, justice principle, and Islamic ruler principle are examples of legal regulations that Islam has setup and the have remarkable impact on preserving environment.

5. Economic solution: signing contracts to delegate the environmental resources preconditioned with preservation of environment, supervision on enterprises in using clean technology and not destroying environment, encouraging policies and punishment concerning enhancement and destruction of environment.

References

Bahrami Ahmadi, H. "Political-legal policy of the Islamic Republic of Iran in protecting the environment", Danesh-e-Syasi 5th year, no.1, 2009.

Bonfeau, Edward, Reconciliation of Man and Nature, Tr. By Salah al-Din Mahallati, Tehran: Center for Academic Publishing, 1996.

Firuzi, M. The right on the environment, Tehran: Publishing House for Jihad Daneshgahi, 2005.

Ghasemi, A. "Seyyed Hossein Nasr's Views on the Crisis of the Environment and its Solutions", Hikmat Moaaser no.3, 2011.

Ghasemzadeh, R. "Assessing dimensions of the environmental rights with emphasis on environmental pollution prevention", Allameh Quarterly.

Haddadi M. "Religions and the environment", Religious News no.12, 2005.

Haught, John F. Science and Religion, Tr. By Batul Najafi, Qum: Ketab Taha, 2003 (originally in 1982).

Hendi, Alaa al-din, Kanz al-O'mmal fi sunan al-qwal va al-af'al, vol.3, Maktabe al-turath al-Islami, 1397 AH.

Horr Aameli, Mohammad ibn Hasan, Vasael-al-shia, Qum: Ahl-al-bait Institute, 1409AH.

Husseini Khamenei, Ali, Statements, "a message on the occasion of Environmental Rights of Iran", Tehran: Office of Publishing, 2003.

Majlisi, Mohammad Bagher, Bahar Al-anwar, Al-Wafa Institute, 1403 AH.

McKeiben, B. "The role of religion in saving the environment", Syahat-e- Gharb No. 17.

Mohmmadi Rayshahri, Mohammad, Mizan Al-Hikmah, 2nd review, vol.2, Qum: Dar al-Hadith, 1416 A.H.

Motahari, Mortaza, Philosophy of ethics, Tehran: Sadra, 1993.

Motahari, Mortaza, Seiri Dar Nahjol Balagha, Tehran: Sadra, 1987.

Motahari, Murtaza, Man in the Qur'an: An Introduction to the Islamic Worldview, vol4, Tehran: Sadra, 1994.

Moussavi Khomeini, Ruh-Allah, Sahifeh Nour, Tehran: Institute for publishing of Imam Khomeini's works, 2000.

Movassaghi, H. "Environmental rights: past, present and future", Journal for Vokala-e-Dadgostari Association, no.16, 2009.

Najandimanesh, H. "The necessity of establishing the International Court of Justice", Political Economic Information no.247-248, 2008.

Nasr, Hussain, Religion and the system of nature, Tr. By M. Ghafouri, Tehran: Hikmat, 2000.

Nouri, Mirza Hussein, Mustadrak Al-Vasael, Qum: Al-Albeit Institute, 1408 AH.

Razi, Al-Sharif Abolhasan Mohammad, Nahj al-Balaghah, Sobhi Salah, Qum: Al-Bohoth al-Islamiyah Center, 1997.

Schumacher, Ernest F. The little is beautiful, Tr. by A. Ramin, Tehran: Soroush, 1993.

Simbar, F. "Environmental degradation and its consequences for developing countries", Syasi Eghtesadi Journal, no.203-204.

Tabatabaii, Mohammad Hussein, Al-Mizan fi Tafsir-alQur'an, vol.2, Qum: Jameae Modarresin, 1417AH.

Majid Reza'ei Davani

Chapter 10: Business Ethics

1 Introduction

Financial markets are among the most important institutions of any economic system. They channel savings into investment, reduce the costs of financial transactions, pool risk, and supply liquidity. The Islamic Economic System improves upon traditional financial markets by implementing policies, based on Islamic principles, that better align the functions of private financial markets with the needs of society at large.

An Islamic economy is designed within the framework of Islamic jurisprudence, laws, and ethics. The economic behavior of participants in the economy are shaped in accordance with Islamic *Sharia* and the concepts of faith and ethics. Islamic ethics and ideology determine and explain fundamental concepts such as profit, loss, fairness, and the privileges of the parties in any transaction. While both religious and secular economies share certain goals: reducing risk, properly distributing liquidity, reducing costs, determining prices, and satisfying the financial interests of market players, the two systems are distinguished by both their objectives and methods of achieving those objectives.

In a secular economy, the "future" is defined entirely in terms of worldly existence and so the aim is to only maximize returns during the life of a person. In contrast, an Islamic economy presupposes the existence of an afterlife and so aims to structure savings in such a way that it maximizes returns in both the present and future, for both the individual in the afterlife as well as for other members of society in the material future.

For Muslims, the primary purpose of savings as, indeed, for all activities, is to please the Almighty. Doing so involves both living off a licit/halal income oneself as well as helping others, including family, the needy, and society at large. The spending of Muslims can be divided into three general categories: 1)personal consumption, 2) social participation, and 3)savings and investments.[1] Personal consumption expenses include the money spent on food, clothing, dwelling, marriage, transport and leisure of the person and his family members. Social participation expenses are funds used by the individual for public affairs voluntarily, e.g. helping the needy, construction of mosques and schools. Savings comprise the portion of present-day earnings set aside for future consumption, some of which is channeled into investments

The following describes Islamic financial ethics in an Islamic economy; it is covered under two headings viz. ethics of financing the needy and ethics of investment.

1 See *Optimal Consumption Pattern within the Framework of Islamic Income Allocation Model*; pp. 13–16.

https://doi.org/10.1515/9783110593419-010

2 Ethics of Financing the Needy

Three methods exist for financing the needy.

2.1 Usury-free Money Lending

While alms and Zakat can be used to directly help the needy, they can also be used to support favorable loans to the poor. Such financial loans are zero interest and called *Qard-ul-Hassana*. These loans are usually allotted to the needy and the motive for providing them is charitable rather than profit seeking. Quaranic verses and Hadiths point to the importance of *Qard-ul-Hassana*.[2] If Muslims give away part of their earnings as alms to the needy, they can surely set aside a greater portion in form of *Qard-ul-Hassana*.This is because *Qard-ul-Hassana* financing can cover an important part of the requirements of the needy and allows financing of various projects at a lesser cost. In other words, charitable loans are a form of "reusuable alms."

Allotting *Qard-ul-Hassana* depends upon the amount of faith of the individuals in a society. In a truly religious society, the faith of the people is at a suitable level. Thus an important part of the capital needs of the under-privileged, whose income is low, can be supplied through *Qard-ul-Hassana* and productivity will form at lower costs. Smaller capitals for small-scale units will be provided by loans and the needy will have priority in allotments. Therefore, less profitable projects will also find a chance to get implemented. Usury-free *Qard-ul-Hassana* loans have lower risk than the lending in the interest-based system.

2.2 Loan Remission

One of the ethical issues of *Qard-ul-Hassana* is that if the debtor could not repay the loan, he should be given time. Remission of the loan is considered a noble feat. In verses related to usury, Holy Qur'an states:

وَإِنْ كَانَ ذُو عُسْرَةٍ فَنَظِرَةٌ إِلَى مَيْسَرَةٍ وَأَنْ تَصَدَّقُوا خَيْرٌ لَكُمْ إِنْ كُنْتُمْ تَعْلَمُونَ (البقره: 280)

> If any debtor suffers hardship, them postpone [repaying] it until conditions become easier [for him]; while if you treat it as an act of charity, it would be better for you, if you only knew! (Al-Baqara: 280)

This Qur'anic verse reiterates that while postponing repayment for incapable debtors is necessary, the remission of a loan is considered an act of charity. Moreover, according

2 See *VasayelAl-Shia*; *Ketab-ul-Qard*, Part 6; Vol. 12; p. 87.

to *Al-Toba*: 60,[3] a part of *Zakat* can be utilized to repay the loans of insolvent debtors. Therefore, in case the debtors are not able to repay their loans, lenders can regard the amount as their *Zakat*.

2.3 Moderateness in Financing the Needy

In describing true believers, Holy Qur'an states:

وَالَّذِينَ إِذَا أَنفَقُوا لَمْ يُسْرِفُوا وَلَمْ يَقْتُرُوا وَكَانَ بَيْنَ ذَلِكَ قَوَامًا (الفرقان: 67)

> *Who when they spend, give neither too lavishly nor yet hold back, and keep to a happy medium.* (*Al-Forqan*: 67)

Lavishness, even in giving away and helping others is not permissible. God's distinct subordinates spend neither extravagantly nor parsimoniously. Moderateness in worshiping is appraised, and a balanced plan is necessary. Benevolence has also its limits and charitableness must be stable and consistent.

3 Ethics of Investment

Saving and investment were of great importance in the economic conduct of religious leaders. Considering the vastness of *Waqf* (endowments) and the copiousness of its products may help in comprehending the prominence of such investments. No doubt, accumulation of such colossal amounts of capital was not possible without apprehension of saving and investment. It can thus be said that a considerable portion of the earnings and amenities has been directed towards investment. Another way to apprehend the efforts spent in investment is to compare the income and expenditures of the religious leaders. Efforts towards enhancing the income level on the one hand, and frugality and thrift on the other, point to their focusing on investment.

Another fact is that Muslims are obliged to utilize their amenities and capabilities in making lands habitable. If the society needs employment but investment is not profitable and just covers the costs, the financiers do not withhold their investments for the benefit of all. Such act is very similar to lending money to the needy without expecting a share in the profit (*Qard-ul-Hassana*). However, it differs in that the financier is also among the users of the investment benefits. A farmer who cultivates his own land will not stop his work because his earnings just cover the costs incurred.

---

3 Charity is [meant] only for the poor, the needy, those working at [collecting and distributing] it, those [possible converts] whose hearts are being reconciled [to yours], for freeing captives and debtors, in [striving along] God's path, and for the wayfarer, as a duty imposed by God. God is Aware, Wise. (*Al-Toba*: *60*)

This holds even if nothing remains as the profit on his investment in the land. Since *Zakat* on property merely includes the accounting costs and not the opportunity costs, is does not include the wages of a person working on his own land. As a result, the profitability of a project in excess of the accounting costs and/or the opportunity costs are not taken into consideration.

In addition to the legal and real limitations imposed on investments, a faithful religious investor also observes ethical issues of Islamic economics. These may develop in relation to the Almighty, society, or nature. Since stagnation of capital is disadvantageous, personal wealth will flow and massive investments will be made. Presence of faith, employment benefits, benevolent incentives and desirability of investment activity will all help in directing the capitals towards all sorts of projects, even those with very low returns. Extension of investment will increase the production level which in turn will lead to cost reduction and more rational distribution of income.

The ethical issues of investment are as follows:

3.1 Desirability of Labor and Profit Earning Before God, and the Necessity of Utilization of Assets

In view of religion, utilization of assets and earning income is a commendable deed. It satisfies God and is considered a form of worship. According to religious scripts, *Halal* (licit) economic activity is inherently desirable. On the one hand, laboring provides income, livelihood, dignity and independence, and on the other hand it is commendable and is greatly insisted upon by the religion. *Halal* economic activity is admirable and the faithful must never abandon it, even if their income is more than that they need. The religion does not limit the extent of the labor, but asks everyone to work harder and earn more. It also shows the right ways to spend income. The faithful are urged to earn more in order to enhance their living standards, improve their livelihood, and prosper. They must engage in charitable deeds, endow the deprived, and help the mendicants. Beneficence is recommended repeatedly in Holy Qur'an.[4] The faithful believe in God and accordingly engage in good deeds. Any deed recommended by religion is benevolent. Worships such as prayers, donations, Haj pilgrimage etc. are also among good deeds, but benevolence is not limited to them. It includes craving for *Halal* earning. According to *Hadith*,[5] "*Halal earning is the greatest worship.*" This is also comprehended from the *Hadith*'s that follow:

4 E.g. *Al-Baqara*: 25, 62, 82 and 277; *Al-Maeda*: 9, 69 and 93.
5 *Ma'āni Al-Akhbar*; p. 262.

1. Imam Baqer used to go to the suburbs of Medina and engage in agricultural work in very hot weather. A man asked him: "Are you after worldly earning in this weather condition? What if God takes away your life?" Holy Imam replied:[6]

   لو جاءنی الموت و انا علی هذه الحال جاءَنی و انا في طاعة الله عز و جل اكفّ بها نفسی و عيالی عنك و عن الناس

   "If I die under this condition, I will die while worshiping God, because I am trying to make myself and my family free from other's obligation."

2. Imam Sadeq gave 1,700 dinars to one of his disciples and ordered him:[7]

   اتّجر بها ثم قال: اما انّه ليس لی رغبة في ربحها و ان كان الربح مرغوباً فيه و لكنی اجببت ان يرانی الله جلّ و عزّ متعرضاً لفوائده

   "Do business with this asset; I am not rejoiced by the secular returns of this business, though making profit is the main incentive for any business; but I would like to benefit from its spiritual returns from God."

The disciple made a profit of 100 dinars. Imam told him to add it to the capital.

3. Ima m Sadeq said:[8]

   انّی لا عمل في بعض ضياعی حتی اعرق و انّ لی من يكفينی ليعلم الله عزّوجلّ انی اطلب الرزق الحلال

   "I work hard on my own land so as I perspire, although there are people who can do the job for me. My aim is that God will see me in earning Halal livelihood."

4. Imam Sadeq said:[9]

   ما يُخْلِفُ الرَّجُلُ بَعْدَهُ شَيْئاً اَشَدُّ عَلَيْهِ مِنَ الْمالِ الصّامِتِ، قالَ: قُلْتُ لَهُ: كَيْفَ يَصْنَعُ بِهِ؟ قالَ: يَجْعَلُهُ في الْحائِطِ وَ الْبُسْتانِ وَ الدّارِ

   "Hardest [worst] thing that may be left from someone is unused and stagnant capital." He was asked that what should be done with it. He replied: "It must be invested in construction of a building, a garden or a house."

5. Imam Sadeq said:[10]

   اِصْلاحُ الْمالِ مِنَ الْايمانِ

   "Rectification of property is a sign of faith."

These are all examples of many anecdotes/apothegms (*Ravayat*) that consider Halal labor as worship and commendable. Although there are economic returns in labor, but it is commended by the Almighty and is desired by the faithful. Labor is of various

6 *Kãfi*; p. 73.
7 *ibid*. pp. 76–77.
8 *ibid*. p. 77.
9 *Vasayel Al-Shia*; *Ketab-ul-Qard*, Part 6; Vol. 12; p. 44.
10 *Kãfi*; Vol. 5; p. 87.

types, and investment in all types of activities, including financial markets has been described in many anecdotes/apothegms as valuable as worship.

Various objectives of laboring are as follows:

1. Being considered as worship, economic activity is even viewed as *Jihad*, if carried out within its limits.
2. Economic activity satisfies the needs, eliminates the requirement to beg from others, and helps the feeling of self-respect and personal worth.
3. It makes the person responsible for his livelihood.
4. Social responsibility of the person requires him to work, even if he is not in need. The faithful must put their efforts to alleviate social shortcomings.Others my benefit from his feats and the person will get the satisfaction from his deeds.
5. Muslims do not only think of saving other people and availing worldly endowments, but strive for existence of all other kinds of creatures. If their deeds result in satisfactory outcomes for animals and sustaining their lives or the nature, it is accounted for them as charity. Holy Prophet said:[11]

   مَا مِنْ مُسْلِمٍ يَغْرِسُ غَرْساً أَوْ يَزْرَعُ زَرْعاً فَيَأْكُلُ مِنْهُ إِنْسَانٌ أَوْ طَيْرٌ أَوْ بَهِيمَةٌ إِلَّا كَانَتْ لَهُ بِهِ صَدَقَه

   "Charity will be written for a Muslim who plants a tree or cultivates a land so that human beings, birds or other animals benefit from it."

6. Rehabilitation of land is one of the main aims of economic activities. The Almighty has ordered human beings to rehabilitate land:[12]

   هُوَ أَنْشَأَكُمْ مِنَ الْأَرْضِ وَاسْتَعْمَرَكُمْ فِيهَا

   "He has produced you from the earth and let you settle down on it."

7. Engaging in economic activity by itself is good for the faithful, even if he, his family, or other creatures do not benefit from it. Holy Prophet (PBUH) said:[13]

   إِنْ قَامَتِ السَّاعَةُ وَ فِی يَدِ أَحَدِكُمُ الْفَسِيلَهُ فَإِنِ اسْتَطَاعَ أَنْ لَا تَقُومَ السَّاعَهُ حَتَّى يَغْرِسَهَا فَلْيَغْرِسْهَا

   "If any of you had a date seedling in his hands and the Judgment Day came, and if you are able toplant it, do not hesitate."

Although Holy Prophet (PBUH) was aware that no one may benefit from such deed, but he considered the benevolence which should never be abandoned.

11 *Mostadrak Al-Vasayel*; Vol. 13; p. 460.
12 *Hūd*; 61 (in part).
13 *Mostadrak Al-Vasayel*; p. 460.

3.2 Beneficial Cooperation and Mutual Collaboration

According to the general principle empathized from Holy Qur'an, the faithful must collaborate in benevolence and moral excellence, and assist one another. Holy Qur'an states:[14]

وَتَعَاوَنُوا عَلَى الْبِرِّ وَالتَّقْوَى

"Co-operate with one another for virtue and heedfulness."

The meaning of this verse points to the importance of collaboration in benevolence, virtue and righteousness. It commends the faithful to cooperate in benevolence. Cooperation and group work is not obligatory and people can work independently; but if they are engaged in collaborative work, the criterion is benevolence and moral excellence.[15] The verse can also be interpreted as recommending cooperation and group work, but voluntary collaboration must also be based on benevolence and moral excellence. Markets are controlled by supply and demand, both of which are necessary ingredients and neither can be omitted. Social works also demand collaboration. Governing countries, defending borders, public services, collecting taxes etc. all demand peoples collaboration. Social systems would not exist without public collaboration. Moreover, carrying out large economic projects without such cooperation is impossible in today's world.

The question is "What if people participate in large projects just to gain profit? Can such collaboration be considered as beneficent and worthy?" Constructing dams will lead to public welfare, and growth and development of the country. To construct a dam, participatory notes may be issued, and people may invest. Although the investors may be after the profits from their capital, but their collaboration is benevolent and virtuous. If a deed is not sinful or illicit, it is altruistic and noble. And if it does not sow enmity, it will lead to consensus and unity of the society.These are all signs of virtue. The growth and development of Islamic states is in need of strong financial markets. Authoritative banks and transparent stock markets are the fundamental elements in economic development of any country. Participation of investors, even for profiteering, will assist in betterment of the society.The investors are all partners of the benevolence and will be rewarded. Buying and selling of the stocks and shares is also looked at similarly. When the aim is benevolence, collaboration is coveted. The only thing is that collaboration, buying and selling of stocks and shares, and investments must not be intended to harm others or devastate their assets.If smaller companies merge together in financial markets, the act should not be aimed at expelling competitors.Otherwise the collaboration is considered monopolistic in which there is

14 *Al-Mā'ede*; 2 (in part).
15 *Al-Anavin*; Vol. 1; p. 564.

no benevolent motive. The regulations must not allow monopolistic mergers that are harmful to the economy.

3.3 Possessing Fraternal and Friendly Intents

According to the Holy Qur'an, the faithful are like brothers and must observe fraternal rights.

إِنَّمَا الْمُؤْمِنُونَ إِخْوَةٌ فَأَصْلِحُوا بَيْنَ أَخَوَيْكُمْ وَاتَّقُوا اللَّهَ لَعَلَّكُمْ تُرْحَمُونَ (الحجرات: 10)

> "Believers merely form a brotherhood, so reconcile your brethren and heed God so that you may find mercy." (Al-Hojorat: 10)

Many Hadiths have been quoted about the fraternal relationship between Muslims. Any Muslim must observe the rights of other Muslims, relieve their difficulties, and be kind to them. He must wish the same as he desires for himself or others as well, and must not harass or disoblige others. Helping and supporting Muslim brethren is more valued than non-obligatory fasting and seclusion.[16] Every market player aspires for the profit of all and does not find any conflict of interest between his gains and that of others'.He does not cause economic trouble and harassment for others in order to make himself a profit or economic gain.He does not look for his own gain in others' losses. Although there exists competition within the markets, but it is for beneficence, enhancement of market environment, and offering of improved goods and services. Development of such sacred spirits will no doubt reduce conflicts and struggles in the market environment. One can make money and gain profit in a truthful and legitimate manner, and achieve economic prosperity.

3.4 Avoiding Deceits and Avowing for Testifying the Quality of Goods

Many anecdotes/apothegms (*Ravayat*) imply the impropriety of buying and selling in obscurity and consider concealing the defect of the product as a kind of betrayal of Muslims. It is believed that cheating in trade will entail divine torment. These anecdotes/apothegms point to the importance of veracity and honesty in trading and avoiding avowal to the Almighty. They assert on desirability of buying and selling proper products. There must be complete information available about the product, so that no loss occurs on the part of the customer for the lack of it.

16 See *Al-Hayat*; Vol. 5; pp. 99–106.

3.5 Contribution to Profit and Loss

People who cannot work with their own capital may participate in the economy with the capital of others. Trading, agriculture and the like can be carried out in participation of the financier and the laborer. In such instances, the costs of managing and the opportunity costs of the capital are not considered in overall costs of the project. That is because both parties benefit from the profits of the project and divide it according to a prior agreement. The criteria of the agreement are based on the conditions of the society and the parties. Depending on the bargaining power of the parties as well as their requirements, their shares of the profit is decided. If the expected profit is nil, participation will not be realized due to the fact that the laborer must receive his wage from the profit. Unless the laborer is ready to work for free, and the financier does not expect any profits, which are possible only under exceptional circumstances, the expected profit must at least suffice the wage of the workforce. A financier, who is able to buy and sell merchandize in markets at credit, must have a share of the profit equal to the interest rate. Excepting cases where the financier is willing to help others altruistically, his expected share of the profit must be sufficient to cover his minimum livelihood expenses. Under assurance conditions, there is no difference between labor and capital opportunity costs and paying the share of profit. In any case, participatory projects must provide a minimum profit enough to compensate for the efforts of both the laborer as well as the financier.

In such arrangements, profit is nothing but the wage paid to the laborer and the participation share of the capital. As stated before, the financier owns the capital, and because his capital is involved in the economic activity, gets his share of the profit. The laborer is not involved in financing, but is responsible for the loss of capital, if any. Therefore both parties are considered owners of the capital and are thought of as one and the same person who has invested his own capital. The share of the profit, however, must be bargained between the parties. Although this deal is similar to that between an investor and a borrower, but the financier is also involved in the project. Therefore, he is also considered as a partner. The case is similar to that when a number of people have put their capitals together to finance a project. Under the given circumstances each party might have bargained some conditions in proportion to his share of capital. Therefore, if the financier is also involved in the production activity, then both parties who are engaged in *Mudharaba*, *Musaqat* and *Muzara'a* contract agreements will be considered as investors. This point has been neglected till date.

There are numerous types of agreements for transactions and the contracts can be arranged according to the criteria of the partners. Either both parties contribute to profit and loss, or one of them alone bears the losses. Participatory contracts are such that profit and loss are shared by both sides. If the economy enters recession, both will bear its effects.And when the boom comes, the benefits accrue to both parties. In dividing the profit between the financier and the laborer, each side tries to determine his share of the profit reasonably without distressing the other.

3.6 Ease of Transaction

The anecdotes/apothegms (*Ravayat*) indicate that the Holy Prophet counseled easy and simple transactions. He has been quoted saying:[17]

إِنَّ اللَّهَ يُحِبُّ الْعَبْدَ أَنْ يَكُونَ سَهْلَ الْبَيْعِ وَسَهْلَ الشِّرَاءِ وَسَهْلَ الْقَضَاءِ وَسَهْلَ الِاقْتِضَاءِ

> "God adores a person who sells easily, buys easily, pays back his debt easily, and asks for his dues easily."

Firstly, trustfulness must govern the market environment, and secondly cumbersome regulations must be waived. While exactitude and vigilance are essential, excessive bargaining must not cause the waste of time and the neglect of more important matters. On the one hand, Holy Qur'an states that liabilities should be clearly inscribed in the presence of witnesses so as to prevent the impingement of anyone's rights. Even the longest verse of Holy Qur'an[18] has been assigned to this, elaborating the details for protection of assets e.g. not delegating to ignorant people and not trusting uncommitted and guilty people.[19] On the other hand, however, people are called upon to carry out transactions easily.Lest the spirit of greed and voracity overcomesthe person so as to forget the objective of life. One should not be deceived, but must not be annoyed about others' gaining. This will lead to the conclusion that the regulations of the financial markets must be watchful of people's assets, as well as be straightforward and smooth not to waste people's time.

3.7 Adhering to Worship Time

A number of *Hadith*s have been quoted about not intermingling the trading time with that of worshiping, and that a separate time other than that of worshiping must be assigned to business; Verse 37 of Al-Noor has been interpreted as follows:[20]

رِجَالٌ لَا تُلْهِيهِمْ تِجَارَةٌ وَلَا بَيْعٌ عَنْ ذِكْرِ اللَّهِ وَإِقَامِ الصَّلَاةِ وَإِيتَاءِ الزَّكَاةِ يَخَافُونَ يَوْمًا تَتَقَلَّبُ فِيهِ الْقُلُوبُ وَالْأَبْصَارُ

> By men whom neither business nor trading distracts from the remembrance of God, keeping up prayer, and paying Zakat; they fear a day when their hearts and eyesight will feel upset.

So people who are not diverted by worldly matters and dealing from thinking of the Almighty, prayers and *Zakat*, would leave their businesses at the time of worshiping.[21]

---

17 *Vasayel Al-Shia*; Vol. 12; p. 332.

18 *Al-Baqara*: 282.

19 *Al-Nesa*: 5; *Al-Hayat*; Vol. 6; pp. 198–208.

20 *Al-Noor*: 37.

21 *Vasayel Al-Shia*; Vol. 12; pp. 8 and 297.

In another instance it has been mentioned "Not to neglect prayers and recalling the Almighty at the time of trading."[22]

From all these anecdotes/apothegms (*Ravayat*) it can be concluded that in spite of the fact that Islam considers economic activity as a religious duty and mentions many rewards for it, but does not expect a society to wholly sacrifice spiritual needs for economic ones. It is appropriate to regulate the working time of markets (including the financial market) in harmony with the religious rituals and reserve a special place (i.e. a mosque) for praying and other religious orders within the markets.

3.8 Teaching Market Rules

In an Islamic economy, entering the market requires not only economic and financial expertise but also ethical/religious instruction. Such knowledge is necessary for everyone in order to distinguish between licit (*Halal*) and illicit (*Haram*), lest they may enter doubtful or illicit transactions, or even get involved in usury.[23] Imam Ali stated:[24]

اَلفِقه ثُمَّ المَتجَرُ

"First learn jurisprudence and then engage in business."

Financial markets which are involved in trading securities, foreign exchange and gold are in great need of learning usury guidelines. Thus license for trading in such markets should require passing of the appropriate training courses.

3.9 Reduced Mediation

Excessive mediation will lead to more costs and higher prices for goods and services. In the past, people used to purchase merchandise from dealers' caravans on the suburbs of cities and sell them in the city markets (تَلَقّی رُکبان). He Holy Prophet strongly forbade such acts. His Holiness also forbade the selling of alien goods by residents (لا یَبیعُ حاضِرٌ لِبادٍ), adding that "allow people to get their livelihood from one another" (دَعوا اَلنّاسَ یَرزُقُ اَللّهُ بَعضَهُم مِن بَعضٍ).[25] Extreme mediation will result in higher prices and interfering in market trends, thus destabilizing the environments. Consequently, reduced mediation is a necessary component among the ethics and moralities of trading any merchandise in the markets, including financial markets.

22 *ibid.* pp. 303–305.
23 *ibid.* p. 283.
24 *ibid.* p. 282.
25 *Vasayel Al-Shia*; Vol. 12; pp. 326–328.

3.10 Informing the Other Party

If there is any defect (either apparent or imperceptible) in the merchandize that the faithful investor trades, it is appropriate that he inform the other party. Understandably, such acknowledgments are signs of perfection of benevolence and integration of faith. It points to the fact that no losses are acceptable on the part of the opposite party due to ignorance.

3.11 Avoiding Interference in Others' Transactions with the Purpose of Cancelling the Deal or Supporting One Party

The believers must not interfere in the transactions of his Muslim brethren. Repugnance and illegitimacy of such an act becomes obvious when a third party intrudes in a deal that has been agreed upon mutually between two others, and revokes it.

3.12 Proportionality in Duration of Market Attendance

Islam addresses all aspects of life and aims to progress human beings in every facet. It views both the temporal and spiritual worlds and provides appropriate plans for them. A faithful person would proportionally divide his time between various activities necessary for his livelihood. Numerous sayings have been quoted in this regard, a few of them are mentioned in the following.

Imam Ali stated:[26]

لِلْمُؤْمِنِ ثَلَاثُ سَاعَاتٍ فَسَاعَةٌ يُنَاجِي فِيهَا رَبَّهُ وَ سَاعَةٌ يَرُمُّ مَعَاشَهُ وَ سَاعَةٌ يُخَلِّی بَيْنَ نَفْسِهِ وَ بَيْنَ لَذَّتِهَا فِيمَا يَحِلُّ وَ يَجْمُلُ وَ لَيْسَ لِلْعَاقِلِ
أَنْ يَكُونَ شَاخِصاً إِلَّا فِی ثَلَاثٍ مَرَمَّةٍ لِمَعَاشٍ أَوْ خُطْوَةٍ فِی مَعَادٍ أَوْ لَذَّةٍ فِی غَيْرِ مُحَرَّمٍ

> "The faithful has three time periods in his life: a period in which he worships the Almighty; a period when he engages in sustenance of his life; and, a period in which he licitly and entertainingly vivifies. It is worth for the thoughtful to follow only three matters: ordering and regulating his living; pursuing afterlife and resurrection; or, relishing legitimate deeds."

In order to balance between the various affairs of life, the faithful spends some of his daily timeearning money and providing for his livelihoodthrough labor and effort. The amount of work must suffice to alleviate his needs. Another part of his time is passed on worshiping, spiritual excellence and communicating with the Almighty. Paying attention to the desires of life constitutes a third part, such as recreation The balance in the behavior of the faithful will thus be worshiping, working and enjoying, while avoiding illicit deeds.

---

26 *Nahj Al-Balaqa*; Hekmat390; p. 432.

A Hadith has been quoted from Imam Kazem with a similar connotation:[27]

اِجْتَهِدُوا فِي أَنْ يَكُونَ زَمَانُكُمْ أَرْبَعَ سَاعَاتٍ سَاعَةٌ لِمُنَاجَاةِ اَللَّهِ وَ سَاعَةٌ لِأَمْرِ اَلْمَعَاشِ وَ سَاعَةٌ لِمُعَاشَرَةِ اَلْإِخْوَانِ وَ اَلثِّقَاتِ اَلَّذِينَ يُعَرِّفُونَكُمْ عُيُوبَكُمْ وَ يُخْلِصُونَ لَكُمْ فِي اَلْبَاطِنِ وَ سَاعَةٌ تَخْلُونَ فِيهَا لِلَذَّاتِكُمْ فِي غَيْرِ مُحَرَّمٍ وَ بِهَذِهِ اَلسَّاعَةِ تَقْدِرُونَ عَلَى اَلثَّلاَثِ سَاعَاتٍ لاَ تُحَدِّثُوا أَنْفُسَكُمْ بِفَقْرٍ وَ لاَ بِطُولِ عُمُرٍ فَإِنَّهُ مَنْ حَدَّثَ نَفْسَهُ بِالْفَقْرِ بَخِلَ وَ مَنْ حَدَّثَهَا بِطُولِ اَلْعُمُرِ يَحْرِصُ اِجْعَلُوا لِأَنْفُسِكُمْ حَظّاً مِنَ اَلدُّنْيَا بِإِعْطَائِهَا مَا تَشْتَهِي مِنَ اَلْحَلاَلِ وَ مَا لاَ يَثْلِمُ اَلْمُرُوَّةَ وَ مَا لاَ سَرَفَ فِيهِ وَ اِسْتَعِينُوا بِذَلِكَ عَلَى أُمُورِ اَلدِّينِ فَإِنَّهُ رُوِيَ لَيْسَ مِنَّا مَنْ تَرَكَ دُنْيَاهُ لِدِينِهِ أَوْ تَرَكَ دِينَهُ لِدُنْيَاهُ

"Try to divide your time into four parts: a period of worshiping the Almighty, a period for laboring and meeting livelihood, a period for associating with Muslim brethren and trusted people,who sincerely point your weaknesses, and a period for availing of the licit (Halal) pleasures that will recreate you and allows you to attend to other affairs (worshiping, work and association). Avail of the pleasures of the world and supply the licit (Halal) sensual demands to a degree that does not harm your manhood (adulthood) and is not wasted or in excess. This way you will consolidate your religious deeds, because it has been quoted from my ancestors that 'he, who neglects the world for the religion, or the religion for the world, is not a believer (aide or supporter) of Ahl al-Bayt.'"

According to this *Hadith,* time can be divided into four different portions which, in addition to prayer, labor and leisure, includes another allocation for social relationships with friends. It insists that if a part of daily time is not spent on licit (*Halal*) pleasure, the person would not be able to attend to other affairs such as worshiping and labor. Division of time into three or four portions is a reflection of important deeds which human beings must perform in their daily lives. Durations of the portions need not be equal, because it may vary according to the season of the year, age of the individual and other specific conditions. For example, the faithful will spend more time praying in the month of *Ramadan* and less time for leisure; or in winters his relaxing time is more as compared to summers. Importance lies in attending all aspects of life; not only praying and depending on others for livelihood, or not only working and accumulating wealth so as to alienate with spirituality and the aims of creation. He must combine the world and the afterlife or else will not be considered among the true disciples of the Holy Prophet.

There are other anecdotes/apothegms (*Ravayat*) suggesting that if an individual does not sleep and keeps working throughout the night, his business is illicit (*Haram*). Two *Hadith*s have been quoted from Imam Sadeq:

مَنْ بَاتَ سَاهِراً فِی كَسْبٍ وَ لَمْ يُعْطِ الْعَيْنَ حَظَّهَا مِنَ النَّوْمِ فَكَسْبُهُ ذَلِكَ حَرَامٌ

"The business of an individual who keeps awake through the night to earn livelihood, and does not relax his eyes, is illicit (*Haram*)."[28]

27 *TohfaUl-Oqul*; p. 409.
28 *Kãfi*; Vol. 5; p. 127.

الصنّاع إذا سهروا اللّيل كله فهُوَ سحت

"If manufacturers keep awake the whole night, their business is illicit (*Haram*)."[29]

In jurisprudential and anecdotal/apothegm texts,[30] such *Hadith* have been interpreted as providing guidance. They suggest that people should pay attention to their health and not deprive themselves of sleep in the pursuit of business. The word "illicit" has been used in some anecdotes/apothegms (*Ravayat*) to emphasize a hygienic mandate or to prevent harm to the body. Although the meaning is not the jurisprudential illicitness, but "avoidance" or "advice/guidance" is destined. There are numerous *Hadith*[31] which encouragethe faithful "to act moderately in craving for daily sustenance; to avoid rapacity in secular needs; neither be fallible nor greedy" point to the maintaining balance in earning livelihood. An individual who only thinks about making profit will become a materialist and will not spend his acquired possessions in the right way; he will be hooked to worldly concerns and will lose his spiritual life.

3.13 Transactions with Inattentive Individuals

One of the ethics of trading is refusal to transact with stingy and neglectful people. Moreover, investing in suspicious/problematic shares or bonds is not considered ethical.

3.14 Assisting the State

Under conditions where the main requirements of society are not properly supplied or when higher prices of essential commodities create difficulty for the general public, it is benevolent for investors to enter production of such supplies. This, however, may be less profitable than producing other commodities. When the state is in dire need of economic *Jihad* and sacrifice, and its foundations require to be reinforced, the congruence of the financiers with the national objectives constitutes a satisfactory ethical principle.

29 *ibid.*

30 *VasayelAl-Shia*; Vol. 12; p. 118; and, *Jawaher Al-Kalam fi Sharh-e Sharaye-el Islam*; Vol. 22; p. 470.

31 *VasāyelAl-Shia*; Vol. 12; p. 30.

3.15 Not Undervaluing Others' Assets (Preserving the Real Value of Commodities and Services)

Among the basic principles of Islamic markets is lack/absence of *Bakhs*.It literally means decrease, reduce or diminish. An imperfection in quantity or quality, or a defect of the merchandize is also called *Bakhs*.[32] The Almighty quotes from Prophet Shu'aib to his clan:

وَيَا قَوْمِ أَوْفُوا الْمِكْيَالَ وَالْمِيزَانَ بِالْقِسْطِ وَلَا تَبْخَسُوا النَّاسَ أَشْيَاءَهُمْ وَلَا تَعْثَوْا فِي الْأَرْضِ مُفْسِدِينَ (هود: 85)

> And, O my people! Give full measure and weight with all fairness, and do not cheat men of their belongings, nor cause havoc on earth as mischief makers do. (*Hūd*: 85)

Remaining loyal to delivering the real amount of the merchandize and not reducing it will reform the society, while exploitative decrement in amount or value will subvert the society. One of the major types of corruption is short-weighing and betrayal in measuring. This verse of Holy Qur'an points to consequences of short-weighing practices:

وَيْلٌ لِلْمُطَفِّفِينَ (1) الَّذِينَ إِذَا اكْتَالُوا عَلَى النَّاسِ يَسْتَوْفُونَ (2) وَإِذَا كَالُوهُمْ أَوْ وَزَنُوهُمْ يُخْسِرُونَ (3) (المطففين: 1–3)

> It will be too bad for *tricksters*; who insist on receiving everything when they have people measure something out for them; yet whenever they measure or weigh things for others, they give (them) less than their due. (Al-Mottafeffin: 1–3)

A short-weigher receives the price of the commodity he sells, but delivers a lesser quantity. In fact, he sells his merchandize at a higher price by cheating the buyer. Pricing in markets must be proportionate with the reality of the merchandize and *Bakhs* means devaluing commodities or prices. In fact *Bakhs* is a type of illegitimate acquisition of profit/wealth (*AklBil-Batil*) without engaging in any economic activity. It is fraudulence in transactions and inflicting damage to others. *Bakhs* contradicts equity and justice and thus will lead to corruption in transactions and will subvert the economic environment. If Islamic laws and regulations govern the market environment and transactions are realized within the framework of *Sharia*, it will lead to factual equity and truthful justice.

32 *Qamus-e Qur'an*; Vol. 1; p. 170.

3.16 Necessity of Exploiting Wealth and Avoiding Stagnation (*Kanz*)

Holy Qur'an states:

يَا أَيُّهَا الَّذِينَ آمَنُوا إِنَّ كَثِيرًا مِنَ الْأَحْبَارِ وَالرُّهْبَانِ لَيَأْكُلُونَ أَمْوَالَ النَّاسِ بِالْبَاطِلِ وَيَصُدُّونَ عَنْ سَبِيلِ اللَّهِ وَالَّذِينَ يَكْنِزُونَ الذَّهَبَ وَالْفِضَّةَ وَلَا يُنْفِقُونَهَا فِي سَبِيلِ اللَّهِ فَبَشِّرْهُمْ بِعَذَابٍ أَلِيمٍ (التوبه: 34)

> O you who believe! Most surely many of the (Jewish) scholars and (Christian) monks do consume people's wealth to no good purpose, and turn (them) from God's path. Announce painful torment to those who hoard gold and silver and do not spend them for God's sake. (Al-Toba: 34)

Kanz literally means a treasure trove. It refers to abundant wealth, including cash, gold and silver, which has remained unproductive or idle. *Infaq*is translated as spending and consuming wealth. The term "God's Path" (سَبِيلِ اللَّه) has been interpreted in two different contexts in various verses and Hadith. One context refers to processes where no personal interest is involved, and are only aimed at obeying the commands of Almighty. For example, *Jihad* against enemies of God, payment of *Zakat*, and all other paths that will lead to satisfaction of the Almighty. *Kanz* consists of the following:

1. Property that has been accumulated but its taxes, *Zakat* and *Khums* have not been paid;
2. Assets that have not been utilized for helping the needy; and,
3. Cash that has been set aside from the usual trend of capital.

The greater the monetary extent of an economy, the greater would be the significance of *Kanz*, i.e. when money is accumulated and enters the market all of a sudden, it leads to devastating economic impacts. This is true even if it comprises the domestic currency that has been accumulated idly over the years. Islam does not discuss the amount of wealth but is particular about its exploitation. If assets are plentiful, they must be exploited for the needs of the society. Therefore, capital ought to be exploited in economic cycle. *Zakat* is a tax that is levied on stagnant capital. It provides an incentive for non-stagnancy of wealth and its entrance into productive works, bringing about an economic boom. Fakhr-Razi in *Al-Tafsir Al-Kabir* (Vol. 16, p. 41), Tabarsi in *Majma' Ul-Bayan* (Vol. 5, p. 41), Rashid Reza in *Tafsir Al-Minar* (Vol. 10, p. 395),AllameTabataba'ei in *Tafsir Al-Mizan* (Vol. 9, p. 247) and many other scholars agree about the illegitimacy of *Kanz*on the basis of the above-mentioned verse of Holy Qur'an. Moreover, the illegitimacy of *Kanz* in relation to wealth and assets has been reiterated in many *Hadith*. Therefore the provisions for illicitness of Kanz, in spite of all other evidence, can be interpreted as illicitness of accumulation of wealth, and its diversion from the trend of economic affairs.

3.17 Entrusting Property to Proficient Experts

Holy Qur'an forbids entrusting of the property into the hands of feeble-minded individuals (unaware and ignorant about what is assigned to him) and states:

وَلَا تُؤْتُوا السُّفَهَاءَ أَمْوَالَكُمُ الَّتِي جَعَلَ اللَّهُ لَكُمْ قِيَامًا وَارْزُقُوهُمْ فِيهَا وَاكْسُوهُمْ وَقُولُوا لَهُمْ قَوْلًا مَعْرُوفًا (النساء: 5)

> And do not give the feeble-mined your property which God has granted you for (their) support; provide for them out of (the profits of) it, and clothe them and address them decently. (Al-Nesa: 5)

Property (wealth) is important to the wellbeing of society and so has to be protected. Personal and public properties should not be entrusted to unaware individuals, because irresponsibility of such persons and their inability to properly utilize the assets a reconsidered a betrayal of society. An ignorant person cannot look after his own property. Capital belonging to such individuals (like those of others) must not remain stagnant and has to be exploited in the economic cycle, so as to provide their livelihood.

4 Conclusion

An Islamic economy creates greater efficiency than a traditional economy by ensuring that the financial needs of individuals coincide with the greater needs of society. By focusing on not just profits but also on increasing the transparency of transactions, preserving the rights of individuals, improving the condition of the needy, and preventing excessively risky activities, an Islamic economy leads to more effective investment and finance.

References

Holy Qur'an; *translated by* T.B. Irving (Al-Haj Ta'lim Ali); Suhrawardi Research and Publication Center, Tehran-Iran; 2003.

Hor Al-Ameli, Al-Sheikh Mohammad Bin Al-Hassan; *Vasayel Al-Shia*; 20 Vols.; *edited/correctedby* Abdol Rahim Al-Rabani Al-Shirazi; Maktabe Al-Islamiye; 1403 LH.

Harrani, Abu Mohammad Al-Hassan Bin Ali Bin Al-Hossein Bin Sho'ba; *TohfUl-OqulAn Al-ul-Rasul*; *edited/corrected by* Ali Akbar Al-Qaffari; Second Edition; Qum; Islamic Publication Institute; 1363 SH.

Hosseini, Seyyed Reza; *Optimal Consumption Pattern within the Framework of Islamic Income Allocation Model*; Islamic Economy; No. 34; Summer 1388 SH.

Hakimi, Mohammad Reza, Al-Hakimi, Mohammad, Al-Hakimi; *Al-Hayat*; 6 Vols.; First Edition; Islamic Culture Publication Office-Tehran; 1406 LH.

Rashid Reza, Seyyed Mohammad; *Tafsir Al-Minar*; Dar-ul-Ma'rafa Al-Taba'ava Al-Nashr; Second Edition; Beirut; No Date.

Razi, Al-Sharif Abu Al-Hassan Mohammad; *Nahj Al-Balaqa*; translated by Seyyed Jafar Shahidi; Islamic Evolution Teaching Publications; Tehran; 1374 SH.

Saduq, Abu Jafar Mohammad Bin Ali; *Ma'ani Al-Akhbar*; *edited/corrected by* Ali Akbar Al-Qaffari; Islamic Publication; Qum; 366 p.; 1361 SH.

Tabataba'ei, Al-Seyyed Mohammad Hossein; *Al-Mizan fi Tafsir Al-Qur'an*; 20 Vols.; Second Edition; Al-A'lami Al-Matbu'at Institute; Beirut; 1394 LH.

Tabarsi, Abu Nasr Al-Hassan Bin Al-Fazl; *Makarem Al-Akhlaq, TaqiqAla Al-e Jafar*; 2 Vol.; First Edition; Islamic Publication; Qum 1414 LH.

Tabarsi, Abu Ali, Al-Fazl Bin Hassan; *Majma' Ul-Bayan*; 5 Vol. (10 Sections); Islami-ye Publishers; 1380 LH.

Fakhr Raazi; *Al-Tafsir Al-Kabir*; Dar Al-Hayat Al-Terath Al-Arabi; Beirut; No Date.

Qarshi, Ali Akbar; *Qamus-e Qur'an*; Dar Al-KitabIslamiye; First Edition; 1372 SH.

Qarzavi, Yusef; *Dor Al-QayyemVaAkhlaq fi Al-Eqtesad Al-Islami*; First Edition; Al-Resala Institute; Beirut; 1417 LH.

Koleini, Abu Jafar Mohammad Bin Al-Yaqub; *Al-Kafi*; *edited/corrected by* Ali Akbar Al-Qaffari; 8 Vols.; Dar Al-KitabIslamiye; Tehran; 1362 SH.

Maraqi, Al-Seyyed Mir Abd Al-Fattah Al-Hosseini; *Al-Anavin*; First Edition; Islamic Publication Institute; Qum; 1418 LH.

Najafi, Mohammad Hassan; *Jawahir Al-Kalam fi SharhShara'e Al-Islam*; 43 Vols.; Dar Al-KitabIslamiye; Tehran; 1365 SH.

Nouri, Mirza Hassan; *Mostadrak Al-VasayelVaMostanbat Al-Masa'el*; 18 Vol. First Edition; Al Al-Bayt (PBUT) L-Ehya Al-ItrathInstitute; Qum; 1408 LH.

Abdul Khaleq Karimi

Chapter 11: Ethical Model of Business Ethics: Qur'an's View

1 Concepts and Research Literature

A "model" refers to a systematic set of concepts, principles, and laws that refer to a logical structure for explaining and interpreting a system of created beings, phenomena, methods, processes, theories and observations. (Mir Mo'izzi 2010). A model is designed to answer "where" and "how" questions. Therefore, the function of a model is of normative type as it present, as accurately as possible, a picture the system that, should exist. It is expected that any model is based on a theory which is itself based on a specific worldview (Salimifar 2010). On this basis, a model, and the theory associated with it, differ from what is understood in the empirical sciences; a model is not the same thing as an "example."

"Akhlaq" (ethics), in Arabic, is the plural of "Khulq" meaning a stable natural disposition of human personality (Dehkhoda Vol 1, p. 1537) These dispositions are categorized as "good" and "bad" or "virtue" and "vice" traits. Akhlaq, or ethics, is the science that teaches how to cure the human psyche afflicted by "bad" traits and how to convert these into being adorned with "good" traits. It is the science of how to live (including how to behave), how to be (including traits of character), and what to be(including formation of the human nature), (Naraghi: c. 1 p. 32). It responds to the question of how should personality traits and behavior be formed to acquire a reality and identity of value and sanctity (Mir Mo'izzi.2012).

From the perspective of Allamah Mohammad Taghi Jafari, ethics is the flourishing of the human personality on the path of becoming a rational being According to Nyashirazi, ethics is a system of values and dos and don'ts that distinguishes between the "good" and "bad" in individual or organizational behavior (Niashirazy 2016). Relying on ethics, managers are able to decide "right" form "wrong" and "good" from "bad". According to Ibrahiminejad, business ethics is part of applied ethics that studies spiritual, ethical principles and problems in the business environment (Ibrahiminejad, 2015) and determines ways and means of recognizing ethical responsibilities and their actualization in specific areas of life (Nyashirazi 2015).

The term "business ethics" or "business and economic ethics" has been used in a broad sense and includes the entire economic realm of life. Hence, it deals with decision-making processes of individuals economic agents such as workers and managers as well as economic systems, the global economy and financial organizations (Gastafson 2004). According to some writers (Dadgar 2006), Islamic and conventional business ethics are complementary in that the former can be considered a special case of the latter. Nevertheless, they differ in many respects, including fundamental

https://doi.org/10.1515/9783110593419-011

and value foundations, principles and objectives, and in the ways and means and approaches to ethics (Dadgar 2006).

This is while some seriously deny the applicability of religion-based business ethics and some even question its possibility. One position, in this context, argues that "business ethics is the ethics of a game and is different from religious ethics." (Gustafson 2006). This controversy has largely focused on the question of whether it is possible to relate individual and social ethics? On this basis, we confront the question of whether it is at all possible to provide a religion-based model of business ethics? (Tavakoli 2009).

To answer this question, we have attempted – with a systemic view of the subject as well as the requirements of model building (foundations, objective, components, ways and means and institutions) – to provide some thoughts on the question relying on our most important religious source, the Qur'an, using an analytic-descriptive technique combined with examination of related verses of the Qur'an and sacred narrations.

2 Basic Principles of the Business Ethics Model

The basic intellectual-philosophical foundations are in fact the worldview (Mir Mu'izzi 1999). A worldview represents a way of thinking or conception that a particular school of thought provides to explain the world and being in that world which then becomes the foundation of thought of that school (Motahari 1995, p. 714–715). By essential foundation of the model of business ethics here, we mean the application of relevant aspect of Islamic worldview that provide the basis for the principle components of the model: objectives, incentives, indicators and the ruels governing behavior, all of which are are directly related to and influence one another (Mir Mu'izzi 2012). Accordingly, the main foundation of the model of the ethics of business can be defined as: the collection of teachings that is expressed within the framework of beliefs-ethics in the areas of worldview, theology and anthropology in relation to the ethics of business.

2.1 Theology and Cosmology Underlying Beliefs-ethics Relation

The Creator is defined in the Qur'an as: One and Unique (1:112); Ever living (58:25); All Powerful (11:11); Possessor of Infinite Power (106:2); The Best Provider (72:23); The Only Provider (58:51); He is Kind and Compassionate to His creatures (30:3); He is the closest Entity to humans who responds to their needs and wants of His creatures quickly and positively. Everything is in His Hands including help and disappointment, benefit and loss, giving and refusing. He is the Only Mover in the world and everything and everyone returns to Him. Keeping these attributes allows humans to rely on and trust Him alone since no one else can help or hurt them, cannot hear human prayers, does not have the power to provide for them and assist humans in the difficulties, trials and tribulations of life on the earth (14:35; 76:5; 17:29; 63:6). The Oneness (Tawheed, the Unity) and the Uniqueness of the Creator is the basic foundation of ethics and all other knowledge, therefore all human sciences in Islam must exists based on and around the axis of Tawheed (Javadi Amoli, 2007). All the moral perfections of the soul are based on the foundation of the correct understanding of Tawheed and the central axis of cleansing the self are determined by it (Javadi Amoli 2009, p. 388).

Belief in applied Tawheed has given rise to the idea that the Qur'an's notion of the appointment of humans the Khalifah (agent/trustee) of Allah on earth-who serves to benefit his own kind and other creatures under the direct Will, Desire and plan of their Creator—should be the basis of knowledge of humans who possess spirits, separate from their bodies, with divine potentialities. In this context, after the creation of the first human body, Allah says to the angels: "So, when I have made himand have breathed unto him of My Spirit, fall down in prostration to him" (28–29:15). Many interpreters suggest that this prostration is a sign of the respect for the greatness and sanctity of the Spirit of the Creator (Tabatabaei 1997, p. 154). Therefore, based on the Qur'an (30:30), it is argued that human nature has divine qualities which is the source of all ethical virtues (Mir Mo'izzi 2012), including the virtues of business ethics.

The verses of the Holy Qur'an indicate that the source of moral requirements is the revelation and the Divine legislative will of Allah because He is not only the Creator of the universe, but also alone and without any partner, guides the world. He is the One who legislates and prescribes the rules governing the behavior of individuals and societies. These rules are based on the reality of the world of beings considering fully the benefits and harms of human behavior (Janipur 2015). According to the teachings of Islam, business and trade are productive activities and not one of brokerage that lacks any productive dimension as is undertaken solely for profit making. While work is considered a form of worship and adoration of Allah, the Creator has also directed humans to develop the earth (61:11; 15:67).

2.2 Belief-ethical Teachings Related to Anthropology

In the monotheistic view, humans are created by Allah and are His trustees of all of His blessings on earth (38:17) who are regarded as divine beings in whom the divine has manifested itself; a characteristic that distinguishes between humans and other creatures. That is, knowledge of the Creator has been imprinted on the humans' primordial nature which motivate them to seek and Allah and be consumed by His divinity (Javadi Amoli 2010, p. 150). Humans are two-dimensional creatures: a physical dimension, their bodies, and a non-physical dimension, the spirit which constitute their reality (28–29:15) Moreover, the needs and desires of humans have two dimensions (physical and spiritual) as well; human ability to attain perfection depends on the development of these two dimensions.

To overlook the ideal and spiritual human dimension, as is done in capitalism, pulls down humans, in view of teachings of Islam, from their lofty state intended for them by their Creator to an unworthy state. Some of the characteristics of such a person and symptoms of his behavior are described in the Qur'an: he is niggardly and selfish, always seeking his own benefits at the exoense of others (100:17); ignores his own real and long-term benefits (20–21:75); he loves wealth and possessions (8:100); he constantly seeks immediate gratification, has low threshold for tolerating difficulties, therefore, constantly complains when faced with economic difficulties, but when he becomes economically well off, he becomes niggardly, tightfisted, defiant and haughty (19–21:70; 6–7:96; 10:11).

In contrast, a human can be cultured, cleansed of undesirable characteristics and ethical who is the true khalifah (trustee/agent) of Allah on earth (30:2); worthy of the prostration of angels (33–34:2) possessed of especial dignity and honor (70:17; 13:49) who is then the "desired economic human." According to the Qur'an, such a "desirable economic human being" possesses the following attributes: he coordinates his own benefits with those of other and, if necessary, he give priority to the latter (9:59); he has no strong attachment to wealth and spends it to achieve the satisfaction of Allah (256:2) to help the needy (19:51); he is serene, possesses self-control, he is patient and does not complain when in difficulties (35:22); he is not defiant, haughty, and overjoyed when he becomes rich (11:11); he is a deep thinker and considers his long-term future, therefore, uses his wealth in "sanctified trade" as means of achieving long-term and sustained benefits (29–30:35).

According to this view, man is only a traveler in this world and must prepare himself for the world to come, hence, when examining his happiness, his condition in the world to come must be taken into account as well. Since we have no knowledge of that world, we must resort to revelation. Revelation recognizes as rational the innate tendency of man to enjoy pleasure and avoid pain but extends the scope of pleasure beyond material pleasures. Rationality, from the point of view of Islam, means maximizing the sum total of this worldly and otherworldly pleasures (Mir Mo'izzi 1999) In general, the basis and foundations of ethics to be considered are: causation as the bais for the knowledge of being, Tawheed as the basis of knowledge about the Creator, goal orientation, optimal system as basis for cosmology, authenticity and perfection of spirit, needing, having an objective in life, freedom of choice, human capacity to accept responsibility as basis for knowledge of man, and, finally, self-love as basis for ethics and normative theory (Mir Mo'izzi 2012)

3 The Basic Objectives of the Model of Business Ethics

One of the most effective ideas of Islam is "blending ethical values with economics" which is aimed at providing material welfare Here and human felicity in the Hereafter (Iravani, 2004, p. 91). The goal of trade and business ethics is to improve the ethical quality of decisions and actions at all levels of business (Gastafson 2004). The ultimate goal of an Islamic economic system is to provide the necessary basis for humans to achieve the desired perfection. In order to achieve this goal, a series of "intermediate goals" are introduced that, on the one hand, are considered as incentives for productive activities of the Muslim individual and, on the other hand, an introduction to achieving his/her ultimate goal of divine satisfaction by helping to meet the essential needs of the community, and then, and only then, enjoy a fair profit. Business ethics has a balanced framework with a systemic link with other dimensions of the political economy of Islam. In addition to emphasizing efficiency and other elements of economic progress, and has srious intent to strengthen them, its ultimate goal is to preserve humanity and ethics.(Dadgar 2006)

In other words, the ultimate goal of man in all areas is to attain his eternal felicity which is attainable with intermediate goal of achieving a good life with the attributes of social justice, security, growth and comprehensive advancement in all aspect of human life such that while a person becomes empowered to use natural resources and the Creator's gifts in the best possible way, he is also able to achieve spiritual elevation to practice his belief in the Oneness of Allah swt and to actualize it in his own life and behavior (Mir Mo'izzi 2012). In the perspective of the Qur'an, the purpose of human creation is attainment of all humans to attain the station of being the khalifah (trustee/agent) of Allah on earth (30:2) which is possible only when humans accept and acknowledge Allah as their only Lord and Master in order to develop the capacity of manifesting the attributes of the Creator. The ultimate goal of humans is to draw near to Allah (42:53; 27–30:89) which is imprinted on the "Fitrah" or the primordial nature of mankind (Misbah Yazdi, 2001, p. 86). This goal can be operationalized through performing religious duties, providing for needs and achieving relative wellbeing, helping society achieve independence, self-sufficiency and power of self-defense which are the most important goals of the Muslim individual through work and production (Iravani, 2004)

4 The Principles and Elements of the Model of Business Ethics

The basic principles and components of business ethics expressed in the following two parts:

4.1 Principles and Components of the Model of Business Ethics in Conventional Economics

Principles of ethics can be defined as a set of values principles and ideals (Arens 1991, p. 71). According to Islamic scholars, the business and commercial sector in an Islamic economy, like business in other branches and views of conventional economics, has certain ethical requirements and observations (Dadgar 2006). Accordingly, the following principles include values and characteristics that, for most people, signify ethical behavior in conventional economy:

Table 11.1: Ethics in the conventional economy.

Ethics fundamental	Concept
Honesty	Being honest; candid;, not using trickery or having penchant toward fraud; truthful; not given to exaggerations or platitudes.
Righteousness	Being committed to principles, honorable, self-reliant, brave and courageous, acting on the basis of strong beliefs.
Faithfulness to promises	Being trustworthy; carrying out commitments fully; being faithfull to the terms and conditions of contracts.
Loyalty	Avoiding conflict of interests and power playing; focusing on one's abilities and not accepting positions not commensurate with those abilities; being objective in making professional judgements.
Fairness	Accepting one's mistake openly and pleasantly; using one's beliefs and positions in the right time and under right circumstances; being just and fair; treating everyone equally; practicing tolerance and forbearance in dealing with others; and accepting others' opinions and views.
Empathy	Being compassionate and caring sharing in the efforts of others; spending one's wealth to help others; being always ready to serve others; assisting those who are suffering and in need; and not hurting others.
Respect for and valuing others	Being concerned about the dignity of others; respecting others' rights and their decisions that affect their own lives; being polite; respecting promises; being punctual; and respectfully dressed.
Responsible citizen	Obeying laws and rules; objecting to unjust rules clearly openly and courageously, expressing view and exercising private and public democratic rights responsibly through taking part in elections.
Seeking Excellence	Being and doing the best in all of one's affairs; having self-reliance, being serious and committed in performing personal and professional duties; exerting best effort in completing responsibilities; attaining highest level of skill possible and maintaining it; being well prepared and fully informed.
Accountability (accepting responsibility)	Accepting responsibility and being willing to be accountable for decisions; accepting the consequences of one's actions; follow the prophets and the select humans in behavior in order to protect one's good name and reputation of which one is proud.

Source: Arens, 1991, p. 71.

These principles can then be employed to evaluate the influence of organizations (Sonyol 2006).

4.2 Principles and Components of the Basic Model of Business Ethics in Islamic Economics

From Islamic scholars' point of view, there are eight moral virtues: integrity, fairness, trust, respect, empathy, benevolence and accountability. Of these respect, honesty and fairness are components of business ethics. (Ebrahimi Nezhad 2015)

Also, justice (and fairness); transparency and honesty; mutual trust and respect; purity of intentions; assumption of being accountable to Allah; encouragement of work and competition; attention to expanded personal interests; maintaining a balance between production and consumption; being fully aware of prohibition on interest rate -based activities, briberry, speculation and the waste of resources are considered as ethical and ideological institutions in Islamic business (Dadgar 2006). In one classification of business ethics, Rahimi suggests five principles that should govern any profession: serving others and society; respecting and being committed to one's duty; being honest and trustworthy; and constantly updating one's skills. (Rahimi 2012).

From the point of view of the verses of the Qur'an, the principles and components of business ethics are divided into two categories of positive and negative principles and components.

4.2.1 Principles and Components of the Positive Business Ethics

1. Focus on spirituality: This requires constant remembrance of Allah (swt) and the Day of Judgement during business transaction, and performing ritual prayers on time. As the Qur'an says: "Men whom neither trade nor exchange beguiles them from remembrance of Allh and who establish prayers and pay Zakat who fear a day when hearts and eyes will be turned (in fear)" (Qur'an, 37:24).

2. Earning Halal Income: That is, obtaining income through activities not prohibited by religion. Islam has prohibited accumulating wealth and insists that its followers must base their financial means on "pure Iman and Taqwa" and earn their sustenance through ways and means that is desirable to healthy nature and the intellect while concurrently considered as permissible by Allah (swt). The Qur'an directs humans thus: "Eat of that which Allah has made lawful and good for you, and keep your duty to Allah in Whom you believe" (88:5).

3. Establishing justice: Justice is a very comprehensive doctrine of Islam. According to Shahid Motahari: in the Qur'an, from Tawheed to the concept of Ma'ad (the ultimate return to the origin), from prophethood to imamate and leadership (of Muslim society), and from individual aspirations to social goals, all are based on the axis of justice. Justice in the Qur'an is considered with the same importance as Tawheed, Ma'ad, the objective of prophethood, philosophy of imamate and leadership, and is the standard of personal perfection in individuals and of the health of the society (Motahari, 2000. p 61). According to the Qur'an, the basic purpose of all religions, especially Islam, is the administration of justice: "We verily sent Our messengers with clear proofs, and revealed with them Scripture and the Balance so that mankind may establish Qist (social justice)..." (25:57).

Justice in the field of business ethics is also based on the criteria for giving others their right because, according to one definition of ethics, an ethical model of behavior toward the self an toward others can be derived from the sense of responsibility that one has with respect to one's own and others' rights (Jabbaran 2011). This criterion applies to all relations, including economic, and covers all sectors of production, distribution, trade and consumption.

4. Observance of fairness (Insaf): One of the branches of justice and one of the best, clearest and most precise criteria for the regulation of personal and social relationships is fairness. It requires that if a person's financial capability exceeds his need, he will spend part of it to provide for the maintenance of the needy and the deprived. Therefore, the Holy Qur'an has said: "And those in whose property there is a right for the needy and the deprived" (24 and 25:70).

5. Sacrifice (Ithar) and Benevolence (Ihsan): These two are higher than justice and fairness. Ihsan means to treat others better than we would like to be treated by them and Ithar means to giving others resources we need ourselves. Justice (al-'Adl) and Benvolence (al-Ihsan) are prescribed explicitly by Allah (swt): "Lo! Allah enjoins justice and benevolence..." (90:16). In interpreting this verse, Imam Ali has said that al-'Adl means fairness and al-Ihasn means giving extra beyond what is required behave with us, and to provide ourselves with the means of providing ourselves with the necessary means. Righteousness and Ehsus are God's explicit command: God is right in command of justice and Ehsan (90:16). In the interpretation of the verse, Imam 'Ali, in Nahj al-Bilaghah said: justice means fairness and Ehsan means excess and bounty. (Hurr Amoli, 2008: Vol 16, p. 291).

The Holy Qur'an has considers maldistribution and the emergence of corruption as a rebellion and ungratefulness of human beings (41:30), and among ways to prevent and cure them, it prescribes equality and benevolence (90:16) as well as promoting in the society the culture of being satisfied with reasonable and fair profits, avoiding hoarding, short changing customers (1:83), and engaging in interest-based transactions.

6. Conscientiousness about work: This term means "the tendency to do the right work and job duties without direct supervision" (Kolayni, 1986, Vol. 5, p. 73), signs of which are more and better work, self-control and willingness to accept responsibility. of which the signs, doing more and better, control Internal and responsible. According to Imam 'Ali (as), in Nahj al-Bilaghah, Letter 47, there are several factors contributing to the creation and strengthening of effective work conscience, and which has been emphasized in religious texts, namely, "correcting attitude" or the negation of some of the false and superstitious ideas about the fate of humans and societies (73:28; 67:10; 12:17); "satisfaction with one's work" through the discovery of the spiritual and social value of work) teaching and modeling excellent work ethics (32:43); strengthening sense of responsibility (Koleyni, 1986, p. 127) and others.

7. Work discipline: According to the Qur'an, the universe is a well-organized system and order governed by Allah (164:2; 95–99:6; 20–21:51; 3–4:67) which is perfect and without minutest of defects. It is a system that human beings must move toward the perfect human state in coordination with that ordered system. In Verse 7 of Chapter 55, the Qur'an says: "And He raised the heavens and set the Balance (scale), and immediately follows, in Verse 8 with the imperative: "Do not transgress the Balance (scale) implying that humans are part and parcel of this universe and they too must have system, order and balance. Without rules and balance (scale or equilibrium of values and actions), the universe would not exist. Similarly without a system, order and balance human life would not be sustained (Makarim, 1995. vol. 23, p. 108).

Discipline and time management are among the most important instruments of optimal utilization of resources hence, in addition to emphasizing the need for an ordered system (Nahj al- Bilaghah, Letter 47), the characteristics of discipline in economic activities are also emphasized. Some of these indicators are: "optimal allocation of time" (73:28; 67:10; 12:17); division of labor based on individuals' capabilities and expertise (32:43); respect for moderation in work by avoiding laziness or greed (Koleyni, 1986, p. 34); and respect for moderation with the goal of expressing gratitude for physical and mental health as well as the ability to perform other duties.

8. Perseverance: Among the principles governing work ethics is perseverance and-continuity until the job is finished other wise even if the work is of good quality if it remains unfinished, the expected results are not attained. Obviously, one must persevere even if faced with difficulties and barriers. Without such perseverance and with weak will and laziness, efforts will be defective and without results. The Qur'an says in this context: "And if they would persevere on the right path, We would give them abundant water to drink (as a symbol of abundant blessing of the Creator) with which we would then test them" (16–17:72)

9. Good Disposition in Business: The Holy Qur'an considers **good disposition as** one of the factors in the success of the Honored Prophet in the management and fulfillment of his mission and in Verse 159 of Chapter 3 says addressing the Messenger: "It was by the mercy of Allah that you were lenient with them, for if you were stern and fierce in your heart they would have abandoned you..." Having this characteristic of good disposition (of leniency, tolerance and being considerate of others feelings and sensitivities) in business dealings can be considered as desired goal of the Qur'anic model of business.

4.2.2 Negative Principles and comonents of Business Ethics

1. Prohibition of Shortchanging of Customers: This practice is forbidden in Islamic Fiqh and is considered an injustice to the rights of others. Allah (swt) has chastised it severely: "Establish the balance (scale) in fairness and do not shortchange it" (9:55). As well in Verses 1-7: Chapter 83, Allah has promised those who shortchange their customers with severe punishment.

2. Prohibition of Bribery: Bribe is one of the great sins. Islam condemns bribes severely. The Holy Qur'an says: "Do not consume your property vainly and do not use it to bribe the judges (or rulers), so that you may knowingly devour a portion of the property of others wrongfully (188:2).

3. Prohibition of Riba: Riba (interest) is the amount of money that a creditor receives, in addition to the amount of the loan, from the debtor, or the amount of the additional poor quality merchandise that in exchange for a higher quality good of the same kind is charged by the seller of better quality merchandise. Riba-based transaction and income proceeds from such transactions are rejected in Islam. These kinds of transactions are considered as declaration of war by Allah (279:2). In this and in Verse 275: Chapter 2, the Qur'an with a an extremely serious tone commands the believers to set aside immediately any Riba-based dealing and what a debtor owes them Riba from previous dealings. And warns those who continue transacting in Riba of the declaration of war by Allah against them: "O you who believe! Observe your duty to Allah and give up what remains from Riba, if you are (true) believers. And if you do not, then be warned of war (against you) from Allah and His Messenger. And if you repent, then you have your principal (without interest). Do not be unjust and injustice will not be done to you" (278–279:2).

4. Prohibition of Coveting the Property of Others: Righteous Muslim leaders have always warned their followers against the indignities of asking, begging or desiring material or financial assistance. They have always tried to acculturate them and habituate them to have self-respect, honor and self-esteem. They would encourage them to provide for their life needs and become financially independent from others through honorable work and effort (Rokni, 2012). To covet property or possessions of others is considered a contemptable attribute of human personality. A person must work hard and expend effort in economic activities and earn legitimate income commensurate with his abilities to provide for himself but never have a greedy eye toward others' possessions and scheme to somehow usurp them. A number of the verses of the Qur'an condemned this characteristic. For example, Verse 131 of Chapter 20 saya: "And do not strain your eyes toward blessings We have bestowed on some wedded pairs among them to enjoy the flower of the life of the world so that thereby We may try them. Provisions of your Lord is better and more lasting."

5. Prohibition of Earning One's sustenance from Haram Sources: The Qur'an condemns engaging in prohibited economic activities to earn a living and considers it as following the Satan as in Verse 168: Chapter 2: "O mankind! Eat of that which is lawful and wholesome in the earth, and do not follow the footsteps of the Satan. Lo! he is your open enemy." Similarly, in Verses 42 and 62 of Chapter 5, the Qur'an prohibits illicit gains.

5 Institutions of the Model of Business Ethics

In the model of Islamic business ethics, work is one of the main institutions of the economic system, and if we consider the economic system one of the four basic components of the social system, work is influential in all social aspects and is, itself, influenced by other social institutions including education and training, the value system and norms and, consequently has an effective influence on the social system and the changes and developments that take place in that system (Moyedfar 2007). Allah (swt) considers work and economic activities seeking of divine grace and calls the believers to work after having had communion with Him: "And when the prayer has ended, then disperse in the land and seek Allah's grace (bounty), and remember Allah much, so that you may be successful (10:62).

The divine bounty is the same as the economic work that should be pursued after performing acts of worship, such as Friday's congregational prayers. Work should not interfere with the time set aside for worship but after that work is encouraged strongly as seeking the grace and bounty of the Creator. Imam al-Sadiq explains to his followers: "I move to fulfill a need for which Allah is sufficient and my intention is that Allah witnesses my efforts in earning Halal sustenance. Have you not heard Allah saying that 'And when the prayer has ended, spread on earth and seek Allah's bounty'" (Tabersi, 1994, Vol. 10, p. 289). Also, the structure of the market, mechanism of the market, private property, priority of social to private rights, Qardh Hasan (loan without interest), Waqf (trust endowments), risk and profit sharing, tax charges like Khums (one-fifth on income) and Zakat (about 2.5% on wealth), Sadaqat (payments in support of the poor, needy and the destitute) and others are considered legal and organizational institutions of business, according to the teachings of Islam (Dadgar 2006).

6 Actualization of the Goals of the Business Ethics Model

To achieve the goals which the Qur'an, the primary source of teachings on ethics, envisions for humans – such as the strength of the ordered system, justice, attaining felicity Here and in the Hereafter – certain "dos and don'ts" are prescribed and required compliance with or violation of which carry consequences such as reward or punishment (Janipur 2015).

On the other hand, considering the systemic nature of Islamic economy, the productive dimensions of the business ethics are not separate from that of its value dimensions. Therefore, both mutually reinforce each other Since, on the one hand, doing normal work is part of the ethics of business (the value of every man is the excellence of his work), and on the other hand, Shari'ah rejects any type of business that distorts the elements of ethics. Therefore, it is forbidden to earn income through trickery in trading, providing misleading information to the customer, hoarding, monopolizing, bribing, engaging in Riba-based transactions, and the like. These activities damage the ethics of the society and sources of injustice to the members of the society (Dadgar, 2006).

As a comprehensive and complete religion, Islam has the potential to develop, expand and institutionalize genuine business ethics. One of the main policies offered in Islamic texts is the attempt to create a religious identity for business owners. This approach is a subtle point that has been taken into account in recent years in applied ethics studies. Based on these studies, ethical beliefs are manifested in people's behavior when they are deeply entrenched in the identity of individuals. The main sign of the creation of moral identity of businessmen is the recognition of the Creator as the axis of words and deeds in the sense that the essence of behavior and disposition of the individual in all aspects of his life is strong consciousness of the presence of Allah (swt). The stronger this presence in the life of the individual, the more his activities, including those in trading and exchange, are imbued with divine coloring. In this context, the Qur'an asks: "...And who is better at coloring than Allah?" (138:2).

Other signs of creating an ethical identity in businessmen and other professionals is to note the interpretation of these people as friends of Allah (swt) as described in narrations from the Messenger (sawa). When businessmen and other professionals consider that they are given this honorable status they will try hard to maintain it by ensuring that they comply with divine standards in their activities. In this vision, internalizing Islamic ethics by a businessman or other professionals becomes the means of protecting their identity as friends of Allah and not to make more profits.

Another policy of the Holy Qur'an is to open human's eyes towards the broader horizon of life and focus on the life in the Hereafter, the status of the Creator's trustee on earth, and imbuing business behavior with the divine coloring which results from conceiving of these activities as acts of adoration of the Creator. Islam sets out a just system of rewards and punishments that empowers an internal motivation and control system which, through prevention of transgressions against individuals and the society, moves the individual to perform his duties toward himself, other humans and nature. The internal system urges him to do good deeds to earn eternal value and worth as the Qur'an says: "Wealth and children are an ornament of life of the world. But the good deeds that endure are better in your Lord's sight for reward, and better in respect of hope" (46:18).

Such logic is rationalized through a decision process that has a much wider horizon of trade and exchange activities that the conventional approach to business ethics because it encourages the believers to engage in trade and exchange with Allah which is much more profitable than usual approach to these activities. In this context, the Qur'an asks: "O you who believe! Shall I show you a trade that will save you from a painful doom?" and then proceeds: "Believe in Allah and His Messenger, and strive in the way of Allah with your wealth and lives. That is better for you, if you only knew" (10–11:61). In this trade, Allah has purchased the lives and the wealth of the believers with the price of felicity in the life to come (see also 111:9). This ethical and ideological vision, extended to activities undertaken with intentions of drawing near to Allah including those of trade and exchange, implies that business activities can would not need to be considered as "win-lose" but "win-win" games because even a loss incurred serving a good cause – say in consideration for the weak, poor, needy or destitute – is, in reality of trading with the Creator, a "win."

Such a view can, in addition to preventing economic and social tensions in the market, pave the way for the emergence of many ethical virtues in the business environment. This framework of thought can provide the basis for the formation of genuine customer-orientation and elevated ethics of business, based on a genuine approach to business ethics which transcends the material-results-oriented approach to business ethics. This orientation attempts to institutionalize such values as fairness and sacrifice in the market and expresses the elevated transcendental approach of Islam to business ethics which is among the objectives of the economic system and a beginning stage in the process of achieving the ultimate goal (Tavakoli, 2009).

Accordingly, the expansion of the values of Islamic business ethics in society must be achieved through non-instrumental internalization of values and ethical motivations for business using religious education tools. This is to ensure implementation guarantees in the busines environment whose members search for short-term profits by ignoring rules and priciples of ethics. This approach can be effective in preparing business ethics codes, organizing ethics training courses for professionals, marketing and advertising policies, and the orientation of institutions active in the field of professional ethics. In particular, the mutual responsibility among the owners of the professions and customers can be rationalized through the use of the concept of khilafah, according to which the blessings of the Creator have been placed in trust in trust, thus giving rise to the responsibilities of humans to their Creator (Tavakoli 2009).

7 Summary and Conclusions

A "model" consists of concepts, foundation, goals, strategies and policies that are needed to explain and design a model of any phenomenon. "Ethics" is the science of what to be, how to be and how to live in a rational life. The processes involved in the design of a model must consider these issues. Ethical issues related to business include problems, positions, or good or bad opportunities that an individual or an organization must addressed. (Ebrahimi Nezhad 2015).

In Islam's view, ethics of business is part of the overall economic and social system and its effectiveness depends on coordination with other parts of the system. For example, its framework is balanced as it involves coordination between consideration of spiritual and the life in the Hereafter, on the one hand, and the material and worldly life, on the other (Dadgar 2006). As well, the framework establishes systemic relation between dimensions of the economy and the macro components of the ethics of business, which include foundations, objectives, principles and components. The fundamental axis of ethical concepts in the Qur'an is the belief in the One Creator and the life in the Hereafter. Ignoring these two axioms, either explicitly or implicitly, causes retardation of growth and spiritual elevation of human beings as well as destruction of individual incentives to do good deeds. The ultimate objective of Islamic model of business ethics is to institutionalize ethical values compliance with which allows humans to attain to the state of human perfection and drawing near to their Creator. It is on this basis that the positive and negative principles and components of ethics find meaning and in terms of compliance with the positive and avoidance of negative principles. The most important institution in this model is work within the context of it being an act of worship. Fundamental to actualization of the objectives of the model are creation of a religious identity in business owners and non-instrumental internalization of ethical values and their empowerment through appropriate incentives and internal controls.

Bibliography

Aghanazari. H. and M. khatibi. 2013. *Methodology of the jurisprudence of economic theories from the viewpoint of Martyr Sadr*, Economic Knowledge 2(8): 5–28.

Bagheri, Khosrow. 2008. *Religious Identity*, Tehran: Ministry of Culture and Islamic Guidance.

Blali, I. And Jafari R. 2015. *Economic Socialization and Savings Behavior among Social Science Children*. Ferdowsi University of Mashhad. SB. 26: 247–270.

Bruno, Hvlnagl. 2004. *regulate the behavior of the economy*, Translator: Hussein Baher. the banks and the economy. 50: 58–59.

Dadgar, Yadollah. 2006. *Business Ethics (and Business) from the Point of View of Islamic Economics and Economics*, Commercial Research Letter. 38: 87–120.

Dehkhoda, Ali Akbar. 1994. *Dehkhoda Dictionary*, Tehran: Tehran University.

Ebrahimi Nejad, Mahdi. 2015. *to review and assess the relationship between business ethics and customer satisfaction,* research and the public administration.28: 87–108.
Ezzati, Morteza. 2009. *The Effect of Religious Capital on Consumption, Modification of the Pattern of Consumption*, by the Excellence of Seyyed Hossein Mir moezzi, Tehran: Research Center for Islamic Culture and Thought.
Gastafson, Andrew. 2006. *Supporting Ethical Holisticism, Response to Religious Approaches in Business Ethics*, translated by Mohammad Hosein Norouzi, Tehran, Center for Globalization Studies.
Hadavi Tehrani, Mehdi. 1999. *Islamic School of Economics, the Cultural Institute*, Qom.
haghiqat, Seyyed Sadegh. 2012. *Methodology of Political Science*, Qom, Mofid University Press, Third.
Hakim, Seyyed monzar. 2009. *Mutafa Fayyad and Tradition of Al-Shihid*, Mohammad Baqir al-Sadr, Tehran, Almaghma al-Takrahib, between Almakhah al-Islamiyah.
Hosseini, Seyyed Reza. 2009. *Optimal Consumption Patterns in the Framework of the Islamic Income Allocation Model*, Islamic Republic of Iran Islamic Economics Quarterly. 8 (34):7–38.
Hurr Amoli, Mohammad ibn Hasan. 2008. *Wasejal al-Shi'a*, Qom: Al-Alibit institute (PBUH): Vol 16.
Ibn Faris, Ahmad. 1984. *Mojtaba Maqayes al-Laghah*, Qom: School of Ala'al al-Islam.
Ibn Manzor.Abu al-Fadl Jamal al-Din. 1988. *Lassan al-Arab*, Beirut, Dar al- 'Arti al-Arabi.
Iman, Mohammad Taqi & Ahmad Kalateh Sadaty. 2013. *Methodology of Humanities for Muslim thinkers*, Qom, Research Institute of Universities and Universities.
Iravani, Jawad. 2012. *An Economic Man from the Viewpoint of the Qur'an, Qur'anic teachings,* Razavi Islamic University of Science, Vol. 15.
Izotsu, Toshichiko. 1999. *Religious Ethical Concepts in the Holy Qur'an, Translation by Fereidoun Badrachi*, Tehran: Farzan Publishing.
Jabbaran. Mohammad Reza. 2011. *The necessity of orbital ethics in the production of science based on the sources of Islamic ethics*. Premiums, 62: 156–178.
Jafari, Mohammad Taghi. 1994. *Explanation of Nahj al-Balaghah*, Tehran: Islamic Culture Publishing.
Janipur, Mohammad & Lotfi, Seyed Mehdi.2015. *The Role of Qur'anic Qur'anic Verses in Developing Personal and Social Guidance Systems*, Qur'anic and Hadith Studies » Summer. 12(26):27–54.
Javadi Amoli, Abdullah. 2007. *Qur'an in the Word of Ali (AS)*, Qom: Islamic Publications.
Koleyni, Mohammad ibn Yaghoub. 1986. *Al-kafi,* Tehran: Islamiyah Publications.
Makarim Shirazi, Nasser and others. 1994. *Sample Interpretation*, 4th c., Tehran, Dar al-Tabl al-Islam, 17th edition.
Mashayekhipour, Mohammad Ali. 2011. *The Principles of Work ethic from the Viewpoints of Imam Ali (AS)*, Two Journal of Scientific and Research Management of Islamic Management, 19(1): 37–65.
Masoumiiniya, Gholamali. 2007. *Economic Ethics, Basis of Vision, Teachings, Works*, Islamic Economics Quarterly. 26: 119–146.
Meanian. D. and Hengameh Eskandari, *trans*. 2006. *Introduction to Organizational Behavior. By* Alice. D. Steve. P. Tehran: Literature.
Mesbahi Moghadam, Gholamreza. 2010. *A step toward developing an Islamic model of progress in Iran*, the first book of strategic ideas, the Islamic Model of Progress in Iran, the Secretariat of the Strategic Thought Meeting.
Mir Ma'zi, Seyyed Hossein. 2010. *Model of the progression and Islamicization of the humanities*, the first book of strategic ideas, the Islamic model of progress in Iran; the Secretariat of the Strategic Thought Meeting.
Mir Ma'zi, Seyyed Hossein. 2010. *The Patterns of Progression and Islamicization of the Humanities*, Recovery in. 2014/11/29. from the Information Base of the Office for the Preservation and Publication of the Works of Ayatullah Seyed Ali Khamenei.

Misbah Yazdi, Mohammad Taghi. 1998. *Ethics in the Qur'an*, Qom: Imam Khomeini Research Institute, Qom.
Mohammadi Rey Shahri, Mohammad. 2001., *Al-Tamieh al-Etissadiyah Fiqatake and al-Sunnah*, in collaboration with Seyyed Reza Hosseini. Qom, Dar al-Hadith.
Motahari, Morteza. 1995. *Divine justice, collection of works*, Vol. 1, Tehran, Sadra Publishing House.
Motahari, Morteza. 2000. *Collection of works* (Vol. 2). Tehran, Sadra.
Moyedfar, Saeed. 2007. *Work ethic as a social issue*, Cultural Engineering. 14:6–18.
Musavi Isfahani, Jamaloddin. 1995. *Economic Qur'anic Messages*; Islamic Culture Publishing House.
Naraqi, Mohammad Mahdi. 2008. *Jamee al-Sa'adat*, Qom, Ismaili Publications, Sept. 7.
Nyashirazi, Hamid Reza. 2016. *Ethics in Business and Ethics*, Ethical Research 24: 23–36.
Parsaniya, Hamid. 2009. *Methodology of Humanities with Islamic Approach*, Research. 1(2): 39–53.
PourAhmadi, Hossein. 2010. *economic approaches to the necessity of changing patterns of production and consumption, emphasizing the role of the media,* research on the relationship of the. 17 (61): 31–58.
Qaramlaki, Ahmad. 2003. *Professional Ethics*, Tehran: Bashra Cultural Research Institute.
Qaramlaki, Faramarz. 2004. *The Origin of Research Ethics*, Unfinished, Unfair.
Ragheb Esfahani, Mohammad ibn Husain. 1996. *Almfrdat al-Fah al-Qur'an al-Karim*, Safwan's research, Adnan Davoodi, Dar al-Alam, Damascus.
Rahimi, Alireza. 2012. *The Ratio of Business Ethics,* Interviewer: Vahab Gilich,New Economy. 136: 154–156.
Rajaee, Seyyed Mohammad Kazem. 2003. *The theme of Qur'anic verses*; Imam Khomeini Institute of Educational and Research Institute.
Rashad, Ali Akbar. 2009. *The Logic of Understanding Religion*, Tehran, Publishing Organization of the Research Institute for Islamic Culture and Thought,
Razavi, Alireza. 2002. *Economic behavior of Islamic government agents from Imam Ali's point of view, Master's dissertation*, Imam Khomeini Institute of Educational Studies, Qom.
Rezaei, Majid. 2004. *doing business in the light of the vision and values of the Islamic*, Islamic Economics. 13: 11–31.
Rezaei, Majid. 1998. *the supply of labor based on the principles governing the Islamic labor market.* Qom, University of Moody.
Rezaeian. Ali. And Abdollahi nesiyani. A 2007. *presentation and explanation of the systemic model of human behavior from the point of view of the Holy Qur'an*, the perspective of public administration. 16: 98–113.
Sadouq, Ibn Baboieh Qomi. 1943. *Personality*, Ali Akbar Ghaffari, Qom: The Society of Teachers.
Sadr, Mohammad Bagher. 1978. *Eqtesadona*, Volume II, Translation: AS. Espahbodi, Second Edition, Tehran: Islamic Publishers.
Salimifar, Mostafa. 2010. *Introduction to the Pattern of Islamic Development in Iran*, The First Book of Strategic Thought, The Islamic Pattern of Progress in Iran; Secretariat of the Strategic Thought Meeting.
Sen, Amartya. 1998. *Ethics and Economics*, Translation by Hasan Fesharaki, Tehran, Shiraz Publishing.
Sonyol. 2006. *Managing Director Credits, Business Ethics, Covenant Managers,* August. 13: 60–63.
Tabarsi, Fadl ibn Hassan. 1994. *Al-Bayan Complex in the Interpretation of the Qur'an*, Beirut, The Institute of Publications.
Tabatabaei, Seyyed Mohammad Hussein. 1996. *Al-Mizan Fi Tafsir Al-Qur'an*, p. 5, Islamic Printing Office, Qom, Fifth Edition.
Tavakoli, Mohammad Jawad. 2010. *An Introduction to the Philosophy of Ethics of Business with Islamic Approach*, Quarterly Journal of Economic Knowledge, First Year, First Issue
Tavassoli, Mohammad Esmail. 2004. *Business Ethics*, Islamic Economics Magazine, Spring. 4 (13): 155–183.

The Holy Qur'an
Thranyzadh, Amir, & Afrough, Seyyed Reza. 2014. *Review of Studies of Islamic economics Sadr realist critical magazine: the methodology of the humanities*; Spring. 78.
Tusi, Nasir-al-Din. 1993. *Ethics of Nasarei*, corrected by Mojtaba Minavi Salmieh Islamiyah Publication.
Yousef Zadeh, Hassan and Mohammad Ali Nazari. 1394. *Comparison of Shahid Sadr and Izetsu Methodology*, Islamic Humanities Research Journal. 3: 16–37.
Yousefi, Ahmad Ali. 2002. *Methods of Inference of the Islamic Economic System*, New Exploration in Jurisprudence, Nos. 33 and 34: 287–327.

Junaid Qadir, Amana Raquib, and Hafiz Saeed Ahmed

Chapter 12: Spiritual Excellence (*Iḥsān*) for Professionals: A *Ḥadīth*-Based Perspective

1 Introduction

1.1 What is Iḥsān?

The word *Iḥsān* literally means excellence or to do things or make things better or beautiful. Imam Rāghib al-Isfahāni, a leading Arabic linguist, explains that *Iḥsān* stands for "*the creation of beauty in one's conduct, which is achieved through beauty in knowledge and beauty in action.*" (al-Isfahāni, 1992[1]).

According to a famous *Ḥadīth*, often referred to as *Ḥadīth* Jibrīl (AS) (*Muslim, Book 1 (Book of Faith), Ḥadīth 1*), there are *three* levels of the Islamic faith called *Islām*, *Imān*, and *Iḥsān*. The first level is *Islām*, this deals with the rituals of *Islām* including the proclamation of faith (*Shahādah*), and the fulfillment of Islamic obligations such as the five daily prayers (*Salah*), the annual charity (*Zakāh*), the annual month of fasting during the holy month of *Ramadān*, and making the pilgrimage to Makkah once in life (subject to conditions such as being financially and physically capable). The second higher level is *Imān*, which refers to the entering of strong faith into the heart. *Imān* involves believing in God, His angels, His books, His messengers, the Last Day with a strong conviction, and in the God's Decree. Total belief in God's omniscience and omnipotence and recognizing God's Lordship in creation (*Khalq*) and in affairs (*Amr*). The highest level of the Islamic faith, and the focus of this proposed book chapter, is *Al-Iḥsān*. This level entails the worship of God as if one is seeing God, and knowing that while one is not able to see Him, He truly sees us. The relevant excerpt of *Ḥadīth* Jibrīl is produced below:

> "(...) Then he (the man) said, "Inform me about Iḥsān." He (Prophet Muhammad[2] (PBUH)) answered, "It is that you should serve Allah as though you could see Him, for though you cannot see Him yet (know that) He sees you (...)" (Muslim, Book 1 (Book of Faith), Ḥadīth 1)[3].

Attaining *Al-Iḥsān* requires striving towards excellence in conduct, morals, and God's awareness. This level entails the worship of God with full God-awareness and with

1 English translation used as quoted in "Quranic Foundations and Structure of Muslim Society" of Dr Fazlur Rahman Ansari.

2 In what follows, we often follow to Prophet Muhammad (PBUH) simply as the Prophet (PBUH) for brevity.

3 The translations of *Ḥadīth* (slightly paraphrased in some cases) and referencing of *Ḥadīth* as per the format followed by the online website Sunnah.com.

https://doi.org/10.1515/9783110593419-012

spiritual excellence. Although the concept of *Iḥsān* is directly emphasized in the *Qur'ān* in various places, the concept is unraveled in all its different manifestations and hues in the narrative *Ḥadīth* literature where the various facets of virtues and excellent conduct are expounded.

1.2 Ḥadīth: Why a Ḥadīth Based Perspective?

In this book chapter, we explain spiritual excellence using the Islamic perspective guided by the *Ḥadīth,* which refers to the reports documenting the sayings (*Aqwāl*), actions (*Afʿāl*), or tacit approval (*Taqrīr*) of the Prophet Muhammad *peace and blessings of Allah be upon him (PBUH)*[4] and as such covers his verbal statements and practical guidance in general. *Ḥadīth* along with *Qurān* constitutes the basic canon of Islamic law with the understanding of the former (i.e., the understanding of the Sunnah or the way of the Prophet (PBUH) acting as a demonstration, interpretation, and elaboration of the latter. Although we refer to *Qur'ānic* verses as well in this chapter but our emphasis is on using *Ḥadīths* to clarify and further elaborate the meanings of these *Qur'ānic* verses.

God describes the Prophet as the best example for all Muslims to follow (*Qur'ān Al-Azhāb 33:21*) and in another verse has made the following of the Prophet (PBUH) the key for obtaining God's Love and Forgiveness. (*Qur'ān Ale-ʿImrān* 3:31). Islamic scholars agree that an appropriate understanding of *Qur'ānic* ethics can only be obtained in the light of the Prophetic Conduct or Sunnah by combining *Qur'ān* and the *Ḥadīth* and that the most complete embodiment of *Qur'ānic* ethics is in the person of the Prophet (PBUH).

> When someone asked ʿĀyesha (RA),[5] the wife of the Prophet (PBUH) about the character of the Prophet, she said: "Don't you read the Qur'an? I said: Yes. Upon this she said: The character of the Messenger of Allah was the Qur'an" (Muslim, Book 6 (Book of Prayer of Travelers), Ḥadīth 168)

4 Traditional salutations offered by Muslims whenever the name of the Prophet Muhammad (peace and blessings of Allah be upon him) is mentioned. This is a translation of the Arabic term "*ṣallā llāhu ʿalayhi wa-sallam*", abbreviated as SAW. In what follows, we often follow to Prophet Muhammad (PBUH) simply as the Prophet (PBUH) for brevity.

5 According to the Islamic tradition, whenever the name of a companion of the Prophet (PBUH) is mentioned, it is recommended to add the suffix *Radi Allahu Anhu* (May God be pleased with him), *Radi Allahu Anhu* (May God be pleased with him), *Radi Allahu Anhuma (*May God be pleased with them both*), Radi Allahu Anhum (*May God be pleased with them all*)* depending on whether a single male, single female, two companions, or multiple companions are referred to. We use the acronym RA to encompass all of these as per the context.

Islamic scholars have focused their efforts on developing a highly rigorous discipline for the collection, checking, and verification of the accuracy of the *Ḥadīth* corpus to ensure that something is not wrongly attributed to the Prophet. The authentic *Ḥadīth* anthologies also serve along with their righteous interpreters and scholars as an impediment to deviant innovations in religion (*Bidʿah*).

The essential need of Sunnah steps from the fact that mere injunctions and commandments are never sufficient for effectively engendering ethical conduct; furthermore, while the commandments in the *Qur'ān* are divine, our understanding is human and prone to deficiencies unless the right conduct is interpreted by someone divinely guided who practically demonstrates and implements the God-provided guidance. The importance of the Sunnah was aptly described by the Islamic scholar Muhammad Asad in the following words: "The Sunnah is the iron framework of the House of Islam; and if you remove the framework of a building, can you be surprised if it breaks down like a house of cards?" (Asad, M.,1982)

1.3 Organization of the Chapter

In this chapter, we will initially introduce the concept of *Al-Iḥsān* and describe what it means and why it is important, particularly for professionals working in the field of Islamic finance by leveraging predominantly the *Ḥadīth* corpus. The relationship of *Al-Iḥsān* with Islamic ethics will also be highlighted. In particular, in Section 2, we will motivate the need for incorporating *Iḥsān* and describe the benefits it can bring to Muslim professionals; in Section 3, we will describe the seven ways someone can become a person of *Iḥsān* (*Al-Muhsin*). We discuss thereafter in Section 4 how the concepts we discuss are relevant in the context of modern society and what value the Islamic concept of *Iḥsān* can bring to the modern ethical practice and discourse. Finally, the chapter is concluded in Section 5.

2 The Importance of Iḥsān in Islamic Ethics: Why Incorporate Iḥsān in Life?

After discussing *what Iḥsān* is, we want to now motivate *why* should one incorporate *Iḥsān* in one's life particularly in the business transactions. Broadly speaking, the two main motivations are (1) to attract the pleasure of God and to follow his injunctions; and (2) for the human, economic, and social welfare that such an attitude accrues in the development of a civilized society. We discuss these points in separate subsections next.

2.1 To Attract the Pleasure of God

"… And do good; indeed, Allah loves the doers of good (Al-Iḥsān)." (Qur'ān Al-Baqarah 2:195)[6]

As described in the *Qur'ānic* verse *(Ayah)* above, God loves the doers of *Iḥsān (Muhsinīn)*. In many places in the *Qur'ān* and the *Ḥadīth*, we find prescriptive divine imperatives commanding believers to strive for spiritual excellence.

"Indeed, Allah orders justice and good conduct and giving to relatives and forbids immorality and bad conduct and oppression. He admonishes you that perhaps you will be reminded." (Qur'ān An-Nahl 16:90)

"Verily Allah has prescribed Iḥsān (perfection) in all things. Thus if you kill, kill well; and if you slaughter, slaughter well. Let each one of you sharpen his blade and let him spare suffering to the animal he slaughters." (Muslim, Book 34 (Book of Hunting, Slaughter), Ḥadīth 84)

We also see that God loves beauty and actions done well and with consummate perfection. In a *Ḥadīth*, it is stated that

"Verily, Allah is Graceful and He loves Grace. Pride is disdaining the truth (out of self-conceit) and contempt for the people." (Muslim, Book 1 (Book of Faith), Ḥadīth 171)

We also find that God will reward those who performed actions of *Iḥsān* and exerted beyond doing the mandatory actions to attain to spiritual excellence.

"Certainly, We shall not make to be lost the reward of anyone who does his (righteous) job in the most perfect manner (ahsana ʿamala)" (Qur'ān Al-Kahf 18:30)

"And My servant does not draw near to Me with anything more loved to Me than the religious duties I have obligated upon him. And My servant continues to draw near to me with nafil (supererogatory) deeds until I Love him. When I Love him, I am his hearing with which he hears, and his sight with which he sees, and his hand with which he strikes, and his foot with which he walks. Were he to ask (something) of Me, I would surely give it to him; and were he to seek refuge with Me, I would surely grant him refuge." (Bukhāri, Book 81 (Book of Softening of the Hearts (Ar-Riqāq)), Ḥadīth 91)

"Allah is good and only accepts that which is good." (Muslim, Book 12 (Book of Zakat), Ḥadīth 83)

2.2 To Promote Human and Social Welfare

Some people asked Allah's Messenger (PBUH), "Whose Islam is the best? i.e. (Who is a very good Muslim)?" He replied, "One who avoids harming the Muslims with his tongue and hands." (Bukhāri, Book 2 (Book of Belief), Ḥadīth 4)

6 The translation of the Quran used is *Saheeh International*, available online on http://quran.com.

Allah SWT is the benevolent God of all mankind (*Rabbin Naas*) (*Qur'ān An-Nās* 114:1) and of all the worlds (*Rabb ul-ʿAlamīn*) (*Qur'ān Al-Fātihah* 1:2) and not only Muslims.

Shariah, which is based on divine all-encompassing wisdom, provides guidelines for all activity within an Islamic society and these rulings always have underlying beneficial purposes that promote the welfare of people (*Maslahah*). Imam Al-Shātibi, the great Andalusi scholar of the science of the objectives (*Maqāṣid*) of Shariah, described this in the following words:

> "Shariah stands for justice, mercy, wisdom, and good. Thus, any ruling that replaces justice with injustice, mercy with its opposite, common good with mischief, or wisdom with nonsense, is a ruling that does not belong to the Shariah, even if it is claimed to be so according to some interpretation." (cited in Auda, 2008).

The Shariah was bestowed upon mankind through the Last Messenger of God, Muhammad (PBUH), who the *Qur'ān* refers to as a Prophet for all People (*Kāfatul Lil An-Nas*) (*Qur'ān As-Saba'* 34:28) and a mercy to all the worlds (*Rehmatul Lil ʿAlamīn*) (*Qur'ān Al-Anbiyah* 21:107). *Qur'ān*, the basic canon of Islam and the firm foundation of Shariah, is described by God as the guidance for all mankind (*Huda Lil An-Nās*) (*Qur'ān Al-Baqarah* 2:185). Finally, the Ummah of the Prophet Muhammad (PBUH) is referred to as the best of the communities since it has been deputed towards all humanity (*Ukhrijat Lil An-Nās*) (*Qur'ān Ale-Imrān* 3:110) to bring all kinds of worldly and other-worldly benefits to them with the duty of conveying God's guidance to them and living with the *Qur'ānic* ethics.

Therefore, we find that attaining spiritual excellence requires that human beings be able to bring benefit to the entire humanity and ward of all kinds of harm.

3 How to Become a Person of Iḥsān

> "Is there any reward for goodness (Al-Iḥsān) other than goodness (Al-Iḥsān)?" (Qur'ān Ar-Rahmān 55:60)

To become a person of *Iḥsān*, a Muslim professional should (A) be sincere and have the correct intention; (B) embrace the character traits of the people of *Iḥsān*; (C) have a vision of a meaningful pioneering life; (D) do justice and excel in one's professional work; (E) have a mastery orientation and a professional outlook; (F) be social useful and beneficial for people; (F) live a productive life that attracts the blessings of God (*Barakah*). These qualities are next described in separate subsections, with backing references from *Qur'ān* and *Ḥadīth*.

3.1 The Importance of Sincerity and Intention

The intention is very important in Islam.

"Actions are according to intentions, and everyone will get what was intended (...)" (Agreed Upon: Bukhāri, Book 83 (Book of Oaths and Vows), Ḥadīth 66; Muslim, Book 33 (Book on Government), Ḥadīth 222)

In addition to having the right intention (of doing an action for the pleasure of God), one should also be sincere to humanity in general and the larger Muslim Ummah.

Prophet (PBUH) said, "The religion is nasīhah (sincerity)." We said, "To whom?" He (PBUH) said, "To Allah, His Book, His Messenger, and to the leaders of the Muslims and their common folk." (Muslim, Book 1 (Book of Faith), Ḥadīth 103)

This also has implications for Muslims in their professional life. One should strive to excel in the worship of God and also consider professional excellence as a religious duty.

Prophet (PBUH) said, "Goodness and comfort are for him who worships his Lord in a perfect manner and serves his master sincerely." (Bukhāri, Book 49 (Book of Manumission of Slaves), Ḥadīth 33).

A Muslim should also prioritize the reward of the hereafter over worldly gains and strive for the home of the hereafter, consistent with the divine imperative seen in the following verse.

"And seek, through which Allah has given you, the home of the Hereafter; and (yet), do not forget your share of the world; and do good (Iḥsān) as Allah has done good (Iḥsān) to you." (Qur'ān Al-Qaṣaṣ 28:77)

A similar message can also be seen in the following *Ḥadīth*.

Prophet (PBUH) said "Whoever makes the ʾĀkhirah (Hereafter) his concern, Allah will gather together his affairs, place contentment in his heart and the world will come to him despite his reluctance. And whoever makes the Dunyah (World) his concern, Allah will scatter his affairs, put poverty before him and nothing of the world will come to him except what Allah has written for him." (Tirmidhī, Vol. 4, Book 11, Ḥadīth 2465)

We find in Islamic tradition that the real reward is according to the intention and similar looking action may get very different rewards and an apparently auspicious action may be wholly rejected due to defects in the intention (e.g., the intention of a ritual worship done for public display is not rewarded by God for God does not condone polytheism (*Shirk)* in any way).

Prophet (PBUH) reported that, "Verily, the first people to be judged on the Day of Resurrection will be a man who was martyred. He will be brought; the blessings of Allah will be made known and he will acknowledge them. Allah will say: What did you do about them? The man will say: I fought in your cause until I was martyred. Allah will say: You have lied, for you fought only that it would be said you were brave, and thus it was said. Then, Allah will order him to be dragged upon his face until he is cast into Hellfire. Another man studied religious knowledge, taught others, and recited the Qur'ān. He will be brought; the blessings of Allah will be made known and he will acknowledge them. Allah will say: What did you do about them? The man will say: I learned religious knowledge, taught others, and I recited the Qur'ān for your sake. Allah will say: You have lied, for you studied only that it would be said you are a scholar and you recited the Qur'ān only that it would be said you are a reciter, and thus it was said. Then, Allah will order him to be dragged upon his face until he is cast into Hellfire. Another man was given an abundance of blessings from Allah and every kind of wealth. He will be brought; the blessings of Allah will be made known and he will acknowledge them. Allah will say: What did you do about them? The man will say: I did not leave any good cause beloved to you but that I spent on it for your sake. Allah will say: You have lied, for you spent only that it would be said you are generous, and thus it was said. Then, Allah will order him to be dragged upon his face until he is cast into Hellfire." (Muslim, Book 33 (Book on Government), Ḥadīth 218)

3.2 Embracing the Excellent Prophetic Character Traits

The people of *Iḥsān* have beautiful character.

Messenger of Allah (PBUH) said, "I was sent to perfect good character." (Al-Muwaṭṭa' 1614)

"The best of you in Islam are those who are most excellent in character as long as you deeply understand the religion." (Musnad Aḥmad, Book Musnad of Abu Hurairah)

The people of *Iḥsān* are characterized by properties of patience, preservation, and deliberation.

"Man was created of haste. I will show you my signs, so do not impatiently urge Me" (Qur'ān Al-Anbiyah 21:37)

Prophet (PBUH) said to Ashajj, of the tribe of 'Abdul-Qais: "You possess two qualities which are liked by Allah: forbearance (Al- Ḥilm) and deliberateness (Al-Anāh)." (Muslim, Book 1 (Book of Faith), Ḥadīth 25; Tirmidhī, Book 27 (Book on Righteousness And Maintaining Good Relations With Relatives), Ḥadīth 117)

"Deliberation is of Allah, and haste is of Satan." (Tirmidhī Book 27, Ḥadīth 118; graded by Tirmidhī as sound (Ḥassan))

The people of *Iḥsān* are additionally characterized by their total reliance on God (*Tawakkul)*

"Certainly, Allah loves those who put their trust (in Him)." (Qur'ān, Al-Imran 3:159)

"And put your trust in Allah, if you are believers indeed" (Qur'ān Al-Maida: 5:23)

Prophet Muhammad (PBUH) said: "If only you relied on Allah a true reliance, He SWT would provide sustenance for you just as He SWT does for the birds: They fly out in the morning empty and return in the afternoon with full stomachs." (Tirmidhī Book 36, Ḥadīth 41; Ibn Mājah Book of Zuhd)

The Prophet (PBUH) also clarified the right way of relying on God and showed how *Tawakkul* is done after adopting the means while relying on the success being achieved through God.

> Anas (RA) reported that a person asked the Prophet (PBUH), "Should I tie my camel and have Tawakkul (trust in Allah for her protection) or should I leave her untied and have Tawakkul." The Prophet (PBUH) replied, "Tie her and have Tawakkul." (Tirmidhī Book 37 (Book of The Description Of The Day Of Judgment, And Ar-Riqaq, And Al-Wara'), 2517)

The people of *Iḥsān* are moderate and eschew extremism in all its forms (*Qur'ān* describes the Muslim community as the balanced middle community (*Ummat Al-Wasat*) (*Al*-Baqarah 2:143). The following *Ḥadīth* emphasizes the need to follow the Prophetic way of authentic moderation.

> "A group of three men came to the houses of the wives of the Prophet asking how the Prophet worshipped (Allah), and when they were informed about that, they considered their worship insufficient and said, "Where are we from the Prophet as his past and future sins have been forgiven." Then one of them said, "I will offer the prayer throughout the night forever." The other said, "I will fast throughout the year and will not break my fast." The third said, "I will keep away from the women and will not marry forever." Allah's Apostle came to them and said, "Are you the same people who said so-and-so? By Allah, I am more submissive to Allah and more afraid of Him than you; yet I fast and break my fast, I do sleep and I also marry women – So he who does not follow my tradition in religion, is not from me (not one of my followers)."" (Bukhāri, Book 67 (Book of Marriage), Ḥadīth 1)

The people of *Iḥsān* are people who seek out wisdom and knowledge.

> "Seeking the (obligatory) religious knowledge is an obligation upon every Muslim." (Ibn Mājah 224).
>
> "The wise saying is the lost property of the believer, so wherever he finds it then he has a right to it." (Tirmidhī, Book 41 (Chapters on Knowledge), Ḥadīth 43; Ḥasan Ḥadīth according to As-Suyuti)

The people of *Iḥsān* have positive thinking (*Ḥusn Zann)* and interpret everything positively and accept the good and the afflictions from God and do not despair of God's mercy during failures and difficulties.

> "Verily with hardship, there is relief" (Qur'ān Alam Nashrah 94:6)
>
> "O Allah, I seek refuge in you from anxiety and grief" (Bukhāri, Book 80 (Book of Invocations), Ḥadīth 66)
>
> "The affair of the believer is amazing! The whole of his life is beneficial, and that is only in the case of the believer. When good times come to him, he is thankful and it is good for him, and when bad times befall him, he is patient and it is also good for him" (Muslim, Book 55 (Book of Zuhd and Softening of Hearts), Ḥadīth 82)

Looking at the positive side allows one to excel despite (and sometimes because of) adverse circumstances.

The people of *Iḥsān* love God more than anything else – more than their family members, more than their wealth, more than dwellings. God says in the *Qur'ān*:

> "Say, If it be that your fathers, your sons, your brothers, your mates, or your kindred; the wealth that you have gained; the commerce in which you fear a decline; or the dwellings in which you delight – are dearer to you than Allah, or His Messenger, or the striving in His cause – then wait until Allah brings about His Decision: and Allah guides not the rebellious." (Qur'ān At-Taubah 9:24).

3.3 The Importance of Having a Life Vision and Leading a Pioneering Life

The people of *Iḥsān* recognize the life is purposeful and work towards establishing a productive legacy.

The Prophet said: "When a person dies, his deeds are cut off except through three: continual flowing charity, knowledge which others benefit, and a pious offspring that supplicates for him." (Muslim, Book 25 (The Book of Wills), Ḥadīth 20)

The people of *Iḥsān* also have leadership qualities (Beekun & Badawi, 1999) and use it to lead people towards praiseworthy matters and desirable ends.

> "You are the best nation produced (as an example) for mankind. You enjoin what is right and forbid what is wrong and believe in Allah." (Qur'ān Ale-ʿImran 3:110))

> The Prophet says, "He who introduced some good practice in Islam which was followed after him (by people) he would be assured of reward like one who followed it, without their rewards being diminished in any respect." (Muslim, Book 47 (Book of Knowledge), Ḥadīth 26)

> "The upper hand is better than the lower hand. The upper hand is one that gives and the lower hand is one that takes." (Agreed Upon: Bukhāri, Book 24 (Book of Zakāh), Ḥadīth 32; Muslim, Book 12 (Book of Zakāh), Ḥadīth 122)

The people of *Iḥsān* are responsible, trustworthy, and take ownership of what they have been entrusted with.

> The Prophet (PBUH) said: "Each of you is a shepherd and each of you is responsible for his flock. The Amīr (ruler) who is over the people is a shepherd and is responsible for his flock; a man is a shepherd in charge of the inhabitants of his household and he is responsible for his flock; a woman is a shepherdess in charge of her husband's house and children and she is responsible for them; and a man's slave is a shepherd in charge of his master's property and he is responsible for it. So each of you is a shepherd and each of you is responsible for his flock." (Abu Dawūd, Book 20 (Book on Tribute, Spoils, and Rulership), Ḥadīth 1)

> "The trustworthy, honest Muslim merchant will be with the Prophets, the honest men, and martyrs on the Day of Resurrection." (Tirmidhī, Book 14 (Book of Business), Ḥadith 7)

The people of *Iḥsān* have leadership qualities and lead the people entrusted to them with integrity and sacrifice.

> Anas bin Malik narrated from Abu Talhah who said: "We complained to the Messenger of Allah (PBUH) of hunger and we raised (our garments) from our stomachs (exposing) a stone (on each of us). So the Messenger of Allah (PBUH) raised (his garment exposing) two stones (indicating that the Prophet (PBUH) led from the front and sacrificed more than the common man)." (Tirmidhī, Book 36 (Book on Zuhd), Ḥadīth 68)

The people of *Iḥsān* are people of great fortitude *(Ḥimmah Aliyah)* and high determination *(High Azm)*

> "And that there is not for man except that (good) for which he strives" (Qur'ān An-Najm 53:39)

> The Messenger of Allah said: "... If you ask Allah for Paradise, then ask him for Al-Firdaws, for it is the highest part of Paradise, in the middle of Paradise, and from it spring the rivers of Paradise, and above it is the (Mighty) Throne of the Most Merciful." (Bukhāri, Book 97 (Book of Oneness of Allah (Tawheed)), Hadith 51)

The people of *Iḥsān* are amenable to manual work and possess hands on skills and are not wary of manual work.

> "Nobody has ever eaten a better meal than that which one has earned by working with one's own hands. The Prophet of Allah, David (upon him be peace) used to eat from the earnings of his manual labor." (Bukhāri, Book 34 (Book of Sales and Trade), Ḥadīth 25)

The people of *Iḥsān* are proactive, activists, and have a bias for action:

> "By Him in Whose Hand my life is, it is better for anyone of you to take a rope and cut the wood (from the forest) and carry it over his back and sell it (as a means of earning his living) rather than to ask a person for something and that person may give him or not." (Bukhāri, Book 24 (Book of Zakāh), Ḥadīth 73).

> The Prophet (PBUH) said, "Whosoever of you sees an evil, let him change it with his hand; and if he is not able to do so, then (let him change it) with his tongue; and if he is not able to do so, then with his heart – and that is the weakest of faith." (Muslim, Book 1 (Book of Faith), Ḥadīth 84)

The people of *Iḥsān* have a spirit of enterprise and hasten towards good and the beneficial.

> "For every nation, there is a direction to which they face, so hasten towards all that is good" (Qur'ān Al-Baqarah 2:148)

> I heard Allah's Messenger (PBUH) saying "From among my followers, a group (of 70,000) will enter Paradise without being asked for their accounts, their faces will be shining like the moon." 'Ukasha bin Muhsin Al-Asadi got up, lifting his covering sheet and said, "O Allah's Messenger (PBUH) Invoke Allah for me that He may include me with them." The Prophet (PBUH) said! "O Allah! Make him from them." Then another man from Al-Ansar got up and said, "O Allah's Messenger (PBUH)! Invoke Allah for me that He may include me with them." On that Allah's Messenger (PBUH) said, "Ukasha has anticipated you." (Bukhāri, Book 77 (Book of Dress), Ḥadīth 29; Muslim Book 1 (Book of Faith), Ḥadīth 428)

The people of *Iḥsān* value their time and are not lazy.

"Take advantage of five matters before five other matters: your youth, before you become old; and your health, before you fall sick; and your richness, before you become poor; and your free time before you become busy; and your life, before your death." (Shu'ab al-Imān 9575; Saḥīḥ (authentic) according to Al-Albani)

Abdullah ibn Umar (RA) reported that the Prophet (PBUH) took me by the shoulder and said, "Be in this world as though you were a stranger or a wayfarer." And Ibn Umar (RA) used to say, "In the evening do not expect (to live until) the morning, and in the morning do not expect (to live until) the evening. Take (advantage of) your health before times of sickness, and (take advantage of) your life before your death." (Bukhāri, Book 81 (Book of Heart Softeners (Ar-Riqāq)), Ḥadīth 5)

3.4 Doing Justice and Excelling in One's Work

The people of *Iḥsān* are meticulous in fulfilling the rights of people (of other people and above all of God) over them.

"O believers! Stand firmly for justice, giving witness for Allah, may be therein your own loss, or of your parents or of your relations. Against whom you be a witness, he be a rich or be a poor, in any case Allah has more power than anyone over them, therefore follow not passion lest you may be far away from justice; and if you distort or turn your face, then Allah is aware of your doings." (Qur'ān Al-Nisā 4:135)

The fulfillment of rights is emphasized highly the Prophet (PBUH) as we see in the following *Ḥadīth*.

"The best among people are those who are best in fulfilling (rights)." (Musnad Aḥmad, Book Musnad of Abu Hurairah)

While it is true that human beings have many different roles, and one is right to prioritize some over the others, *Iḥsān* entails the need to fulfill the rights of everyone and everything that has a right over them.[7]

'Abdullah bin 'Amr bin Al-'As (RA) narrated that the God's messenger (PBUH) said, "O 'Abdullah! Have I not been informed that you fast all the day and stand in prayer all night?" I said, "Yes, O Allah's Messenger!" He said, "Do not do that! Observe the fast sometimes and also leave them (the fast) at other times; stand up for the prayer at night and also sleep at night. Your body has a right over you, your eyes have a right over you and your wife has a right over you." (Bukhāri, Book 67 (Book of Marriage), Ḥadīth 133)

7 In the "The Meaningful Life Framework" booklet (Ahmer, 2019), the author expounds this concept by describing that human beings have numerous *mandated* and *elective* roles and it is necessary to satisfy certain minimum performance levels (MPL) for these and that it is not desirable that one attains excellence in some roles by remaining deficient in other essential roles.

This entails holding on the highest standards of professional ethics and avoid any apparent or hidden deception and betrayal.

> "And give full measure when you measure, and weigh with an even balance. That is the best (way) and best in result." (Qur'ān Al-Isrā 17:35)

> "Every traitor will have a banner on the Day of Resurrection and it will be said: This is the betrayer of so-and-so." (Muslim, Book 32 (Book of Jihad and Expeditions), Hadith 16)

> "God said: There are three whom I will oppose on the Day of Resurrection: a man who gave his word and then betrayed it; a man who sold a free man into slavery and kept the money; and a man who hired someone, benefited from his labor, then did not pay his wages." (Bukhāri, Book 34 (Book of Sales and Trade), Ḥadīth 174)

In a professional context, this is especially relevant to leaders and people of responsibility.

> "Your slaves are your brothers and Allah has put them under your command. So whoever has a brother under his command should feed him of what he eats and dress him of what he wears. Do not ask them (slaves) to do things beyond their capacity (power) and if you do so, then help them." (Agreed Upon: Bukhāri, Book 2 (Book of Belief), Ḥadīth 23; Muslim, Book 27 (Book of Oaths), Ḥadīth 61)

> The Holy Prophet said: "Any man whom Allah has given the authority of ruling some people, and he does not look after them in an honest manner, will never feel even the smell of Paradise." (Bukhāri, Book 93 (Book of Judgments), Ḥadīth 14)

Justice is an also an important component, rather the primary objective, of an Islamic economic system – and its defining characteristic. It is stated in the *Qur'ān* that the purpose of sending divine messengers to different people is to establish humankind on justice (*Qur'ān, Al Hadīd* 57:25). This is in contrast with the modern secular western economic system – in particular, the capitalistic system – which has the acquisition of wealth as its prime objective (Zaman, A., 2017).

The people of *Iḥsān* are also particular about permissible (*Halāl)* and impermissible (*Harām)* and have *Taqwa* of Allah.

> "A time will come when people will no longer care about whether their wealth has been lawfully or unlawfully acquired." (Bukhāri, Book 34 (Sales and Trade), Ḥadīth 36)

> "... Every person starts his day as a vendor of his soul, either freeing it or causing its ruin." (Muslim, Book 2 (Book of Purification), Ḥadīth 1)

The people of *Iḥsān* recognize that this world is a world of toil (*Qur'ān Al-Balad 90:4)* and striving and a place for doing actions.

> "Say, "Do (what you do); Allah will see your deed, as will the Messenger and the believers. And you shall be returned to the Knower of the Seen and the Unseen, then He will tell you what you have been doing." (Qur'ān At-Taubah 9:105)

"And those who strive for Us – We will surely guide them to Our ways. And indeed, Allah is with the doers of good" (Qur'ān Al-Ankabūt 29:69)

"This life is but a tillage for the next, do good that you may reap there; for striving is the ordinance of God and whatever God hath ordained can only be attained by striving."

The people of *Iḥsān* are not lazy as this is a sign of hypocrites (*Munāfiqun*) (*Qur'ān An-Nisā 4:142)* and something that the Prophet (PBUH) sought refuge of God from in the following words.

"O Allah, I take refuge in You from anxiety and sorrow, *weakness and laziness*, miserliness and cowardice, the burden of debts and from being over powered by men." (Bukhāri, Book 80 (Book of Invocations), Ḥadīth 66)

The people of *Iḥsān* recognize that one is ethically responsible (*Mukallaf*) for trying one's best.

"The best of earnings is the earning of a person's hand as long as the person was sincere (Nasaḥa)." (Musnad Aḥmad, Chapter Musnad of Abu Hurairah, Ḥasan)

"Whoever fears traveling at night – and whoever travels at night reaches his destination – Allah provides him with the most precious of goods, and indeed Allah's goods are but Paradise." (Tirmidhī, Chapter Day of Judgement, Ar-Riqaq, and Al-Wara')

The people of *Iḥsān* also recognize that excellence is a continuous journey.

"A believer never satisfies doing good until he reaches Jannah." (Tirmidhī, Book 41, Ḥadīth 42)

3.5 Having a Mastery Orientation and Preferring Quality over Quantity

In the Islamic worldview, the concept of *Iḥsān* is autotelic – and one must continue to do the actions without being satisfied by doing good.

"Whoever recites the Qur'ān and masters it by heart, will be with the noble righteous scribes (in Heaven). Moreover, whoever recites the Qur'ān and stutters with it, and it is difficult for him, will have a double reward." (Muslim Book 6 (The Book of Prayer – Travellers), Hadith 290)

The people of *Iḥsān* loves meticulous/ professional action/ completion of a job and taking honor in one's work.

"Allah loves to see one's job done at the level of Itqān." (Bukhāri and Muslim)

The word *Itqān* occurs also in the Qur'ān and refers to 'excellence', 'mastery', and 'proficiency' and it is in its most complete form attributed to God Most High. God says:

> "An act of Allah who has **perfected (atqana)** everything. Surely, He is All-Aware of what you do" (Qur'ān An-Naml 27:88).

> "Allah is pleased with the task performed by you in which both the action and duty are sound and which is performed well. (Tabarani, Al-Mu'jam Al-Awsat; 1/275)

> And those who strive for Us – We will surely guide them to Our ways. And indeed, Allah is with the doers of good. (Qur'ān Al-Ankabūt 29:69)

The people of *Iḥsān* are regular in their actions. The people of actions complete and continue their actions that they start and do not become dabblers in matters in which they start an affair and then lose steam and leave the action.

> "... the best deeds are those done regularly even if they are few." (Ibn Mājah, 4240)

> Prophet (PBUH) is reported to have said, "If the Final Hour comes while you have a palm-cutting in your hands and it is possible to plant it before the Hour comes, you should plant it." (Al-Adab Al-Mufrad, Book 27, Ḥadīth 479)

People of *Iḥsān* are committed to excellence and are not complacent. In the works of Stephen Covey (Covey, 1989), one must periodically renew one's self, remain vigilant, and "sharpen the saw" to maintain peak productivity.

> Prophet (PBUH) said: "The likeness of the one who memorizes the Qur'ān is that of the owner of a hobbled camel. If he tends to it regularly, he will keep it, but if he lets it go, he will lose it." (Bukhāri, Book 66 (Book of Virtues of the Qur'an), Ḥadīth 53).

The people of *Iḥsān* prioritize quality over quantity.

> "(God is He) who created death and life to test you (as to) which of you is best in deed – and He is the Exalted in Might, the Forgiving" (Qur'ān Al Mulk 67:2)

> "Competition in (worldly) increase diverts you" (Qur'ān At-Takāthur 102:1)

> "There is nothing in the world which is better than thousands of its own kind except man", (Al-Jami' Al- Saghir, No. 5394)

It is not that quantity does not matter but it only counts when accompanied by quality

> "The best among people are those who live the longest and excel in their deeds, whereas the worst of people are those who live the longest and corrupt their deeds." (Tirmidhī, Book 36 (Book of Zuhd), Ḥadīth 27)

We find in various *Ḥadīths* that the reward of actions is according to its quality (in terms of intention, attention, humility, submissiveness, etc.). Prophet Muhammad (PBUH) confirms the importance of having solemnity and full submissiveness in the prayer and keeping the heart fully concentrated. The Muslim will be rewarded for his prayer as much as he accomplishes this.

> "There are people who fast and get nothing from their fast except hunger, and there are those who pray and get nothing from their prayer but a sleepless night." (Ibn Mājah, Book of Fasting)

> The Prophet was asked, "What deeds are loved most by Allah?" He (PBUH) said, "The most regular constant deeds even though they may be few." He (PBUH) added, "Don't take upon yourselves, except the deeds which are within your ability." (Bukhāri: Book 81 (Book of Heart Softeners (Ar-Riqāq)), Ḥadīth 54)

We find that in the Islamic tradition, it is not wealth and things that are valued but the development of honorable upright human beings, which are considered as the greatest assets of a society.

> "Real men are as rare as a reliable strong camel that can endure the burden of long trips; you can hardly find one in a hundred" (Bukhāri, Book 81 (Book of Heart Softeners (Ar-Riqāq)), Ḥadīth 87)

> The Prophet (PBUH) said: "People are like gold and silver; those who were best in Jahiliyyah (Pre-Islamic Period of Ignorance) are best in Islam, if they have religious understanding." (Muslim, Book 45 (The Book of Virtue, Enjoining Good Manners, and Joining of the Ties of Kinship), Ḥadīth 205)

We also find this example in the righteous followers of the Prophet (PBUH). It is reported that once 'Umar ibn Al-Khattab (RA), the second Caliph of Islam, was sitting with a group of his companions. He asked them (RA): "Make a wish", one of them said, "I wish to have as much gold as would fill this whole house, so that I could spend it in *Jihād*"; then again 'Umar (RA) asked: "Make a wish", another man said, "I wished that this house was full of jewels and pearls so that I could spend it all in *Jihād* and charity for the sake of Allah"; 'Umar asked for the third time: "Make a wish", his companions said: "We don't know what to say, O leader of the believers"; There upon 'Umar (RA) said, "I wish that this house was full of men like Abu 'Ubaydah Ibn Al-Jarraah, Mu'ādh bin Jabal and Sālim Mawla Abu Hudhayfah[8] in order to use them to spread the word of Allah".[9]

3.6 Importance of Being a Giver (and Being Socially Useful)

Islam places a lot of importance on being socially useful and to bring benefit to people. The famous Islamic theologian Al-Ghazali recognized the broader concept of *Maṣlahah* as furthering the ultimate purposes of Shariah, which are to safeguard the following five things: (1) their faith; (2) their life; (3) their intellect; (4) their posterity; (5) and their wealth. Shah Waliullah Ad-Dehlawi, another great Islamic scholar, further adduced that *Maṣlahah* conveys yet a broader sense of the salutary purpose of

---

8 These are all honorable companions of the Prophet who were the highest examples of high-quality men.

9 Narrated in Al-Mustadrak of Al-Hakim in the mention of the virtue of Sālim Mawla Abu Hudhayfah.

the divine injunctions and said that all of the divine injunctions have underlying salutary benefits and the Shariah of God is not like that of a King who imposes arbitrary orders on people to see who obeys the injunctions and who does not – on the contrary, every ruling in Shariah has an underlying salutary benefit, which exists even if we are not able to comprehend it.

The foremost duty for a person of *Iḥsān* in this regard is to avoid harm and avoid reciprocating harm.

"There should be neither harming (darar) nor reciprocating harm (dirār)." 'Arbaīn Nawawi, Ḥadīth 32.

In particular, Muslim professionals should avoid all forms of cheating, deception, short-charging, and fraud.

"O you who have believed, do not consume one another's wealth unjustly but only (in lawful) business by mutual consent" (Qur'ān An-Nisā 4:29).

"Whoever bears arms against us is not one of us, and whoever cheats us is not one of us." (Muslim, Book 1 (Book of Faith), Ḥadīth 189)

According to another report, the Prophet passed by a pile of food in the market. He put his hand inside it and felt dampness, although the surface was dry. He said: "O owner of the food, what is this?' The man said, 'It was damaged by rain, O Messenger of God.' He said, 'Why did you not put the rain-damaged food on top so that people could see it! Whoever cheats us is not one of us." (Muslim, Book 1 (Book of Faith), Ḥadīth 190)

This means engendering magnanimity in one's person and to not envy what people have.

"A man came to the Prophet (PBUH) and said, "O Messenger of Allah, direct me to an act which, if I do it, (will cause) Allah to love me and the people to love me." So He (PBUH) said, "Renounce the world and Allah will love you, and renounce what the people possess and the people will love you." (Ibn Mājah; 'Arbaīn Nawawi, Ḥadīth 31)

People of *Iḥsān* are people who cooperate and facilitate and bring ease to people

Prophet Muhammad (PBUH) said to his companion Mu'adh bin Jabal (RA) on deputing him towards Yemen, "Facilitate things for the people (treat the people in the most agreeable way), and do not make things difficult for them, and give them glad tidings, and let them not have aversion (i.e. to make the people hate good deeds)" (Bukhāri, Book 78, Ḥadīth 151)

The Prophet (PBUH) said, "Make things easy for the people, and do not make it difficult for them, and make them calm (with glad tidings) and do not repulse (them)". (Bukhāri, Book 78 (Book of Manners (Al-Adab)), Ḥadīth 152)

"Kindness is not to be found in anything but that it adds to its beauty and it is not withdrawn from anything but it makes it defective." (Muslim, Book 45 (The Book of Virtue, Enjoining Good Manners, and Joining of the Ties of Kinship), Ḥadīth 100)

> "He who is deprived of tenderly feelings is in fact deprived of good." (Muslim, Book 45 (The Book of Virtue, Enjoining Good Manners, and Joining of the Ties of Kinship), Ḥadīth 97)

People of *Iḥsān* do community service and bring benefit to mankind and to all creations of God.

> "... that which benefits people remains on the earth ..." (Qur'ān Ar-Ra'd 13.17)

> "The best of people are those that bring most benefit (Anfa'uhum) for mankind." (Tabarani, Al-Mu'jam Al-Awsat)

> Prophet Muhammad (PBUH) said: "If any Muslim plants something or sows seed from which a man, a bird or an animal eats, it counts as a charity for him." (Bukhāri, Book 41 (Book of Agriculture), Ḥadīth 1)

3.7 Living a Productive Life by Attracting Barakah

If spiritual excellence is named *Iḥsān*, then spiritual productivity is *Barakah*. The concept of productivity is different in secular world and in Islam. In Islam, *Barakah* (translated as blessing) is the endowment of blessings in something by God such that all kinds of benefits are accrued from little. Imam Rāghib al-Isfahāni defined *Barakah* as the attachment of Divine goodness to a thing, so if it occurs in something little, it increases it; and if it occurs in something abundant, it further increases the benefit.

The question remains how does one attract *Barakah*. We find guidance in this regard from the *Qur'ān* and the authentic *Sunnah* that there are numerous ways to attract such *Barakah*.[10]

An important way to attract *Barakah* is to fulfill the rights of others, of one's family, and to perform charity.

> The Prophet (PBUH) reported that, "While a person was in the wilderness he heard a voice from the cloud (commanding it thus): Irrigate the garden of so and so. (After that the clouds slinked aside and poured water on a stony ground. It filled a channel amongst the channels of that land and that person followed that water and he found a person standing in the garden busy in changing the course of water with the help of a hatchet. He said to him: Servant of Allah, what is your name? he said: so and so. And it was that very name which he had heard from the clouds. and he said to him: Servant of Allah, why do you ask me my name? He said: I heard a voice from the clouds of which is the downpour, saying: Water the garden of so and so, like your name. What do you do (for the favor) shown to you by Allah in this matter? He said: Now as you state so. I look what yield I get from it, and I give one-third as charity out of it and I and my children eat one-third of it and one-third I return to it as investment." (Muslim, Book 55 (The Book of Zuhd and Softening of Hearts), Ḥadīth 56)

10 https://productivemuslim.com/18-sources-of-barakah/.

We also see from the *Ḥadīth* above that another source of attracting Barakah is to do good actions consistently and regularly (the farmer regularly gave out one-third of his harvest as charity) and of moderation (the farmer was not reinvesting all of the harvest, or giving away all the harvest in charity, or consuming all the harvest – instead the farmer was moderate in spending in all the due places).

Finally, the people of *Iḥsān* are people that are thankful and grateful.

The Prophet (PBUH) was forgiven for any of his 'sins' but he exerted himself in the worship of God saying that "Should not I be a grateful Slave?"

> 'Āyesha (RA) asked the Prophet (PBUH), "Why do you undergo so much hardship despite the fact that Allah has pardoned for you your earlier and later sins?" He (PBUH) responded, "Should I not prove myself to be a thankful servant?" (Muslim, Book 52 (Characteristics of the Day of Judgment, Paradise, and Hell), Ḥadīth 78)

Another way to attract *Barakah* and attain spiritual excellence is to focus on important things related to one and to avoid idle matters or things unrelated to a person and thereby fully utilize one's time.

> "Indeed, your efforts are diverse" (Qur'ān Al-Layl 92:4)

> "Surely, of the excellence of a person's Islam is that he leaves what does not concern him." (Tirmidhī, Book 36 (Book of Zuhd), Ḥadīth 15)

People of *Iḥsān* can make monumental achievements that astound people and make them wonder how some people are able to achieve so much in so little time. One major reason for this is that they value their time and have a system for managing their time and making in productive.

> "There are two blessings, and most people evaluate these blessings incorrectly: health and free time." (Bukhāri, Book 81 (Book of Softening of Hearts (Ar-Riqāq)), Ḥadīth 1)

People of *Iḥsān* also leverage times at which their energies are at their peak. We find in the Prophetic tradition an encouragement to start work early in the morning and to sleep after the night prayer (*Isha*).

> Prophet (PBUH) said: "O Allah, bless my nation in their early mornings (i.e., what they do early in the morning)." (Ibn Mājah, Book 12, Ḥadīth 2236)

Naps are also well known in the productivity literature and it was also a *Sunnah* of the Prophet (PBUH).

> Anas ibn Malik (RA), a companion of the Prophet (PBUH), said, "They used to gather and then take a midday nap." (Al-Adab Al-Mufrad 1240)

The people of *Iḥsān* are masters at prioritizing and focusing on the most important and relevant tasks for the moment.

Prophet Muhammad (PBUH) said: "The best of' the deeds or deed is the prayer at its proper time." (Muslim, Book 1 (Book of Faith), Ḥadīth 162)

Prophet (PBUH) is reported to have said, "The first matter that the slave will be brought to account for on the Day of Judgment is the prayer. If it is sound, then the rest of his deeds will be sound. And if it is bad, then the rest of his deeds will be bad." (Tabarani, Al-Mu'jam Al-Awsat)

Another rich source of *Barakah* is to avoid all *Haram* and to have God-consciousness (*Taqwa*), which means guarding oneself from Allah's displeasure. There are many benefits of *Taqwa* including *Barakah* and the expansion of sustenance (*Rizq*), which refers to all aspects of a person's subsistence and livelihood, including but not restricted to, wealth, status, business and children.

"And if only the people of the cities had believed and feared Allah, We would have opened upon them blessings from the heaven and the earth; but they denied (the messengers), so We seized them for what they were earning." (Qur'ān Al-ʿArāf 7:96)

"And whoever fears Allah – He will make for him a way out. And will provide for him from where he does not expect. And whoever relies upon Allah – then He is sufficient for him. Indeed, Allah will accomplish His purpose. Allah has already set for everything a (decreed) extent." (Qur'ān At-Talāq 65:2–3)

Prophet (PBUH) is reported to have said: "The person who (sincerely) relies on God, God will suffice for all the responsibilities of that person. Rizq will be received from such sources, whence it cannot be imagined. The one who relies on the (material) world, God hands that person over to the world." (Hayāt ul Muslimīn)

Another rich source of *Barakah* is establishing good relationships with one's close relatives and with the whole Muslim community.

The Prophet (PBUH) said, "Whoever is pleased to have his provision expanded and his life span extended, then he should keep good relations with his family." (Agreed Upon: Bukhāri, Book 34 (Book of Sales and Trade), Ḥadīth 20; Muslim Book 45 (The Book of Virtue, Enjoining Good Manners, and Joining of the Ties of Kinship), Ḥadīth 23)

"The believers in their mutual kindness, compassion and sympathy are just like one body. When one of the limbs suffers, the whole body responds to it with wakefulness and fever." (Riyadh As-Salihīn, Book 1 (Book of Miscellany), Ḥadīth 224; Agreed Upon (Bukhāri & Muslim))

4 What Iḥsān Can Bring to Contemporary Ethical Discourse and Practice

One of the most significant observation in the area of behavioral ethics is that although most people think of themselves as ethical, everyday professionals (even those who are highly educated) often cheat and resort to unethical means to get what they want when they can get away with it (Bazerman & Gino, 2012). Research has shown that this is not an atypical occurrence and dishonesty is common globally (Ariely, 2012); furthermore, research has indicated that modern business and economics education rather than making students more ethical instead makes them *less likely* to act ethically (Anand, Ashforth, & Joshi, 2004).

The alienation of human beings from moral judgement and responsibility has wrought on many of the modern crises including the ones that periodically afflict the financial arena due to which human beings can operate without empathy and due regard for the pain and sufferings of others. No wonder the 2011 Financial Crisis Inquiry Commission probing into the global financial crisis in 2008 highlighted the "systemic breakdown in accountability and ethics" as one of the six major causes of the crisis (Mirakhor, 2014).

There are various reasons why modern education has not helped improve ethical standards. Apart from the fact that humanities and ethics are rarely given the attention given to technical courses, it is also the case that merely providing the knowledge does not automatically engender the moral intent or drive in students to act ethically especially when it is in their interest to cheat a little. We need both an increased emphasis on ethics but also a stronger moral incentive for the people to act ethically.

With the advancement of science and technology, there is an increased need to develop ethical excellence since scientific knowledge may be likened to a two-edged sword that can be used for construction or for demolition. Historically we know of no other force as effective as religion and spirituality for cultivating the conscience that can motivate ethical behavior and motivate people towards the fulfillment of their moral duties even when they are not being observed. We believe that an infusion of Islamic ethical teachings can improve this situation by motivating professionals – especially Muslim professionals who already have religious belief (*Iman*) in the divine nature of *Qur'ān* and the revealed nature of *Ḥadīths* – to develop higher levels of personal accountability, moral consciousness, and social responsibility.

In particular, the Islamic ethical tradition of spiritual excellence (*Iḥsān*) provides not only normative legal guidelines through the Qur'ān but also provides practical instruction on how to live the life of *Iḥsān* through the *Ḥadīth* literature, which has captured the sayings, actions, and implicit approval of the Prophet Muhammad (PBUH), who most perfectly embodied the spiritual excellence loved by God. A Muslim is not an otherworldly person who only lives for the hereafter for God says that there is no sin on one who seeks the grace of God (*fadhl*) (through trade) (*Qur'ān*. 2:198) In line with the *Qur'ānic* instructions of not forgetting one's share in this world while preparing for the hereafter (*Qur'ān* 28:77), a Muslim possessing the quality of *Iḥsān* is an active dynamic person of toil and production who contributes proactively to the development of earth, civilization, and society and aims to achieve both in worldly matters and those matters that relate to the hereafter.

5 Conclusions

Islam is the divine religion that offers a complete code of ethics that can guide humanity towards greater wellbeing, effectiveness, and productivity. In particular, the spirit of spiritual excellence *(Iḥsān)*, in all its multifaceted manifestations, can bring upon a system of justice, beauty, excellence, magnanimity, and egalitarianism in which human beings will live in great harmony and attain joy in this world while attaining ultimate felicity and the pleasure of God in the hereafter. In this book chapter, we relied upon the *Ḥadīth* literature to expound on the *Qur'ānic* imperative of living a life of *Iḥsān* (*Qur'ān* 2:195) to qualify for God's good pleasure (*Qur'ān* 55:60). By adopting the Islamic concept of spiritual excellence, Muslims will be able to become the standard bearer of *Qur'ānic* morality and a witness to the truth before mankind (*Shuhadah 'alan-Naas*) (*Qur'ān* 2:143). Furthermore, adoption of *Iḥsān* leads to human development, felicity, spiritual productivity (*Barakah*) both in this world and in the hereafter (*Al-Akhirah*).

References

Ahmer, Suleman (2019). The Meaningful Life Framework. Online document. Retrieved from http://www.timelenders.com/doc_view/65-the-personal-organizational-effectiveness-book on 15th February 2019.

Asad, Muhammad. Islam at the Crossroads. Dar Al-Andalus, 1982.

Al-Isfahāni, Rāghib (1992). Al-Mufradat fi Gharib al-Quran. Damascus: Dar al-Elm.

Ariely, D. (2012). The (honest) truth about dishonesty. New York, NY: Harper Collins Publishers.

Auda, J. (2008). Maqasid al-shariah: A beginner's guide (Vol. 14). International Institute of Islamic Thought (IIIT).

Anand, V., Ashforth, B. E., & Joshi, M. (2004). Business as usual: The acceptance and perpetuation of corruption in organizations. Academy of Management Perspectives, 18(2), 39–53.

Bazerman, M. H., & Gino, F. (2012). Behavioral ethics: Toward a deeper understanding of moral judgment and dishonesty. Annual Review of Law and Social Science, 8, 85–104.

Beekun, R. I. (1997). Islamic business ethics. International Institute of Islamic Thought (IIIT).

Beekun, R. I., & Badawi, J. A. (1999). Leadership: an Islamic perspective. Beltsville, MD: Amana.

Covey, S. (1989). The 7 Habits of Highly Effective People, Free Press.

Faris, Mohammed (2016). The Productive Muslim: Where Faith Meets Productivity. Claritas Books; 1st edition (January 1, 2016).

Mirakhor, A. (2014). The starry heavens above and the moral law within: on the flatness of economics. Econ Journal Watch, 11(2), 186–194.

Qadir, J., & Zaman, A. (2018). The Ends of Development in Islam: Seven Overlapping Concepts. Journal of Islamic Banking and Finance, Volume 35, No 3, 2018.

Qadir, J. (2017). The Islamic Worldview and Development Ideals. Journal of Islamic Banking and Finance, Volume 35, Number 1, Jan–Mar 2018, pp 33–44.

Zaman, A., & Qadir, J. (2017). Putting Social Justice First: The Case of Islamic Economics. Journal of Islamic Banking & Finance. Oct–Dec 2017, Vol. 34, Issue 4, pp 87–99. 13p.

Majid Habibian Naghibi

Chapter 13: Human and Role of Ethics in His Interactions in *Makarim-ul-Akhlaq* Prayer by Ali bin Hussain (PBUH)

1 Introduction

Sometimes in Islamic teachings and even in the approaches attributed to the Muslim and non-Muslim thinkers we come across some points that apparently seem to be incompatible with material intellect. The main reason for such approach is the difference of opinion on definition of man. In other words, if we correct our conception of man, we will undoubtedly confirm the compatibility of these rules and recommendations with human perfection. Therefore, at the outset of this paper, we intend to clarify what we mean by man and mankind.

On the other hand, the ultimate goal of religions and even the primary purpose of prophecy, have been correcting the behavior of this man on earth for the sake of his perfection, discernment of what is right and accomplishment of his duties. Human behavior on earth must be arranged, indeed, in such a way as to be in line with fulfilling his duties in a time- and place-bound mission. On this basis, and to meet this goal, certain principles such as dignity, justice, fairness and freedom must govern man's interactions with others.

In this paper, we will review the essential moral laws of human behavior while giving a clear picture of the concept of man. Reviewing Makarim ul-Akhlaq Prayer from Sahifeh Sajjadieh (as one of the authentic Islamic sources), we have tried to extract and propose recommendations – as far as possible – in line with the role of ethics in interactions and business activities.

In brief, this paper has been authored for two specific goals: 1) Opening up an avenue for right approach toward the humanity of man on earth and defining an economic man; 2) Creating responsiveness and boosting attention to Sahifeh Sajjadieh prayers attributed to the Fourth Imam of Shia Muslims Hazrat Zeyn al-Abedin Ali bin Hussain (AS). The author of these lines is satisfied with even minimum achievement concerning the two goals.

2 The Concept of Man

The meaningful differences of opinion in humanities come from the disagreement in the concept of man as the most important subject, tools and the goal in this science. Perhaps, creation of a common language is the most important issue for scientific

https://doi.org/10.1515/9783110593419-013

discussions in humanities. Therefore, at the outset of this paper, it is better to clarify what we mean by the concept of man.

As a matter of fact, the principal question of this paper and the majority of research works on humanities is this: What is the concept of man? The response to this question may seem to be easy yet difficult to clarify. In other words, the majority of people think the answer to this question is very easy. They claim there is no ambiguity and the man living on earth is what we mean by the concept of man. Some, however, do not take it for granted. They avoid oversimplification and answer more analytically. In this part, we will first provide a lengthy introduction in search of an appropriate answer to the question on the concept of man who has become the focus of attention of humanities in various schools of thought.

Undoubtedly the "man living on earth" is the concept we mean. We use this sentence to pose two questions: 1) In view of the spatial vastness, what proportion of material world does the earth constitute? 2) In view of the life span and life of mankind, and also in view of the time length, what proportion of the material world and even the earth belongs to the human generation of Adam the father of mankind?

In response to the first question, we can say in brief that according to scientific studies the average[1] diameter of earth is less than 13,000 km, that in comparison with the distance from the recently discovered galaxy (13.5 million light year) it is a trivial figure of like 10^{-13}.[2] Therefore, the earth on which human beings, i.e. the human generation (that is our target population) live, is trivial even in material terms. It is like a drop in the ocean and there should be no merely material approach toward all the creatures of the universe.

In a brief response to the second question, we can say that Islamic texts have not determined a precise date for the history of the recent generation of mankind (the children of Adam). Of course, the literature related to Judaism, says the history of mankind is about seven thousand years. Muslim scholars such as the late Allameh Tabatabaei (Tabatabaei, 1417, Vol. 4, p. 223) have accepted the figure. Therefore, even if we consider a maximum 10 thousand years for this generation of mankind, the life of this generation in comparison with the estimated life of earth (i.e. 4 billion years) and the life of universe (i.e. 13.5 billion years) in particular, will be trivial. As a result, the target population in these types of research works is very limited and small in time even in material terms.

A further study shows that we are talking about the kind of man for whom - even in the developed nations - the life expectancy is significantly below a hundred years. It is interesting to note that forecasting models in their best possible form and based on the gathered data, make projections for shorter times, while ignoring increasing

1 The earth is not perfectly round. Today, precise measurements show that the equatorial diameter of earth (12,756 km) is 43 km more than its polar diameter (12,713 km).

2 It must be noted that we merely mean the material world. Of course, we know that over 90 percent of this material world is still unobservable and unidentifiable with the existing devices.

restrictions and all biases toward the realities. Advanced research centers for future studies are constantly putting before researchers, decision-makers and policymakers a spectrum of diversified probabilities based on various scenarios. But who is this man who has upstaged all the aspects and warp and woof of humanities?

We all know that mothers feel like carrying merely a spiritless and independent thing in their womb when the embryo is below four months old. The "blowing of spirit" (or whatever you believe in) into this flesh marks the beginning of a period the movements and pauses of the fetus is not necessarily under the mother's control. Also, at the end of his life on earth, when the soul leaves the body (whatever it may be), nothing remains but a carnal body that shows no motion and has no power. In this time lapse (between the incarnation and departure of the soul), the majority of the cells constituting the body, change form for many times, but the humanity of the individual is still there, although it experiences some stages of perfection or probably inferiority. This may explain the meaning of the famous saying that "The world is a farm for the Hereafter" (Molla Saleh Mazandarani, Vol. 7, p. 120).

The "soul" which we call it humanity is indeed blended into the body to accomplish its mission with all restrictions of the material body in this world. Any man is born with a responsibility to fulfill in this world. This responsibility is exclusive to him and no other man can ever accomplish this mission. Of course, it is very difficult to identify this mission, and perhaps its accomplishment is more difficult than its recognition. In any case, the ways and means for recognition and perfection of man have been confined to material tools and ways. Of course, the material and spiritual powers are always in constant competition. Boosting the ways and means for recognizing spiritual aspect of man will offer vast and rich capacities and capabilities for him that may dominate many material affairs. The more bodily power is strengthened and the more material demands are addressed, the lesser will be the spiritual power. The best ever state for dominance of the spiritual power is manifested when the body comes to its knees and bows before God.

Of course, we should note that due to the inseparable union of the material and spiritual powers, it is essential to address minimum material demands to help boost the spiritual power. As such, material power is reinforced upon meeting the spiritual demands. This is the Achilles' heel and the critical point for including ethics in human behavior, including its impact on business, based on which this paper has been developed.

Therefore, the story is all about the man with two material and spiritual aspects whose reality is the spiritual aspect encompassed by the material constraints. This man is in pursuit of perfection, all his behaviors are at the service of his perfection, and his perfection lies in his spiritual aspect. The ever-changing material aspect of man paves the ground for perfection of humanity (spiritual aspect).

Human perfection primarily depends upon right recognition of his mission and accomplishment of this mission in the restricted and transient material world. Further, all capacities and issues related to humanities must be at the service of man to recognize his mission and accomplish it. Therefore, the issue of man and the role of ethics in business environment must be also reviewed in this connection.

Following, we will review some basic principles governing human behavior and continue with paraphrasing Makarim ul-Akhlaq Prayer of Sahifeh Sajjadieh for correcting the behavior of human beings in business environment.

3 Moral Laws of Human Behavior

With respect to the definition of man, there should be some rules governing his behavior in the material world and the observation of these rules is also essential in business environment. Ignoring these rules and principles is a practice against humanity of mankind. Of course, this does not mean observing all these principles by all individuals in the society through the entire life of humanity in behaviors and interactions with others. We should note that observing these principles must be manifested in behavior of man with God, behavior of man with himself, behavior of man with other people and in his behavior with other creatures and the material world. It is only under such circumstances that man becomes moderate in behavior, something that the entire community will be entitled to. As for brevity, in this paper we will take a glance at some of these principles that are more important in view of the author of these lines. Undoubtedly, the principles governing human behavior are not confined to these examples and we hope there would come another time and opportunity for further research on these.

As a matter of fact, some of these principles are meta-religious and meta-ritual, i.e. such principles as justice, human dignity, human freedom, and right of ownership are among the principles that any common sense admits their importance and necessity even if religions and Islam do not endorse and place emphasis on them. Therefore, the acknowledgement of the religions may be interpreted as *ershadi* (rule of wisdom and Sharia) not *mawlawi* (binding) rule. Of course, the difference of opinion on this, will not have any significant effect on our discussion (principles governing human behavior).

It may be claimed that the majority of these principles are observed in contracts and interactions among the intellectuals in the form of terms and conditions. However, it is a reality that the ordinary relations among individuals and probably the invisible hands, are incapable of covering them qualitatively and quantitatively in full. The existence of numerous contracts and transactions lacking these principles in various societies is a solid evidence for this claim.

3.1 Dignity

Dignity is among the essential qualities of man and the Holy Qur'an has attributed it to the generation of mankind: "And We have certainly honored the children of Adam."

(Surah Isra, 70) The verse gives some examples for honoring man and says perfection of human dignity means his superiority over the majority of creatures on earth (and preferred them over much of what We have created, with [definite] preference. Surah Isra: 70) Also, Verse 4 of Surah al-Tin (We have certainly created man in the best of stature.) may refer to this quality of man.

Dictionaries define dignity as the state or quality of being worthy of honor or respect, and an opposite to meanness. There are of course many connotative meanings for the word. (Khalil bin Ahmad Farahidi, 1410) In this connection, it has been said that: Generosity is either material dignity or moral dignity. Generous is a noun attributed to a thing or a man who possesses all laudable and good qualities. It is the opposite of mean. This quality is usually attributed to human beings. (Al-Ayn, Vol. 5, p. 371)

Although dignity is the same as avoiding meanness and inferiority, generous is different than great and grand. *Karim* (generous, noble) is a word that may not have clear-cut comprehensive equivalent in other languages. Therefore, we must put together a few words to clarify its meaning. For instance, a magnanimous and immaculate soul is called generous. (Javadi Amoli, 1988)

Some are of the opinion that there are three types of dignity throughout the creation: a) Celestial dignity: This type of dignity is merely supernatural and attributed to the angels of God, Throne of Heaven, servants of the Throne of Heaven, etc. b) Natural dignity: It is related to the natural creatures encompassing a spectrum of precious stones to the plants. And c) Universal human dignity: It is created by juxtaposition of natural and supernatural dignities and comes from the union of celestial dignity and natural dignity. Therefore, human dignity can be classified as 1- Inherent God-given dignity, and 2- Acquired dignity. All people possess the God-given dignity and the natural prestige, this noble quality, as far as on their choice they do not deprive themselves of this dignity by practicing treachery and committing crime against oneself and others. The acquired dignity is attained by employing talents and positive forces inside human being and by efforts and endeavors toward human perfection and doing pious acts. This dignity is acquired and optional, and man's ultimate and sublime value depends on this dignity. (Javadi Amoli, 2002)

Religiousness, piety, patience, gentleness, cheerfulness, bridling the tongue, virtue, forgiveness, lack of jealousy, forbearance, thankfulness and trust are among the criteria of dignity. Attaching less significance to materiality, seeking justice, generosity, good morals, happy end, minimizing discord with others, good deed and creed, tolerance, increased sustenance, satisfaction of God, and greatness before others are some of the aftereffects of dignity. To attain dignity one must attach greater significance to persistence in his acts, trust in God, God's satisfaction, doing good in material world as provisions for the Hereafter, and no complaint of God before the people in all his deeds and creeds.

Furthermore, the individual must be careful his interactions with himself and with others must not go counter with any type of dignity. As such, when forgiveness is offered somewhere or when peace is made or something is bought, the dignity of the other party must be preserved. In this connection, the Holy Qur'an says: "O you who have believed, do not invalidate your charities with reminders or injury." (Surah Baqarah: 264) Extracts from the Makarim ul-Akhlaq Prayer attest to this point, which we will review later in this paper.

3.2 Justice as an Ethical Principle in Interactions

Undoubtedly justice is one of the most important and essential principles governing human behavior and interactions. Thinkers and intellectuals belonging to different philosophies and schools of thought in any type of government have placed its realization among their basic goals. The concept of justice, of course, is easy yet difficult to clarify. It may seem as a simple and clear-cut concept to everyone at first glance, while a more precise look at the concept, indicates complexity of its understanding and aspects. At any rate, justice may be considered as old as the social life of humanity that the children of Adam recognized it from the outset of human civilization and tried to establish it on earth.

Lexicographers have defined justice as justness, fairness, righteousness and orderliness (Ibn Manzour, Vol. 11, p. 432) and as it was mentioned earlier, the majority of thinkers have opined on justice. Plato in his "The Republic", Sheikh Tousi in "Al-Mabsout", and Allameh Tabatabaei in "Al-Mizan" have included valuable materials on justice where attaining merits and indeed, the ethical approach toward justice is very outstanding. They have considered justice as an ethical concept, saying all the factors affecting the ethics in any nation are effective in discerning oppression. There are two famous definitions on justice, whose ethical interpretation is simple: 1) Justice is putting everything in its proper place; 2) Any force deserves the right to be placed in its deserving place.

Justice is not necessarily synonymous with equity and the goal of justice is not always realization of equity among the individuals. It is important to observe proportion and moderation between the risk and efficiency in interactions. This has been referred to in the principle of "He who enjoys benefits, must also accept losses." Justice is realized in time-bound exchanges, when either of the contract parties fails to get rich at the cost of the other party's poverty or gains both-end interests. As a matter of fact, there is no significant difference in the general concept of justice. The differences arise when they embark on making secondary rules and bring them into conformity with the exterior realities. This is what we mean by easiness and difficulty of the concept of justice.

However, we should admit that the concept of "equity" as the essence and basis of justice is preserved in all these differences of opinion. In other words, "horizontal justice" and "vertical justice" can be collective aspects for various points of view. Therefore, it can be said that due to the existence of differences, man needs a sort of justice inside himself. Everyone experiences such a feeling of justice more or less. Therefore, justice is an ethical concept (Nayini, Vol. 2, p. 190) and all the factors affecting the morality of any nation are effective in the distinction of justice and injustice. (Katuzian, p. 311) Of course, the rules of justice are not innate and fixed and it is not enough to rely on the power of intellect to distinguish them; rather, ethics, values and sentiments have each a considerable share in justice.

A glance at the transactions and the dominant rules and regulations shows that observing justice in them has been an indisputable principle to the intellectuals, something that Islamic Sharia law has endorsed too. For instance, the consolidation of options (right to cancellation of transaction) in case of the fault in price and considerations, cancellation of the contract or collecting compensation and upon enjoying the right of cancellation of transaction in case of unusual overcharging with option of lesion, the creation and expansion of justice in business are pursued. Also the need for mental maturity (having wisdom for livelihood and the power of transaction) as the minimum general terms and conditions for players in business market, prevents any oppression and abuse of rights. Welcoming the caravans before their arrival in the city is another evidence for existence of a comprehensive and convergent system to prevent abuse of faulty or biased information.

3.3 Fairness

Fairness is a concept with positive connotation in common sense, particularly in businesses. The Islamic sharia law has endorsed observing fairness in business. In dictionaries, fairness means impartial and just treatment or behavior without favoritism or discrimination. Fairness is achieved when a man reduces his bias in favor of others or grants in transactions half of his right to the other party willingly, the same amount of right he intended to collect for himself. (Kitab al-Ayn, Vol. 7, p. 132 and Lisan al-Arab, Vol. 9, p. 330) "Love for others whatever you love for yourself" (Nahjul Balagha, Letter No. 31)

Observing fairness and neutrality paves the ground indeed for realization of justice. Fairness leads to justice. A fair person is someone who accepts any truth revealed to him. He never tends to apparent wrong. Fair people must safeguard the rights of the oppressed and help justice and fairness translated into their rights.

Justice, however, is different from fairness. Justice has a typical concept and it must not be mistaken with fairness that is an ethical sentiment. Fairness is needed when enforcement of law probably leads to undesirable results and ethical conscience intends to correct it. There is a hidden point in fairness that is absent in justice. In fairness, man puts himself in place of others to see how he likes to be treated, then he treats the other people in the same way. If he likes to be cooperated with, then he cooperates with others and if he likes to be forgiven, he forgives others.

The Holy Qur'an (verses 135 and 152 of Surah Nisa) and traditions point to and place emphasis on this issue. As it has been brought in Islamic sources, it is a sign of fairness for man to admit the right when it is revealed (Bahar al-Anwar, Vol. 75, p. 80). And fairness toward the subjects is an instance of wisdom (Ghurar ul-Hekam, p. 59).

Fairness is a type of social manner and one of the outstanding qualities of the believers that boosts man's respect (Extracts from Mizan al-Hikmah, p. 378, Tradition 4229). "Do to others whatever you would like them to do to you, and do not do to others whatever you wouldn't like them to do to you" (Vasael al-Shia, Vol. 15, p. 287). Observing fairness has been considered as the highest level of faith (Truly the highest level of faith is when man observes fairness, Ghurar ul-Hekam, p. 88) that leads to constant affection and friendship (Mizan al-Hikmah, Vol. 13, Tradition 20196), uproots differences and promotes the culture of friendship and amity in the society (A fair person has many friends and followers, Mizan al-Hikmah, Vol. 13, T 20206) and can bestow upon the individual and the society comfort and welfare.

Fairness can be discussed from various points of view such as fairness toward oneself (Ghurar ul-Hekam, p. 394), fairness in what is due to God (Al-Kafi, Vol. 8, p. 352) and fairness toward other human beings (Mustadrak al-wasā'il, Vol. 11, p. 164; Man lā Yahduruhu al-Faqīh, Vol. 2, p. 623). It is interesting to know that observing fairness has been regarded as the Zakat of power for rulers (Mustadrak al-wasā'il, Vol. 7, p. 46; Da'a'im al-Islam, Vol. 1, p. 353). In brief, it can be said that observing fairness is one of the important and influential principles in business environment and in man's economic behaviors.

3.4 Freedom and Its Moral Backing in Business

As we know, people are free in selecting manners of concluding contracts. According to Islamic thinkers, they are also fully free in selecting a new reasonable form of contract. Indeed, the most important rule included in the principle of freedom of contract is this that people are authorized to include their mutual consent in the framework of imperative law and under any title they like to freely determine the results and effects of this innominate or private contract. On this basis, the projections by certain institutions in transactions (nominate contract) do not necessitate people to select either of them for agreement; rather, people are legally authorized to select from among a wide spectrum of forms and ways including nominate and innominate to draw up their financial and contractual relations (Katuzian, 2004, Vol. 1, p. 146).

It is a reality that the principle of freedom of contract forms in transactions enjoys an ethical basis. For more on this, we should know that some Islamic thinkers consider promise as a type of command not a tradition or statement (Majlesi, 1984, Vol. 11, pp. 29, 116; and Vol. 14, p. 422), and therefore, it does not involve obligation and recognizance, thus its enforcement is not obligatory according to Sharia law. However, fulfillment of one's promise upon the existence of the possibility to fulfill is religiously recommended and ethically mandatory.[3] According to jurists, binding obligation is the obligation to do an act that is not religiously prohibited or leaving an act that is not religiously obligatory. Fulfilment of one's binding obligation is religiously obligatory and the one who fails to fulfill his obligation has indeed committed a sin for which he has to make an atonement. Agreement in dictionaries has been put against dissolution. This has been also referred to as binding agreement and authentic agreement (Nayini, 1418 H., Vol. 1, p. 186 and Vol. 3, p. 7). It might be said (Mohammadi & Fallah, 2015) that the need to fulfill one's promise, obligation and agreement enjoys moral backing. This is because, first, the ethical incumbency (not religious incumbency) of fulfilling the obligation has been stipulated. Secondly, fulfilling the obligation and agreement that has been deemed as religiously mandatory are ethically obligatory a fortiori. In other words, the wellness of fulfilling one's commitment or agreement or indecency of violating them is not because it needs telling lies, rather, it is because the intellect rules on the wellness of fulfillment and decency of violation upon considering ethical principles (Majlesi, 1983, Vol. 11, p. 30).

Therefore, any individual selecting either a nominate or innominate contract with full freedom, enters a business over the assurance that the other party will stay loyal to the terms and conditions of the contract. The other party, too, does the same. The necessity for fulfilling one's promise that is the basis for free and fair entry of the individuals into a business, is more moral-based than legal- and jurisdiction-based.

4 Corporate Ethics in Makarim ul-Akhlaq Prayer by Imam Sajjad

Sahifeh Sajjadieh is a collection of prayers and supplications attributed to the fourth Imam of Shia Muslims, Ali bin Hussain (AS) mostly known as Sajjad. Known as the "Psalms of the Dynasty of Muhammad (PBUH)" and the "Gospel of the Infallible Household of the Prophet (PBUH)", it is third in importance to the Shia scholars after the Holy Qur'an and Nahjul Balagha, so that even some Sunni scholars and thinkers have admired its rhetoric and eloquence (Balaghi, p. 37). In his Az-Zaree'a, Agha Bozorg Tehrani has cited 50 commentaries on Sahifeh Sajjadieh, the most well-known of which is Riaz al-Salekin by Seyyed Alikhan Shirazi. In addition to Farsi, Sahifeh Sajjadieh has been also translated into English, French, Turkish, Urdu, Spanish, Bosnian, and Albanian languages. Under certain circumstances in his time of Imamate, Imam Sajjad had to expound on many sciences in the form of prayers.

The 20th prayer of Sahifeh Sajjadieh, known as "Makarim ul-Akhlaq", contains 22 phrases each of which begins with expressing greetings to Muhammad

3 Moghniya, w/d, Vol. 13, p. 10; Khunsari, 1405 H., Vol. 3, pp. 147, 408; Nayini, 1418 H., Vol. 3, p. 247.

(PBUH) and his household. In each phrase, Imam Sajjad asks for granting some good qualities or seeks protection from moral vices to hereby introduce values and anti-values. Due to valuable themes in these phrases, they have been paid serious attention by the thinkers who have written and published commentaries on the book.[4]

The basis of requests made in this prayer, indicates a sort of special attitude toward man in material world and his mission and responsibility in this world. The reason for incompatibility of some cases with our material intellect is because we have made an incorrect definition of man. If we correct our understanding of man, we will definitely admit compatibility of these rules and recommendations with human perfection. Some phrases of this prayer referring to correcting attitudes toward man are the following: 1) O God, put all moments of my life in line with fulfilling the mission You have assigned for me (Let me pass my days in that for which Thou hast created me!); 2) Paying attention to this essential approach that life on earth must be toward proximity to the perfect qualities of the Almighty God (Let me live as long as my life is a free gift in obeying Thee,); 3) Human perfection must not be confined to material gain, and the worldly wealth or ranks of other people must not arouse our envy (Tempt me not with ingratitude!)

In the transient world, man should heed passing through a few steps in order to realize how he should behave according to his dignity: 1) Cleansing the self and spiritual purification; 2) Doing desirable activities and avoiding undesirable behavior; 3) Good interaction with other people in business environment; 4) Seeking good ending as the ultimate goal of man in his life and in his transactions. Of course, as it was mentioned earlier, it is necessary to observe such important principles as justice, dignity, fairness and freedom along with practicing the above-said steps. There are very important and valuable phrases in Makarim ul-Akhlaq Prayer with the centrality of human ethics in business, some of which will be brought hereunder.

A: Human Self-Purification

It is a reality that without self-purification one must not expect desirable behavior from man. Self-purification is undoubtedly one of the major goals of the Divine religions for the guidance of man in this transient world. In his Makarim ul-Akhlaq Prayer, Imam Sajjad (AS) has placed special emphasis on this in various phrases.

A/1: Asking for the most perfect faith (Make my faith to be the most perfect faith,): In the Holy Qur'an, the rank of faith is high above the rank of Islam (Surah Hujurat: 14). Perhaps faith is the most pivotal human quality in his path toward spiritual perfection and for his right fulfillment of his duties. All other good behaviors come from one's faith.

4 Some of the commentaries are the following: 1).

A/2: Requesting the best of the intentions: The correction and purity of intentions enjoy special status in discussions on ethics. The famous tradition by the Prophet (PBUH), i.e. "Actions are judged by Intentions" has been narrated by both Shia and Sunni Muslims.[5] Moreover, according to Islamic teachings the acceptance of many acts of worship and non-worship depends upon right intention (for proximity to God). In the beginning of Makarim ul-Akhlaq Prayer, Imam Sajjad requests the best of the intentions from the Gracious God, where he says "take my intention to the best of intentions." As a matter of fact, self-purification and wellness of intentions are related to internal and spiritual affairs of man, although with varying degrees based on human behavior. Such a difference indicates the existence of various levels of self-purification and purity of intention. This stage of qualities shows its influence on other stages indeed.

B: Desirable Activities and Avoiding Undesirable Behaviors

In this part, we will focus on individual behaviors and interaction with others will come in the next part. Man should ponder upon his dignity and human value without any comparison with others to do acts that are compatible with his dignity. This has been expressed in various phrases of the Makarim ul-Akhlaq Prayer by Imam Sajjad (AS).

B/1: The best of deeds: Good deed or an act that is compatible with dignity is one of the human virtues. Of course, good deeds come from good intentions. In the first phrases of the Makarim ul-Akhlaq Prayer, Imam Sajjad (AS) requests the best of the deeds from the Gracious God (Take my deeds to the best of deeds.) There are, however, preconditions for attribution of such quality, the most important of which is remembrance of God in all moments of one's life, something that the Imam requests in another phrase (Incite me to remember Thee in times of heedlessness.)

B/2: Testing man in financial matters (by his properties) is undoubtedly more difficult than testing his life. According to the Islamic teachings, Islam attaches great significance to the life, properties and dignity of the individuals (Jawahir al-Kalam, Vol. 2, p. 16). It is very difficult for a man to devote each one of the three and of course, financial test, i.e. success in financial Jihad, is more difficult than devotion of life. Taking this important point into consideration, the Imam asks for financial affordability (Give me moderation in economy) and greater sustenance (Expand Thy provision toward me). He continues with requesting God to put him among the righteous and resilient people (Make me into one of the people of right behavior), and among the pious people (And the servants of righteousness) to enjoy salvation in the Hereafter (and provide me with triumph at the place of Return and safety from the Ambush). Apparently financial Jihad is a very difficult endeavor few people can make success in. That is why the Imam requests God's help in passing the test successfully. This phrase is indeed a

5 Shia scholars: 1- & Sunni scholars.

warning to the human beings not to ignore good behavior and the financial test at a time they enjoy wealth, and they must work more and strive to gain a success in it.

B/3: Right economic management and avoiding prodigality and oppression: Success in the important test on one's wealth and properties requires some steps that Makarim ul-Akhlaq Prayer has paid due attention to. The Imam clearly requests right management and good economic guardianship (Place in me excellent guardianship) and avoiding oppression (Let me not be wronged). There is an important warning and admonition toward the concept of ownership that says all the properties on earth belong to God and He can easily take them away from us (While Thou art powerful over holding me back).

Undoubtedly, such an approach toward the world and the issue of property ownership will lead to good behaviors that are in full compatibility with the principles discussed in previous section (dignity, fairness, justice and freedom). On this basis, the Imam requests another important quality, i.e. needlessness to other peoples' properties and wealth (And tempt me not with ingratitude! Exalt me and afflict me not with pride). Needlessness is one of the important attributes the Islamic teachings have always paid attention to, so that the Prophet (PBUH) says "The dignity of man lies in his needlessness from people." (Tanbih al-Khawatir, p. 69) It must be however, taken into consideration that the dignity of the believers in not dependent upon richness, rather, it lies in their needlessness of the properties and wealth of the others.

B/4: Correcting undesirable ethical qualities: There are recommendations in Islamic teachings that indicate man's efforts to avoid undesirable qualities in his personal and social behaviors and interactions. In some phrases of the Makarim ul-Akhlaq Prayer, this key issue has been taken into consideration, where it is asked from the Gracious God to keep the man safe from undesirable qualities (O God, deposit in me no quality for which I will be faulted, unless Thou set it right), and complete the qualities that are compatible with human dignity (No deficient noble trait, unless Thou completest it). It seems that success in this test is also very difficult that is impossible to make without the help of the Almighty God; thus, the Imam requests the Gracious God not to leave him alone in this path (O God, deposit in me no quality for which I will be faulted).

Seeking power, dominance and prodigality are among the undesirable qualities that can make man fail to pass the financial and economic test. The Makarim ul-Akhlaq Prayer contains precise reference to this where it says "Let me not be insolent while from Thee comes my wealth", that refers to this important fact that the existence of man on earth and his nature belong to God. Upon such an approach to man and humanity, mutiny and ignoring limits and boundaries with such undesirable behaviors as prodigality, will be a big oppression and an unforgivable sin, something the Imam asks for God's help to be away from it (Hold me back from prodigality). It is important to know that there is a difference between prodigality and squandering. Prodigality refers to extravagance in consumption while squandering refers to over-consumption and splurging.

C: Constructive Interaction with others in Business Environment

Undoubtedly creating an appropriate approach in interaction with others is one of the principal goals of Islamic Sharia and its teachings in addition to self-purification of human beings. Hereunder, we will cover some phrases from Makarim ul-Akhlaq Prayer that pay attention to this.

C/1: Preparations for a desirable interaction: If human beings respect dignities and human prestige of one another, their relations will become humane too. All good qualities can be institutionalized in social behaviors. Imam Sajjad in Makarim ul-Akhlaq Prayer requests paying attention to the dignity and prestige of human beings and avoiding faultfinding (Suffice me against the burden of shame toward the servants), avoiding distrust and suspiciousness toward others (The suspicion of the people of righteousness with trust). As we know, trust is one of the most important indicators for social capital and various economic systems have argued its importance (Folland, Sherman; Rocco, Lorenzo, eds. 2014). Perhaps its importance is more than physical and human assets. Islamic teachings, too, shun any attempts for destroying trust and social capital, and instead, encourage avoiding accusations (He who subjects himself to infamy and accusation must not blame the one who is suspicious to him; Saying 151, Nahjul Balagha). In this connection, it is mentioned in Makarim ul-Akhlaq that envy must be turned into friendship (Replace the envy of the people of insolence with affection). According to the phrase, instead of unfair competition, people should seek gaining precedence in doing good (Precedence in reaching excellence, preferring bounteousness). Perhaps, it is a clear reference to a verse in the Holy Qur'an that asks people to race for good (For each [religious following] is a direction toward which it faces. So race to [all that is] good. Wherever you may be, Allah will bring you forth [for judgment] all together. Indeed, Allah is over all things competent; Baqarah: 148)

C/2: Desirable interaction: Following citing sufficient preparations before integration into community life, Makarim ul-Akhlaq Prayer has paid special attention to desirable behavior in interactions with others. Some phrases in this book emphasize good interaction and behavior with others (Repay him who separates from me with gentle devotion) as well as observing social and ethical codes (Make everything he causes to pass over my tongue, - the indecent or ugly words, the maligning of good repute, the false witness, the speaking ill of an absent man of faith or the reviling of one present, and all things similar). Man should respond undesirable behavior by other people with desirable behavior in his interactions, thus the Imam requests good counsel in view of those undesirable behaviors (And point me straight to resist him who is dishonest toward me with good counsel). Such a behavior turns animosity, hostility and unfair competition into friendship and amity; therefore the Imam asks for turning animosity by the close associates into friendship (The enmity of those close with friendship) and compassion of the flatterers into real affection (The attachment of flatterers with love set right).

It is interesting to know that the Imam seeks all these graces for more and better service rendering to the individuals in the community (The rejection of fellows with generous friendliness), as if serving the community is a major and universal responsibility of all human beings in this mission to the transient material world. The Imam also seeks avoiding faultfinding with others (Refraining from condemnation), while paying attention to his shortfalls and saying he is not free from faults himself. He requests, then, desirable conditions to be immune against other people's attempts to find fault with us (Suffice me against the burden of shame toward the servants). This means faultfinding on either side is disagreeable.

Perhaps the Holy Qur'an's verse "Woe to every scorner and mocker" (Surah Al-Humazah, 1) is the origin of this phrase of Makarim ul-Akhlaq Prayer. It should be noted that the Holy Qur'an in the outset of its two chapters used the word "*Wayl*" as rebuke, one of which is specifically related to business interactions, where in rebuke of shortchanging the Holy Qur'an warns of punishment (Woe to those who give less [than due]; Surah Al-Mutafeffin: 1). Although shortchanging by definition clearly refers to exchange of goods, it can be consciously generalized to cover rendering services as well.

Replacing the animosity with friendship is another request at this prayer book (And replace for me the animosity of the people of hatred with love). We know that the principle of pride is a jurisprudential principle in transactions that is essential for creation and sustainability of wholesome market. This means that any loss incurred via treachery or deception by either party in the contract, must be compensated by the other party who is held accountable for this. It may perhaps include other cases such as misrepresentation of goods and services for selling higher than real prices. There are, of course, options for revocation of transaction due to defect or lesion that promote security and instability of transactions in the market.

C/3: Centrality of justice in transaction: A glance at the pertinent phrases of Makarim ul-Akhlaq shows that the dominant attitude in transactions and various man-to-man behaviors must be based on justice. To that end, a phrase in the prayer book says "adorn me with the adornment of the righteous" to highlight observing a pattern of behavior and required orientation toward boosting the culture of justice. At the same time, there is an emphasis on rejecting oppression and suppression (Let me not do wrong while Thou art powerful over holding me back, let me not be misguided while Thou art able to guide me,) and on attempting to fight oppression. The Imam, then, seeks sufficient power to fight oppression that is a precondition for establishing peace in the society, restoring calm and correcting the community (Appoint for me a hand against him who wrongs me, a tongue against him who disputes with me).

D: Good Ending, Ultimate Objective of Interactions

All human affairs and activities must be in line with certain objectives and based on what has been mentioned in the first part of the paper. The main objective behind human behaviors, is fulfilment of responsibilities in the limited mission in this material world. Some phrases of Makarim ul-Akhlaq Prayer contain considerations on secondary goals, while paying attention to the major issues. Undoubtedly unconditional long material life is not desirable in view of Islam. A long life, in view of Islam, is desirable only when it is in line with fulfilling one's responsibilities and with human perfection. Therefore, the Imam in this prayer book seeks a sort of life to be spent on obeying God the Almighty (Let me live as long as my life is a free gift in obeying Thee, but if my life should become a pasture for Satan, seize me to Thyself before Thy hatred overtakes me or Thy wrath against me becomes firm.) The phrase points out that the major goal of an economic man in view of Islam shall not be merely maximization of material gains.

To that end, the book prescribes inattention to wealth accumulation by others (And tempt me not with ingratitude! Exalt me and afflict me not with pride). Of course it is not desirable to be in need in the closing years of one's life. That is why financial affordability (Give me chance to enjoy moderation in spending) and greater sustenance (Appoint for me Thy widest provision in my old age) are among the important requests in this book of prayer. The desirable end for life, after all, must be the one with Divine forgiveness (O God, seal my term with Thy pardon) and protection from the wrath of God (And protect me through Thy mercy "from the chastisement of the Fire").

5 Summary and Conclusion

Surveying in brief the life of man on this material world that has attracted all branches of humanities, this paper claims that humanity of mankind is related to his spiritual and celestial aspects that are associated and blended with material and physical constraints. The paper has also reviewed in brief such important principles as dignity, justice, fairness and freedom – that must be paid due attention vis-à-vis human behavior – with an ethical approach to show that ethics and these principles interchangeably affect one another. The paper continued with extracting and elaborating ethical recommendations from Makarim ul-Akhlaq Prayer of Sahifeh Sajjadieh attributed to the fourth Imam of Shia Muslims, Hazrat Ali bin Hussain (Zeyn al-Abedin (AS)) and showed their impact on human life in business environment.

The principal goal of this paper was opening up a window toward creation of a right image of the humanity of mankind and introducing Makarim ul-Akhlaq Prayer in brief. If this paper brings about even minimum reference to the valuable book of "Sahifeh Sajjadieh" by the researchers and thinkers, it has realized indeed the goal it was after.

References

Alavi Qazvini, Seyyed Ali, and Masoudianzadeh, Seyyed Zabihollah. "Men Lah ul-Ghanam Fe'liya al-Gharam". *Legal Thoughts Research Quarterly*, Winter, 2014.

Al-Bukhari, Abu Abdallah Muhammad ibn Ismai. Sahih al-Bukhari. Damascus-Beirut: Dar ibn Kathir.

Al-Najafi, Muhammad Hassan. Jawahir al-Kalam fi Sharh Shara'i' al-Islam. Beirut: Dar Ehya' Al-Turath Al-Arabi, 1925.

Al-Tusi, Muhammad bin al-Hassan. Al-Mabsut fi Fiqh al-Imamiyya. Tehran: Al-Maktab al-Mortazaviya Publishing House, 2008.

Ansarian, Hossein. Land of the Lovers: Detailed Commentary on Sahifeh Sajjadieh, Vol. 2. Tehran: Payam Azadi, 1993.

Falsafi, Mohammad Taqi. Commentary on and Interpretation of Makarim ul-Akhlaq Prayer. Tehran: Islamic Culture Publishing House.

Farahidi, Khalil bin Ahmad. Kitab al-Ayn. Dar al-Hijrah Institute.

Hatami Mousavi, Akram. Ethical Concepts in View of the Most Elegant Worshipping Soul. Tehran: Kavosh Qalam Publishing House, 2007.

Hosseini Tabatabaei, Seyyed Mohammad Hossein. Tafsir al-Mizan. Qum: Eslami Publishing House, 1997.

Ibn Fars, Ahmad bin Fars bin Zakariya. Miqayees al-Lughat. Qum: Dar al Kutub al Iilmiyah Publishing House, Ismailian.

Ibn Majah, Abu Abdallah Muhammad ibn Yazid al-Qazvini. *Sunan Ibn Majah, research by Muhammad Fuad Abd el-Baqi.* Dar Ehya al-Kotob al-Arabiya.

Ibn Manzur, Jamaluddin Muhammad ibn Mukarram. (n.d.), *Lisan al-Arab*. Beirut: Dar al kotob al ilmiyah Publishing House.

Javadi Amoli, Abdollah. *Dignity in Qur'an*, Second Edition. Tehran: Raja Center for Cultural Publications, 1988.

Javadi Amoli, Abdollah. *The Image and Conduct of Man in Qur'an*, Second Edition. Qum: Asra Institute, 2002.

Kahf, Munzar. *"A Review of Islamic Economy Patterns"*, Translated by Seyyed Hossein Mir Moezzi: Islamic Economy Quarterly, Series 6, No. 21, 2006.

Katouzian, Nasser. *Family Civil Rights*. Tehran: Enteshar & Bahman Borna, 1999.

Kulayni, Muhammad bin Yaqub. *Al-Kafi*. Tehran: Ilmiya al-Islamiya Bookstore.

Mamdouhi Kermanshahi, Hassan. *Intuition and Cognition* (Translation and interpretation of Sahifeh Sajjadieh, Second Edition. Qum: Boostan-e Kitab, 2006.

Mazandarani, Muhammad Salih bin Ahmad. *Sharh al-Kafi (Al-Osul va al-Rowzah)*. Al-Maktaba al-Islamiya le al-Nashr val al-Towzi', 1968.

Mohammadi Reyshahri, Mohammad. *Mizan al-Hekmah*. Qum: Dar al-Hadith Scientific and Cultural Institute, 2010.

Mohammadi Sam, and Fallah Mahdi. "Ethical Foundations of the Principle of Freedom of Titles in Iranian Jurisprudence and Law". *Research Quarterly on Private Law*, Allameh Tabatabaei University, Series 4, No. 12.

Nahjul Balagha

Nayeeni, Mohammad Hossein. *Maniyya al-Talib fi Sharh al-Makasib, authored by Al-Sheikh Musa bin Muhammad al-Najafi al-Khonsari*. Qum: Al-Nashr al-Islamiya affiliated to Society of Seminary Teachers of Qum.

Nouri, Mirza Hassan. *Mustadrak al-Wasa'il*. Qum: Aal al-Beit le-Ehya al-Torath Institute, First Edition, 1987.

Sahifeh Sajjadieh

Shushtari, Sheikh Muhammad Javad bin Sheikh Muhammad. *Sharafat al-A'amaal fi Sharh-e Makarim ul-Akhlaq men al-Sahifeh Sajjadieh.*

The Holy Qur'an

Tonekaboni, Mohammad bin Suleyman. *Commentary on Sahifeh Sajjadieh, First Edition*. Qum: Shams ul-Zoha Publishing House, 2005.

Zu Elm, Mohammad Hossein. *Noor al-Afaq, Commentary on Makarim ul-Akhlaq Prayer*, Tehran: Rayeheh Etrat Publishing House, 2004.

Mohammad Javad Nourahmadi

Chapter 14: Shaheed Sadr's Perspective on Property Rights in Islam

1 Introduction

The existence of conflicts between private interest and public interest and also between selfishness and altruism as well as between efficiency and equity, or between economic growth and justice are issues that have engaged the minds of the greatest thinkers in human history who sought to resolve conflicts between these concepts and to coordinate them in a way that promotes the growth and progress of social systems. These issues have always been among the main concerns of philosophers, theologians, lawyers, political scientists and economists. The key concept and the connector between these topics is ownership rights.

Shaheed Sadr[1] believes that there exists in humans a natural tendency to possess the results of his work to himself, which is expressed in the social concept of ownership. But the nature of the rights that result from this ownership are not established in accordance with a natural tendency. It is the social system that determines it in accordance with its own ideas and interests. For instance, is it the right of the worker, who owns the commodity at work, to use his goods in vain as long as it is his private wealth? Or is it his right to exchange it for another commodity or to trade and develop his wealth by means of making it a commercial or usurious capital? The answer to these questions and the like is given by the social system which determines the rights of private ownership and is not related to the basic human nature and instinct.[2]

Because of this, Islam intervened in determining these rights, rejecting some and accepting others in accordance with its own values and ideas. For instance, it rejected the owner's right to waste their own property or squander in the field of charity, but established his right to utilize it without being wasteful or squander. It denied the owner the right to accumulate wealth which he owned by means of usury, but allowed him to increase the wealth through trade within special limits and conditions and in accordance with its general prescriptions governing distribution which we shall soon discuss in the coming sections.[3]

---

1 Martyr Ayatullah al-Sayyid Muḥammad Bāqir al-Ṣadr (Arabic: السيد محمد باقر الصدر) (b. 1353/1935 – d. 1400/1980) was a *faqih* (jurisprudent), Interpreter of the Holy Qur'an, thinker and also a political activist in *Iraq*. To learn more about his economic books, refer to the attachment.

2 Shaheed Seyyed Mohammad Baqir. Al-Sadr, *Iqtisaduna*, Vol. I, Part. II (Tehran, Iran: World Organization for Islamic Services, 1984), 123.

3 Al-Sadr, *Iqtisaduna*, 124.

https://doi.org/10.1515/9783110593419-014

The pursuit of desire to possess, is not undesirable in itself, and it provides the basis for increased efficiency and economic growth by creating the incentive for work, effort and productivity, savings and investment. But the desire for possession is infinite and insatiable and has the potential to threaten public interest, undermining ethics and incentives for altruism, leading eventually to the emergence of economic inequalities and injustice in social systems through violation of the interests of others, ignoring the needs of fellowmen, and unbalanced accumulation of wealth in the society and to leading to domination over others.

If everything was found in the nature in abundance, that is, if there was no scarcity, there would be no problem, or if there was a limit to all human needs and wants, it would not be a matter of concern. But the wealth and the benefits of nature are not unlimited, and therefore humans battle and compete for possession.[4] The most important question facing great scholars throughout the history has been how should the ownership structure be designed and how property should be distributed among the population in a way that is both efficient and fair, serving both individual and public interests, while satisfying selfish desire to possess property without undermining altruism, while promoting economic growth with justice.

Ownership has several components:[5]

1. **Objects of Property**: What can be owned? Material assets include physical and objective assets such as cars and land. They also include nonmaterial assets, such as patents, known as intellectual property.
2. **Subjects of Property**: Who may own it? Assets can be privately owned or owned privately by the members of the society or by the state.
3. **Articulation of Use or** "Property rights", i.e. rights to usufructs of what is owned. It stipulates what can be done with property. Property rights include many features that are presented as a package or set of rights each of which represents a different aspect of property ownership. These features include the right to use (and thus benefit from) an asset, the right to prevent others from using property and the right to transfer assets to others.
4. **Enforcement of Rights:** The social rules that constitute property rights are neither self-evident nor self-enforcing in and of themselves. Who specifies and enforces these rules? Property rights may be formally determined by the country's legislative system or determined unofficially according to social customs and traditions. Thus, the acquisition of property rights is subject to the rule of law and the institutional framework governing the country.

4 Mohammad Ali. Movahed, *In Search of Right and Justice* (Tehran: Karnameh Publishing, 2002), 27.

5 Bruce G. Carruthers., and Laura. Ariovich. "The Sociology of Property Rights," Annul. Rev. Social, no.30 (2004).

5. **Transfer of Rights**: Property rights are established and extinguished, and move between owners. Today, many transfers are accomplished through market exchanges, but other types of exchange also occur.

Different dimensions of ownership, characterize the ownership structure in theories and economic systems. In this paper, the ownership concept is synonymous with the ownership structure, property rights institution and ownership system, which covers the various dimensions mentioned above. Ownership in all economic systems has a central role in the dualities such as economic growth and distribution of income and wealth, freedom and justice, as well as government and markets.

There is no disagreement among scholars about the existence of the ownership institution and the need for precise definition and protection of property rights as an economic institution providing discipline and security in economic systems. But there is a serious disagreements over the various aspects of the ownership structure. The root answer to these issues is given in ethical, legal, and political systems, based on the specific definition of the social justice. It should be noted that justice itself is also defined on the basis of prevalent anthropology and ontology in social systems. Thus, the difference between economic systems relating to the optimal structure of ownership is derived from the different anthropology and ontology that exists in each system and leads to different conceptions of justice.

In this paper, In addition to presenting an explanation of the ownership structure, we will seek to answer two important questions based on the views of Shaheed Sadr:

1. What is the ethical basis of ownership structure in Islamic economic system?
2. What are the consequences of a fair and ethical ownership structure in the Islamic economic system? In other words, how does a moral and fair ownership structure play a role in the realization of economic justice, which is the main objective of the Islamic economic system?

2 Explaining the Concept of Ownership Structure

Ownership, property rights, and ownership structures are highly relevant concepts. "Ownership" refers to the attribution of an asset or the ability (control?) of a real or legal person over a period of time.[6] Sir William Blackstone famously defined property as: ". . . that sole and despotic dominion which one man claims and exercises over the external things of the world, in total exclusion of the right of any other individual in the universe."[7] Therefore, the Power to exercise control over an asset or resource is

6 Mohsen. Renani, *Bazar and Na bazar* (Tehran: Planning and Budget Organization, 1997), 287.

7 W. Blackstone, *Commentaries on the Laws of England*, Vol. 2., (Chicago: Univ. Chicago Press, 1766 (1979)). Quoted from Bruce G. Carruthers., and Laura. Ariovich. "The Sociology of Property Rights," Annul. Rev. Social, no.30 (2004).

regarded as ownership. Often defined also as the residual rights of control, meaning that ownership confers on the owner the right to exercise control over the resource only within certain limits determined by the legal system and/or contractual obligations.[8] But "property rights" stipulate how to benefit from or do harm through ownership of an asset or the possession of the power to the owners themselves or to others. In fact, all decisions, forecasts and plans of individuals and units for communicating with others, engaging in economic activity, such as exchange and others, are carried out in accordance with and in the context of the requirements that constitute "property rights".[9]

About the right of ownership, I. Fisher said: "A property right is the liberty or permit to enjoy benefits of wealth while assuming the costs which those benefits entail… property rights are not physical things or events, but are abstract social relations. A property right is not a thing."[10] Therefore, property rights are relations among men that arise from the existence of scarce goods and pertain to their use. By the term "property rights," economists usually mean private property rights. However, there are other forms of property rights, such as collective property rights, for example, ownership of a lake or a forest that everyone has the right to use, but not the right to prevent others from using them. There are also state property rights that exist in socialist economic systems in which government agents control the use of resources.[11]

Ownership can be viewed as a "bundle of sticks," composed of the following rights:[12]

C: The right to *control* the asset and decide on its use.
V: A claim to the *value* the asset generates.
E: The right to *exclude* others from using the asset.
T: The right to *transfer* the bundle *C*, *V*, *E*, *T* to another holder.

The right of ownership contains the following four elements:[13]
(i) the right to use an asset (usus)
(ii) The right to capture benefits from that asset (usus fructus).

8 Syed B. Hussain, *Encyclopedia of Capitalism* (New York: Golson Books, Ltd, 2004), 629.
9 Renani, *Bazar and Na bazar*, 287.
10 I. Fisher, *Elementary Principles of Economics* (New York: Macmillan, 1923), 27. Quoted from Svetozar. Pejovich, *The Economics of Property Rights* (Dordrecht, the Netherlands: Kluwer Academic Publishers, 1990), 27.
11 Svetozar. Pejovich, *The Economics of Property Rights* (Dordrecht, the Netherlands: Kluwer Academic Publishers, 1990).
12 Dennis C. Mueller, *The Oxford Handbook of Capitalism* (Oxford: Oxford University Press, 2012).
13 Svetozar. Pejovich, *The Economics of Property Rights* (Dordrecht, the Netherlands: Kluwer Academic Publishers, 1990), 28.

(iii) the right to change its form and substance (abusus), and
(iv) The right to transfer all or some of the rights specified under (i), (ii), and (iii) to others at a mutually agreed upon price.

The most important components of the bundle of rights that define ownership are exclusivity and alienability. Exclusivity refers to the right to determine who may (and who may not) use the resource in a particular way. Alienability refers to the right to reassign ownership to someone else, including the right to offer for sale at any price.[14]

It is important to understand that property rights do not regulate the relationship between the owner and his or her property but the relationship between the owner and other persons, with respect to the property. Unlike contract, which regulates the relationship between specific parties, property rights are rights against the world. Owners of property can be individuals, groups of individuals, organizations, or the state. And property owned can be tangible, such as personal property or real property (land), or intangible, such as corporate stock or intellectual property. Furthermore, property rights may or may not be formally recorded and may be granted perpetually or over a limited duration (e.g., patents, copyrights).[15]

3 The Ethical Basis of the Ownership Structure in the Islamic Economic System from the Viewpoint of Shaheed Sadr (RA)

To understand the ethical basis of the ownership structure[16] in the Islamic economic system, it is first necessary to examine the bases of Islamic anthropology and ontology. As we will see, the starting point of Islamic economic thought, instead of focusing on the scarcity of natural resources, is to pay attention to some of the moral vices of man, such as greed and injustice, which leads to unfairness and inefficiency in the economic system. The shift from a material to a spiritual and monotheistic and moral vision of man, based on the two concepts of *Khilafah* (vice regency) and the guidance of man through revelation and prophecy, will be the basis for the formation of a fair ownership structure. In the following, we will describe anthropology and ontology underlying the ownership structure in the Islamic economic system from the perspective of Shaheed Sadr (RA).

---

14 Hussain, *Encyclopedia of Capitalism*, 629.
15 Mueller, *The Oxford Handbook of Capitalism*.
16 To study the ownership structure in relation to the concepts of justice and economic growth in the development of economic thoughts, you can refer to Nourahmadi (2013).

3.1 Is the Root of Economic Problems to be Found in the Scarcity in the Nature or in the Excessive Wants and Desires of Man

From Sadr's point of view, the economic problem according to the capitalist system is that "the natural resources of wealth cannot keep pace with the growth of civilization to ensure satisfaction of all the needs and desires that are ever growing."[17] On the other hand, the economic problem according to the Marxism is the "contradiction between the mode of production and distribution relations. Therefore, whenever there is consistency between the two, stability in the economic life is the result, irrespective of the social system resulting from the agreement between the mode of production and distribution relations."[18]

According to Shaheed Sadr, In Islam, the real problem relates to man himself, not to nature, and not to the mode of production because, as the Qur'an declares: "And He gives you of all that you ask Him; and if you count Allah's favors, you will not be able to number them; most surely man is very unjust, very ungrateful: "إن الانسان لَظلومٌ كَفّار.[19] Shaheed Sadr says: "Thus man's unjust behavior in his practical life and his ingratitude of the Divine bounty are the real causes of the economic problems in man's life. Man's injustice in the economic field is due to mal-distribution while his ingratitude of Divine bounty lies in his exploitation of the nature and in his negative attitude towards it. So when injustice in the social relations of distribution is removed and the abilities of humans are collectively mobilized to take employ natural resources to meet the need of all, the economic problem disappears. Islam is, indeed, committed to the eradication of economic injustice by means of the solutions it has proposed in the areas of distribution and circulation of wealth. It has also addressed the issue of ingratitude by prescribing concepts and rules that govern production and consumption."[20]

In the fourth part of this paper, we will describe the distribution, exchange and production theories of Shaheed Sadr.

3.2 Spiritual View and Human Ethical Training: Solution to Economic Problems

Shaheed Sadr believes the only solution to the economic problem is to shift the understanding of living and life away from a materialistic conception of life. According to Sadr, Islam does not reject private property. On the contrary, it guarantees it within

---

17 Shaheed Seyyed Mohammad Baqir. Al-Sadr, *Iqtisaduna,* Vol. I, Part. II (Tehran, Iran: World Organization for Islamic Services, 1984), 108.
18 Al-Sadr, *Iqtisaduna,* 109.
19 Holy Qur'an, Surah Ibrahim, Verse: 34.
20 Al-Sadr, *Iqtisaduna,* 110.

the society without any contradiction. Islam rejects the materialist interpretation and offers a new understanding of existence and life in this universe. Islam considers attaining Divine satisfaction and approval – the authentic ethical measure by which human action is judged – as the most fundamental objective of human life.[21] Shaheed Sadr believes that religion unifies indicators individuals' perception of their personal interests and what is considered (by religion) as worthy to be followed in order to ensure felicity, wellbeing, and justice in human life.[22] This unification occurs through two methods. Using the first method, religion provides its vision of correct way of living and explains that life on earth constitutes a beginning stage of life everlasting. The efforts that a person exert in this life toward achieving Divine satisfaction become source of benefit and felicity in the life to come. Accordingly, while the ethical standard, Divine satisfaction, ensures individual interests, it, concurrently, contributes to actualization of societal objectives. Islam takes the individual by the hand and leads him/her to cooperation with others to achieve social benefits and social justice, hence, Divine satisfaction. According to the logic of Islam, any effort exerted and any activity performed by the individual to promote social benefits will, simultaneously, the individual's Own interests. Islam shifts the perception of individuals regarding their self- interests such that they will perceive a binding connection between their own interests and those of the humanity as a whole, structured according to the vision of Islam.[23]

The second method utilized by religion to coordinate and collate internal motivations and values and interests of society is through specific cultivation of ethics that elevates human sympathies, empathies and ethical sensitivities in the individual. Additionally, since, on the one hand, there are materialistic and base motivations and desires that are constantly in motion within the human nature, and, on the other hand, human nature also contains, spiritual potentialities, capabilities and desires, religion elevates this facet of human nature by nurturing it through cultivation, education and training of its various dimensions.[24] It is natural for man that left to himself, his materialistic and base instincts dominate his spiritual needs. Religion nurtures sympathies and sensitivities and edifies humans such that ethical values become part of their preference orderings to the point that when these values are actualized they experience pleasure.[25] There are, therefore, these two elements of "spiritual cognition of human life" and "ethical nurturing of human psyche" that together obliterate deeply rooted social malaise. They, acting in tandem, ensure a fair individual and social life and lead humanity to truth, goodness and justice.

---

21 Shaheed Seyyed Mohammad Baqir. Al-Sadr, *Islam and Economic Schools* (Qum: Mehr Printing, 1976), 34.

22 Al-Sadr, *Islam and Economic Schools*, 36.

23 Al-Sadr, Islam and Economic Schools., 37.

24 Al-Sadr, Islam and Economic Schools, 38.

25 Al-Sadr, Islam and Economic Schools, 38.

3.3 Human Agency and the Testimony and Witnessing of the Prophets of Allah: Two Pillars of Formation of a Unified Society and Just Social Life

Such a life as described in the last paragraph, in Shaheed Sadr's view, is grounded on two pillars: human agency (*Khilafah*) on earth and "the testimony of the Prophets." Allah (swt) has gifted humans with the honor of being His agency/trusteeship on earth.The office of agency is the gift of Allah by which humans are distinguished from the rest of creation earning the acknowledgement of the angels who as a sign of this acknowledgement made *Sujud*[26] to Adam (as). The *Khilafah*, or human agency and stewardship means that God Almighty has given the human community, Governing the people and Administration of Community Affairs and leading the world and Natural and social development of the earth.

Broadly, the following elements and attributes define the concept of human collective agency:[27]

1. Identification of human collectivity by its association with and belief in the axis of the One and Only Creator, Ruler, and Owner of all Creation. This is the concept of pure *Tawhid*[28] based upon which Islam is founded.
2. Establishment of social relations based on the concept of acknowledgement of perfect servitude to the Creator and the liberation of man from the bondage to titled and named powers that are manifestations of all kinds of exploitation, ignorance and tyranny.
3. Actualization of the spirit of brotherhood among all members of humanity in all social aspects after elimination of all exploitation and domination.
4. Khilafah, stewardship or agency means conferring trusteeship to human collectivity. For this reason, the Qur'an refers to Khilafah as *amanah*[29], "trust" meaning that the office of agency has associated responsibilities and obligations.

Responsibility is a two-way relationship: On the one hand, responsibility requires commitment. The human community must judge fairly and through implementation of the rules of behavior – prescribed by the Creator – among the members of society as prescribed by the Creator, demonstrate its divine trusteeship. On the other hand, responsibility implies that humans are free beings since without freedom, responsibility is not meaningful. Allah has appointed a being as His trustee or agent who has

---

26 *Sujūd* or sajdah is an Arabic word meaning prostration to God (Arabic: الله Allah) in the direction of the Kaaba at Mecca.

27 Shaheed Seyyed Mohammad Baqir. Al-Sadr, *Al-Islam yaqud al-hayat* (Qum: Dar al-Sadr Publications, 2015), 151.

28 *Tawḥīd* (Arabic: التَّوحيد), or *monotheism* is the most fundamental doctrine in Islam, which means believing in the oneness and uniqueness of God and not ascribing any partners to Him.

29 Holy Qur'an, Surah Al-Ahzab, Verse: 72.

free choice to engage in good or corrupt activities on earth and who, using his own free will and choice, determines the results of actualization of his choices. There can, however, be no expectation that such a being with free will and choice and with the powers invested in him as the agent of the Creator on earth, upon whose will humanity's course of history could well depend and whose compliance with prescribed rules are not guaranteed, would always avoid bad, malicious and corrupt activities.[30]

It should be noted that the freedom of the being whom Allah has chosen to serve as His agent on earth does not mean that he is left all to his devices, it only means that he has different means of guidance of this being is different from all others in the creation. Instead of guiding him through immutable, unchanging and non-violable laws which guide the movements plants, stars, and every atom in the universe, He has provided a clear and unerring Book through which the human being is nurtured to elevate himself toward the highest state of excellence that His Creator has intended for all humans. Thus he is given the freedom to choose to shape his own destiny. Allah (swt) has prescribe the law of evolution toward perfection through another means in tandem with the responsibility of agency and stewardship. That means is the testimony that implements divine leadership and the divine guiding light on earth.[31]

The divine *Khilafah* of the human community, according to its characteristics, as already mentioned, has its own nature, eliminates all artificial and constraining barriers that waste human energies and talents, thus, provides real and genuine opportunity for progress of human beings. The true growth and development according to Islam is that human beings – the Khilafah of Allah on earth – internalizes the values that he believes are collectively and in unity present in his Creator who has appointed him as his agent and trustee placing him at the helm of the course of existence. Therefore, attributes and characteristics with which Allah (swt) defines himself (such as justice, knowledge, power, kindness towards the oppressed, and retribution against tyrants, and endless forgiveness) are indicators and objective of human behavior in the Khilafah society; a society in which all members consider themselves as agent and trustee of the Creator. In Hadith it is stated: "تشبهوا باخلاق الله", that is, adopt the attributes of Allah. Since these values are absolute and unlimited in the Divine nature, and on the other hand, the human Khilafah of the Lord is a limited creature (with limited abilities), it is natural that the process of actualization these values in man is a continuous and endless movement towards that Absolute Being.[32]

To the extent that man can ascend toward Allah in actualizing His attributes – such as justice, power, mercy, forgiveness and confronting oppression – he will draw nearer to Allah. The fact that justice is considered second among the principles of religion, and thus distinguished from other divine attributes, is an indication of the

30 Al-Sadr, *Al-Islam yaqud al-hayat*, 152–153.
31 Al-Sadr, Al-Islam yaqud al-hayat, 154–155.
32 Al-Sadr, Al-Islam yaqud al-hayat, 156.

importance of the practical manifestation of the role of this crucial attribute of Allah in directing humans' forward and upward movement. Justice is the fundamental precondition for actualization of all other excellent values in the ascension of individual toward highest level of human state founded on the idea of social justice, one without which society lacks the ecosystem necessary for the emergence growth of other high values and talents. Khilafah, therefore, is a continuous movement towards high values of justice and empowerment, one without a specific stopping point since it is a movement towards the Absolute.[33]

Allah has coupled testimony and witnessing with Khilafah, and this Divine intervention is meant to protect the Khilafah human from going stray and in order to give him a compass to move toward perfection of Khilafah state. Allah knows the temptations of the human psyche, the talents and the sensitivities of human soul, how temptations and base drives influence him, and the weaknesses that lead him to failure.[34] The Holy Qur'an[35] divides witnesses into three classes: prophets, the *rabbis* and the *priests*. The *priests* (*Ahbar*) are the scholars of the pathways prescribed by Allah (*shari'ah*, rules governing human behavior) and the *Rabbis* (the *Rabbanioon)* occupy a middles position between the prophets and the scholars, i.e. they are the *Imams*.[36]

In general, the common role of witnessing among the three classes is:[37]

1. Learning the celestial mission and protecting it
2. Care and oversight of human activity in order to play its role in the actualization of the function of Khilafah and guiding humans to that end
3. Intervention to prevent deviation and to take any action possible for the wellbeing of the path of evolution-toward-perfection of Khilafah

Shaheed Sadr mentions Four stages for the human Khilafah and for the testimony of the Prophets:[38]

The first stage is the stage of the primordial nature (*Fetrat*) that grants governance of the human society to humans themselves. The role of prophets at this stage is to guide, set directions for and supervise humans.

The second stage is that of the emergence of exploitation, conflict of interests, ignorance and injustice as the result of which Prophets raise up and revolt in order to lead the society to the *Fitri* path (the path imprinted on the primordial nature), based on Divine revelations, and eradication of exploitation and injustice. Prophets do this by inviting people to mount two types of jihad. One is the *jihad of Akbar* (the greatest struggle) in which the weak and oppressed restructure and remake themselves

33 Al-Sadr, Al-Islam yaqud al-hayat., 156–157.
34 Al-Sadr, Al-Islam yaqud al-hayat., 159.
35 Holy Qur'an, Surah Al-Ma'idah, Verse: 44
36 I Al-Sadr, Al-Islam yaqud al-hayat., 160.
37 Al-Sadr, Al-Islam yaqud al-hayat., 161.
38 Al-Sadr, Al-Islam yaqud al-hayat., 171–190.

through an internal struggle to conquer their whims, temptations and weaknesses in order to become leaders well prepared and empowered for creating major changes in the society. The other is the minor struggle (*Jihad Asghar*) to remove exploiters and oppressors from their position to create the type of society intended by the Creator, that is the Khilafah Society. At this stage, the Prophet takes the leadership of the Khilafah society that Allah has granted the people on earth.

The third stage is the continuation of the prophet's revolution by the Imam. At this stage, Imam is witness of and a testifier to the behavior of people as well the agent and trustee (*Khalifah*) of Allah on earth.

The fourth stage is that *of religious* authority (*Marja'iyyah*; مرجعيت) or the third level of witnessing and testifying. When a society is governed by tyranny, the general trusteeship (*Khilafah 'Aammah*) of the society belongs to the religious authority (*Marja'*). However, when the governance of tyrants and oppressors is eradicated, Khilafah is returned to the people collectively.

3.4 The Human *Khilafah* and its Implications for Ownership and Justice

Islam considers Allah as the original owner of all things. In accordance with this principle, the Creator has given humans the role of trustee (*Khilafah*) of all resources on earth in order to manage the affairs of the world. These resources All resources on earth.[39] Therefore, humans are obligated to use these resources, which are placed with them in trust by the Original owner, according to the rules prescribed by the Creator. Shaheed Sadr believes: "If this specifically Islamic way of thinking governs Muslim society, it will, much like a guiding force, control actions and behavior of people and, like a binding constraint, make the human owner comply with the Divine prescribed rules."[40] Also: "Once this idea spreads, social relations strengthen and mitigate selfish ownership," moderates the behavior of the rich, and creates dynamism within social and economic life.[41]

Allah, then, is the Original owner and has appointed humans as the Khilafah, trustee, of all resources and wealth in existence.[42] He says in the Qur'an: "It is He who has appointed you agents/trustee in the earth; so he who disbelieves, his disbelief be on his own head. Their disbelief does not bring them anything more than abhorrence

39 Shaheed Seyyed Mohammad Baqir. Al-Sadr, *A Picture of Islamic Economics* (Tehran: Roozbeh Publication, 1980), 13.

40 Shaheed Seyyed Mohammad Baqir. Al-Sadr, *Iqtisaduna*, Vol. II, Part. I (Tehran, Iran: World Organization for Islamic Services, 1984), 171.

41 Al-Sadr, *Iqtisaduna*, Vol. II, Part. I, 172.

42 Shaheed Seyyed Mohammad Baqir. Al-Sadr, *Al-Islam yaqud al-hayat* (Qum: Dar al-Sadr Publications, 2015), 49.

of their Lord. For the disbelievers, their disbelief brings nothing other than loss."[43] It is Allah who has appointed humans as agent/trustee and if He wills, this appointment will be revoked "...if He Wills, He will remove you and, thereafter, appoint whom He wills as agent/trustee."[44]

It is embedded in the nature of the agency/trusteeship to imposes an obligation on the trustee to perform, to the best of his/her ability, the duties of trusteeship.[45] Allāh says: "Believe *in Allāh and His Messenger, and spend of that unto which He has made you trustee. And those of you who believe and expend shall have a mighty reward."*[46] A consequence of agency/trusteeship is that the trustee is accountable to the trustor regarding the way the trustee has used the resources entrusted to her/him. Hence Allah (swt) says: "Then we appointed you viceroys in the earth so that we might see how you behave."[47]

Shaheed Sadr believes that, in principle, the office of Khilafah belongs to the human collectivity because the objective is to create enabling condition for the use of the created resources for the benefit of mankind[48] as is declared in the Qur'an: "It is *He who has created for you all things that are on earth.*"[49] The second phase of human *Khilāfah*, from Shaheed Sadr's perspective, is the Khilafah of individuals who have gained private property legitimately, based on *Fiqhi* and legal rules. This Khilafah is trusteeship, conferred on the individual by the society.[50]

Since the office of *Khilāfah* (general trusteeship) is conferred by Allah upon human society as a whole and since individual property ownership is an aspect of the Khilafah (individual trusteeship) conferred upon individuals by the society, neither the connection, of the Original Creator nor that, of the society to property of individuals ever terminate; the supervision responsibilities of the society, with respect to property, continues. As an example, the society is obligated to protect the property in possession of mentally challenged individuals against abuse since the latter is unable to perform the responsibilities of trusteeship.[51] In this context, Allāh (swt) says: "Do not entrust your property that Allah has made means of support for you *to those weak of understanding; but use (part of it to) feed and clothe them and speak to them words of gentleness.*"[52] This imperative is addressed to the human society as a whole, for the *Khilāfah* (trusteeship, stewardship or agency) belongs to human collectivity prohibiting allowing abuse, hoarding or squander of resources and wealth, that are intended

43 Holy Qur'an, Surah Fatir, Verse: 39
44 Holy Qur'an, Surah Al-An'am, Verse: 133
45 Al-Sadr, *Al-Islam yaqud al-hayat*, 50.
46 Holy Qur'an, Surah Al-Hadid, Verse: 7
47 Holy Qur'an, Surah Yunus, Verse: 14
48 Al-Sadr, *Iqtisaduna*, Vol. II, Part. I, 173.
49 Holy Qur'an, Surah Al-Baqarah, Verse: 29
50 Al-Sadr, *Al-Islam yaqud al-hayat*, 52.
51 Al-Sadr, *Iqtisaduna*, Vol. II, Part. I, 173.
52 Holy Qur'an, Surah An-Nisa, Verse: 5

to serve the interests of humanity, in the hands of those who are "weak of mind." It is therefore the human society which has the responsibility of Khilafah. Then, if private ownership is unable or unwilling to serve this objective, society must perform its responsibility of ensuring that resources and wealth are indeed utilized in ways that benefit the whole society.[53]

In summary, according to Shaheed Sadr's view, a person sees himself as responsible to the Creator in his use of his resources and wealth. Additionally, the individual is responsible to the society as well. The fundamental question is what are these responsibilities to Allah in the context of his role as Khilafah? To answer this question, Shaheed Sadr investigates (34:14): "And He Gave you everything you asked Him, and if you (try to) count the bounty of Allah you cannot reckon it. Lo! The human indeed wrong-doer, an ingrate."[54] The Verse refers to two human deviations: being unjust and being ungrateful to his Creator for all His blessings. Shaheed Sadr believes that, in the context of this Verse, injustice means misdistribution of wealth and misallocation of resources among members of the society. This is injustice which parts of the society commit against other segments. Ingratitude, again in the context of this Verse, Shaheed Sadr believes, means the failure of human society to actualize the potential abilities and talents gifted by the Creator to individuals or, in other words, failure to create opportunities for scientific discoveries, inventions and innovations. This is an injustice the society commits against itself.[55]

According to his understanding of the Verse, Shaheed Sadr specifies two duties humans have toward Allah: (1) Justice in the distribution of wealth meaning that any access to societal wealth is consistent with the general Khilafah of collective humanity; just as, by the same token, respecting the right of Khilafah in all of creation is necessary; and (2) justice in protection as well as the expansion of wealth of the society, meaning that the growth of wealth must take place through utilization of the totality of all of human abilities in use of natural resources and Divine blessings to develop the earth.[56]

3.5 Social Justice: The Purpose of Divine Standards Related to Wealth and Ownership

According to Shaheed Sadr's view, the Creator has appointed humans as His trustee, agent or steward on earth and has given them two responsibilities: (1) implementing justice in the distribution of wealth; and (2) protection and expansion of wealth. He has also provided the human Khilafah (His trustee, agent or steward on earth)

53 Al-Sadr, *Iqtisaduna*, Vol. II, Part. I, 174.
54 Holy Qur'an, Surah Ibrahim, Verse: 34.
55 Al-Sadr, *Iqtisaduna*, Vol. I, Part. II, 110.
56 Al-Sadr, *A Picture of Islamic Economics*, 15.

guidance by means of nurturing and training of the human trustee through the instrumentality of the testimony and the witnessing of the Prophets, the Imams, and religious authorities so that they are empowered to establish a just society on earth. Shaheed Sadr believes that Islamic economics means implementation of Islam's rules that governing wealth and responsibility for actualization of Islam's conception of justice on earth in compliance with the Will of Allah.[57]

By reviewing the principles of Islam, Shaheed Sadr addresses the plan of God to establish a divine society based on right and justice: The five principles, or axioms (1. *Tawhid* meaning that there is only one and unique Creator; 2. *Prophethood*; 3. *'Adl*, justice; 4. *Ma'aad*, Return to origin and accountability before the Creator for the deeds done in this world; and 5. *Imamah*, the Leadership of the Community) are considered to constitute the foundation of Islam, and the essential content of the Divine mission, can best objectify, outline and design for humanity the vision of the social revolution of the prophets and make available to humans the idea of the general Khilafah on earth. From a social perspective, the first among these five principles, *Tawhid*, means that the ownership of all things belongs to the Creator and no other imagined deity. The second fundamental principle means that Prophets are assigned the task of communicating to humans the optimal rules of behavior compliance with which guarantees wellbeing on this plane of existence and felicity in the Hereafter as well as the task of guiding social revolutions when and where necessary. The third principle, *'Adl*, means that the right of possession of the blessings, resources and wealth provided by the Creator is transferred to the worthy and virtuous society as a whole in which no one or group has priority over anyone else or other groups in accessing these resources. The third principle, *Ma'aad*, represents the foundation stone of belief in ultimate accountability and preference for accumulation of good deeds that bring reward in the Hereafter rather than focus on wealth, pleasures and possessions of this world. Finally, the fifth principle, *Imamah*, refers to the leadership of the society after Prophets and continuation of their revolution until the society achieves the desired objective in its role as the Khilafah of Allah. The third principle represents the foundation stone of belief in accountability and concern for the immortality of the human essence which is to be preferred to focus on wealth and possessions in the transitory life of this world.[58]

According to Shaheed Sadr, "Islam has come to regulate the economic life and set up a system based on social justice worthy enough to serve as the basis of economic life."[59] Thus, Islamic economics represents justice from the point of view of Islam and the just method of organizing the life of the economy. "Islam has clarified the domain of justice and has prescribed rules that govern in all facets of social life including

57 Ibid., 22.
58 Al-Sadr, A Picture of Islamic Economics, 17–22.
59 Al-Sadr, *Islam and Economic Schools*, 166.

production, exchange, and distribution of wealth. Any incidents of ignorance of and noncompliance with these rules and the domain established for justice is considered transgression against the rights of others and, therefore."[60] Therefore, Islam has based the framework of the Islamic economic system on the foundation of justice. Consequently, social justice in Islam is not a dry and empty conception amenable to a variety of rationalization and interpretation. To actualize this crucial concept, Islam has proposed a clear and specific framework that could be implemented in a live and dynamic society.[61]

4 Implications of the Fair Ownership Structure for the Realization of Justice in the Islamic Economic System

As we noted, the value-base of the structure of ownership is itself founded on the concept of Khilafah (trusteeship, stewardship or agency) of man on earth and his guidance by Divine and religious teachings. The most important goal of religions, especially Islam, is the realization of justice and fairness in social and economic systems. Islam's principle of social justice is embodied in the conception of production, distribution and exchange of wealth in the Islamic society.[62] Since, in Shaheed Sadr's view, exchange – which is a secondary tier of distribution through property ownership – is part of distribution, rules governing wealth in Islam can be investigated within the framework of production and distribution. In what follows, theories of distribution and production and the relationship between these and conceptions of property ownership and justice in the thoughts of Shaheed Sadr will be discussed.

4.1 The Distribution Theory of Shaheed Sadr: Equitable Distribution of Income and Wealth

Throughout history, humans have suffered injustice and inequity in various systems of distribution of income and wealth. These inequities were, at times, due to the individual-based nature of the wealth-distribution system which led to transgressions against the interests of the public. At other times, inequities emerged because the wealth-distribution system was excessively focused on public interests thus

60 Al-Sadr, A Picture of Islamic Economics, 176.

61 Mohammad Ali. Taskhiri, *Fifty Lessons in Islamic Economics* (Tehran: Publishing the Middle East Culture, 2003), 190.

62 Al-Sadr, *Islam and Economic Schools*, 175.

individual rights were violated and their interests threatened. Shaheed Sadr argues that distributive system, organized according to Islamic teachings, is such that the interests of the public and the individual are protected. He asserts that the basis of wealth distribution system has two components: (1) Work; and (2) Need which are together instruments of the initial wealth distribution. In his view, ownership constitutes the secondary instrument.[63] The next section discusses the thoughts of Shaeed Sadr relating to his theories of distribution before and after production, exchange and redistribution.

4.1.1 Obtaining Work-Based Ownership in Distribution Theories Before and After Production and Exchange Theory

Labor is considered as the fundamental basis of ownership in the distribution system, according to the teachings of Islam. According to Shaheed Sadr "work allows labor to own what he produces indicating man's natural desire to own and control what he produces as well as the benefits that accrue from that ownership and control. Therefore, work-based ownership is the natural right of man which originates in his natural sentiments."[64] In Shaheed Sadr's view, since, based on natural human sentiments, Islam considers labor as the foundation of property ownership, two important consequences follow:

(1) since work is the foundation of ownership and the results of individual labor belongs to the worker, private property ownership is valid. An important point that Shaheed Sadr notes is that while a person owns what he produces, rights associated with this ownership are no longer related to natural sentiments. Instead, they are determined by the social system based on public interests. This is the reason Islam intervenes in the determination of the rights that govern private property ownership. For example, Islam forbids unlimited or wasteful spending on consumption. Another example, Islam does not permit wealth accumulation through Riba-based transactions while allowing the owner to do so through economic activities within a specific framework and under specified conditions.[65]

(2) Private property ownership has limitations since work is the foundation of ownership, private ownership can only be exercised by a person if his work has indeed been involved in the production of the property. Consequently, private ownership does not extend to property in whose production human work has had no role. On this basis, there are two types of wealth: (a) Private; and

63 Al-Sadr, *Iqtisaduna*, Vol. I, Part. II, 111.

64 Al-Sadr, Iqtisaduna, Vol. I, Part. II, 114.

65 Al-Sadr, *Iqtisaduna*, Vol. I, Part. II, 123. And Taskhiri, *Fifty Lessons in Islamic Economics*, 447.

(b) public wealth. The former covers property in whose production involves human labor either through direct. This can happen in two ways: a product is produced directly through exertion of human labor, such as the production of agricultural or textile products, or through indirect human effort, such as digging for water or oil. The latter are properties in producing of which man has not been involved like land and mines. Therefore, these kinds of property do not fall within the purview of private property. They belong to the public as a whole.[66]

4.1.1.1 Ownership and Distribution Before Production

The distribution of the wealth takes place at two levels: productive resources and produced wealth. The former includes: nature, capital and labor.[67] In his theory of "distribution before production," Shaheed Sadr sets aside consideration of capital and labor to focus only on the way ownership of natural resources is acquired.

According the Shaheed Sadr, in capitalism, distribution of natural resources is under the control of the powerful members of the society. Hence individuals can own natural resources and expropriate the products these resources produce. In Marxism, resulting output of each production cycle is related to the mode of production: there is an inevitable relation between production and distribution. The focus of Islam is on the individual human needs that must be met. For this reason, the ownership of natural resources takes three forms: private, public and government.[68] Sadr develops the proposition that "labor is the origin of rights and private ownership of natural resources." Two factors influence the position of labor within this framework: Kind of labor and the associated rights. These two factors differ depending on circumstances. For example, taking possession of a piece of land is not considered work, but possession of rocks gathered in the wilderness is considered work and can be owned privately. Similarly, working in a mine allows private ownership of what that labor produces but not the mine itself.[69]

Sadr refers to two kinds of work in Islam and states that in Islamic economics, there must be distinction between "useful" and "non-useful" work. From the point of view of Islam, the former leads to acquiring rights but not the latter. For example, collecting dry firewood is useful work but not the conquest of land. The second factor, acquisition of private property rights on natural resources, requires continuous commitment by the owner to work with natural resources to create new

---

66 Al-Sadr, *Iqtisaduna*, Vol. I, Part. II, 124–125.

67 Taskhiri, *Fifty Lessons in Islamic Economics*, 268.

68 Taskhiri, Fifty Lessons in Islamic Economics, 269.

69 Al-Sadr, *Iqtisaduna*, Vol. II, Part. I, 62-65 and 140–141.

productive opportunities. Once this work terminates so will the right of ownership.[70] For example, when a person reclaims a piece of unused land, farms it, he acquires private property rights in the use of land. Fairness demand this right and the priority in the use of land. However, if the famer terminates work on that farm and allows it to go to waste, he loses his private property rights on that land.[71]

Shaheed Sadr believes that the ownership of belongs to the Imam and the government of a Muslim society. For this reason, he believes that a person who reclaims an unused piece of land and farms it, does not acquire private ownership of the land itself but a priority right to use the land and, from a *Fiqhi* point of view, Imam has a right to levy taxes on that land.[72] {Shaheed Sadr believes in the existence of three types of land ownership. For the detail discussion of this topic, see the second volume of the English translation of his classic book *Iqtisaduna* (Our Economy) with the title: Our Economics in two volumes}.

According to Sadr, mines are owned by the public as a whole jointly and individuals cannot acquire private ownership on underground resources.[73] Also, sea waters, rivers, springs and other sources of water that run naturally on the surface of the earth are in the public domain and the private sector cannot owned them, except insofar as it is allowed on the basis of before-production distribution theory where private individuals, through their own work find access to a source of water on a piece of land they have reclaimed and are farming.[74]

4.1.1.2 Post-Production Distribution: Distribution of Income among Production Factors

The concept of "post-production distribution" deals with the distribution of income from the proceeds of selling goods produced among the factors of production (it is secondary distribution after the primary distribution of natural resources).[75] In capitalist economy, income from production is distributed as wages, interests, rents and profits.[76]

According to Shaheed Sadr, Islam does not treat factors of production, in terms of their importance in production, the same as doe's capitalism; it does not accept the notion that distribution is determined by the law of supply and demand for each and every factor of production. According to the concept of post-production distribution, products and the revenues accrued from them belongs to those who have exerted their

---

70 Yadollah. Dadgar., and Seyed Mohammad Baqir. Najafi, *Islamic jurisprudential principles of Islamic economics* (Kermanshah: Razi University, 2001), 128.

71 Al-Sadr, *Iqtisaduna,* Vol. II, Part. I, 150 – 151.

72 Al-Sadr, *Iqtisaduna,* Vol. I, Part. II, 106 – 107.

73 Al-Sadr, *Iqtisaduna,* Vol. II, Part. I, 120.

74 Dadgar., and Najafi, *Islamic jurisprudential principles of Islamic economics*, 124.

75 Taskhiri, *Fifty Lessons in Islamic Economics*, 268.

76 Al-Sadr, *Iqtisaduna,* Vol. II, Part. II, 9–10.

labor directly in the production process. Other factors of production, land and capital, do not have a share in the proceeds other than rent for the duration of their service in production. Islam considers that the product and its resulting proceeds (income from its exchange or sale) belong to the person who, by hiring machinery, equipment and natural resources, has produced the product through the use of his labor.[77]

Difference between capitalism and Islam, according to Sadr, is that in the former, human is only an instrument at the service of production and, therefore, it has the same role as any other factor of production. Like them, he receives a share of the product. In the latter, however, Islam is the objective of production not and not its instrument. Production, and its factors, are for humans to use to meet their needs. Islam does not treat human labor the same as other owners of other factors of production.[78]

An important difference between capitalism and Islam is that in the former, capitalists has the right to hire as many workers and use as much of natural resources in exchange for wages. The only benefit which accrues to human labor force is his wages. The capitalist is the owner of the product, resulting from human labor, and the income from the selling it. According to the teachings of Islam, however, such production relations are impermissible since direct labor exerted on natural resources is an ownership condition, the capitalist is not permitted to own all the product produced by hiring labor. Sadr argues "the result of implementation of rules of Islam governing production and distribution is eradication of any possession of property by anyone without exertion of direct labor. These rules reject capitalist exploitation, meaning capital accumulation with exertion of direct labor."[79] He explains that, based on the 'concept of post-production distribution, the person who produces a product exerting his own labor has the right of ownership to the result of his work in which other factors of production have no share other than rewards (rents) that the worker-producer pays them for their services.[80]

4.1.1.3 Theory of Exchange: Acquiring Ownership Through Transfer

As discussed earlier, Islam considers labor as the primary means of acquiring ownership rights. The secondary means is through transfer of ownership rights acquired through exchange, for example through trade which is governed by specific set of rules prescribed by Islam so that this activity does not contradict the commitment of Islam to social justice. It must be kept in mind that, in accordance with spiritual

77 Al-Sadr, Iqtisaduna, Vol. II, Part. II 10.
78 Al-Sadr, Iqtisaduna, Vol. II, Part. II 11–12.
79 Al-Sadr, Iqtisaduna, Vol. II, Part. II 13.
80 Al-Sadr, Iqtisaduna, Vol. II, Part. II 42–43.

values and societal interests, Islam has imposed limitations on private ownership rights.[81]

To explain Islam's theory of exchange, Sadr first focuses on the etymology of the term "trade" which, he argues, means transfer of a thing from one place to another. Traditionally, however, it refers to transactions that take place through contracts of exchange (such as contract of al-Bay'). Trade is considered a productive activity in that it gives opportunity for added value through transfer of property ownership. Legally, however, trade means transfer of property rights from one person to another.[82]

From an historical point of view, trade and exchange arose as the result of division of labor and specialization which led to surplus production beyond the immediate need of the specialized producers. Trade, direct or through brokers, made it possible for the surplus to be sold through transfer of ownership of the surplus product from the producer to the buyer in exchange for surplus product of other producers or for money.[83]

Through time, motivation for trade and exchange became dominated by self-love and selfishness, especially in the present form of capitalism, forcing this activity away from its initial impetus and motivation of responding to actual and logical human needs. As a result, characteristics of productive and useful no longer apply to trade and exchange, hence, the motivation behind these activities has become the seeking of prophets without the sellers performing any productive activities. Consequently, only the transfer of property rights has become the source of prophets, whereas before it was the productive activity of exchange which was the primary source of prophets in trading. For this reason, Sadr argues, the view of Islam which considers exchange as part of the process of production contradicts trading activities of the currently dominant capitalism.[84]

The root of the problems of unequal and unjust relations in current trade and exchange system originates with the use of money as means of additional wealth and its accumulation and concentration instead of serving the role of an intermediary between production and consumption thus facilitating exchange. In order to solve the problems of exchange and the unjust relations resulting from this abuse of money, Islam has prescribed rules governing fair exchange, some of which follow:[85]

(1) Islam has prohibited hoarding of money and has imposed Zakat on idle money. If this Zakat were to be paid in full, it would undermine the incentive to hoard money. This is one way in which Islam ensures the role of wealth in production and consumption.

---

81 Al-Sadr, *Iqtisaduna*, Vol. I, Part. II, 127.

82 Al-Sadr, *Iqtisaduna*, Vol. II, Part. II, 111.

83 Al-Sadr, *Iqtisaduna* 112.

84 Al-Sadr, *Iqtisaduna* 113.

85 Al-Sadr, *Iqtisaduna*, Vol. I, Part. II, 137–138.

(2) Islam has prohibited Riba, which causes devastating results in distribution and disequilibrium in the economy, unequivocally. Similarly, Islam has negated the Riba-orientation of money which by itself also leads to increase wealth. On the other hand, Islam has returned to money its genuine and natural role, meaning general representation of goods and services, measure of value and means of exchange.
(3) Islam has empowered the government of an Islamic society to have a comprehensive control and supervision of exchange and trade market in order to mitigate its domination by illegitimate individualism, without causing harm an instability to economic life.

In summary, Islam considers trade and exchange as useful and productive activities the resulting profits of which are productive income and not income from simple transfer of property rights. Therefore, trade and exchange profits must be based on work performed and not simply a purely legal entitlement without exertion of labor effort.

4.1.2 Redistribution: Acquiring Property Rights Based on Need, in Accordance with the Principles of Social Security and Balance

As noted above, work is the foundation of property rights and the fundamental first instrument of distribution in Islam. Need is the second instrument. Together, work and need constitute the function of distribution in an Islamic society.[86]

To illustrate, Sadr divides the members of the society into three groups:[87]
(1) The first group is made up of those with physical, mental and intellectual power who use these abilities to provide for a comfortable life for themselves.
(2) The second group are those that are unable to work due to lack of physical or mental abilities.
(3) The third group are those who can only meet their basic necessities through work.

The first group have the right of ownership of the results of their work, even if their income is higher than their needs, so long as their activities are within the framework prescribed by Islam. For this group work is the measure of distribution of wealth. For the second group, need becomes the measure of distribution since they are unable to work. For the third group, the measure of distribution is a combination of work and need in order to have relative wellbeing.

---

86 Al-Sadr, *Iqtisaduna* 116.
87 Taskhiri, *Fifty Lessons in Islamic Economics*, 245.

Sadr believes that, Islam recognizes work as being the instrument of the distribution besides the need and entrusts to it a positive role in this regard and thereby it opens the way in the economic life for the appearance of all the powers and talents and the development thereof somewhat on the basis of competition and rivalry and urges the talented individuals to expend all their potentialities in the field of civics and economy.[88]

But contrary is the case with Communism because by basing the distribution on the need of the worker alone, irrespective of the nature and activity of his work, it leads to freezing of natural incentives in man which make him work hard and be active. As a matter of fact what induces one to hard work and activity is but his own interest and therefore when work is stripped of its being an instrument of distribution and the need alone is adopted as the criterion of the share of every individuals, as does Communism, it means a death blow to the most important power that pushes the economic system ahead and moves it more upward.[89]

In capitalism, need is none of the positive instruments of distribution. Thus the greater it is with the individuals the lesser becomes their share in the distribution so that decrease in the share leads ultimately to a large number of them with-drawing from work and distribution. Therefore, the need in the capitalist society means withdrawl of the individual from the field of distribution and it was not an instrument of distribution.[90]

In contrast, need in an Islamic economy is an instrument of distribution which ensures a general level of economic wellbeing for all three groups – based on the principle of "guaranteed" meaning commitment to social security and social balance which are, Sadr argues, the general principles of establishing social justice in Islamic system. In what follows we will discuss the principle of "guarantee" and social security.

4.1.2.1 Social Security

In Islamic thought on the economy, principle of social security is set up on the two bases of the Islam's doctrine of economics and receives or draws its doctrinal (economic) justification from them both. The first of these two bases is a public reciprocal responsibility, and the other is, the right of the society to the public resources of the State. The principle of public reciprocal responsibility is the first basis of the principle of social security. Islam has prescribed it for the Muslims as a *fardu 'l-kifāyah* (a common duty). The implication is that members of the society have a mutual and reciprocal obligation to protect one another. In economic terms, it means each person must ensure that others have minimum degree of economic security, at least,

88 Al-Sadr, *Iqtisaduna,* Vol. I, Part. II, 117–118.
89 Al-Sadr, *Iqtisaduna,* Vol. I, Part. II 118.
90 Al-Sadr, *Iqtisaduna,* Vol. I, Part. II 121–122.

in meeting his/her basic needs. Basic needs are understood as those without which lives are endangered.[91]

The second principle of social security in Islam relates to the responsibility of the government to ensure that those who are economically unable to achieve a "*Muta'arif*" (common) living standard – a "*Muta'arif*" standard of living means that level which a common individual or family considers as sufficient. This is flexible concept which varies with the general standard of wellbeing and welfare of the society. The measure of the "common" standard of living increases as the level of wellbeing and welfare of the society as a whole increase. According to teaching of Islam, it is the obligation of the government to ensure that each member of the society is able to meet his/her basic needs for food, housing and clothing. Meeting these needs means that individual has sufficient resources for a dignified living in accordance with current common standard of living. Beyond that, the government must ensure that the secondary needs of the members of the society which emerge as the general standard of living in the society increases are also met.[92]

The basis for this government obligation is the rights members of society possess over the wealth of the society which has its root in Verse 29 of Chapter 2 of the Qur'an in (part of) which the Creator declares that He has created all the resources for the human collectivity: "He is Who Has created all that is on the earth for all of you..." Therefore, every human being has a right in the created resources. This includes those who cannot fend for themselves economically. Their share has to be redeemed. Not doing so leads to injustice in distribution of wealth and its concentration in the hands of a few.[93] It then becomes government's responsibility to ensure that those unable to exercise the physical and/or mental capacities to use their share of resources, receive their rightful share of what is produced.[94]

4.1.2.2 Social Balance

Social balance refers to the balance among members of the society with respect to their standard of living. Sadr rationalizes the existence of two phenomena in Islamic teachings related to wealth distribution: (a) disparity in wealth holding among members of the society; and (b) Islam's tolerance of this disparity. He argues that the former emerges due to natural differences in spiritual, mental and physical abilities among individuals. The second relates to the view of Islam regarding wealth distribution which considers work as the primary source of acquiring ownership and property rights. In combinations, these two lead to acquiescence of Islam to existence of

---

91 Al-Sadr, *Iqtisaduna,* Vol. II, Part. II, 125–126. And Dadgar., and Najafi, *Islamic jurisprudential principles of Islamic economics*, 170.

92 Al-Sadr, *Iqtisaduna,* Vol. II, Part. II, 128.

93 Dadgar., Najafi, *Islamic jurisprudential principles of Islamic economics*, 171.

94 Al-Sadr, *Iqtisaduna,* Vol. II, Part. II, 128–131.

differences in wealth holding among individuals. Natural differences make it possible for individuals to have different level of access to natural resources, like land, in combinations with their own abilities, to gain different results. Social balance implies a general level of standard of living that is shared equally by all members of the society such that resources and opportunities are available equally to all to gain access to common and balanced economic life through their own efforts. In an Islamic society, this means a comfortable "common" standard of living for all. *Fiqh* (jurisprudence) defines a poor family as one unable to support themselves at the level of society's "common" standard of living. It is mandatory that this shortfall be compensated by Zakat and other resources specified by religious rules.[95]

The objective and the duty of the government is to spending all efforts to ensure that all members of the society have a "common" level of standard of living; a sufficient and comfortable level of standard of living. Islam has provided governments ways and means commensurate with this obligation of achieving the objective of general wellbeing and social balance which can be summarized as follows: (1) revenues earmarked for the achievement of social balance sourced from constant and continuous taxes on income and wealth (*Khums*, one-fifth of income; and *Zakat*, about 2.5% of wealth); (2) revenues generated from assets that Islam has placed at the disposal of the government (*Anfal*, windfalls gained from resources belonging to the Imam, i. e. government), like revenues from unused land belonging to the government that has been made available to private farmers to cultivate for profit-sharing with the government). The purpose here is for the government to use this revenue for social balance, but also make unused resources available for production; (3) prescribed rules of Islam that help the government of an Islamic state to establish social balance such as rules against the hoarding of wealth, *Riba*, laws of inheritance that break up wealth at the time of the passing of wealth holders, permission to the state to legislate laws deemed necessary to help establish social balance, rejection of exploitation of natural resources the way it is done in capitalism. Given these views and positions of Islam, it would seem unlikely that the economic activities of the private would dominate production, exchange and trade to the extent that would endanger social balance because Islam, from its inception, has always tried to mitigate the emergence of causes of social conflicts and contradictions.[96]

4.2 Views of Sadr on Fair Growth of Wealth

As mentioned earlier, Sadr believes that ingratitude and lack of appreciation of the blessings of the Creator is one of the main root causes of economic problems and

95 Dadgar., and Najafi, *Islamic jurisprudential principles of Islamic economics*, 174–175.
96 Al-Sadr, *Iqtisaduna*, Vol. II, Part. II, 139, 145–145.

believes that the solution is in to ensure justice in the preservation and growth of societal wealth. Moreover, he believes that there is a consensus among all schools of economic thought on the use of natural resources to expand production, but emphasizes that Islam rejects ways of doing so that come into conflict with fair distribution and ideas that demand justice.[97] Islam has a comprehensive view of opportunities and conditions for economic growth and use of natural resources and has prescribed rules and procedures governing these processes, some of which have their roots in nurturing and acculturation while others are ways and means of implementation by the government within the general framework of rules governing the Islamic economy. These include: (1) intellectual and cultural instruments; Islam encourages humans to work and produce and has placed great value on human effort to the point that it is honored by Allah and even by the intellect; (2) legal instrument; to prepare the ground for the growth of production, Islam has prescribed various and coordinated rules some which are:

a. If a piece of land is left unused, it is removed from the control of the individual possessing it and turned over to someone else to reclaim and make it productive;
b. Profligacy and wasteful production and consumption are forbidden;
c. laws of inheritance are in place to avoid transfer of accumulated wealth to only one offspring of the deceased;
d. Prohibition of the act of possession of land without making it productive (holding it for speculative purposes) but simply building walls around it to signify ownership;
e. Prohibition of income from non-beneficial activities such as *Riba*, gambling and bribery;
f. Impressibility of allowing possession of opportunities and resources, like land, by mentally challenged individuals, those who would abuse resources;
g. Prohibition of hoarding wealth;
h. Prohibition of the concentration of wealth in the hands of a few.

In discussing the position of schools of thought relating to increase in wealth, Sadr points to two major differences. One is the final objective of doing so (why produce wealth?) and the other it's in the life of the society (what is the role of wealth?) Schools differ in their response to these two issues depending on their worldview. Capitalism, Sadr argues, is the most important manifestation of materialism philosophy, "usually the goal and ultimate objective of economic activities is the growth of capital; matter has a super position beyond all other values and no objective other than material wealth and its growth is recognized. Therefore, individuals expend their efforts to gain wealth and material wellbeing. Capitalism decouples increase in capital and distribution. Its supporters believe that social welfare and poverty alleviation occur

97 Al-Sadr, *Iqtisaduna*, Vol. II, Part. II 78.

automatically through increase in total national wealth. This objective is served when higher levels of economic activities increases national wealth, even if as a result of fierce competition, the activities of small firms terminate and the firms themselves are destroyed. To the supporters of capitalism recurring crises are caused by lower levels of production, shortage of raw material and insufficient supply. The only solution, according to this view, is greater exploitation of natural resources and increased volume of production."[98] Contrary to this view, Sadr argues, growth of production and wealth is not the ultimate objective of economic activities in Islam; it is one objective among others and it is accepted as such, in the teachings of Islam, in conjunction with its own view of distribution. It rejects the idea that economic problems are caused by reduction in the volume of production. Instead, it conditions increased production on fair distribution and social welfare and wellbeing.[99]

In his research of religious texts relating to the role of wealth in Islam, Shaheed Sadr classifies them into two categories: those that consider a level of wealth and worldly comfort sufficient to meet life's needs a good opportunity for acquiring the means of felicity in the Hereafter and those texts that, on the contrary, consider pursuit of wealth and worldly comfort as the source of undesirable characteristics and behavior harmful to the objective of achieving felicity in the life to come. To reach a clear understanding of the position of Islam on wealth, Sadr believes that there are two limits to wealth determined by the psychological and spiritual conditions of individuals. On the one hand, wealth can become an instrument serving the objective of nurturing ethical excellence that enable an individual to perform well his function as Khilafah (agent/trustee). In this case increase in wealth is useful in securing felicity in the Hereafter. However, if increase in production and wealth are sought solely for themselves and become the only reason for human activity, then they become the source of all misconduct that force humans away from their Creator, cause their spiritual desires to deviate from their correct path, intensify the love of material life, and harm their pursuit of the goal of establishing justice in the world. Islam's goal is to encourage humans to work hard to ensure social wellbeing for all, establish the virtues of the brotherhood of man and actualization of universal justice, and strengthen the relationship between man and his Creator. Therefore, Islam calls for and encourages any activities that promote attainment of these goals.[100]

---

98 Al-Sadr, *Iqtisaduna,* Vol. II, Part. II., 75.
99 Al-Sadr, *Iqtisaduna,* Vol. II, Part. II 75–82.
100 Al-Sadr, *Iqtisaduna,* Vol. II, Part. II 80–102.

5 Summary and Conclusions

In this paper, we sought to study the ethical dimensions of the ownership structure in the Islamic economic system based on Shaheed Sadr's views. To this end, the concept of ownership structure was first studied in general. Then, the value and ethical basis ownership structure in the Islamic economic system were examined based on the views of Shaheed Sadr. For this purpose, anthropology and ontology s were first studied from the perspective of Islam. We saw that, from the point of view of Islam, man's unjust behavior in distribution and his ingratitude and thanklessness for Divine bounties are the real causes of the economic problems. The solution of Islam to this problem is to shift human perception (away from material orientation) to spirituality and ethics. Islam considers humans as the trustee/agent of the Creator on earth and the appointment of Messengers and Divine revelations have the responsibility of facilitating this shift in perception. The objective of this guidance is to establish fairness and justice in human society. Islam's teachings on ethics and its prescribed rules governing property, wealth and ownership are all relate to realization of justice. Hence, the structure of property ownership in Islamic economic system is oriented toward actualization of economic justice based on Islam's conception of fairness and justice.

As explained earlier, Shaheed Sadr argues that economic justice has two dimensions: justice in production (or economic growth) and justice in distribution of income and wealth. Property ownership is the major source of income and wealth. Shaheed Sadr argues that, based on Islamic teachings, work is the basis of ownership which is a natural and instinctive right of humans and Islam specifies the conditions governing ownership. He further argues that that private property ownership is limited to what is produced by the work the owner has expended directly in its production. All other property that are produced without involvement of work belongs to the society collectively. Sadr asserts that the fundamental difference between capitalism and Islam relating to distribution of income and wealth is in their conception of the role of humans in production. The former considers human beings as instruments of production only whereas Islam considers humans and their wellbeing as the final objective of all activities. Whereas in capitalism human beings are treated same as other factors of production and are given the same consideration, in Islam labor is the genuine and fundamental factor of production.

In view of Shaheed Sadr, money and its abuse is at the root of all problems of unjust relations in exchange and trade. To mitigate these problems and to render exchange fair, Islam prescribed rule, such as the obligation of Zakat, prohibition of its idle accumulation and Riba. According to Sadr, Islam, through its support for work and need as the two basis for distribution of income and wealth, on the one hand, creates the necessary foundation for the flourishing of creativity, work incentives and production while, on the other hand, it creates an appropriate social environment for attainment of justice in distribution. While Islam acquiesces in existence of inequality among members to due to their natural differences, it does its utmost to create social balance and a general standard of living for all. It is worth noting that the rules and laws of Islam are such that to prevent emergence of large inequalities in income and wealth from the start. Sadr argues that Islam rejects modes and methods of growth of production and wealth that come into conflict with its view on distribution and it orientation toward justice. Only those method of growth of production and wealth are accepted that fall within the framework just distribution of income and wealth.

In summary, ownership structure in Islamic economy is such that it guarantees economic growth and just distribution of income and wealth (economic justice). Such results are possible with full implementation of Islamic economic system in a social environment in which spirituality and ethical values prevail. In other words, these results with implementation of the teachings of Islam in individual and social lives which are fully aware of attuned to the Day of Returning and Accountability as well as the life in the Hereafter.

References

A) Persian and Arabic sources

Al-Sadr, Shaheed Seyyed Mohammad Baqir. *A Picture of Islamic Economics*, Translated by Jamal Mousavi, Tehran: Roozbeh Publication, 1980.

Al-Sadr, Shaheed Seyyed Mohammad Baqir. *Al-Islam yaqud al-hayat* (Islam Directive to Life). Translated by Mahdi Zandieh, Qum: Dar al-Sadr Publications, 2015.

Al-Sadr, Shaheed Seyyed Mohammad Baqir. *Fadak in History*. Translated by Mahmoud Abedi. Tehran: Roozbeh Publication, 1981.

Al-Sadr, Shaheed Seyyed Mohammad Baqir. *Human Khilafah (vice regency) and the Testimony of the prophets*. Translated by Jamal Mousavi. Tehran: Roozbeh Publication, 1980.

Al-Sadr, Shaheed Seyyed Mohammad Baqir. *Iqtisaduna (Our Economics): Discovery Attempt on Economic Doctrine in Islam*. Vol. I, Part. I. Translated from Arabic to English by World Organization for Islamic Services. Tehran, Iran: World Organization for Islamic Services, 1984.

Al-Sadr, Shaheed Seyyed Mohammad Baqir. *Iqtisaduna (Our Economics): Discovery Attempt on Economic Doctrine in Islam*. Vol. I, Part. II. Translated from Arabic to English by World Organization for Islamic Services. Tehran, Iran: World Organization for Islamic Services, 1984.

Al-Sadr, Shaheed Seyyed Mohammad Baqir. *Iqtisaduna (Our Economics): Discovery Attempt on Economic Doctrine in Islam*. Vol. II, Part. I. Translated from Arabic to English by World Organization for Islamic Services. Tehran, Iran: World Organization for Islamic Services, 1984.

Al-Sadr, Shaheed Seyyed Mohammad Baqir. *Iqtisaduna (Our Economics): Discovery Attempt on Economic Doctrine in Islam*. Vol. II, Part. II. Translated from Arabic to English by World Organization for Islamic Services. Tehran, Iran: World Organization for Islamic Services, 1984.

Al-Sadr, Shaheed Seyyed Mohammad Baqir. *Islam and Economic Schools*. Translated by Mohammad Nabi zadeh. Qum: Mehr Printing, 1976.

Al-Sadr, Shaheed Seyyed Mohammad Baqir. *Our Philosophy*. Translated by Seyyed Mohammad Hasan Marashi Shooshtari. Tehran: Sadr Library, 1972.

Dadgar, Yadollah., and Seyed Mohammad Baqir. Najafi. *Islamic jurisprudential principles of Islamic economics*. Kermanshah: Razi University, 2001.
Hamadah, Khaldun. *Banking without Riba in Shaheed Sadr's Works*. Qum: International Congress of the Grand Ayatullah Shaheed Sadr, 2000.
Kia al-Husseini, Seyyed Ziaeddin. *Proceedings and lectures at the International Conference on Shaheed Sadr Economic Thoughts*. Qum: Mofid University Press, 2007.
Movahed, Mohammad Ali. *In Search of Right and Justice: from Natural Rights to Human Rights*. Tehran: Karnameh Publishing, 2002.
Nourahmadi, Mohammad Javad. *A Review of the Book of Al Islam Yaqud Al-Hayat*. Special Issue of the Second International Conference on the Study of Economic Thoughts of Ayatollah Shaheed Sadr. Qum: Mofid University, 2006.
Nourahmadi, Mohammad Javad. *Religious Economics from the perspective of Muslim and Christian Economic Thinkers*. Tehran: Imam Sadegh University, 2010.
Nourahmadi, Mohammad Javad. *Ownership, Justice and Growth in the Process Development of Economic Thoughts*. Tehran: Imam Sadiq University, 2013.
Renani, Mohsen. *Bazar and Na bazar: examining the Institutional Barriers to the Efficiency of the Market Economic System in Iranian Economy*. Tehran: Planning and Budget Organization, 1997.
Taskhiri, Mohammad Ali. *Fifty Lessons in Islamic Economics*. Tehran: Publishing the Middle East Culture, 2003.

B) English Resources

Blackstone, W. *Commentaries on the Laws of England*, Vol. 2. Chicago: Univ. Chicago Press, 1766 (1979).
Carruthers, Bruce G., and Laura. Ariovich. "The Sociology of Property Rights.", Annul. Rev. Social, 2004,30:23–46.
Fisher, I. *Elementary Principles of Economics*. New York: Macmillan, 1923.
Hay, D. *Economics: A Christian Critique*. Leicester, England: Apollos, 1989.
Hussain, Syed B. *Encyclopedia of Capitalism*. New York: Golson Books, Ltd, 2004.
Mueller, Dennis C. *The Oxford Handbook of Capitalism*. Oxford: Oxford University Press, 2012.
Pejovich, Svetozar. *The Economics of Property Rights: Towards a Theory of Comparative Systems*. Dordrecht, the Netherlands: Kluwer Academic Publishers, 1990.

Attachment: Introducing the Important Economic Works of Shaheed Seyed Mohammad Baqir as-Sadr (RA)

Allameh Shaheed Ayatollah Seyyed Mohammad Baqir Sadr – ه ش 1313–1359 / 1980–1933 AD), from the great Shiite Imam References, from the geniuses of Islamic scholars, from the Forerunners of the revival of the social philosophy of Islam and from the most influential Islamic writers in the fields of jurisprudence, Principles of Islamic jurisprudence, philosophy, *Tafsir*,[101] *'Ilm al-Kalām*[102] and economics in the twentieth century. "Shaheed Sadr was born in the original and famous family and was educated in the school of Prophet *Muhammad* (PBUH) and *Ahlul-Bayt* (AS), And with firm conviction, deep knowledge and certainty to salvation of the teachings of Islam, he has tried to present the views of this religion in different fields of society in a new way, looking at society and managing it. God's mercy with God's talent and his tireless efforts came to be seen in the form of literary works in this field, which today are the authoritative sources for the scholars of the Islamic world and ultimately signed his alliance with the god with his own blood. "(Kia al-Husseini, 2007, p. 19)

Martyr Sadr at a time when socialism and capitalism was dominated on global thoughts At the same time, they criticized both theories and, with a solid and scientific statement, revealed their shortcomings and dishonesty, completing the principles and policies of Islam in various fields of philosophy, politics, economics and ethics. (Sadr, 1972)

The most important works of martyr Sadr on social issues, and in particular on economics, are *Fadak in History* (1954), which deals with the formation of the political and social system of Islam. (Sadr, Ibid) In *our philosophy* (1959), whose translation of the full title is "Fundamental studies of various philosophical schools, in particular the philosophical school of Islam and the dialectical materialism of Marxism," addressed philosophical issues between religious philosophers and materialists and criticized the dialectical materialism school and rejects it. (Sadr, 1972). *Our Economy* (1961), whose translation of the full title is "An Investigative Study Including Critique and Discussion on the Principles of Thought and the Explanation of the Economic Systems of Marxism, Capitalism, and Islam" (Sadr, 1984.a) at age 27, was elaborated by him. And indicates his domination of jurisprudence and his method of *Ijtihad*,[103] and seeks to provide a model for the school and the economic system of Islam with the aim of social justice. (Kiaalhosseini, 2007, p. 15). *Our economy* consists of three major parts. The first part deals with the critique of competing schools of socialism and capitalism. The second part is devoted to the generalities and foundations of Islamic economics, and the third part is the theory of Islamic economics, which is presented in three sections: distribution before production, distribution in the production and distribution after production, and the role of government in Islamic economics. (Sadr, 1984.a)

Al-Banak al-Larabo Fi'l-Islam, whose full title is: "Banking without usury in Islam, A Plan for *Riba* Replacement, And a Study of Different Banks Activities In The Light Of Islamic Thinking". This book is the second most important economic activity of

101 (Arabic: تفسير, translit. *Tafsīr*, lit. 'interpretation')
102 (Arabic: عِلم الكَلام, literally "science of discourse")
103 ***Ijtihad*** (Arabic: اجتهاد *ijtihād*, lit. effort, physical or mental, expended in a particular activity) is an *Islamic* legal term referring to independent reasoning or the thorough exertion of a jurist's mental faculty in finding a solution to a legal question.

Martyr Sadr, which was carried out at the request of the Board of Directors on Kuwait's financial plan, and was published in Beirut in the early 1980s. Shaheed Sadr, in this book, describes the principles of Islamic banking in countries where religious laws and ordinances are not fully implemented, although in this book, he describes the concept of Banking without usury in implementing governments of Islamic rulings. (Khaldun, 2000, p. 14)

The Book of *El Salam Yaqud al-Hayah* or Islam, Guidance on Life (1979) is one of the precious works of Martyr Sadr in the late years of their life. This work was written at the beginning of the victory of the Islamic Revolution in Iran. The main purpose of this book is to provide a general framework for the elaboration of the political and economic system of Islam. In his book, the main reason for the lack of development in Islamic countries considered their distancing from Islam. By explaining the social image of Islam, Islam considers as a program of life and the only way for the formation of Islamic societies. By distinguishing fixed phenomena from the changing phenomena and explaining the concept of the *al-Fraqah district,* Islam introduces a living framework that is capable of solving the political and economic problems of contemporary times. By emphasizing the fundamental concept of the caliphate, the purpose of God toward the creation of man and the sending of prophets and imams, Introduces the establishment of a monotheistic community on earth and monotheism as the true basis of justice and freedom. (Nourahmadi, 2006) Some other works of martyr Sadr, which contain social issues from the Islamic perspective, include *Trends of History in Qur'an* and *Al-Madrasah al-Islamiyyah.*

Considering that jurisprudence is the most important specialty of *Allameh* Shaheed, there are many innovations in jurisprudential analysis or theorizing with the aim of extracting social systems of Islam In this way, while adhering to the original *fiqh,* he is seeking to discover the individual and partial rulings, laws and social system of Islam. (Kiaalahsinī, 2007, p. 15).

Omar Fisher

Chapter 15: Significance of "Trust" in Capital Formation in Islamic Finance

1 Framework

As our world becomes increasingly globalized, we are compelled to deal with strangers – whether in business, at school or for delivery of services to the home. Those who utilize resources online via internet to search for information, book a trip or hotel, or simply order groceries or pizza are keenly aware that such services and products will be fulfilled by faceless people, unfamiliar persons in call centers, or perhaps delivered to our front door by total strangers. Many people are now working from home and interacting with suppliers or customers whom they never meet. Successful corporations are adopting a social enterprise business model whereby group work and wide spread stakeholder collaboration, sometimes with strangers, is fast becoming a norm. The collaborative economy is rapidly emerging globally.

The need for *trust* arises urgently due to our interdependence upon others and the swift emergence of an interconnected digital and sharing economy. There is also an element of *risk* embedded into trust, we cannot compel others to cooperate with us nor do our bidding exactly as we want. Hence key questions often arise: what is human trust in such an environment? How to engender trust between known and even unknown persons? If broken, what is the process to repair and re-establish trust?

One can identify three dimensions to trust:

1. trust in one's self (i.e. self awareness and beliefs)
2. propensity to trust others
3. trustworthy behavior

Dimension 1 above is beyond the scope of this paper. Suffice to say that self-trust involves self-knowledge leading onto predictable and consistent behaviors; i.e. "doing the right thing." This dimension does not consist of reciprocity, but rather concentrates on self-belief, confidence and calmness in one's self as well as a measure of self-forgiveness (i.e. living with no regrets). In this chapter, our focus is rather on interaction between people, the ethics arising in both human interactions and commercial transactions – enveloped by a sharing economy and money capital as encompassed by Dimensions 2 and 3.

1.1 Taxonomy

Figure 15.1 shows how a taxonomy of trust might look like.

https://doi.org/10.1515/9783110593419-015

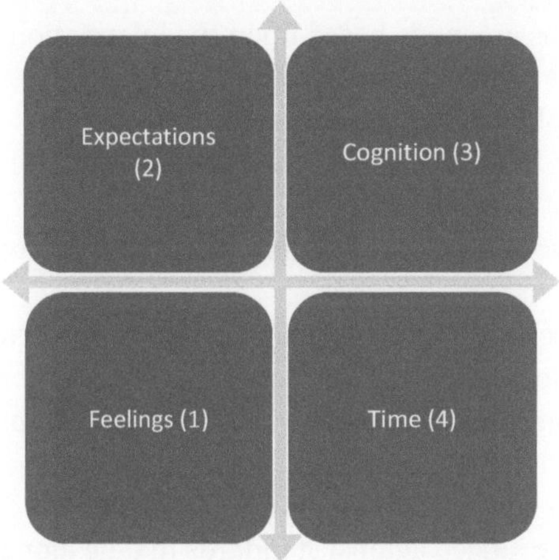

Figure 15.1: Segments of Recognizing and Building Trust.

Segment No. 1 "Feelings" includes:
- Use of language – verbal and non-verbal to help us translate "feelings" of trust into a bond or relationship with another person. Communications between people – verbal and non-verbal – add to a sense of trust, or conversely detract from a sense of trust (i.e. mistrust or even suspicion) when a mis-alignment occurs in words and deeds.
- Respect – display of manners and tolerance towards others. Degree of fairness and commitment to standards helps to create a safe zone whereby a bond or relationship can begin.
- Benevolence – assessment of the "goodness" of another person, their concern for our well-being, and how honest actions can make a positive contribution to our shared lives.

Segment No. 2 "Expectations" includes:
- How probable (likely) are the actions of others? What are the visible (physical/non-verbal) and invisible (verbal) clues to consistency, which underlie the human interaction. When there starts to emerge a recognizable pattern of speech or behavior, then a bond of trust might commence.
- How predictable are the outcomes to my expectations? Recurrent themes, patterns and verbal cues are comforting and offer fertile soil for seeds of trust.
- Are the experiences authentic? Fulfillment of intentions (Expectations) may be insufficient to engender trust – the outcomes must also be genuine and truly authentic.

Segment No. 3 "Cognition" includes:
- Information to reinforce the initial impressions and patterns that you see in others. How does this information get received and stored: aural, seeing, tactile, taste, etc.

- Understandings emerge and associations are made based upon the information, insights and related emotions which the rational mind perceives.
- Assessment of competence and ability of others to perform as promised.

Segment No. 4 "Time" includes:
- Sense of time – how we feel and what we believe here and now, in the moment of interaction with the other.
- Longevity – how we feel and what we believe over time, which is also referenced to our Expectations (No. 2); does our independent experiences of the other vary or remain consistent during passage of Time? The latter reality underscores a deepening of trust.

These four (4) segments are constantly being judged against standards that lie along a continuum as to level of Sincerity and Integrity (Z axis) of the actions, pledges and speech of the other person. This adds a 3rd dimension to our personal experiences of the other and to the four (4) elements that comprise a *sense of trust*. Therefore, a two (2) dimensional grid is inadequate and should be expanded to incorporate a third (Z) axis to assess the level of Sincerity and Integrity that we experience over a period of time.

Shown in Figure 15.2 is a three (3) Dimensional image of what adoption of trust might look like.

Of course, external events in the real world impinge on the relationship that can accelerate trust, or alternatively erode the trust bond. Thus, we all use our Feelings, Expectations and Cognition inputs about another person and intuitively judge these as to **Likelihood** of occurrence and **Impact** on our lives. It is obvious that ethics, our personal notions about personal Truth and standards in our world, shades our

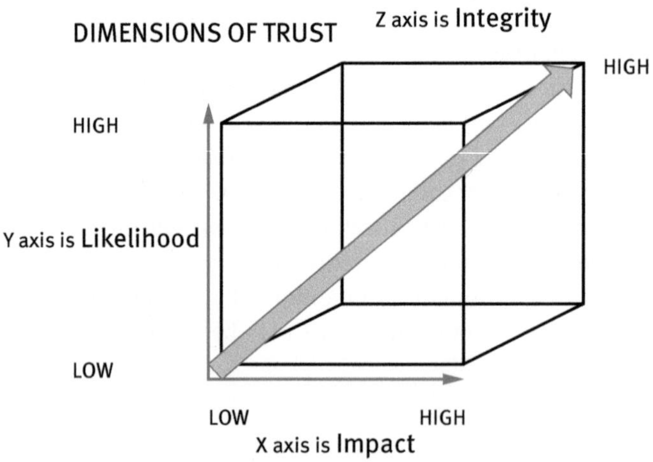

Figure 15.2: Dimensions of Trust.

perceptions – both of **Integrity** in action and in the level of **Impact in our lives**. The more often our assessments are proven true, that is the *likely outcomes* and/or the *expected favorable impacts* actually happen to our personal satisfaction, then a bond of trust can be strengthened. Conversely, in the event that trust is established and then for some reason broken between two parties, the transition from broken trust to renewed trust may not be linear as when first established but rather halting – a pattern of "stop and go". Meaning that one or both parties must test and re-test the bond of trust as it is being reasserted, and this may take an extended Time period (segment 4).

1.2 Propensity to Trust Others

Why do we trust? What motivates each of us to place trust in another person? Some researchers[1] explain that when we trust, we feel "good", the brain releases the hormone oxytocin, producing pleasurable emotions associated with safety and security. A *presumptive tendency* to trust is related to such factors[2] as: similarity and resemblance, physical contact, facial expressions.

However, tendency to trust others is also bounded by cultural factors and conditioning, according to cross-cultural studies[3] done by Richard D. Lewis. Nationalities move within a triangular model with three poles when developing trusted relations: a) *Linear-active* (Nordic/USA/Latin America)- where people trust institutions, b) *Multi-active* (Mexico/South EU/Middle East/Far East Asia)- where people depend upon in-group affinity where compassion and truth are flexible, and c) *Reactive* (Japan/Singapore/Canada)- where people rely upon reciprocity, protecting "face" and extended eye contact is avoided. Hence, cultural upbringing and societal factors influence also the process by which trust is established. It is this final aspect – cultural upbringing and socialization – where ethics gets inserted.

Purposes for building trust seem fairly universal – comfort, safety, security as well as efficiency, performance and self-fulfillment. Nevertheless, human judgments derived from physical cues or perceived character traits can be ill-founded, erroneous, with sometimes disastrous consequences.

A question presents itself here: is building trust linear or non-linear? As with many social interactions among humans there appears to be multi-valence conditions of "complexity and chaotic" relations impressed by asymmetrical information and

---

1 For example, Paul Zak demonstrates that oxytocin is associated with positive emotional states, social connections and trusting (HBR, Rethinking Trust, Roderick Kramer, June 2009).

2 IBID, HBR, p. 3.

3 Cultural Types: The Lewis Model, Richard D. Lewis, www.crossculture.com, from "When Cultures Collide", 1996.

perceptions. However, human behavior can be measured using standards[4] of trust and resilience of the bonds of such relations. In summary, we can adopt here an approach to *trust* (or Theory "T") which can be explained in sequential stages that evolve or devolve and where the four (4) Segment inputs blend together so to be adjudged by us along a continuum of **Integrity** (the 3rd-dimensional Z axis- Figure 15.2).

On the other hand, it is apparent that a rupture of trust leads us to experience frustration, anger, disappointment, a range of negative emotions wherein we may feel victimized in some ways. Violations of trust by others causes us to blame the other person or to doubt ourselves, which invariably leads on to mistrust in many other human relations thereafter. Degree of perceived "harm" affects the Cognitive assessment of trust (segment 3) and affects the Feelings (segment 1) assessment as well. If severe enough divergence of outcomes from our Expectations occurs, then consequences result in *mistrust* that might transform into suspicion, retaliation, revenge behaviors and irreparable damage to possibilities of trust in/with that person.

Rebuilding trust once broken involves simultaneous resolution of two parts: i) dealing with stress and negative emotional impact caused by the rupture of trust, and ii) reconciling that future trust violations can somehow be dealt with. A full measure of maturity is required in segments of Cognition and Feelings in order to restore shared trust between people. In addition, often forgiveness is a necessary condition to re-start the process of building trust. Nonetheless, if trust can be repaired the resultant bond of trust relationship may be stronger than before and more resilient.

1.3 Features of Being Trustworthy

Research completed at the psychology department of New York University in 2014[5] concludes that most people's brains make snap judgments to trust another "almost instantaneously."

Trustworthiness is always a tough call but a new study suggests our brains make that decision on a stranger almost instantly, just by sizing up their face. A related study done earlier had determined that there are certain facial features that most people tend to perceive as trustworthy, such as a u-shaped mouth and larger, baby-like eyes. However, this new study suggests researchers are now claiming that they have discovered at exactly what point we make the decision on trustworthiness, and it's almost instantly.

"Our findings suggest that the brain automatically responds to a face's trustworthiness before it is even consciously perceived," explains Dr. Jonathan Freeman,

4 Basic standards assessed include: fairness, fulfillment of promises, truthfulness, setting-honoring deadlines, consistency of behaviors, etc. Refer to: "Trust and Trust Building", Roy J. Lewicki, Edward Tomlinson, article Dec. 2003.

5 "Our Brains Judge a Face's Trustworthiness'" www.nyu.edu, Aug.5, 2014.

an assistant professor of psychology at New York University and the study's senior author. "The results are consistent with an extensive body of research suggesting that we form spontaneous judgments of other people that can be largely outside awareness. The study specifically focused on the region of the brain called the **amygdale**, the part known to play a key role in our decision-making and emotional behavior."

It would seem that placing trust in another person can be a "confusing mix": it is associated with our perceptions of their inner character, yet intimated by our judgments of outward appearances as well. Our assessment is affirmed or undercut by passage of Time and the degree to which our Expectations are realized in reality. Our personal assessment of both inner character and outward appearances and behaviors are anchored in our personal beliefs about ethics.

A recent survey of Americans on the features of trusted personalities and leaders reveals[6] that key character traits are associated with trustworthy behaviors; namely:
- Integrity and character
- Exceptional talent and drive for person excellence
- Moral compass
- Honesty
- Exudes leadership

Progressive studies on collaboration conducted by the Quality Institute (www.thecqi.org) confirm that meaningful enterprise value is created when employees and stakeholders use collaboration – in high trust situations – as opposed to conditions of conflict, confrontation and mis-trust. Refer to Figure 15.3. Leaders who are perceived to be trustworthy inspire their enterprises to compete more effectively and fashion more collaborative, fulfilling work environments within their organizations. What about the role of capital that drives the financial aspects of that same company? Is there a correlation between capital and brand image, or to the underlying *ethics of the enterprise*?

2 Trust and Capital

Capital is a noun derived from the Latin "capitalis" or "caput" meaning head or chief. Originally capital described the cap of a pillar or a major city area. Gradually, usage included the "chief" assets of any enterprise; i.e. capital stock or goods. Common meanings today refer to the rights of owners of a business to its goods, assets and paper shares that signify ownership in these properties.

6 Readers' Digest, Survey by Wagner Group: "Why do we trust at all?" Courtenay Smith and Alison Caporimo, June 2013.

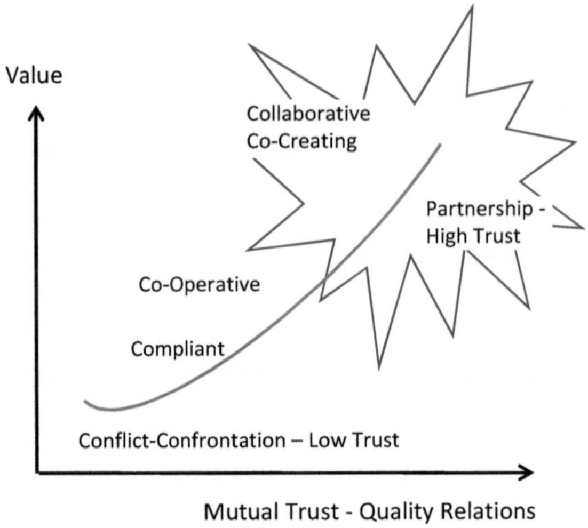

Figure 15.3: Relationship journey equates trusting collaboration with value creation in human endeavor.
Source: Thecqi.org, 2014.

Typically, capital does not reference its sources nor its end-use in terms of any ethics or non-economic values. Thus, capital is an intermediate good whose value is the result of labor. One important role of capital today is its exchange value between different goods – yet notice that an inference is generally accepted that capital is also a reservoir of monetary value [thus idle capital deserves interest accruals]. In short, modern economic theory splits Real Capital (goods/services) from Monetary Capital (fiat money).

This decoupling permits manipulation of money capital through fractional banking and creation of credit (thru debt financing). One consequence is expansionary monetary policies by nation states through deficits and debts financing by global banks. Another is opening a door to "asset" securitizations of debts (Asset-Backed-Securities) which can be credit card debts, auto loans and home loan mortgages. Moreover, financial engineering has produced Credit Derivatives and Credit Default Swaps which places a "bet" on the risk of default by borrowers and then trades that derivative contract for a premium price. Notice that the matter of ethics in proliferation of credit capital, other types of capital and its usufruct is silenced, or declared irrelevant.

2.1 Islamic Capital and Trust

An alternative to contemporary binary "capital" is **Islamic capital,** which fundamentally is a form of faith-based finance – hence ripe with ethical considerations. Core elements start with intention (Nea'a) for the user to fulfill his/her religious duties, to consciously purify personal actions and to align financial actions with end goals of community well-being and broad social justice. Individual motivations revolve around awareness of man-God relationship (al-Taqwa) and accountability for how commercial relationships are structured and executed to be permissible in the fulfillment of duties and trusts. Unlike contemporary finance, the Ends do not justify the Means when one chooses Islamic capital. To explain this difference, we need to probe the functions of "capital".

Our relationship to capital (money) features five cardinal facets:

1. How capital is earned
2. How capital is spent
3. How capital is saved and/or invested
4. How capital is donated
5. How capital is inherited and/or delivered as a legacy to next generation

Trust intrudes into each facet. Yet the influence of trust rather dominates in areas 2, 3, and 5. A person applies himself to his job throughout the month without weekly salary payment, due to a trust engendered with an employer that the payroll will be distributed at the end of every month. As is apparent, the level of Sincerity and Integrity of an employer is central to each employee's willingness to work for deferred wages.

On the other hand, typically every person is highly cautious in spending capital for personal consumption to assure that their Expectations are satisfied at the moment of purchase and, indeed, in after-sales performance of the purchased item. Gaps in fulfillment or unsatisfactory experiences with purchased items inevitably lead on to erosion of trust with the brand and eventually to switching to a new product or alternative brand.

Likewise, saving and investing financial assets requires an assessment over time to ascertain the efficacy of the service or product and the degree to which the sales' promises can be trusted. A mutual fund or pension scheme might require +10 or 20 years of patience to finally conclude that a trusted relationship during a lifetime is justified with an anticipated financial outcome finally being fulfilled.

Conversely, capital distributed through inheritance laws, trusts and estates requires a kind of "blind trust" because the ultimate disposition of that capital occurs after the demise of the person. In substitution, we place our trust in an Executor or Trustee appointed to execute our will at the appropriate time. One exception is a Living Will Trust or Legacy whereby the capital is deployed into whatever charity or activity as desired by the person who is still living to witness that the intended outcomes do in fact happen.

2.2 Features of Islamic Capital

Our relationship to capital and money is quite often influenced by an intermediary as money manager – typically a bank or asset manager. Banks can safeguard our capital as savings and can be trusted to assist us with a variety of investment options developed to accelerate our savings rate. Today's banking system, however, is characterized by ideology that largely reflects capitalistic values and appeals to those people who trust materialistic and utilitarian viewpoints (one popular understanding of ethics).

It may be noted that nearly one quarter of the world's population espouses a differing viewpoint and trusts non-conventional values of capital and money – referring to so-called "Islamic" banking and the real economy. Simply put, Muslims adhere to ethical principles and values relating to how capital is earned, how it is spend, how it is donated and finally how distributed through inheritance laws that are "halal" or permissible. In short, this means avoidance of certain actions and items – riba, gharar, maisir, pork, munitions, tobacco, pornography, and other vices as prohibited by Shariah laws described in the Holy Quran and Sunnah.

Although a rapport and sense of familiarity can be established between capital managers and Muslim customers if an institution is established using Islamic principles and operates consistent with main Shariah (Islamic laws) rules, a bond of trust is not automatic nor guaranteed, but rather must conform indeed to the above segments of Expectations fulfillment, mutual understanding (Cognition) and consistent habits over Time.

Interestingly, in the conventional banking space premium prices and high quality services tend to reinforce a brand image and aid transition by customers towards a fully trusting relationship. Surveys report that less than 20% of Muslims will accept a premium Price despite lesser Quality of services as simply the "cost of being Muslim" provided this assures their compliance with religious tenets. Conversely, most Muslims believe that neither a premium Price nor an Islamic label assure that the banking transaction is "halal" and many even shun Islamic banks as untrustworthy financial partners. The unique challenge here is that Christians, Jews and other non-Muslims do not feel accountable to the sources and end-uses of the capital whereas Islamic doctrines insist that staunch Believers have individual accountability to God after death that their capital must be handled as "halal" in all financial transactions and every person should die debt-free. This trust (or amanah) is integral to a covenant with the Creator and cannot be assigned or delegated to an intermediary – even an Islamic Bank.

3 Islamic Viewpoint on Trust

Trust is a cardinal virtue and central to a truly human experience of living. Divine revelation in the Holy Quran makes clear that God Almighty as Creator of the Universe (Allah-swt) enters into a covenant with each and every creature that is obligatory to uphold in exchange for the miracle of life. We can understand this covenant more accurate as containing two parts: a **Primary Covenant** between each human being and his/her Creator, and a **Secondary Covenant** amongst members of same family, tribe, community and nation. A Primary Covenant exists to acknowledge and worship the One God, to be grateful and to preserve and improve on the gifts and talents (body, intellect, children, property and assets) bestowed upon each of us. Concomitantly, each person is responsible and will be accountable for fulfilling this covenant and behaving with obedience to its guidance.

In addition, a Secondary Covenant exists whereby each person, within their means and resources, must employ these gifts (including capital on hand) for positive personal and social impact (i.e. productive usufruct) through capital sharing transactions and collective risk sharing. Such actions are understood to result in employment generation, innovation, commercial trading, etc. which enable trust and growth among community members, a pre-requisite for nation-building.

The scope of trust in the Holy Quran circumscribes three areas:

1. Role-based trust i.e. the **Primary Covenant**, and under the **Secondary Covenant** both trustworthy behaviors;
2. between an individual and others in the community which should be trustworthy behaviors; and
3. between an individual and his/her work or livelihood – honesty of efforts (i.e. pursuit of excellence).

Guidance and injunctions for each area is clearly stated:

1. Role-based trust mentions include:

At the time of creation of Mankind, God Almighty offered "trust" first to His primordial elements, yet they declined to accept the mandate and heavy responsibility. Mankind, however, accepted it. The Quran states:

> "We did indeed offer the Trust to the heavens, and the earth and the mountains; but they refused to undertake it being afraid thereof. But man assumed it." (AlAhzab, 33:72)

Elsewhere, the Quran counsels that:

> "On no soul does Allah place a burden greater than it can bear." (AlBaqarah, 2:286)

It can be assumed that Mankind due to limited Free Will is uniquely equipped to undertake the Trust which involves acting consciously as Vice Regent of the known temporal Universe, a task that heavens and earth were unwilling or incapable to perform. Hence, the conscious act and deliberate behavior of obedience to the guidance of the Covenants are uniquely spiritual and uniquely human acts. Every such action consistent with this Trust elevates man towards universal perfection in reference to what he is entrusted to do and be, whereas actions that deviate or frustrate this Trust conversely lowers man into purely selfish, vain and self-centered performance.

Verses that portray the **Primary Covenant** include:

"Our Lord comprehends all things in His Knowledge. In Allah is our trust." (9:89)

"Say: 'Nothing will happen to us except what Allah has decreed for us; He is our Protector', and on Allah let the Believers put their trust." (9:51)

"Why we should not put our trust on Allah? Indeed He Has guided us to the Ways we (follow). We shall certainly bear with patience all the hurt you may cause us. For those who put their trust should put their trust on Allah." (14:12)

"But if they turn away, Say" (Allah) sufficeth me: there is no god but He, on Him is my trust – He is the Lord of the Throne Supreme!" (9:129)

"Those who faithfully observe their trusts and their covenants; And who (strictly) guard their prayers; These will be the heirs,/Who will inherit Paradise: they will dwell therein forever." (23:8–11)

"And put thy trust in Allah, and enough is Allah as a disposer of affairs." (33:3)

Equally important are the **Secondary Covenants,** whereby each person is called to practice trustworthy behaviors and to safeguard all promises, pledges and property entrusted to him generally towards the community, and more specifically at his/her work to sustain trustworthy behaviors.

"Surely Allah commands you to make over trusts to their owners and that when you judge between people you judge with justice; surely Allah admonishes you with what is excellent; surely Allah is Seeing, Hearing." (4:58)

"O you who believe! Be not unfaithful to Allah and the Messenger, nor be unfaithful to your trusts while you know." (8:27)

"O ye that believe! Betray not the trust of Allah and the Messenger, nor misappropriate knowingly things entrusted to you." (9:27)

"And those who respect their trusts and covenants/And those who stand firm in their testimonies/And those who (strictly)guard their worship;/Such will be the honored ones in the Gardens of Bliss." (70:32–35)

"...Then, when thou hast taken a decision put thy trust in Allah. For Allah loves those who put their trust (in him)." (3:159)

"Allah: there is no god but He. And on Allah, therefore, let the Believers put their trust." (64:13)

Allah defines Believers as ones who uphold their trusts, including the public and private trusts, as well as the covenants they undertake in all the issues related to their public and private lives. When a trust is betrayed, ignored, or neglected that person is considered to be "unfaithful to Allah-swt", to His Prophets and His Message in both their public and private lives.

From a sermon narrated by Imam Al-Baqir once said: "There are three things which Allah, the Mighty and the Glorious, has not permitted anyone to forsake: returning a trust to its owner, irrespective of whether he is a good person or an evil one; fulfilling one's promises and covenants, irrespective of whether it has been made to a good person or an evil one; being good and kind towards one's parents, irrespective of whether they are good or evil."

3.1 Contrast of Islamic Viewpoint of Wealth

Islamic viewpoint on money and wealth may be succinctly summed up:

Islamic capital bifurcates into (A) Individual Capital and (B) Social Capital. (A) Individual Capital derives from Real Assets and the transformation of goods/service by human intelligence and labor into "added value". Return to capital follows human endeavor and the taking of business risks. This contrasts with the demand for interest accruals on (passive) money as "returns on capital", or certificates of deposit, for example. The central concepts are support to human dignity from Labor/Work and the fact that fiat/paper money cannot be a storehouse of value.

Whereas Social Capital (B) is connected to an over-arching principle of Social Justice, whereby common goods (parks, trash disposal, minerals, roads, fire brigade) and natural assets (rivers, clean air) are a Social Right (like Capital Stock) and must be preserved not exploited. Hence, the surrounding society has a claim on private Individual Capital to contribute towards a higher goal: which is *"greatest good for the greatest number of the community"*.

In this interpretation, Individual Capital and Social Capital are distinct functions yet become intertwined:

> "As for man, when his Lord tries him by giving him honour and gifts, then he says (puffed up): 'My Lord has honoured me.' But when He tries him, by straitening his means of life, he says: 'My Lord has humiliated me!' Nay! But you treat not the orphans with kindness or generosity! And urge not on the feeding of the poor! And devour inheritance – all with greed! And you love wealth with a great love!" (Surah al-Fajr, 89:15–20)

> "You shall certainly be tried and tested in your wealth and properties and in your personal selves, but if you persevere patiently and become Al Muttaqun (pious), then verily that will be a determining factor in all affairs." (Al Imran, 3:186).

3.2 Risk Capital

To live is to encounter risk. Increasing Wealth and Real Assets brings about concerns for preservation of such Assets from damage, theft, loss, disappearance and even injury – if related to our human health. When such losses occur, then we must use our "Risk" Capital to repair or replace the Asset unless we have exchanged the risk exposure with others; i.e. procure insurance. Conventional insurance trades the risk exposure for a Price (premium) from the Insured to the Insurer (Stock corp. model). By contrast, an Islamic insurance alternative (Takaful) model provides risk sharing, or risk pooling by the owners of the covered risks and results in mutual indemnification.

Once again deployment of Islamic Capital aims to achieve a dual purpose: individual risks are protected against through donations (tabarru) into a common funds pool, and social ends are advanced by spreading of such risks among the community of Takaful members, whereby the fortunate are giving financial assistance to the misfortunate hit by calamity.

3.3 Should We Trust Islamic Capital?

Among the salient features of Islamic capital – faith-based finance – are:

Table 15.1: Features of Islamic Capital.

Features	Islamic capital as compared to Conventional capital
Guiding Principles	Less religious capital than ethical capital; meaning guided by principles and rules rather than solely by rate of return
Asset-based	Asset-based not asset-backed ... real tangible assets and "true" ownership not simply paper ownership: e.g. like Credit card securities ... rights to cash flows from servicing debts
For Profit	Islamic capital is profit-driven, not charitable funds, similar to conventional capital
Respects Private Rights	Islamic capital respects private property and rights of ownership, trusts and inheritance
Transparent	Islamic capital can and should deliver transparency, full disclosure and symmetry of information
Risk-sharing	Islamic capital requires risk-sharing and not risk transfer nor full guarantees of principal and profits (like home loan mortgages)
Real Economy	Islamic capital prohibits short-selling, hoarding and market manipulation – elements the capitalists claim promote a "free" market when in reality such elements permit unfair advantages to certain parties over other parties in market exchanges
Re-balances risk capital and supports entrepreneurship	Islamic capital is inherently more just and fair-minded to entrepreneurs (new businesses) as losses in business (except for gross negligence) are born by Agent (Mudareb-Rab Al Mal-capitalist) whereas the entrepreneur loses his/her labor/time only; equates human capital to money capital
Rates of Return	Islamic capital balances risk-reward with no pre-set limitations, whereas conventional capital typically benchmarks to LIBOR or similar interest rates and references to weighted cost of capital; i.e. linked to time value of money, a notion that money itself carries intrinsic value.
Universal- not for Muslims only	It is noteworthy that Islamic capital can be employed by anyone as the finance and banking system is not meant solely to serve Muslim believers.

Thus, Islamic capital when correctly practiced secures the rights of all parties, assures full transparency and equality of information, promotes equitable risk sharing and safeguards a private return to capital (profits) that is fairly priced as determined by market forces.

4 Conclusions

Trust is an essential human trait and set of behaviors that supports our survival and continued evolution. Trust is not something that can be gifted – it must be mutually accepted as a social connection and, while research suggests trust may be instantaneous, generally it must be earned over time. A taxonomy of elements of trust includes: Feelings, Cognition, Expectations and Time. Measurement of trust exists on two dimensions, but a third axis (Z) captures how we intuitively judge Integrity and authenticity of a trusted person's behaviors towards us, whereby trust in that relationship either evolves or devolves over time. Ethics become embedded in each individual based upon cultural upbringing and socialization, which influence each person's interpretation of Integrity for actions of self and others.

Islamic capital and Islamic banking emerged and was codified in the 7th to 9th centuries, some +700 years before the advent of Italian mercantile finance, which is the forerunner of modern day conventional finance. Although the moniker is synonymous with one of the world's five great religions – Islam – it can be understood as ethical or interest-free finance that strikes a middle ground for local commerce and global financial transactions between opposing goals of maximum profit-making and social justice.

In today's era of finance dominated by program trading in nano-seconds, mobile banking, financial engineering of debt securities, crypto-currencies and credit default swaps, is there a role for Islamic capital? Moreover, blue-chip commercial banks and private wealth brands instill confidence and promote images of trustworthy icons. Islamic banks and Shariah compliant capital is a relative upstart: barely $2.5 Trillion dollars under management globally (2019) in contrast to $100 Trillion dollars of commercial debt and finance worldwide and in excess of $700 Trillion in notional value of CDOs and credit default swaps issued. Is it too early to trust the Islamic capital brand as a nascent alternative to conventional finance?

Firstly, perhaps we should re-think the trust that is invested in the contemporary conventional banking system – because of the egregious poor risk management and loose credit underwriting which precipitated a global financial banking crisis 2007–2011 with a stunning loss of private wealth and stock exchange valuations exceeding $65 Trillion dollars. Personal bonus incentives and greed of bankers aggravated this crisis and pushed financial institutions to over-leverage and under-capitalize the portfolio of risks they carried. Issues associated with "too-big-to-fail" banks and regional systemic risks of bankruptcy still persist as largely unredressed still nine (9) years on.

Hence, the preemptive trust we might be extending to "respected" bank brands needs immediate re-assessment.

Secondly, the conventional materialistic finance tools and techniques are advancing ever greater income inequality[7] that further concentrates capital in hands of a wealthy few. Concomitantly, despite this wealth there is little effective contribution to resolve pressing social issues for many millions of people across MENA region, Eastern Europe and Africa especially; for example, we can see massive youth unemployment which drains hope and precipitates social strife.

Thirdly, purveyors of Islamic capital must do better in explaining and promoting the benefits of their products and services. Despite the virtues of Islamic capital (noted in Table 15.1), many Muslims and non-Muslims alike are skeptical and mis-trusting of the underlying value proposition, the genuineness of financing structures, impact on social justice and justification for a pricing premium when compared with costs of conventional financing. Restoration of trust in Islamic capital requires that Islamic banks, asset managers and Takaful operators follow the latest research[8] in building trust:

- Know yourself – Islamic financial institutions need total overhaul and re-engineering of processes and "customer touch points" to genuinely incorporate ethical values and practices. Walk the walk.
- Trust entails risk – start with smaller tasks and interactions with intended customers to deliver on "lots of small trusting acts" which provides signal that Islamic institution is seriously interested in building up and sustaining a trustworthy relationship
- Aim for stronger and consistent message and acts – reinforce communications and delivery of values of fairness, honesty, integrity and transparency. Also where possible seek to personalize such messages to strengthen the social bonds around your brand.
- Cultivate role-based trust – in addition to personalized experiences that engender trust, the Islamic financial institution must focus on its processes, technology and documentation of transactions to assure congruence and alignment of non-personal aspects with the espoused ethical/Islamic values. Any gaps here will be spotted immediately by intended customers and erode trust due to the perceived "double-standards".

Finally, we must remain vigilant – because trust is continually earned and poised in flux between positive evolution or devolution towards mis-trust. Humans seek certainty and closure in relationships. Thus, Islamic financial institutions need to

7 Refer to Davos Report on Global Inequality (2015), "Income Inequality in USA", Piketty and Saez (2003), and "Global Wealth Report", Credit Swiss Research Institute (2010).

8 Adapted from steps described in HBR article on "Rethinking Trust", Roderick Kramer, June 2009.

continuously evaluate the status of trusting bonds with stakeholders (customers, suppliers, employees and board of directors) to judge effectiveness of formative ethical and trust-building experiences. What is working well? What now requires adjustments or refinement? Certainly, very important questions, as trust capital is never static.

References

Paul Zak and Kramer, Roderick (2009), "*Rethinking Trust*", Harvard Business Review, June, https://hbr.org/2009/06/rethinking-trust.

Lewis, Richard D., "When Cultures Collide", 1996 and www.crossculture.com, The Lewis Model, 2014.

Lewicki, Roy J. and Edward C. Tomlinson (2003) "*Trust and Trust Building*." Beyond Intractability. Eds. Guy Burgess and Heidi Burgess. Conflict Information Consortium, University of Colorado, Boulder. Posted: December 2003. https://www.beyondintractability.org/essay/trust_building.

Smith, Courtenay and Alison Caporimo, "*Why do we trust at all?*", Survey by Wagner Group: Readers' Digest, June 2013, 3rd Ave., New York City, NY USA.

Davos Report on Global Inequality (2015)

Piketty, T., and E. Saez (2003), "*Income Inequality in the United States, 1913–1998,*" Quarterly Journal of Economics, 118(1), 2003:1–39.

Credit Suisse Research Institute, "Global Wealth Report 2010–2018", Credit Suisse, Zurich, Switzerland.

Behrouz Mohammadi Monfared and
Mohammad Esma'eil Tavassoli

Chapter 16: Principle of Human Dignity: The Criteria for Ethical Assessment of Business Relations in Islamic Economy

1 Introduction

According to Islamic thought, assessment of the rightness or wrongness of conducts of economic behavior, work and business activities (kasb), such as transactions, options (Khiaraat), warranties (Dhamanaat) and usury (Riba) are based on whether the behaviors are confirmed by the teachings of revelations or not. A major part of jurisprudence, called "*Al-Makasib*," (ways of earning income) deals with methods of recognition of properness or improperness of such conducts. Of course, expressions (applied to categories of actions) like *Mubah* (permissible by religion), *Makruh* (disliked; reprehensible) and *Haram* (forbidden) replace the terms properness or improperness in jurisprudence. In fact, the sources of awareness about permissibility or proscription of such conducts can be traced to the Qur'an, *Rawayat* [narrations of the sayings from the Prophet or the Imams (as)] and the intellect. It is the responsibility of the Fuqaha (experts in jurisprudents, "Mujtahids") and their followers [those who follow ("Taqlid") the opinions of Fuqaha] to understand and then comply with related rules. Therefore, recognition of *Mubah*, *Makruh* or *Haram* conducts is a result of the jurisprudential perspective individuals. In Islamic teachings, it is also possible to assess rules governing ethics of work and business conducts from the point of view of ethics/morality and judge their appropriateness rationally in accordance with their beneficial or adverse results for the society. This assessment will consider the benefits and adverse results of actions in this world and in the Hereafter and then rules on their rightness or the wrongness. Thus, the difference between ethical and jurisprudential perspectives about properness or improperness of conducts within business realm is that in jurisprudential approach rules of Fiqh are followed strictly, without searching for underlying causes, to decide whether an action is appropriate or not. On the other hand, in making such decisions within an ethical framework, we search for rational indicators that allow determination of whether voluntary actions. are good, bad, virtuous or vicious in terms of human welfare. In this paper, and notwithstanding the conflicting views in determination or design of various indicators of ethical values, we are attempting to identify a criterion for understanding appropriateness of voluntary actions relating to work and business activities in Islamic economics. While it is possible to rely solely on criteria of such determination provided by religious rules, intellect ('Aql) too can be utilized to make such determination. That is,

https://doi.org/10.1515/9783110593419-016

intellect too can determine the ethical appropriateness of voluntary actions based on their beneficial or detrimental effects on human welfare, with the help of teachings of the revelation.

In view of the authors, actualization of dignity or ignominy in human behavior within the realm of work and business activities can be employed as a criterion or indicator for understanding the ethical appropriateness of behavior (that is, if such conducts are compatible with human dignity, they are righteous, else they are considered unrighteous). Accordingly, two aspects of any conduct are of significance in the determination of ethical appropriateness of work as well as economic and business behavior: 1) actualization or non-actualization of human dignity, based on the resulting benefits (or damage) of work and business conduct accrued to human welfare, constitutes the benchmark or indicator of appropriateness of behavior; and 2) whether the agent's intention was focused on the actualization of human dignity. Given these considerations, it can be claimed that behaviors such as "Ihtikar" (hoarding) and charging "Riba" ("ususry") are considered reprehensible and deserve the title of unethical conducts because they contradict personal and social human dignity and affect them adversely. Moreover, the ethical principles derived provide criteria for resolving the ethical challenges and conflicts facing work and business activities.

This paper attempts to answer three queries: (1) how can human dignity, in its variety of forms, serve as a benchmark, criterion or indicator for understanding values and anti-values? (2) What role does actualization of (acquired and social) dignity play in understanding ethical appropriateness of voluntary behavior in realm of work and business? And, (3) how does social dignity affect the process of identification of ethical appropriateness of such conducts? It must be noted that the discussion of "ontological/intrinsic dignity," constitutes the underlying and preliminary discourse for the relevance and acceptability of acquired and social dignities and plays the role of facilitating the interrelationship between the ontological/intrinsic human dignity and the acquired and social dignities.

2 Human Dignity as a Criterion for Understanding of Value

The worldview (*Weltanschauung*) of any school of thought inspires and proposes its own ethical. The ethical system of a divine worldviews is totally different from that of materialist worldviews. The ethical insights of an individual who believes that the universe is a creation of the wise Will of Allah and humans are Divine Breath is different from that of an individual who considers the universe aimless without any defined objective (Motahari, 2009 [1388], pp. 16–17). In Shi'a philosophy, 'Aql (intellect) has a special status in understanding good (ethical) and bad (unethical) behaviors.[1] Moreover, divine teachings like the Qur'an and Sunnah (doings and sayings of the Prophet) play roles in understanding of ethical appropriateness of conduct. Presently, we want to search for a general criterion for understanding the goodness (ethicality) and badness (unethicality) of behavior. From the point of view of authors, an important criterion for this purpose is whether actions lead to enforcing or weakening human dignity. Accordingly, we focus on the role of human dignity in understanding what constitutes value.

Verses of the Qur'an point to three types of dignity: ontological/intrinsic, acquired and social dignity for human beings. Every one of these types, in one way or another, help in understanding the effects of goodness, badness, and appropriateness of voluntary behaviors of individuals, including those related to work and business activities. Ontological/intrinsic dignity means that human beings are more respected than other created beings because they possess intelligence ('Aql), freedom of choice (Ikhtiar) and a primordial nature (Fitrah) which others lack. Honored Qur'an states:

وَلَقَدْ كَرَّمْنَا بَنِي آدَمَ وَحَمَلْنَاهُمْ فِي الْبَرِّ وَالْبَحْرِ وَرَزَقْنَاهُمْ مِنَ الطَّيِّبَاتِ وَفَضَّلْنَاهُمْ عَلَى كَثِيرٍ مِمَّنْ خَلَقْنَا تَفْضِيلًا (الإسراء: 70)

And, surely We have dignified the children of Adam, and transported them around on land and at sea. We have provided them with good things, and have favored them especially over many of those whom We have created (Al-Asra', 17:70)

لَقَدْ خَلَقْنَا الْإِنْسَانَ فِي أَحْسَنِ تَقْوِيمٍ (التِّين: 4)

We have certainly created man with the finest stature (Al-Teen, 95:4)

Taking into account these two verses, it can be deduced that the ontological/intrinsic dignity refers to preeminence of human beings over other beings of the world, and that is the reason why the Almighty has designated human beings as his successors on the earth (Al-Baqara, 2:30). It is clear that human beings have no volition in attaining this kind of dignity, because they cannot impart the reality of intelligence, will and free choice to themselves, but have received them from the Almighty at time of creation. It must be noted that responsibility for cognition of this kind of dignity is with theoretical wisdom. The question that arises is: How does ontological/intrinsic dignity affect the understanding of ethical values? The fact is that the possession of the instruments of this kind of dignity, i.e. intelligence, will and the primordial nature (Fitrah) by human beings has led to formation an array of "dos" and "don'ts" to be attached to the individual. Otherwise, if humans were not given intelligence ('Aql), will and free choice, we could not attribute ethicality or non-ethicality to them or to their behavior. This because attributing ethicality or unethicality to human action is precisely because of his possession of power of intellection, cognition and free will. For this reason, humans also are capable of achieving and enjoying individually

1 For Shia's thought believes it is wisdom that primarily recognizes virtues and evils. However, where wisdom cannot distinguish, divine revelation will preside.

acquired and social human dignity as derivatives of the ontological/intrinsic human dignity granted by Allah. Consequently, without determining the sources of the ontological/intrinsic dignity, it is not possible to determine the ethical goodness or badness of voluntary human actions. In addition, the criteria for many rights bestowed upon human beings are based on their ontological/intrinsic dignity to the point that it constitutes the foundation of human rights principles.

The acquired dignity is realized when the individual willingly engages in conducts that draw him nearer to the Almighty and achieve spiritual excellence personal felicity thereby progress beyond other humans who are deficient in such conducts or distinctions. Holy Qur'an states:

إِنَّ أَكْرَمَكُمْ عِنْدَ اللَّهِ أَتْقَاكُمْ (الحجرات: 13)

The noblest among you before Allah is that one of you who best performs his duty (Al-Hojarat, 49:13)

This verse points to acquired dignity. It is through acquired dignity that Taqwa (excellence of virtues that are acquired through complete compliance with the rules prescribed by Allah swt in the Qur'an) is achieved. The benchmark, indicator or criterion of closeness to Allah and getting ahead of other humans whose actions do not correspond to behavior expected from them. Therefore, any action that draws a human near to Allah will lead to acquired dignity. On the other hand, any action that leads to preserving human dignity, deserves the label of "praiseworthiness" and "goodness." The role of acquired dignity in determination of ethical propriety of any behavior can be presented in the following framework:

Premise 1: There are many Qur'anic verses and Rawayat [sayings of the Prophet (sawa) and the Imams of his progeny (as)] about human behavior that draw humans near to the Almighty and lead them toward achieving human perfection and acquired dignity. Therefore, there is a direct relationship between acquired dignity, "Taqwa" and nearness to the Divine[2] are the final objectives of the creation of mankind; this is also evident in the last-mentioned Qur'anic verse which considered nearness to the divine as the only indication of superiority of any individual human over others. Imam Baqer (PBUH) has mentioned:

وَ مَا خَلَقَ اللَّهُ عَزَّ وَ جَلَّ خَلْقاً أَكْرَمَ عَلَى اللَّهِ عَزَّ وَ جَلَّ مِنَ الْمُؤْمِنِ لِأَنَّ الْمَلَائِكَةَ خُدَّامُ الْمُؤْمِنِينَ وَ أَنَّ جِوَارَ اللَّهِ لِلْمُؤْمِنِينَ وَ أَنَّ الْجَنَّةَ لِلْمُؤْمِنِينَ وَ أَنَّ الْحُورَ الْعِينَ لِلْمُؤْمِنِين

"Allah, the most cherished and the most magnificent, has not ever created any more adored being than the faithful (mu'min), because the angels are servants of the faithful and divine proximity belongs to the faithful." ['Arousi, 1412 AH (1991 AD, Vol. 3, p. 189, H 302)].

2 Divine proximity in Islamic thought can be considered as the ultimate level of excellence. That is the reason discussion of human excellence is always looked upon as propinquity with the Almighty.

In essence, an individual's highest excellence is not separate from nearness to Allah, firstly, and his acquired dignity, secondly. Therefore, human excellence is the indication of the desired result of ethical principles. Thus, if actual felicity and excellence are attained by human beings, then the dignity acquired (in the same way as divine propinquity) will be of intrinsic value. An important worth noting is that human excellence and acquired dignity can be thought of as an objective of the way of Islamic Shari'ah. This important point can be observed in the emphasis placed (in the sacred sources) on the need for actualization of acquired dignity.

Premise 2: Any behavior that results in proximity to the Almighty as a result of which the individual is honored (Karamah) by Allah justifiably earns the title of "goodness" and "appropriateness." Contrarily, any behavior that distances the individual from Allah and reduces the intensity of the honor with which Allah considered him, deserves the title of "badness" and "inappropriateness."

Conclusion: Actualization or non-actualization of acquired dignity are results of voluntary actions and lead us to the understanding of their "appropriateness" or "inappropriateness." In other words, an indicator of appropriateness of action is whether such behaviors lead to attainment of acquired dignity? If they do, then they are ethically appropriate, otherwise they are ethically inappropriate.

Turning to social dignity, this concept refers to the rights of the members of the society to respect and dignity. Concurrently, it also means that no individual has the right to insult, disrespect, dishonor and disregard the dignity of another member of the society. The rule covers life, possessions, family, reputation and character of the individual members of the society. To generalize this rule, Prophet Mohammad (sawa) called the individuals who do not respect others as evil and despised.

عَنِ اَلنَّبِيِّ صَلَّى اَللَّهُ عَلَيْهِ وَ آلِهِ قَالَ: أَذَلُّ اَلنَّاسِ مَنْ أَهَانَ اَلنَّاسَ

He (sawa) said: The most despised among the humans is the one who dishonors other humans" (Majlesi, Bihar al-Anwar, Vol. 75, p. 52).

Islamic thought considers mutual respect and preservation of others dignity as an intrinsic social value and principle. Based on this principle, it requires that individuals must have self-respect so that others are not allowed to dishonor or disrespect him (Mottahari, 1388 SH; p. 127). Imam Sadiq (as) stated: "Be moderate in socializing; neither be too harsh, rough, irritating, and uncordial that people avoid you, nor be so weak that people humiliate you" (Mottahari, ibid. p. 154). Therefore, Islam is against violating the dignity of others and considers it as destructive to social cohesion. Thus, social dignity has intrinsic value. By extension, many other despised practices such as lying, and backbiting and slandering are considered counter-values. Consequently, actualization of social dignity, and whatever proceeds from it, can be considered as criteria for determination of the ethical goodness or badness of many voluntary actions. We can organize this discussion with the help of the following framework:

Premise 1: Social dignity is one the objectives and criteria for actualization of proper behavior according to Islamic Shari'ah and possesses intrinsic value. In Islamic legal system, the person who violates human dignity of others is held responsible and must compensate for the material and spiritual damages incurred by the victims (see Naqibi, 1386 Solar (2008 AD), p. 150). That social dignity possesses intrinsic value can be observed in the emphasis that many verses of the Qur'an and Rawat {narration of related sayings [of the Prophet (sawa) and the Imams of his Ahlul Bayt (his family)]} place on the instruments of social dignity, such as preservation of life, possessions, family and reputation of the faithful (Mu'mineen).

Premise 2: Ethical behaviors such as respect, benefaction and kindness to others, as well as self-esteem require social dignity, i.e. their existence in human society means that social dignity has actualized in the society. Contrarily, widespread presence of violations of human dignity through slander and humiliation of individuals contradict social dignity.

Premise 3: In general, observing existence of a phenomenon indicates that it's accompanying instruments too exist. This means that once it is observed that social dignity possesses intrinsic value of goodness, instruments that accompany it and help the society to attain it, such as mutual respect and beneficence are also of value and considered good.

Conclusion: Observing social dignity in a voluntary behavior can be a criterion for determination of the goodness of that behavior. Moreover, absence of social dignity in any behavior serves as a criterion for conceiving its badness.

It is clear that actualization of either of the acquired or social types of dignity would lead to realization of the other. Additionally, discovery of any of the two in any behavior would mean the observation of the other dignity as well. When acquired dignity and propinquity to the Almighty are realized for the members of a society, everyone will respect all others, and social dignity will also actualize as a consequence. On the other hand, if members of a society mutually honor and respect, it means that acquired dignity too has been actualized since social dignity is welcomed by Allah. In brief, within the dominant Islamic thought, although the goodness and evilness of the voluntary conducts of intelligent creatures are considered intrinsic, but in case of human beings these qualities are truly actualized only if it leads to appreciation of his value and the nearness to the Almighty is ensued and acquired dignity is achieved. That is, a behavior is good and admirable basically because, in the first stage, it leads to perfection and ultimate felicity, which is nothing but nearness to the Divine, the same way that verses of the Qur'an consider being far from Allah as the first cause of despicable behavior such slander, backbiting. Additionally, characteristics such as fairness, beneficence, and justice, as constituting elements of social dignity, play and important role in legitimizing the title of "goodness" attached to action. This claim is verified through inductive logic applied to divine teachings, that is, verses of the Qur'an and Rawayat (sayings of the Prophet (sawa) and the Imams of his household (Ahlul Bayt)).

At this instant, three points are worth noting: (1) although the reality of acquired and social dignities possess intrinsic values, some voluntary actions of human beings, such as justice, beneficence and kindness are the prerequisites of this dignity. In this view, any behavior that culminates in justice, benefaction or kindness, would actualize social and acquired dignities as well; (2) the actualization of acquired and social dignities through any voluntary action are not the sole cause of achieving the title of goodness for that action; (3) in this discussion, our reference to the term "voluntary actions" is comprehensive in that it includes all voluntary action of individuals including work and business activities. Hence, in this case too work or business activities that result in attainment of acquired and social dignity can allow us to apply labels of "goodness" and "appropriateness" to such actions. Therefore, it is possible to consider economic behavior such as "warranties", "options", "Riba" and "Ihtikar" within an ethical framework in addition to a "Fiqhi" framework. Early discussions provided us with criteria according to which "good" and "bad" actions could be understood in general and thence provide a framework to extend to work and business activities.

3 Acquired Dignity as a Criterion for Business Ethics

In the opinion of authors, actualization of acquired dignity through any of voluntary actions in the realm of business can serve as a benchmark, indicator or criterion for determination of ethical goodness and propriety of that behavior. In this view, actualization of acquired dignity is not the principal cause and ultimate objective for goodness of such behaviors, but only helps in determining their ethical goodness and badness; it indicates only helps in understanding attribution of "goodness" and "badness" to the doer of voluntary actions. In order to achieve a clear and precise understanding of the nature of acquired dignity as indicator of "goodness" or "badness" of work and business activities we need logical framework of reasoning to establish the validity of its premises in order to reach desired results. For this purpose, consider the following framework of reasoning:

Premise 1: Based on Islamic thought trade, work and business activities are considered sanctified and virtuous acts of worship as is reflected in the Hadith (Sheikh Horr Al-Ameli; 1376 (1998); Vol. 2; p. 233):

العِبَادَة سَبعُونَ جُزءاً أفضَلُهَا طَلَبُ الحَلالِ

"Worshiping consists of 70 different parts, the best among them is Halal earning."

Also, in a number of Rawayat earning one's livelihood through Halal work and business activities is considered as Jihad (struggling in the way of Allah). This principle has been emphasized in the sayings attributed to the honored Prophet (sawa) and Imam Ali (PBUH) are said to have considered those who earn Halal livelihood the same as those who participated in Jihad (Mohaddith Al-Nouri; 1991 AD; Vol. 13; pp. 12–13). Therefore, if work and business activities – performed in order to earn Halal livelihood for the person and his family – has been considered as worship along with other acts of worship such as Jihad, then it will also bring about nearness to the Almighty in the same way as do other acts of worship and are emphasized as such by divine teachings. Moreover, some voluntary behaviors in the realm of business, such as principles of warrants and options, help remove ambiguity and doubt from transactions leading to Halal gains to both sides of the transactions. Under such circumstances warrants and options serve as instruments for earning Halal livelihood, and in the same way that Halal work and business activities are praiseworthy and lead to nearness to Allah, these instruments too lead to nearness to Allah. In this view, application of warranties and options in appropriate time and remaining faithful to their requirements – while relying on Fiqhi teachings – makes it possible to attribute sanctity to these actions so that they too lead to nearness to Allah as do Halal work and business activities.

On the other hand, many voluntary behaviors in realm of work and business activities, such as Riba (Al-Baqara, 2: 278–279, 275–276), short-changing customers (Al-Asra, 17:35 and Al-Rahman, 55:8), and hoarding (Bin Haivan, 1385, p. 35) can be thought of as confronting the Almighty and result in distancing from Him and eternal suffering. Holy Qur'an states:

يا أَيُّهَا النَّاسُ كُلُوا مِمَّا فِي الْأَرْضِ حَلَالًا طَيِّبًا وَلَا تَتَّبِعُوا خُطُوَاتِ الشَّيْطَانِ إِنَّهُ لَكُمْ عَدُوٌّ مُبِينٌ (البقره: 168)

> O humans! Eat the lawful and good things that exist on earth, and do not follow the footsteps of Shaytan; surely, he is your manifest enemy (Al-Baqara, 2:168).

In this and many other similar verses of Holy Qur'an, the Almighty commands utilization of Halal goods and services in this world; it is obvious that currently this cannot be achieved except through proper work and business activities and its implementation of instruments such as warranties and options to earn the livelihood. Concurrently, the verse emphasizes not following Shaytan; i.e. not trading in harmful products such as alcoholic beverages and narcotics; not taking Riba ("usury") for more profit; not engaging in short-selling or hoarding since all such activities represent confrontation with the Almighty and are therefore *Haram*. The outcome of first premise is that with the help of divine teachings, we can conclude that some kind of work and business activities lead to the nearness of the Almighty while some others result in estrangement from and confrontation with Allah.

Premise 2: Employing an inductive logical view of numerous verses of the Qur'an and Riwayat as well as the relationship between acquired dignity and voluntary activities – discussed in the previous section – if voluntary activities relating to work and business lead to nearness to the Almighty, they will gain acquired dignity and are hence conceived as good and proper, else they will culminate in the absence of acquired dignity. For instance, if work and business activities are undertaken intending nearness to Allah and to earn means of living for oneself and one's family and are not confronting Allah (violating rules of behavior prescribed in the Qur'an). On the other hand, engaging in transactions involving products whose trading has been forbidden by Allah or participating in transactions involving Riba deprives the agent from acquired dignity and his actions is considered as "reprehensible". In other words, there is close relationship between "permissibility" or "impermissibility" of a voluntary action in working or in business activities and their desirability. This means that complying with the teachings of Fiqh in work and in business activities allows the agent to move toward attaining acquired dignity and actualize his ethical mission as a human being. For example, the following Verse of the Qur'an emphasizes general permissibility "*Mubah*" nature of work and business activities in earning one's sustenance. At the same time, the Verse warns that this permissibility must not lead the individual to exceed proper bounds of behavior by violating the rules prescribed by the Sahri'ah. It is worth noting that the term "يَحْلِلْ" in the following Verse obviously points to rational/reasonable permissibility (*Halal*). [In other words, it seems reasonable that any behavior that violates prescribed rules deserves disapproval of Allah (swt)]:

كلُوا مِنْ طَيِّبَاتِ مَا رَزَقْنَاكُمْ وَلَا تَطْغَوْا فِيهِ فَيَحِلَّ عَلَيْكُمْ غَضَبِي وَمَنْ يَحْلِلْ عَلَيْهِ غَضَبِي فَقَدْ هَوَى (طه: 81)

> Consume the good things We have provided you and do not act arrogantly while doing so, lest My wrath come upon you; and whomsoever My wrath comes upon will surely perish (Taha, 20:81)

Premise 3: From the above, we learned that there is a direct relationship between "Taqwa" (compliance with prescribed rules) and nearness to the Almighty, on the one hand, and acquired dignity, on the other. Just as devoutness (Taqwa) and the nearness to Allah possess intrinsic values, so does acquired dignity. In fact, the intrinsic value of acquired dignity is confirmd through Qur'anic verses like Verse 13: Chapter 49: "The the most honored among you to Allah are those who are most rule-compliant": "إِنَّ أَكْرَمَكُمْ عِنْدَ اللَّهِ أَتْقَاكُمْ". Such verses consider "Taqwa" and nearness to Allah as the criteria of dignity. Since this honor and dignity is attained directly from Allah without an intermediary, it can be concluded that acquired dignity has intrinsic value. In this view, whatever leads to actualization of acquired dignity has instrumental value and, therefore, is desirable. Question arises whether the intellect, assisted by the Qur'an and Riwayat, is capable of recognizing differences between ethically desirable and undesirable behavior that lead to attainment of acquired dignity. Answer to this question determines the ethical appropriateness of a given behavior. It follows that all work and business activities that lead to the nearness to Allah and attainment of acquired dignity also have instrumental intrinsic value. Accordingly, if we observe a behavior that possesses acquired dignity, we can apply to it the title of desirability and goodness.

Conclusion: Based on Islamic thought and with the help of Qur'anic verses and Riwayat, if any voluntary behavior in the field of work and business acitivities establishes acquired dignity, apprehension of such quality can culminate in recognizing its goodness and properness. In this view the acquired dignity possesses intrinsic value and other behaviors that lead to its establishment will also possess value and are titled "good".

It must be stressed here that we consider observance of acquired dignity in work and business activities will only be instrumental in understanding and recognizing ethical appropriateness of a particular behavior and not the original cause of considering its goodness. In principle, observing the presence of acquired dignity and actualization of nearness related to voluntary work and business activity cannot be considered as the main cause of their ethical propriety, but only help in understanding it. In other words, if we understand that "usury" (Riba) or Ihtikar (hoarding) will lead to loss of nearness to Allah and hence loss of acquired dignity, it becomes clear why these two activities earn the title of "badness".

4 Social Dignity as a Criterion for Work and Business Ethics

So far, we have understood that actualization of acquired dignity through work and business activities can help in understanding their ethical "goodness". However, the ethical "goodness" or "badness" such activities can also be understood by considering whether they lead to social dignity. In order to employ social dignity as a criterion of judgement of ethicality of work and business activities, consideration of Qur'anic verses and Riwayat, based on which such activities in the field of work business are evaluated, will suffice. As it can be seen, some activities in the field of business, such as warranties (Dhamanat) and options (Khyarat), will directly lead to attainment and preservation of social dignity, and some other activities, such as Riba ("usury") and Ihtikar (hoarding), lead to absence of acquired of social dignity. To elaborate further, in the next section we focus on the reasoning behind permissibility and ethical "goodness", in principle, of trade, philosophy underlying Khyarat and Dhamanat, and prohibition of activities such as Riba and Ihtikar.

4.1 Principle of Exchange and Trade (*Al-Tijara*)

As discussed earlier, in Islamic thought, exchange and trade, in principle, is considered trading was considered as 'Ibadah (acts of worship and adoration of Allah) that leads to nearness to Allah and thereby attain social dignity. Hence, such activities can carry the title of "goodness". Here, we wish to argue logically that, in principle, trade and exchange activities are ethically "good" since they make it possible for humans to attain acquired dignity. We present the premises and conclusion of our logical argument below:

Premise 1: In the first place, trade, work, and business activities are aimed at earning the livelihood requirements of individuals – and their families –, their independence from others, and maintaining their self-esteem. Imam Sadeq (as) stated:

"مَنْ طَلَبَ اَلتِّجَارَةَ اِسْتَغْنَى عَنِ اَلنَّاسِ".

"Individuals who engage in business will not be in need of other people" (Sheykh Hurr al-'Amili, 1376 (1998), Vol. 2, p. 233); meaning that whoever engages in trading, will not need to appeal to others for help and support himself and his family with his own efforts.

Clearly, not having to need others' help to support oneself and one's family would lead to attainment of self-esteem and social dignity. If all members of the society consider it a duty and an obligation to work and engage in business activities to earn livelihood for themselves and their family, hardly any individual would be insulted or disrespected for her/his poverty and social dignity of everyone will be preserved. Moreover, based on Qur'anic verses and Riwayat, the most important criterion of ethical propriety of any trading and exchange activity – which is carried out to support livelihood of the person and his family – is the satisfaction of both sides of the transaction. Consider the following Verse of the Qur'an:

"يَا أَيُّهَا الَّذِينَ آمَنُوا لَا تَأْكُلُوا أَمْوَالَكُمْ بَيْنَكُمْ بِالْبَاطِلِ إِلَّا أَنْ تَكُونَ تِجَارَةً عَنْ تَرَاضٍ مِنْكُمْ وَلَا تَقْتُلُوا أَنْفُسَكُمْ إِنَّ اللَّهَ كَانَ بِكُمْ
رَحِيمًا" (نساء, 4: 29)

O you who believe! Do not squander your wealth among yourselves in vanity, except for trading by mutual consent, and do not kill one another; surely Allah is ever Merciful towards you (Al-Nisa', 4:29).

Based on this Verse, work, trading and exchange will only be considered proper if both sides of the transaction are satisfied, and this cannot be achieved except through balance and justice between the parties. Therefore, it will not be proper if an individual is forced to engage in a transaction. It should be clear that mutual satisfaction here refers to mutual contentment of participants in a transaction meeting the conditions of Shari'ah governing transactions, consequently, satisfaction of minors, mentally incapacitated, or inebriate is not valid. Stipulation of "satisfaction" in properness of business activities is important because merchandize or assets of any party of the deal must not be seized by the other; respecting the properties of an individual is the same as esteeming that individual. In other words, the condition for satisfaction of both parties is to maintain respectability of the individuals and their properties, and from here social dignity of the parties will follow.

Premise 2: The principle of social dignity of human beings and their properties possesses intrinsic value. If voluntary actions in working or engaging in business activities of individuals are aimed at alleviating the need to appeal to others for livelihood as well as preserving respect, and if binding condition of mutual satisfaction is fulfilled, then such actions are considered as instruments of preservation of the social dignity of individuals and their assets.

Conclusion: The principle of trading and exchange can be considered as ethically "good" if such activities are undertaken to help independence from others in earning livelihood and preservation of the social dignity of individuals, and if the binding condition of mutual satisfaction of parties to transaction is met, then one can apply the title of ethical "goodness" to these activities.

4.2 Principle of Warranties (*Al-Ḋhaman*)

It is clear that not all trades and transactions are dealt in cash, and inevitably, the principle of trading and transaction may lead to indebtedness of one the parties. Under such circumstances, the creditor who wants to be assured of repayment of what he is owed, or to protect his assets, may ask for warranty, in form of personal guarantee contract ('Aghd Dhaman) or property mortgage (Rahn), from the debtor. Therefore, the principle of warranty (Dhaman) provides a collateral for consolidation and confirmation of the principle of trading as well as a guarantee for fulfilling the promise to repay; i.e. the creditor can be hopeful to claim the rights to the property owed to him with the help of the financial guarantees such as a mortgage or a promissory note. This will increase the hope that the debtor will abide by his promise in completing the transaction, and maintain the stature of the property of the creditor as well as his self-esteem. In fact, if abiding by the promise in repayment of the debt were to be fully guaranteed, there would be no need for a collateral; but to secure the liabilities of the debtor towards the deal he has entered, to assure his abiding by the promise to repay, and to observe the rights of the other party in transaction, collaterals become necessary. Accordingly, the criterion for understanding the ethical "goodness" of warranties can be considered as actualization of human dignity and respect for human rights. The following section provides our logical reasoning for this claim:

Premise 1: Realization of warranties (Dhaman) is for assuring the possibility of complete fulfilment of the rights of the creditor as well as fulfillment of the debtor's promise to repay.

Premise 2: Social dignity of an individual and respect for his property rights possess intrinsic value and so do their requirements possess instrumental value.

Conclusion: Obtaining complete rights of the creditor and abiding by a promise are actualized based on dignity and stature for the property of the individual, and thus, the principle of warranties is conceived as ethically "good" voluntary behavior because it provides the means to gain social dignity for a transaction.

Consequently, it is obvious that one of the criteria which serves for apprehension of properness and goodness of principle of warrants is that it preserves respect for the property of the creditor and hence maintains his social dignity.

4.3 Principle of Options (*Al-Khyarat*)

In the terminology of Islamic jurisprudence, "options" are considered as one of the causes for revocation of some transactions, so that final confirmation of the deal has been placed at the disposal of the party who has the right to revoke the transaction. Of course, there are a number of options, reviewing of which requires a long discussion, but as an instance, in case of "defect option" (*Khiyar Al-'Aib*), if after the transaction is completed, the merchandize or the property turns out to be defective/damaged, the buyer can revoke the deal or can ask for compensation to cover the incurred damages [Ja'fari Langaroudi; 1384 (2006); p. 269]. Similarly, in case of "fraud option" (*Khiyar Al-Qabn*), if any party has incurred losses as the result of fraudulent features in the product or the contract, the buyer is entitled to remedies.

One of the criteria for understanding the ethical "goodness" of these options is that individuals who complete a transaction will separate with full satisfaction (Mohaddith Al-Nouri; 1991; Vol. 13; p. 297). Such satisfaction of parties will result in elimination of ambiguity about the transaction, and if any problems arises later on in the principle of trading, it may be resolved straightforwardly on the basis of principle of options. In fact, these options are meant to obviate any possible losses and thereby safeguarding the interests/assets of both the parties from any probable damages. It is obvious that the consequence of satisfaction of both the parties will be that they will not engage in any altercation or dispute for incurring losses, damages or defects, and their stature and dignity will be maintained. Now, consider the following deduction:

Premise 1: Availability of different types of options including "defect option" (*Khiyar Al-Aib*) and "fraud option" (*Khiyar Al-Qubn*) for any of the parties of the transaction will result in:

1. Contentment of both the parties about the principle of trade, because both will envision that they have attained their financial rights, and if any time they think that they have incurred any loss or damage, can easily claim their financial rights.
2. Preparing the ground for obviating possible financial damages, which may be revealed to any party in a later occasion, because none of the parties is sure about not incurring losses, and thus reserves the option for the party/ parties to rescind the deal within the same contract agreement.

In Islamic thought, there is a principle called "necessity for repulsing probable damages" which is considered as a fundamental, jurisprudential and even a Kalami (polemical) rule. This principle usually refers to otherworldly losses and afterlife punishment. However, since the earthly deeds provide the ground for afterlife punishments, the authors are of the opinion that the scope of "damage" can be expanded to encompass the worldly affairs as well. That is the reason why many solely material affairs, such as life, wealth and chastity have been so important in divine view. Accordingly, the probable damages due to failure in establishing human dignity as a result of violation of the rights of one the parties and his oppression, must be circumvented, because it brings about afterlife punishment for the other party (oppressor). Therefore, the outcome of the principle of options is satisfaction and contentment of the parties as well as repulsing any probable financial damages.

Premise 2: Satisfaction and contentment of the parties to a deal as well as repulsing any probable financial damages of transaction are considered as important material practicalities which is formulated through principle of options. The significant outcome of this vantage is that the social dignities of both parties to the deal are maintained and possibilities of insults and quarrels after the deal are ruled out.

Conclusion: Options including "defect option" (*Khiyar Al-Aib*) and "fraud option" (*Khiyar Al-Qabn*) are for preserving respect and dignity of individuals, and as social dignity which possesses intrinsic value. Whatever action or instrument that makes social dignity possible, also possesses intrinsic value, properness and ethical "goodness". Therefore, one of the important criteria for apprehension of goodness of principle of options is the principle of observing the rights of others.

Up to now, we have referred to few verses of the Qur'an and Riwayat which in principle are addressed to actualization of social dignity of individuals through balance, generosity and respect of others leads to preservation of his own rights and that of his property. Here we refer to verses that prohibit certain activities, such as Riba, short-selling, hoarding (Ihtikar), which create enmity and hatred among people and lead ultimately to disregard for their social dignity. For example, consider the following Verse:

يَا أَيُّهَا الَّذِينَ آمَنُوا إِنَّمَا الْخَمْرُ وَالْمَيْسِرُ وَالْأَنْصَابُ وَالْأَزْلَامُ رِجْسٌ مِنْ عَمَلِ الشَّيْطَانِ فَاجْتَنِبُوهُ لَعَلَّكُمْ تُفْلِحُونَ (٩٠) إِنَّمَا يُرِيدُ الشَّيْطَانُ أَنْ
يُوقِعَ بَيْنَكُمُ الْعَدَاوَةَ وَالْبَغْضَاءَ فِي الْخَمْرِ وَالْمَيْسِرِ وَيَصُدَّكُمْ عَنْ ذِكْرِ اللَّهِ وَعَنِ الصَّلَاةِ فَهَلْ أَنْتُمْ مُنْتَهُونَ (٩١) (المائده)

O you who believe! Liquor and gambling, idols and raffles, are only the filthy work of Satan; turn away from them so that you may prosper. Satan only desires to cast enmity and hatred among you by means of liquor and gambling, and to hinder you from the remembrance of Allah and from praying. So, will you then stop? (Al-Ma'ida, 5:90–91)

According to these verse, such prohibited activities like earning a living from trading in wine and gambling are despicable evil behavior. These verses attribute the source of such behavior to Satan who wishes to create enmity, hatred and grudges among humans so that disrespect, insults and mutual humiliation spread in the society. Consequently, such behaviors are prohibited. Hence, it can be deduced that enmity and grudge in the first place, and desecration of social dignity of individuals in the second, are improper behaviors and consequently, obtaining property by prohibited (Haram) methods, such as trading liquor or gambling are improper and forbidden. To illustrate, we will consider two examples of work and business activities which are considered as ethically "bad" activities.

5 Riba ("Usury")

Based on Islamic thought, one of the prohibited business activities is Riba. The most important reason why it is considered as ethically "bad" activity is that it damages human rights and social dignity of individuals. Ethical reasoning behind prohibition of Riba as an indicator of social dignity is given as follows:

Premise 1: Taking into account various verses of the Qur'an and Riwayat, it can be observed that the reason for the prohibition of Riba is its role in inflicting discord (Fitnah) in the society to the extent that Imam Ali (as) called those who charge Riba as "Ahl al-Fitnah", the people of discord (Mohaddith Nouri; 1991; Vol. 13; p. 329). These people are sources of discord because they do not extend even a minimum dignity and respect to human beings and their rights. In reality, Riba leads to injustice and hatred between those who charge Riba and those who are forced to pay it. Consider the following verses:

الَّذِينَ يَأْكُلُونَ الرِّبَا لَا يَقُومُونَ إِلَّا كَمَا يَقُومُ الَّذِي يَتَخَبَّطُهُ الشَّيْطَانُ مِنَ الْمَسِّ ذَلِكَ بِأَنَّهُمْ قَالُوا إِنَّمَا الْبَيْعُ مِثْلُ الرِّبَا وَأَحَلَّ اللَّهُ الْبَيْعَ وَحَرَّمَ
الرِّبَا فَمَنْ جَاءَهُ مَوْعِظَةٌ مِنْ رَبِّهِ فَانْتَهَى فَلَهُ مَا سَلَفَ وَأَمْرُهُ إِلَى اللَّهِ وَمَنْ عَادَ فَأُولَئِكَ أَصْحَابُ النَّارِ هُمْ فِيهَا خَالِدُونَ (البقره: 275)

Those who swallow Riba will never stand up, except as one whom Satan has knocked down with a fit rise up again. That is because they say: "exchange is just like Riba" Yet Allah has allowed exchane and forbidden Riba. Those who receive such an admonition from his Lord, and stops doing so, he shall keep whatever (capital) there is from the past, and his affair is in the hands of Allah; and those who return (to charging Riba) will become the inmates of the Fire; they shall remain there forever (Al-Baqara, 2:275).

يَا أَيُّهَا الَّذِينَ آمَنُوا اتَّقُوا اللَّهَ وَذَرُوا مَا بَقِيَ مِنَ الرِّبَا إِنْ كُنْتُمْ مُؤْمِنِينَ (البقره: 278)

O you who believe! Be conscious of (your duty to) Allah and give up anything that remains (due to you) from Riba, if you are (true) believers (Al-Baqara, 2:278)

فَإِنْ لَمْ تَفْعَلُوا فَأْذَنُوا بِحَرْبٍ مِنَ اللَّهِ وَرَسُولِهِ وَإِنْ تُبْتُمْ فَلَكُمْ رُءُوسُ أَمْوَالِكُمْ لَا تَظْلِمُونَ وَلَا تُظْلَمُونَ (البقره: 279)

But if you do not do so, then be warned of war from Allah and His Messenger. And if you repent, then you shall retain your capital (without the Riba); neither shall you do injustice nor will injustice be done to you (Al-Baqara, 2:279)

On the basis of these verses, the main reason for the prohibition of Riba is that it is an unjust behavior in which the usurer, disregard of dignity of another human being and unjustified usurpation of his (the debtor) property. As it is clearly mentioned in part of the verse that if the usurer repents, and writes off the amount with the extra interest, then he can retain the capital since he has committed no injustice and no injustice is done to him. In a narration from al-Imam al-Ridha (as), the cause of the prohibition of Riba is given as its unjust nature:

عِلَّةُ تَحْرِيمِ اَلرِّبَا ... وَ لِمَا فِي ذَلِكَ مِنَ اَلْفَسَادِ وَ اَلظُّلْمِ وَ فَنَاءِ اَلْأَمْوَالِ ...

"Reason for prohibition of Riba [...] (is that it leads) to corruption, injustice and destruction of property." However, it is worth noting that, according to Islamic thought, prohibition of Riba does not apply to lending between father and his children as well as between husband and wife as they can take interest from each other. It is clear that non-prohibition of such Riba is because it does not lead to injustice or discord. And, should such Riba exist (between the parties mentioned), we do not expect that the honor and human rights of anyone would be violated.

Premise 2: Affairs that are considered as those that create discord and cause violations of human rights and cause the suffering are ethically repugnant and lead to non-actualization of human social dignity. Hence, since non-actualization of human social dignity is despicable, whatever leads to this result is also despicable.

Premise 3: Charging Riba is the corroborating example of activities that lead to discord, injustice and human suffering and which undermine preservation of human social dignity.

Conclusion: It is clear that Riba leads to discord and injustice and, therefrom, results in non-actualization of human social dignity. Since this result is repugnant, its cause, i.e. Riba, is ethically repugnant as well.

The gist of this section is that one indicator of why Riba is considered as a prime example of ethically "bad" activities is that it is a source of suffering and injustice resulting in disregard of the esteem and honor of the debtor who pays higher sum to the creditor than he borrowed. In contrast, Islamic thought recommends Qard

Hasan (beautiful loan: loan given by a creditor to a debtor without charging interest). Because such a loan preserves human dignity, it has intrinsic value.

6 Ihtikar (Hoarding)

Constituting one of the voluntary behaviors in the field of business, hoarding is conceived as an improper and ethically "bad" activity. The reason is that it is irrational and leads to adverse effects such as inflicting financial suffering on people. Impropriety of this activity is logically argued in the following framework:

Premise 1: According to Islamic thought, hoarding bears numerous adverse and negative consequences, the most important of which are financial suffering and hardships due to scarcities on part of other members of the society. Imam Ali (as) stated:

مِن طَبائعِ الأغمارِ إتعابُ النُّفوسِ في الاحتِكارِ

"Imposition of suffering on people through hoarding, is characteristic of ignorant individuals." (Tasnif Qarar Al-Hikam va Dorar Al-Kalam; 1410 LH (1990) p. 361)

Premise 2: Imposing suffering on others go hand-in-hand with dishonoring them and disregarding their human dignity.

Conclusion: Result of this analysis is that activities such as Riba and Ihtikar lead to the disregard of human dignity since these activities create considerable financial problems for them and imposes difficulties on them. Therefore, observing violation of the esteem and dignity of people leads us to conclude that such activities lack propriety.

7 Summary and Conclusion

It was shown that if a voluntary behavior in field of business results in establishment of acquired and social dignities for human beings, it will be titled ethically good and proper. Therefore, actualization of human dignity in any manner can be a criterion for apprehension of ethical "goodness" or "badness" of the voluntary activities in the field work of business. The important point is, however, that simple observance of acquired or social dignities cannot serve as a general acknowledgement of goodness and properness of business conducts, but merely provides a criterion apprehension of their goodness. The outcomes of the present research indicate that recognition of acquired and social dignities plays a pivotal role in coordinating Islamic economic system because it helps in evaluating the properness or improperness of any voluntary behavior in realm of Islamic economy. More significantly, it is not necessary to rely on usual criteria of consequentialist or deontological approaches in to determine the ethical propriety of activities. It suffices to relay on cognition of the principles of acquired and social dignity related to these activities to determine their ethical propriety.

References

Holy Qur'an; *translated by* T.B. Irving (Al-Haj Ta'lim Ali); Suhrawardi Research and Publication Center, Tehran-Iran; 2003.

Arousi Howeizi, Abd Ali Bin Joma'; *Tafsir Nur Al-Thaqalein*; Vol. 3; Qum; Ismaeilian Institute; 1412 LH.

Bin Haivan, No'man Bin mohammad Maghrebi, Daaem aleslam va zekro lhalal va lharam va lghazaya va lahkam, publisher: Al lbeit, Qum, 1385 gh.

Horr Al-Ameli, Al-Sheikh Mohammad Bin Hassan; *Afsul Al-Mohema fi Osul Al-A'ema*; Qum; Imam Reza Islamic Education Institute; 1376 SH.

Ja'fari Langroudi, Mohammad Ja'far; *Legal Terminology 15*; Ganj Danesh Library; Tehran; 1384 SH.

Majlesi, Mohammad Baqer; *Behar Al-Anwar*; Dar Eh'ya Al-torath Al-Arabi; Beirut: 1403 LH (1993).

Mohaddith Al-Nouri (Nouri Al-Tabarsi), Mirza Hossein; *Mostadrak Al-Vasayel Va Mostanbat Al-Masa'el*; Al Al-Bayt (PBUT) L-Ehya Al-Itrath Institute; Qum; 1411 LH; Vol. 13.

Motahari, Morteza; *Philosophy of Ethics*; Tehran; Sadra Publishers; 1388 SH.

Naqibi, Seyyed Abolqasem; *Spiritual Damages in Islamic Law*; Iran and Contemporary Legal Systems; Tehran; Amir Kabir Publishers; 1386 SH.

Razi, Al-Sharif Abu Al-Hassan Mohammad; *Nahj Al-Balaqa*; translated by Seyyed Jafar Shahidi; Islamic Evolution Teaching Publications; Tehran; 1374 SH.

Tamimi Amedi, Abd Al-Wahed Bin Mohammad; *Tasnif Qarrar Al-Hekam va Dorrar Al-Kalam*; *researched and corrected by* Derayati, Mostafa; Islamic Publicity Office; Qum; First Edition; 1366 SH.

Imam Ali, *Tasnif Qarar Al-Hikam va Dorar Al-Kalam*, Gatherer: Abdolvahed Bin Mohammad, Qum, Dar o lketab Al Slami, 1410 LH (1990).

Seyyed Mohammad Kazem Raja'ee and
Mostafa Kazemi Najafabadi

Chapter 17: Domains of Probity ("*Sidaqat*") in Islamic Markets

1 Introduction

Leaning on revelatory teachings and focusing on ethics in the market, Islam has provided grounds for the realization of probity in the marketplace. Providing justifications and establishing discipline through emphasis on certain criteria will lead to availability of all effective information to the parties to a transaction. The criteria include ascertained price and quality of goods;[1] definitive subject, type and terms of the transaction contract;[2] and the time of invoicing/payment, delivery and appropriation, registering and recording of such cases in the contract. Furthermore, ethical recommendations to marketers and providing the individual who has been betrayed, or has received the defective goods, with the privilege to rescind the contract, will minimize the fraud motives. Besides, following the advice of the Holy Prophet of Islam and Imam Ali for guiding and protecting the markets, the Islamic government is obliged to apply appropriate and effective policies for upholding the probity in the market. This can be achieved either directly or indirectly, in order to promote market efficiency. Methods that improve market efficiency include:

a) Strengthening faith and piety of the effective elements in the market by institutionalizing truthfulness and trustworthiness;
b) Abiding by promises and rules of fairness;
c) Insisting on the principle of "learning religious decrees (jurisprudent) of transaction before engaging in trade and business;"[3] and,
d) Avoiding cheating and excessive speculation. (*Bai' Al-Gharar*)[4].

The Islamic market renders a strong motivational system for revealing information to all parties to a transaction. By incorporating spiritual motivations into a private actor's calculus in making business decisions, the Islamic market can help reconcile personal and societal needs. Consequently, it seems that such a market will

1 Al-Ameli; *Vasayel Al-Shia*; Vol. 17; p. 376; H. 22785.
2 Al-Koleini; *Al-Kafi*; Vol. 5; p. 206.
3 اَلْفِقْهُ ثُمَّ الْمَتْجَرُ
4 *Al-Gharar* Literary means hazard, chance or risk. It refers to sale of a thing that is not present at hand; or the sale of a thing whose consequence or outcome is not known; or a sale involving risk or hazard in which one does not know whether it will come to be or not, such as a fish in the water or a bird in the air.

https://doi.org/10.1515/9783110593419-017

have the capacity to avail of stronger honesty and greater transparency, leading to establishment of probity.

2 Domains of Probity ("Sidaqat")

Probity in the Islamic market depends on the kinds of interactions between its various agents, i.e. suppliers/vendors, demanders/purchasers, physical atmosphere, illuminations/advertisement, and placement of goods. In other words, the overall atmosphere of the market must reflect the reality, so that deviation from reality must not occur. If it occurs, for any unintentional reason, the market must possess the necessary flexibility to recompense it.

Accordingly, it can be stated that probity in Islamic markets can be manifested in the intention, determination, and impression of the market factors/agents, their behavior or the structure of the market. Consequently, the domains of the market comprise conceptual, cognitive, structural, or behavioral.

Within the conceptual domain, probity in an Islamic market emerges as beliefs, the foremost among them being faith in God, faith in resurrection and the afterlife, legitimacy/authenticity of divine prophets as well as their directive role established by the Almighty. In the domain of cognition, market agents are obligated to acquire sufficient knowledge on religious decrees, legal regulations and ethics of transactions. The legitimacy and discipline governing the market and recognition of its various factors help in comprehending the structural domain of probity. Emphasis on learning religious decrees (jurisprudent) of transaction before engaging in trade and business, expresses the endeavors of Islam in recognition and knowledge of religious laws governing the market. Institutionalization of truthfulness through the adoption of ethical virtues such as abiding by promises, trustworthiness, non-involvement of market agents in prevarications (e.g. cheating and collusion), as well as implementation of religious decrees (e.g. options) will contribute to the behavioral domain of probity.

2.1 Conceptual Dimensions

If devotion to the Almighty truly exists, probity in the Islamic market will be reflected by honesty in intention, speech and behavior. The Holy Qur'an considers lack of conviction as the source for fabrications. Abbas Bin Helal recalls: While speaking about a liar, Imam Reza (PBUH) recited this Qur'anic verse:

إِنَّمَا يَفْتَرِي الْكَذِبَ الَّذِينَ لَا يُؤْمِنُونَ بِآيَاتِ اللَّهِ وَأُولَئِكَ هُمُ الْكَاذِبُونَ (النحل: 105)

Only those who do not believe in signs of God forge falsehoods; such men are liars (Al-Nahl: 105)

Imam Ali stated:[5] "The sign of faith is to tell the truth, even if it harms, and do not tell lies, even if it benefits. Never speak of anything beyond your knowledge and information. Fear God and never talk behind others' back." His Holiness has also expressed:[6] "People will never taste the sweetness of faith, unless they abandon lies, whether it is uttered humorously or seriously." Still in another instance, he advised:[7] "Be truthful, since God adores truthfulness. Avoid falsehood, because it contradicts faith. Truthfulness saves people from blunders and dignifies them, but falsehood brings about collapse and destruction of human's life."

2.2 Cognitive Dimension

Sufficient knowledge and cognition about religious decrees, ethics as well as rules and regulations of the market are essential and have been emphasized in the anecdotal and jurisprudential literatures. In addition, lack of cognition about divine legitimacy (Halal) and prohibition (Haram) has been considered as a sign of falsehood. Mu'awiya Bin Wahhab quotes Imam Sadiq saying:[8] "The sign of a liar is that he talks about east and west, about the earth and the sky. But if questioned about divine legitimacies and prohibitions, he does not know anything."

2.3 Behavioral Dimension

The fields of religious decrees, ethics and culture can be differentiated from one another in the domain of behavior. Religious decrees refer to dos and don'ts that must be observed by market agents. There has not been any precise research on the distinction between ethics and religious decrees, or jurisprudence and work ethics. Moreover, such analyses are beyond the scope of the present article.[9] Culture points to continuity and sustainability of market agents and enculturation of honesty. AmroBin Abu Al-Moghdam describes: "When I first met Imam Baqer (PBUH) he recommended me neither to utter any words nor narrate a Hadith, until I acquired truthfulness." Moreover, Imam Baqer has quoted Ali Bin Al-Hossein (i.e. his holy father) to have always advised his children: "Avoid falsehood, and never utter any oaths, neither major nor minor, for carrying out important or ordinary matters. If an individual tells

5 Nahj Al-Balaqa; p. 556.

6 Al-Koleini; *Al-Kafi*; Vol. 2; p. 340.

7 Al-Majlesi; *Behar Al-Anwar*; Vol. 69; p. 260.

8 Al-Majlesi; *Behar Al-Anwar*; Vol. 69; p. 248.

9 However, it is worth noting that many ethical rules have been dictated in form of religious orders. If we consider obligatoriness (*Wajib*) and prohibition (*Haram*) as religious orders, then recommendableness (*Mustahab*) and reprehensibleness (*Makruh*) have the status of ethical teachings.

a lie for an ordinary matter, he dares to do the same even in important matters as well. Haven't you heard that the Holy Prophet said: 'a servant can behave honestly, so that God considers him as exuberantly truthful ("*siddiq*"). Else he will always indulge in falsehood, so that God considers him as a prevaricator'."[10]

Imam Sadiq was asked whether an individual who tells a lie about something is called "*kazzab*" (mendacious). Imam answered: "Not at all! Any individual may make a mistake and tell a lie; but '*kazzab*' refers to an individual whose nature is intermingled with falsehood."[11]

Ahmad Bin Mohammad Hamedani quotes Imam Javad (PBUH), who has quoted his ancestors (PBUT) about the Holy Prophet stating: "Do not be deceived by the plentitude of their prayers and fasting, going for Haj pilgrimage, their deeds, staying awake at night and reciting Holy Qur'an. Look if they are truthful and oblige trustiness."[12]

Also, Ishaq Bin Ammar narrates Imam Sadiq saying: "Do not be fascinated by their prayers and fasting, since people become eager for prayers and fasting at times, because of their fears. Test them in their honesty and trustiness."[13]

2.4 Structural Dimension

The Islamic market has a legitimate structure with a special discipline and order. This legitimacy defines a significant part of the domains of probity in the Islamic market. Therefore, practices that are illegitimate are precisely identified.

2.4.1 Legitimacy and Discipline

In the Islamic market, every transaction must be carried out in the form of a specific contract. Each agreement contract has an exact lexical articulation which is subject to proposal (*Ijab*) and countenance (*Qabul*) of the parties to that contract. The type of goods, their exact or approximate amount, and their price; the quality of the goods; and the required schedule along with the terms and conditions of the contract are precisely determined within the agreement contract. In addition, the market is physically well-organized. In Islamic jurisprudence, emphasis has been placed on precise detection and accurate determination of each of the above-mentioned factors. Therefore, the ambiguity in any of the variables that may culminate in ignorance leading to conflict/quarrel, would make the transaction unpredictable. A legitimate and disciplined market is one in which all of its variables are predetermined. The Islamic

---

10 Al-Koleini; *Al-Kafi*; Vol. 2; p. 338.
11 Al-Koleini; *Al-Kafi*; Vol.; pp. 340 and 341.
12 Sheikh Sadouq; *Al-Emali*; p. 303.
13 Al-Koleini; *Al-Kafi*; Vol. 2; p. 104.

market is obligated to the set terms and conditions of the agreement contract and the market elements must fully comply with it. Registration of these items in the agreement contract has been accentuated repeatedly. In the following, the desirable details of legitimacy and discipline variables are explained briefly. It must be borne in mind, however, that legitimacy and discipline fall within the structural dimension of the Islamic market, whereas their implementation by market agents is a matter of the behavioral dimension.

2.4.1.1 Type of Transaction

In each transaction, the parties must have sufficient information about the type of transaction. Each trading party must enter into the contract under a specified condition. Imam Musa Kazem quotes Amir Al-Mu'minin: "If during a sales transaction, the seller proposes two different prices for cash and installment payments, and proposes to mention both in the agreement contract, only the lower price can be written in the contract, even if the payment will be in installments." His Holiness continued: "Any seller who trades with two prices, one for cash payments and one for installment payments, must specify any one of the types of transaction prior to signing the contract."[14]

Some jurisprudents believe that if there are differences between the parties in relation to the realization of the title or type of transaction, this dispute will rescind the contract.[15] The meaning of this statement is that the parties must agree on the type of agreement contract based on which the transaction is going to take effect, and such consent is only achieved by defining the title of contract for both parties.

Moreover, the jurisprudents consider the proposal (*Ijab*) and countenance (*Qabul*) as necessary steps in agreement contracts. Although *Bai'Al-Mu'atah*[16] allows appropriation of the transacted commodities, but most jurisprudent scholars believe that it will not transfer the ownership. Further, one of the conditions of the transaction is compatibility of proposal with countenance, meaning that both the parties to the transaction will have the same perception about the type of the contract. Therefore, countenance/acceptance must be based on what has been proposed. If the seller asks "dealt?" (بعت) and the buyer responds "accept the donation," (قبلت الهبه) the former proposes to sell, while the latter believes that the commodities are donated; naturally, it can be concluded that the type of transaction has not been clearly defined for the parties.[17]

---

14 Al-Koleini; *Al-Kafi*;.; Vol. 5; p. 206.

15 Mousavi Al-Khomeini; *Kitab Al-Bai (taqrirat)*; Vol.1; p. 367.

16 A sales contract whereby the buyer picks up the goods and the seller accepts the price without any explicit bargaining.

17 Mousavi Al-Kho'ei; *Mesbah Al-Fiqaha'*; Vol. 3; pp. 71–72.

2.4.1.2 Parties to the Transaction

General conditions of the contract puts the responsibility of the transaction on the shoulders of those who are obligated and capable of carrying out the deal dutifully. Such legitimacy makes it impossible for individuals who are immature, insane and incapacitated, and thus prone to financial dupery, to enter the Islamic markets. Therefore, the chances of deception, insecurity and unreliability are reduced. In addition, authentication of the ownership of the supplying party in the transactions will result in minimization of the instances of selling others' property or selling a single property to several individuals. In the answer by Imam Zaman to Hamiri, it is stated: "Selling of goods is not permissible except by the owner, under his order or with his consent."[18] In the jurisprudential literature, the condition of ownership is one of the essential criteria of the transaction.[19]

2.4.1.3 Type of Goods/Commodity

In Islamic jurisprudence, it is necessary that the subject of a transaction is clearly determined and specified before composing the agreement contract. The parties to the transaction must be aware of what they are trading. If the type of goods are not specified in the contract, so that the parties agree to carry out the transaction without knowing the type of goods involved,the transaction is void based on Islamic jurisprudence;[20] e.g. when the goods are determined by act of chance, such as throwing a stone etc. (ignorance about the type of goods is common in all such deals).[21] Specificity of the type of the merchandise to be transacted is so important that if the buyers tell the seller: "Of the thousand different commodities, I buy one hundred, and will choose them after the completion of the deal;" the transaction is again void from the point of view of Islamic jurisprudence, because of the ignorance about the type of commodity at the time of composing the contract.[22]

There are many anecdotes (Hadith) about the definitive nature of the type of goods to be traded, wherein certain kinds of transactions are proscribed due to indeterminateness of the goods. For example, the Holy Prophet has prohibited"*Bai'*

---

18 Mousavi Al-Kho'ei; *Mesbah Al-Fiqaha'*; p. 337; H. 22699.

19 Bahjat; Mohammad Taqi; *Ja'me Al-Masa'el*; Vol. 2; p. 506.

20 Sheikh Sadouq; *Ma'ani Al-Akhbar*; p. 278.

21 Such kinds of transaction were very common prior to Islamic Era; today, the stock basket combination of many capital bonds available in the stock markets is not known.

22 Al-Ameli; *Vasayel Al-Shia*; Vol. 17; p. 360; H. 22745; Esfahani Majlesi (the Second); *Mer'at Al-Oqul fi Sharh Akhbar Ale' Al-Rasoul*; Vol. 19; p. 259.

Al-Munabadhah,"[23] "*Bai' Al-Mulamasah*"[24] and "*Bai' Al-Hasah.*"[25] Such transactions which were very common in pre-Islamic era, and are prohibited in Islam due to the indefiniteness of the goods that aretraded.[26] Furthermore,Mohammad Bin Sanan narrates that Imam Baqer reprehended two types of transaction: "First is the 'Pay and Take' deal, in which the customer pays an amount (without discussing with the salesman about the commodity), and takes the good. And the second is buying something without sighting it."[27] In addition to lack of prior consent and agreement about the subject of transaction in such deals, there is no information about the quantity and quality of the merchandise.

Determining the type of each commodity must be in accordance with its characteristic specifications. If a product is intended to taste well, then it can be authenticated by the customer by tasting it.[28] A product whose odor is to be desirable, should be smelled by the customer prior to the transaction. Emphasis on savoring and smelling for the goods whose taste and odor are to be desirable, respectively, points to the need for customer satisfaction about the quality of the product and its direc tinfluence on the pricing. Therefore, the market agents must be able to test goods, with the permission of the other party, to prevent subsequent losses and difficulties.

2.4.1.4 Quality of Goods/Commodity

No act which obscures or conceals the quality of the merchandize is acceptable in transactions, and accordingly Islam has strongly condemned instances of deception, suppression of defect and dissimulation (*Tadlis*), because they obfuscate the quality of the merchandize.

Definitiveness of the quality of the goods is so important that in some anecdotes (Hadith) even payment of adulterated,[29] infrequent[30] and problematic[31] cash for transaction has been prohibited. This is primarily due to the uncertainty of the characteristics and quality of traded items (in this case, cash) in the transaction.

---

23 A contract of sale prevalent in the days of the Prophet in which the seller or the buyer would throw a piece of cloth towards the other and this very act of throwing finalized the deal.

24 A form of sale prevalent in the days of the Prophet in which the buyer or the seller used to touch a piece of cloth and this very act of touching finalized the deal.

25 A type of business transaction in pre-Islamic Arabia where the contract was concluded by the buyer throwing pebbles towards the merchandise, the one hit by the pebble becoming the object sold.

26 Al-Ameli; *Vasayel Al-Shia*; Vol. 17; p. 358; H. 22747.

27 Al-Ameli; *Vasayel Al-Shia*; Vol. 17.; p. 376; H. 22785.

28 Al-Ameli; *Vasayel Al-Shia*; Vol. 17H. 22783.

29 Al-Ameli; *Vasayel Al-Shia*; Vol. 18; p. 186; H. 23452.

30 Al-Ameli; *Vasayel Al-Shia*;; p. 187; H. 23456.

31 Al-Ameli; *Vasayel Al-Shia*;.; H. 23457.

One of the religious decrees that indicates the importance of definitiveness of the quality of goods to be traded is that of *Bai' Al-Salam*.[32] It is a sale agreement that involves advance payment for goods that are to be delivered later, provided the goods are defined, price is paid in advance and the date of delivery is fixed. The quality of the objects of this sale should not change over the course of time.[33]

2.4.1.5 Quantity of Goods/Commodity

The necessity of knowing the quantity of the goods that are traded in a transaction has been emphasized in a number of anecdotes/apothegms (Hadith). This vehemence is greater in case of weighed and volumetrically measured commodities.[34]

Some jurisprudential decrees such as appended transactions (e.g. *Bai' Al-Laban Fi Duru' Al-An'am*[35] and *Bai' Al-Thimar*[36]) are also allowed, but only if the goods are measured and the price is charged for the actual measured quantity. Ambiguity in the quantity of goods is not acceptable. In addition, the definitiveness of the quantity of merchandize and the time of delivery in *Bai' Al-Salam*, indicates the importance of transparency of the quantity of goods in the Islamic market.[37]

One of the reasons for the prohibition of the sale of fruit before ripening and pigmentation[38] is the fact that the quantity of the goods is undetermined (since it is unclear that at the time of delivery of the goods, how much remains). According to the same anecdotes/apothegms (Hadith), one of the essential conditions for the correctness of the transactions, is the definitiveness of the quantity of goods.[39]

2.4.1.6 Price of Goods/Commodity

There are a number of anecdotes/apothegms (Hadith) that explicitlyemphasize the necessity of having a definite price in transactions. Imam Sadiq is quoted in an anecdote/apothegm (Hadith) saying: "If an individual expresses that he sells his goods for 10 dinars (gold coin) minus 1 dirham (silver coin), to be paid later, the transaction is not correct, because the conversion rate of dirham and dinar at the time of clearing the debt is unknown, and the price is ambiguous."[40] Therefore, the type of currency

---

32 Al-Ameli; *Vasayel Al-Shia*; p. 284; H. 23674.
33 Al-Ameli; *Vasayel Al-Shia*;.; p. 287; H. 23684.
34 Al-Ameli; *Vasayel Al-Shia*; .; Vol. 17; p. 342; H. 22706.
35 Sale of milk in the udders of the animals. Al-Ameli; *Vasayel Al-Shia*;.; p. 349; H. 22723.
36 Sale of fruit on tree prior to ripening. *ibid.*; Vol. 18; p. 210; H. 23512; and p. 219; H. 23538.
37 *i* Al-Ameli; *Vasayel Al-Shia*;.; p. 288; H. 23686; p. 289; H. 23690; p. 285; H. 23676 and H.23678.
38 Al-Ameli; *Vasayel Al-Shia*;.; p. 210; H. 23514.
39 Najafi Mohammad Hassan Bin Baqer; *Jawaher Al-Kalam fi Shara'e Al-Islam*; Vol. 22; p. 417; 5th Condition.
40 Al-Ameli; *Vasayel Al-Shia*; Vol. 18; p. 81; H. 23198, H.23196 and 23197.

used for the transaction (if different currencies exist) must be precisely defined in the contract.[41]

Also, in credit and installment sales transactions, where goods are delivered but the payments are deferred, the amount as well as the exact time of payments must be clearly defined in the contract. Rent/lease contracts are also required to have a definite amount and date of payment. There is a specific chapter on this topic which delineates the terms and conditions for type of property, duration of rent/lease, amount of rent/lease and mode of payment. When Imam Baqer was asked: "Is it correct to rent an animal for a definite distance at a definite price, and mention that if the animal covers an extra distance, there will be extra payment?" His Holiness replied: "If the amount of extra payment is defined clearly, it is correct."[42]

The late Sheikh Ansari was of the opinion that the main reason for the invalidity of transactions where the price is not defined is the renowned Hadith of "Nullityof Aleatory Sale" (*Naf'ye Al-Gharar*).[43] Accordingly, all jurisprudents[44] consider the definitiveness of price in terms of amount, type and specifications of currency as the main criterion for correctness of the transactions.[45]

The prohibition of the following acts are all indications that any act that violated the pricing ambience of the transaction is undesirable/disagreeable from Islamic point of view:

1. Purchasing merchandise from dealers' caravans on the suburbs of cities and selling them in the city markets (تَلَقّی رُکبان);
2. Touting with no intention to purchase in order to increase the price (*Najsh*); and,
3. Baulking while intending to purchase in order to reduce the price (*Tada'bor*).

The prices of commodities is not known to the caravan travelers who are entering the cities, and those who approach the caravans on the suburbs of cities can abuse ignorance about prices, purchase the goods and sell them at a higher profit margin in the city markets (تَلَقّی رُکبان).[46]

In cases of *Najsh* and *Tada'bor*,[47] collusion of a third party (who does not intend to make a transaction) with one of the parties to the transaction will obscure the price

41 Al-Ameli; *Vasayel Al-Shia*;.; p. 96; H. 23228.

42 Al-Ameli; *Vasayel Al-Shia*; ; Vol. 19; p. 112; H. 24260.

43 Ansari, Morteza Bin Mohammad Amin; *Al-Makasib*; Vol. 2; p. 213.

44 Ansari, Morteza Bin Mohammad Amin; *Al-Makasib*; Vol. 2; p. 213.

45 Najafi Mohammad Hassan Bin Baqer; *Jawaher Al-Kalam fi Shara'e Al-Islam*; Vol. 22; pp. 405 and 406.

46 Al-Ameli; *Vasayel Al-Shia*; Vol. 17; p. 443; H. 22949; and, p. 444; H 22950.

47 Al-Johari, Ismaeil Bin Hammad; *Al-Sah'hah*; Vol. 3; p. 1021; and, Vol. 2; p. 655.

and lead to dishonesty, forcing either the buyer (in case of *Najsh*) or the seller (in case of *Tada'bor*) to err; this constitutes the reason for their prohibition in Islam.[48]

2.4.1.7 Invoicing/Payment and Delivery

It is necessary to precisely define the times of payment and delivery of goods in Islamic markets. Imam Kazem was asked about the sale of dates still on the palm tree. His Holiness replied: "If the dates are sold annually, it must be postponed till ripening of the fruit."[49]

Imam Reza answered the same question saying: "Selling of palm dates prior to fruit coloration (pigmentation) is not permissible;"[50] while Imam Sadiq responding to the same query has considered the criteria of "pigmentation" necessary for permitting the transaction.[51] Furthermore, His Holiness added in this relation: "It is not permissible to sell the dates of a one-year palm tree, unless the fruit reaches a level that protects it from pests."[52]

It is also conceived from some jurisprudential decrees that because of the ambiguity about time of invoicing/payment and delivery in Islamic markets, appended transactions (e.g. *Bai' Al-Abd Al-Abiq*,[53] *Bai' Al-Laban Fi Duru' Al-An'am*,[54] *Bai' Al-Thimar*,[55] *Bai' Al-Samak Fil Ma'*,[56] *Bai' Habal Al-Habala*[57] and all other types of *Bai' Gharar*) may result in conflict and rescinding of the contract. Therefore, such transactions are strictly prohibited.

Based on the time of payment and delivery, the transactions can be divided into three categories: 1. Cash/Spot,[58] 2. Deferred/Installment[59] and 3. "Salam."In spot sale for cash, the timing of payment and delivery is immediate at the meeting which leads to the transaction. In installment sale, the delivery time of the goods is simultaneous with the transaction, but payment for it is deferred to a future time which is decided by the consent of the parties. *Bai' Al-Salam* involves advance payment for goods that are to be delivered later, at a time agreed by the parties. The common feature of all these categories of transaction is that the goods are defined, the price is fixed, and the

---

48 Al-Ameli; *Vasayel Al-Shia*; Vol. 17; p. 458; H. 22991; and, p. 459; H. 22993.

49 Al-Ameli; *Vasayel Al-Shia*; Vol. 18; p. 210; H. 23511.

50 Al-Ameli; *Vasayel Al-Shia*; H. 23513.

51 Al-Ameli; *Vasayel Al-Shia*; H. 23514.

52 Al-Ameli; *Vasayel Al-Shia.*; p. 212; H. 23522.

53 Sale of a slave who has escaped his master. It was prohibited by the Prophet.*ibid.*; p. 349; H. 22723.

54 Sale of milk in the udders of the animals.*ibid.*

55 Sale of fruit on tree prior to ripening. *ibid.*; Vol. 18; p. 210; H. 23512; and p. 219; H. 23538.

56 Sale of fish in the water.*ibid.*; Vol. 17; p. 354; H. 22735.

57 A type of business transaction prevalent in pre-Islamic Arabia where the unborn child of a camel was sold while it was still in the womb of the she-camel.*ibid.*; p. 352; H. 222730; and, Al-Koleini; *Al-Kafi*; Vol. 5; p. 191; H. 5.

58 *Al-Bai' Al-Najiz*

59 *Al-Bai' Li-'Ajal*

date of payment and delivery are decided by the consent of the parties. For example, in "Salam" transactions where the delivery of goods is postponed to a future time, it has been emphasized that the quality, quantity and time of delivery must be definitely described, otherwise, the transaction is invalid. On a question about the permissibility of "Salam" transactions for non-agricultural products, Imam Sadiq has been quoted: "If the quantity and delivery time of the goods is precisely mentioned, it is permissible."[60]

2.4.2 Physical Order

As described earlier, the market which was confirmed by the Holy Prophet of Islam, and further evolved in Islamic civilization, constituted a place where suppliers were located next to each other with the merchandize being produced in their backyards. When the production institutes of a particular industry form a specialized circle and position in a single location, and supply specific and relatively similar merchandize in that place, numerous demanders will also crowd that place. Consequently, the ground for honesty is gradually provided. This will also result in performing market activities openly and will lead to transparency of the market. In such markets no secretiveness or concealment of information is possible. Some jurisprudents have clearly recommended this kind of physical order in the Islamic markets:

"Since most demanders are present in the specific market of a commodity, and the prices offered there are more reasonable and more transparent, it is desirable that every commodity be traded in its own specific market. Thus paper must be traded in the paper market, cloth and textile in the cloths market, carpets in the carpet market, and any commodity in its respective market."[61]

Transparent setting of sales centers and manufacturing institutes (marts), mosques, educational centers, and the type of market architecture, tile works and appropriate and sufficient lighting, can be effective in consolidating the market ethics and providing grounds for honesty.

60 *Al-Bai' Al-Najiz*; Vol. 18; p. 289; H. 23686–23689; and, p.290; H. 23690.Al-Koleini; *Al-Kafi*; Vol. 5; p. 208. Esfahani Majlesi (the Second); *Mer'at Al-Oqul fi Sharh Akhbar Ale' Al-Rasoul*; Vol. 19; p. 259.
61 *Al-Mabsut fi Fiqh Al-Imamiya'*; Vol. 7; p. 270.

3 Compare Complete Information and Probity ("Sidaqat") in Islamic Market

Prevailing theories in conventional economics do not tolerate idealistic considerations. In this economy, the non-concealment of information is interpreted as transparency. William Stanley Jevons (1871) introduced the idea of complete information in competitive markets in his book titled "The Theory of Political Economy," through amalgamation of the concepts of market and competition. In addition to the knowledge of businessmen about the criteria of supply and demand and the prices of transactions, Jevons considered a fully competitive market as the requirement for realization of complete information.

Stiglitz emphasized that the competitive model of markets can only be achieved in view of complete transparency of the market, but in reality, the outside world suffers from incompleteness of information. While economists confess that most markets are influenced by incomplete competitive conditions and the Walras' equilibrium is vagarious, there is no way other than accepting the asymmetry of information in the markets.

Economists have put forward various strategies including signaling by suppliers, designing institutions, and managing and controlling information by the government in order to compensate for the lack of market information. The capitalist economy seems to be inherently disadvantaged by deficits and concealment of information, and is unable to repair this defect.

A basic problem of the capitalist economy lies in its foundations, i.e. the move towards an exclusive focus on capital and authentication of profiteering by *Homo economicus*. This problem is unlikely to be resolved by intervention and supervision of governments, who themselves are founded on the basis of the same concepts. If personal interests demand that institutions be formed by the production enterprises, and governments are established by those institutions, there would be no supervising authority for overseeing the conduct of such institutions and the state, excep the same powerful production enterprises. It seems that this school of thought cannot resolve the existing difficulties facing societies where goods are generally not homogeneous and a large number of buyers and sellers exist for a myriad of goods with vast ranges of quality. Assuming the focus of personal interest and the goal of profit maximization, the question would be what measures are necessary to confront the enterprises who are sending false signals, through dissemination of false advertisements, tagging and warranties, to achieve the aforementioned objectives.

Taking into account the preconditions of the competitive market, if greater profits can be earned by concealing defects, collusion, dissimulation and misrepresentation, and there exists no concerns about divine instructions and guiding by the Almighty, the hidden power of spiritual motives, or the benefits and losses of the afterlife, as well as no intervention by the Government, nothing can prevent production enterprises from concealment of information. And capitalism as the prevailing school of economic thinking has no remedies for the resultant conditions.

In the Islamic market, on the contrary, the individuals who pursue a superior and persistent life in the hereafter have realized that the pleasures of afterlife are of greater quality and more persistent than those of world. Consequently, probity will routinely be established in Islamic markets by durable and eternal/unworldly personal interest. Through the values it creates, it not only builds confidence and establishes security and assurance, but renders the capacity to produce information in excess of what is required by the market and is effective in pricing. As a result, the information asymmetry in the market is systematically reduced and the Islamic market will benefit from probity.

4 Conclusion

Delusive advertisements, false product labels, fabrication, fraud, cheating, collusion, breaking promises, perfidy (betraying the trust), and unfairness are all signs of a lack of probity in Islamic markets. Absence of probity among suppliers and demanders will incur heavy costs in the market and leads to various damages to the market and hence the society.

Probity in Islamic market depends on the kinds of interaction between its agents, i.e. suppliers/vendors, demanders/purchasers, physical atmosphere, illuminations/lightings, and placement of goods. In other words, the overall atmosphere of the market must reflect the reality, so that deviation from reality or reversing of facts must not occur under any circumstances. If it occurs, for any unintentional reason, the market must possess the necessary flexibility to recompense it.

Accordingly, it can be stated that probity in Islamic markets may be manifested in the intention, determination, and impression of market factors/agents, their behavior or the structure of the market. Consequently, the domains of the market comprise conceptual, cognitive, structural or behavioral. Nonetheless, the measures for achieving probity can be categorized into grounding, process-related, or options/compensatory, based on the respective influence in preparing the ground, the realization of the operational processes of transactions, or recompensing the market defects.

From the Islamic perspective, probity in markets can be achieved in various domains by a number of measures. A review of Islamic literature reveals that the domain of probity in Islamic market includes type, quality, quantity and price of commodity as well as type of transaction, invoicing/payment and delivery times, parties to the transaction and the governing rules and regulations of the market.

In the Islamic market, the individuals who pursue a superior and persistent life in the hereafter have realized that the pleasures of the afterlife are of greater quality and quantity than those of this world. Consequently, probity will routinely be established in Islamic markets by durable and eternal/unworldly personal interest. Through the values it creates, it not only builds confidence and establishes security and assurance, but renders the capacity to produce information in excess of what is required by the market and is effective in pricing. As a result, the information asymmetry in the market is systematically reduced and the Islamic market will benefit from probity.

References

Holy Qur'an; *translated by* T.B. Irving (Al-Haj Ta'lim Ali); Suhrawardi Research and Publication Center, Tehran-Iran; 2003.

Razi, Al-Sharif Abu Al-Hassan Mohammad; *Nahj Al-Balaqa*; translated by Seyyed Jafar Shahidi; Islamic Evolution Teaching Publications; Tehran; 1374 SH.

Ibn Manzur; Mohammad Bin Mokarram; *Lesan Al-Arab*; 15 Vol.; Beirut, Lebanon; Dar Sa'd; 1414 LH.

Esfahani Majlesi (the Second), Mohammad Baqer Bin Mohammad Taqi; *Mer'at Al-Oqul fi Sharh Akhbar Ale' Al-Rasoul*; 26 Vols.; Dar Al-Kotob Al-Islamiya'; Tehran, Iran; 1404 LH.

Mousavi Al-Khomeini, Ruhollah; *Kitab Al-Bai (taqrirat)*;Institute for Compilation and Publication of Imam Khomeini's Works, Tehran; 1376 SH.

Ansari, Morteza Bin Mohammad Amin; *Al-Makasib*; The Great Sheikh AnsariCommemoration Conference, Qum; 1415 LH.

Bahrani, Seyyed Hashem; *Al-Borhan fi Tafsir Al-Qur'an*; researched by Be'that Foundation Research Bureau; Qum; 1416 LH.

Bolaghi Najafi, Mohammad Javad; *A'al' Al-Rahman fi Tafsir Al-Qur'an*; Be'that Foundation Research Bureau; Qum; 1420 LH.

Bahjat, Mohammad Taqi; *Ja'me Al-Masa'el (L'il Bahjat)*; No Date; No Place.

Tavakoli; *An Introduction to Moral Philosophy of Commerce with Islamic Approach*; Economic Teachings; Vol. 1; pp. 7–31; 1389 SH.

Jawaheri; Ismaeil Bin Hammad; *Al-Sohah*; Beirut, Lebanon; Dar Al-Elm L'il Molla'ein; 1407 LH.

Raja'ei, Seyyed Mohammad Kazem; *Thematic Lexicon of Economic Verses of Holy Qur'an*; Qum, Publications of Imam Khomeini Education and Research Institute; 1382 SH.

Saduq, Abu Jafar Mohammad Bin Ali; *Al-Amali*; Islamiya' Publishers; Tehran; 1362 SH.

Saduq, Abu Jafar Mohammad Bin Ali; *Ma'ani Al-Akhbar*; *edited/corrected by* Ali Akbar Al-Qaffari; Islamic Publication; Qum; 366 p.; 1361 SH.

Tabataba'ei, Al-Seyyed Mohammad Hossein; *Al-Mizan fi Tafsir Al-Qur'an*; 20 Vols.; Second Edition; Al-A'lami Al-Matbu'at Institute; Beirut; 1394 LH.

Tousi, Mohammad Bin Hassan; *Al-Tebyan fi Tafsir Al-Qur'an*; edited by Ahmad Qasir Al-Ameli; Beirut, Lebanon; Dar Al-Ihya Al-Torath Al-Arabi; No date.

Hor Al-Ameli, Al-Sheikh Mohammad Bin Al-Hassan; *Vasayel Al-Shia*; 20 Vols.; A'l Al-Bait (PBUT) Institute; Qum; 1409 LH.

Majlesi, Mohammad Baqer; *Behar Al-Anwar*; Wafa Institute; Beirut, Lebanon; 1404 LH.

Jaberi, Ali; *Conventional Economic Science and Hedonistic Egoism*; Economic Teachings; Vol. 1; No. 1; p. 163–184; No date.

Al-Ayyashi, Mohammad Bin Masoud; Kitab Al-Tafsir; researched by Seyyed Hashem Rasouli Mahallati; Tehran, Elmiya' Printing Press; Vol. 2; p. 23; 1380 LH.

Ghaffari, Hadi; *Economic System of Early Islamic Era*; Tehran, Payam Noor University Press; 1386 SH.

Ghara'ati, Mohsen; *Tafsir Al-Nour*; Lessons of Qur'an Cultural Center; 1389 SH.

Al-Koleini, Abu Jafar Mohammad Bin Al-Yaqub; *Al-Kafi*; *edited/corrected by* Ali Akbar Al-Qaffari; 8 Vols.; Beirut, Lebanon; Dar Al-Azwa; 1405 LH.

Gonabadi, Soltan Mohammad; *Tafsir Bayan Al-Sa'ada' fi Maqamat Al-Ibada'*; Beirut, Al-A'lami L'il Matbu'atSecond Ed.; 1408 LH.

Team of Translators; *Translation of Tafsir Jawame' Al-Jame'*; with an introduction by Ayatollah Vaez zAdeh Khorasani; Mashhad, Islamic Research Foundation, Astan Qods Razavi; Second Ed. 1377 SH.

Team of Translators; *Translation of Maj'ma' Al-Bayan fi Tafsir Al-Qur'an*; research by Reza Sotudeh; Farahani Publishers; Tehran 1360 SH.

Nouri, Mirza Hassan; *Mostadrak Al-Vasayel Va Mostanbat Al-Masa'el*; 18 Vol. First Edition; Al Al-Bayt (PBUT) L-Ehya Al-Itrath Institute; Qum; 1408 LH.

Mousavi Al-Kho'ei, Seyyed Abolqasem; *Mesbah Al-Fiqaha'*; edited by Sheikh Mohammad Ali Tohidi; No Date; No Place.

Makarem Shirazi, Naser; *Tafsir Nemoune'*; Qum; Dar Al-Kotob Islamiya'; 1374 SH.

Najafi, Mohammad Hassan Bin Baqer; *Jawahir Al-Kalam fi Sharh Shara'e Al-Islam*; researched and edited by Sheikh Abbas Ghoochani; Beirut, Lebanon, Dar Al-Ihya Al-Torath Al-Arabi; No Date.

Naraghi, Mohammad Mahdi; *Jame' Al-Sa'adat*; edited by Seyyed Mohammad Kalantar; Beirut, Al-A'lami L'il Matbu'atSecond Ed.; 1408 LH.

North, Douglass C.; *Transaction Costs, Institutions, and Economic History*; Journal of Institutional and Theoretical Economics; Vol. 140; pp. 7–17; 1984.

Stiglitz, Joseph E.; *Information and the Change in the Paradigm in Economics*; The American Economic Review; Vol. 92, No. 3 (Jun., 2002), pp. 460–501; 2002.

Seyyed Mohammad Kazem Raja'ee and Mostafa Kazemi Najafabadi

Chapter 18: An Index of Islamic Market Probity ("*Sidaqat*")

1 Introduction

The word "Index" refers to any instrument which is used for quantifying and evaluating a specific variable at a certain time in a certain place. For evaluation and assessment of multi-dimensional concepts that cannot be quantified by a single definite measure/scale, composite indices are utilized. (Tabataba'eian 2011, p. 114)

Since economic analysis and planning requires devising various kinds of economic indicators, a wide spectrum of indicators have been utilized by different statistical and academic institutions in various countries covering extensive range of economic themes. Among the most important categories of such indicators, from an Islamic viewpoint, are market indicators which provide credible, standard and reliable information about the conditions and trends of markets.

"Probity Index" is a composite index comprising various indicators of Islamic market which combines a set of differently-weighted variables to measure the veracity of market transactions. Three of these possible variables may be referred to as grounding, process-related, or options/compensatory which encompass conceptual, structural or behavioral aspects of market behavior. Utilization of this index, along with other indices, may allow evaluation of the prevailing conditions of the market and its compliance with the desirable model of the Islamic market. Examining the status of probity in the existing markets and scrutinizing the variables that affect it, can help. authorities adopt the right policies. The present article attempts to recognize various criteria and indices of the markets based on primary Islamic literature including the Holy Qur'an and Hadith (sacred narrations). In addition, views of jurisprudents and interpreters are also scrutinized through validity analysis method and independent reasoning (*Ijtihad*). For determining the weights of each indicator, the technique of "Analytic Hierarchy Process" (AHP) is used. Since the outcomes of this technique are totally dependent on the opinion of the researcher/expert, this paper has incorporated the views of the scholars who are familiar with the primary Islamic and jurisprudential literature relating to markets and also teach various economic subjects. In other words, the variables were obtained from Holy Qur'an, Hadith and viewpoints of jurisprudents, while their weights were determined using Holy Quran, Hadith and jurisprudential and ethics literature. The "Probity Index" has been assessed and evaluated through "interview," "questionnaire," and "reviewing the available documents" during the field study.

https://doi.org/10.1515/9783110593419-018

2 Background

Transparency of information and its special connotation does not possess the required capacity to define the conceptual significance of the strong transparency which is expected to govern Islamic markets. The term "probity" ("*sidaqat*") better explains such connotation. Reference to the concept of probity and non-concealment/non-cloaking of information is observed throughout Hadith, jurisprudential and ethics literature, as well as the Shari'ah. Although transparency is greatly discussed in economic literature, there has been no research on the concept of probity in the markets. The structure and specific features of Islamic markets have been investigated by many, some of which also refer to the concept of truthful exchange of information and transparency. Zara'Nejad (2002), Karami (1996), Ghaffari (2007) and Raja'ei (2011) have considered the spiritual/divine motives of the Islamic markets as the main cause of avoidance of cloaking/concealment of information. They all assign the efficiency of Islamic markets to the resultant "transparency." To answer the question of how to measure market, the present article attempts to arrive at a quantitative index as a measure for probity in an Islamic market. After empirically testing it in a specific market, it will introduce a "Indicator of Probity" for the Islamic markets.

3 Terminology and Etymology of "Sidq"

The word "*sidq*" (صِدق or truthfulness) is the antonym of "*kezb*" (كِذب or untruthfulness) and means "consistency of the information with the reality of the subject/affair." In Islamic viewpoint, this is interpreted as the conformity to what has been preserved in "the Guarded Tablet" (فِي لَوْحٍ مَحْفُوظٍ); e.g. saying "Mr. X is in the house," when Mr. X is actually in the house. A person who is truthful in his words is called "*sadiq*" (صادِق). When *sadiq* is used as proper noun, however, it refers to Imam Ja'far Bin Mohammad Al-Sadiq (Tarihi 1996, p. 199).

Any information or news may be described by the syntactical adjectives truthful or false/untruthful; e.g. when a pagan unbelievingly says: "Prophet Mohammad (sawa), the Messenger of Allah," it is truthful since it conforms to reality. But at the same time, it is false/untruthful, for it is not uttered with sincerity and does not comply with the belief and conscience of the utterer(Raqib Isfahani 1991, p. 478). Holy Qur'an impugns the hypocrites who testify that the Prophet is the Messenger of Allah:

إِذَا جَاءَكَ الْمُنَافِقُونَ قَالُوا نَشْهَدُ إِنَّكَ لَرَسُولُ اللَّهِ وَاللَّهُ يَعْلَمُ إِنَّكَ لَرَسُولُهُ وَاللَّهُ يَشْهَدُ إِنَّ الْمُنَافِقِينَ لَكَاذِبُونَ (63: 1)

> Whenever hypocrites come to you, they say: "We profess that you are most surely Allahs's Messenger;" Allah already knows that you are most surely His Messenger, while Allah testifies that the hypocrites are surely liars. (1:63).

The term "*siddiq*" (صدّيق) connotes a person of exuberant truthfulness. A number of scholars have opined that the habitual indulgence of "*siddiq*" in truthfulness prevents him from being involved in prevarications. According to some others, "*siddiq*" is a person who is truthful in speech, belief and practice.

"*Sidq*" and "*kezb*" can also apply to beliefs which are characterized as "true" or "false" in virtue of the truth or falsity of the propositions that are believed. Moreover, they can sometimes be used to describe behaviors and deed. For example, truthfulness of an individual in a battle refers to sincere endeavor by the individual to do whatever is necessary and fulfil all the covenants.

The Holy Qur'an introduces Allah as the most truthful in narration/speech (4:87) and most truthful in allegiance/commitment. (4:122) In addition, Abraham, (19:41) Idris (Enoch), (19:56) Mary (5:75) and others who are allegiant/loyal to Allah's messengers (4:69) are also considered the most truthful ("*siddiq*"). "*Sidq*" has been used with different connotations in the Holy Qur'an which includes: praising the messengers of Allah, (33:24) praising the faithful, (33:24, in part: ... لِيَجْزِيَ اللَّهُ الصَّادِقِينَ بِصِدْقِهِمْ) as well as praising the non-human entities such as the Holy Qur'an itself (76:92), the archangels (2:31) and the hoopoe (27:27). Moreover, it is used to imply honesty (17:80) and abiding by promises/commitment (33:23). It also connotes implicit suggestion of truthfulness in faith, commitment and probity (2:177), and explicit definition of truth (29:3 and 33:8 and 24).

4 Probity (صِداقَت "Sidaqat") in an Islamic Market

Based on what was explained in the previous section, the chief principle in the concept of "*sidq*" is integrity and perfection, avoidance of transgressions mistakes, and having the right on one's side always. However, this primary meaning changes depending on the use in context (*Mostafavi* 1981, p. 213).

Considering the lexical meaning and scholars' terminological usage, the concept of "*sidaqat*" can be defined as: "A multi-faceted acquired ethical virtue of an individual which is manifested in interaction with the self, Allah, other members of society, or the environment. It is internalized deeply by the individual and settles to become a strong habit. Consequently, an equilibrium is created within the individual between his inward/outward character and manifested in his speech, writing and other behavior."

Accordingly, the probity of the markets depends on the factors that influence the workings of the market – meaning sellers and buyers and the interaction between them, physical ambience, lighting, display of goods and the general attitude within the market – will reflect the true reality fully and transparently in a way that no deviation from the truth and reality of aspects of market transactions would be possible. And if, for any reason, such deviations occur, the market has the resilience needed to correct such failures. Persistence of the character of probity, and its influence on various market factors, will be manifested in all aspects of the market so that the market itself will acquire the character of probity. It then becomes possible to measure the degree of the probity of such market.

Probity is fundamental in social relations of the market including supply and demand. False advertising, untrue labels, prevarication, deception, cheating, collusion, breach of contract, perfidy (betrayal of trust) and unfairness are all signs of absence of probity in the market. Lack of probity within the community of producers and consumers will impose significant transaction costs and damages on the market and, ultimately, on the society. Absence of probity in labor market and among factors of production will lead to cover ups, shirking, shortchanging market participants, stealing, irresponsibility, opportunism (self-seeking), and, finally, to quality degradation and reduced production efficiency.

5 Types of Probity Indicators

Various types of indicators can be defined for measurement and evaluation of probity in the market. These include: indicators of grounding, process-related, or options/compensatory. The first, "Grounding Indicator," prepares the ground for probity of the market. The second is the indicator which measures the realization of the operational processes of transactions and is called "Process-related Indicator" (or "Prompt flow of information Indicator"). While the third, "Options Indicator," will recompense the market failure in discovering information or deliberate withholding of information by one of the parties to a transaction.

5.1 Grounding Indicator

The greater the knowledge of the parties to a transaction about rules, regulations and ethics of the market, the greater their understanding of the nature of the transaction and easier the contract negotiations. Although value- and ethics-based governance per se can be considered among factors that prepare the ground for probity, market ethics and what is considered here as positive and negative indicators refer to probity of the process of market exchange. Therefore, ethics that govern the market, in and of itself, provide the basis for probity, in addition to being an indicator of timely flow of information. On the one hand, the extent to which market participants abide by the governance of ethical principles is considered among causal factors and prepares the ground for probity in the market. On the other hand, the existence of such indicators in itself conveys probity and prompt flow of information.

Acquisition of knowledge about rules, regulations and ethics of transactions is referred to here as cognition. Emphasis on learning jurisprudential rules governing transactions (Fiqh) before engaging in trade and exchange (Al-Ameli 1988, p. 381 and 382; H. 22794 and 22795) indicates the importance Islam attaches to attainment of knowledge and familiarity with the rules of the market. Knowledge of the rules governing the market, and their application to actual cases, attained by market participants leads to religiously approved (Shar'ii) transactions while protecting the participants from involvement in Riba-based transactions, cheating and other prohibited activities. Knowledge of the rules is necessary for the awareness of permissible and prohibited transactions. A significant portion of rules and ethics of the market target information related to transactions. In the rules and regulations of Islam, a number of variables need to be defined and explained clearly and transparently so that market participants can understand them, otherwise their implementation becomes problematic. Knowledge of rules and ethics provides the foundation of Probity in implementation of rules, behavior in compliance with rules and ethical principles of Islam.

Knowledge of rules is in fact a kind of preventive measure against engaging in Gharar (creating moral hazard for others by withholding information from them or providing them with false information leading them to take risks which they would not have taken had they been provided fully transparent and correct information), unlawful acquisition of wealth (*Akl Bil Batil*) and entering in any type of forbidden business. Awareness of buyers and sellers about their rights, terms and conditions of contract, and rules governing transactions avoids losses due to lack of knowledge. Additionally, awareness rules enhances incentives to comply with them and helps individuals avoid suspicious transactions that are detrimental to the transparency of the market (Al-Ameli 1988, p. 382 and 383; H. 22795 and 22797).

Knowledge of Islamic ethics and etiquette of the market is an absolute requirement for their implementation in transactions. Moreover, awareness of the ethics of business will provide the grounds for practical commitment to ethical virtues. While the goodness of the truthfulness (Al-Ameli 1988, Vol. 12, p. 285; H. 4), abiding by promises and commitments (17:34 and 5:1) and fairness (Al-Koleini 1984, Vol. 2, p. 14) is obvious, consideration of the role of ethical virtues in human felicity and happiness, on the one hand, and the role of ethical vices, such as prevarication, lies, deception and injustice in human degradation, on the other, will lead to enhanced motivation for individuals to act ethically.

Cognition can be measured by use of the following three indicators:

1. Level of information about fundamentals, principles, obligations and prohibition of transactions;
2. Level of information about recommended, the reprehensibility, and the ethics of transactions; and,
3. Level of information about official (governmental) rules and regulations governing markets in the country.

The weighted average of these three information indicators constitutes the "Cognition Indicator." The "Cognition Indicator" with its own weight contributes as a variable to the weighted average of "Probity Index."

5.2 Process-Related Indicator

On the one hand, the "Process-related Indicators" (or timely flow of information indicator) demonstrate how timely the information in the transaction process is provided to buyers and sellers. On the other hand, they indicate the extent to which the barriers to probity and provision of information have been removed. "Indicator of compliance with the rules and the discipline governing the market" as well as "Positive Ethics Indicators" in the Islamic market demonstrate the timely exchange of market information. Lower levels of cheating and collusion in the market point to greater removal of the barriers to disclosure of information.

5.2.1 Compliance with Rules and the Discipline Governing the Market

This concept refers to the requirement that in an Islamic market every transaction must be carried out in the form of a specific contract. Each contract has its own specific terms and conditions, and is entered into with the consent and approval of the parties. In an Islamic market, it is necessary that the terms and conditions of the contract are clear in its minutest details. The principles and criteria of the contract as well as the terms and conditions of the transaction must be agreed upon with the consent of the parties. The type of contract, price, quantity and quality of goods, the timing of invoicing and payment as well as delivery, and the timing of other services must be specified. The terms of the contract must be defined and the precise specifications of the goods must be expressed clearly, the goods and their full characteristics must be visible to both sides of the contract so that the contract is designed based on full information. Finally, the text of the contract must be written with the consent of the parties. Consequently, the parties to the transaction will enter into the deal with complete knowledge of important criteria of the transaction and the role they play in determining the price.

Many of the inadequacies of market information, which are the source of disturbance in market probity and cause distrust of market agents, are outcomes of lack of accurate recording of details transactions and obligations associated with the them. Lack of agreement on the basis of mutual satisfaction of the parties and absence of written contracts and covenants between individuals will lead to disagreements and creates grounds for distrust and uncertainty about the other party. This in turn diminishes human relationships, and disrupts market discipline.

Based on the lengthiest verse of the Holy Qur'an (282:2), which is about documenting and recording of liabilities, it is clear that detailed coverage and recording of liabilities,[1] determining the exact time of repayments of debts,[2] naming of a fair third party to ensure the resolution of possible future disagreements between the parties,[3] pious preparation of the contract document ensuring that none of the parties are exploited,[4] and protecting the rights of those parties to the contract who do not possess full mental and physical capacity,[5] will bring the market closer to justice.[6] Hence, compliance with these requirements prescribed in the Verse strengthens market exchange and increases the confidence of market participants and reduces distrust.[7] As a result, market atmosphere for probity sterngthens.

> يَا أَيُّهَا الَّذِينَ آمَنُوا إِذَا تَدَايَنْتُمْ بِدَيْنٍ إِلَى أَجَلٍ مُسَمًّى فَاكْتُبُوهُ وَلْيَكْتُبْ بَيْنَكُمْ كَاتِبٌ بِالْعَدْلِ وَلَا يَأْبَ كَاتِبٌ أَنْ يَكْتُبَ كَمَا عَلَّمَهُ اللَّهُ فَلْيَكْتُبْ وَلْيُمْلِلِ الَّذِي عَلَيْهِ الْحَقُّ وَلْيَتَّقِ اللَّهَ رَبَّهُ وَلَا يَبْخَسْ مِنْهُ شَيْئًا فَإِنْ كَانَ الَّذِي عَلَيْهِ الْحَقُّ سَفِيهًا أَوْ ضَعِيفًا أَوْ لَا يَسْتَطِيعُ أَنْ يُمِلَّ هُوَ فَلْيُمْلِلْ وَلِيُّهُ بِالْعَدْلِ وَاسْتَشْهِدُوا شَهِيدَيْنِ مِنْ رِجَالِكُمْ فَإِنْ لَمْ يَكُونَا رَجُلَيْنِ فَرَجُلٌ وَامْرَأَتَانِ مِمَّنْ تَرْضَوْنَ مِنَ الشُّهَدَاءِ أَنْ تَضِلَّ إِحْدَاهُمَا فَتُذَكِّرَ إِحْدَاهُمَا الْأُخْرَى وَلَا يَأْبَ الشُّهَدَاءُ إِذَا مَا دُعُوا وَلَا تَسْأَمُوا أَنْ تَكْتُبُوهُ صَغِيرًا أَوْ كَبِيرًا إِلَى أَجَلِهِ ذَلِكُمْ أَقْسَطُ عِنْدَ اللَّهِ وَأَقْوَمُ لِلشَّهَادَةِ وَأَدْنَى أَلَّا تَرْتَابُوا إِلَّا أَنْ تَكُونَ تِجَارَةً حَاضِرَةً تُدِيرُونَهَا بَيْنَكُمْ فَلَيْسَ عَلَيْكُمْ جُنَاحٌ أَلَّا تَكْتُبُوهَا وَأَشْهِدُوا إِذَا تَبَايَعْتُمْ وَلَا يُضَارَّ كَاتِبٌ وَلَا شَهِيدٌ وَإِنْ تَفْعَلُوا فَإِنَّهُ فُسُوقٌ بِكُمْ وَاتَّقُوا اللَّهَ وَيُعَلِّمُكُمُ اللَّهُ وَاللَّهُ بِكُلِّ شَيْءٍ عَلِيمٌ (2: 282)
>
> O you who believe! Whenever you contract a debt for a stated period, write it down. Let some literate person write (what goes on) between you with fairness; no literate person should refuse to write it down, just as has taught him, so let him write it down, and let the borrower dictate. May he (the recorder of the contract) heed Allah and not omit any part of it. If the borrower is feeble-minded or incapacitated or cannot manage to dictate himself, then let his guardian dictate it in all fairness, and seek out two witnesses from among your men-folk to act as witnesses. It there are not two men (available), then one man and two women (may serve) as witnesses from anyone you may approve of, so that if either of them should slip. up, then the other woman may remind (her). Witnesses must not refuse (to serve) when they are called upon, nor try to get out of writing anything down whether it is small or large, along with its due date. Such (procedure) is more equitable so far as Allah is concerned and it makes for more valid testimony, as well as reducing the chances for doubt; unless it is some transaction handled on the spot that you pass around among yourselves, in which case it will not be held

---

1 يَا أَيُّهَا الَّذِينَ آمَنُوا إِذَا تَدَايَنْتُمْ بِدَيْنٍ إِلَى أَجَلٍ مُسَمًّى فَاكْتُبُوهُ
O you who believe! Whenever you contract a debt for a stated period, write it down ...

2 أَجَلٍ مُسَمًّى
... for a stated period ...

3 وَلْيَكْتُبْ بَيْنَكُمْ كَاتِبٌ بِالْعَدْلِ
... let some literate person write (what goes on) between you with fairness ...

4 وَلْيَتَّقِ اللَّهَ رَبَّهُ وَلَا يَبْخَسْ مِنْهُ شَيْئًا
... May he heed Allah and not omit any part of it ...

5 فَإِنْ كَانَ الَّذِي عَلَيْهِ الْحَقُّ سَفِيهًا أَوْ ضَعِيفًا أَوْ لَا يَسْتَطِيعُ أَنْ يُمِلَّ هُوَ فَلْيُمْلِلْ وَلِيُّهُ بِالْعَدْلِ
... If the borrower is feeble-minded or incapacitated or cannot manage to dictate himself, then let his guardian dictate it in all fairness ...

6 ذَلِكُمْ أَقْسَطُ عِنْدَ اللَّهِ
... Such (procedure) is more equitable so far as Allah is concerned ...

7 وَأَقْوَمُ لِلشَّهَادَةِ وَأَدْنَى أَلَّا تَرْتَابُوا
... and it makes for more valid testimony, as well as reducing the chances for doubt

> against you for not writing it down. Call in witnesses whenever you engage in trade, and let no literate man nor any witness feel obligated if you do so; that would be immoral on your part. Heed Allah, for Allah teaches you! Allah is Aware of everything. (282:2)

The "Indicator of compliance with rules and the discipline that govern the market" is one of the most important measures that demonstrates the level of probity in the market. Sacred narrations and Islamic jurisprudence emphasize the importance of determining the various dimensions of any exchange. This indicator is derived from the weighted average of the items to be specified in the transaction, namely the existence of a written contract; definition of the type of transaction, and naming the parties of the transaction; defining the price, quantity and specifications of the goods; and, the physical order of the market.

5.2.2 Ethics Governing the Market

Ethics, along with beliefs and governing, constitute the three foundations of Islam. In Islamic teachings, the economy and the market are inseparable from spirituality and ethics. Ethics in the Islamic market is a concept compliance with which allows individuals attainment of human excellence, nearness to Allah (swt), and benefit from the rewards in the Hereafter. The religious-minded individual – focused on the vast expanse of life (87:16 and 17),[8] the divine endowments entrusted to man(33:24),[9] (Tabataba'ei 1974, Vol. 8, p. 93) as well as the fair accountability system of rewards and punishments in the Hereafter – will be equipped with an internal incentive-motivation and control system which by preventing individual and social transgressions and errors, not only call him to perform his duties towards himself, other individuals, and even the surrounding environment, (17:37)[10] but also leads him to perform benevolent deeds (18:46).[11] The prevalence of such attitude in the Islamic market would culminate in the honest behavior of participants and induces market transparency.

Islam aims at conversion of the atmosphere of market activities into one where such actions become deeds of worship. and adoration of the Creator through expansion of the consciousness of individual participants to focus on the eternal dimension of life, their trusteeship. regarding the divine endowments and giving market

---

8 بَلْ تُؤْثِرُونَ الْحَيَاةَ الدُّنْيَا (16) وَالْآخِرَةُ خَيْرٌ وَأَبْقَى (17)
Instead you prefer the worldly life, (16) whereas the hereafter is better and more enduring (17)

9 ... وَآتُوهُمْ مِنْ مَالِ اللَّهِ الَّذِي آتَاكُمْ ...
... and give them of the wealth of Allah which He has given you ...

10 ... وَلَا تَمْشِ فِي الْأَرْضِ مَرَحًا
And do not go about in the land exultingly ...

11 ... وَالْبَاقِيَاتُ الصَّالِحَاتُ خَيْرٌ عِنْدَ رَبِّكَ ثَوَابًا وَخَيْرٌ أَمَلًا
... and the ever-abiding, the good works, are better with your Lord in reward and better in expectation

activities religious identity. Attempt to institutionalize values such as fairness (Al-Majlesi 1984, Vol. 74, p. 112) and sacrifice (Al-Majlesi 1984, p. 133) within the market reflects the transcendental approach of Islam towards business and work ethics. Institutionalization of these values can only be achieved by expanding the visions of the faithful towards business. Accordingly, the faithful have been asked to enter into transaction with Allah, a trade that is much more profitable than the worldly businesses. (61:10)[12] They can reap. the divine rewards through virtuous transactions. (*Nahj Al-Balaqa* 1995, Qesar Al-Hekam 113) With this orientation, the act of trading by the virtuous becomes an act of worship. which gains access to Paradise as the most valuable reward. (9:111)[13] Such deliberate thinking will not only prevent economic and social tensions in the market, but will trigger the emergence and manifestation of many ethical virtues in the business environment. (Tavakoli 2010, p. 7–31)

The Islamic approach to probity within the market can be deduced from the application of ethical rules governing trade. Faithful are advised to be truthful in the transaction (Al-Majlesi 1984, Vol. 100, p. 95), abide by the promises, covenants and contracts (Al-Majlesi 1984, Vol. 72, p. 94 and 171), be trustworthy and fair (Al-Majlesi 1984, Vol. 88, p. 235), contented (Majlesi 1984, Vol. 74, p. 45; and Vol. 68, p. 346), and magnanimous and chivalrous. Moreover, activities such as cheating (Majlesi 1984, Vol. 100, p. 82), touting with no intention to purchase in order to increase the price (*Najsh*) (Majlesi 1984, Vol. 72, p. 189, and Vol. 73, p. 348), charlatanism and creating illusions (*Tadlis*) (Al-Koleini 1984, Vol. 5, p. 153), concealing defects (Al-Majlesi 1984, Vol. 100, p. 82), and appearing to cutoff negotiations with true intention of forcing a reduction in the price (*Tadabor*) Al-Ameli 1988, Vol. 17, p. 459, H 22993) are strictly prohibited. These are all indications that Islam supports ethical excellence in the business and work environment which allows, in addition to full transparency, probity to govern the market.

The issue of ethics in the business environment has recently attracted the attention of Western economists, some of whom emphasize the role of ethics as an important factor in fostering a healthy environment for business activities. However, ethics in conventional economics is understood as "not violating" laws, norms and regulations only. Conventional economics gives no consideration to the relationship. between ethics and belief in the origin of the creation and its final destination (when each human is held accountable for deeds while on earth) (Nahavandian 2006, p. 45–64). For reasons of its limited and constrained grounding on epistemological and cosmological foundations, therefore, its limited anthropology enhanced by its insistences on materialism, conventional economics, in principle, does not have the

12 يَا أَيُّهَا الَّذِينَ آمَنُوا هَلْ أَدُلُّكُمْ عَلَى تِجَارَةٍ تُنْجِيكُمْ مِنْ عَذَابٍ أَلِيمٍ
O you who believe! Shall I lead you to a bargain that will save you from painful torments?
13 إِنَّ اللَّهَ اشْتَرَى مِنَ الْمُؤْمِنِينَ أَنْفُسَهُمْ وَأَمْوَالَهُمْ بِأَنَّ لَهُمُ الْجَنَّةَ ...
Surely, Allah has bought up. their persons and their property from believers, so they shall have the garden (instead) ...

capacity for cognition and understanding ethics derived from transcendental consideration of the origin of the creation and its finality as well as lack of cogitation on the concept of "nearness to Allah" as the objective of actions.

5.2.2.1 Positive Ethical Rules Governing the Market

In Islamic teachings, the economy and markets are inseparable from spirituality and ethics. In Islamic teachings, the market, ethics and Fiqh (jurisprudence) have been kneaded and formed together throughout the history of Muslim civilization.

It is natural to expect that ethical virtues and excellent qualities will exert positive influence on the proper behavior of the parties to exchange. The individual who possesses such virtues will be less avaricious, compared to those who have less of these virtues, and more diligent in avoiding non-transparency and prevarication. The most prominent ethical virtues that directly affect market probity, viz. truthfulness, abiding by promises and commitments, trustworthiness and fairness, have a significant direct weight in probity of the market. These virtues are considered hereunder as the indicators of the extent to which ethical rules govern the market as measure of probity.

5.2.2.1.1 Truthfulness

This term encompasses truthfulness in communication, advertisement, registering the specifications of goods, tags and weightage in an Islamic market. The greater the degree of truthfulness, the lesser the degree of non-transparency, and stronger the extent of market probity.

To measure the truthfulness of the market, the following indicators are proposed: (1) the degree of compatibility and coordination of the transaction with the contract (in terms of type of goods, weight, price, time and conditions); (2) the degree correspondence between the product tag and the actual characteristics of the product (in terms of weight, price, quality, ingredients); and (3) the degree of accuracy of advertisements of the product with its actual quality.

The weighted average of these three indicators comprises the "Truthfulness Indicator." This indicator, with its own weight, constitutes one of the variables of positive ethics which is, in turn, one of the main variables in calculating the weighted average of probity and transparency of information.

5.2.2.1.2 Faithfulness

The degree of faithfulness to one's obligations is an indicator of the actualization of probity of the market mechanism and constitutes a solid principle of market transactions, which can even be used as evidence in the event of disputes between the parties to a transaction.

The degree of commitment to abiding by promises in the market can be measured by the following variables: prompt delivery of goods and transfer of funds (cash and credit; differences in the timing of the invoice and the delivery of goods or the price; the amount of deferred payments, and payment default measured by the amount of bad checks), after-sales service and other obligations (general and contingent). The weighted average of these three indicators represents the "Commitment Indicator." This indicator, with its own weight, constitutes one of the variables of positive ethics, which in turn is one of the main variables in calculating the weighted average of probity.

5.2.2.1.3 Trustworthiness

A component of probity of the markets is trustworthiness (Tamimi Amadi 1987, H 2083) which is a characteristic of righteous (Tamimi Amadi 1987, H 2335) and worthy individuals (70:32). Trustworthiness can be measured by timely payment and timely delivery of goods, the degree of care for the product during after-sale servicing, and accuracy in measurement to avoid fraudulent in weighing and measuring (1:83)[14]. The weighted average of these three indicators represents the "Trustworthiness Indicator." This indicator, with its own weight, constitutes one of the variables of positive ethics, which is, in turn, one of the main variables in calculating the weighted average of probity and transparency.

5.2.2.1.4 Fairness

This term connotes placing one's conscience as the arbiter in the sense that what is considered good for oneself is extended to others as well and what is considered as reprehensible for oneself is also considered as reprehensible for others as well. Indeed, no party in the marketplace expects other parties to a transaction to betray him, lie to him, conceal the defects of products from him. With this definition of fairness, every individual will put himself in place of his counterpart and will avoid lies, betrayal, concealing defects, collusion, and other misconducts. Every party to transaction will contribute to probity of the market by honest interaction with others.

Another definition of fairness connotes contentment with low profit (Tamimi Amadi 1987, p. 391, H 8981). When satisfaction for justifiable profit is institutionalized within the market, the motivation for deception and concealment of information is minimized, thus, the level of probity and market transparency are enhanced. The "Fairness Index" is measured by various indicators comprising the rate of profits, types of fraudulent in weighing and measuring, committing prohibited acts (charging interest, cheating, charlatanism and dissimulation), and praising one's own products while bad-mouthing those of others'. This indicator, with its own weight, constitutes one of the variables of positive ethics which is, in turn, one of the main variables in calculating the weighted average of probity and transparency of information.

---

14 وَيْلٌ لِلْمُطَفِّفِينَ

5.2.2.2 Negative Ethical Rules Governing the Market

In addition to encouraging the acquisition of ethical virtues, the Islamic market prohibits such vices as cheating in transaction, charlatanism and swindle (*Tadlis*), touting with no intention to purchase in order to increase the price (deception, *Najsh*), and baulk while intending to purchase in order to reduce the price (misdirection, *Tada'bor*). All such behaviors have their roots in chicanery, trickery and deception. Ethical vices have many dimensions, each of which somehow intensifies the mentality of profiteering and voracity in human beings. Nonetheless, cheating, which also includes charlatanism and dissimulation (*Tadlis*) as well as collusion of any party to the transaction, is a kind of negative ethics affecting probity. These vices have noteworthy and significant direct effects on probity and transparency, and for this reason, they have been used as indicators of probity and transparency of information. Naturally, due to the negative relationship. between cheating and collusion with probity, their level reflects lack of probity in the market.

5.2.2.2.1 Deception

All types of deception are considered incompatible with probity and are exactly like lying in general. Islam is opposed to all kinds of deception, including charlatanism and swindle (*Tadlis*) (Al-Koleini 1984, Vol. 5, p. 153), hiding defects(Al-Koleini 1984, p. 151), and adulterating quality goods with cheaper products (in an indiscernible manner) (Al-Koleini 1984, p. 183).

Islam considers all transactions in which there is doubt and possible fraud, for example, selling goods in places without sufficient lighting (Saduq Qomi 1993, Vol. 3, p. 272, H 3980), as potential deception and has prohibited sellers to give any thought or consideration to committing such acts (Saduq Qomi 1993, Vol. 4, p. 15). The strong emphasis on avoidance of deception in sacred narrations (Ahadith) are indicative of their significant influence rendering market atmosphere. High rate of deception in the market points to lack of probity and hence absence of transparency in the market.

Taking into account the concept of deception and related jurisprudential discussions, the following variables are considered for measuring the level of deception:

1. The amount of the fraudulent in weighing and measuring (short-weighing of the package; lesser input of raw material than expected by the customer; and lower quality);
2. The amount of adulteration of products indiscernible to the general public. Sacred narrations (Ahadith) and jurisprudential discussions describe three kinds of adulteration:
   a. mixing of superior products with cheaper qualities, e.g. mixing of milk with water;
   b. mixing goods with worthless substances, e.g. wheat with sand and gravel; and,
   c. mixing goods with harmful substances, e.g. adding chemicals for greater attraction);

3. The level of deceptive advertising (glamorous lighting; eye-catching appearance and appealing design and packaging; use of striking colors and/or additives); and,
4. The extent of incorrect information provided (use of fake brands, deceptive packaging, incorrect information on the product, not mentioning the dates of production and expiry, wherever required).

The weighted average of these four indicators constitutes the "Deception Indicator." This indicator, with its own weight, constitutes one of the variables of negative ethics, which is, in turn, is one of the main variables in calculating the weighted average of market probity and transparency of information.

5.2.2.2.2 Collusion

Exploiting existing legal loopholes, various economic entities in the market can collude with each other to create falsehoods in order to benefit from ensuing market chaos.

Such abusive practices have been carefully addressed in many sacred narrations (Hadith) and two of the most important issues of collusion in the market, i.e. deception (*Najsh)* and misdirection (*Tadabor),* are strongly condemned. The individuals who engage in such activities, are deprived from the mercy of the Almighty (Al-Ameli 1988, Vol. 17, p. 458, H 22991 and p. 459, H. 22993). *Najsh* (deception) occurs when an individual, either in collusion with the salesman or independently, touts about a commodity. Despite of having no intention to purchase the commodity, he offers to pay an unreasonably higher price in order to persuade others to purchase it with no bargaining. *Tada'bor* (misdirection) is the opposite to *Najsh* and happens when an individual, either in collusion with the customer or independently, while having no intention to purchase the commodity, offers to pay a lower price and then baulks, in order to force the seller to reduce the price. Both *Najsh* and *Tada'bor* are considered as self-serving promotional acts and contrary to market probity. They not only result in disruptions in the workings of the market information system, they are themselves the results of flaws and disorderliness in the information network.

In addition to *Najsh* and *Tada'bor,* which are kinds of collusion at micro level, the economic enterprises can disrupt the flow of rapid information exchange at macro level. Since they find their maximum benefit in concealing market information, they push the market towards monopolization. Therefore, the higher the number of monopoly firms, the lesser the timely flow of information, as a result of which the market loses its transparency.

The level of collusion in the market can be measured by the following variables: the number of monopoly manufacturing units (except natural monopolies); the amount of collusion among seller (*Najsh*); and the amount of collusion among buyers (*Tadabor*). This index, with its own weight, is one of the variables of the negative ethics indicator, which in turn constitutes a variable to the weighted average of Probity Index.

5.3 Options and Compensation Indicator

The term *Al-Khiyar* is grammatically a gerund and connotes "option to rescind a contract of sales by either party to a transaction within a certain period after the conclusion of a bargain." (Ibn Manzur 1993, Vol. 4, p. 267) In the civil law of the Islamic Republic of Iran, following Fiqhi texts, a general position on khyaraat (options to declare a transaction null and void) which does not exist in other countries' civil law. In the provision number 396 of the Civil Code of the Islamic Republic of Iran ten types of Khyaraat (options) have been defined as follows:

1. *Khiyar al-Majlis*, the condition of withdrawing from the contract while the two parties are still at the place of transaction.
2. *Khiyar al-Haiwan*, the option to rescind the contract of purchasing animals within a period of three days, if they are unhealthy.
3. *Khiyar al-Shart*, conditional option, where one of the parties stipulates certain conditions, failing to meet it would grant a right to the stipulating party to rescind the contact.
4. *Khiyar al-Ta'khir thaman*, where the seller has the option to cancel the contract if the buyer does not pay cash up. to a certain agreed date.
5. *Khiyar al-Ru'yah*, option of rescinding the transaction for the individual who has not seen the merchandize, but has purchased it based on the description provided by the seller, and, therefore, has the right of rejection after seeing the product, due to lack of specified features.
6. *Khiyar al-Ghabn*, the option of the buyer to cancel the contract if the seller has sold it at a price higher than what an independent evaluator assesses.
7. *Khiyar al-'Aib*, the option to rescind the contract on discovery of a defect in the subject of sale.
8. *Khiyar al-Tadlis*, option to rescind the contract if the seller perpetrates a fraud causing loss to the buyer.
9. *Khiyar Tafarruq al-safaq*, the right of the buyer to reject part of the contract of sale due to defect in some of the goods, irrespective of cause of the defect.
10. *Khiyar al-T'ayin*, where a person having purchased two or three things of the same kind, stipulates a period to make his selection.

The existence of options is considered a special distinction of Islamic market and is an important measure for its probity. Trading laws and regulations are designed in a manner to provide the ground for establishment of probity at the time of the transaction. In case of incurring losses due to lack of information, existence of options can be compensatory. Existence of the above-mentioned options also indicate that Islam considers as paramount the importance of honest dealing and availability of comprehensive market information before the transaction, e.g. if a customer has seen 99% of the goods and only 1% has not been seen, Khiyar al-Ru'yah, or the option of rejecting the goods purchased after seeing it, still holds valid (Al-Ameli *1988*, Vol. 18, p. 28 and 29, H 23065).

Options will, to some extendt, obstruct the ways to circumvent probity so that no party to a transaction will be able to gain from the ignorance of the other party. In order to complete the transaction, the parties are obliged to deal honestly with each other and to provide complete information about the goods to each other. This will lead to awareness and satisfaction of both the parties makes possible the spread of information among the buyers and the sellers (Ghaffari 2007, p. 175).

6 Probity Index in Islamic Market

The various indicators of "Probity Index" can be divided, in terms of their status in transactions, into categories of grounding, process-related, or option/compensatory indicators. They can also be differentiated as conceptual, cognitive, structural or behavioral according to their fields of influence. Both classifications have the same outcomes in determination of Probity Index.

The appearance and application of faith and piety of a market participant must be sought in his trustworthiness and truthfulness. In other words, market participants' internal views must be reflected in their the behavioral and structural indicators. Furthermore, the cognitive indicator can be summarized in terms of the knowledge of rules, norms, regulations and ethics governing the market. Structural indicator can be introduced by compliance and discipline indicator, while option/compensatory indicator and behavioral indicator point to the governing ethics and avoidance of ethical vices.

There may be occasional non-transparency of information during a transaction. The sacred Islamic Sharia has availed various options to rescind a contract on the basis of variety of clearly expressed conditions in order to compensate for market shortcomings in discovering information or concealment by one of the parties to transaction. Implementation of options can compensate for market defects with respect to probity or deliberate concealment of information.

A summary of the indicators that are used as variables in the design of the proposed Probity Index along with their respective weights are presented in Table 18.1.

Probity Index is a composite index comprising "Cognition Indicator" with a weight of 0.193; "Compliance and Discipline Indicator" with a weight of 0.246; "Net Ethics Indicator" (positive ethics minus negative ethics) with a weight of 0.322; and "Options Indicator" with a weight of 0.214. Each of these indicators have their

Table 18.1: Probity Index and its different indicators along with their respective weight.

Sr. No.	Indicator: Main	Indicator: Subcategory	Weight	Variables	Weight	Type of Indicator
1	**Cognition (Rules, Norms, and Regulations; Ethics;)**		**0.193**	Amount of information on fundamentals, principles, obligations and proscriptions of transactions	0.52	Grounding
				Amount of information about recommended and reprehensible transactions and market ethics	0.13	
				Amount of information about civil laws and regulations related with markets	0.34	
2	**Compliance and Discipline**		**0.246**	Existence of contract, type of transaction, and the parties to the transaction	0.34	Process-related or Prompt Flow of Information
				Price determination, quantity and specifications of goods	0.23	
				Physical order	0.41	
3	**Governing Islamic Ethic (Net) (0.322)**	**Truthfulness**	**0.38**	Compatibility of transaction and contract with reality (in terms of type of goods, weight, price, time and conditions)	0.1	
				Compatibility of specifications or the contents of the tag (weight, price, quality and ingredients) with reality	0.31	
				Compatibility of advertisements with reality	0.55	
		Abiding by the promise	**0.12**	Prompt payment of the price (cash and credit) and timely delivery of goods	0.31	
				Commitments about after-sale service	0.35	
				Other commitment (general commitments and criteria mentioned in the contract)	0.33	

		Trustworthiness	**0.29**	Prompt payment of cash and credit	0.28	
				Care of goods after payment and delivery and during the servicing and repair	0.1	
				Absence of Short-selling	0.61	
		Fairness	**0.18**	Interest rate	0.11	
				Observing equity (Absence of various types of short-selling)	0.31	
				Committing illicit acts (charging interest, deception, charlatanism and dissimulation)	0.46	
				Promoting one's merchandize and disapproval of others'	0.06	
4	**Governing Islamic Ethics (negative)**	**Cheating**	**0.55**	Short-selling (various types)	0.38	Process-related or Prompt Flow of Information
				Adulteration of products indiscernible to the general public	0.33	
				Deceptive advertisements	0.15	
				Providing false and misleading information	0.17	
		Collusion	**0.44**	Number of monopolized manufacturing units (excepting for natural monopolies)	0.48	
				Amount of collusion among sellers (*Najsh*)	0.31	
				Amount of collusion among buyers (*Tada'bor*)	0.18	
5	**Options**		**0.214**	Knowledge of parties to transaction about options	0.28	Compensatory (Recompensing market defects and concealment of information
				Status of options in the legal system of the country	0.28	
				Consent about options in market tradition	0.36	

respective variables, each of which has its own weight. The average weight of the variables of each sub-indicator defines the role it plays in the main indicator, and the average weight of the main indicators contribute to the composite Probity Index.

7 The Structure of the Probity Index: Formulae and Calculations

Cognition Indicator = (Information on fundamentals, principles, obligations and proscriptions * 0.52) + (Information on recommended and reprehensible transactions and market ethics * 0.13) + (Information about civil laws and regulations related with markets * 0.34)

Compliance and Discipline Indicator = (Existence of contract, type of transaction and the parties to the transaction * 0.34) + (Price determination, quantity and specifications of goods * 0.23) + (Physical order of the market * 0.41)

Governing Islamic Ethics (Net) = (Positive Islamic Ethics * 0.322) – (deception * 0.55) – (Collusion * 0.44)

Governing Islamic Ethics (Positive) = (Truthfulness * 0.38) + (Abiding by promises * 0.12) + (Trustworthiness * 0.29) + (Fairness * 0.18)

Truthfulness = (Compatibility of transaction and contract with reality * 0.1) + (Compatibility of specifications or the contents of the tag with reality * 0.31) + (Compatibility of advertisements with reality * 0.55)

Abiding by the promise = (Prompt payment of the price * 0.31) + (Commitments about after-sale services * 0.35) + (Other commitment * 0.33)

Trustworthiness = (Prompt payment of cash and credit * 0.28) + (Care of goods after payment and delivery, and during the servicing and repair * 0.1) + (Absence of fraudulent in weighing and measuring * 0.61)

Fairness = (Interest rate * 0.11) + (Observing equity * 0.31) + (Absence of illicit acts * 0.46) + (Promoting one's merchandize and bad-mouthing of others' * 0.06)

Deception = (fraudulent in weighing and measuring* 0.38) + (Adulteration of products * 0.33) + (Deceptive advertisements * 0.15) + (Providing false and misleading information * 0.17)

Collusion = (Number of monopoly manufacturing units * 0.48) + (Amount of collusion among sellers* 0.31) + (Amount of collusion among buyers * 0.18)

Options = (Knowledge of parties to transaction about options * 0.28) + (Status of options in the legal system of the country * 0.28) + (Consent about options in market tradition * 0.36)

Probity Index = (Cognition * 0.193) + (Compliance and Discipline * 0.246) + (Governing Islamic Ethic – Net * 0.322) + (Options * 0.214)

8 Measuring Probity Index: Application

The Probity Index in the Islamic market constitutes one of the measures designed to assess the market characteristics in terms of proximity to Islamic values. The dairy products in Iran are of prime importance because of their direct relevance to the health of the people and are considered as an essential nutritional commodity. This market has been selected for measuring its probity in order to illustrate the application of the Probity Index for the first time.

The value chain within the dairy market, like any other market, consists of several diverse entities. The transactions between the producers, as the suppliers of the products, and the wholesalers, as the purchasers of the dairy products, were selected because of their greater access to information and complete attentiveness of these two groups to the overall market conditions.

The most important and challenging issue in empirical evaluation of the Probity Index in this market was the methodology or approaches to accessing information as well as the procedure of calculating the index. Therefore, after assessing all the available techniques to access information, it was decided to use “interview,” “questionnaire,” and “reviewing the available documents” during the field study.

In order to calculate the Probity Index in the dairy market, various indicators were considered individually, and after analyzing the details of the Probity Index in Mashhad (a major city in North East Iran) dairy market, the Probity Index was computed as follows:

Probity Index = (Cognition * 0.193) + (Compliance and Discipline * 0.246) + (Net Islamic Ethics * 0.322) + (Options * 0.214)

Net Islamic Ethics = (Truthfulness * 0.38) + (Abiding by the promise * 0.12) + (Trustworthiness * 0.29) + (Fairness * 0.18) – (Deception * 0.55) – (Collusion * 0.44)

Net Islamic Ethics = (72.700 * 0.38) + (92.100 * 0.12) + (92.341 * 0.29) + (79.844 * 0.18) – (76.685 * 0.55) – (0 * 0.44) = 27.626 + 11.052 + 26.779 + 14.379 – 42.177 – 0.0 = 37.679

$$\text{Probity Index} = (63.438 * 0.193) + (100 * 0.246) + (37.659 * 0.322) + (93.76 * 0.214) = 12.244 + 24.600 + 12.126 + 20.065 = 69.035$$

As it can be seen, the Probity Index in the dairy market of Mashhad city is equal to 69.035 out of 100 or 69.035 percent.

Taking into account the results of interviews with dairy industries experts and practitioners, the most important factors in reducing the Probity Index of the dairy industry was found to be the inappropriate culture of the consumption of dairy products and the outdated livestock breeding. Therefore, proper enculturation as well as the design and implementation of appropriate policies for the modernization and industrialization of breeding farms would lead to significant increase in the Probity Index of the dairy market.[15]

9 Brand and Indicator of Probity

Brand is the legal title for a trademark, a design, a symbol, a phrase, a name, and the like that provides services or sells a particular product through which a product or a service differentiates itself from other similar products. The distinguishing mark, or the hallmark of a brand is what creates mental awareness of the traits and attributes of the product in a visual, audible, or sensual manner in the consuming public. The brand will have to be registered to ensure its property rights.

The guarantee of authenticity would be meaningful only when consumers who observe the registered brand on goods or services are assured that the quality of the product or the service they are purchasing is that associated with the firm to which the brand name belongs. In fact, the aim is to prevent deception of the general public. The value of a hallmark is closely related to the success rate of the products that are provided under its brand. This makes clear the importance of registering the brand in the target markets and attracting the attention of consumers.

Considering that the design of a Probity Index was modeled in this paper and applied empirically to a specific market and given the positive role that brand names can play, the study suggests that Muslim countries officially recognize a "Mark of Probity" in the same way that the mark of Halal is recognized presently. As a result, people around the world can differentiate between various commodities from the point of view of conscience and probity. In addition, manufacturers who seek a greater

15 This section is a summary of the operational section of the research project titled "Probity Index in Mashhad city Dairy Products Market", which was conducted at the Pishgaman-e Pajoohesh Research Institute under the auspices of the Institute for Technological Studies of the Presidential Office, and was presented at the "Ethics and Economics Conference" by Dr. Seyyed Kazem Raja'ee and Saeed Khadivi Rofougar. The research was later published in the Journal of Economic Knowledge, No. 9.

share of the market would also try to obtain the Mark of Probity, and consequently, greater efficiency of the market will be assured. Once such mark is recognized, manufacturers will lose their incentives for dishonesty, because the benefits from having the probity mark would be much greater than that of not having it. Implementation of thios proposal will assure that markets progressively approach the ideal Islamic market.

10 Conclusion

Relying on revelatory teachings and focusing on ethics in the market, Islam has provided grounds for the actualization of probity in the marketplace. Preparing the groundwork, and establishing discipline through emphasis on ascertained price and quality of goods; Clear definition of the subject, type and terms of the transaction contract; clear specification of timing of invoicing and payment, delivery; and registering and recording of these items in the contract, will allow the parties to a transaction access to all available information related to the transaction. Furthermore, ethical recommendations to market participants and giving those who have been defrauded or have received defective goods the right to rescind contracts, will minimize the strength of incentives to swindle. In the same way, market discipline too will reduce such incentives. Additionally, to enhance the efficiency of the market, Islamic government – following the traditions and the teachings of the Prophet and Imam Ali in guiding and protecting markets – is obliged to design and implement, directly or indirectly, appropriate and effective policies for upholding probity as the governing principle in the market in order to promote market efficiency.

Strengthening the faith and piety of the effective elements of the market by institutionalizing truthfulness and trustworthiness; abiding by the promises and observance of fairness; insisting on the principle of "learning Fiqhi rules governing market behavior before engaging in trade and business;"[16] avoiding deception, cheating and aleatory sale (*Bai' Al-qarar*); will all provide the ground for avoiding non-transparency, preventing unlawful acquisition of wealth (*Akl Bil Batil*) and averting losses due to ignorance, and ultimately improve market efficiency. Through the strengthening of spiritual incentives, linking the interests of the society to that of the individuals and combining internal and external supervision Islamic market creates an incentive structure for non-concealment of facts and provision of correct information, and protecting other market participants from incurring losses. According to the results of the current research, a Probity Index for measuring and evaluating the extent of probity prevailing in the market is proposed as a composite index whose variables would be grounding, process-related, or options/compensatory. These

16 اَلْفِقهُ ثُمَّ الْمَتْجَر

would encompass the conceptual, the structural or the behavioral elements. Implementation of this index along with other indicators can help. in assessing the current market situation and its compliance with the desirable Islamic market. The probity of the markets can be considered to depend on various factors, such as suppliers, consumers, kinds of interactions, physical ambience, lighting, and placement of goods. That is, the overall atmosphere of the market must reflect the reality, so that deviation from the reality of the market or misrepresentation of fact must not occur in any circumstances. If it occurs, for any unintentional reason, the market must possess the necessary flexibility to recompense it.

Probity is a fundamental issue in social relations of the market including supply and demand. False advertisements, untrue labels, prevarication and fabrication, deception, cheating, collusion, breach of contract, perfidy (betrayal of trust) and unfairness are all signs of absence of probity in the market. Lack of probity within the community of producers and consumers in the market will impose significant costs and inflict severe damages on the market and on the society. Absence of probity in job market and among production agents will lead to coverups, stealing from work and fraudulenting in weighing and measuring, irresponsibility, opportunism (self-seeking), and finally quality degradation and reduced efficiency.

Because of the importance of ethics in efficiency of the markets in general and that of probity in particular, policy-makers and authorities of the market, especially those at the Ministry of Commerce, are advised to expend efforts at design of indicators for measuring probity. They ought to attempt to identify factors that influence affecting the probity of markets so that, by designing and implementing appropriate policies, markets move gradually toward becoming Islamic. Furthermore, establishing a procedure for official recognition of "Mark of Probity" similar to mark of Halal can inspire the producers to comply with ethical principles of production.

References

Holy Quran. 2003. *translated by* T.B. Irving (Al-Haj Ta'lim Ali); Suhrawardi Research and Publication Center, Tehran-Iran.

Razi, Al-Sharif Abu Al-Hassan Mohammad. 1995. *Nahj Al-Balaqa*; translated by Seyyed Jafar Shahidi; Islamic Evolution Teaching Publications; Tehran.

Ibn Manzur; Mohammad Bin Mokarram. 1993. *Lesan Al-Arab*; 15 Vol.; Beirut, Lebanon; Dar Sa'd.

Ibn Sina. 1984. *Al-Isharat va Al-Tanbihat*; corrected by Mahmood Shahabi; Tehran University Press.

Abolhassani Niaraki, Fereshteh. 2010. *Analyzing the Concept of Honesty and its Varieties*; Honesty Conference; Tehran University; Abstract Volume.

Akrami, Abolfazl. 1996. *Markets in Islamic Civilization*; Research Quarterly Journal of Imam Sadeq University; Vol. 1; No. 3.

Budden, Lewis. 1961. *History of Economic Thought*; translated by Houshang Nahavandi; 193 p.; Tehran, Morvarid Publishers.

Layard, Peter Richard Grenville, and, Walters A.A. 1998. *Microeconomic Theory*; translated by Abbas Shakker; Nei Publishers.

Begg, David, Fischer, Stanley, and Dornbusch, Rudiger. 2006. *Economics*; translated by Mohammad Hossein Tizhoush; Tehran, Jangal.

Bahmanyar Bin Marzban Azarbaijani. 1970. *Al-Tahsil*; corrected by Morteza Motahhari; Tehran University Press.

Pindyck, Robert, and Rubinfeld, Daniel. 2002. *Microeconomics*; translated by Ahmad Zihajjehzadeh; Tehran, Samt.

Preston McAfee, Rudolph. 2008. *Introduction to Economic Analysis*; translated by Kambiz Peikarjoo and Ali Sayyadzadeh; Tehran, Kavir Publications.

Tavakoli. 2010. *An Introduction to Moral Philosophy of Commerce with Islamic Approach*; Economic Teachings; Vol. 1; pp. 7–31.

Jorjani, Mir Seyyed Sharif. 1938. *Al-Ta'rifat*; Misr Publishers.

Harvey, Jack. 2009. *Modern Economics*; translated by Mohammad Baqer Nobakht and Farid Nobakht; Tehran, Expediency Council of I.R. Iran; Strategic Research Center.

Raqeb Isfahani, Hossein Bin Mohammad. 1991. *Al-Mofradat fi Qarib A-Quran*; corrected and researched by Adnan Davood; Beirut, Suri; Dar Al-Elm Al-Dar Al-Shami.

Raja'ei, Seyyed Mohammad Kazem. 2011. *Islamic Market Features in Theory and Practice*; Economic Teachings; Vol. 2; No. 1(3).

Raja'ei, Seyyed Mohammad Kazem. 2003. *Thematic Lexicon of Economic Verses of Holy Quran*; Qum, Publications of Imam Khomeini Education and Research Institute.

Sheikh Eshraq. 1988. *Hekma' Al-Eshraq*; translated by Seyyed Jafar Sajjadi; Tehran University Press; Vol. 5.

Tabataba'ei, Al-Seyyed Mohammad Hossein. 1974. *Al-Mizan fi Tafsir Al-Quran*; 20 Vols.; Second Edition; Al-A'lami Al-Matbu'at Institute; Beirut.

Tabataba'eian; Seyyed Habibollah, Naghizadeh, Reza and Naghizadeh, Mohammad. 2011. *Methodology of Establishing Composite Indicators for Assessing Innovation in Accordance with Islamic-Iranian Pattern of Development*; Economic Teachings; No. 4.

Tarihi, Fakhroddin. 1996. *Majma' Ul-Bahrain; researched by* Seyyed Ahmad Hosseini; Tehran; Mortazavi Books.

Tamimi Amadi, Abdolwahid Bin Mohammad.1987. *Qarar Al-Hekam va Dorr Al-Kalam*; H. 2083.

Hor Al-Ameli, Al-Sheikh Mohammad Bin Al-Hassan. 1988. *Vasayel Al-Shia*; 20 Vols.; A'l Al-Bait (PBUT) Institute; Qum.

Majlesi, Mohammad Baqer. 1983. *Behar Al-Anwar*; Wafa Institute; Beirut, Lebanon.

Nouri, Mirza Hassan. 1987. *Mostadrak Al-Vasayel Va Mostanbat Al-Masa'el*; 18 Vol. First Edition; Al Al-Bayt (PBUT) L-Ehya Al-Itrath Institute; Qum.

Ghazzali. No Date. *Me'yar Al-Elm fi Fann Al-Mantiq*; Dar Al-Andelos; Lebanon.

Ghaffari, Hadi. 2007. *Economic System of Early Islamic Era*; Tehran, Payam Noor University Press.

Farahanifard, Saeid. 2002. *Role of Governments in Economy*; Tehran; Islamic Culture and Thought Research Institute, Publication Center.

Al-Koleini, Abu Jafar Mohammad Bin Al-Yaqub. 1984. *Al-Kafi; edited/corrected by* Ali Akbar Al-Qaffari; 8 Vols.; Beirut, Lebanon; Dar Al-Azwa.

Tabibian; Mohammad. No date. *Advance Microeconomics: Theoretical and Applied Concepts*; 418 p.

Mostafavi, Hassan. 1981. *Al-Tahqiq fi Kalamat Al-Quran Al-Karim*; Tehran, Translation and Publication Enterprise.

Al-Majlesi. 1984. *Behar Al-Anwar*; Vol. 100.

Zara'Nejad, Mansour. 2002. *Considering Market Characteristic from the Islamic Viewpoint and History*; Economic Research Quarterly; Vol. 1; No. 5–6.

Mankiw, Gregory. 2003. *Principles of Economics*; translated by Manouchehr Asgari; Tehran Kuhsar Publications.

Qadr Applied Studies Institute. 2010. *Islamic Republic of Iran Resolution.*

Hadavi Nia; Ali Asghar. 2003. *Homo economicus from the Islamic Perspective*; Qum, Iclamic Culture and Thought Research Institute.

Akerlof, George A. 1970. *The Market for 'lemons': Quality Uncertainty and the Market Mechanism*; Quarterly Journal of Economics; Vol. 84.

Durluf, Steven N., and Blume, Lawrence E. (Editors). No date. *The New Palgrave Dictionary of Economics*; Second Edition.

Mirman, Leonard J.; In. 1987. *The New Palgrave Dictionary of Economics*; *edited by* John Eatwell, Murray Milgate and Peter Newman; Volume 3; Japan, Maruzen Company Limited.

Mohammad Bin Ali Bin Babeveih (Saduq Qomi).1993, *Man La Yahzarah' Al-Faqia'*; Vol. 3; p. 272; H. 3980.

Nahavandian, Mohammad.2006. *An Introduction to Business Ethics in Global Environment*; pp. 45–64.

North, Douglass C., and Thomas, Robert Paul. 1979. *The Rise of the Western World*; Cambridge University Press.

North, Douglass C. 1984. *Transaction Costs, Institutions, and Economic History*; Journal of Institutional and Theoretical Economics; Vol. 140; pp. 7–17.

Stigler, George J. 1957. *Perfect Competition, Historically Contemplated*; Columbia University Press; The Journal Of Political Economy; Volume 65; Number 1.

Stigler, George J. 1961 *Prize Lecture: The Economics of Information*; The Journal of Political Economy; Vol. 69; No. 3.

Stigler, George, J. 1987. *Competition*; In: The new Palgrave Dictionary of Economics; edited by John Eatwell, Murray Milgate and Peter Newman; Volume 3; Japan, Maruzen Company Limited.

Abulfazl Pasebani Some'eh

Chapter 19: Fair Wages in Islam

1 Introduction

One of the most important issues in economics is the concept of labor market and the analysis of its supply and demand which, in addition to affecting and being affected by other markets, it enjoys a two-way relationship with its previous levels, the system of governance as well as formal and informal institutions associated with labor (Williamson, 2000). Furthermore, since wages and employment are considered significant issues by the majority of citizens (either employees or employers), they must be investigated more intensely. On the other hand, because of the significance of the individual and his behavior in the labor market, ignoring the optimal performance of this market will bring about economic, political and even security consequences.

In addition, as Simon argues, due to the final outcome of bounded rationality in contracts, including the exchange of work for wage, it is not completely possible to investigate the optimal performance of this market; therefore, arriving at a mutually satisfactory wage contracts becomes doubtful. However, it is possible to avoid the pitfalls of full reliance on bounded rationality and achieve sustainable equilibrium in the labor market if the participants on the two sides of the contracts resort to revealed teachings agreed to by both sides.

Therefore, the present article investigates the literature of the subject in the mainstream economics, examining the teachings of Islamic economics with the aim of exploring Islamic attitudes towards justice regarding the issue of fair wages. It also illustrates various stages required for the Islamic fair wages to go through at all levels of institutional analysis.

2 Review of Literature and its Evolution

The fundamental issue in examining each of the four core markets in the economy is how the equilibrium quantities and prices are formed. In the labor market concern is with equilibrium wages and labor which in the labor market is synonymous with the formation of the balanced wage and actualized employment. Of course, to the question: "how are wages determined?" Classical economists regarded the market mechanism as the determining factor (McConnell, 1970, p. 7). The neoclassical economists stressed the concept of "wage equal to the value of the marginal product of labor." Marx and his various followers maintained that, in practice, the wages are paid close to the minimum standard of living which means capitalists exploit surplus value of

https://doi.org/10.1515/9783110593419-019

labor. This unfairness leads workers not to willingly participate in the production process. This sense of being unfairly exploited forms the basis of class conflict.

In contrast to these one-sided and confrontational attitudes, another group believes in partnership solution which guarantees the payment of the minimum wage, in order to fight the stagflation, but paying the workers a share of the profit & losses of the firm. (Weitzman, 1984). Nevertheless, generally employers provide amenities and services that make wages higher than their Walrasian market-clearing wages (Snowdon; Vane; Wynarczyk; 2004, p. 308; Romer, 1385, p. 644), which also causes involuntary unemployment (Mankiw-Romer, 1991).

In the meantime, the investigation of Hawthorne phenomenon[1] showed that the workers were not a machine and want to be treated humanely and appreciated for their efforts, therefore, they reject low wages (Akerlof, 1984). Therefore, not only the environmental conditions but also the employees' morale affect productivity, and wages higher than the Walras' level create incentives for increase in labor productivity even though these higher wages increase costs of production initially and labor contracts are not complete, the increased costs will be compensated by additional labor productivity (Reynolds 1948, PP 289–301, reprinted in McConnell, Campbell R, 1970, p. 63).

The evolution of the discussion on wages has been enriched by economists such as George Akerlof. In his article "Gift Exchange & Efficiency – Wage Theory: Four Views" (1984), through analyzing sociological and psychological foundations, the economic behavior of the gift exchange and the theory of efficiency wage, he suggested that the firm, contrary to classical views, pays wages higher than the market-clearing wage with the expectations that the workers will work harder. This higher-than-the-equilibrium wage leads to higher productivity. On the other hand, paying lower wages leads to higher costs of production because of lower productivity (Yellen 1984, Kats 1986).

In collaboration with his wife, Yilin (1990), Akerlof also explored the Fair Wage-Effort Hypothesis and Unemployment" and its applications. According to this hypothesis, workers have a sense and cognition of fair wages in their minds and, when they receive lower real wages, they tend to reduce effort proportionately. With the help of these articles as well as other analytic papers such as "Fairness and Unemployment" (Akerlof and Yellen, 1988), and "Labor Contracts as Partial Gift Exchange" (Akerlof, 1982) and "The Identity and Economics of Organizations" (Akerlof & Kranton, Winter, 2005), he and his co-authors showed the role of a number of factors that play a role in the determination of "fair wages." In addition, the concept of cognitive dissonance provided the basis for Akerlof to explore the issue of wage differentiation due to work safety and difficulty (Akerlof, & Dickens, 1982, pp. 307–319).

1 Hawthorne, a Western Electric company in Illinois, led by George Elton Maui of Australia, a psychologist, sociologist and theoretician of the organization. By explaining the theory of human relationships, he asked the managers to pay attention to the emotional needs of the staff.

Despite these valuable efforts, some vital issues remained unresolved, including the definition of the "fair wage" and the possible difference in the minds of the parties to the work contract, issues which Abulfazl Pasebani Some'eh and Ja'far Ebadi addressed in their article "The Most Important Factors Affecting Fair Wage in Iran" (2013) presenting 38 main factors involved and categorizing them in to 5 groups. These factors are effective in the general formation of fair wages and achieving them. These authors also addressed specifically the characteristics of the labor force in the formation of fair wages in their article: "The Characteristics of the Labor Force and Their Role in Fair Wages" (2014). In another article: "Analysis of the Grounds and Reasons for the Emergence and the Need to Investigate Fair Wage", Pasebani, Ebadi and Dadgar, (2015), provided answer to the question of why it is important to investigate the various dimensions of the concept of the "fair wage" and the causes of its emergence.

In this context, while Pasebani (2010) dealt with the benefits of paying fair wages, based on Islamic teachings as well as the ideas of the Charter of Human Rights in his article "The Benefits of Fair Wages as A Human Right", the subject of fair wages and work has not been investigated properly in the literature of Islamic economics. We hope that the present paper can fill the gaps to some extent. Other sources that have dealt tangentially with this topic will also be reviewed.

In three different articles in the book called "The Ethics of Work in divine and Oriental Faiths", Pelikan, Kitagawa, and Nasr (2001) have briefly highlighted the role and influence of work and work ethic in Eastern religions and divine religions (Judaism, Christianity and Islam) and look for a kind of divinity of work in the context of religious doctrines and in the worldview of their followers.

In a study titled: "On the Supply of Muslim labor Force", Rezaee argues that because Allah is active and creative, and the duty of man is to achieve divine attributes, therefore, work is a righteous deed that must satisfy a legitimate need. Hence, spending an inordinate amount of time in acts of worship and voluntary unemployment are rejected by Islam. Unquestionably, the employer must pay wages proportionate to the amount and quality of work and avoid oppressing and exploiting workers.

In his article "Theoretical Review of Wage Theories – Human Resource Productivity in Islam," Rostami (2005) argues that the relationship between fair work and fair wages leads to the latent talents of the labor come to the surface leading to increase in productivity.

The findings of the second wave of research by the National Research Council of the Ministry of Culture and Islamic Guidance, called the Survey of Values and Attitudes of Iranians (2002 and 2004), while explaining the concept of justice, suggested that in considering wages, some of Iranian workers look at the nature of the work and a great many of them look at the expertise and few of them consider labor needs as important factor. Also, the majority of Iranians think most of the organizations do not pay enough attention to expertise and experience while, according to the Constitution of the Islamic Republic of Iran, the government has a responsibility to provide all persons with the possibility of employment and equal conditions to find jobs. According to Part 9 of Article 3 of the Constitution, the government is assigned the task of: "Eliminating undue discrimination and creating just opportunities for all in every material and spiritual area."[2]

3 A Glance at Other Religious Societies' Views on Fair Wages

The investigating of the concept of justice and fair wages in various religions can create many advantages to elaborate a comprehensive theory. Such research will demonstrate similarities, important and trivial differences in the view of various systems of thought and how the views of different religions have evolved while discovering the historical roots of the topic of fair wages. Given the importance of the topic, this paper briefly points to elements that can provide a general view of how other religions view fair wages.

The first evidence for the regulation of labor relations date back to the Hammurabi era (1792–1750 BC) in Babylon[3] with a listing of wages for various work performed and the required minimum wage for each.[4] Akerlof and Yellen show that relation between jealousy and punishment as well as that between equality and performance are not an original discovery of psychologists and sociologists by referring to the story of Yusuf (AS),[5] reported in the Old Testament, and argue that Yusuf's policy represents a failure of management due to unfair wage policy.[6]

On the other hand, the successful experience of Kibbutz or the collective community has been due to a tendency to celebrate work by dividing and sharing it. The original belief of such collectives was "religion of hard work and labor," and they performed religious rites on the fields, and the hardest work was the most rewarding psychologically and socially.[7]

Interesting evidence has also been found regarding labor force in the ancient Iranian history based on discoveries of about 180 tablets and stone inscriptions from Persepolis which deal with the relationship between the worker and the employer,

2 Sobhani, 2009, p. 56.

3 Batrow, Jan, 2003, p. 159.

4 Batrow, Jan, 2003, p. 7.

5 He was born around 1600 BC.

6 According to the Genesis of the Torah, Joseph spoke to his father about the wrongdoings of his brothers. Also, Joseph, who was the son of his father's old age, was more favored by Jacob than the other brothers, and so Jacob made a colorful crochet for Joseph. When the brothers realized that his father loved him most, they bore a grudge against him. (Genesis 37: 3 and 4). However, the story of Yusuf (AS), based on Islamic teachings, is only a narration about the jealousy of the brothers.

7 Walser, 2010, p. 289–288.

indicating the basic principles governing the community and the regulation of relations, in particular the relationship between the wage of the worker with work and its payment at certain intervals. An interesting point is the names of boys and girls as wage earners.[8] It also includes issues such as division of labor, working age, daily work, and the equality of wages for male and female workers.

In the medieval economic system, fair wages were not based on market conditions but on the basis of scholastic ethics which expected that wages would be sufficient to support the standard of living commensurate with that of all wage earners. This definition of wages, along with other teachings, created a society in which there was no class conflict between employers and workers during the medieval period.[9] In those days, it was believed that a kind of divine, ethical, and objective law governed economic relations. Everything, including work, had a fair value and a fair price, and receiving or paying less than what was deemed fair was considered a sin. In this regard, Saint Thomas Aquinas[10] (1225–1274) believed that the worker had to receive a payment in return for his services that would adequately provide the necessary facilities for his life and his family. In addition, the working conditions must be humane and it should not be forgotten that the worker is also human and not a machine.[11] In his opinion, the matching of the selling price of anything with the employed labor and the producer's cost was a fair price.[12]

According to the preaching of the Puritan preachers,[13] all the good jobs and useful deeds were equal before God. But in the following centuries, increasing attention to fair wages systematized the infrastructure of all professions and state-owned enterprises.[14] Baxter,[15] one of Puritan religious scholars, argued: "If God shows a way by which one can gain more money without hurting oneself or others, he will and if one refuses to take the opportunity, one of the goals of the Lord has been violated. As a result, he has turned down divine blessings which could be used in His path, and has deprived him from getting closer to God."[16]

This attitude towards the issue of wages existed in the religious societies and classically it was believed that whenever there was unlimited labor supply, the workers had to be paid the minimum competitive wage which Lassalle called "Iron Wage" to lower the expenses of the firms and maximize its profits, creating the ground for more savings and consequently more investments (in this view, human beings were

8 Ronagh, 2005, p. 4.
9 Namazi, 2008, p. 47.
10 Thomas Aquinas.
11 Tamadon, 1983.
12 This definition was the first theory of the value of labor, which John Locke, Adam Smith and David Ricardo later completed, and was used by Karl Marx.
13 The Christian sect which dates back to the 16th and 17th centuries.
14 Robertson, 1999, p. 109.
15 Richard Baxter
16 Robertson, 1999

machines which could be regulated). However, the practical outcome of this attitude was the spreading of conflict which had no ultimate result but to waste a remarkable part of the limited resources. As time passed, it became obvious that productivity would increase by allowing labor force time for leisure assumed that rational employers would find the limit of adequate time for leisure. Undoubtedly, this attitude towards the welfare of the labor was based on foresight or efficiency-seeking but not justice.

The important point is that any understanding of the relationship between labor and wages, which is based on even meager historical document, included both work and leisure. Consequently, people like Marx were able to uncover the unfairness and false reasoning of contemporary defenders of 12 hours of daily work and 7 days of weekly work by pointing to countries that sanctify the Sabbath[17] (like England, in the 1840s and 1850s), but did not extend it to the workers, as a purgatory of deviation from their religious beliefs.[18]

In this context and as time passed, the dimensions of fair wages, including equal pay, for women and men as well as for minorities(of various races and religions, for equal work, were included in the Constitution of the International Labor Organization (established in 1919) and were supported by the membership of ILO.[19]

4 The Necessity and Importance of Investigating Justice and Fair Wage

Before directly discussing the fair wage issue, it is necessary to briefly address the issue of justice as its root.

It is clear that the accepted theory of justice, through the establishment of a relationship between values[20] and their logical and sustainable interaction, provides for the possibility of social organization, organizing the basic values of society (freedom, efficiency, property rights, tolerance, equality and spirituality), and prevents conflicts among them.

17 According to the book of the Deuteronomy in the Old Testament, the Sabbath was set to commemorate their escape from Egypt. The slaves used to work constantly, but Bani Israel considered the Sabbath as the first sign of the liberated people whose members had a fixed day for rest. Indeed, the divine command, based on the account of book of the Deuteronomy, was firstly addressed to the slaves of the Israelites: "But the seventh day of the week belongs to me, Thy God. No one should work that day, neither you nor your children, nor your cows or donkeys, nor even those strangers who live in your cities, so that your servant and maids can relax as you can" (Deuteronomy, 14: 5)

18 Walser, p. 314.

19 Mojtaba, 1993, p. 416

20 Theodor, Smith, 2012, p. 25

On another level of discourse, and considering that the rich and poor, powerful and powerless have not always had a fixed position,[21] prevention of violations of justice in contracts when one of the parties becomes more powerful as well as rational and sustainable management of societies require exposition and implementation of an unbiased theory of justice.[22] Moreover, since the great majority of contemporary humans do not wish to observe the permanency of deprivations, in order to prevent chaos and conflicts, on the one hand, the chosen justice theory must be superior to other theories and, on the other hand, decisions made must be in compliance with such a theory.

It is inevitable that theories of justice would have shortcoming due to human cognitive limitations. Nevertheless, even a minimum level of justice is preferable to complete injustice. Therefore, resorting to a theory of justice (even if it evokes criticism) may make possible (theoretically at least) clear understanding of existing injustices, agreements on the need to remove them, allowing the society to approach achieving justice as well as emergence of fair wages.

Arrow (1974) and Rader (1979) explained how moral virtues, such as honesty and trustworthiness, had an impact on increased economic efficiency under conditions of uncertainty.[23] By referring to empirical evidence from societies like Japan, it can be suggested that avoiding selfish behavior, acting responsibly, loyalty and goodwill play a major role in industrial success.[24] Under such circumstances and given the moral commitment of workers to perform the assigned tasks to the best of their ability, workers are assured that they will continue to receive their wages when sick and unable to work.[25]

By reviewing the values and work culture of various communities and carefully studying some of the Iranian proverbs one of which says "whatever you do, either good or evil, comes back to you", it can be observed that most people believe that working hard will bring about blessing and not doing so can be detrimental, and even employers who treat their workers justly and positively will enjoy the blessings as well.

According to the religious teachings, Allah the Just commands justice.[26] This implies the possibility of understanding what justice is and how it can be implemented. Violation of justice, in contrast, leads to injustice in various forms and degrees which, in the context of work performance, means reduced incentive to work hard, non-cooperation, objections to management and even voice and exist from

21 See the interpretation of the verse: Such days (of varying fortunes) We give to men and men by turns:

22 Sen, 2011, p. 317.

23 Sen, 2011 p. 103.

24 Sen, p. 20.

25 Iraqi, p. 233.

26 إعدِلوا هُوَأقرَبُ لِتقوى "do justice, it is closest to righteousness." The Qur'an, Verse 8: Chapter 5.

employment. As a result, the society and government will be deprived of the services of their most important resource, their labor productivity effort.

Social sciences also place great importance one quality and non-discrimination as the axis of social relations. The moral principle of "equal rights and opportunities for everyone" as a basis for the modern economy is of special importance. In this regard, equality is good because it is needed to consolidate the brotherhood among the community members. As a result, not only equality becomes an instrument of actualization of economic objectives, it has ethical importance by its very nature.[27]

However, since the employers and employees have two different understanding regarding justice, liberty and morality[28] depending on circumstances,[29] question arises whether there is a third position and Meta paradigm from which the other two paradigms can be judged?[30]

5 Explanation of Islamic View, Based on the Teachings of Imam Ali (AS)

Islamic teachings and their emphasis on human equality in terms of their origin and creation[31] are expressions of the fundamental role of justice in the strength of social life.[32] While the definition and measurement of justice is not an easy task,[33] when human knowledge is evolutional by understanding the teachings of the revelation and sufficient will, it prevents errors of judgment, due to the bounded human rationality, that lead to lack of empathy and sympathy and brings human behavior closer to the realization of justice.

Thus, despite the wide-ranging debates on the nature of justice, religious teachings, including Islamic teachings, can be studied in the search for definition of what constitutes a just imperative. In this regard, Nahj al-Balaghah, containing formal speeches and sermons as well as other pronouncements Imam Ali (As) which represent theory and application as well as evidence of authentic Islamic teachings (and a common ground of all Muslim schools of thought). It is important to note, in the context of discussion of Islam's view of justice, that the Imam (as) was martyred and his martyrdom is interpreted as to have been caused by his ardent and strong

27 Hausman, McPherson, Pages 204–201.
28 Based on the psychology of individuals, they impose a degree of force in different situations.
29 Soroush, 2005, p. 234.
30 Soroush, 2005, p. 244.
31 Hujarat, verse 13. Seyyed Qutb, 2000, p. 91.
32 Ali (AS), al-Adl Hayat al-Hokkam, Gharar al-Hakam, p. 30.
33 Sen, 2011, p. 42.

emphasis on justice. For these reasons, focus on his thoughts and actions provides guidance in search for understanding justice and fairness.

On the other hand, as Imam al-Sadigh (AS) speaks about the knowledge of the Ahlul Bayt, their understanding of the heavens and the earth, and the past and future, is derived from the Qur'an: "*We have sent down to thee the Book explaining all things.*"[34] And basically, the Qur'an, in general, contains principles and rules pertaining and governing all things subject to debate among humans.[35] Therefore, it becomes doubly necessary to pursue the issue of justice and fair wage in this context.

There can be little doubt that when people believe in respecting their mutual rights and obligations to establishing Qist (interpersonal justice and fairness),[36] it can be expected that informal institutions and, moreover, the formal institutions and governance work harder in the interests of justice, and the ground is paved for cooperation to create the necessary consensus for the administration of justice.

Search for of justice and fair wage in the Qur'an and sacred narratives can be related to prohibition of Israf (prodigality), Tabdheer (squandering), injustice, and corruption. Additionally, there are three important Islamic principles of: (1) Being faithful to giving exact weight and measure and not undervaluing or degrading peoples' goods and services;[37] Severe warning to Muttaffifeen (those who defraud others);[38] and (3) That man can have nothing but what he strives for.[39] These prohibitions and warnings can be extended to the labor market which at least among Muslims have sufficient basis for their acceptance by both sides of labor contracts and thus help provide a unified definition of fair wages.

In this context, Imam Ali (AS), commenting on the benefits of respecting justice states: on the path to moderation or the Divine's Straight Path,[40] being just attracts friends and allies and enemies will be defeated.[41] Moreover, lack of respect for the truth and justice also has nothing but deviation and humiliation,[42] and quite naturally reduces friendships and increases the number of enemies.

Seeking to transform justice into a widespread norm, he states: the greatest obligatory responsibility is the rights which are due to the ruler over the people who have entered into a contract to govern and the rights of the people over the ruler which Allah has made the motivation of the bond between the two sides of the contract and thus has sanctification of their religion. Hence, there is a mutual dependence of

34 Ayazi, 1399, pp. 32–33.
35 Kolaini, 1980 Vol. 1, p. 60.
36 Hadid, verse 57.
37 Araf, 85.
38 Mutafifin, verse 1.
39 Najm, verse 39.
40 Imam Ali (AS), Nahj al-Balaghah, 1999, p. 18.
41 Imam Ali (AS), Nahj al-Balaghah, 1999, p. 398.
42 Imam Ali (AS), Nahj al-Balaghah, 1999, p. 363.

the wellbeing of people on the righteousness of the rulers while the latter, in turn, depends on the righteousness of the people. Therefore, justice between the rulers and their people gains great importance and the evidence of justice become clear. If, (on the other hand), people revolt against the ruler or if the ruler is unjust toward the people, conflicts and indications of injustice appear and that is when the righteous are degraded and unrighteous valued. Therefore, it is your duty to advising each other about this issue and valuing the right of cooperation. No one, no matter how little others think of him and his opinion, is so small to be incapable of helping others or be helped by others.[43] Accordingly, Imam Ali (AS) considered observing and respecting all aspects of mutual rights in all the areas of the relationship between people and authorities as a sign of justice and he asked everyone to establish justice.

In explaining the essence of justice, while stressing on the things in which contain benefits for all people equally, the Imam (As) advises: abstain from claiming something just for yourself in which all have equal share.[44] In addition to referring to property rights (Tasleet) rule,[45] Imam Ali (AS) emphasizes rights of benefiting from Bayt Al-Maal (the resources of public treasury). For instance, he states: this property (resources of public treasury) belongs neither to me nor to you but to all the Muslims to strengthen their sword (to defend their religion). If you assist them in this task, you can receive your share of resources otherwise you are not entitled to what belongs to them.[46] Hence, while Islam recognizes legitimate differences, it has established various rules and regulations to ensure that, without deviation, greater justice, though not absolute equality, in distribution is achieved.[47]

In this context, the Prophet (sawa) distributed all of the resources gained from the confrontation with the tribe of Bani al-Ndheer among Mohajereen (emigrants) and two poor members of Ansars (Helpers) to create some sort of balance in property possessions among his followers.[48] In a letter to his governors regarding poverty alleviation and prioritizing public spending, Imam Ali (As) commands: Look into Allah's resources that has been accumulated in your hands and give it away to families with many children and the hungry around you who are in desperate need and send the rest to us to share it with those around us.[49] Disapproving of the way previous Caliphs handled the distribution of public treasury (as many people had become very wealthy as the result of discriminatory and unequal distribution of public funds), he states: By Allah! If I live, I will distribute the public treasury equally among the people.[50] When

43 Imam Ali (AS), Nahj al-Balaghah, 1999, pp. 9–248.
44 Imam Ali (AS), Nahj al-Balaghah, 1999, p. 340.
45 People have control over their own properties.
46 Sermon 232 Nahj al-Balaghah, pp. 5–264.
47 Thirteen Muslim economists, 1996, p. 522.
48 Qutb, 2000, p. 181.
49 Letter 67 of Nahj al-Balaghah, 352.
50 Imam Ali (AS), Nahj al-Balaghah, 1999, p. 57.

he was criticized why he had given everyone an equal share of the public treasury, he replied: if even it were mine, I would give everyone an equal share let alone (the fact that this is) Allah's property. Remember that giving the resources of the public treasury to someone who does not deserve is the same as Tabdheer and Israf.[51]

Imam Ali (AS), therefore, believed in merit, equality of all and giving priority to the poor as criteria in distribution of the resources of public treasury. The Imam (AS) was asked: "Which is better, benevolence or justice?" The Imam replied: "justice puts everything in its rightful place but benevolence does otherwise. Justice benefits all while benevolence benefits a few. Therefore, justice is more honorable and virtuous than benevolence."[52]

On this basis, pursuing the objective of establishing justice requires, on the one hand, equal treatment of all in basic rights on the one hand and a discriminatory attitude (towards the deserving due to their contribution to the value added or for the purpose of preserving innate human dignity), on the other. Hence, it is unacceptable that ethical worth or the innate value of a person declines proportionately when the demand for his labor declines or when he is unable to supply his labor.[53] The story of an old Jewish man who was disabled and had nothing to offer to the labor market and Imam Ali (As) ordered that he was to be provided sufficient means of living from the public treasury, arguing that throughout his life, the man had contributed to the society and now that he is unable, it is the responsibility of the society to take care of him, is an example of the application of this principle. In other words, changing demand and supply conditions in the market cannot be the only determining factor for fair wages. However, ignoring changes in the labor market can lead to long term distortions in micro and macro management of the economy.

In reference to the attitude and behavior of authorities toward people while implementing the laws, Imam Ali (AS), in a letter addressed to Aswad bin Qutaybah, whom the Imam had appointed as the governor of Hulwan, declared: "Be aware that) various temptations may prevent a ruler from being just. Therefore, you must treat people's rights (in things that are the concern of the ruler) equally, making sure that justice is replaced by injustice, hence, treat people as you would like to be treated."[54]

Imam Ali (AS) believed that the Islamic ruler and government had a number of responsibilities including the punishment of law breakers and ensuring that each member of the society receives his share of public treasury.[55] It should be noted that Islam, in addition to stressing the government's responsibility in implementing justice, has also paid attention to public duties and has elaborated on the principle of mutual obligations and caring (Takaful) among the members of the society in all its

---

51 Imam Ali (AS), Nahj al-Balaghah, 1999, p. 124.
52 Imam Ali (AS), Nahj al-Balaghah, 1999, p. 440.
53 Rawls, 2003, pp. 67–466.
54 Letter 59 of Nahj al-Balaghah, p. 344.
55 Imam Ali (AS), Nahj al-Balaghah, 1999, pp. 98–97.

dimensions, including obligations one has towards himself, his relatives, society and other nations, his generation and the future generation.[56]

Imam Ali (AS) tried to induce governors and officials to conduct people's affairs based on respect for their rights and consensus with reliance on moderation while condemning governance based on deception, resorting to force, fear, and selfishness. For instance, he advised the Zakat collectors: "Fear Allah and do not frighten any Muslim! Do not reprimand the Zakat payer if he is not pleased! Do not ask them to pay more than Allah's share. When you arrive at the area where a tribe lives, get off your horse (and stay in the vicinity of the central area) near their water well and do not go to their houses. Then go among them slowly and peacefully, when you approach them greet them warmly[57] and do not confiscate what they need in their day-to-day living."[58]

Based on these instructions, one can surmise that when fairness is defined as observing equality in all the significant affairs among all people, respecting the merit of those producing value, prioritizing the eradication of poverty, ethical reform of the judicial system and clearly defining its responsibilities and emphasizing moderation, then there can be an expectation of full agreement and faithfulness to compliance with the terms and conditions specified in contracts made between members of the society. Even after all dimensions of just behavior, including fare wages, are defined and clarified, there is still a need for conscious internalization of standards of justice that are integrated with personal judgments if there is going to be the hope and expectations of gradual implementation of justice. In this regard, Imam Ali (AS) advises his son Imam al-Hassan (AS): My son! Consider yourself as a scale (of value) in the relationship between you and others, therefore, wish for others what you wish for yourself and vice versa.[59]

6 Detailed Investigating of Work in Islamic Teachings

While commanding establishment of justice and Qist (fairness in interpersonal relationships),[60] Allah (SWT) has depicted human beings in a state of suffering and endeavor towards their Creator Whom they shall eventually meet.[61] In Arabic, Kadh

56 Imam Ali (AS), Nahj al-Balaghah, 1999, p. 104.

57 Imam Ali (AS), Nahj al-Balaghah, 1999, p. 286.

58 Sayyed Qutb, p. 345, quoted from al-Khurjar Abu Yusuf's book.

59 Letter 31, Nahj al-Balaghah, p. 301.

60 –We sent aforetime our messengers with Clear Signs and sent down with them the Book and the Balance (of Right and Wrong), that men may stand forth in justice, Hadid / 25.

61 O thou man! Verily thou art ever toiling on towards thy Lord- painfully toiling, – but thou shalt meet Him.Inshiqaq/6.

is defined as excruciatingly hard and rigorous work, as a result, life is accompanied by hardships and any improvements towards perfection and meeting our Creator can be actualized through endeavor.[62] Islam condemns laziness, shirking in work, and monasticism even under religious pretexts. There is nothing more humiliating than being in need.[63] While sanctifying work in a narration, the Prophet (SAWA) states: "Allah loves those faithful servants who have chosen a career or occupation and no one can ever eat anything better than what he himself has worked hard for". As a result, the wage of the worker has been regarded as sacred in Islam[64].

Also, in other narrations, worshiping and adoring Allah has been divided into 70 parts, the best part of which is gaining Halal (legally and lawfully gained) income. Allah loathes oversleeping and long periods of voluntary idleness. That is why the religious leaders lived on their own income rather than relying on others despite their continuous struggle against infidelity, injustice and their efforts to manage and educate the Islamic nation. They prohibited themselves receiving Zakat and Sadaqaat), and took pride in earning Halal incomes. In other words, shirking and negligence in working has been seriously reprimanded while hard work and perfection in doing one's job has been emphasized. It is narrated that the Prophet sanctifies hard work (SAWA) when he kissed the hands of a worker. This can be interpreted as an incentive for people to organize their economic affairs[65] and strengthen and purify their bodies and souls through work and endeavor.[66]

With regard to high-quality work, it is reported that the Prophet (SAWA) filled a crack of the grave with his own hands while burying his son Ibrahim, saying: "Whenever you do something, do it with uttermost perfection.[67] I know that this corpse will soon decay but Allah loves those who do with uttermost perfection whatever they are assigned to do.[68] Therefore, it can be inferred the labor force should carry out whatever assignments they have been given perfectly with the highest possible quality. Undoubtedly, this way of performing good and commendable work in every position and situation must be receive wages and rewards based on merits and worth of the work performed.

In addition, when the Qur'an states that all the actions and deeds are observed by God[69], individuals get highly motivated to work hard and accurately[70] because

---

62 Bazargan, 1999, p. 79.

63 Qutb, former, p. 84.

64 Imam Ali (AS), Nahj al-Balaghah, 1999, p. 189.

65 Sobhani, 2009, pp. 122–121.

66 Qutb, p. 191.

67 اذا عَمِلَ أحدكم عملًا فليَتقِن -1 Abu Jafar Mohammad bin Ya'qub al-Kolaini, Volume 3, p. 262.

68 انی لَاعلمُ انه سیبلی و یصل الیه البلی و لکنّ الله تعالی یحب عبداً اذا عمل عملًا فَاَحکَمَه -, al-Hur al-Amli, Volume 2, p. 883 and Rezai, 1998, pp. 24–23.

69 And say: "Work (righteousness): Soon will Allah observe your work, and His Messenger, and the Believers", Tawba, 105.

70 Qutb, p. 188.

everybody will gain rewards proportionate to their deeds.[71] Therefore, the society and individuals' materialistic and the spiritual benefits depend on work. Every person becomes the owner of something over which he gains property rights. In this regard, the holy Qur'an states: "mankind gains nothing but the outcome of his efforts."[72] Also, nobody is punished because of somebody else's sins[73] so that everybody is rewarded according to what they produced.[74] The holy Qur'an also emphasizes that the work performed by experts and scholars or those of skillful people and the inexperienced or untrained individuals are not to be treated the same[75] nor should they be valued the same.[76] However, Islam considers it having an opportunity to work as a right of individuals which must be made available.[77] Hence, Islam gives priority to right to life, through work to earn sufficient income, over the right to property.[78] Moreover, inability of some members of the society to produce value added commensurate with their needs is not a reason for the society to ignore their life requirements. Also, it is recommended in Islam to honor elders[79] and compares the materialistic individuals who do not provide for or dishonor the weak and the aged to predators chasing their prey; the powerful devour the weakest and the youngest prey.[80] It is also necessary to consider the opinions of experts and the prudence of experienced elders more valuable and more favored than the efforts of the young[81] because every experience is the result of a lifetime journey and experimenting various stages of life and can be regarded as half of knowledge which may create more productivity. Based on what has been said thus far, the following primary criteria to for unequal treatment according to Islam can be presented: (1) Knowledge and understanding; (2) age; (3) poverty and need; and (4) experience and skills.

During the temporal leadership of the Messenger (SAWA), as well as during the time of the first ruler who took power after the Prophet (SAWA), resources of the Bayt al-Maal (public treasury) were distributed equally and without the exercise of any criteria of discrimination. However, during the time of the second ruler (when there was a high inflow of resources into the public treasury as the result of conquests, government positions became a source of personal gains and accumulation of immense wealth), the rule governing distribution changed from equal to unequal distribution

71 To all are degrees (or ranks) according to their deeds.
72 Najm / 39. (There are interpretative differences, but many commentators (including Javadi Amoli) have expressed the same idea presented in this article.
73 No bearer of burdens can bear the burden of another, Isra / 15.
74 And in order that each soul may find the recompense of what it has earned, Jathiya / 22.
75 Zemar (39) Verse 9.
76 Qutb, p. 190.
77 Qutb, 2000, p. 343.
78 Qutb, p. 286.
79 Mahallati, 1399, p. 223, quoted from Imam Ali, Gharir al-Hikam and Derer al-Klamm.
80 Letter 31 Nahj al-Balaghah, 2009, p. 303.
81 Attaran, 2005, pp. 228–227.

based on the timing of a person's Islam. This meant that those who claimed or were considered as having accepted Islam earliest gained seniority and received the most from the public treasury. Money under the pretext.[82] Consequently, the way was paved for the emergence of a new social class and idle rich people who received an income from the public treasury without any effort and hard work.[83]

However, during his rule, Imam Ali (AS) reverted to the distributive criteria as established by the Prophet (SAWA) and followed by the first ruler after him. Thus the discriminatory distribution practice was abandoned (at least for a time) while the Imam (AS) tried to reform the mentality of the greedy. To discourage idleness, the Imam argued that it is the duty of everyone to work to provide for themselves and their dependents and provided a rule for allocation of one's time during the day-night cycle: a part allocated to devotion to and adoration of Allah, a part allocated to work to earn a living, and a part for rest and permissible enjoyment of blessings.[84]

These efforts, combined with the remarks of the Prophet (SAWA) regarding the treatment of slaves have implications for treatment of workers. While the Qur'an and the tradition of the Prophet (SAWA) encourage freeing slaves as pleasing to Allah, the Prophet commands that: Slaves are your brothers whom Allah has placed in your care. Therefore, share with them what you eat and wear and do not impose on them work beyond their ability (either too many hours of labor or work that is so hard that it may endanger their safety and security).[85] Accordingly, the workers must not be abused and extremely demanding jobs (long hours or seriously hard work threatening the life of the worker) must not be imposed on them or when there is an excess supply of labor force and the workers cannot haggle, the employers cannot inflict heavy work on them or ignore providing them with convenient facilities.[86]

The actualization of these results requires a formal agreement to reduce the chances of violation. It has been narrated that Imam Reza (AS) witnessed his servants building a barn with the help of a black man. The servant explained that the man helps us and in the end we pay him some. The Imam asked them whether they had settled on his wages at the beginning of the work. They replied no, whatever we give him he accepts. This reply angered the Imam who told his companion (a man named Suleiman): I have told them repeatedly not to hire anyone without having agreed on his wage in advance. Know that when someone performs a task without his wage having been set before the start of the job, will be unhappy after the work is complete even if you pay him three times what his wage would have been whereas if you pay him what has been agreed upon before the start of the work, he will be satisfied. And if you give him even a grain of wheat in addition to his agreed wages, he will know

82 Shahidi, 2006, p. 47.

83 Qutb, p. 334.

84 Quotations 390, 1378, p. 432.

85 جعلهم اله تحت ايديكم فمن كان اخوه تحت يده فَليَطعِمهُ مما يَأكُل و ليَكسِهِ مما يَلبَس و لا يُكلِّفه ما يَغلِبه فان كلفه ما يغلَبه فَليُعنِه

86 Rezaei, p. 39.

that you are paying him more than his wages.[87] According to this narration, it is necessary to determine the amount of compensation to be paid to the workers before the start of work.

Of course, care must be taken that both parties to an agreement are satisfied with its terms and conditions[88] otherwise any contract of exchange that involves duress or reluctance of either party is considered null and void.[89] Trapped by certain circumstances, some workers have no option but to consent to work with a low wages and seemingly they are not forced by their employers to work and such an arrangement is not based on reluctance. The worker is desperate to exchange his labor for minimum wage to feed himself and his family. Not to worse his condition (not to prolong his suffering), Fiqh (jurisprudence) allows such urgent agreements,[90] however, the government tries to remove such problems through legislating new laws, giving the possibility of expression of worker complaints and collective bargaining so that the employers cannot abuse their workers.[91]

As Ibn Khaldon argued, violating people's property rights discourages their efforts to produce and accumulate wealth and, importantly, challenges the stability of the economy and security of the country (which depends on justice and fairness).[92] On the other hand, ignoring the virtue of justice promotes two vices of injustice and inequity[93] and lawful business relations will not be subject to three important conditions of avoidance of abuse, humiliation and degradation of others.[94] There will be no incentive for people to try to work hard to improve their living standards which is the most pleasing characteristic of humans.[95] To avoid this outcome, justice, in all its dimensions, must become the foundation.[96] One such dimension of justice is natural justice meaning that "when one class of the society become victorious over others and gain good fortunes (material and non-material), it should give more to those who assisted them in their victory and less to others."[97]

---

87 Hor al-Amoli, Wasa'l al-Shi'a, 1383, AH, p. 245.
88 And trade by mutual good-will, Nisaa / 29.
89 Reluctance is defined as a threat to do harm.
90 Rezaei, p. 45.
91 Tamadon, p. 3.
92 Ibn Khaldun, 1987, p. 72.
93 Nasir al-Din Tusi, 2008, p. 120.
94 Nasir al-Din Tusi, 2008, p. 211.
95 Nasir al-Din Tusi, 2008, p. 212.
96 Pasbani, 2008.
97 Farabi, 1982, p. 329.

7 Various Aspects of Fair Wages in Islam

Islamic teachings in the Qur'an, such as Verse 85: Chapter 7; Verse 183: Chapter 26; and Verse 90: Chapter 16 and the guidelines of the Prophet (SAWA) and the Imams (AS)[98] explain the concept of fair wages. For example, the Prophet (SAWA) has been quoted as saying: O people! Whoever underpays a worker must prepare him for hellfire.[99] When Allah (SWT) ordained that we must return to the owner anything that has been entrusted to us, we can infer that a reasonable wage is something that the employers must pay to the worker as soon as possible (immediately upon finishing his work), that abusing workers (short-changing them or delaying their pay) is considered a capital sin,[100] and that, in principle, every type of unemployment has been rejected by Islam.[101]

Using inductive logic and reliance on direct and evidence from the verses of the Qur'an and sacred narrations, it can be inferred that "fair wages" can include: (a) wage amount stipulated in a contract no more, no less;[102] (b) the wage rate commensurate with the level prevailing in the labor market and tradition; (c) wage commensurate with the effort of the worker; (d) wage equal to the marginal product of labor; and (e) the wage sufficient to meet the basic needs of the labor.

As mentioned earlier, Islam considers work and productivity constitute the foundation of property rights and the basic principles of wage determination. In addition, based on Islamic laws, every worker has the right to social security and he must not be worked beyond his stamina or forced to do something reluctantly or be harmed. He also has the right fair wages in exchange for the work he performs. Also, workers are entitled to leisure time, rewards, and promotion while duty-bound to perform their assigned tasks in the most careful and best form possible and respect the rights of the employer as defined legally and religiously.[103]

Since for all humans, in one form or another or at one level or another, being considered as part of the labor force of the society in relation to a higher authority in the hierarchy of social existence is a common characteristic they all share, it is natural that they all would want to treated fairly. As was pointed out earlier, Smith, Ricardo and Marx stressed the labor theory of value as the foundation of price theory in mainstream economics, concepts of demand and supply and marginal utility. However, those who advocate old institutionalism, such as Hodgson, believe that the prices are social conventions which are strengthened through habits and are institutionalized.

---

98 Hakimi, al-Hayat, Vol. 1 to 8, 1977 to 2009, Vol. 4, p. 456.

99 Hakimi, al-Hayat, Vol. 4, p. 457 and Vol. 5, p. 547.

100 Hakimi, al-Hayat, Vol. 4, p. 457.

101 من انتقص اجيراً اجره، فليتبوا مقعده من النار

102 Hakimi, al-Hayat, Volume 4, pp. 456 and 457.

103 Montazeri, 2006, p. 54

Undoubtedly, with the power some of the groups have in the governments[104] or the power the leisure class has in shaping the institutions,[105] the wages can be structured completely unequally and become institutionalized. Of course, these are unequal pays, which are assumed to maintain class differentiations among groups, classes and races, will result in nothing but social disharmony and discord leading to political upheavals.

Since there is a significant relationship between the worker's efforts and their attitudes toward the fairness of their employers, if they think they are receiving fair wages, their productivity and loyalty increase and their voice and exit rates decline. Also, since the production process is the result of the teamwork, more harmonious and coordinated work relationships emerge increasing output per worker. Considering the fact that the most important issue in human rights is the eradication of discrimination among human beings, agreeing on the formal rule of "equal wage under equal working conditions" (horizontal and vertical equality) within the firm eliminates one of bases of comparison of internal and external wages.

While it is beneficial to institutionalize the above rule as a right, efforts must be made to reform cultural and value mindsets toward understanding that paying fair wages does not increase costs of production rather it enhances factors of production leading to increased efficiency and secures the interests of the firm. If this legal right is recognized, then it should be supervised and measures must be taken to implement it but when it is strengthened enough to become a norm, the right to fair wages works autonomously and without additional costs.

8 Informal Institutions (Religious Teachings, Work Culture, Convention And Customs)

It is not very difficult to understand why the wages do not decrease, even though some are unemployed, when there is bargaining. Considerable evidence exist to demonstrate the role of social contract in the labor market which should not be surprising considering the explanation provided by the theory of clubs.[106] As the theoreticians of labor market maintain, the workers and employees have some ethical beliefs that affect the wage bargaining.[107] For example, individuals feel a sense of pride when they perform a benevolent act for others.[108] Also, if the employers treat their employees respectfully and decently, they have better chances at hiring noble and decent

104 See the doctrine of choice at the Social Convention.
105 Pasbani Some'eh, Motavaseli, 2011.
106 Harguzip, Shan.P, pp. 161 and 162.
107 Hausman, McPherson, p. 304.
108 Hausman, McPherson, p. 308.

workers who will behave honorably toward their employer as well. Honesty and fairness that help the economic systems to perform well require that economists too take into account the importance of these highly valuable ethical resources (honesty and fairness) and to strengthen and enhance them.[109]

Moreover, existence of transparent legislation and legal institutions addressed to the implementation of fair wages by themselves cannot solve all the problems associated with fair wages. Therefore, it is important to strengthen informal institutions that are helpful in enhancing actualization of fair wages. In a developed society with an institutionalized working culture, workers make greater effort with higher quality and employer pay fairer wages. In this framework, it would be expected that, autonomously, employers and employees would not violate the rights of others, depending on the strength of their beliefs and religious ethical teachings. Therefore, religion promotes ethics, ethics promotes justice, and justice places constraints on exercise of various kinds of power.[110]

In this context it worth noting that in Verse 32: Chapter 43 of the Qur'an, Allah (SWT) asks: "Is it they who apportion the mercy of thy Lord? We have apportioned among them their livelihood in the life of the world, and raised some of them above others in rank so that some of them may employ others; and the mercy of thy Lord is better than (the wealth) that they amass. Also, in Verses19–25: Chapter 70 Allah declares: "Lo! Man was created anxious; Fretful when evil touches him; And niggardly when good reaches him; Not so those devoted to prayer; Those who remain steadfast in their prayers (are in continuous communion with their creator); And those in whose wealth is an acknowledged right; For the destitute (needy) and the deprived." On this basis, it can be expected that stronger belief of employers will not permit them to dismiss their workers as soon as they incur losses and, when they earn profits, they set aside a share for their workers.

In addition, Imam Ali's[111] remarks regarding efforts at earning Halal sustenance and its associated difficulties[112] can help establish fair relationships in business transactions in which both efforts and wages would be fair. Otherwise, the ground is paved for Haram earnings. In advising that one should not be "among those who desire felicity in the world to come without making any effort; those who become arrogant when they become rich while if they become needy, they are discouraged, depressed, and hurt; when they work, they shirk in their duties and when ask for wages, they ask for much," the Imam (AS) is recommending that expectations should be commensurate

---

109 Hausman, McPherson, p. 311.

110 Soroush, p. 144.

111 There comes a time when a scar by the sword is easier to tolerate for a believer than to obtain lawful money. The time when the recipient of the money receives more rewards than the donor because he receives to stay alive, but the donor does not care if his money is legal or ill-gotten.

112 Sermon 187 Nahj al-Balaghah, 1999, p. 204.

with efforts.[113] Also, he advised his son, Imam al-Hassan (AS): "Do not violate the right of your brother (in religion or in humanity), make sure that your behavior towards them does not make them miserable. The reward of someone who pleases you is not mistreatment. Whosoever turns away from justice, becomes unjust."[114]

Also, considering the fact that Islam frowns upon laziness and condemns voluntarily unemployed, work is considered a norm with a value equivalent decades of worship. Therefore, an individual who believes in this cultural and ethical institution is source of labor power with well-defined objective. Hence, if in a society there exists unemployment due to idleness or due to discriminatory practices toward labor, it can be taken as indication of unethical and non-religious nature of the economic system. Consequently, it is necessary to combat problems of shirking, idleness which may have resulted from absolute job security and guaranteed wages. Within the framework of religious teachings and their institutionalization, the relationships between the employers and employees are designed in a way to prevent the violation of the rights of both parties, the practice of justice becomes customary, and the behavior of economic agents is influenced indirectly in a way that ensures fair dealings in the market and injustices are avoided.

It is noteworthy that according to expert interpreters of the Qur'an Allah's command in Verse 1: Chapter 5: "O ye who believe! Fulfill (the terms and conditions of) contracts" refers to all contracts including those between humans and Allah, between each human and his/her self, and between each individual and others.[115] Therefore, employers and employees must fulfill all the terms and conditions of contracts between them which are based on justice and responsibility. Such an employer treats his employees kindly and generously and in return the employee works as hard as possible to earn Halal wages and fulfill his responsibility toward Allah and his employer.[116]

An important point in the view of Islam regarding work relationships is that work ethics is not considered solely on the basis of economics alone (for example, the view that treating workers as human beings increases labor productivity performance[117]) but involves human, ethical, and divine dimensions. Economic activities without ethical considerations based on justice are regarded as illegitimate.[118] In addition, combining the work environment and markets with to mosques (as is done in many Muslim countries), to an extent, provides external religious assurance in protecting ethical conditions necessary for religiously oriented work. Nevertheless, the most important guarantee in these cases is the conscience of the Muslims and

113 Quotations 150, 1999, p. 389.
114 Letter 31 Nahj al-Balaghah, 1371, p. 306.
115 Nasr, pp. 72–70.
116 Nasr,, p. 75.
117 Corman, p. 232.
118 Nasr, p. 77.

their internalized religious values.[119] The necessity of respecting the rights of others creates an expectation that Muslims have a strong sense of responsibility regarding the mutual duty of being faithful to terms and conditions of contracts.

There is no doubt that the norms which are learned, formally and informally, create ethical obligations that change behavior of the teach people. In addition, generalization of what and how of others behavior influence how individuals think about their own behavior. For example, when human behavior is modeled as if it is being motivated by short-term, material self-interests, inevitably, it justifies and strengthens selfishly-motivated behavior of individuals.[120]

Therefore, if today the labor force agrees to work 16 hours a day and receive a bowl of soup and a pillow in return, even if it is considered voluntary, rational and according to the terms of employment contract, based on today's accepted values, most people will consider such an arrangement as abusive and unfair.[121] In some places emergence of such situation is prevented by legal means and in other places through non-legal means. For example, in France problems resulting from collective contracts were resolved through legal guarantees and in England through social guarantees.[122]

Naturally, some of the main components constituting fair wages[123] need to become culturally institutionalized and turned into norms for which Islamic and national teachings can be beneficial. Some other components need to be reflected in national and international laws to make tracking of payment of fair wages as well as supporting their formation possible.

It should be noted that some of the components of fair wage are not only influenced personal position by individual behavior but also strongly by customs. Therefore, the question arises as to which criterion must be used to judge the fairness of customs and habits and their legitimacy?[124] Perhaps, various understandings of existing customs might be formed in the minds of the parties to the contract which might contradict each other regarding fair wages. However, it seems that through evolutionary path and unbiased negotiations, a more accurate correspondence between the views of the two parties may be achieved.

9 Formal Institutions of the Labor Market

According to Islamic teachings regarding work and wages, in addition to improving the conditions of informal institutions, formal institutions (negative and positive

119 Nasr,, p. 79.
120 Hazeman, McPherson, p. 310.
121 Ibid, p. 36.
122 Tamadon, p. 25.
123 Ebadi, Pasban, 1391.
124 Rawls, p. 76.

norms) should be established and informed so that they can dominate the labor market in the Islamic community to prevent imposition of harsh working conditions and make possible living wage. Some of the most important of these institutions are:[125]

1. The Rule of No Harm: Laws of the labor market determined by the government or based on mutual agreements should not cause any harm to the parties.
2. The Rule of No Waste: The time of the labor force should not be wasted through non-payment of wages nor should labor waste its time through shirking in performance of assigned duty, after the contract is agreed upon.
3. The Rule of No Hardship and Anguish: No one should is responsible to work beyond his ability[126] and difficult terms causing undue hardship should be abolished or compensated appropriately.
4. The Rule of Rejection of Earnings from Forbidden Activities: Prohibition of earnings through theft, expropriation, and other non-permissible activities.[127]
5. The Rule Rejecting Profligacy (Israf): Israf can lead to negation of other rules by the employer or the worker through undue stimulation of demand and has been prohibited in 25 versus of the Qur'an.[128]
6. The Rule of Respecting Muslims' property and work
7. The Rule of Trust; if a person enters into something and gets injured, that person is not the guarantor.
8. The Rule of Negation of Forced Imposition of Duties or Work that Labor is Reluctant to Perform; Do not force someone to do the wrongdoing.
9. The Rule of Rejection of Monopolization Behavior such as Hoarding (Ihtikar)[129]
10. The Rule of Rejection of Duress:[130] Due to threatening and intolerable conditions, one does not lead to inaccurate activity.
11. The Rule of Full Commitment to Terms and Conditions of Agreements

10 Appropriate Management System Needed for the Implementation of Fair Wages

The more the above-mentioned rules are implemented, the higher the expectation that the ground for emergence of productivity and fairness will be prepared through

---

125 Rezaei, 2005, p. 63.

126 Baqara verses 185–286, Hajj, verse 78 and Maedeh verse 6.

127 Sadr, 2008, p. 63.

128 Sadr, 2008, p. 62.

129 Rezaei, pp. 79–74.

130 In this regard, Ali (AS) quotes the Prophet (PBUH): "Do not deal with the needy out of emergency. Quotations 468, 1378, p. 444.

evolution and cooperation and not through confrontation and enmity.[131]As a result, it is necessary to have an appropriate system of management which can assume the responsibility of implementing these rules; otherwise they will only be documented on paper but not allowed to govern market behavior.

The government, NGO and the people are responsible to prevent any exploitation of labor force, especially the unskilled that are exploited more than others, and prevent the violation of their rights through supervising implementation of the terms and conditions of employment contracts. In this regard, Imam al-Sadegh (AS) narrates that in his last moments, the Prophet (SAWA) advised Imam Ali (AS) to prevent any injustice against farmers and to prevent workers from being humiliated. This advice to Imam Ali (AS), who had assumed many responsibilities for the affairs of the Muslims before and after he accepted to be drafted as the ruler, indicates the importance of the duty of the management of the implementation of a fair system for people.

In this context, Islamic teachings offer valuable insights. For example, as the Prophet recommends us to pay the wage of the worker before his sweat runs dry, it is necessary for the governance systems to adopt policies which ensure the payment of fair wages on time. If this important issue is overlooked and the wage is not paid in due time, the time value of the wage is eroded and, in addition, the workers may lose faith in their employers which might lead to less productivity. As Imam Ali (AS) states, human soul experiences various emotions at various times, therefore, the wage of the worker should be paid at the expected time to motivate them and improve their sense of loyalty.[132]

Another policy that can make firms more successful is development of human relations and consultation with others in the organization which can be possible through mutual respect among the employees. Through this approach, employers can attract the consensus of the employees regarding decisions which may have not have been supported previously.[133]In this context, Imam Ali (AS) addressing Malik Ashtar in a letter appointing the latter as Governor advises: "Do not say 'I have been appointed (as the Governor), I command expecting obedience.' This leads to hardness of the heart and erosion in belief, causes loss of blessing and brings tribulation and disaster."[134] These remarks indicate that while dealing with subordinates one should not use force or apply shear power. This idea is reflected in a poem: The wise man listens to his subordinates; the head cannot go where the legs refuse to go.

Imam Ali (AS) also speaks about the division of various tasks by saying: "Assign each of your workers to a task so that everyone will know their specific duties which they will perform without passing it onto others. In addition, pay them their wages

131 Qutb, p. 55.

132 Hearts could be both willing and reluctant, try to hire the ones who are willing to work because if they do not wish to work, they will not pay any attention to you! Quotations 193, 2009, p. 394.

133 Giddens 2008, pp. 323–321.

134 Letter 53 Nahj al-Balaghah, 1378, p. 326.

and bonuses completely and properly."[135] Therefore, one of the significant aspects of every policy related to wage payment is setting and implementing regulations that determine the kind of work and the wage and salary scale of the employees so that wage differentials will be determined by the nature of the work and the amount of effort as well as the quality of the work performed.[136] As a result, by eliminating personal biases, fair judgment becomes possible, as Rumi said: If the scale had any interest in the commodity being weighted, how would it ever reveal the true weight?"

11 Summary and Conclusion

The present paper, after reviewing related literature and its evolution, looked at the place of fair wages in other religious societies and argued the necessity of investigating the relationship of justice and fair wages. In this context, it also considered the view of Islam related to work and investigated various dimensions of fair wages through institutional analysis levels.

Now, in the final parts of the paper, it is worth considering remarks made by Arthur Schopenhauer who, in his book called "the Art of being Right," argued that in many confrontations and debates, there is no interest on the part of the participants to the discovery of truth. Keeping this in mind, question arises whether it is realistic to claim, as some economists do, that, regardless of institutional requirements, the result of competition in the market (with no regards to its health and fairness) is improved quality through elimination of low-quality agents and firms and is, fair and useful? Has any strategy for eliminating other parties in this debate not employed? When rules of ethics in religion teachings and philosophy are taken into account, undoubtedly, there are differences between "free competition" and fair, ethical and legitimate competition (in which end does not justify the means, and the means are legal, ethical and fair themselves).

There is no doubt that paying fair wages prevents class conflicts in the society by creating stable relationship among employee and employer while reducing poverty. These results are obtained when there is true motivation to pay fair wages. In this context, it is necessary to make rules governing rights are made transparent, hidden borders of apparent logic are removed, organic relationship between rights and ethics is enlightened by conception of justice, and, finally, in addition to such order, there is high motivation and the will for establishing justice, in the first place. This way, and with the agreement of both sides, wages will be determined based on contract stipulation, commensurate with the level of general wages prevailing in the market, proportionate to the effort exerted, sufficient to meet the needs of the worker, and equivalent

135 Attaran, p. 238.
136 Budi, Web, pp. 71–72.

to the marginal product of labor. To implement such system, its components must be institutionalized (as formal or informal institutions) and reflected in the management system of the society. This, then, would give rise to expectation that actualization of this ethical set up will lead to a more productive economy.

Components that, based on the teachings of Islam as well as rational and empirical considerations, are influential in the formation of fair wages considerations have a variety of dimensions which, in a general view, include: (a)characteristics of the employees(literacy, skill, experience, responsibility, social status, marginal product, innovativeness, etc.); (b) The conditions of other workers, work and employer (wages in other firms, goals of the firm, social status of the work, etc.); (c) labor market situation (unemployment rate, hours of work, time of work, the degree of difficulty of work, etc.); (d) compliance with institutional rules (poverty lines, general welfare, human rights, habits, rule of law, etc.); and(e) other market conditions (share of capital owners in production, prices level, business cycles, inflationary expectations, productivity shocks (organizational, institutional and technological evolution...).

References

English References

Akerlof, George A., Gift Exchange & Efficiency – Wage Theory: Four Views, Pittsburgh, the American Economic Review, 1984.

Akerlof, G, A., the Market for Lemons: Quality Uncertainty and the Market Mechanism, Cambridge, Quarterly Journal of Economics, 1970.

Akerlof, G. A. & Dickens, W. T, the Economic Consequences of Cognitive Dissonance, Pittsburgh, the American Economic Review, 1982.

Akerlof, G. A. & Janet L. Yellen, Fairness and Unemployment, Pittsburgh, the American Economic Review, 1988.

Akerlof, G. A. & Kranton Rachel, Identity and the Economics of organizations, Pittsburgh, The Journal of Economic Perspectives, 2005.

Akerlof, G. A. & Janet L. yellen, the Fair Wage- Effort Hypothesis and Unemployment, Cambridge, the Quarterly Journal of Economics, 1990.

Akerlof, G. A., Labor Contracts as Partial Gift Exchange, Cambridge, the Quarterly Journal of Economics, 1982.

Hodgson, Geoffrey M, the Approach of Institutional Economics, Pittsburgh, Journal of Economic Literature, 1998.

Marx, Karl, Critique of the Gotha program, Rockville, Maryland, Wildside press, 1973.

Pasbani Someeh, Abolfazl, the Advantages of Paying Fair Wages as a Human Right, International Workshop, human Rights and Business, Syracuse, Italy, 2010.

Pasbani Someeh, Abolfazl, Child Labor Prohibition: Flexibility or Rigidity?, International Migration, Women's Employment, and Child Labor, An International Expert Round Table, Louaize, Lebanon, Notre Dame University, 2011.

Rawls, John, a Theory of Justice, Harvard, Harvard University Press, 2003.

Williamson O. E., The New Institutional Economics: Taking Stock, Looking Ahead"; Pittsburgh, Journal of Economic Literature, 2000.
Yellen, JL, Efficiency Wage Models of Unemployment, Pittsburgh, the American Economic Review, 1984.

Persian References

The Holy Qur'an
Imam Ali (AS), Nahj al-Balaghah, Translated by, Shahidi, Jafar, Tehran, Scientific and Cultural Press, 1999.
Abu Ja'far Muhammad bin Ali al-Sadouq, Ma'ani al-Akhbar, Translated by, Ghafari, Ali Akbar, Qum, Islamic publication, 1982.
al-Hur al-Amli, Muhammad ibn al-Hassan, Wesayel al-Shi'a, vol. 20, Tehran, Maktobe al-Islamiyah, 2004.
Attaran, Ali Asghar, the Roles and Rights of Children in Organizations in the Viewpoint of Imam Ali (AS), Qum, Boostan e Ketab, 2005.
Ayazi, Seyyed Mohammad Ali, the Comprehensiveness of Qur'an, Rasht, Ketab e Mobin, 1999.
Bazargan, Mehdi, Collection of works vol 8, Work in Iran, Tehran, Publication Co, 1999.
Betro, Jean, Badamchi, Hussein, the Advent of Legislation, History of Ancient Mesopotamian Law, Tehran, Tarh-e-Nou, 2003.
Blake Moore, Ken, Introduction to Social Policy, Translated by, Saeedi, Ali Asghar, Sadeghi Jegheh, Saeed, Tehran, Social Security Research Institute, 2006.
Buvi, Angela, M, J. H Web, Payment Based on Output-Based Systems, Manchester, 1990.
Corman, Abraham. K, Industrial and Organizational Psychology, Translated by, Shokrkon, Hossein, Tehran, Roshd, 2002.
Drucker, Peter, Future Manager, Translated by, Rezai nejad, Tehran, Rasa, 1994.
Ebadi, Jafar, PhD dissertation on microeconomics, Justice and Government Interference, Tehran, 2006.
Ebadi, Jafar, Dadgar, Yadollah, Pasbani Some'eh, Abolfazl, Analysis of The Grounds and Reasons for The Occurrence and Need for Fair Wage Processing, Tehran, Planning and Budget, 2015.
Ebadi, Jafar, Pasebani Some'eh, Abolfazl, The Most Important Factors Affecting Fair Wage in Iran, Tehran, Economic Research, 2013.
Ebadi, Jafar, Pasebani Some'eh, Abolfazl, The Characteristics of the Labor force and Their Role in Fair Wages, Qom, Economic policies, 2014.
Eyraud Francois, Catherine Saget, the Fundamentals of Minimum Wage Fining, Translated by, Isa Zadeh, Saeed, Saeednia, Peyman, Tehran, Labor and Social Security Institute, 2007.
Farabi, Abu Nasr, Thoughts from Utopia, Translated by, Sajjadi, Jafar, Tehran, Taheri, 1982.
Giddens, Anthony, Sociology, Translated by, Sabori, Manuchehr, Tehran, Nashr e Ney, 2008.
Haguzip, Shan.P, New Keynesian Macroeconomics, Translated by, Taghavi, Mehdi, Tehran, Islamic Azad University, 2000.
Hakimi, Al-Hayat, Volume 1 to 8, Ahmad Aram, Tehran, Islamic Culture Publishing House, Qum, Dalil-e-Ma, 1997 to 2009.
Hausman. D. M, McPherson. M.S, Economic Analysis and Ethics Philosophy, Translated by, Dadgar, Yadullah, et. al., Tehran, Institute for Research and Development of the Humanities, 2007.
Hirotakatukuchi, Management in Japan, Translated by, Afshin Mansesh, Hossein, Tehran, Iran Tire Co, 1986.
Ibn Khaldun, Abd al-Rahman, Introduction, Translated by, Gonabadi, Parvin, Tehran, Scientific and Cultural Press, 1987.

Iraqi Ezatollah, Labor Rights Course, Volume 1, Tehran, National University of Iran, 1979.
Jalal al-Din Muhammad Balkhi Rumi, Masnavi Spiritual, Tehran, Scientific and Cultural, 1997.
Japan's Office of Labor and Employment, Salary System in Japan, Translated by, Arabs, Seyyed Mohammad, Tehran, Trading and Publishing Company, 1995.
Kaleini Razi, Mohammad Ibn Yaghoub ibn Isaac, Osol Kafi, Volume 1, Translated by, Mostafavi, Javad. Qum, Islamic Publications, 1978.
Katouzian, Nasser, Introduction, Civil Society Philosophy, Tehran, Enteshar Public Joint Stock Company, 2005.
Lambatan, A.K.S, Landlord and farmer in Iran, Tehran, Scientific and Cultural, 1960.
Minimum Wage Regulations, enacted in 1968 by Wages Department, 1969/9/23.
Ministry of Culture and Islamic Guidance, Evaluating the Values and Attitudes of Iranians, 2001 & 2003.
Mojtabavi Naini, Seyyed Mehdi, Dictionary of Labor and Social Welfare,Tehran, Labor and Social Security Institute,1993.
Montazeri, HosseinAli, a Law Dissertation, Qum, Arghavan Danesh, 2006.
Muvaffaghian, Nasser, Floating Employment Theory, Tehran, Social Security Quarterly, 2006.
Naghizadeh, Mohammad, the Basics of Japan's Economic and Developmental Thoughts, Tehran, Enteshar Public Joint Stock Company, 2007.
Namazi, Hussein, Economic Systems, Tehran, Enteshar Public Joint Stock Company,2008.
Pasebani Some'eh, Abolfazl, Extracting the Focal Variable in the Theory of Islamic Justice, Tehran, ACECR, 2005.
Pasebani Some'eh, Abolfazl, Motevasseli, Mahmud, Conspicuous Consumption in the Thorestein Veblen's Opinion and Saving, Tehran, Journal Economic Research, No. 98, Faculty of Economics, University of Tehran, 2012.
Patrick Walker, Angela. M. Buvi, Job Evaluation and the Discrimination between Male and Female Employees, Manchester, 1990.
Pelikan, Jaroslav, Kitagava, Joseph, Nasr, Seyyed Hussein, Work Ethics in Eastern Religions and Rituals, Translated by, Movathaghi, Sayyid Ahmad, Tehran, Institute of Labor and Social Security, 2001.
Planning Deputy, Population and Manpower Office, Wage Report (productivity, wages and prices in Iran), 1976.
Rasulli Mahallati, Seyyed Hashem, Imam Ali (AS), Tehran: Islamic Culture Publishing House, 1999.
Rezaee, Majid, Supply of Labor Force Based on the Principles Governing the Islamic Labor Market, Mofid University, 1998.
Rezaee, Majid, Work and Religion, Tehran, Andisheye Jawan Center, 2003.
Rezaee, Majid, the Effects of Some Laws on the Labor Market, Qum, Journal of Islamic Economics, 2005.
Robertson, James, Future Work, Translated by, Alwani and Danaeifard, Tehran, Nashr e Ney, 1994.
Ronagh, Yuseph, Wages and Benefits of the Labor and Social Security Law in Iran, Tehran, Farmanesh Publication, 2005.
Rostami, Mohammad Zaman, Theoretical Review of Wage Theories – Manpower Productivity from the Viewpoint of Islam, Tarbiat Modarres University, 2005.
Sadr, Seyyed Kazem, Islamic Economics in the beginning, Tehran, Shahid Beheshti University, 2008.
Sayyid Qutb, Social Justice in Islam, Translated by, Gerami, Mohammad Ali, Khosroshahi, Seyyed Hadi, Tehran, kolbeye Shrogh, 2000.
Schopenhauer, Arthur, the Art of Being Right, Translated by, Sabeti, Erfan, Tehran, Qoqnus, 2015.
Sen, Amartya, the Idea of Justice, Translated by, Mahmoudi, Vahid, Homayounpour, Hormuz, Tehran, Kondokav, Clear book, 2011.
Shahidi, Seyyed Ja'far, Ali described by Ali, Tehran, Publishing House of Islamic Culture, 2006.

Sobhani, Hassan, Justice-Based Economics, Tehran, Soroush, 2009.
Soroush, Abdolkarim, the Manners of Power and Justice, Tehran, Sirat, 2007.
Tabatabai, Mohammad Hussein, Shia in Islam, Qum, Bostan e Ketab, 2008.
Tamadon Jahromi, Mohammad Hussein, The History of Economics Ideas' textbook, Tehran, Tehran University, 1982.
Tamadon Jahromi, Mohammad Hussein, Speeches in Economics, Social Sciences, and Knowing Scientific Methods, Tehran, Institute for Humanities and Social Studies, ACECR, 2010.
Tamadon Jahromi, Mohammad Hussein, inedited, Collective Labor Agreements, (comparative study of French and British law).
Tarow, Leicester, Great confrontation, Translated by, Kiawand, Aziz, Tehran, Didar, 1998.
Tavasoli, Gholam Abbas, the Sociology of Work and Occupation, Tehran, 1975.
Thirteen Muslim Economists, Topics in Microeconomics (Islamic Attitudes), Translated by, Sadeghi, Hossein, Tehran, Economics Research Center, Tarbiat Modarres University, 1996.
Tusi, Nasir al-Din, Naseri Ethics, Translated by, Mojtaba Minavi-Alireza Heidari, Tehran, Khwarizmi, 2008.
Walzer, Michael, Spheres of Justice, Translated by, Najafi, Saleh, Tehran, Thaleth, 2010.
Weitzman, Martin L, the Share Economy (Conquering Stagflation), Translated by, Yasseri, Ali, Tehran, Central Bank, Center for Banking Studies, 1989.

Mojtaba Baqeri Tudeshki

Chapter 20: Ethics and the Acknowledged Right of the Destitute in the Qur'an and Hadith

1 Introduction

The new economic theories have arrived at a consensus that not all economic problems can be resolved through market mechanisms and by the intervention of the government. Although many of such difficulties may be resolved by observing engineering features such as maximizing utility, welfare and profit, and minimizing costs, many others that concern the public sector, economic institutions and environment can only be facilitated through personal ethics and non-profit incentives.[1] For instance, when the government has collapsed, or is facing extreme budget deficit and cannot collect taxes, and the society is seriously engulfed by poverty, only ethics and altruism can resolve the economic difficulties that are created due to poverty.

According to Amartya Sen, economics has two distinct origins: one relates to ethics and the other relates to engineering. He believes that there are at least two central issues that bond ethics with economics: first is the relationship between ethics and human motivation, for ethical deliberations cannot be totally inconsequential to actual human behavior. The second issue concerns the desired and ultimate economic happiness which according to Sen cannot be based only on efficiency alone and must include ethical dimension as well.[2]

In cases of market failure, incidence of poverty and maldistribution of wealth, Islamic economy, aside from duties of government, relies on public ethics, and considers strengthened ethics through enhancing faith (Iman) as solution to these economic problems. The Qur'an considers the perfection of ethics/morality (of individuals and societies) as the objective of appointment of messengers.[3] Moreover, in the Riwayat it is declared: "The noblest among you from the viewpoint of faith is that one of you who has the best morality/ethics."[4] Concurrently, faith is associated with 'Amal Salih (acting in compliance with the rules prescribed in the Qur'an) and helping

1 Amartya Sen, *On Ethics and Economics*, translated by Hassan Fesharaki (Tehran: Shirazeh, 1377 SH), 3–8.

2 Amartya Sen, *On Ethics and Economics* (New York: NY, Basil Blackwell 1987).

3 Mohammad Baqer Majlesi, *Behar Al-Anwar*, Vol. 68, (Beirut: Dar Eh'ya Al-torath Al-Arabi, 1403 LH), 382 and Ahmad Bin Hossein Beihaqi, *Al-Sonan Al-Kobra*, Vol. 10, (Beirut: Dar Al-Kotob Al-Elmiya1424 LH), 323: "عن أبى هُرَيْرَة، قال: قال رسول الله (ص): إِنَّمَا بُعِثْتُ لِأُتَمِّمَ مَكَارِمَ الْأَخْلَاقِ".

4 Ibn Sho'ba Harrani, *Tohf Ul-Oqul An Al-ul-Rasul*, edited/corrected by Ali Akbar Qaffari, (Qum: 1363 SH), Hadith 303588 and Mohammad Baqer Majlesi, *Behar Al-Anwar*, Vol. 74, 150.

https://doi.org/10.1515/9783110593419-020

the poor. Therefore, in an Islamic society composed of believing individuals, resolves many problems related to poverty and distribution of wealth through morality/ethics.

Two verses of the Qur'an and a number of Riwayat point to existence of an "acknowledged right" in the wealth of the believers. The status of this right seems to be different than that of Khums, Zakat and resources of Islamic government that provide support for the livelihood of the poor. On the one hand, the philosophy of imposition of Zakat is provision for the needs of the society, including that of the poor and the destitute. On the other hand, the Qur'an also establish an obligatory "acknowledged right" in the wealth of the Abrar (the righteous) and believers to support of the deprived and mendicants, which appears to be from Zakat on property. Consequently, there are differences of opinion among the Fuqaha (jurisconsults) and interpreters (of the Qur'an) regarding the meaning of these verses which necessitate further investigation in Islamic literature to distinguish this kind of right from other financial obligations and its operational guarantee or its enforcement.

Using a bibliographic and descriptive methodology, the present article attempts to analyze the status of "acknowledged right" the verses of the Qur'an and Riwayat related to this right from the point of view of jurisprudents and exegetists. Further, it will be argued the "acknowledged right" is an obligatory (*Wajib*) duty as is the obligatory Zakat. Moreover, it will be shown that morality/ethics sanction or enforce the implementation of this right.

To establish the validity these claims, the article begins with an introductory discussion about the definition of ethical conduct and its sanctioning. Then, the view of scholars regarding the implications of Qur'anic verses and Riwayat about "acknowledged right" are presented. The status of "acknowledged right" among other resources for funding the livelihood of the poor are subsequently deliberated and it is concluded that "acknowledged right" is an obligatory duty different from Zakat. It depends on public donations to resolve poverty issues at the time of shortage of Zakat and other financial resources available to the government. Finally, the relation between ethics and "acknowledged right" is explained and it is shown that "acknowledged right" can only be sanctioned/enforced by ethics.

2 Ethical Conduct and its Sanctioning (Enforcement)

2.1 Definition of Ethical Conduct

Different definitions that have been provided for ethical acts are classified by Morteza Motahhari, in the book titled *Education and Training* as follows:

1. Ethical act is an act that runs counter to human nature, therefore any act that contradicts demands of our nature is ethical.

2. Criterion and measure of an ethical act is that it is based on "other-loving" (or "other-regarding") and not "self-love." This means that an act whose motive is to benefit the self or avoid a loss to the self only is not ethical. If an act is motivated primarily to benefit "the other" only it is ethical.
3. Criteria for an ethical act is "other-loving" but it must be an acquired love or regard and not natural. Thus, there are two kinds of "other-loving" (or "other-regarding"): (a) natural "other-loving" like maternal affection, racial/ethnic and familial attachments; and (b), acquired "other-loving" meaning the kind of love for others that is not governed by human nature but is volitionally gained. If one develops a love for others the same way that a mother loves her child, this becomes an acquired "other-loving" characteristic and a derived (secondary) excellence/perfection in his personality.
4. Ethical conducts are those which possess intrinsic goodness while unethical conducts are inherently repugnant. Thus, an ethical conduct is performed based on rational reasoning. As well, ethical humans are those individuals whose entire being is ruled by rationality where anger passions and fear play no role in ruling their existence (this is the view of the thinkers of the old).
5. An ethical act is pure (absolute), i.e. an individual performs it for its own sake and has no other motivation (it is not, for example, self-serving). It is done as a duty whose source is the conscience of the individual.

It can be argued that all these views share something in common: to be ethical means to transcend the self. This means that any action that is intended to be self-serving (benefiting the self or avoiding a loss to the self) cannot be termed "ethical."[5] Hence, helping the poor based on an acquired "other-loving," conscience, and duty is an ethical action.

2.2 Conscience and Faith Sanction/Enforcement of Ethical Conduct

Obeying the laws other than ethical rules is motivated either by material self-interest of the individual or an external command/force. A clear example of external command relates to government enforcement of many of the legislated laws. An external command, however, cannot create an ethical rule. The origin of ethical duties arises from the very being of a human being and the inner call of her/his conscience which constitute the foundation of ethics.[6]

5 Morteza Motahhari, *Education and Training in Islam*, (Tehran: Sadra Publications, 1370 SH), 67 and Morteza Motahhari, *Methodical and Cultural Foundation*, (Tehran: Sadra Publications, 1382 SH), 67.
6 Immanuel Kant, *The Metaphysical Elements of Ethics*, translated by Hamid Enayat and Ali Qeysari, 107.

Enforcement of most of the laws, whether legal or criminal, are clear. The enforcer of the laws (government, for example) ensures compliance through use of force, courts, imprisonment, exile, denial of social rights and execution. Guarantor of enforcement of ethical/moral norms however, is the ethics of individuals which varies among individuals and is dependent on the circumstance, degree of shame that the action evokes in a person's conscience, belief in the punishment of the Day of Judgement, and the reproach of peers.

3 Status of "Acknowledged Right" in Islamic Economy

3.1 Obligatory Nature of "Acknowledged Right" According to the Views of some Scholars

The Qur'an and Riwayat refer to an "acknowledged right" whose strength as an obligatory duty and its determination are contested among Fuqaha (jurisconsults) and interpreters who have different views and Ijtihadi opinions (opinions arrived at through rational religious reasoning). Convergence of these views requires more in-depth analysis.[7] This paper attempts to demonstrate the obligatory nature of this duty with the help of Ijtihadi reasoning and, thereby, strengthen the other-than-Zakat nature of this right of the poor in the wealth of the rich. Based on this reasoning, the paper will show the place of this right in an Islamic economy. In doing so, the paper relies on the works of those scholars whose views support and strengthen these arguments.

Among Sunni scholars,[8] Ibn Abbas Sha'bi, Mujahid and Ibn Omar have considered "acknowledged right" as an obligation other than Zakat.[9] In *Tafsir (interpretation of the Qur'an) Dorr Al-Manthur*,[10] from Beyhaqi is narrated that Fatimah Bint Qays

---

7 There is disagreement on compulsiveness or recommendability of "acknowledged right", as well as its inclusion in Zakat or not, overall, three views currently exist: 1. It is the same as obligatory Zakat, 2. It is a recommended charity/donation different than obligatory Zakat, and, 3. It constitutes another obligation in addition to Zakat.

8 Some of Sunni scholars, like Ibn Abbas, Hassan Basri, Ibn Sirin, Qattade' and Tabari, believe that "acknowledged right" is the same as obligatory Zakat, while some other, like Ata', Mujahid and Nakhaei, consider it as a recommended charity/donation (Abolfotuh Razi, *Tafsir Al-Razi*, Vol. 30 (Beirut: Dar Al-Kotob Al-Elmiya), 115).

9 Abolfotuh Razi, *Tafsir Al-Razi*, Beirut, Vol. 30, (Beirut: Dar Al-Kotob Al-Elmiya), 115.

10 The renowned views of erstwhile Shia jurisprudents and raconteur scholars, such as Saheb Jawaher, Sheikh Hor Ameli, and contemporary jurisprudents, such as Ayatollah Kho'ei and Ayatollah Montazeri indicates that this right is a recommended charity/donation (Hossein Ali Montazeri, *Kitab Al-Zakat*, Vol. 1, (Qum: Dar Al-Fikr Publications, 1409 LH), 20). As stated earlier, there are different views that can be classified into 3 groups.

quoted the Prophet (sawa), when asked about the "acknowledged right" as saying: "In wealth, there are rights other than Zakat," thus pointing to the obligatory nature of "acknowledged right" I the words of the Prophet (sawa).[11]

Among contemporary Sh'ii exegetists, 'Allameh Tabataba'ei,[12] Sadeqi Tehrani[13] and Makarem Shirazi,[14] have considered "acknowledged right" an obligation other than Zakat, while Shahid Sadr in his book *Eqtisadona* considers it is an obligatory general Takaful (mutual responsibility, mutual commitment to joint support among people), aimed at alleviating people's severe needs.[15]

In what follows, the paper attempts to substantiate the view that "acknowledged right" is an obligation other than Zakat. Its amount is determined by the individuals themselves rather than the government, based on the essential livelihood requirements of the poor. To establish this claim, the paper relies on reasoning based on the verses of the Qur'an and Riwayat. To keep the paper within reasonable length, the paper does not focus on opposing views in the text of the paper.

3.1.1 "Acknowledged Right" of the Poor in the Qur'an

Two verses of the Qur'an mention "acknowledged right:" Verse 24 of Chapter 70 (Al-Ma'arij) and Verse 19: Chapter 51 (Al-Zariyat). In the former, the word "Haqq" (right" is introduced by adjective of "Ma'lum" (acknowledged, recognized) while in the latter Verse, "Haqq" does not have an adjective. Verses 19–25 of Chapter 70 explains that humans are created "Halu'a" (impatient, greedy) so that when experiencing adversity, he complains. When experiencing a good blessing (in terms of wealth), they hold on to it strongly (want it all for themselves and refuse to use it help others). Except "Musalleen," those who are constantly in "Salat" (those who are in constant connection, in constant communion with Allah), and who recognize a right (for the poor) in their wealth.

A. "Acknowledged Right" of the Destitute in Al-Ma'arej

Holy Qur'an states:

إِنَّ الْإِنْسَانَ خُلِقَ هَلُوعًا (19) إِذَا مَسَّهُ الشَّرُّ جَزُوعًا (20) وَإِذَا مَسَّهُ الْخَيْرُ مَنُوعًا (21) إِلَّا الْمُصَلِّينَ (22) الَّذِينَ هُمْ عَلَى صَلَاتِهِمْ
دَائِمُونَ (23) وَالَّذِينَ فِي أَمْوَالِهِمْ حَقٌّ مَعْلُومٌ (24) لِلسَّائِلِ وَالْمَحْرُومِ (25) (اَلمعَارِج: 19–25)

11 Shia exegetists, such as Sheikh Tousi in *Tebyan* and Sheikh Tabarsi in *Majma' Al-Bayan*, have considered it as recommended.

12 Mohammad Hossein Tabataba'ei, *Tafsir Al-Mizan*, Vol. 20, (Qum: Jama'ate Al-Modarresin fi Al-Howza Al-Elmiya fi Qum Al-Moqaddaseh), 16.

13 Mohammad Sadeqi Tehrani, *Fi Tafsir Al-Forqan*, Vol. 29, (Beirut: Mo'assesa Al-A'lami l-Al-Matbou'at), 130.

14 Naser Makarem Shirazi, *Tafsir Nemoune'*, Vol. 25, (Qum: Dar Al-Kitab Islamiya), 95.

15 Al-Seyyed Mohammad Baqer Sadr, *Eqtesadona*, (Maktab Al-E'lam Al-Islami, 1417 LH).

> Surely man has been created greedy (19), when they are afflicted, they complain severely (20), but when they are fortunate, they become niggardly (21); except those who are steadfast in their Salat (prayers of communion with Allah) (22), and are constant at their prayer (23), and those whose wealth comprises an acknowledged right (24), towards the destitute and the deprived (25) (Al-Ma'arij, 70:19–25).

i. Hints for Understanding of the Verse of Haqq Ma'lum (Recognized, Acknowledged Right)

a. Meaning of "Impatient, Greedy" ("هَلُوع")

Indeed, human beings have been created greedy/covetous. The greediness is interpreted in the following two verses in the sense that when evil comes upon human beings, they get impatient and panicky. However, when good befalls them, they become grudging, and do not leave it or share it with others.

b. View of Exegetists on the Connotation of Adjective "Greedy" for Human Beings

According to the interpretations provided by most of exegetists, this verse is a reproach for human beings. It criticizes the rapaciousness of man. Based on Zamakhshari in *Dorr Al-Manthur*,[16] "man has been created greedy" is a metaphor which does not point to the original creation of man and his covetous nature. It indicates that human beings have a strong tendency for rapaciousness. Therefore, Holy Qur'an does not mean to say that human beings have been created covetous. This is like it is said in describing certain abilities of individuals with exceptional talents that the individual "has been thus created."

c. Modification of "Greedy" with Prayers and Bounteousness

It is thus conceived from the verses that all human beings possess the quality of rapaciousness, which is a despicable ethical quality, unless they are real supplicants (prayers); i.e. they set aside and pay the "acknowledged right" from their wealth. Consequently, the less the greediness and profiteering, the more the "acknowledged right."

B. Right of the Poor in Chapter 51 (Al-Zariyat)

The Holy Qur'an describes the "Righteous" ("الْمُتَّقِينَ") as follows:

> إِنَّ الْمُتَّقِينَ فِي جَنَّاتٍ وَعُيُونٍ (15) آخِذِينَ مَا آتَاهُمْ رَبُّهُمْ إِنَّهُمْ كَانُوا قَبْلَ ذَلِكَ مُحْسِنِينَ (16) كَانُوا قَلِيلًا مِنَ اللَّيْلِ مَا يَهْجَعُونَ (17)
> وَبِالْأَسْحَارِ هُمْ يَسْتَغْفِرُونَ (18) وَفِي أَمْوَالِهِمْ حَقٌّ لِلسَّائِلِ وَالْمَحْرُومِ (19) (الذَّارِيَات:15–19)

16 Mohammad Hossein Tabataba'ei, *Tafsir Al-Mizan*, Vol. 20, 16. *ibid*.

> Surely, the righteous shall live in gardens and fountains (15) receiving their reward from their Lord. They had been beneficent people before the Day of Judgment (16). They slept very little during the night (17), and sought forgiveness in the early dawn (18). They assigned a share of their wealth for the destitute and the deprived (19) (Al-Zariyat, 51:15–19).

i. Points Related to the Right of the Poor in Al-Zariyat

a. Unremitting Support for the Poor by those who are "Beneficent" ("الْمُحْسِنِينَ")

The sacred verses indicate that the righteous individuals pray and seek forgiveness of the Lord throughout the night in their worldly life. They also assign a share of their wealth for the poor and the deprived. That is the reason for assigning them the quality of "beneficence" and calling them "beneficent."

b. Meaning of a "Beneficent" Person ("مُحسِن", Muhsin)

The word is used in Holy Qur'an to refer to those who "do good" for others and always refers to those who perform their deeds with motives other than gaining profit or personal interests motivated by "other-regarding". It is therefore necessary to consider the characteristics of these individuals in the Qur'an.

c. Characteristics of those who are "Beneficent" ("الْمُحْسِنِينَ")

1. Those who are "Beneficent" are individuals who spend their wealth for the cause of Allah in times of prosperity as well as adversity.[17]
2. They control their anger.[18] They do not break their covenants and practice forgiveness.[19]
3. They forgive the transgression of others.[20]
4. they pay (at least part) the dowry of their wives even if the marriage has not been consummated (but ends in divorce).[21]

---

17 الَّذِينَ يُنْفِقُونَ فِي السَّرَّاءِ وَالضَّرَّاءِ وَالْكَاظِمِينَ الْغَيْظَ وَالْعَافِينَ عَنِ النَّاسِ وَاللَّهُ يُحِبُّ الْمُحْسِنِينَ (آل عمران: 134)
Who spend (for others) throughout happiness and hardship, and suppress their anger and overlook what other people do. God loves the benefactors (Ale Imran: 134).

18 Mohammad Hossein Tabataba'ei, *Tafsir Al-Mizan.*

19 فَبِمَا نَقْضِهِمْ مِيثَاقَهُمْ لَعَنَّاهُمْ وَجَعَلْنَا قُلُوبَهُمْ قَاسِيَةً يُحَرِّفُونَ الْكَلِمَ عَنْ مَوَاضِعِهِ وَنَسُوا حَظًّا مِمَّا ذُكِّرُوا بِهِ وَلَا تَزَالُ تَطَّلِعُ عَلَى خَائِنَةٍ مِنْهُمْ إِلَّا قَلِيلًا مِنْهُمْ فَاعْفُ عَنْهُمْ وَاصْفَحْ إِنَّ اللَّهَ يُحِبُّ الْمُحْسِنِينَ. (المائده: 13)
Since they broke their covenant, We have cursed them and planted a hard shell over their hearts. They lift words out of their context and have forgotten a portion of what they should have memorized. Except for a few of them, you will always catch come of the committing some act of treachery. Yet pardon them and overlook it, God loves those who act kindly (Al-Ma'eda: 13).

20 Mohammad Hossein Tabataba'ei, *Tafsir Al-Mizan.*

21 لَا جُنَاحَ عَلَيْكُمْ إِنْ طَلَّقْتُمُ النِّسَاءَ مَا لَمْ تَمَسُّوهُنَّ أَوْ تَفْرِضُوا لَهُنَّ فَرِيضَةً وَمَتِّعُوهُنَّ عَلَى الْمُوسِعِ قَدَرُهُ وَعَلَى الْمُقْتِرِ قَدَرُهُ مَتَاعًا بِالْمَعْرُوفِ حَقًّا عَلَى الْمُحْسِنِينَ. (البقره: 236)

5. They are those who practice patience (in avoiding transgressions, in bearing afflictions, and in practicing compliance (with the rules of behavior prescribed in the Qur'an).[22]
6. They are renowned for their benevolence and generosity without expecting reciprocity (from those who are subject of their beneficence).[23]

The above-mentioned verses of the Holy Qur'an are all indicative that the characteristic of beneficence in individuals transcends them beyond those who seek their own interests and want to maximize their profits in all their transactions and deals. Helping others during hardships such as famine, forgiving others, paying part of the dowry to their wives even if the marriage has not consummated, are patient during adversities, and avoiding whatever causes disunity, damages social solidarity and leads to loss of more important benefits, all in all point to the fact that those who practice beneficence acknowledge a right for the poor without expecting reciprocal benefits from them in return.

d. Recognition of those who Practice Beneficence and their Rewards in the Created Order

In accordance with His Sunnah (His established way of doing), Allah rewards those who practice beneficence beyond what the physical world possesses and beyond usual causes and means. He guides them to an incredible path which is unimaginable from a scientific and intellectual point of view. He saves them from natural catastrophes, does not diminish the rewards due them because of their material sacrifices they made in order to help others, rewards them, both Here and in the Hereafter, more than their good actions deserve, and arranges the divine rules such that some of their transgressions committed with the intention of doing good will not be burdens deserving punishment.[24]

It will not be held against you if you divorce women when you have never had any contact with them, nor assigned them any living. Provide for them, the well-to-do according to his means and the straitened according to his means, an assignment is due in all decency from those who act kindly (Al-Baqara: 236).

22 وَاصْبِرْ فَإِنَّ اللَّهَ لَا يُضِيعُ أَجْرَ الْمُحْسِنِينَ (هُود: 115).

Act patiently, God does not ignore the reward of those who do good (Hud: 115).

23 ... إِنَّا نَرَاكَ مِنَ الْمُحْسِنِينَ (يوسف: 36)

... we see you are someone who acts kindly (Yusef: 36, in part).

24 Rewards in paradise:

إِنَّ الْمُتَّقِينَ فِي ظِلَالٍ وَعُيُونٍ (41) وَفَوَاكِهَ مِمَّا يَشْتَهُونَ (42) كُلُوا وَاشْرَبُوا هَنِيئًا بِمَا كُنْتُمْ تَعْمَلُونَ (43) إِنَّا كَذَٰلِكَ نَجْزِي الْمُحْسِنِينَ (44) (المرسلات: 41–44).

Surely, the heedful will be in shady nooks by springs (41) and have whatever fruit they may hanker for: (42) "Eat and drink at leisure because of what you have been doing." (43) The We reward those who act kindly. (Al-Morsalat: 41–44).

e. Presence of the Term "Right" and the Associated Obligation of Performing it as a Duty

Occurrence of the term "right" in the two verses mentioned indicates that the faithful are obligated to be mindful of the situation of the poor and the meaning of the word "Ma'lum" (known, acknowledged) is the amount of assistance that the individual

---

لَهُمْ مَا يَشَاءُونَ عِنْدَ رَبِّهِمْ ذَلِكَ جَزَاءُ الْمُحْسِنِينَ (الزُمِر: 34)
They will have anything they wish from their Lord, this is the reward for those who act kindly (Al-Zomer: 34) Forgiving the sins and rewarding more than deserved:
وَإِذْ قِيلَ لَهُمُ اسْكُنُوا هَذِهِ الْقَرْيَةَ وَكُلُوا مِنْهَا حَيْثُ شِئْتُمْ وَقُولُوا حِطَّةٌ وَادْخُلُوا الْبَابَ سُجَّدًا نَغْفِرْ لَكُمْ خَطِيئَاتِكُمْ سَنَزِيدُ الْمُحْسِنِينَ (الاعراف: 161)
When they were told: "Settle down in this town and eat wherever you wish in it, and say: 'Relieve (us)!' Enter the gate (walking) on your knees. We will forgive you your mistakes, We will give even more to those who act kindly." (Al-A'raf: 161)

Increased worldly blessings:

Bestowing unimaginable judgment and knowledge
وَلَمَّا بَلَغَ أَشُدَّهُ آتَيْنَاهُ حُكْمًا وَعِلْمًا وَكَذَلِكَ نَجْزِي الْمُحْسِنِينَ (يوسف: 22)
And when he became of age, We gave him discretion and knowledge, thus We reward those who act kindly. (Yusef: 22)

Unbelievable rescue from catastrophes
وَلَقَدْ نَادَانَا نُوحٌ فَلَنِعْمَ الْمُجِيبُونَ (75) وَنَجَّيْنَاهُ وَأَهْلَهُ مِنَ الْكَرْبِ الْعَظِيمِ (76) وَجَعَلْنَا ذُرِّيَّتَهُ هُمُ الْبَاقِينَ (77) وَتَرَكْنَا عَلَيْهِ فِي الْآخِرِينَ (78)
سَلَامٌ عَلَى نُوحٍ فِي الْعَالَمِينَ (79) إِنَّا كَذَلِكَ نَجْزِي الْمُحْسِنِينَ (80) (الصافات: 75–80)
Noah called out to Us, and how gracious was the Hearer of his prayer. (75) We saved him and his family from serious grief, (76) and set his offspring up as survivors. (77) We left (mention) of him among later generations: (78) "Peace be upon Noah throughout the Universe!" (79) Thus We reward those who act kindly. (Al-Sa'fa't: 75–80)

Inclusion of minute benevolent deeds
مَا كَانَ لِأَهْلِ الْمَدِينَةِ وَمَنْ حَوْلَهُمْ مِنَ الْأَعْرَابِ أَنْ يَتَخَلَّفُوا عَنْ رَسُولِ اللَّهِ وَلَا يَرْغَبُوا بِأَنْفُسِهِمْ عَنْ نَفْسِهِ ذَلِكَ بِأَنَّهُمْ لَا يُصِيبُهُمْ ظَمَأٌ وَلَا نَصَبٌ وَلَا مَخْمَصَةٌ فِي سَبِيلِ اللَّهِ وَلَا يَطَئُونَ مَوْطِئًا يَغِيظُ الْكُفَّارَ وَلَا يَنَالُونَ مِنْ عَدُوٍّ نَيْلًا إِلَّا كُتِبَ لَهُمْ بِهِ عَمَلٌ صَالِحٌ إِنَّ اللَّهَ لَا يُضِيعُ أَجْرَ الْمُحْسِنِينَ (التوبه: 120)
The inhabitants of the city of Medina and the desert Arabs dwelling around it were not supposed to disobey the Messenger of God or to give priority to their own lives above that of the Prophet. For if they had given priority to the life of the Messenger of God, they would not have experienced the hardships of thirst, fatigue, or hunger in their struggle for the cause of God, nor would their travelling have enraged the disbelievers and they would not have received any injury from enemies that God would not record for them as a virtuous deed. God does not ignore the reward of those who do good. (Al-Toba': 120)

Finding unpredictable events tolerable
فَلَمَّا أَسْلَمَا وَتَلَّهُ لِلْجَبِينِ (103) وَنَادَيْنَاهُ أَنْ يَا إِبْرَاهِيمُ (104) قَدْ صَدَّقْتَ الرُّؤْيَا إِنَّا كَذَلِكَ نَجْزِي الْمُحْسِنِينَ (105) إِنَّ هَذَا لَهُوَ الْبَلَاءُ الْمُبِينُ (601) وَفَدَيْنَاهُ بِذِبْحٍ عَظِيمٍ (107) وَتَرَكْنَا عَلَيْهِ فِي الْآخِرِينَ (108) سَلَامٌ عَلَى إِبْرَاهِيمَ (109) كَذَلِكَ نَجْزِي الْمُحْسِنِينَ (110) (الصافات: (110–103
When they both had committed themselves peacefully (to God) and he had placed him face down, (103) We called out to him: "Abraham, (104) you have already confirmed the dream!" (105) Thus We reward those who act kindly. (106) This was an obvious test. (107) We ransomed him by means of a splendid victim, (108) and left (him to be mentioned) among later men: "Peace be upon Abraham!" (109) Thus We reward those who act kindly. (110) (Al-Sa'fa't: 103–110)

performing the duty determines for himself/herself or the amount determined by the level of poverty estimated by the Islamic government (as absolute poverty line) in order to estimates the tax rate (Zakat and other charges) which the government imposes on the economically able and provides to the poor. The rule governing the Haqq Ma'lum (acknowledged right), however, relates to the situation where this amount is not sufficient in covering the livelihood of the poor necessitating additional assistance (beyond Zakat and other dues) that must be provided by people.

f. The Difference Between the Destitute ("سَّائِلِ", Sa'il) and the Deprived ("مَحْرُوم", Mahrum)

Holy Qur'an uses the terms destitute ("سَّائِلِ") to refer to the needy who begs openly for assistance with his livelihood and thus easily identified. The word deprived ("مَحْرُوم", Mahrum)), however, refers to those who feel shame in expressing their needs and therefore continue to live with deprivation. In some Riwayat the term "deprived" (Mahrum) is interpreted as a businessman who has gone bankrupt because such individuals do not display their impoverishment.

3.2 "Acknowledged Right" in the Riwayat of Ahl Al-Bayt (the "People of the House" of the Messenger (Sawa)

There are many Riwayat exist that indicate the Almighty has obligated the faithful believers to remit the "acknowledged right," as an additional duty beyond Zakat. In several instances, it has been referred to as Zakat Al-Batin, the inner Zakat, thus clarifying the obligatory nature of this duty. A few of these narrations are reported here:

1. Sama'ah Bin Mehran narrates from the Imam al-Sadiq (as) saying: "But Allah (swt) has imposed rights in the wealth of the rich other than Zakat. He (swt) has Said: 'And those in whose wealth there is known right due to the destitute and the deprived,' and the known right is other than Zakat. It is a duty that the individual imposes on himself to transfer from his wealth in accordance to his ability and the extent of his wealth. He can do so every day of the week or on each Friday or at the end of the month as he wishes."[25]
2. The position of the Messenger (sawa) on this issue was cited from Tafsir of Dorr Al-Manthur which reports a Hadeeth [saying narrated from the Messenger (sawa)]

25 Mohammad Hassan Al-Horr Al-Ameli, *Vasayel Al-Shia*, Vol. 9, (Qum: A'l Al-Bayt (PBUT) L-Eh'ya Al-Torath, 1416LH), 5–52.
وَ عَنْ مُحَمَّدِ بْنِ يَحْيَى عَنْ أَحْمَدَ بْنِ مُحَمَّدٍ عَنْ عُثْمَانَ بْنِ عِيسَى عَنْ سَمَاعَةَ بْنِ مِهْرَانَ عَنْ أَبِي عَبْدِ اَللَّهِ عَلَيْهِ اَلسَّلاَمُ قَالَ فِي حَدِيثٍ: وَ لَكِنَّ اَللَّهَ عَزَّ وَ جَلَّ فَرَضَ فِي أَمْوَالِ اَلْأَغْنِيَاءِ حُقُوقاً غَيْرَ اَلزَّكَاةِ فَقَالَ عَزَّ وَ جَلَّ وَ اَلَّذِينَ فِي أَمْوٰالِهِمْ حَقٌّ مَعْلُومٌ لِلسّٰائِلِ، فَالْحَقُّ اَلْمَعْلُومُ غَيْرُ اَلزَّكَاةِ وَ هُوَ شَيْءٌ يَفْرِضُهُ اَلرَّجُلُ عَلَى نَفْسِهِ فِي مَالِهِ يَجِبُ عَلَيْهِ أَنْ يَفْرِضَهُ عَلَى قَدْرِ طَاقَتِهِ وَ سَعَةِ مَالِهِ فَيُؤَدِّي اَلَّذِي فَرَضَ عَلَى نَفْسِهِ إِنْ شَاءَ فِي كُلِّ يَوْمٍ وَ إِنْ شَاءَ فِي كُلِّ جُمْعَةٍ ، وَ إِنْ شَاءَ فِي كُلِّ شَهْرٍ.

narrated by Fatimah Bint Qays to the effect that there are rights in the wealth other than Zakat,[26] thus confirming that the redemption of the rights of the poor, destitute and deprived in one's wealth is an obligatory duty.

3. Abi Basir recalls a meeting with the Imam al-Sadiq (as), where some wealthy people were also present and mentioned Zakat to which the Imam responded: "Payment of Zakat does not bring its payer praise because it is paid in the open by the payer, it saves his blood from being shed while he is called a Muslim while its non-payment makes his prayers (Salat) unacceptable. Indeed, there is for you other duties than Zakat in your wealth." Abi Basir reported "I then asked him, what else is ordained for us in our wealth other than Zakat? The Imam responded: "Allah be praised, have you not heard Allah (swt) saying in His book 'And those in whose wealth there is a known Haqq (right) for the destitute and the deprived'? I then asked him what is this known right? He replied: "it is the amounts an individual (remits to the poor) from his wealth every day of the weak or on every Friday or in a month or more and he perseveres in doing so continuously."[27]
4. Sadouq narrated, without mentioning the name of the transmitters, and Sheikh Tousi narrated, relying on Koleyni, from Imam al-Sadiq (as) who stated: "Do you think that the Almighty has obligated you to pay only Zakat from your wealth? Obligations other than Zakat that Allah has ordained to be paid out of your wealth is beyond Zakat and which must be paid to your poor relatives and to whomsoever that comes to you and asks you for assistance.[28]
5. Isma'il Bin Jaber inquired from Imam al-Sadeq (as) about the Verse of the Qur'an on "acknowledged right" and whether it is distinct from Zakat. The Imam responded: "The Almighty has bestowed individuals with riches out of which he

---

26 Mahmoud Bin Zamakhshari, *Tafsir Kashaf*, Vol. 4, (Beirut: Dar Al-Kitab Al-Arabi), 611.
اَخْرِج اَلْبِيهَقَى فِي سُنَنَه عَنْ فاطَمه بِنْت قِيْس إنَّهَا سَألَتَ اَلنَبِيَّ هَذه اَلأيَه (وَ فِي أَمْوَالِهِمْ حَقٌّ مَعْلُومٌ) قَالَ فِي اَلْمَالِ حَقٌّ سِوَى اَلزَّكَاةِ.

27 Mohammad Hassan Al-Horr Al-Ameli, *Vasayel Al-Shia*, Vol. 9, (Qum: A'l Al-Bayt (PBUT) L-Eh'ya Al-Torath, 1416LH), 45–52.
وَ عَنْ عَلِيِّ بْنِ إِبْرَاهِيمَ عَنْ أَبِيهِ عَنِ اَلْحُسَيْنِ بْنِ سَعِيدٍ عَنْ فَضَالَةَ بْنِ أَيُّوبَ عَنْ أَبِي اَلْمَغْرَاءِ عَنْ أَبِي بَصِيرٍ قَالَ: كُنَّا عِنْدَ أَبِي عَبْدِ اَللَّهِ عَلَيْهِ اَلسَّلاَمُ وَ مَعَنَا بَعْضُ أَصْحَابِ اَلْأَمْوَالِ فَذَكَرُوا اَلزَّكَاةَ فَقَالَ أَبُو عَبْدِ اَللَّهِ عَلَيْهِ اَلسَّلاَمُ ، إِنَّ اَلزَّكَاةَ لَيْسَ يُحْمَدُ بِهَا صَاحِبُهَا وَ إِنَّمَا هُوَ شَيْءٌ ظَاهِرٌ إِنَّمَا حَقَنَ بِهَا دَمَهُ وَ سُمِّيَ بِهَا مُسْلِماً وَ لَوْ لَمْ يُؤَدِّهَا لَمْ تُقْبَلْ لَهُ صَلاَةٌ وَ إِنَّ عَلَيْكُمْ فِي أَمْوَالِكُمْ غَيْرَ اَلزَّكَاةِ فَقُلْتُ أَصْلَحَكَ اَللَّهُ وَ مَا عَلَيْنَا فِي أَمْوَالِنَا غَيْرُ اَلزَّكَاةِ فَقَالَ سُبْحَانَ اَللَّهِ أَ مَا تَسْمَعُ اَللَّهَ عَزَّ وَ جَلَّ يَقُولُ فِي كِتَابِهِ وَ اَلَّذِينَ فِي أَمْوَالِهِمْ حَقٌّ مَعْلُومٌ لِلسّٰائِلِ وَ اَلْمَحْرُومِ قَالَ قُلْتُ مَا ذَا اَلْحَقُّ اَلْمَعْلُومُ اَلَّذِي عَلَيْنَا قَالَ هُوَ اَلشَّيْءُ اَلَّذِي يَعْمَلُهُ اَلرَّجُلُ فِي مَالِهِ يُعْطِيهِ فِي اَلْيَوْمِ أَوْ فِي اَلْجُمْعَةِ أَوْ فِي اَلشَّهْرِ قَلَّ أَوْ كَثُرَ غَيْرَ أَنَّهُ يَدُومُ عَلَيْهِ.

28 Mohammad Hassan Al-Horr Al-Ameli, *Vasayel Al-Shia*, Vol. 9, (Qum: A'l Al-Bayt (PBUT) L-Eh'ya Al-Torath, 1416LH), 45–52.
وَ عَنْ عِدَّةٍ مِنْ أَصْحَابِنَا عَنْ أَحْمَدَ بْنِ مُحَمَّدٍ عَنْ عَلِيِّ بْنِ اَلْحَكَمِ عَنْ مُثَنًّى عَنْ أَبِي بَصِيرٍ فِي حَدِيثٍ قَالَ: قَالَ أَبُو عَبْدِ اَللَّهِ عَلَيْهِ اَلسَّلاَمُ: أَ تَرَوْنَ أَنَّمَا فِي اَلْمَالِ اَلزَّكَاةُ وَحْدَهَا مَا فَرَضَ اَللَّهُ فِي اَلْمَالِ مِنْ غَيْرِ اَلزَّكَاةِ أَكْثَرُ تُعْطِي مِنْهُ اَلْقَرَابَةَ وَ اَلْمُعْتَرِضَ لَكَ مِمَّنْ يَسْأَلُكَ. وَ رَوَاهُاَلشَّيْخُبِإِسْنَادِهِعَ نْمُحَمَّدِ بْنِيَعْقُوبَ؛ وَ رَوَاهُاَلْمُفِيدُ فِي اَلْمُقْنِعَةِمُرْسَلاً.

spends a thousand dirhams, two thousand, or even three thousand or more or else to cover the needs of their relatives or unburden an encumbrance of the society."[29]

6. Qasim Bin 'Abd al-Rahman Al-Ansari narrates from Imam al-Baqir (as) that a man approached his father Ali Bin Hossein (as) and asked the meaning of the Verse of the Qur'an about "acknowledged right." The Imam told him: "The 'acknowledged right' is the amount, which is neither Zakat nor Sadaqah (obligatory transfer payments other than Zakat) that is remitted from one's wealth." The man then asked: "If it is neither of those obligations, then what is it?" Imam answered: "It has to be set aside by the individual from his wealth either more or less than he can afford." The man further asked: "What is then done with it?" The Imam replied: "It can be spent on (economically less able) relatives, or to support the needy, assist the weak, remove a burden (from others), or use it to establish contact with a brother in faith or help him in overcome a calamity." Upon hearing this response, the man exclaimed: "Allah knows where best to place His Message (meaning that Allah has chosen the Ahl al-Bayt as the receptors of His message)."[30]
7. In a narration by Mofadhdhal, a companion of the Imam al-Sadiq (as), states that a man asked Imam al-Sadiq (as) about the amount of Zakat. The Imam asked: "Which kind of Zakat do you want to know about, Zakat Al-Zahir (apparent and obligatory) or Zakat Al-Batin (the inner/non-apparent Zakat)?" The man replied: "I want to know both." The Imam responded: "In case of Zakat Al-Zahir, it is 25 dirhams per every 1,000 dirhams of wealth. But for Zakat Al-Batin, you should never keep for yourself that which your brother (in faith) needs more than you (i.e. there is no exact amount and it depends on the needs of the poor and the ability of the giver)."[31]
8. Koleyni cites Sama'ah Bin Mehran who narrated form Imam al-Sadiq (as) saying: "The 'acknowledged right' is not the same as Zakat. It consists of the amount that

29 Mohammad Hassan Al-Horr Al-Ameli, *Vasayel Al-Shia*, Vol. 9, (Qum: A'l Al-Bayt (PBUT) L-Eh'ya Al-Torath, 1416LH), 45–52.
وَ عَنْ عَلِيِّ بْنِ مُحَمَّدِ بْنِ عَبْدِ اَللَّهِ عَنْ أَحْمَدَ بْنِ مُحَمَّدِ بْنِ خَالِدٍ عَنْ عُثْمَانَ بْنِ عِيسَى عَنْ إِسْمَاعِيلَ بْنِ جَابِرٍ عَنْ أَبِي عَبْدِ اَللَّهِ عَلَيْهِ اَلسَّلاَمُ: فِي قَوْلِ اَللَّهِ عَزَّ وَ جَلَّ وَ اَلَّذِينَ فِي أَمْوٰالِهِمْ حَقٌّ مَعْلُومٌ لِلسّٰائِلِ وَ اَلْمَحْرُومِ، أَ هُوَ سِوَى اَلزَّكَاةِ فَقَالَ هُوَ اَلرَّجُلُ يُؤْتِيهِ اَللَّهُ اَلثَّرْوَةَ مِنَ اَلْمَالِ فَيُخْرِجُ مِنْهُ اَلْأَلْفَ وَ اَلْأَلْفَيْنِ وَ اَلثَّلاَثَةَ اَلْآلاَفِ وَ اَلْأَقَلَّ وَ اَلْأَكْثَرَ فَيَصِلُ بِهِ رَحِمَهُ وَ يَحْمِلُ بِهِ اَلْكَلَّ عَنْ قَوْمِهِ.

30 Mohammad Hassan Al-Horr Al-Ameli, *Vasayel Al-Shia*, Vol. 9, (Qum: A'l Al-Bayt (PBUT) L-Eh'ya Al-Torath, 1416LH), 45–52.
وَ عَنْهُ عَنْ أَحْمَدَ بْنِ مُحَمَّدٍ عَنِ اِبْنِ مَحْبُوبٍ عَنْ عَبْدِ اَلرَّحْمَنِ بْنِ اَلْحَجَّاجِ عَنِ اَلْقَاسِمِ بْنِ عَبْدِ اَلرَّحْمَنِ اَلْأَنْصَارِيِّ قَالَ سَمِعْتُ أَبَا جَعْفَرٍ عَلَيْهِ اَلسَّلاَمُ يَقُولُ: إِنَّ رَجُلاً جَاءَ إِلَى أَبِي عَلِيِّ بْنِ اَلْحُسَيْنِ عَلَيْهِمَا اَلسَّلاَمُ ، فَقَالَ لَهُ أَخْبِرْنِي عَنْ قَوْلِ اَللَّهِ عَزَّ وَ جَلَّ وَ اَلَّذِينَ فِي أَمْوٰالِهِمْ حَقٌّ مَعْلُومٌ لِلسّٰائِلِ وَ اَلْمَحْرُومِ، مَا هَذَا اَلْحَقُّ اَلْمَعْلُومُ فَقَالَ لَهُ عَلِيُّ بْنُ اَلْحُسَيْنِ عَلَيْهِمَا اَلسَّلاَمُ ، اَلْحَقُّ اَلْمَعْلُومُ اَلشَّيْءُ يُخْرِجُهُ مِنْ مَالِهِ لَيْسَ مِنَ اَلزَّكَاةِ وَ لاَ مِنَ اَلصَّدَقَةِ اَلْمَفْرُوضَتَيْنِ قَالَ فَإِذَا لَمْ يَكُنْ مِنَ اَلزَّكَاةِ وَ لاَ مِنَ اَلصَّدَقَةِ فَمَا هُوَ فَقَالَ هُوَ اَلشَّيْءُ يُخْرِجُهُ اَلرَّجُلُ مِنْ مَالِهِ إِنْ شَاءَ أَكْثَرَ وَ إِنْ شَاءَ أَقَلَّ عَلَى قَدْرِ مَا يَمْلِكُ فَقَالَ لَهُ اَلرَّجُلُ فَمَا يَصْنَعُ بِهِ فَقَالَ يَصِلُ بِهِ رَحِماً وَ يُقَوِّي بِهِ ضَعِيفاً وَ يَحْمِلُ بِهِ كَلاًّ أَوْ يَصِلُ بِهِ أَخاً لَهُ فِي اَللَّهِ أَوْ لِنَائِبَةٍ تَنُوبُهُ، فَقَالَ اَلرَّجُلُ اَللَّهُ أَعْلَمُ حَيْثُ يَجْعَلُ رِسَالاَتِهِ.

31 Mohammad Hassan Al-Horr Al-Ameli, *Vasayel Al-Shia*, Vol. 9, (Qum: A'l Al-Bayt (PBUT) L-Eh'ya Al-Torath, 1416LH), 45–52.
مُحَمَّدُ بْنُ عَلِيِّ بْنِ اَلْحُسَيْنِ فِي مَعَانِي اَلْأَخْبَارِ عَنْ مُحَمَّدِ بْنِ اَلْحَسَنِ عَنْ أَحْمَدَ بْنِ إِدْرِيسَ عَنْ مُحَمَّدِ بْنِ أَحْمَدَ عَنْ أَبِي عَبْدِ اَللَّهِ اَلرَّازِيِّ عَنْ نَصْرِ بْنِ صَبَّاحٍ عَنِ اَلْمُفَضَّلِ بْنِ عُمَرَ قَالَ: كُنْتُ عِنْدَ أَبِي عَبْدِ اَللَّهِ عَلَيْهِ اَلسَّلاَمُ فَسَأَلَهُ رَجُلٌ فِي كَمْ تَجِبُ اَلزَّكَاةُ مِنَ اَلْمَالِ فَقَالَ لَهُ اَلزَّكَاةَ اَلظَّاهِرَةَ أَمِ اَلْبَاطِنَةَ تُرِيدُ فَقَالَ أُرِيدُهُمَا جَمِيعاً فَقَالَ أَمَّا اَلظَّاهِرَةُ فَفِي كُلِّ أَلْفٍ خَمْسَةٌ وَ عِشْرُونَ دِرْهَماً وَ أَمَّا اَلْبَاطِنَةُ فَلاَ تَسْتَأْثِرْ عَلَى أَخِيكَ بِمَا هُوَ أَحْوَجُ إِلَيْكَ مِنْكَ.

you set aside from your wealth, either on each Friday (weekly) or monthly." At the end of the narration, the Imam said: "In the Verse "And in their wealth there is an 'acknowledged right,' the "right" is other than Zakat. It refers to an amount that the individual makes obligatory on himself in his life and wealth which must be redeemed based on his ability and extent of his wealth."[32]

9. Ammar Sabbati narrated that Imam al-Sadiq (as) once asked me: "O Ammar! Do you have much assets?" I responded: "Yes, may I be ransomed for you." The Imam then asked: "Then do you pay all your Zakat dues punctually?" "Of course, I said." The Imam then asked: "And do you also set aside 'acknowledged right' from your wealth as well?" "Yes, I responded." The Imam asked: "Do you then give it to your brothers?" Yes, I said. The Imam then said "O Ammar! Remember that wealth will vanish; human bodies will decompose; but deeds persist, only the Almighty is ever-living and does not die."[33]
10. In another Riwayah, Sheikh Tousi, relying on his own documentation, narrates from Mojasha'ei who quotes the Imam al-Ridh narrating from his forefathers that the Messenger (sawa) was once asked: "O Prophet of Allah is there any other any other right in wealth than the Zakat?" He replied: "Yes, kindness to a relative who has lost his wealth and social status and assistance to the neighbor!" He then said: "Does not believe in me he who sleeps nights with a full stomach when his neighbor spends the night in hunger."[34]
11. 'Ayyashi in his book *Tafsir* narrates from Sama'ah bin Mehran that I asked Imam al-Sadiq (as) about the Verse of the Qur'an "وَالَّذِينَ يَصِلُونَ مَا أَمَرَ اللَّهُ بِهِ أَنْ يُوصَلَ" (Al-Ra'd, 13: 21; in part: "And those who connect/join what Allah has ordained to be connected/joined". The Imam replied: "It is what Allah has ordained an individual to spend, other than Zakat, from his wealth (on his needy relatives); anyone

---

32 Mohammad Hassan Al-Horr Al-Ameli, *Vasayel Al-Shia*, Vol. 9, (Qum: A'l Al-Bayt (PBUT) L-Eh'ya Al-Torath, 1416LH), 45–52.
وَ بِإِسْنَادِهِ عَنْ سَمَاعَةَ عَنْ أَبِي عَبْدِ اَللَّهِ عَلَيْهِ اَلسَّلاَمُ قَالَ: اَلْحَقُّ اَلْمَعْلُومُ لَيْسَ مِنَ اَلزَّكَاةِ هُوَ اَلشَّيْءُ تُخْرِجُهُ مِنْ مَالِكَ إِنْ شِئْتَ كُلَّ جُمْعَةٍ ، وَ إِنْ شِئْتَ كُلَّ شَهْرٍ وَ لِكُلِّ ذِيفَضْلٍ فَضْلُهُ وَ قَوْلُ اَللَّهِ عَزَّ وَ جَلَّ وَ إِنْ تُخْفُوهَا وَ تُؤْتُوهَا اَلْفُقَرٰاءَ فَهُوَ خَيْرٌ لَكُمْ فَلَيْسَ هُوَ مِنَ اَلزَّكَاةِ وَ اَلْمَاعُونُ لَيْسَ مِنَ اَلزَّكَاةِ هُوَ اَلْمَعْرُوفُ تَصْنَعُهُ وَ اَلْقَرْضُ تُقْرِضُهُ وَ مَتَاعُ اَلْبَيْتِ تُعِيرُهُ وَ صِلَةُ قَرَابَتِكَ لَيْسَ مِنَ اَلزَّكَاةِ وَ قَالَ اَللَّهُ عَزَّ وَ جَلَّ وَ اَلَّذِينَ فِي أَمْوٰالِهِمْ حَقٌّ مَعْلُومٌ، فَالْحَقُّ اَلْمَعْلُومُ غَيْرُ اَلزَّكَاةِ وَ هُوَ شَيْءٌ يَفْرِضُهُ اَلرَّجُلُ عَلَى نَفْسِهِ أَنَّهُ فِي مَالِهِ وَ نَفْسِهِ يَجِبُ أَنْ يَفْرِضَهُ عَلَى قَدْرِ طَاقَتِهِ وَ وُسْعِهِ.

33 Mohammad Hassan Al-Horr Al-Ameli, *Vasayel Al-Shia*, Vol. 9, (Qum: A'l Al-Bayt (PBUT) L-Eh'ya Al-Torath, 1416LH), 45–52.
مُحَمَّدُ بْنُ عَلِيِّ بْنِ اَلْحُسَيْنِ بِإِسْنَادِهِ عَنْ عَمَّارٍ اَلسَّابَاطِيِّ أَنَّ اَلصَّادِقَ عَلَيْهِ اَلسَّلاَمُ قَالَ لَهُ: يَا عَمَّارُ أَنْتَ رَبُّ مَالٍ كَثِيرٍ قَالَ نَعَمْ جُعِلْتُ فِدَاكَ قَالَ فَتُؤَدِّي مَا اِفْتَرَضَ اَللَّهُ عَلَيْكَ مِنَ اَلزَّكَاةِ فَقَالَ نَعَمْ قَالَ فَتُخْرِجُ اَلْحَقَّ اَلْمَعْلُومَ مِنْ مَالِكَ قَالَ نَعَمْ قَالَ (فَتَصِلُ قَرَابَتَكَ) قَالَ نَعَمْ قَالَ فَتَصِلُ إِخْوَانَكَ قَالَ نَعَمْ قَالَ عَلَيْهِ اَلسَّلاَمُ يَا عَمَّارُ إِنَّ اَلْمَالَ يَفْنَى وَ اَلْبَدَنَ يَبْلَى وَ اَلْعَمَلَ يَبْقَى وَ اَلدَّيَّانَ حَيٌّ لاَ يَمُوتُ يَا عَمَّارُ أَمَا إِنَّهُ مَا قَدَّمْتَ فَلَنْ يَسْبِقَكَ وَ مَا أَخَّرْتَ فَلَنْ يَلْحَقَكَ. وَ رَوَاهُ اَلْكُلَيْنِيُّ عَنْ أَحْمَدَ بْنِ مُحَمَّدِ بْنِ عَبْدِ اَللَّهِ وَ غَيْرِهِ عَنْ أَحْمَدَ بْنِ أَبِي عَبْدِ اَللَّهِ عَنْ أَبِيهِ عَنْ عَبْدِ اَللَّهِ بْنِ اَلْقَاسِمِ عَنْ رَجُلٍ مِنْ أَهْلِ سَابَاطَ قَالَ: قَالَ أَبُو عَبْدِ اَللَّهِ عَلَيْهِ اَلسَّلاَمُ لِعَمَّارٍ اَلسَّابَاطِيِّ: وَ ذَكَرَ مِثْلَهُ وَ رَوَاهُ أَيْضاً عَنْ عَلِيِّ بْنِ مُحَمَّدِ بْنِ بُنْدَارَ وَ غَيْرِهِ عَنْ أَحْمَدَ بْنِ أَبِي عَبْدِ اَللَّهِ: مِثْلَهُ.

34 Mohammad Hassan Al-Horr Al-Ameli, *Vasayel Al-Shia*, Vol. 9, (Qum: A'l Al-Bayt (PBUT) L-Eh'ya Al-Torath, 1416LH), 45–52.
اَلْحَسَنُ بْنُ مُحَمَّدٍ اَلطُّوسِيُّ فِي مَجَالِسِهِ بِالْإِسْنَادِ اَلسَّابِقِ فِي مَنْعِ اَلزَّكَاةِ عَنِ اَلرِّضَا عَنْ آبَائِهِ عَلَيْهِمُ اَلسَّلاَمُ قَالَ: قِيلَ يَا نَبِيَّ اَللَّهِ فِي اَلْمَالِ حَقٌّ سِوَى اَلزَّكَاةِ قَالَ نَعَمْ بِرُّ اَلرَّحِمِ إِذَا أَدْبَرَتْ وَ صِلَةُ اَلْجَارِ اَلْمُسْلِمِ فَمَا (آمَنَ بِي) مَنْ بَاتَ شَبْعَاناً [شَبْعَانَ] وَ جَارُهُ اَلْمُسْلِمُ جَائِعٌ ثُمَّ قَالَ مَا زَالَ جَبْرَئِيلُ يُوصِينِي بِالْجَارِ حَتَّى ظَنَنْتُ أَنَّهُ سَيُوَرِّثُهُ.

who obeys Allah's command has indeed complied with what has been ordained for him."[35]

12. In another Riwayah reported by Koleyni, 'Aamer Bin Juza'ah narrated that someone approached the Imam al-Sadiq (as) and asked: "Can you loan me some money until the time I am able to repay it?" The Imam asked: "Do you own any cereal which you can sell me in exchange for the loan?" The mean said no. The Imam asked: "Can you engage in any trade with the proceed of which you can repay the debt?" The man said no. The Imam asked: "Is there any kind of transactions you can undertake with the proceeds of which you can repay the debt?" The man sad no. The Imam then said: "You are the of those for whom Allah has ordained a right in our wealth." The Imam then ordered that a sack in which there were some money to be brought to him out of which the Imam took a handful and gave it to the man. The Imam then told the man: "Fear Allah, do not be wasteful in your spending nor spend too little because strength and stability lie between these two extremes. Indeed, extravagant spending is also wasteful."
13. Koleyni cites Safwan Bin Jammal who had inquired from Imam al-Sadiq (as) about the terms destitute ("سَّائِلِ") and deprived ("مَحْرُومِ"). The Imam replied: "The term "deprived, Mahrum" refers to an individual whose earnings from an occupation is not sufficient to cover his livelihood."[36]
14. Koleyni quotes Imam al-Baqir (as) and Imam al-Sadiq (as) without documentation: "The deprived denotes an individual who is not irrational but one whose sustenance has not expanded."[37]

3.3 "Acknowledged Right" (Zakat Al-Batin) and its Criteria in the Riwayat

From the above-mentioned Riwayat, the following deductions are possible:

1. It can be inferred from narrations 1–4, 6 and 8–10, as well as the Verse of the Qur'an quoted above that "acknowledged right" is an obligation other than

35 Mohammad Hassan Al-Horr Al-Ameli, *Vasayel Al-Shia*, Vol. 9, (Qum: A'l Al-Bayt (PBUT) L-Eh'ya Al-Torath, 1416LH), 45–52.
اَلْعَيَّاشِيُّ فِي تَفْسِيرِهِ عَنْ سَمَاعَةَ قَالَ: سَأَلْتُهُ عَنْ قَوْلِ اَللَّهِ عَزَّ وَ جَلَّ وَ اَلَّذِينَ يَصِلُونَ مٰا أَمَرَ اَللّٰهُ بِهِ أَنْ يُوصَلَ، فَقَالَ هُوَ مَا اِفْتَرَضَ اَللَّهُ فِي اَلْمَالِ غَيْرَ اَلزَّكَاةِ وَ مَنْ أَدَّى مَا اِفْتَرَضَ اَللَّهُ عَلَيْهِ فَقَدْ قَضَى مَا عَلَيْهِ.

36 Mohammad Hassan Al-Horr Al-Ameli, *Vasayel Al-Shia*, Vol. 9, (Qum: A'l Al-Bayt (PBUT) L-Eh'ya Al-Torath, 1416LH), 45–52.
وَ عَنْهُ عَنِ اِبْنِ فَضَّالٍ عَنْ صَفْوَانَ اَلْجَمَّالِ عَنْ أَبِي عَبْدِ اَللَّهِ عَلَيْهِ اَلسَّلاَمُ: فِي قَوْلِ اَللَّهِ عَزَّ وَ جَلَّ لِلسّٰائِلِ وَ اَلْمَحْرُومِ، قَالَ اَلْمَحْرُومُ اَلْمُحَارَفُ اَلَّذِي قَدْ حُرِمَ كَدَّ يَدِهِ فِي اَلشِّرَاءِ وَ اَلْبَيْعِ.

37 Mohammad Hassan Al-Horr Al-Ameli, *Vasayel Al-Shia*, Vol. 9, (Qum: A'l Al-Bayt (PBUT) L-Eh'ya Al-Torath, 1416LH), 45–52.
قَالَ اَلْكُلَيْنِيُّ وَ فِي رِوَايَةٍ أُخْرَى عَنْ أَبِي جَعْفَرٍ وَ أَبِي عَبْدِ اَللَّهِ عَلَيْهِمَا اَلسَّلاَمُ أَنَّهُمَا قَالاَ: اَلْمَحْرُومُ اَلرَّجُلُ اَلَّذِي لَيْسَ بِعَقْلِهِ بَأْسٌ وَ لَمْ يُبْسَطْ لَهُ فِي اَلرِّزْقِ وَ هُوَ مُحَارَفٌ. وَ رَوَاهُ اَلشَّيْخُ بِإِسْنَادِهِ عَنْ مُحَمَّدِ بْنِ يَعْقُوبَ وَ كَذَا اَلَّذِي قَبْلَهُ.

Zakat. It is inferred from the narration 6 that this right is different from Zakat Al-Fitr (Zakat on body paid, for example after the end of the Month of Ramadhan) or Zakat Al-Zahir, while the narration 7 refers to "acknowledged right" as Zakat Al-Batin. Further, narration emphasizes that there are other obligations than Zakat like "acknowledged right." For instance, *Al-Ma'un* (small household articles that neighbors or friends borrow from each other for temporary use without any consideration), *Al-'Ariyah'* (to allow another person receive benefit from one's property without any consideration), *Qardh* (Loan of money with the stipulation to return the principle only in the future) and *Silat' Al-Rahim* (being in touch with relatives and assisting them financially if they are in need of such help) which either jointly or individually can be considered as examples of the "known right."

2. Narration 3 mentions that the Zakat Al-Zahir is collected by the government mandatorily (similar to tax collection and if someone evades payment, he would be chastised or, if his refusal to pay his Zakat becomes violent, he may lose his life). Hence, the Imam (PBUH) stresses that paying the ordained Zakat does not earn any praise for the payer. Payment of Zakat results in person's affiliation to Islam, but "acknowledged right" does not concern the government and is an obligation that depend on the commitment and the ethics of individuals. That is why it is called "Zakat Batin" meaning that the inner dimension of individuals is involved in meeting this obligation.
3. From narrations 1, 3 and 9 it can be inferred that the amount of this obligation depends on the ability of the individual and the extent of his wealth independent of government intervention.
4. That the amount of "acknowledged right" depends on the individuals' capability and wealth is inferred from narrations 1 and 6.
5. Narrations 1, 3 and 9 suggest that the time for redemption of "acknowledged right" is not annual like Zakat, but it can be paid daily, weekly or monthly. Furthermore, the payment must be consistently carried out throughout the year, depending on the need of the poor (narration 3). From narration 4, we learn that the timing of redemption is when the poor ask for help or the time the person realizes that the person becomes aware that a deprived person is ashamed of asking for help. From narration 7, it can be inferred that when a number of needs in relation to resources, the necessary needs of the poor and those of one's brother in faith must take priority.
6. It is deduced from narration 7 also that "acknowledged right" does not have any definite measure or limit (the way Zakat is determined by its limit or the payments of taxes which are determined by the government). It depends on the requirements of the Muslims, while anecdote/apothegm 5 puts its amount as high as thousands of dirhams.

7. It can be inferred from narrations 4, 5, 9 and 11 that the obligatory *Silah Al-Rahim (maintaining familial ties)* and "acknowledged right" can be combined to support the needy in one's family.
8. From narrations 13 and 14, that redemption of "acknowledged right" is generally applicable to all types of poor including those who solicit openly as well as those who are employed but their earning are not sufficient to cover their livelihood but nevertheless try to maintain the best face and not openly ask for assistance (indicating that, as Islam ordains, one must at all times be aware of the needs of one's family, neighbors and acquaintances).

Overall, it can be concluded that "acknowledged right" is an obligation whose amount is decided by the individual according to his ability and wealth, as well as the needs of the poor. It is different from Zakat and the tax that is mandated by the government.

3.4 Status of "Acknowledged Right" Besides Other Financial Resources for Supporting the Poor

A. Status of Other Financial Resources for Supplying the Destitute

Each and every financial resource of the government includes a special designation devoted to the financing of the needs of the poor and are different than that of "acknowledged right." These are discussed in the following sections:

i. Zakat Al-Amwal (Zakat on Property/Zakat Al-Zahir)

The Almighty has commanded Zakat tax levied on all private or public wealth to be used for specific purposes. There are some differences among the Fuqaha as to what types of wealth and assets are subject to Zakat. There are two principle views. The first is the well-known position that Zakat is levied on only the traditional 9 items (wheat, barley, dates, raisins, gold, silver, camels, cows, and sheep) that were subject to Zakat in the earliest period of Muslim history. The second view argues that Islam is a universal message with rules applicable to all times and places and Zakat, as one of these rules, must be relevant to time and place. This view argues that the basis of Zakat, therefore, must be appropriately designed appropriately. Consequently, this view suggests that the decision on items that must be subject to Zakat must be left to the Muslim state.[38]

38 See Hossein Ali Montazeri, Vol. 2 Ketab Al-Zakat, (Qum: Dar Al-Fikr Publication, 1409 LH), 145.

Accepting the more expansive view raises various points as follows:

1. The items on which Zakat can be levied, as well as its amount, must be defined by the Muslim state on an annual basis which requires new analysis of components of subjects involved in the discussions of Zakat.
2. Taking into account the annual periodicity of Zakat, and the fact that part of it must be utilized to facilitate the livelihood of the poor, the Muslim State must estimate the annual livelihood of the poor as well as other demands to be supplied by Zakat resources (based on the Verse 60 of Chapter 9, Al-Tobah[39]). The state must then designate the assets that will be subject to Zakat. Therefore, the state must estimate revenues and expenditure for each upcoming year, as has been reported in a number of narrations, to ensure there is sufficient Zakat resources.
3. Verse of the Qur'an (60:9) that lists specific items for which Zakat resources are used shows that all assets of the society constitute the basic source of Zakat. This means that the state must estimate the amounts of financial resources it needs to ensure that the livelihood expenses of the poor are met in the coming year and then decide which items of wealth must be subjected to Zakat to ensure sufficient resources for meeting the needs of the poor. There is therefore no difference between estimating the revenue-expenditure for the general annual budget of the state and that of estimating the annual financial requirements to meet the estimated livelihood needs of the poor.

ii. Zakat Al-Fitrah

This type of Zakat, also interpreted as Zakat on bodies (Zakat Al-Abdan), is calculated per head of family members, with the hope to contribute to the healthiness of the head and the members of family. It is aimed at alleviating part of the requirements of the needy and constitutes one of the obligatory financial assistance provided by the public which can either be given to the Imam (the state) or be spent on the poor by the Zakat payer. Zakat Al-Fitrah must be utilized to provide for basic needs of the poor, such as food. Muslim State must estimate this type of Zakat into its budgetary estimates for supporting the needy, and then levy Zakat Al-Amwal (Zakat on assets) accordingly. Zakat Al-Fitrah provides a good practice for per capita support and attending to the bodily health as well as paying Zakat in Muslim society.[40]

---

39 Al-Toba': 60.
إِنَّمَا الصَّدَقَاتُ لِلْفُقَرَاءِ وَالْمَسَاكِينِ وَالْعَامِلِينَ عَلَيْهَا وَالْمُؤَلَّفَةِ قُلُوبُهُمْ وَفِي الرِّقَابِ وَالْغَارِمِينَ وَفِي سَبِيلِ اللَّهِ وَابْنِ السَّبِيلِ فَرِيضَةً مِنَ اللَّهِ وَاللَّهُ عَلِيمٌ حَكِيمٌ
The obligatory charity is (meant) only for the poor, the needy, those working at (collecting and distributing) it, those (possible converts) whose hearts are being reconciled (to yours), for freeing captives and debtors, and in (striving along) God's way, and for the wayfarer, as a duty imposed by God. God is Aware and Wise.

40 See Majid Reza'ei, *Public Finance in Islam*, (Tehran: Samt Publications, 1389SH), 104.

iii. Al-Khums

This constitutes one of the financial obligations which is, under certain conditions, levied on some properties. Holy Qur'an states (Verse 41: Chapter 8) the amount of this levy as one-fifth of unexpected and windfall gains (*Qana'im*) incomes must be paid:[41]

" وَاعْلَمُوا أَنَّمَا غَنِمْتُمْ مِنْ شَيْءٍ فَأَنَّ لِلَّهِ خُمُسَهُ... "

> And know that whatever thing you gain, a fifth of it belongs to Allah and the Messenger and close relatives, the orphans, he destitute, and the wayfarer... (Al-An'fal, 8: 41; in part)

Qanimah (windfall gain) is therefore the prime type of gains that are subject to Al-Khums, but, in the course of time, other types of asset have also been added on the basis of various Riwayat. For instance, jewelry found accidentally at sea; a treasure trove found hidden on land; incomes and profits in excess of annual expenses of an individual; land sold to non-Muslim and other than "People of the Book" (i.e. monotheists consisting of Jews, Christians and Zoroastrians); and assets mixed inseparably with those of others which are of illicit (Haram) origin.[42] Consequently, it can be deduced that Al-Khums is a type of tax levied in order to rectify the insufficiencies and shortages in the economy. The detailed description and discussion of these is, however, beyond the scope of the present paper.

The poor and destitute are included in allocating the resources mobilized from this levy. Therefore, it is necessary that this kind of levy should be included in the annual determination of the rate of Zakat levy and the type of assets that are to be subject of its imposition.

iv. Al-Kharaj (Tribute)

One of the most important financial resources of Muslim government throughout the history has been Al-Kharaj. It is levied on properties and asset acquired by the government as a result of wars and the like and then has been leased to Muslims and non-Muslims in the private sector in order to generate revenues for the state.[43]

---

41 The etymological root of the term "Qanima'" ("غَنيمَت") is "Qanam" ("غَنَم") meaning "effortless and stress-free income which is greater than the expectations." Thus Qanima' indicates an easily-gained profit in excess of the anticipations of the individual and does not apply to ordinary profits, it is in fact greater in amount than that imagined or supposed. It is the antonym of Qaram ("غَرَم") which points to "compensation for an accidental loss."

42 See Majid Reza'ei, *op. cit.*

43 See Hossein Ali Montazeri, *Darasat fi Velayat Al-Faqih and Fiqh Al-Dolat Al-Islamiya*, Vol. 3, (Qum: Dar Al-Fikr Publications, 1411 LH), 363–499, and, Majid Reza'ei, *op. cit.*, 120.

Government, while estimating the Zakat al-Amwal levy, must take into consideration the revenues from Al-Kharaj in the budgetary estimations at the commencement of the fiscal year. Al-Kharaj can also be use for alleviation of poverty.

v. Al-Jizyah (Compensations from Non-Muslims)

It is a compensation for the security and protection extended to the the non-Muslims who live in Islamic territories. The Islamic government mandates such individuals to pay Al-Jizyah for protection of their lives and properties without any obligations to fight Muslim wars or to pay Zakat. Muslims living in Islamic territories are obligated to pay Zakat as well as other types of taxes, but "People of the Book" (i.e. monotheists consisting of Jews, Christians and Zoroastrians) who accept the rule of Islam and live under the protection of Islamic government are exempt. Instead, they participate in the costs of establishing community security and the rule of law by contributing Al-Jizyah. According to some anecdotes/apothegms, the Islamic ruler is obliged to bear the expenses of the protection of "People of the Book."[44]

vi. Al-Anfal (Spoils of War) and Al-Fai (Gains from Enemy without War)

Al-Anfal and Al-Fai are considered among the public properties withheld by the Islamic government and can be used to supply the financial needs of the destitute and the deprived. Etymologically, the term "Anfal" is rooted in "Nafl" ("نَفْلْ" or "نَفَلْ") meaning "excessive." It refers to properties which are either in excess of the properties being exploited by the private sector but are not being used in the private sector or are additional resources that is not in the public interest to allow their uses by the private sector or are those developed resources which have been gained by Muslims without doing any work on them. Al-Anfal can also be utilized for the benefit of the poor by the Islamic government.[45]

vii. "Acknowledged Right" in Alleviating Poverty

Zakat Al-Zahir, Al Khums and other financial resources as well as "acknowledged right" have all been established to provide for the livelihood of the poor. However, the Islamic government must first estimate the essential requirements of the poor along with other expenditures for administrating the state prior to the commencement of the fiscal year. Then, it can accordingly decide about the amount of Zakat Al-Zahir, Al-Anfal, Al-Kharaj etc. Nonetheless, if there is still insufficient resources, the economically able segment

44 See Hossein Ali Montazeri, *op. cit.* p. 373, and, Majid Reza'ei, *op. cit.*, p. 104.

45 See Majid Reza'ei, *op. cit.*, p. 104, and, Hossein Ali Montazeri, *op. cit.* pp. 194–256.

of the population must undertake the task of providing additional resources needed to satisfy the needs of the society. This obligation constitutes the "acknowledged right" which is similar to "enjoining good and forbidding wrong," and is classified under the category of "general public obligations" ("واجب کفایی"). Such obligatory acts are considered as a general responsibility upon the society, and if any individual performs them, the rest of the society are exempted. As a rule, all the inhabitants of the society must participate in meeting such demands in accordance to their affluence and amenities.

It can be concluded that the budgetary allocation of the Islamic state comprises a portion to cover the needs of the destitute, and the collected Zakat resources also include the share for poverty alleviation. However, "acknowledged right" is used for the unprecedented needs which have no budgetary allocations, such as the following:

1. The unconsidered essential needs of individuals.
2. The unforeseen essential needs of individuals that accidentally emerge during the fiscal.
3. The essential needs of individuals which are outside the capacities of the Islamic government to meet.

All such requirements are the instances for the use of "acknowledged right" for which Muslim community is responsible. Therefore, although Al-Khums, Zakat, Al-Kharaj and other financial resources of the Islamic government along with additional financial obligations by individuals are paid for supplying the livelihood of the poor, but if essential needs are still unmet, the obligations of of members of the society to provide resources for this purpose remains. Therefore, the "known or acknowledged right" of the poor in the wealth of the rich is an obligation imposed on all Muslims and is not part of resources that is not included in the budget of the government. The next section argues that ethics is the guarantee of implementation of this duty. well-to-do inhabitants of the society are not exempt.

3.5 Sanctioning of the "Acknowledged Right" by Ethics

As stated earlier, Zakat Al-Zahir, Al-Kharaj, Al-Jizyah, Al-Khums etc. constitute the financial resources ordained to provide for the expenditures of the Islamic government and must be determined prior to the commencement of the fiscal year. They are estimated based on the predicted government expenditures whether for the needy or any other purpose. While all the aforementioned types of financial obligations are ethically binding on inhabitants of the society, the Islamic government has been designated as the guarantor of their implementation. also endorsed rules and regulations. It can employ all the necessary means at its disposal to ensure implementation. However, "acknowledged right" differs in the sense that the guarantor of its implementation is the conscience of individual who are aware of the fact that it is duty ordained by Allah (swt). As a result, if other financial obligations of the people do not suffice to cover the essential needs of the poor, the members of the society are not exempt from the obligation of poverty alleviation. This obligation is similar to those such as Hijab, not lying, not back biting, and others whose implementation, when conditions are not exceptional, is left to the conscience of the individual. Therefore, ethics, conscience, and the fact that it is Allah who has ordained this duty guarantee the implementation of this duty as is also emphasized by the Qur'an.

3.5.1 Ethical Deed, The Motive for Paying "Acknowledged Right" in Holy Qur'an

Individuals who obliterate their greed and covetousness and they act without considering their own interests and listen to the voice of their conscience and therefore undertake to help others motivated by "other-loving" and for the interests of others as well as those who respond to the call of conscience, act ethically as was discussed above in presentation the two verses of the Qur'an (viz. Al-Ma'arij: 24, and Al-Zariyat: 19).

3.5.2 Diminution of the Self-interest as a Guarantor of Implementation of the "Acknowledged Right" as Deduced from Al-Ma'arij: 19–25

The redemption of obligatory "acknowledged right," as mentioned in the Verse 24 of Al-Ma'arij, intends to reduce greed and covetousness through perseverance in prayers and payment of the "acknowledged right." Both these actions are contrary to self-interests. When widespread poverty exists, self-interest runs contrary to attempts at alleviation of poverty. The Holy Qur'an implicitly points out that redeeming the rights of the poor in the wealth of rich is an ethical act whose guarantor is individual's conscience and a divine duty and not the government.

3.5.3 Enhancing "Other-Loving" Motive as a Guarantor of the Implementation of the Duty of Redeeming the "Acknowledged Right" as Deduced from Al-Zariyat: 15–19

Holy Qur'an recognizes payment of "acknowledged right" as a sign of beneficence in Al-Zariyat 19 and mentions that these individuals sleep very little during the night (spending the night in communion with their Creator) and seek forgiveness (from their Lord) in the early dawn during their prayers. They also assign a share of their wealth for the "acknowledged right." Doing good toward others indicates an incessant ethical act with "other-loving" motive as a characteristic of Muhsineen (those who do good for others without a self-interest motive). Therefore, in this Verse too there is an implicit acknowledgement that performing the duty of redeeming the right of the poor is ethical and the guarantor of its implementation is ethics.

4 Conclusion

It can be concluded that, in an Islamic society, "acknowledged right" is closely linked to ethics and can cover shortfalls in the government's role in the society. The government and the people can act in tandem as do the two wings of a bird in flight to compensate for market failure, in alleviation of poverty and in distribution of wealth. The Islamic government must estimate its revenues and expenditures first and then enact Zakat tax accordingly. If the government efforts as the main pillar to correct market failure, reduce poverty and reduce imbalance in distribution of wealth are insufficient, ethics and faith of the people mobilize additional support to supplement government efforts. Hence, the collective ethics of the citizenry becomes the second essential pillar of the society. Those who have complied with the rules of Islam and have ascended spiritually through prayers and who have distanced themselves from greed and no longer want everything for their own enjoyment become capable of to supplement the efforts of the government in avoiding market and state failure. This too depends on the degree to which the society has internalized Islamic teachings and ethics.

References

Holy Qur'an. translated by T.B. Irving (Al-Haj Ta'lim Ali). Tehran: Suhrawardi Research and Publication Center, 2003.

Abu Obaid, Al-Qasem Bin Salam. *Kitab Al-Amval*. Beirut: Dar Al-Kotob Al-Elmiya, 1406 LH.

Abu Yusef, Yaqub Bin Ibrahim. *Kitab Al-Kharaj*. Beirut: Dar Al-Ma'refa'. 1399 LH.

Al-Hakimi, Mohammad Reza, Mohammad Al-Hakimi, Al-Hakimi. *Al-Hayat*. 6 Vols. First Edition. Tehran: Islamic Culture Publication Office, 1406 LH.

Beihaqi, Ahmad Bin Hossein. *Al-Sonan Al-Kobra*. Vol. 10. Beirut: Dar Al-Kotob Al-Elmiya1424 LH.

Hadifar, Davood. *Regulatory Legal Organizations. Structure and Administration*. Etrat No' at the order of Privatization Organization, 1389 SH.

Harrani,Ibn Sho'ba. *Tohf Ul-Oqul An Al-ul-Rasul*. edited/corrected by Ali Akbar Qaffari. Qum: 1363 SH.

Hor Al-Ameli, Al-Sheikh Mohammad Bin Al-Hassan. *Vasayel Al-Shia*. Vol. 9. Aal Al-Bayt Publishers. 1416 LH.

Kant, Immanuel. *The Metaphysical Elements of Ethics*. translated by Hamid Enayat and Ali Qeysari, without date.

Mahmoud Bin Zamakhshari. *Tafsir Kashaf*. Vol. 4. Beirut: Dar Al-Kitab Al-Arabi.

Majlesi,Mohammad Baqer. *Behar Al-Anwar*. Vol. 68. Beirut: Dar Eh'ya Al-torath Al-Arabi, 1403 LH.

Majlesi,Mohammad Baqer. *Behar Al-Anwar*. Vol. 74. Beirut: Dar Eh'ya Al-torath Al-Arabi, 1403 LH.

Makarem Shirazi, Naser. *Tafsir Nemoune'*. Vol. 25. Qum: Dar Al-Kitab Islamiya.
Montazeri, Hossein Ali. *Darasat fi Velayat Al-Faqih and Fiqh Al-Dolat Al-Islamiya*. Vol. 3 and 4. Tafakkor Publications, 1411 LH.
Montazeri, Hossein Ali. *Kitab Al-Zakat*. Vol. 1. Qum: Markaz Al-Nashr. Maktab Al-E'lam Al-Islami, 1409LH
Montazeri, Hossein Ali. *Kitab Al-Zakat*. Vol. 2. Qum: Markaz Al-Nashr. Maktab Al-E'lam Al-Islami, 1409 LH
Motahhari, Morteza. *Education and Training in Islam*. Tehran: Sadra Publications, 1370 SH.
Motahhari, Morteza. *Methodical and Cultural Foundation*. Tehran: Sadra Publications, 1382 SH.
Razi, Abolfotuh. *Tafsir Al-Razi*. Vol. 30. Beirut: Dar Al-Kotob Al-Elmiya.
Reza'ei, Majid. *Public Finance in Islam*. Tehran: Samt Publications and Mofid University, 1389SH.
Sadeqi Tehrani, Mohammad. *Fi Tafsir Al-Forqan*. Vol. 29. Beirut: Mo'assesa Al-A'lami l-Al-Matbou'at.
Sadr, Al-Seyyed Mohammad Baqer. *Eqtesadona*. First Edition. Maktab Al-E'lam Al-Islami. 1417 LH.
Sen, Amartya. *On Ethics and Economics*. New York, NY. Basil Blackwell, 1987.
Sen, Amartya. *On Ethics and Economics*. Translated by Hassan Fesharaki. Tehran: Shirazeh, 1377 SH.
Tabarsi, Abu Ali Al-Fazl Bin Hassan. *Majma' Ul-Bayan*. 5 Vol. (10 Sections). Islami-ye Publishers. 1380 LH.
Tabataba'ei, Al-Seyyed Mohammad Hossein. *Al-Mizan fi Tafsir Al-Qur'an*. 20 Vol. Second Edition. Beirut: Al-A'lami Al-Matbu'at Institute, 1394 LH.

Hassan Abedi Jafari, Pooya Pirmaleki and
Mostafa Kazemi Najafabadi

Chapter 21: Influence of Piety (Taqwa) on Ethical Decision-makings in Business: Integration of Religious and Scientific Views

1 Introduction

The existing approaches for studying religion in the realm of business include philosophical, Religious(Theological) and scientific (empirical) (Chan-Serafin, Brief, and George 2013). In spite of the persistent prevalence of the philosophical approach, recent years have witnessed an expansion of Religious and scientific approaches, which, for various reasons, would be expected to continue to grow in the future (Melé 2015). Within Religious approach (normative/conceptual studies) business ethics is investigated from the perspectives of different religions (i.e. the ideal, theoretical aspects are discussed), while the scientific approach (descriptive/empirical/quantitative research) takes into account the impact of various aspects of religiosity on ethical decision-making in business.

The first part of this article explores the Islamic approach, from among various Religious approaches, towards business ethics (ethical decision-making), and attempts to illustrate the pivotal role of the concept of "piety" in strengthening the four-stage process of ethical decision-making in business. "Islamic Business Ethics" is growing into a specialized field of research (e.g., Al Arkoubi 2013, Ismaeel and Blaim 2012, Sidani and Al Ariss 2015, Richardson, Sinha, and Yaapar 2014, and Syed and Metcalfe 2015).

The last part of the article analyzes and synthesizes empirical research to put forth a model (Figure 21.1) for determining the impact of Intrinsic religiosity (piety) on ethical decision-making (awareness, judgment, intention and ethical behavior) in business. The empirical investigations that evaluated the impact of religion on ethical decision-making have conceptualized and evaluated religion in contrasting ways. This has created divergent results of its positive, neutral or negative impact in the process. For instance, some research evaluated the influence of a single or a combination of few attributes of religious commitment (e.g. beliefs, rituals, emotions and religion consequences, and importance of religion in the mind of individual) on ethical decision-making (e.g., Greenman 2012; Emerson and Mckinney 2009; Oumlil and Balloun 2009; Parboteeah, Hoegl, and Cullen 2008), Others have considered and evaluated the effects of Religious identity (Peterson et al. 2010), type of religion(Wimalasiri 2001), View of God (Alshehri, Fotaki, and Kauser 2016), belief in God (Smith, DeBode, and Walker 2013), pantheistic vs. monotheistic conception

https://doi.org/10.1515/9783110593419-021

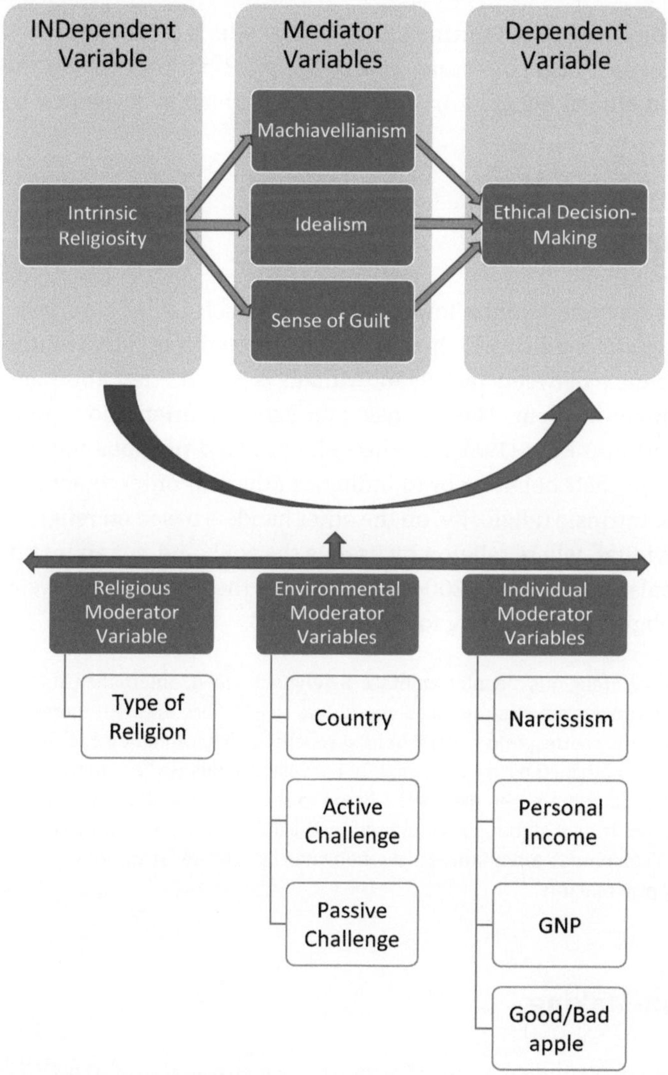

Figure 21.1: A hybrid model for explaining the impact of Piety (Taqwa) on Ethical Decision-makings in Business: scientific view.
Source: current research finding.

of God (Graafland, Kaptein, and Mazereeuw – van der Duijn Schouten 2007), religious training (or religiosity of the parents) (Flurry and Swimberghe 2016), Religious schema (Proios and Proios 2017), vertical and horizontal religiosity (Saat, Porter, and Woodbine 2009) and religious atmosphere (Du et al. 2016) on ethical decision-making. However, most of the research carried out in this field have examined the impact of intrinsic religious orientation on ethical decision-making in business. The analyses are based on the concept of "Intrinsic Religiosity" which is developed by Allport and Ross (1967), which also constitutes one of the principal concepts in the theory of "Religiosity and ethical behavior in organizations" which is developed by Weaver and Agle (2002).

1.1 Intrinsic Religiosity

There can be three different orientations towards religion which include *intrinsic, extrinsic,* and *Quest orientation*, all of which exist in any devoted individual simultaneously. The only difference between various individuals is which orientation prevails and is more prominent in them. The intrinsic and extrinsic orientations were first introduced by Allport and Ross (1967). Extrinsically oriented religious individuals use religion to explain their behavior or to influence others in order to achieve their non-religious goals. Intrinsic religiosity, on the other hand, is based on religious belief system of the individual, where religion by itself is the goal, and not an instrument to achieve other goals. Masters et al. 2004, describe well the difference between intrinsic and extrinsic religiosity: According to them:

> These individuals [intrinsic religious people] embrace a religious creed, internalize it, and attempt to follow it. Other needs are regarded as being of less significance and are, therefore, met only to the extent that they correspond with the religious beliefs. Their attendance at church may be thought of as being motivated by spiritual growth. Extrinsic religiosity (ER), on the other hand, is characterized by individuals who use their religion to serve some utilitarian purposes such as enhancing their security or status, providing self-justification for actions, or promoting social or political aims. Their church attendance is less motivated by a desire for spiritual growth and more influenced by other factors.

1.2 Ethical Decision-Making

It is a four-step process comprising awareness (recognizing a moral action in a situation); judgment (deciding or judging whether the action or decision is ethical); intention (making a goal of moral action); and behavior (engaging in ethical actions). These steps have been conceptualized by Rest (1986). The ability of individuals to recognize that they are faced with an ethical situation requiring ethical judgment, is much varied. Unless the individual recognizes the ethical situation, other steps are insignificant, and the ethical behavior cannot be manifested. It is only after the recognition of the ethical situation that the ability of the individual to judge or evaluate the situation gains importance. At this stage, the individual must visualize and evaluate a variety of possible options and choose the most ethical one. Individuals differ in terms of their ability to morally judge and evaluate various ethical options.

After one chooses any of the evaluated scenarios as a moral scenario, the priority level of ethical values over other values becomes highly determinative and defines the intention of individual to act ethically (i.e. according to the scenario chosen in the previous step). If the individual passes through the previous three steps, and has the ability to carry out the selected scenario, then the ethical behavior will be manifested.

To the best of our knowledge, the empirical research efforts that have measured the impact of Intrinsic religiosity on ethical decision-making in business have not been thoroughly and systematically reviewed, analyzed and integrated till now. Consequently, the purposes of the present research are:

1. to discover the Islamic approach to the influence of Intrinsic religiosity (piety *or Taqwa* "تقوى") on ethical decision-making based on authentic Islamic literature,
2. to demonstrate how this influence has been reported (positive, negative or neutral) in various empirical investigations as a whole, and,
3. to explain various processes through which such influence is actualized (in terms of mediator and moderator variables).

2 Islamic View of Influence of Intrinsic Religiosity on Ethical Decision-making

Since the present article seeks to investigate the influence of Intrinsic religiosity on ethical decision-making both theoretically and practically, attempt is made here to first provide definitions for Intrinsic religiosity and ethical decision-making based on conventional literature and then to introduce their lexical equivalents in Islamic culture. In the next step, the viewpoint of Islam in this field is investigated. This is followed by the analysis of Empirical studies in which Intrinsic religiosity constituted the independent variable (either mediator or moderator), and their dependent variable comprised one or more of the four stages of ethical decision-making in business. This will methodically illustrate the practical outcomes of the application of theoretical investigations.

3 Intrinsic Religiosity and Its Stages of Progression According to the Islamic Viewpoint

In the lexicon of Qur'an and Islamic tradition ("*Sunnah*"), the concept of "Intrinsic religiosity" is connoted by the word "*Taqwa*" ("تقوى") or "piety" which has various levels. As is the case of all prophets and Messengers of Allah, the Prophet and the *Ahl al-Bayt*[1] are considered infallible and pure. As such, they occupy the highest level of piety. An individual who has attained Intrinsic religiosity is known to be "pious" or "*Mottaqi*" ("متقی").

Etymologically, "*Taqwa*" is from the Arabic root "*Waqaye*"" ("وقایه") meaning "prevention, forbearance, fear and protective abstinence." It refers to an instrument or a cause by the help of which human beings are protected from the evils.[2] From the point of view of sacred verses of Holy Qur'an and the reports of sacred narrations (*Riwayat*), piety (Taqwa) has various levels and stages:

3.1 First Level of Intrinsic Religiosity

This level is realized through abandoning the forbidden deeds ("*Haram*") and performing the obligatory deeds ("*Wajib*").[3] Imam Ali expressed (Tamimi Amedi 1366 SH, p. 87)

اَلمُتَّقی مَنِ اِتَّقَی الذُّنُوبَ

> *"A pious person (who is mindful of Allah) is the one who protects himself by avoiding the commitment of sins."*

Prophet stated (Majlesi 1404 LH, p. 196)

اِعْمَلْ بِفَرَائِضِ اَللَّهِ تَكُنْ أَتْقَی اَلنَّاسِ

> *"Perform all the obligatory deeds ("Wajib") prescribed by Allah (and) you will become the most pious of the people."*

---

1 In Shia Islam the Ahl al-Bayt are central to Islam and interpreters of the Quran and Sunnah. Shias believe they are successors of Muhammad (Wikipedia).

2 Farahidi, Raqeb Isfahani, under the title/entry of "Waq'y" ("وقی").

3 The "practical commandments" of Islam, which specify the duties of human beings in carrying out or keeping away from certain deeds, are referred to as "*Ahkam*" (decrees/rulings). Every act of human beings has its respective specific decree, and there are five different types of decrees that define the responsibilities of human beings: 1. Obligatory ("*Wajib*") deeds are those compulsory and their abandoning results in punishment; e.g. praying and fasting; 2. Forbidden ("*Haram*") acts comprise those which are to be abandoned and performing them is a sin and results in punishment; e.g. lying and oppressing; 3. Recommended ("*Mustahab*") deeds are those that are benevolent and their performance carries rewards (but are not compulsory), and their abandoning does not lead to punishment; e.g. greeting others and giving alms; 4. Reprehensible ("*Makruh*") refer to those behaviors whose abandoning is recommended, but performing it does not result in retribution 5. Neutral ("*Mubah*") acts which have no consequences (reward or punishment), whether done or left undone; e.g. walking and sitting.

3.2 Second Level of Intrinsic Religiosity

Performing all the recommended deeds ("*Mustahab*") and abstaining from the reprehensibles ("*Makruh*") takes the pious individual to second level of Intrinsic religiosity. It must, however, be borne in mind that performing the recommended deeds must not prevent the individual from doing obligatory deeds. Imam Ali stated (Tamimi Amedi 1366 SH, p. 31):

إِذَا أَضَرَّتِ النَّوَافِلُ بِالْفَرَائِضِ فَارْفُضُوهَا

"If performing the recommended deeds prevents you from carrying out the obligatory deeds, leave aside the former."

And another important topic which has been reiterated by the Imam (as) is (Tamimi Amedi 1366 SH, p. 251)

إِنَّ لِلْقُلُوبِ إِقْبَالاً وَ إِدْبَاراً فَإِذَا أَقْبَلَتْ فَاحْمِلُوهَا عَلَى النَّوَافِلِ وَ إِذَا أَدْبَرَتْ فَاقْتَصِرُوا بِهَا عَلَى الْفَرَائِضِ

"For hearts, there is a state of desire (coming forth) as well as a state of reluctance (turning back); when your heart desires, perform the recommended deeds, and whenever your heart does not desire, just perform the obligatory deeds."

3.3 Third Level of Intrinsic Religiosity

This level is achieved when the individual performs all the permissible deeds, such as eating, drinking, sleeping and others not just to enjoy them but performs them with the intention to gain sufficient bodily strength to better serve Allah, Islam and society. As the Prophet expressed (Majlesi 1404 LH, p. 212; and, Reyshahri; *Reyshahri* 1416 LH, H 6570)

إِنَّمَا الأَعْمَالُ بِالنِّيَّاتِ

"The value of deeds depend on the intentions behind them."

And on another occasion he stated (Reyshahri 1416 LH, H 6562)

يُبْعَثُ اَلنَّاسُ يَوْمَ اَلْقِيَامَةِ عَلَى نِيَّاتِهِمْ

"In the Judgment Day, people will be resurrected (and held accountable) based on their intentions (behind their actions) in life."

The Qur'an and sacred narrations (Ahadith) enumerate various qualities for the pious individuals who have internalized fully and strongly their religious beliefs such that these qualities are manifested in their personal and social behavior. The personal manifestation of Intrinsic religiosity includes theocentricism (2:177), faith in divine prophets, (2:177) faith in resurrection (and it accountability), (2:177) faith in the Divine books (2:4), faith in angels (2:177), treasuring the divine rites (22:32), performing the good deeds, (Majlesi1404 LH, p. 282) paying Zakat (2:177), preparing their last will and testament (2:180), expressing gratitude for the blessings they receive (3:123), believing in the Divine Guidance (2:5), the duty of controlling bodily organs, (Nahj Al-Balaqa; Sermon 193) the duty of controlling behavior, (Nahj Al-Balaqa; Sermon 193) cleansing of the self, (Nahj Al-Balaqa; Sermon 193) repentance, (Harrani 1363 SH, p. 232) avoiding suspected deeds or materials, (Nahj Al-Balaqa; Sermon 193) acquiring knowledge, (Nahj Al-Balaqa; Sermon 193) being orientated towards seeking wisdom (2:197), having patience and fortitude (2:177), having certitude, (Nahj Al-Balaqa; Sermon 193) being honest (2:177), practicing asceticism, (Nahj Al-Balaqa; Sermon 204) being spiritually tranquile (7:35), being humble, (Nahj Al-Balaqa; Sermon 193) having good disposition, (Deilami 1371 SH, p. 121) being beneficent (2:177), experiencing ease in resolving difficulties in his affairs (65:4), being mindful in performing acts of worship reverentially (Nahj Al-Balaqa; Sermon 193) and believing in the possibility of achieving felicity in the Hereafter (2:5).

The social manifestation of Intrinsic religiosity by an individual who has internalized his religious beliefs comprises, for example, faithfulness to the terms and conditions of promises, contracts and covenants, commitment to social solidarity and unity, being trustworthy, (Nahj Al-Balaqa; Sermon 193) accepting religious responsibility, and being devoted to maintaining contact and communication with relatives and being ready to help them when and if needed. As a sign of the importance of the qualities displayed by Intrinsic religiosity (Taqwa), it suffices to not that Islam considers it as “the best and permanent provision” (2:197) for the Hereafter and promises Paradise as the ultimate reward for Taqwq (15:45).

As mentioned earlier, ethical decision-making possesses four stages each of which can be influenced by internal religiosity (piety). The four stages include recognition of the ethical situation, judgment, inclination and ethical behavior. In Islamic teachings, there is a great deal of evidence that Intrinsic religiosity impact each of these four stages which will be further investigated in the following paragraphs.

3.4 First Stage of Ethical Decision-Making: Recognition of the Ethical Situation

In the Islamic worldview, a pious (Motaqi) or Intrinsically religious person possesses an accurate view of the material world. In his vision, the material world is a place for being tested and his success in the tests will provide him with felicity in the Hereafter. Such a view sensitizes the Intrinsically religious individual to see himself as subjected to Divine trial at all stages of decision-making and, therefore, strives to make the best moral decisions in order to achieve felicity. The greater the depth of Intrinsicness of religiosity, the greater the level of individual sensitivity towards the decision-making. It must be remembered that this kind of insight and attitude is only achieved in the light of Qur'anic teachings for the faithful. The second verse of the Chapter of *Al-Ankabut* (the Spider, Chapter 29 of the Qur'an) emphasizes that human beings would not be spared testing in this world just because they say "we believe;" they will, indeed be constantly tested by Allah:

أَحَسِبَ النَّاسُ أَنْ يُتْرَكُوا أَنْ يَقُولُوا آمَنَّا وَهُمْ لَا يُفْتَنُونَ (29:2)

> *"Do people reckon that they will be left alone just because they say: 'We believe,' and they will not be tested?" (2:29)*

Having this kind of attitude, Intrinsically religious individuals consider all decisions in field of business as Divine trials and become sensitive towards their choices of action. For instance, if an individual is not Intrinsically religious, he will consider his own interests at the time of paying his employee's salary and will determine the wage based on supply and demand. But an Intrinsically religious individual conceives such decision-making as an ethical choice and seeks to comprehend the situation correctly and make the fairest possible decision.

Moreover, the Qur'an uses the term "do not draw nigh to" ("وَلَا تَقْرَبُوا") while referring to a number of sins (6:151 and 6:152). According to exegetists of the Qur'an, in these cases the emphasis is that the individuals must not even think of indulging in a sin, or must not bear any feeling in their mind.

. . . وَلَا تَقْرَبُوا الْفَوَاحِشَ مَا ظَهَرَ مِنْهَا وَمَا بَطَنَ . . . (6:151)

> *... and do not draw nigh to indecencies, those of them which are apparent and those which are concealed ... (6:151, in part)*

This interpretation is a lot different than "do not indulge in sins," and emphasizes "not entering the realm of proscriptions prescribed by Allah" and "not even contemplate performing such deeds." This kind of understanding insists strictness of Allah's prohibition, and as a consequence, the sensitivity of Intrinsically religious individuals is provoked intensely. They will be contended to make the best ethical decisions in all aspects of life and would not approach the realms forbidden by the Allah.

Piety will lead to opening of the gates of the Transcendental consciousness, awareness and wisdom by the Allah on the Intrinsically religious individual. In Qur'anic literature, piety and internalization of religion are considered to increase the spirituality of individuals.

. . . وَاتَّقُوا اللَّهَ وَيُعَلِّمُكُمُ اللَّهُ . . . (2:282)

> *... observe your duty to Allah (be mindful of Allah) and Allah Will illuminate you (give you wisdom or transcendental consciousness) ... (2:282, in part)*

This wisdom or transcendental consciousness has been interpreted in some sacred narrations (Hadith) as a beam of light by which the Allah illuminates the hearts of the *Motaqi*, so that they employ the necessary sensitivity for making ethical decisions (Majlesi 1404 LH, p. 224).

3.5 Second Stage of Ethical Decision-Making: Judgment

Some verses of the Qur'an emphasize that if one succeeds in internalizing religion and attains piety, Allah will bestow on him the "*Forqan*," i.e. the standard and measure for distinguishing the right/good ("حق") from the wrong/evil ("باطل").

يَا أَيُّهَا الَّذِينَ آمَنُوا إِنْ تَتَّقُوا اللَّهَ يَجْعَلْ لَكُمْ فُرْقَانًا ... (8:29)

> *"O you who believe! If you are mindful of Allah, He will grant you(the power of) discrimination (between right and wrong)" ... (8:29, in part).*

Attaining truthfulness in human beings is an outcome of piety, and thus, the Allah endows the Intrinsically religious individuals with the distinguishing power ("*Forqan*") to discriminate between the right and the wrong. Therefore, in decision-makings and judgments, they will not be confused between right and wrong.

The Quran states:

إِنَّ الَّذِينَ اتَّقَوْا إِذَا مَسَّهُمْ طَائِفٌ مِنَ الشَّيْطَانِ تَذَكَّرُوا فَإِذَا هُمْ مُبْصِرُونَ (7:201)

> *"Surely those who are mindful of Allah (and perform their duties as prescribed by Allah), bring Allah to remembrance, whenever some impulse from Satan bothers them, and so they are granted insight."*

The way for the righteous to overcome the satanic enticements/temptations, according to the above sacred verse, is to remember Allah (and his endless blessings) as well as the dreadful consequences of sins (painful punishments by Allah). Then the right path will be illuminated before the faithful (and the dark clouds of temptation will be pushed aside from their hearts). Such verses indicate that the Intrinsically religious individuals are careful not to allow evil enter their minds and hearts. And in the decision-making process, they are not unaware of their Lord and will be safe from the evil enticements. Therefore, they would prefer ethical decisions in business, and the Allah provides them with correct verdicts.

Also, in other Verse of the Qur'an, those who have Intrinsic religiosity are described as those whom business activities will not take their attention away from Allah (for example):

"رِجَالٌ لَا تُلْهِيهِمْ تِجَارَةٌ وَلَا بَيْعٌ عَنْ ذِكْرِ اللَّهِ . . . " (24:37)

> *"Men whom neither business nor trading diverts them from the remembrance of Allah"*

Even in their own business, the Intrinsically religious individuals are not heedless of Allah and, in making decisions, they always opt for the decision that is closer to the remembrance citation and gratification of Allah.

3.6 Third Stage of Ethical Decision-Making: Intention

As stated earlier, the third step of the ethical decision-making process commences after the individual becomes aware of and sensitive to the ethics of a situation and capable of correct judgement regarding his choice. The next step involves development of an intention to implement the choice. In the Islamic literature, several basic factors influence the development of Human intention, which are described below.

3.6.1 Awareness Factor

Individuals acquire a sincere desire and intention in accordance with their knowledge about the options they have. Just as the common people never desire eating unclean and discarded waste (say human waste) because of their awareness and understanding of the nature of the material, the Intrinsically religious and the pious individual loses the desire for committing sins because of his full awareness regarding the nature of such acts and their consequences. Therefore, if the individual internalizes his religion, Allah provides him with the required skill and knowledge to easily discern the nature of the possible consequences resulting from his decisions, and accordingly enhances the intention towards the correct act.

Piety will lead to the opening up of the gates of knowledge by the Allah upon the pious and Intrinsically religious individual. There are several illustrations of the different aspects of committing sins in the Qur'an and in the reported sacred narrations (Hadith); e.g. the Verse that describes backbiting as "eating of the dead brother's flesh," (49:12)

Therefore, the desires of the pious and Intrinsically religious individuals are far different from that of the others. This is due to their awareness and knowledge, part of which has been acquired by the individual and the other part has been bestowed upon him by the Allah.

3.6.2 Conducts and Behavior

Some scholars are of the opinion that sins change the source of human desires, and sometimes a single sin can change the destiny of an individual. This is because every sin which is committed by a person will result in a defect in his character and a shadow of darkness befalls his heart. And as the person persists on committing sins, the darkness expands gradually until it covers all his heart.

Imam al-Baqer stated:

إِذَا أَذْنَبَ الرَّجُلُ خَرَجَ فِي قَلْبِهِ نُكْتَةٌ سَوْدَاءُ فَإِنْ تَابَ انْمَحَتْ وَ إِنْ زَادَ زَادَتْ حَتَّى تَغْلِبَ عَلَى قَلْبِهِ فَلاَ يُفْلِحُ بَعْدَهَا أَبَداً

> *"There is a bright spot in the heart of every human being, which will be covered by a dark shadow when he commits a sin. If one persists on sinning, the darkness will prevail and the bright spot disappears. In such a case, the individual will never reach salvation."*

Thus it can be seen that committing sins gradually transforms the inner self of human beings. These changes of heart and mind are progressively accumulated and modify the direction of the movement of the heart and human desires. Having lost the purity of the heart and its natural health, the holder of such an altered heart misses many spiritual privileges including sensitivity and astuteness of his heart in the process of making his business decisions. Sensitivity and awareness of the heart are the outcomes of Intrinsic religiosity, and it is a great blessing that prevents the individual from being indifferent toward right ("حق") and wrong/evil ("باطل"). Consequently, in the process of business decision-making, if the individual tends towards wrong/evil and makes a wrong decision in difficult dilemmas, he immediately regrets and corrects his course of action. But since this awareness and consciousness is either reduced or eliminated due to spiritual alteration, one becomes indifferent to the right and wrong (or excellence and imperfection) and even one's internal sensitivity in all fields including business becomes impaired to the point that the individual is unable to make the right decision. As a result, he will not be inclined toward appropriate ethical decisions.

3.7 Fourth Stage of Ethical Decision-Making: Behavior

After the above-mentioned three steps, the stage for manifestation of the behavior is reached. In Islamic teachings, various behaviors in the field of business have been enumerated for the Intrinsically religious or pious individuals which can be categorized as Theocentricism, individual ethics, business ethics, Shari'ah/religious considerations, managerial considerations, marketing and sales considerations, and concerns for financial facilities.

3.7.1 Theocentricism

One of the main characteristics of the Intrinsically religious individuals in the field of business is Theocentricism. About those who consider the Creator as the center of all existence, including their own, Imam Ali stated:

عَظُمَ اَلْخَالِقُ فِي أَنْفُسِهِمْ فَصَغُرَ مَا دُونَهُ فِي أَعْيُنِهِمْ

> *"Allah is so majestically present in their consciousness that everything else is insignificant in their view."*

Therefore, considering this characteristic of the Intrinsically religious individuals, they would always view Allah in all their decision-makings, would remain theocentric and would be grateful to the Allah (16:121). In business, such individuals only look for blessings from Allah only (65:3), are only choose Halal business (2:168), and do not ignore learning the religious rules governing business (Al-Koleini 1362 SH, p. 150). They abstain from swearing by taking the name of Allah in vain in business activities (2:224), avoid corruption and illicit trading (41:49 and 70:19), and try not to allow work to interfere with acts of worship. Thus they opt for the best ethical choices at every decision-making opportunity.

3.7.2 Individual Ethics

The Intrinsically religious and pious individual possesses an honest(9: 119), trustworthy (4:58), fair (5:44–47), and magnanimous (18:10) personality, abides by his promises (9:111) and abstains from cruelty, lies (24:7), and betrayal of trust (4:58). Consequently, having internalized all these traits, the individual will always prefer truth over falsehood, fairness over unfairness, magnanimity over inequity, abiding by a promise over breaching it, and trustworthiness over perfidy and makes ethical decisions.

3.7.3 Business Ethics

Based on Islamic teachings, Intrinsically religious and pious individual will abstain from the following: interfering in others' dealings/trading; (Sahih Bukhari, p. 28) acting deceptively; (Jawama'Al-Faqih, p. 14) concealing the defect of merchandize; (Kenz Al-Emal, p. 59) abusing others' trust, or benefiting from others' encumbrances; short-changing others (83:1–3); fraudulent acts; (Hor Al-Ameli 1403 LH, p. 376; H. 22785) hoarding goods/merchandize (9:34); cheating; (Majlesi1404 LH, p. 134) hedging or postponing deals; and acting as a broker when such function is not unnecessary (Hor Al-Ameli 1403 LH, p. 443; H. 22949). Therefore, He will always make the right decision, keeping away from the aforementioned malefactions, getting closer to Allah's satisfaction and approval.

3.7.4 Shari'ah/Religious Considerations

According to Quranic verses and sacred narrations reported (*Riwayat*), the Intrinsically religious individual pays the obligatory dues (Khums and Zakat) (2:43) as well as voluntary (alms and charities) payments (2:261), and abstains from Riba (30:39), bribery (2:188), discriminatory pricing (*Jawama' Al-Faqih*; p. 528), profiteering (11:84), unreasonable price hiking, and after-sale bargaining. Therefore, in the difficult decision-making situations, he always chooses the path endorsed by the Shari'ah.

3.7.5 Managerial Considerations

In Islamic thinking, the Intrinsically religious individual associates himself with the obligation to partner with creditable individuals, and documents and records all his contracts (2:282). Therefore, he will avoid dealing with ignorant and disreputable individuals in his business decision-makings.

3.7.6 Marketing and Sales Considerations

According to Islamic teachings, pious or Intrinsically religious individuals always strive to obtain the satisfaction of their customers in an appropriate way and never use false advertisements (9:119; 16:105 and 16:116). They do not negatively propagandize about competitors and consider quality enhancement and respect for customers as the main slogan of their business. Therefore, in making business decisions, they always opt for divine satisfaction as against personal benefit in order to make ethical decisions.

3.7.7 Financial Facilities

The pious individual avoids any sever behavior (*Al-Kafi* 1362 SH, p. 151; H 3) and his business strategy revolves around receiving fair and reasonable profit in trade. As a result, He/she warmly welcomes those who have buyers' remorse after the completion of the deal (Reyshahri 1416 LH, p. 523).

4 Theoretical Foundations of Empirical Studies

As it was stated in the previous sections describing the levels of Intrinsic religiosity, depending on whether the Intrinsically religious individual is in the first, the second or the third level, his commitment to the above-mentioned behaviors is determined. This is because some of these affairs fall in the category of obligatory ("Wajib") or forbidden ("Haram"), while some others are considered as recommended ("Mustahab") or reprehensible ("Makruh").

From the set of issues discussed in this section one can comprehend that Islam has taken into account the role of Intrinsic religiosity or piety in all four stages of ethical decision-making. Therefore, a pious individual in the business environment can always make ethical decisions because his virtue helps him throughout the whole process. However, the question is whether the empirical evidence confirms the above-mentioned propositions? To find the answer, we must review the results of the empirical studies about the effects of Intrinsic religiosity on ethical decision-making to perceive the practical influence of Intrinsic religiosity on ethical decision-making. The best studies that could complement this discussion would have been the Islamic investigations, but due to lack of such works, researchers have moved to make Religious studies the basis of their assertions. In this article, the empirical research that have investigated the impact of Intrinsic religiosity on ethical decision-making in business are systematically searched. Thirty-three studies which satisfied the specific conditions based on definite criteria were selected, and by combining them, a model (Figure 21.1) is presented to explain the process by which Intrinsic religiosity influences decision making. The results suggest that Intrinsic religiosity, either directly or indirectly, improves the process of ethical decision-making in business through strengthening idealism, enhancing the sense of guilt caused by unethical behavior, and weakening of Machiavellian morality. Majority of empirical research (about 80%) have found the influence to be positive and meaningful. Influence is greater among consumer group as compared to senior managers and specialists, while it is weaker in the more narcissistic, wealthier, and the ill-natured individuals as well as those with active ethical challenges. At the end, it is suggested to take greater advantage of longitudinal/experimental/interventional methods in future empirical research instead of segmental studies and use of questionnaires alone. Moreover, use of variable such as "love of money", "commitment to ethical improvement" and "perceived moral intensity/strength," as the mediators, as well as variables such as "degree of formalness," "type of organization," "social pressure for religiosity," "cognitive abilities" and "opportunities for unethical behavior" as moderators are proposed.

Most empirical research in the field of management and organization, which have focused on the influence of religion on behavior, are rooted in Weber's thesis. It combines economic sociology and the sociology of religion, as elaborated in his book titled *The Protestant Ethic and the Spirit of Capitalism*.[4] According to this thesis, religious beliefs and values have an impact on behaviors (including ethical behaviors), and consequently on economic performance.

In his well-known book *An Inquiry into the Nature and Causes of the Wealth of Nations*,[5] Adam Smith also opines that one of the most economically significant functions of religious belief is to provide strong incentives to follow moral foundations that help support civil society, that is, honesty, benevolence, restraint against violence, and so forth (Nath 2007).

Having a functional/social approach towards religion, Durkheim considered that the religious beliefs and rituals constitute the basis for ethics in society. The results of empirical research by William James also indicate that religion is the source of positive emotions, helping others, increasing resistance and tolerance, self-esteem, and

4 Max Weber, 1930.
5 Adam Smith, 1776.

many other positive psychological characters in individuals. By creating these positive emotions, religion exerts a positive influence on the ethical behavior of human beings (James 1910).

The findings of Kohlberg's empirical research, however, showed no relationship between moral development and religious beliefs. In fact, the stages of moral development of children in different religions are similar. Nonetheless, he did not rule out the connection between religious experience and moral development, but overall, the results of his research indicated that religion is not an important factor in moral development (Kohlberg 1976; quoted by Rest 1979, p. 266).

In "General Theory of Marketing Ethics," (Hunt Vitell 1986; Hunt and Vitell 2006) religion is introduced both as a cultural factor as well as one of the personal characteristics in ethical decision-making within the business environment. Religious people possess more powerful norms which exert a greater influence on their ethical judgments. Weaver and Agle (2002), applied the Concept of intrinsic Religiosity, that had been earlier introduced in field of psychology of religion, to organizational and management studies. They presented the theory of influence of religion on ethical decision-making in organizations. In this theory, Intrinsic religiosity plays a moderator role through influencing religious identity salience and religious motivational orientation in ethical decision-making. From the viewpoint of Religious Orientation Theory,[6] Intrinsic religiosity contrasts with extrinsic religiosity in its kinship with positive psychological characteristics (e.g. altruism and unselfishness) (Allport and Ross 1967).

5 Methodology of Empirical Studies

Accumulation of primary studies necessitates secondary studies or literature reviews. Although such reviews could lead to production of new knowledge, but in the past, scientists usually did not carry out the process of collection and accumulation of primary studies methodically and scientifically. No proper method for synthesizing the primary studies existed by the beginning of the 20th century, and most of the development occurred in the last two decades of the past century(Chalmers, Hedges, and Cooper 2002). One of the reasons for slow emergence of theorizing and modelling in organizational and management studies as compared to other branches of science is the ampleness of primary research that have not been synthesized. In other words, the researchers in the fields of management and organization have shown little willingness to synthesize the primary research (Hoon 2013). One of the numerous methods of literature reviews, which has increasingly been utilized in recent years due to the emphasis on enhanced quality of secondary studies, is the systematic approach. The prominent features of the systematic approach in analyzing the literature comprise:

6 Allport and Ross, 1967.

1. Existence of a specific query;
2. Comprehensiveness, transparency and repeatability of the searching process for primary research;
3. Specific criteria for selection of primary research (in order to determine the quality and relevance of research query); and
4. Theory-based understanding of the phenomena of research (Gast, Gundolf, and Cesinger 2017).

In the present article, the influence is initially analyzed from the viewpoint of Islam on the basis of Quranic verses and sacred narrations (*Riwayat*), i.e. the Religious approach. Then the manner in which Intrinsic religiosity influences ethical decision-making in business is defined using the scientific (empirical) approach. Finally, these two approaches are compared with a synthesizing methodology. Therefore, the research methodology is described in two distinct parts (viz. the Religious approach and the scientific approach).

The methodology of the first part (Religious approach) comprised review of Islamic scriptures (Verse of the Qur'an and Riwayat with an analytical-descriptive attitude. But in the second part (scientific approach), the empirical literature were first analyzed and synthesized using the systematic literature review, in order to answer the research query. The specific query in the scientific approach is how Intrinsic religiosity influences ethical decision-making process in business. The research variables (intrinsic religiosity and ethical decision-making) are based on the "Religious Orientation Theory,"[7] and the four stages of ethical decision-making.[8] In line with these two theories, the keywords were identified and searched in internationally recognized scientific databases,[9] and search results were screened according to specific criteria. At the end, a total of 33 primary articles or researches were selected.

General religious keywords[10] along with specific keywords of the leading religions,[11] and general keywords related to ethical decision-making,[12] as well as the specific keywords associated with the four stages of ethical decision-making drawn from Lehnert, Park, and Singh (2015), which include several instances,[13] were searched in

7 Allport and Ross, 1967.

8 Rest, 1986.

9 Google Scholar, Springer, Academy of Management Journals, SAGE, Taylor & Francis, Emerald, ScienceDirect, JSTOR, EBSCO, ABI Inform/ ProQuest, Wiley Online Library, and Palgrave.

10 religion, religiosity and religious.

11 Christianity, Islam, Judaism, Hinduism, Buddhism, Confucianism.

12 ethical decision making, business ethics, moral, morality, ethical, ethics, ethic.

13 1. ethical sensitivity, perceived/perception of ethical problems, and awareness/recognition of ethical issues; 2. make a moral/ ethical judgment, moral reasoning, tolerance, identification of ethical scenarios or models, responses to rule-based scenarios, ability to perceive/judge ethical actions, and/ or trade-offs; 3. behavioral intention, and likely behavior or engagement; and, 4. (Moral/Ethical) action/behavior/character.

international scientific databases. The primary articles found were screened, and 33 of them were ultimately selected on the bases of the following criteria.

1. Research is of empirical (quantitative) nature.
2. "Intrinsic religiosity"[14] constitutes an independent, mediator, or moderator variable of the research.
3. The dependent variables of the research comprise one or more stages of the four-stage ethical decision-making process (awareness, attitude or judgment, intention, and ethical behavior).[15]
4. The journal where the article is published is peer-reviewed.

Primary research articles were categorized and analyzed based on factors such as year of publication, authors (researchers), journals, sample, religions, use of mediator and moderator variables, ethical decision-making stages, and the findings of the research. In other words, the sample and geographical location of research, the religions which were focused on, the moderator and mediator variables used, and the stage of the ethical decision-making process were clearly defined in each case. Finally, a hybrid model (Figure 21.1) based on the framework of "independent variable-mediator and moderator variables-dependent variables" was presented.

6 Findings

The result of systematic search carried out is the 33 quantitative studies that have examined the influence of Intrinsic religiosity on one or more stages of the ethical decision-making process in business. These studies are listed in Table 21.1 based on the authors; year of publication; religions; the identity of the sample; the country and the number of the sample; components of ethical decision-making (awareness 'A', attitude/judgment 'J', intention 'I', and behavior 'B' or 'AJIB'); the result of the research; and, the mediator 'ME' variables/moderator 'MO' variables.

7 Investigated Religions and Geographic Distribution of Research

About two-thirds of the 33 research studies were carried out in the United States and over two-thirds are focused on Christianity. Two studies were in Australia, and two in Europe (the Netherlands and Germany). The sample in four cases exclusively com-

14 Allport and Ross, 1967.

15 Rest, 1986.

Table 21.1: Empirical quantitative research in the field of Intrinsic religiosity and ethical decision-making in business.

Sr. No.	Author(s), Year	Religion(s)[19]	sample (Identity)[20]/Country/ No of Individuals)	AJIB[21]	Result(s)	Mediator Variables (ME)/ Moderator Variables (MO)
1	Arli, 2017	C	Co/Australia/517	Judgment	Positive, significant	Type of ethical issue (MO)
2	Arli and Pekerti, 2017	ICBH	Co/Australia and Indonesia/1200	Judgment	Positive, significant	Type of ethical issue; type of the country (MO)
3	Sims, 2017	C	Ro/United States/372	Awareness	Positive, significant	Intrinsic religiosity (MO)
4	Sauerwein, 2017	C	Es/United States/156	Judgment	Ineffective/Insignificant	N.A.
5	Voegel and Pearson, 2016	C	St/United States/300	Intention	Positive, significant	Idealism (ME)
6	Flurry and Swimberghe, 2016	C	Co/United States/250	Judgment	Positive, significant	Type of ethical issue (MO)
7	Walker, Jones-Farmer, DeBode, Smither and Smith, 2015	C	Ce/United States/212	Judgment	Ineffective/Insignificant	N.A.
8	Mazereeuw, Graafland and Kaptein, 2014	C	Sm/The Netherlands/473	Judgment and Behavior	Mixed	N.A.
9	Arli and Tjiptono, 2014	ICBH	Co/Indonesia/356	Judgment	Positive, significant	N.A.
10	Karami, Olfati and Dubinsky, 2014	I	Ve/Iran/263	Judgment	Positive, significant	N.A.

(continued)

16 Christianity(C), Islam(I), Hinduism(H), Buddhism(B).

17 identity of the samples: consumers ('Co'), vendors ('Ve'), students (mainly in Management courses) ('St'), common employees ('Ce'), senior managers ('Sm'), experts/specialist ('Es'), and staff of religious organizations ('Ro').

18 Four stages of ethical decision-making (awareness 'A', attitude/judgment 'J', intention 'I', and behavior 'B' or 'AJIB').

Table 21.1 (continued)

Sr. No.	Author(s), Year	Religion(s)[19]	sample (Identity)[20]/Country/ No of Individuals)	AJIB[21]	Result(s)	Mediator Variables (ME)/ Moderator Variables (MO)
11	Putrevu and Swimberghek, 2013	C	Sm/United States/600	Judgment and Intention	Positive, significant	N.A.
12	Singhapakdi, Vitell, Lee, Nisius and Yu, 2013	C	Sm/United States/205	Intention	Positive, significant	N.A.
13	Chai and Tan, 2013	I	Co/Malaysia/184	Judgment	Positive, significant	N.A.
14	Jamali and Sdiani, 2013	CI	Sm/Lebanon/149	Judgment	Ineffective/Insignificant	Type of religion (MO)
15	Cooper and Pullig, 2013	C	St/United States/385	Judgment	Positive, significant	Narcissism (MO)
16	Chen and Tang, 2013	C	St/United States/359	Judgment	Positive, significant	Machiavellianism (ME) and Personal Income (MO)
17	Smith, DeBode and Walker, 2013	C	St/United States/275	Judgment	Positive, significant	N.A.
18	Bakar, Lee and Hazarina, 2013	I	St/Pakistan/276	Judgment	Mixed	Sense of Guilt (ME) and Type of ethical issue (MO)
19	Walker, Smither and DeBode, 2012	C	Ce/United States/216	Judgment	Positive, significant	Intrinsic and extrinsic religiosity (MO)
20	Patwardhan, Keith and Vitell, 2012	C	Co/United States/314	Judgment	Positive, significant	N.A.
21	Swimberghe, Flurry and Parker, 2011	C	Co/United States/531	Judgment and Behavior	Positive, significant	Judgment (ME)
22	Schneider, Krieger and Bayraktar, 2011	IC	Co/Turkey and Germany/471	Judgment	Positive, significant	Type of religion (MO)
23	Tang and Tang, 2010	C	St/United States/266	Intention	Positive, significant	Machiavellianism (ME) and Good/Bad apple (MO)

24	Kum-Lung and Teck-Cha, 2010	I	Ce and St/Malaysia/269	Judgment	Positive, significant	N.A.
25	Ho, 2010	ICBH	Sm/Malaysia/1500	Awareness	Positive, significant	Type of ethical issue and Nationality (MO)
26	Jewe, 2008	C	St and Ro/United States/561	Judgment	Positive, weak	N.A.
27	Burks and Sellani, 2008	C	St and Ro/United States/490	Judgment	Ineffective/Insignificant	N.A.
28	Vitell, Singh and Paolillo, 2007	C	Co/United States/127	Judgment	Positive, significant	N.A.
29	Vitell, Paolillo and Singh, 2006	C	Co/United States/127	Judgment	Positive, significant	N.A.
30	Vitell, Paolillo and Singh, 2005	C	Co/United States/114	Judgment	Positive, significant	N.A.
31	Knotts, Lopez and Mesak, 2000	C	St/United States/226	Judgment	Positive, significant	N.A.
32	Pavri, Jalil and Wimalasiri, 1996	--[22]	Sm and St/Singapore/157	Judgment	Positive, significant	N.A.
33	Clark and Dawson, 1996	C	St/United States/144	Judgment	Positive, significant	N.A.

19 The religion of participating individuals is not mentioned, and cannot be guessed either considering the multi-religion society of Singapore.

prised Muslims (two in Malaysia, and one each in Iran and Pakistan). The samples in five researches conducted in Malaysia, Lebanon, Indonesia, Singapore, Hong Kong, Turkey and Germany, were a combination of two or more religions (Islam, Christianity, Hinduism, Buddhism, Taoism and Confucianism).

8 Analysis of Results and the Impact of the Nature of Statistical Population on the Findings

Except for two studies[20] where Intrinsic religiosity has a moderating role, the latter constitutes an independent variable in the rest of researches. Its impact on ethical decision-making has been direct, either without using mediator and moderator variables (in about 60%) or with the use of them (in about 40%). As shown in Table 20.1, in about 80% of the reviewed literature (26 out of 33), the overall impact of Intrinsic religiosity on ethical decision-making in business has been reported positive and significant. Only in seven studies[21] this impact has been reported as insignificant, weak, neutral or mixed. The samples of the researches include: consumers ('Co') in 13 cases; vendors ('Ve') in one case; students (mainly in Management courses) ('St') in 10 cases; common employees ('Ce') in three cases; senior managers ('Sm') in five cases; experts/specialist ('Es') in one case; and staff of religious organizations ('Ro') in two cases. Three[22] out of six studies conducted in the community of senior managers ('Sm') and experts/specialists ('Es) have reported Intrinsic religiosity to be uninfluential on ethical decision-making.

Sauerwein who had deliberately selected the statistical community from among accounting managers and experts, reported that ethical decision-making was unaffected by Intrinsic religiosity.[23] Mazereeuw-van der Duijn Schouten et al. recounted that Intrinsic religiosity of senior executive officers had either positive or negative impacts on different aspects of organizational social responsibility.[24] Jamali and Sdiani also reported the uninfluential nature of Intrinsic religiosity of Lebanese executives towards social responsibilities of the organization.[25] Nonetheless, as shown in Table 20.1, in other samples (consumers, common employees, etc.), only four out of 27 studies have reported Intrinsic religiosity as uninfluential. Consequently, it can be deduced that the positive impact of Intrinsic religiosity on ethical decision-making is weaker among senior executives and experts than other groups (consumers, common employees, etc.).

20 Sims, 2017; and, Walker et al., 2012.

21 Sauerwein, 2017; Walker et al., 2017; Mazereeuw-van der Duijn Schouten et al., 2014; Bakar et al., 2013; Jamali and Sdiani, 2013; Joe, 2009; and, Burks and Sellani, 2008.

22 Sauerwein, 2017; Mazereeuw-van der Duijn Schouten et al., 2014; and, Jamali and Sdiani, 2013.

23 Sauerwein, 2017.

24 Mazereeuw-van der Duijn Schouten et al., 2014.

25 Jamali and Sdiani, 2013.

9 Comparative Studies

In four studies, the effect of Intrinsic religiosity on ethical decision-making in business in different countries and religions have been compared: Australia and Indonesia;[26] India, China, and Malaysia;[27] Turkish Muslims and German Christians;[28] and Lebanese Muslims and Christians.[29] The results of these investigations showed greater influence of Intrinsic religiosity on ethical decision-making of the Australians than the Indonesians; the Indians than the Chinese, and the Turkish Muslims than the German Christians; but no difference between the Muslims and the Christians in Lebanon was reported.

10 Mediator Variables of Research

In just four of the studies, Machiavellianism,[30] idealism (deontology),[31] and sense of guilt[32] have been reported as mediator variables in the relationship between Intrinsic religiosity and ethical decision-making. In other words, these four studies show that with increasing Intrinsic religiosity, the Machiavellianism of the individuals decreases, while their idealism and sense of guilt (towards unethical acts) increases. As a result, the unethical attitude and tendency diminishes while the incidence rate of ethical behavior increases. It should be noted that various researches show the positive effect of idealism on ethical decision-making in business.[33]

Only seven out of 33 studies have reported the impact of Intrinsic religiosity on ethical decision making in business as not positive and not significant. One of the characteristics of all these studies is the non-utilization of mediator variables. For example, while reporting Intrinsic religiosity to be directly uninfluential on ethical decision-making, Bakar et al. have considered the impact of "sense of guilt" as a mediator variable and that of the "type of unethical behavior (either active or passive)" as a moderator variable to be positive and significant.[34]

26 Arli and Pekerti, 2017.
27 Ho, 2010.
28 Schneider et al., 2011.
29 Jamali and Sdiani, 2013.
30 Tang and Tang 2010; Chen and Tang, 2013.
31 Voegel and Pearson, 2016.
32 Bakar et al., 2013.
33 For example: Arli and Pekerti, 2017; Voegel and Pearson, 2016; Oumlil and Balloun; 2009; Vitell, 2001; Singhapakdi, 1999.
34 Bakar et al., 2013.

11 Moderator Variables of the Research

The moderator variables have been utilized to a greater extent than the mediator variables. The moderator variables used in these researches can be grouped into three categories: individual characteristics (narcissism, personal income and Good apple/bad apple); environmental variables (type of ethical challenge, legal support of ethical behavior and country); and, religious variables (in these cases, the type of religion). To put it otherwise, Intrinsic religiosity has a stronger impact on moral decision-making among people with less narcissism, lower personal income, and Good apples. The influence of Intrinsic religiosity on ethical decision-makings has been reported to be different in different countries, religions and in case of various ethical challenges.

The type of ethical challenge (scenario) is effective in the mode of influence of Intrinsic religiosity on ethical decision making. For example, Intrinsic religiosity has a positive impact in preventing unethical behaviors (passive ethical challenge), but it is either ineffective or lowly effective in encouraging ethical behaviors (active ethical challenge).[35] In the cases where legal support for an ethical conduct does not exist, the effect of Intrinsic religiosity in persuading individuals to carry out that act is likely to be more.[36] In a cross-cultural study, five different types of ethical scenarios were put forth to a sample of over 1,500 executive managers in three countries, viz. India, China, and Malaysia.[37] It was ultimately found that the level of Intrinsic religiosity of managers had a positive impact on their ability to recognize ethical challenge. Nonetheless, the impact was modified (lowered or heightened) depending on their nationality and the type of ethical challenge faced. For instance, the positive impact of Intrinsic religiosity on the ability to recognize some of the ethical challenges is stronger in the Indians than the Chinese. Moreover, the effect of Intrinsic religiosity on the ethical attitude toward some ethical challenges in a country like Australia with a relatively higher national income is stronger than that of a country like Indonesia whose national income is lower.[38] On the other hand, Chen and Tang identify increased personal income as an undermining factor for the impact of Intrinsic religiosity on attitudes toward ethical behaviors. Therefore, the moderating role of income at the national and the individual levels can be different. The positive effect of Intrinsic religiosity on ethical judgment is low in high incomes males.[39]

Narcissism constitutes another moderating variable. Presenting six unscrupulous business scenarios to 385 management students, Cooper and Pullig showed that

35 Arli, 2017; Flurry and Swimberghe, 2016; and, Bakar et al., 2013.

36 Arli and Pekerti, 2017.

37 Ho, 2010.

38 Arli and Pekerti, 2017.

39 Chen and Tang, 2013.

Intrinsic religiosity had a positive impact on their moral judgments. But this effect dies out in narcissist individuals.[40]

The type of religion is another moderating variable. For instance, Schneider et al. demonstrate that the Turkish Muslim consumers have greater ethical attitudes than the German Christian consumers.[41] On the contrary, Jamali and Sdiani found no difference between the ethical attitudes of the Christian and the Muslim executive managers in Lebanon.[42] "Good Apples and Bad Apples"[43] is another construct whose moderating role has been demonstrated in the studies of Tang and Tang. The good temperament of individuals influences the relation between "Intrinsic religiosity-Machiavellianism-ethical tendencies." Among the "Good Apples," Intrinsic religiosity positively impacts ethical tendencies both directly as well as through reducing Machiavellianism. While in case of "Bad Apples," Intrinsic religiosity has only a positive effect by reducing Machiavellianism, and its direct effect is lost.[44]

12 Synthesizing the Researches and Proposing a Model

The following model can be synthesized through reviewing the results of the above-mentioned investigations and a model for explaining the impact of Intrinsic religiosity on ethical decision-making in business is thus proposed. It is obvious, however, that the model cannot be generalized due to limited number of empirical studies that confirm its components. Consequently, the proposed model needs to be further verified in different samples through future research.

13 Discussion

Parallel synthesis of the results of investigations and the identity of their samples led to the conclusion that the positive impact of Intrinsic religiosity on ethical decision-making in business is a function of individual identities. In other words, this effect is weaker among senior managers and experts than others (consumers, common employees, students etc.). These results can be explained by "Role Morality

40 Cooper and Pullig, 2013.
41 Schneider et al., 2011.
42 Jamali and Sdiani, 2013.
43 Terms used to refer benevolent and malevolent temperament of individuals, respectively. The "Good Apples" have a lower tendency towards unethical behaviors.
44 Tang and Tang, 2010.

Theory"[45] and the importance of the prominence of organizational identity as compared to religious identity.[46] Based on the "Role Morality Theory," when the individuals are performing their professional and organizational role within the organizational framework, they are more likely to behave unethically.[47] In a pilot study, Radtke showed that individuals behave more unethically in making business-related decision than in ordinary decisions.[48] Some studies which have examined the impact of religiosity on ethical decision-making in business have reported differences between senior managers and lower-ranked officers/individuals. For example, Ibraham, Howard and Angelidis reported the impact of religiosity on social responsibility to be weaker among the managers as compared to students.[49] The study by Chusmir and Koberg also shows that the religious commitment of lower-ranked employees is greater than that of managers and higher-ranked officers.[50] The result of this research can be explained by the theory of Weaver and Agle which emphasizes the importance of relative prominence of religious identity in relation to other identities. Based on the said theory, the effect of religiosity on ethical decision-making by managers and specialists is lower than that of the lower-ranks due to the prominence of their organizational and professional identity (in comparison with their religious identity). In other words, the higher the organizational rank of individuals, the greater their organizational and professional identity as compared to their religious identity, and the lower the influence of religiosity on their ethical decision-making. Therefore, it is necessary to consider the type of occupation and the prominence of organizational identity of the individuals compared to their religious identity as an important moderating variables in all future research in the field of "Intrinsic religiosity/ethical decision-making in business."

The present article also analyzed the surveyed investigations based on geographical location and religion. The main focus of most reviewed articles has been on Christianity in United States, which is in accordance with the findings of other secondary studies in field of religion and management. Reviewing the research literature in field of religion and organization (86 papers), Tracey concluded that the focus of such studies has been on Christianity in North America and Europe.[51] Dike reviewed 83 articles in the field of religious management and showed that 46 articles were focused on Christianity, 29 on Eastern religions, and only 4 on Islam. Concentration of the research over a single geographic region and a particular religion is the main obstacle on generalizability of the results of this field of research.

45 Applbaum, 1999.
46 Weaver and Agle, 2002.
47 Applbaum, 1999; pp. 9 and 10.
48 Radtke, 2005.
49 Ibraham, Howard and Angelidis, 2008.
50 Chusmir and Koberg, 1988.
51 Tracey, 2012.

14 Conclusion

Using a Religious approach, this article first attempted to demonstrate how Islamic teachings, worldview and value system can strengthen the four-stage ethical decision-making process through the concept of "*Taqwa*" (Intrinsic religiosity). A pious/devout Muslim, who has Intrinsic religious values, views the world as a place for Divine trials and finds himself at ethical dilemmas in all aspects of life. As a result, his ethical sensitivity is elevated and the ability to recognize ethical situations is strengthened in him (the first stage of ethical decision-making). Abstaining from sinning and committing reprehensible acts ("*Makruh*"), and performing the obligatory ("*Wajib*") and the recommended ("*Mustahab*") deeds, endows the Intrinsically religious individuals with the power of distinction between right and wrong, truth and falsehood ("*Forqan*"). In other words, his ability to make ethical judgment is strengthened (second stage of ethical decision-making), and the source of his desire for unethical behavior is weakened (third stage). Consequently, the possibility of indulging in unethical behavior by pious individual is diminished (fourth stage of ethical decision-making).

In the second part of the article a scientific approach has been utilized. Initially, the equivalent of the concept of "piety" (i.e. Intrinsic religiosity) was recognized in the current empirical research. Then these researches were analyzed and synthesized in order to explain the process of how Intrinsic religiosity can impact ethical decision-making in business. A hybrid model that demonstrates the mode of this impact is also presented.

One of the most important achievements of the present research is the rejection of Kohlberg's theory (the ineffectiveness or low effectiveness of religion on ethical decision-making) by providing empirical evidence (quantitative research). Using a comprehensive and repeatable search methodology, and based on specific criteria and theories (Allport and Ross; Rest), the selection of evidence was systematically performed from among the retrieved research papers. The synthesis of these quantitative studies suggests that Intrinsic religiosity reinforces ethical decision-making in business. This is done both directly and indirectly through strengthening idealism, enhancing the sense of guilt caused by unethical behavior, as well as weakening of Machiavellian morality.

By internalizing religious beliefs, the sense of guilt towards unethical behavior acts as a defense mechanism and reduces unethical judgments and tendencies in the individual. Intrinsically religious individuals largely follow fixed ethical principles and are more idealistic than the result-oriented individuals in terms of ethical philosophy. On the other hand, various studies have demonstrated that idealism positively impacts and reinforces ethical decision-making. Hence, Intrinsic religiosity also strengthens ethical decision-making through reinforcing idealism. Moreover, Intrinsic religiosity has a positive impact on ethical decision-making by weakening Machiavellian morality. There are also background and moderating variables that either weaken or strengthen this relationship (i.e. the relationship between Intrinsic religiosity and ethical decision-making). The organizational and professional identities of the individuals are further strengthened with promotion in organizational rank, and thus the said relationship is weakened. This relationship is also weakened or totally diminished among the ill-tempered, the rich and the narcissists.

References

Al Arkoubi, Khadija. 2013. "The Islamic Faith: Implications for Business Management." In *Handbook of Faith and Spirituality in the Workplace*, edited by Judi Neal, 103–18. New York, NY: Springer New York. http://link.springer.com/10.1007/978-1-4614-5233-1_7.

Allport, Gordon W., and J. Michael Ross. 1967. "Personal Religious Orientation and Prejudice." *Journal of Personality and Social Psychology* 5 (4): 432.

Alshehri, Faisal Ali, Marianna Fotaki, and Saleema Kauser. 2016. "The Effects of Islamic Religiosity on the Ethical Judgment." In *Academy of Management Proceedings*, 2016:17996. Academy of Management.

Abu Obaid, Al-Qasem Bin Salam; 1406 LH. "Kitab Al-Amval"; First Edition; Beirut; Dar Al-Kotob Al-Elmiya.

Chalmers, Iain, Larry V. Hedges, and Harris Cooper. 2002. "A Brief History of Research Synthesis." *Evaluation & the Health Professions* 25 (1): 12–37.

Chan-Serafin, Suzanne, Arthur P. Brief, and Jennifer M. George. 2013. "How Does Religion Matter and Why? Religion and the Organizational Sciences." *Organization Science* 24 (5): 1585–1600.

Du, Xingqiang, Yingjie Du, Quan Zeng, Hongmei Pei, and Yingying Chang. 2016. "Religious Atmosphere, Law Enforcement, and Corporate Social Responsibility: Evidence from China." *Asia Pacific Journal of Management* 33 (1): 229–65.

Deilami, Hassan Bin Mohammad; 1371 SH. "Irshad Al-Qolub"; Qum, Al-Sharif Al-Razi;.

Emerson, Tisha LN, and Joseph A. Mckinney. 2009. "Importance of Religious Beliefs to Ethical Attitudes in Business." *Journal of Religion and Business Ethics* 1 (2).

Flurry, Laura A., and Krist Swimberghe. 2016. "Consumer Ethics of Adolescents." *Journal of Marketing Theory and Practice* 24 (1): 91–108. https://doi.org/10.1080/10696679.2016.1089766.

Gast, Johanna, Katherine Gundolf, and Beate Cesinger. 2017. "Doing Business in a Green Way: A Systematic Review of the Ecological Sustainability Entrepreneurship Literature and Future Research Directions." *Journal of Cleaner Production* 147 (March): 44–56. https://doi.org/10.1016/j.jclepro.2017.01.065.

Graafland, J., M. Kaptein, and C. Mazereeuw – van der Duijn Schouten. 2007. "Conceptions of God, Normative Convictions, and Socially Responsible Business Conduct: An Explorative Study Among Executives." *Business & Society* 46 (3): 331–68. https://doi.org/10.1177/0007650306296085.

Greenman, Cindy Scholten. 2012. *Marital Status, Religiosity, and Experience as a Predictor of Ethical Awareness among Accounting Professionals*. Northcentral University. http://search.proquest.com/openview/cf3393e4816a3afe38cc7658092ff312/1?pq-origsite=gscholar&cbl=18750&diss=y.

Hoon, C. 2013. "Meta-Synthesis of Qualitative Case Studies: An Approach to Theory Building." *Organizational Research Methods* 16 (4): 522–56. https://doi.org/10.1177/1094428113484969.

Hunt, S. D., and S. J. Vitell. 2006. "The General Theory of Marketing Ethics: A Revision and Three Questions." *Journal of Macromarketing* 26 (2): 143–53. https://doi.org/10.1177/0276146706290923.

Hunt Vitell. 1986. "A General Theory of Marketing Ethics." Journal of macromarketing.

Holy Quran; translated by T.B. Irving (Al-Haj Ta'lim Ali). 2003. Suhrawardi Research and Publication Center, Tehran-Iran.

Harrani, Abu Mohammad Al-Hassan Bin Ali Bin Al-Hossein Bin Sho'ba; 1363 SH. "Tohfa' Ul-Oqul An Al-ul-Rasul"; edited/corrected by Ali Akbar Al-Qaffari; Second Edition; Qum; Islamic Publication Institute.

Hor Al-Ameli, Al-Sheikh Mohammad Bin Al-Hassan;1403 LH. "Vasayel Al-Shia"; 20 Vols.; edited/corrected by Abdol Rahim Al-Rabani Al-Shirazı; Maktabe Al-Islamiye.

Ismaeel, Muatasim, and Katharina Blaim. 2012. "Toward Applied Islamic Business Ethics: Responsible Halal Business." Edited by Wafa El Garah. *Journal of Management Development* 31 (10): 1090–1100. https://doi.org/10.1108/02621711211281889.

James, William. 1910. *The Varieties of Religious Experience: A Study in Human Nature*. Longmans Green and Company.

Kohlberg, Lawrence. 1976. "Moral Stages and Moralization: The Cognitive-Developmental Approach." *Moral Development and Behavior: Theory, Research, and Social Issues*, 31–53.

Koleini, Abu Jafar Mohammad Bin Al-Yaqub; 1362 SH. "Al-Kafi"; edited/corrected by Ali Akbar Al-Qaffari; 8 Vols.; Dar Al-Kitab Islamiye; Tehran.

Lehnert, Kevin, Yung-hwal Park, and Nitish Singh. 2015. "Research Note and Review of the Empirical Ethical Decision-Making Literature: Boundary Conditions and Extensions." *Journal of Business Ethics* 129 (1): 195–219. https://doi.org/10.1007/s10551-014-2147-2.

Masters, Kevin S., Robert D. Hill, John C. Kircher, Tera L. Lensegrav Benson, and Jennifer A. Fallon. 2004. "Religious Orientation, Aging, and Blood Pressure Reactivity to Interpersonal and Cognitive Stressors." *Annals of Behavioral Medicine* 28 (3): 171–178.

Melé, Domènec. 2015. "Religious Approaches on Business Ethics: Current Situation and Future Perspectives." *Ramon Llull Journal of Applied Ethics*, no. 6: 137–160.

Majlesi, Mohammad Baqer; 1404 LH. "Behar Al-Anwar"; Wafa Institute; Beirut, Lebanon.

Nath, Sushmit. 2007. "Religion & Economic Growth and Development."

Oumlil, A. Ben, and Joseph L. Balloun. 2009. "Ethical Decision-Making Differences Between American and Moroccan Managers." *Journal of Business Ethics* 84 (4): 457–78. https://doi.org/10.1007/s10551-008-9719-y.

Parboteeah, K. Praveen, Martin Hoegl, and John B. Cullen. 2008. "Ethics and Religion: An Empirical Test of a Multidimensional Model." *Journal of Business Ethics* 80 (2): 387–98. https://doi.org/10.1007/s10551-007-9439-8.

Peterson, Robert A., Gerald Albaum, Dwight Merunka, Jose Luis Munuera, and Scott M. Smith. 2010. "Effects of Nationality, Gender, and Religiosity on Business-Related Ethicality." *Journal of Business Ethics* 96 (4): 573–87. https://doi.org/10.1007/s10551-010-0485-2.

Proios, Miltiadis, and Ioannis Proios. 2017. "The Influence of Religiosity on Moral Judgment in Sport." *Social Sciences* 6 (1): 5. https://doi.org/10.3390/socsci6010005.

Raqeb Isfahani, Hossein Bin Mohammad; 1412 LH. "Al-Mofradat fi Qarib A-Quran"; corrected and researched by Adnan Davood; Beirut, Suri; Dar Al-Elm Al-Dar Al-Shami.

Rest, James R. 1979. *Development in Judging Moral Issues*. Minneapolis: University of Minnesota Press.

Reyshahri, Mohammad; 1416 LH; "Mizan Al-Hekmat"; Qum, Dar Al-Hadith; Second Ed.

Reyshahri, Mohammad. 1986. "Moral Development: Advances in Research and Theory."

Richardson, Christopher, Lalita Sinha, and Md. Salleh Yaapar. 2014. "Work Ethics from the Islamic and Hindu Traditions: In Quest of Common Ground." *Journal of Management, Spirituality & Religion* 11 (1): 65–90. https://doi.org/10.1080/14766086.2013.801025.

Saat, Maisarah Mohamed, Stacey Porter, and Gordon Woodbine. 2009. "Does Religiosity Influence Ethical Sensitivity? An Investigation on Malaysian Future Accountants." *Malaysian Accounting Review* 8 (2): 17–41.

Sidani, Yusuf, and Akram Al Ariss. 2015. "New Conceptual Foundations for Islamic Business Ethics: The Contributions of Abu-Hamid Al-Ghazali." *Journal of Business Ethics* 129 (4): 847–57. https://doi.org/10.1007/s10551-014-2136-5.

Smith, Raymond D., Jason D. DeBode, and Alan G. Walker. 2013. "The Influence of Age, Sex, and Theism on Ethical Judgments." *Journal of Management, Spirituality & Religion* 10 (1): 67–89. https://doi.org/10.1080/14766086.2012.758048.

Syed, Jawad, and Beverly Dawn Metcalfe. 2015. "Guest Editors' Introduction: In Pursuit of Islamic Akhlaq of Business and Development." *Journal of Business Ethics* 129 (4): 763–67. https://doi.org/10.1007/s10551-014-2130-y.

Tamimi Amedi, Abd Al-Wahed Bin Mohammad; 1366 SH. "Tasnif Qarrar Al-Hekam va Dorrar Al-Kalam"; researched and corrected by Derayati, Mostafa; p. 361; H 8200; Islamic Publicity Office; Qum; First Edition.

Weaver, Gary R., and Bradley R. Agle. 2002. "Religiosity and Ethical Behavior in Organizations: A Symbolic Interactionist Perspective." *Academy of Management Review* 27 (1): 77–97.

Wimalasiri, Jayantha S. 2001. "Moral Reasoning Capacity of Management Students and Practitioners: An Empirical Study in Australia." *Journal of Managerial Psychology* 16 (8): 614–34. https://doi.org/10.1108/EUM0000000006303.

Seyyed Ziaoddin Kia al-Hosseini

Chapter 22: The Role of Religious and Ethical Teachings in Designing Social Welfare Function

1 Introduction

Welfare and prosperity are among the ancient desires of human beings and any economic system, though the way a society is led toward achieving welfare is different in various economies. To this end, the economics of welfare is a framework based on which the importance of normative decision making and economic events are evaluated. In order to interpret the results of economic welfare over a phenomenon, one must go beyond the study of positive economics so that the impact of a phenomenon over economic variables (such as price and quantity) could be objectively measurable. The welfare economist would like to specify the desirability of a specific policy, not on account of his own values, but rather on account of an explicit ethical criterion. To evaluate states and policies and make his recommendation, he would need to socially rank different economic position. This will enable him to compare all positions and classify each of them as better, worse, or equal relative to other positions (Bourdy and Bruce, 1993, p. 4). Welfare economists grapple with definition, explanation, and measurement of social and economic phenomena. They aim to clarify or measure specific aspects related to the concept of social welfare. The highest degree of public comprehension of social welfare comes from some considerations such as inequality and poverty in society, extensiveness of rights, liberty, and opportunities provided the people. Therefore, it is natural that welfare economists are interested in the contents of these concepts and measurements. Another goal for welfare economics is to provide methods and criteria for evaluating policy changes. As a result, a fundamental question in welfare economics is what makes a policy change is desirable? Despite considerable research related to this question and presentation of various methods and criteria by economists, law scholars, philosophers, ethical scholars, and politicians, and the like, no completely acceptable answer to this question (one that could command strong consensus) has been offered. Therefore, welfare economics is a multifaceted and interdisciplinary subject and is approached differently depending on visions, ideologies, cultures and even geographies. Hence, ethical and value judgements play an important role in this subject. On the other hand, welfare is sometimes referred to mere economic features such as income, consumption, accommodation, and sometimes takes a more general meaning and includes having an appropriate level of education, health, hygiene, lifespan, and the like. This more general concept is known as well-being. The most extensive definition of welfare, referred to as "happiness and prosperity," involves value concepts

https://doi.org/10.1515/9783110593419-022

such as beneficence, goodness and virtue of individual and society. The emergence of modernity and materialistic approach toward human being, human values and human society ever since eighteenth century, words such as welfare, fortunate, prosperity, and the like refer mostly to purely materialistic this-worldly happiness. In the vision of Islam, however, welfare is interpreted to mean felicity and prosperity and therein lies the essential difference between this vision and that of conventional theories. The present paper is an attempt to explain the impact of religious ethics and teachings on designing social welfare function. To achieve this goal, the next section presents and analyses the history and definition of the concepts of welfare and welfare economics. In the third section, various types of social welfare will be discussed. What is meant by welfare function is a mathematical expression, formed based on the researcher's thinking or on the thinking of a particular school of economics, and includes variables that influence welfare and the ways they exert such influence. Section four deals with the role of ethics and religious values on designing a welfare function. As mentioned, the subject of social welfare is interdisciplinary topic influenced by value judgements. For this reason, the section is divided into two subsections. In the first subsection, teachings, beliefs and rules that influence indirectly the social welfare function are explained and analyzed. Factors that influence the social welfare directly are presented and analyzed in the second subsection. In the conventional economics, three principles govern welfare economics: comparability, anonymity, and symmetry. It appears that by taking into account ethical values and Islamic teachings, three other principles influence the design of the social welfare function: Other-worldly orientation, spirituality, and altruism. The last section of the paper is devoted to summary and conclusion.

2 History of Welfare Economics

For variety of reasons, there are a number of ways to classify theories of welfare. For instance, on the basis of the methods used for social ranking and measuring social welfare, there are two general methods of welfarism, non-welfarism, or meta-welfarism. Welfarism evaluates policies on the basis of their impact on the utility of individuals while non-welfarism considers the impact of policies beyond their effects on individual utility. Alternatively, welfare theories could be classified under three categories on the basis of the measurement criterion of welfare, utility and variables influencing the welfare function (Crisp, 2008). The first category includes those theories that define welfare in terms of elements internal to the individuals such as enjoyment, happiness and the like and are known as "hedonistic theories". The second category is a perspective that defines welfare in terms of satisfaction of preferences and desires that could be called "superficial theory". The third category includes those theories that define welfare in terms of the elements that constitute it (Hausman and Mcpherson, 2006, p. 119). It is apparent that the classification of social states, whatever the criteria, is a normative method and involves value judgement so that any set of adopted value judgements results in a different social ranking. Therefore, there is no objective or unified method of ranking social states. In the following section we analyze and explain these various methods of classification.

2.1 Hedonistic Theory

This theory is the same as welfarism, considers welfare and prosperity as something real and internal to the individual, i. e. pleasure. The advent of this theory goes back to Jeremy Bentham who believed "nature is governing mankind by two potent lords, namely pleasure and pain. Only these two can determine what we must do or what we will do. On the other hand, the criteria of evaluation of goodness or badness is tied to them. (Bentham ,1996, p. 11). The classical economists, following Jeremy Bentham, have simply added individual utilities arithmetically together to arrive at the means to evaluate the welfare impact of a policy in terms of whether the policy has increased or reduced the total utility. This approach, however, has some limitations because it not only assumes that utility can be measured arithmetically but also assumes interpersonal comparability of utility. The hypothesis of comparability and/or arithmetic addition of utility is as meaningless as comparing and/or adding apples and oranges.. One of the problems of this method is reporting on the welfare impact of events and policies. This problem is adding all the individual preferences to arrive at in a meaningful measure of total welfare of the society. This problem was solved in the nineteenth century by utilitarianism which assumed that the amount of pleasure obtained from consumption of each good for each household (such as temperature) is measurable in cardinal numbers (Bourdy and Bruce, 1993, p. 61). Old welfare economics, which was built on the foundation of utilitarianism, had accepted the two hypotheses of carinal utility and its interpersonal comparisons.

There are a few points to mention concerning the theory of welfarism. First, it is not possible to assert that welfare and wellbeing are external to and have no relation or reaction internal to an individual. Second, goodness and badness of somethings are relative in the sense that something may be good for one person and bad for another. Third, the goodness of somethings is not necessarily intrinsic; rather, the thing is an instrument and intermediary step toward obtaining another good thing. For instance, high income is not inherently good in and of itself but rather, presumably, it is good as means to a good life.

Also, the hedonistic theory is based on two concepts. On the one hand, it is presumed that an individual always acts on the basis of pursuing something which gives him the highest utility, which is a psychological hedonism concept. The second concept, on the other hand, holds that hedonism is dictated by practical rational mind. Thus, it is an ethical criterion for measurement and evaluation which is called "evaluative hedonism". Therefore, laws should be designed in a way that would maximize utility and minimize pain. Adherents to this theory believe that the prime goal of punishment is to avoid repetition rather than rehabilitating the criminal which is a different objective (Bentham, 1996 [1789], p. 158–64).

With respect to individual behavior, this perspective believes that people intrinsically and naturally behave the way they must, therefore, naturally and intrinsically human beings are aware that welfare and wellbeing are the same as utility and that is what they want and pursue. There is however something other than the nature of pleasure involved in the utility of things which determines whether it is desirable or undesirable thus making pleasure only an indicator of utility (Nozick, 1991, pp. 42–43; Mcpherson and Hausman, 2006). For example, enjoyment from irrational activities such as use of illicit drugs has negative effect on welfare and wellbeing of the user. With respect to society, if the increasing the level of welfare and wellbeing of society is considered a responsibility of the government, then the latter should design policies and institutions such that the total pleasure in the society is maximized since, according to this view, the welfare of the society is the sum total of the utility of its members. Consequently, this view holds that individuals should be allowed to pursue their own self-interests with no or minimal interference. Hence, government should not intervene in the workings of the economy and only police behaviors of individuals to ensure that there are no violation against the freedom of others. That is why the old welfare economics believed that perfect competition would lead to maximization of social welfare. Any interference in the market, according to this view, would create disturbances in the workings of the market and reduce individual and social welfare.

2.2 Pareto Principle

Vilferedo Pareto was the first person who defined the concepts of social welfare in a way that did not rely on the assumptions of cardinal measurement or interpersonal comparison of utility. Hence he is known as the father of the concept of ordinal utility. His theory involved much weaker assumption and involved a criterion for the measurement of changes in the social welfare that became known as "Pareto Criterion" (Bourdy and Bruce, 1993, p. 61). According to the definition of Pareto criterion, any allocation of goods and services among households is considered an economic state. Pareto criterion allows comparison of two economic states (X and Y) based on their resulting social welfare. According to the strong Pareto criterion, if in state X some people are better off relative to state Y and no one is worse off in state X than in state Y, then state X is preferred because the level of social welfare is better than in state Y. According to the weak Pareto criterion, however, state X is preferable to state Y if one household is better off in state X than in state Y (Bourdy and Bruce, 1993, p. 62).

The Pareto optimalityrefers to a state of economy in which, under a given set of conditions, no can be made better off without making someone else worse off. Such state exists in abundance in the economy. For example, it is possible to imagine a state in the economy where one person possesses the total national income while the rest of the people in the society go hungry or, alternatively, a state in which everyone has equal income. All such states are Pareto optimal but not Pareto comparable and Pareto criterion cannot be used to choose between them (Bourdy and Bruce, 1993, p. 63).

This criterion has some shortcomings. The first one is its imperfect rating through Pareto principle because using this principle, incomparable states of the economy cannot be ranked. For example, it is not possible to evaluate the state in which (as a result of a given policy) some people are made better off and others worse off. In other words, given the Pareto efficiency principle, it is not possible to rank a Pareto optimal allocation preferable to another non-Pareto optimal allocation or even rank two different Pareto optimal allocations relative to one another. One solution to this problem is referred to as the "compensation principle" proposed first by Hicks (1939) and Kaldor (1939). According to the compensation principle, the state B is preferred to the state A if those who gain from a policy would compensate the losers such that at least one person is better off and no one is worse off. However, compensation here is potential not actual in which payment of compensation depends on value judgement. However, the principle of compensation does not have the necessary attraction to become basis of laws since the Hicks-Kaldor rule can lead to unethical consequences by sacrificing the innocent. For example, the utility that a criminal obtains from committing a financial or sexual crime may be more than the loss of utility by the victim. Question then arises whether the society can accept Hick-Kaldor rule of compensation in this or like situations. With due consideration to justice and ethics, the answer is clear. Another problem is the neutrality of Pareto criterion vis-à-vis income distribution. For example, consider a state of the economy in which, as a result of a policy, the rich are better off without the poor becoming worse off. While in this new state of the economy, there is Pareto improvement, income distribution is worse than before. Another criticism of Pareto Optimality has been offered by Sen (1970) who argued that Pareto criterion is in conflict with liberal values in the sense that a Pareto-optimal state may not be liberal. For example, in designing laws dealing with internet crimes, while consideration of impact of these laws on the utility of individuals are important, the freedom and private rights of individuals too has to play a significant role in evaluating the consequences of such laws. The framework of the old welfare economics is very limited when it comes to including these concerns regarding the rights and freedom of individuals, fairness and other human values. In general, considering the Pareto principle as the sole basis of defining the objective of laws is not rational.

2.3 Theories of Happiness and Life Satisfaction as Welfare and Wellbeing

Also called "desire and want" theories was first expounded by Sumner (1996; see also Crisp, 2008) who shifting attention from focus on pleasure to desire and want, argued that what the individuals want is athe actual experience. Either due to their mathematical orientation or a desire to avoid philosophical debates, many economists continue to adhere to the superficial theory of welfare economics. On the assumption that individuals are the best judge of their own interests, securing their own preferences is the same as their serving their own welfare. Therefore, they argue that by observing each individual's preference, their welfare and well-being can be determined. This view reflects the influence of behavioral approach to social sciences or paternalism of liberal thinking.

This conception of welfare is attractive for economists because, on the one hand, it offers a concrete set of measurements, such as dealing with what is possible in the design of a ranking system and welfare functions, on the one hand, and the political compatibility of this conception with the present dominant economic thinking, on the other. Moreover, the dominant thinking argues, planners, legilators and policy makers do not possess as much information about individuals and their situations as do the individuals themselves nor, it can be assumed, worry as much or expected to seek more benefits for individuals that the latter do for themselves. Hence, it is argued, this conception would dictate minimal interference of government in the economic life of individuals; an assertion which is again compatible with the thinking presently dominant in economics.

The simplest form of this theory is that the welfare and prosperity of a person is considered to be within the present preference satisfaction of the person, which is called "present preference satisfaction theory". It is evident that the individual's preference satisfaction does not necessarily provide his welfare and prosperity; rather, sometimes it is possible that it could lead to opposite results (Crisp, 2008, section 2–4). This type of criticism brought attention to the "comprehensive preference satisfaction theory" based on which the welfare and wellbeing of the individual is related to the level of total satisfaction of the preferences of the individual over the lifetime and not limited solely to the present or specifically periodic preferences (Crisp, 2008, section 2–4). Both theories face other shortcomings and limitations. For instance, the individuals' preferences are a function of information available to them, their own calculations, views and beliefs (Sen, 1987, chapter 1).

The "inclusive and informed preference satisfaction theory" was proposed to avoid these limitations. It appears that even this theory has some shortcomings. For example, the individual's preferences, in addition to the variables mentioned earlier, depend on his taste, level of thinking, insight, and will. Therefore, satisfaction and provision of vulgar preferences, preference for expensive and luxury products, preference for harmful products, racist or other anti-social preferences (Hausman and Mcpherson, 2006, p. 127) as well as preferences derived from laziness or idleness do not necessarily serve welfare and wellbeing of individuals nor can general policy making or ethical mandates be justified on the basis of such preferences. To correct for these shortcomings, some consider that welfare and wellbeing relate to preference satisfaction based on rational or fully informed or refined self-interest (Rileton, 1986).

Although there is a great gap between the primary simple theory and that of evolved theory, that is satisfaction of rational preferences with full information and refinement, there is criticism to this latter theory as well. For instance, what is meant by rational or refined? What is the criterion of rationality? By what means does the refinement take place? To avoid these question as well philosophical discussions, economists resorted to the superficial theory but this reduced welfare theories to the level of considering only mechanical behavior. When each individual is considered the best judge of his own best interests and wellbeing analyzed through preference satisfaction, at least in some cases base instincts replace wisdom and rationality of the intellect that has the capability of knowing good and evil whereby the latter is replaced by the thinking instrument slave to base instincts which is calculating and self-centered. As a result, the concepts of welfare and wellbeing, which mean knowing the best human interests and felicity, transform into material and superficial concepts that relate to pleasure or satisfaction of preferences.

2.4 Objective List Theories

These theories search for the objective components of the "good life." Since they attempt to define elements that actually constitute the welfare and wellbeing of individuals, they are considered among realistic (not superficial) theories. They focus on the states internal to the individual such as pleasure and contentment that constitute the good life. While the actualization of a good life for an individual reflects his internal state, the essential question is what are the elements of the list of variable that lead to the good life?

The prominent contemporary economists, Amartya Sen, believes welfare and wellbeing of each individual is determined by his/her capabilities and functionalities. He considers a person's life as the collection of interrelated functionalities. In his opinion, the wellbeing of a person can be judged based on the quality of his life which, according to Sen, depends on total interrelated functionalities available to that person. Functionality of a person includes the kind of work he performs as well as situations or emotions he experiences. Sen argues that a person's functionalities transcend usual activities such as walking, reading, good diet, normal life expectancy to include achievements such as happiness, self-respect, and participation in social activities. As well, Sen believes that the same that a person's budget reflects his ability and his freedom of choice in his consumption behavior, his capabilities in the functionality space reflects his freedom in the choice of the type of life he wants to live (Sen, 1992, p. 31–40). Sen explains the relationship between welfare and capability in two different ways. First, freedom of choice is a valuable part of life and influential component in determining its quality, therefore, the level of welfare is subject to the boundaries of his freedom. Second, freedom is an important element for an optimal social structure. Thus, a good society is the one in which, in addition to other components of the good life, it can also be free (Sen, 1992, pp. 40–41). However, Sen does not provide a list of capabilities since he believes capabilities differ from one society to another depending on the objectives and conditions of societies because, in his view, components of welfare are not constant and change depending on conditions of societies (Sen, 1992, pp. 41–45). In his view, government policies should focus on expanding capabilities rather than on individuals' functionalities directly since the latter depends on individual's choices. Moreover, Sen does not directly explain the philosophical foundation of his theory and does not specify the bases for or the logic of the determination of the components that would constitute the capabilities. In other words, what bases and criteria help us determine functionalities and capabilities of a good life? It appears that he considers the matter to be something traditional and, without entering into this discussion, he refers it to the works of the contemporary philosopher, Nussbaum, with whom he has done joint research in the past (Sen, 1992, p. 39).

Martha Nussbaum explains her theory according to Aristotelian point of view of human virtue and wellbeing. Aristotle believed that the virtue of every being is its perfection and virtue should be something that is inherently desirable. In his opinion, this should be explored in relation to individuals' duties which are different from one person to another depending on their occupation. For this reason, we must search for what all humans share in common. To determine the true nature of felicity one should explore the specific feature of human life which he calls rational life that guides human behavior through human intellect which possesses the power of differentiation between good and bad and which shows humans how to achieve perfection. Of course, this is not the calculating and self-interested intellect that serves human desires (Aristotle, 2007, pp. 16–22). In this perspective, Nussbaum believes that what makes up the welfare and wellbeing of a person is what constitutes his special life as a human being, such as having access to knowledge which brings about the flourishing and perfection of human nature, and are the elements that determine the welfare and wellbeing of humans. Accordingly, Nussbaum presents a list of basic human capabilities which in summary are: having a normal life expectancy, health and fitness, security, decent education that creates the mental and rational health, mental and spiritual health that constitute his emotions, guaranteed freedom of speech and beliefs, ability to envision virtue and goodness, possibility of forming social relationships with others and participation in social interactions, having respect and esteem and the absence of possibility of being subjected to any kind of indignity and contempt (Nussbaum, 2001, pp. 416–418). She believes that the government duty is merely the provision of minimal level of every capability for all citizens which is determined by the internal policy procedures of each country and are protected and preserved by social institutions. Therefore, according to Nussbaum, human welfare and wellbeing is to be found in factors that lead to the growth and flourishing of human potentialities which is the subject of discussion, debate and determination in different societies and cultures.

Undoubtedly, the objective-list theory, especially Sen's theory and that of Nussbaum, is considered as an advancement in welfare theories, but it encounters limitations and problems. First, Sen has not proposed a specific basis for determination of capabilities and functionalities that constitute a good life. Second, the objective-list perspective is founded on the modern conceptual basis of the "self". Human is modeled merely as a materialistic and worldly being for whom freedom and autonomy are original and basic values for a this-worldly life. All other values such as welfare and wellbeing, equality and justice, are preconditioned to redefine the basic values of freedom and autonomy. In addition, the modernistic conceptualization of the "self" here influences conceptions of human perfection and those capabilities and functionalities are emphasized which fully free and autonomous individuals can choose for his lifestyle through achievement of which they can actualize the flourishing of their potential talents. Finally, this perspective a type of cultural plurality in terms of competencies is accepted in line with preservation of individual freedom and autonomy.

3 Types of Social Welfare Functions

Social welfare function is a mathematic form which in summary includes variables that influence social welfare. As indicated before, social welfare is a multifaceted subject and includes value discussions. Therefore, the researchers' perspective can affect the form of the social welfare function. For instance, the formation of a social welfare function proposed by a given researcher can be influenced by the the utility obtained from consumption of goods and services or the underlying philosophical attitude of a researcher or a school of economic thought toward justice. The classical school, first generation of Western economists, believed that the social welfare function was composed of the utility the members of the society obtained from goods and services and proposed the following social welfare function for a society composed of two persons, individual A and individual B:

$$W = W(U^A, U^B) \tag{1}$$

Bergson and Samuelson proposed a modern version of the social welfare function as function as:

$$W=W(C_1, C_2, ..., C_k ; h_1, h2, ..., h_k) \tag{2}$$

In this function, the society is composed of K groups (n number) and work is the only source of income. Individuals divide their time between work and leisure so that the social welfare is a function of leisure (h_i) and consumption (c_i). Maximization of individual utility is subject to the condition that that the marginal product of labor is equal to the marginal rate of substitution between consumption and leisure.

The second modern form of social welfare function was proposed by Kenneth J. Arrow who showed, through exposition of his "impossibility theorem," that a social utility function based on the aggregation of individual welfare based on the free choices of individuals is not possible. Therefore, to compare different social states, he proposed the use of social welfare function composed of individual preferences, R_i. The general form of his social welfare function is:

$$W = F(R_1, R_2, \ldots, R_k) \tag{3}$$

Harsany in 1955 presented a third form of social welfare function by separating individual utilities and social welfare preferences which in his view represented both social preferences (that is, an individual's consideration of the welfare of others) and individual interests. This allows for comparison of welfare between different people as well. Therefore, the social welfare function is defined as the total weighted utility of utility of the ,members of the society as:

$$W = \sum_{i=1}^{n} \alpha_i \beta_i \tag{4}$$

In which α_I is a positive coefficient and the condition to maximize the above function is the following equation:

$$\alpha_i = \frac{U_i}{m_i} = \alpha_j = \frac{U_j}{m_j} \tag{5}$$

Equation (5) shows that the realization of equality between individuals requires that coefficient α should be equal for all individuals.

Due to lack of information concerning individuals' utility function, Atkinson designed the social welfare function based on the level of income of individuals such that by changing the relevant coefficient of equality or inequality, it would be possible to determine the sensitivity of the function to income distribution. In some way, this proposed function does not face the difficulties associated with functions based on utility. The form of this utility is as:

$$W = f(I_1, I_2, \ldots, I_n) \tag{6}$$

In this function, (I) represents individuals or the average income of different groups.

"Utilitarian" social welfare function is a form of functions that was designed by Dalton in order to meet the needs of utilitarianism school. Accordingly, social welfare is the aggregation of individual utilities:

$$W = \sum_{i=1}^{n} U_i(X_i) \tag{7}$$

This function is not sensitive to income distribution; therefore, its coefficient for everyone is equal. Amartya Sen (1973) showed that maximizing welfare according to utilitarianism will lead logically to and equal distribution of income only if all individuals in the society have the same utility function; even if one individual among all the members has a different utility function, increase in the level of social welfare increases income inequality. The condition for maximizing social welfare function, according to utilitarianism, is: $\frac{\partial Ui}{\partial Mi} = \frac{\partial Uj}{\partial Uj}$, that is, marginal utilities derived from income are equal for all individuals.

In contrast to utilitarianism, John Rawls proposed welfare function which is entirely sensitive to income distribution such that social welfare increased only when the state of the poorest people in society is improved. This means that increase in the total welfare of the society depends on the increase in the welfare of the poorest individual such that if his welfare is not improved, any increase in the welfare of others does not mean that the total welfare and the wellbeing of the society has improved. The mathematic form of this welfare function is as follows:

$$W = W(U_1, U_2, \ldots, U_n) = Min\ \{U_1, U_2, \ldots, U_n\} \tag{8}$$

The last social welfare function to be discussed here was proposed by Amartya Kumar Sen who, along with his colleagues proposed that social welfare is a function of the utility of the individual members of the society which is itself, in turn, a function of the social position of the individuals:

$$S(X) = S[U(X_1), U(X_2), \ldots, U(X_n)] \tag{9}$$

Where S is a symmetrical and concave function, and U is also a concave function, that is why to a large extent it looks like Bergson Samuelson social welfare function. If the utility function of every individual is the same, the social welfare function equals the total utility of individuals in the, $\sum_i^n = 1[U(x)] = s(x)\, f(x)\, dx$. In 1974, Sen proposed another form of social welfare function as follows:

$$W(x) = \sum_{i=1}^{n} X_i\, \vartheta_i(X) \tag{10}$$

In this model X_i is the income of the person i, and $\vartheta_i\ (X)$ is the weight given to the person. Now, if it is assumed that (X,i) is a state belonging to the person i in income distribution X which has the income state X_i, the general form of the social welfare function proposed by Sen would be as follows:

$$W(X) = \mu\,(1\text{-}G) \tag{11}$$

where μ is the average income and G is Gini coefficient for income inequality.[1] Finally, η_μ and η_G are sensitivity or elasticity of social welfare function W (x) with respect to average income (μ) (as the economic growth index) and with respect to the state of income distribution and inequality (G), that is:

$$\eta_\mu = 1 \quad \text{and} \quad \eta_G = \frac{G}{1-G} \Rightarrow |\eta_G| < |\eta_\mu| \quad \text{for} \quad G < \frac{1}{2}$$

now if the Gini coefficient is less than 0.5, Sen's social welfare function is more sensitive to average income (economic growth) than to income inequality.

In general, it can be concluded that all the functions discussed briefly here try to measure social welfare and its changes. Most of them consider welfare as having a qualitative characteristic and a function of utility of individuals in the society the quantitative version of which requires constructing a measurement criterion. However, the function proposed by Sen is an exception in that it is already a quantitative function for measuring economic welfare and welfare changes. In Sen's formulation, welfare is a function of per capita income and Gini coefficient. In this context, principles that govern the social welfare function include the following:

1. Symmetry principle (anonymity): a basic principle of most modern value systems is the indifference (anonymity) principle. The principle of reciprocity which states: "Treat others the way you would like others to treat you" means that while judging what person A should do in situations that affect both individual A as well as individual B, one must remain indifferent toward the individuals. Meaning that if, at a point in time, individual A was in a superior position to individual B but the situation was reversed such that individual B was placed in a superior position with respect to individual A, it will not change one's judgement (Layard and Walters, 1985, p. 54).
2. Comparability: it means that the social welfare function should be formed such as to allow comparisons across various economic states. Based on this principle, the welfare function should have the necessary weight to compare various income classes and their population densities. For instance, such a social welfare function would allow us to know enough about the population and their position in the income distribution to identify the poorest member of the society. According to Rawls a policy that would improve this person's welfare while reduce that of the rest of the society is fair and must be implemented. This principle is based

1 Coefficient represents the amount of inequality for income distribution in society and changes between 0 and 1. It means that if it is 0 the whole people are of identical income, and if becomes 1 it means that the entire income of society is for one person or one statistical class of income.

on the idea that one can cardinally measure the welfare of individuals as well as compare it across individuals.

3. Transfer principle: if person A is richer than person B, any income transfer from person A to person B increases total welfare. For any welfare function it seems there is a reasonable and logical condition. The more the people of the society favor income equality the closer the welfare indifference curves of the function approach the vertical axis. In turn, if we are indifferent toward income distribution, the identical welfare curves change into a straight line (Ibid, p. 54).

4 The Role of Ethics and Religious Values in Designing Welfare Function

At the introductory part of this paper it was mentioned that the subject of welfare is not detached from the consideration of values embedded in beliefs, teachings, culture and ethics. Since divine religions, especially Islam, are based on spiritual teachings and ethics, it is natural to consider values in the design and implementation of economic policies, measurement of impact of policies on people's welfare, in judging economic states or in designing the social welfare function for Muslim societies. From the point of view of Islam, welfare and wellbeing are subjects that are dealt with in different domains of the Islamic sources (the Qur'an and Sunnah) and also writings on Ethics, but in this paper we deal with the part of these sources that deals directly with the subject matter of social welfare function. Religious values that influence the design of the social welfare function could be divided into two sections. The first section includes teachings that have indirect influences and those that relate directly to the design of the social welfare function.

4.1 Teachings that have Indirect Impact

Dual dimensionality of human being (matter and spirit) is clear and certain in the Qur'an and Sunnah. Numerous verse of the Qur'an reason that the ultimate objective of the creation of humans is their perfection (see for example, Qur'an, Hijr (15:29). This objective is presented in its various dimensions, such as being an agent or vicegerent (Khalifah) of the Creator on earth (2:30); an expression of the Love of Allah (Walayah) (2:257); life of purity (Hayat Tayyibah) (16:97); the Firm station of Truth (Magham Sidq) near Allah (54:55); the station of Contentment having achieved the pleasure of Allah (3:15; 5:119); and the station of Adoration ('Ubudiyyah) of Allah (51:57). In other words, from the perspective of the Qur'an, a human being achieves ultimate felicity and wellbeing when he/she achieves the station of nearness to the Divine and has earned a life of contentment in Heaven as is reflected in Chapter 11: Verse 108. These examples from the Qur'an indicate that to achieve ultimate wellbeing and felicity or human perfection is a free choice available to humans.

To achieve such a state of welfare and wellbeing the teachings of the Qur'an, the Prophet (sawa) and his family and progeny (as) have enumerated the components of behavior required for this objective. These include: believing in the origin of creation and the final stage of return and accountability, aware adoration of the Creator, avoidance of wasteful use of one's time (23:1–3), purification of the self (87:14; 91:9); remembrance of Allah (87:14; 62:10); repentance and return to Allah (24:31); Consciousness of Allah and exertion of effort in the way of Allah (5:35), all of which represent the other-worldly dimension human wellbeing. In the sacred legacy of the Prophet (sawa) and his family and progeny (as) elements such as certainty; action according to knowledge; belief; perseverance on the path of truth and justice; constant questioning of the self, holding it accountable, and efforts at its purification; love for the Prophet (sawa), his family and progeny (as) and following their teachings; tranquil heart; obedience to intellect (al-'Aql) and disobedience of ignorance (al-Jahl) are all considered as factors thar lead to felicity and wellbeing. Blessings of Allah that constitute elements of worldly wellbeing have been referred to in many verses of the Qur'an and in sacred narrations. These include: Learning the Qur'an and attaining wisdom (2:231); comfortable home (7:74), husband and wife (30:21); righteous children (4:14); provision of sustenance (35:3); good means of transportation (Majlisi, 1992, volume 76, pp. 143–149); good neighbors and companions (Saduq, 1982, pp. 159–207); appropriate occupation (Majlisi, 1992, Volume 103, pp. 5–19), health of body and belief (Nahj al-Bilaghah, Speech 99); and security (Saduq, 1982, pp. 284–334).

4.2 Learnings with Direct Impression

As mentioned earlier, three principles of comparability, anonymity and symmetry govern the design of the social welfare function in conventional economics. These principles, which are self-evident and with which intellect and intellectual agree, are acceptable in Islam as well. However, these three principles don't differentiate social welfare function from personal attitudes leading a welfare function that is based on individualism. One way of correcting for this shortcoming is to introduce supplementary principles derived from religious teachings that would allow us to transcend the focus on the one-dimensionality of individualism and materialism. Islamic belief, teachings and ethics make it possible to design a social welfare function that takes account of the interrelationships among the individuals in the society (for example, the fact that the welfare of individual a influences the welfare of B and vice versa), altruism, empathy, and benevolence, thus reflecting individual's beliefs, ethics and behavior which impact the welfare of other members of the society. Such principles include.

4.2.1 Principle of Altruism

The Qur'an states that believers are brother to one another (49:10), a principle which the Prophet (sawa) implemented among his followers upon entering Medina through the contract of brotherhood between those who accompanied him in his migration from Mecca and the people of Medina. Imam Ali(as) in his letter 45 recommends that a Muslim, especially government agent, has no right to sleep with a full belly while his neighbors are hungry. Or in the letter 53 he reminds Malik Ashtar, whom the Imam appointed as the Governor of Egypt, that the people of Egypt are either his brothers in Islam or are his brothers in humanity living in peace with the Muslims and have rights as human beings. Therefore, he advises Malik, that he must take care that they are not exploited and their properties looted as if they are war booties. This illustrates the great social responsibility that a Muslim has toward his fellow human being whether Muslim and non-Muslim. Of course, tolerating the discomforts of this world leads to etrnal peace and comfort (Sermon, 114). In another Speech, the Imam advises the rich that material wealth is not everlasting and they will not be able to take their wealth with them to the grave. What is everlasting, the Imam said, is the results of good and bad actions in the world. One way to ensure that the results of one's action will have positive results in the Hereafter is to spend one's wealth in the Way of Allah (Infaq) to help the poor which improves the welfare of the person receiving the help Here and that of the person giving in the Hereafter. While the material worth of this type of altruistic spending is finite, it has much larger effect in terms of its impact on total social welfare through demonstration of ethical behavior and respect for human dignity through an act of religious worship.

4.2.2 Principle of Orientation Toward the Hereafter

Over one fifth of the verses of the Qur'an are about resurrection and accountability of human beings for their conducts. Many of these were revealed at the beginning of the appointment of the Messenger (sawa) and became a tool of educating Muslims and directing their behavior. The believers learned that in all their actions, they are transacting with a Creator who owns the entire creation and who gains nothing from this transaction while humans stand to gain everything. Every action of every individual, even if it appears to be the same as those of another, receives different reward or retribution from Allah depending on the conditions under which the act is committed as well as the spirit and essence of the action. surrounding the commission of the action, the spirit and essence. While all actions have consequences, some actions receive multiple returns because of their special circumstance. For instance, in the Verse 261, Chapter 2, the return to spending in the Way of Allah is equal to 700 times the value of what has been spent (meaning that the action is so blissful to resemble a seed of wheat sowed in fertile soil, each grain of which will produce 700 as many seeds. In contrast, Verse 264 of the same Chapter states that if the same spending is done without orientation toward Allah and belief in accountability, then it bears no yield as if the seeds were sowed on a field of granite. Awareness created by this orientation that the every action is counted creates special utility and satisfaction from performing it as well as an incentive to repeat it or undertake to perform other similar actions. This worldview exists in the Qur'an and is reflected in the behavior and conducts of the Prophet (sawa), Ahlul Bayt (his family and progeny), his companions and faithful believers. Prophet (sawa) called this world as a fertile field for the Hereafter. In his letter to his eldest son al-Imam al-Hasan (Letter No. 31, Nahj al-Bilaghah), Imam Ali advises that the real life is not Here, it is only a passage way to the Hereafter. In another letter (Letter No. 55, Nahj al-Bilaghah), the Imam advises that the life Here is not the ultimate goal of human life, it is the beginning of preparation for the eternal life. This way of thinking will certainly affect human behavior. To cut off the roots of attachment to worldly whims, desire and expectation, which are barriers to nearness to Allah, the Prophet (sawa) advises that humans have a very short life span on the earth which passes very rapidly. One fruit of belief in the Hereafter is absence of avarice and intensification of the spirit of generosity as well as happiness in the well-being of others and the approval of their Creator, all of which increases the utility of the believers.

4.2.3 Principle of Orientation Toward Spirituality

According to this principle, that more intense fidelity to religious teachings and higher achievement of spirituality leads to better life Here in addition to felicity in the Hereafter. For instance, spending in the Way of Allah, such as Sadaqah or infaq (transfer payments to help others) not only increases the utility and welfare of the donor Here but that of the society as well. In addition to the verses of the Qur'an mentioned earlier, a number of sacred narrations focus on this issue and emphasize that this type of expenditure such as Zakat, rather than reducing one's wealth, protect it against losses as if Zakat insures wealth and property. The Messenger (sawa) advises: "Protect protect your wealth and property by paying Zakat." Imam al-Sadiq (as) said: "No wealth or property has been destroyed on land or on the sea for no reason other than non-payment of Zakat. Therefore, protect your belongings by Zakat." Imam al-Ridha (as) advised: "If the Zakat of animals is not paid, they die." These narrations indicate that protecting one's property through payment of Zakat has spiritual causation not known to ordinary humans. Spending in the Way of Allah, in general, and Zakat, in particular, increase wealth and property, in addition to protecting them. The Prophet (sawa) advised: "If you want Allah to increase your wealth and property, pay its Zakat." Imam al-Baqir Opined: "Zakat increases sustenance." Imam al-Sadiq advises one of his Companions (a Man named Mufadhdhal): "Tell our friends to pay their Zakat and I will guarantee anything they lose" (indicating the Imam's sense of certainty that Zakat increases, not reduce, wealth and property on which Zakat is paid). There is non-physical and spiritual reason why Allah has placed so much blessing (Barakah) in the payment of Zakat that not only increases the wealth and property of the payer but also increases the purchasing power of the needy whose marginal propensity to consume is high which, in turn, increases demand, production, employment, income and growth of the economy thus increasing the income and wealth of Zakat payers. From Imam Ali's point of view, the element of blessing (Barakah) can influence Muslim individuals so much as to give it a significant role in welfare. In his speech, No. 142 (Nahj al-Bilaghah), the Imam (as) when altruistic transfer payments are made with the intention of drawing near Allah, such generosity increases the respect dignity of the person in the society Here and leads to felicity in the Hereafter. And in his Speech No. 81 (Nahjal-Bilaghah), the Imam (as)in his definition of Zuhd (asceticism) as avoidance of luxuries and hedonism, irrational desires and expectations while being grateful for the blessings of Allah and termination of transgressions as well as commission of prohibited acts. An appropriately structured and righteous society promotes these values.

The important result of these three principles is that in most of the welfare functions, by transferring a portion of his income to the needier members in society the wealthy person helps increase the welfare of others and decrease his own welfare. However, due to the principle of transfer, in general, the overall welfare of society will elevate which is per se Pareto-improvement. (Cannoli and Monero, 2009, p. 67). Thus, in conventional welfare theory income transfers from individual A to individual B leads to reduction in the welfare of the former because his own consumption budget declines. In Islam, however, Infaq (altruistic income transfers as expenditures in the Way of Allah) the welfare of individual A does not decline but, on the contrary, increases (given that the horizon of a Muslim individual extends to the life Hereafter) due to belief in the Hereafter and its priority over the life Here. This is a reflection of the long-run vision of human life in Islam.

To explain, assume there are two persons, A and B who take pleasure when they observe a reduction in poverty. Each of these individuals contemplate contribution 1 monetary unit to poverty reduction which created 0.75 unit of utility. Table 22.1 summarizes the choices and utility rewards for these two individuals. The table gives the payoffs of person A and person B are shown. For instance, if each donates one monetary unit, the total amount donated will be two monetary units, which increases 1.5 monetary unit for person A. But he should deduct the cost of his contribution (one monetary unit), so his payoff out of his donation would be 0.5 monetary unit. Similarly, when he contributes one monetary unit but the person B doesn't, then one monetary unit is donated and one social benefit worth 0.75 monetary unit and one cost worth one monetary unit is created for him, and in short, he loses 0.25. When person B donates one monetary unit, through a free ride, person A can obtain a 1.5

Table 22.1: Analysis of Two-Person Contribution Game.

		Person B	
		Donates 1 monetary Unit	**Donates no money**
Person A	Donates 1 monetary Unit	0.5, 0.5	1.5, −0.25
	Donates no money	−0.25, 1.5	0, 0

monetary unit payoff compared with the payoff of 0.5 monetary unit payoff when he made 1 monetary unit contribution. Now, if person B does not donate, he should not either. The optimal solution for the person B is also no donation which is Nash equilibrium in this game, i. e., no one contributes. In this case, the Pareto optimal solution, with 1 monetary unit contribution from each individual, dominates (Cannoli and Monerro, 2009, p.69).

As is evident, this table is designed for analysis of two-person contribution game in which the individuals see each other's contribution and both benefit from any contribution in this two-member society. From the table, it can be concluded that the cooperative strategy results in social optimum, otherwise the dominant strategy would be Nash equilibrium where no one contributes. (It is to be noted that the above example is based on the assumption that the amount of benefit achieved out of the donation of every person is 0.75 monetary unit for each individual. However, if the benefit is more than 1 monetary unit, then Nash equilibrium is not in non-cooperation. Furthermore, in this example, the benefit of each person is the level of satisfaction that the person receives from his own action. Now, if in addition to personal satisfaction, the satisfaction of Allah is included, Nash equilibrium and the strategy of non-cooperation will not be the answer since in this case every person obtains the satisfaction of Allah for his donation).

In the above example, if there is a three-persons society, every person benefits 0.75 so that the total benefit becomes 2.25. But since every person spends 1 unit, the final benefit that each person obtains would be 1.25 units. And if we assume a four-person society, the benefit of each person would be 3 units but since he spends 1 unit, the net benefit for each person is 2 units. As can be observed, increasing the number of persons, since the amount of donation is assumed to be fixed, leads to the increase in the net benefit of each person. Of course, this result is due to the assumption that people draw satisfaction from observing the altruistic behavior of others and become motivated to become contributors themselves. Although contributions are conditional in this example and is subject to free-riding, it is possible to extend it to cases where participants contribute even when they cannot observe others' contributions. While this model does not face the issue of free-riding nor the issue of Nash equilibrium, that altruism leads to accelerated increase in payoffs from contributions is a shared consequence of both cases.

In view of the teachings of Islam, the three principles mentioned above, and mutual responsibilities among individuals, it would be expected that not only altruism and other-regarding will be more important but that their welfare impact with be greater. In contrast to the assumptions of conventional economics, an individual Muslim, who has in view the Hereafter, need not observe others' giving and contributions in order to become motivated to help the needy. Such individuals, relying on their fundamental values, take pleasure in helping the poor and the needy as they see themselves responsible for the life conditions of the poor and consider that such conditions affect their own wellbeing. Moreover, unlike the view in conventional economics, an individual Muslim does not believe that a 1 monetary unit of altruistic expenditure is a 1unit loss to himself. On the contrary, such expenditures, he considers as being more than compensated in the world-to-come and that even in this life, he will have his own welfare enhanced greater than the amount spent to help others.

According to the teachings of the Qur'an (for example, Chapter 2: Verse 261) a Muslim helps the poor and the needy publically or secretly although doing so secretly has greater rewards. Consequently, a Muslim need no demonstration of others' altruistic behavior in order to become motivated to help the poor. Moreover, knowing that the Creator is the ultimate owner of everything in creation and He is the One who sustains all, a Muslim individual does not consider spending to help the poor and needy as loss to his income and wealth but an enhancement of his own welfare. Such an individual's plan horizon extends to the life everlasting in which the ultimate objective is to achieve nearness to Allah. Therefore, he views expenditure to help the poor and the needy as means of increasing his own welfare toward achieving felicity in the Hereafter as well.

In the end, it should be stated that the conventional economic welfare function is based on the three principles of comparability, anonymity, and symmetry which are necessary in designing the social welfare function as well as in comparative studies. The teachings of Islam with emphasis on ethics and the belief that human life horizon does not end with life on earth, require three additional principles of orientation toward altruism, Hereafter, and spirituality which together add a spiritual dimension to the material one of the conventional welfare theories. This change in thinking changes standards and values which lead to changes in the behavior of individuals toward one another and ultimately to increase in social welfare. The difference between what is proposed here and the conventional welfare theories should lead to consideration of multidimensional nature of welfare. With added consideration of justice and its impact on welfare, direction of the design and implementation of economic policies changes from reliance on classical economics which considers justice only as a tool of optimal allocation of resources.

5 Conclusion

Welfare economics is a branch of economics that deals with the study of welfare in society. Since the economic welfare of a society is based on the judgement of the policy makers, it follows that value judgements play an important role in the judging whether a society's economic welfare is better or worse as a result of implementation of a given economic policy. In the classical theory of welfare, such judgments regarding welfare improvement was based on material wellbeing. However, with the passage of time, other dimensions of human life such as justice and freedom as standards of welfare entered the literature of welfare and included as indicators of the measurement of wellbeing in the social welfare function by scholars such as John Rawls and Amartya Sen. By considering this aspect of human being and criteria inserted in welfare function, three principles are taken into account in designing social welfare function: comparability, anonymity, and symmetry. Comparability in the design of the social welfare function makes judgement and comparison between different welfare positions possible. There is a consensus on anonymity as the basis for constructing social welfare function on the foundation of justice. As for the principle of symmetry, it allows making judgement on whether income transfers increase the total welfare of the society even though it may increase the welfare of some while reducing that of others. Moreover, this principle allows assigning different weights to different groups in order to make value-based judgements.

Importantly, however, the conventional approach to welfare has neglected non-material and ethical dimensions of wellbeing of humans. While this neglect may be due to the fact that the non-material dimension of human life is not an integral part of economics, reality of life and behavior of humans is surely influenced by these dimensions. It is was the purpose of this paper to investigate this dimension and its effects according to Islam and its influence on human behavior in the design of social welfare function. In this context, the teachings of Islam which have direct and indirect influence on the welfare function were enumerated and summarized into three principles of orientation toward altruism, Hereafter and spirituality. Each of these principles lead to higher level of utility and welfare for the individual behavior. These principles govern the design of the social welfare function. The question of to what extent these principles influence the social welfare function relates to the degree and strength of beliefs and fidelity to religious teachings. Further research will have to address the issues that will inevitable be raised including the form the welfare function takes when designed under the influence of these principles, how and in what direction the social welfare function changes and by how much under this influence.

References

Holy Qu'ran.
Imam Ali (As). *"Nahj al-Balagheh"*.
Arrow Kenneth. J. *"Social Choice and Individual Values"* Second Edition, New Haven and Landon, Yale University Press, 1961.
Bentham, Jeremy (1996). *"An Introduction to the Principles of Morals and Legislation"*. Burns, J. H. & H. L. A. Hart (eds.), Oxford: Clarendon Press.
Boadway Robin w. & Bruce Neil, *"Welfare Economics"*. Blackwell Publishers, 1933.
Connolly, Sara. & Alistair Munro. (1999). *"Economics of the Public"* Prentice Hall Europe.
Crisp, Roger (2008), *"Well-Being Stanford Encyclopedia of Philosophy"*. Available at: http://plato.stanford.edu/entries/well-being.
Hausman. D. M. & McPherson, M. S. *"Economic Analysis, Moral Philosophy and Public Policy"* Second Edition, Cambridge University Press, 2006.
Kulayni, Muhammad bin Yaqub. (1984), *"Al-Kafi"*. Tehran: Ilmiya al-Islamieh Bookstore.
Layard, P. R. G. & *Walters*, A. A. (1985) *"Microeconomics"* McGraw –Hill.
Majlesi, Mohammad Bagher. (1992), *"Beharul-Anwar Volume: 76"*. Daroehia Al-Torath Al-Arabi Publication. Beirut, Lebanon.
Mohammad Ben Hasan (Al-Shaykh al-Saduq), (1982). *"Kitāb Man lā yaduruh al-faqīh"* Daftar Tablighat Publication, Qum, Iran.
Mohammad Ben Hasan (Al-Shaykh al-Saduq). *"Al-Khisal"*. Daftar Tablighat Publication, Qum, Iran.
Nozick, Robert (1991). *"Anarchy, State, and Utopia"*. UK: Blackwell Publishers.
Nussbaum. M. & Amartya Sen (eds.). (1999). *"The Quality of Life"*. Oxford: Clarendon Press. (1993).
Nussbaum, Martha (2001), *"Upheavals of Thought"* Cambridge University Press.
Sen Amartya K. (1970). *"Collective Choice and Social Welfare"*. San Francisco: Holden Day; North Holland; n Third printing edition (January 15, 1984).
Sen Amartya K. (1987). *"The Standard of Living"*. (Hawthorne G). Cambridge: Cambridge University Press.
Sen Amartya K. (1992), *"Inequality Reexamined"*. Harvard University Press.
Sumner, L. W. (1996), *"Happiness and Ethics"*. Oxford: Clarendon Press.
Tabatabaei, Seyyed Mohammad Hossein. (1997), *"Tafsir al-Mizan"*. Qum: Eslamieh Publishing House.

Salman Ahmed Shaikh

Chapter 23: Towards an Integrative Framework for Understanding Producer Behaviour in Islamic Economics Framework

1 Introduction

This chapter presents the Islamic approach to production theory in economics by outlining Islamic philosophy and teachings along with their economic effects. Section one outlines Islamic principles on earning a livelihood by presenting the permissible and impressible sources of earning a livelihood and ethical principles governing the production, selling and distribution of goods and services in the Islamic economics framework. Section two reviews theoretical works on the analysis of the behaviour of firms in Islamic economics framework. Section three discusses the approach to methodological integration by isolating economic and non-economic choices. Finally, Section four presents an example of methodological integration through an illustrative mathematical model.

2 Islamic Moral Principles on Earning Livelihood

2.1 Encouragement for Pursuit of Livelihood

In this section, we discuss how Islamic teachings govern the pursuit of earning incomes. The Islamic teachings encourage striving for *Halāl* means of earning as long as the other duties, such as worship to Allah are performed (Al-Qur'an, Al-Jumuah: 10) and impermissible means and ways of earning are avoided, such as interest (Al-Qur'an, Al-Baqarah: 276), bribery (Al-Qur'an, Al-Baqarah: 188), fraud (Al-Qur'an, Al-Mutaffifeen: 1–4), gambling (Al-Qur'an, Al-Maida: 90), theft (Al-Qur'an, Al-Maida: 38), business of intoxicants (Al-Qur'an, Al-Maida: 90) and prostitution (Al-Qur'an, Al-Nur: 19), for instance. In general, barring the above exceptions, the Qur'an allows mutually beneficial and consensual exchange (Al-Qur'an, Al-Nisa: 29). As per Islamic texts, endowments bestowed by Allah are to be used for material goods as well as for societal causes to earn *Falah* (well-being in both worlds). Prophet said: "The truthful and trustworthy businessman will be in the company of Prophets, saints and martyrs on the Day of Judgment." (Jami-al-Tirmizi, Vol 3, Chapter on Business, Hadith Number 1209).

Islam discourages idleness, dependency and unnecessary exit from the labor force. Prophet Muhammad said: "For one of you to go out early to gather firewood

https://doi.org/10.1515/9783110593419-023

and carry it on his back so that he can give charity from it and be free of need from the people, is better for him than to ask a man who may give that to him or refuse. Indeed, the upper hand (giving) is more virtuous than the lower hand (receiving), and begin with (those who are) your dependants." (Jami-at-Tirmidhi, Vol 2, Chapters on *Zakāt*, Hadith Number 680). In another Hadith, Prophet Muhammad explained: "The upper hand is better than the lower hand, and the upper hand is the one that spends, and the lower hand is the one that asks." (Sunan Abu Daud, Vol 2, Book of *Zakāt*, Hadith Number 1648). Prophet Muhammad said that begging is not lawful for the rich and physically fit except for the one who is severely poor or in perilous debt (Jami-at-Tirmidhi, Vol 2, Chapters on *Zakāt*, Hadith Number 653).

2.2 Binary Filter of *Halāl* (Permissible) & *Harām* (Impermissible) in Production

Earlier, we looked at how the Islamic principles govern activities related to earning a livelihood. Now, we discuss what guidelines Islamic texts prescribe for the consumption behaviour of individuals. These teachings are also relevant for Islamic firms to ensure that their product offerings, marketing strategies and sales promotions are consistent with Islamic teachings. Islamic teachings make a distinction between permissible and impermissible goods. Qur'an says "*... Eat of that which is lawful and good on the earth...*" (Al-Qur'an, Al-Baqarah: 168). Thus, impermissible goods are axiomatically excluded from the consumption bundle. Consumption opportunity set will axiomatically filter out the prohibited consumption goods from the consumption set in both contemporaneous and inter-temporal consumption. So, the consumer would only make a choice among *Halāl* consumption and *Halāl* investment options. Thus, the ordinal preferences do not apply to the axiomatically excluded non-*Halāl* goods and services. For instance, Islam forbids intoxicants (Al-Qur'an, Al-Baqarah: 219), the meat of dead animals, blood and flesh of swine (Al-Baqarah: 173). In financial services, Islam forbids interest (Al-Qur'an, Al-Baqarah: 276) and gambling (Al-Qur'an, Al-Maida: 90), for instance.

In the Islamic jurisprudence, we also come across a hierarchy of needs. Al-Raysuni (2013) states that Imam Al-Shatibi has categorized human needs into three groups; i) *Dharuriyah* (necessities), ii) *Hajiyah* (conveniences) and iii) *Tahsiniyah* (refinements). Quoquab (2015) explains that in the hierarchical structure of needs given by Al-Shatibi, necessities include such activities and things that are essential to protect i) *Imān* (faith), ii) *Nafs* (life), iii) *Māl* (wealth), iv) *Aqal* (intellect) and v) *Nasl* (progeny). Thus, Islam recognizes physiological as well as aesthetic needs but requires moderation in consumption.

2.3 Islamic Teachings Governing Conduct of Producer

Endowment inequality and relative abundance of one or the other type of resource in this world does not provide any basis of superiority in Islamic social framework. It is only meant to test thankfulness, patience and fairness in interpersonal and socio-economic relations. Qur'an says: "Is it they who would portion out the Mercy of your Lord? It is We Who portion out between them their livelihood in this world, and We raised some of them above others in ranks, so that some may employ others in their work. But the Mercy (Paradise) of your Lord (O Muhammad – PBUH) is better than the (wealth of this world) which they amass." (Al-Qur'an, Al Zukhruf: 32)

Islam allows trade, but cautions against unfairness, exploitation and deceit. Qur'an says: "Do not devour one another's property wrongfully, nor throw it before the judges in order to devour a portion of other's property sinfully and knowingly." (Al-Qur'an, Al-Baqarah: 1880. In another place, Qur'an says: "Do not devour another's property wrongfully – unless it be by trade based on mutual consent." (Al-Qur'an, Al-Nisa: 29)

Islamic teachings related to commerce also strongly recommend fairness in trade dealings. Qur'an says: "And measure full when you measure. And weigh with an even balance. This is better and its end is good." (Al-Qur'an, Al-Bani-Israel: 35). In another place, Qur'an says: "Woe to those that deal in fraud, those who, when they have to receive by measure from men, exact full measure, but, when they have to give by measure or weight to men, give less than due. Do they not think that they will be called to account?" (Al-Qur'an, Al-Mutaffifin: 1–4). Furthermore, Islam also emphasizes on fulfilling contractual obligations in mutual exchange. Qur'an says: "O you who believe! Fulfil [your] obligations". (Al-Qur'an, Al-Maida: 1)

Islam allows profit motive and using the profits for consumption and further investment. However, it discourages accumulation for the purpose of hoarding. Qur'an says: "They who hoard up gold and silver and spend it not in the way of Allah, unto them give tidings (O Muhammad) of a painful doom." (Al-Qur'an, Al-Tauba: 34).

Islamic teachings related to commerce denounce taking oaths for deceiving others. Qur'an says: "You resort to oaths as instruments of mutual deceit, so that a person might take greater advantage than another; although, Allah puts you to the test through this. Surely, on the Day of Resurrection, He will make clear the truth concerning the matters over which you differed." (Al-Qur'an, Al-Nahl: 92).

In commercial undertakings, Islam encourages documenting the terms of the agreement to mitigate the risk of moral hazard. Qur'an says: "O Believers! Whenever you lend money for a particular period, write and someone among you must write it justly. And the one who can write must not refuse." (Al-Qur'an, Al-Baqarah: 282).

Islamic principles of trade allow credit transactions and debts but condemn defaulting on loans. Prophet Muhammad said: "Any who takes out a loan, having resolved not to pay it back, will meet Allah as a thief." (Sunan Ibn-e-Maja, Vol 3, Chapters on Charity, Hadith Number 2410).

Islamic principles of trade allow mutual bargaining to achieve the best result for oneself but recommend gentleness and softness in executing deals so as to avoid the zero-sum game and undue advantage. Prophet Muhammad said: "May Allah's mercy be on him who is lenient in his buying, selling, and in demanding back his money [or debts]." (Sahih Bukhari, Vol 3, Book of Sales, Hadith Number 2076).

In selling goods, it is highly recommended that deceit is avoided in making and selling of products. Prophet Muhammad said: "It is not permissible for a Muslim to sell his brother goods in which there is a defect without pointing that out to him." (Sunan Ibn-e-Maja, Vol 3, Chapter on Business Transactions, Hadith Number 2246).

In another Hadith, Prophet Muhammad said: "The seller and the buyer have the right to keep or return the goods as long as they have not parted or till they part; and if both the parties spoke the truth and described the defects and qualities [of the goods], then they would be blessed in their transaction, and if they told lies or hid something, then the blessings of their transaction would be lost." (Sahih Bukhari, Vol 3, Book of Sales, Hadith Number 2079).

Deceit in contracts to get an unfair advantage is strongly condemned in Islam. Prophet Muhammad said: "Whoever takes a false oath to deprive somebody of his property will meet Allah while He will be angry with him." (Sahih Bukhari, Vol 3, Book of Watering, Hadith Number 2356).

From the traditions of Prophet Muhammad, it appears that it is encouraged for the price discovery process to be market-driven and without any frictions and hindrances. To ensure that price is determined competitively without information asymmetries, Prophet Muhammad forbade a town dweller to sell on behalf of a Bedouin and to artificially inflate prices (Sahih Muslim, Vol 4, Book of Marriage, Hadith Number 3459). Prophet Muhammad forbade intercepting traders until they reach the markets with their goods. (Sahih Muslim, Vol 4, Book of Financial Transactions, Hadith Number 3821). Furthermore, in bidding for goods, assets or businesses, overbidding without having a genuine intention to buy (*Al-Najash*) is prohibited.

Speculative trades inflate prices and lead to artificial price bubbles and crises when these bubbles burst. To foster genuineness of trades and diminish the speculative motives, Prophet Muhammad said: "He who buys food grain should not sell it until he has taken possession of it." (Sahih Muslim, Vol 4, Book of Financial Transactions, Hadith Number 3836)

In contemporary production processes, often labor is employed to produce the goods. In labor management and relations, Islam, gives due protection and credit to labour. To highlight the importance of fair treatment of labor, Prophet Muhammad said: "I will be a foe to three persons on the Last Day: one of them being the one who, when he employs a person that has accomplished his duty, does not give him his due." (Sahih Bukhari, Vol 3, Book of Hiring, Hadith Number 2270). On timely remuneration to labor, Prophet Muhammad said: "Give the labor his wage before his sweat dries". (Sunan Ibn-e-Maja, Vol 3, Book of Pawning, Hadith Number 2443)

In another Hadith, Prophet Muhammad said: "Those are your brothers [workers under you] who are around you; Allah has placed them under you. So, if anyone of you has someone under him, he should feed him out of what he himself eats, clothe him like what he himself puts on, and let him not put so much burden on him that he is not able to bear, [and if that be the case], then lend your help to him." (Sahih Bukhari, Vol 3, Book of Manumission, Hadith Number 2545).

In monopolistic competition, sellers often devise and execute marketing strategies to increase their product's appeal, demand and hence increase the sales and thereby profits. Advertising also helps them to create brand recall and loyalty. From an Islamic perspective, there are certain principles and broad guidelines that must be followed and taken care of while advertising the products.

False information must be avoided. Persuasive advertising that commits attributes which cannot be provided as promised is deemed immoral. Not acting upon the promise made is a serious sin in Islam. While physiological and aesthetic needs and wants can be targeted through the effective presentation, it must not overly promote consumerism, which is inconsistent with the modesty cherished in the Islamic value system.

Islamic etiquette also does not approve creating appeal for products by representing a culture that does not signify or match with Islamic social etiquette. For instance, advertising for perfume by showing how it can create a positive image before opposite gender is neither necessary nor in line with Islamic social etiquette. Likewise, showing how one can stand out and be envied by others if one buys a particular brand of perfume, car, consumer appliance and clothing is neither necessary nor in line with Islamic etiquette. Finally, the disclosures about products must not be presented in a way to just bypass legal formalities. Rather, the disclosures must be explicit and readable.

3 Review of Firm's Behaviour in Islamic Economic Framework

In this section, we take a brief look at the theory of the firm in Islamic economics and how a firm's objectives and governing framework is different in Islamic economics framework as compared to the neoclassical and value-neutral economic framework.

Alhabshi (1987) reflects on Islamic economic scheme and argues that Islam does not disregard a human's desire for material welfare. It allows the fulfillment of both material as well as spiritual needs. Sattar (1988) argues that even though Islam is not fundamentally opposed to the operation of market forces, but it intervenes by imposing certain limits from the perspective of ethics and morality to achieve fairness and foster cooperation in economic decision making and outcomes.

In addition to that, Amin et al. (2003) explain that in the Islamic economics framework, it is assumed that economic agents are guided by Islamic values. Thus, a Muslim producer, being accountable to Allah, treats the resources at his command as a trust and the production of goods as a duty, and he will base his production decisions on the concept of '*Maslaha*' (public good). The author opines that a producer in an Islamic market could still be profit-driven; but, being governed by the Shariah, the Islamic producer's valuation of economic costs will be modified. Hence, the producer will internalize the externalities in its utility and cost functions.

Hassan (1983) points out that there are some aspects in which the capitalistic system and the Islamic economic scheme have some compatibility. Islam allows the pursuit of profit and private property ownership including the means of production and the freedom of enterprise. On the other hand, it differs from the capitalistic system by its emphasis on cooperation against the competition, social gains against private self-interested behaviour alone and disallowing unfair and speculative means of economic exchange and enterprise, such as *Ribā* (interest), *Maysir* (gambling) and *Gharar* (uncertainty).

Another contrast which comes in the Islamic approach to production theory is in its emphasis on morality in the choice of goods to be produced (*Halāl* vs *Harām*), in the way factors are used (avoiding exploitation, injury and harm), in the way goods are produced (using *Halāl* materials, processes and methods), in the way economic gains are distributed (having fair returns to factors of production and no fixed remuneration to money capital that bears no risk in productive enterprise) and in finally, how the goods are consumed [avoiding *Harām* goods and services as well as *Isrāf* (extravagance) and *Tabzir* (wasteful spending on unlawful things) in consumption].

Discussing the goals of the firm in Islamic economics framework, Hasan (2002) argues that it is important to understand what is being maximized, how, and for what purpose. He says that maximizing survival, employment, equity, or the pleasure of God would probably be welcome to most of the people. Hasan (2002) opines that if the firms fulfill their Islamic duties towards the consumers, the employees, and the society in general in arriving at their total revenue curves, then profit maximization is not objectionable. Hasan (2002) argues for internalizing social costs and benefits to enable the use of profit maximization with requisite modifications and restrictions.

Azid et al. (2007) share the view that competition and cooperation can be a complementary concept on the moral plane. For achieving productivity and avoiding wastage of resources, the pursuit of efficiency is not problematic to achieve the best output to input ratio. On the other hand, when markets do not cater to social problems, ills and negative externalities, ethical and moral behaviour by showing cooperation for social gains is desirable and recommended in the Islamic ethos.

In exploring mathematical modeling of a firm's behavior, Metwally (1997) describes an Islamic firm as one that would seek the maximization of utility which is a function of the amount of profits and the amount of spending on charity or good deeds. The author suggests using the utility as a broad function which includes net profits as well as charity as parameters. However, the amount of profit would, after the payment of all imposed taxes (*Zakāt* and other dues) be no less than a minimum level which is 'safe' to keep the firm in business.

One problem with this way of modelling firms in Islamic framework is that altruism is treated in the utilitarian framework and thus, it affects the purity of altruistic activity and motive. In the Metwally (1997) model, higher payments in charity have supposedly a higher effect on price. If this happens due to improvement in the social image, then the purity of altruistic activity becomes questionable if the sacrifice of profits in charity is recouped through higher prices. Secondly, in an economy where it is not obligatory to pay charity, increasing price by a firm motivated through Islamic principles would not be possible without diminishing its demand, especially in competitive markets with standardized products. Finally, in situations where prices decline, this charity spending which was depending on transfer pricing, would decrease in society when it is needed most in the period of deflating prices when economic investment and employment opportunities decline.

In another mathematical formulation, Bendjilali and Taher (1990) argue that even in an imperfect market structure like a monopoly, if the monopolist is concerned about the social welfare, then he will be willing to partially sacrifice his profits in order to attain efficiency and minimize social welfare loss. Indeed, as discussed above, Islamic principles encourage the firms to uphold moral values and incorporate both positive and negative externalities in their decision making.

Hence, it could be appreciated that several authors have emphasized the ethical and spiritual rationality in the firm's behavior. In a value-neutral framework, there is no cap or mechanism to solve the problem of a human's greed. In fact, a value-neutral framework provides a cover to follow, pursue, harness and practice greed. On the other hand, Islam addresses hearts and first of all, it attempts to purify the heart and encourages compassion and shared responsibility through reminding about afterlife accountability.

4 Methodological Integration by Isolating Economic and Non-Economic Choices

It is a fact that markets exist and people do engage in purposive behaviour. While people might not follow all principles of the standard definition of rationality, it does not mean that they just make random purposeless decisions involving resources which they put to use in the market economy.

In achieving methodological pluralism for realistic analysis, a possible way out is to separate economic decisions in the marketplace and non-economic behaviour outside the marketplace. In modelling, this can be achieved by modifying the constraints of the objective functions. One way of integration is to deduct the income and time from the resource constraint. Even if a person spends 5% of income on self-consumption and 5% of wealth on earning profits on investment,

i) He/she would not buy expensive *Halāl* goods for no reason when a cheap is available (when 5% of his *Halāl* income is spent on self-consumption).
ii) He/she would not choose to buy good A instead of good B if prices of both *Halāl* goods are same and if he/she prefers B more over A (when 5% of his *Halāl* income is spent on self-consumption).
iii) He/she would not choose to engage in behaviour where without any explicit or implicit cost, more profits can be earned than less in a *Halāl* business (when 5% of his wealth is spent on earning incomes).

The implication of this approach is that it will help in avoiding analysis of every behaviour within the utility framework even if it is purely altruistic and pure pro-social behaviour. That is where; this suggested approach avoids the problem of having a market exchange for pure-altruistic and pro-social goods/services.

In this recommended approach, economists would not consider values-based choices as a good to be bought and sold in the market. They would not be compelled to compute elasticity and substitution effects involving pure altruistic or pro-social choices. This approach would respect pure altruism and pro-social preferences as against the stance taken by Andreoni (1989; 1990). Thus, this approach would reduce economics to market-based behaviour of consumption of *Halāl* Goods and earning incomes from market-based *Halāl* sources only.

An implication of profit maximization is that firms try not to lose an opportunity to earn more profits if it is available at no further increase in marginal cost. From an Islamic perspective, there is nothing wrong in seeking endowments if certain conditions are met (Hassan, 2002).

Economists should not comment on non-economic choices, unlike the views of Becker (1976) and Iannaccone (1991, 1992, 1994, 1995, 1997). However, in economic pursuits, constrained profit maximization for firms is a useful framework to analyze why firms advertise, merge, acquire, build new plants, invest in research and development, innovate, introduce new products, re-engineer production processes and give discounts and promotions. Since these decisions and activities routinely happen in the real world, the mainstream framework of constrained profit maximization is one way to contemplate and analyze the outcomes of these particular decisions. Indeed, in the Islamic economics framework, if that framework is adopted, more constraints can be added to incorporate Islamic values and norms in the production set to exclude *Harām* goods, factor returns to exclude fixed compensation to money capital in the form of *Ribā* and cost function to exclude investable resources set aside for *Zakāt*, *Sadqāt* and *Waqf*.

In corporate finance, firms use net present value to decide about major capital expenditure. Firms choose the highest net present value projects in most cases. Such decisions are driven by the profit motive. The profit motive would not be the sole motive and would not be applicable on all the resource endowments of a firm in Islamic economics framework. But, the amount of resources allocated for productive enterprise could be driven by the profit motive. Profits, if and when earned, can be donated and spent on social causes. The motive for donation and contribution to social causes can be pure and spiritual. Such spending when added as expense in accounting reduces the return on equity. Hence, spending with a corporate social responsibility motive still looks at the return on such spending on future profits and customer retention via goodwill. By not considering such spending as part of the allocable cost function, one avoids the opportunity cost of such spending as lost profits.

The job of economics should be to explain the behaviour only in the marketplace. Behaviours can be completely contradictory across time and space. That is why, there can be completely contradictory theories, let alone a theory that will be deterministic or completely follow empirical evidence always. People can be selfish and selfless. Economists should not intervene in considering self-less behaviour as unreal, irrational or irrelevant. Likewise, to expect that people will have absolutely no regards for self-interest is also another extreme not supported by evidence. Islam denies the unrestrained pursuit of self-interest but allows flexibility within the *Halāl* choice set. Within that *Halāl* choice set, a person who does not commit excess in consumption and who pays *Zakāt* and *Sadqāt* generously can flexibly choose a means of transport one likes, the proportion of meat and vegetable in food one likes and so on.

Thus, constrained profit maximization simply means that a company would try to pursue a profit opportunity that is available at no further increase in marginal cost. If a product is *Halāl*; marketing is within Islamic ethics and values; all contracts follow the Islamic law of contracts and exchange; then, it is not a cause of concern if more output is produced when marginal revenue is greater than marginal cost.

5 Modelling Firm Behaviour in Islamic Economics Framework

In this section, a simple illustration is provided to show how a firm's behaviour in Islamic economics framework can be modeled in the integrative framework, which is suggested in the previous section. We know that the total revenue of a firm is defined as the product of price times output:

$$TR(Q) = P * Q \tag{1}$$

The first distinction that comes in the Islamic framework is that the nature of the good that is produced needs to be *Halāl*. Thus, for non-*Halāl* goods, Muslim society shall have missing markets. Secondly, the investable endowments can be used for altruistic and pro-social expenditure as well by the Muslim entrepreneur. The portion of total investable endowments that are kept for earning *Halāl* source of income from the entrepreneurial activity is the cost budget for productive enterprise. The total private business costs are defined as the quantity of labor, L, used multiplied by the price of labor (wage rate), w, plus the value of physical capital, K, used multiplied by the per period rental price of capital, v. The third distinction in the Islamic framework is that instead of a fixed return on money capital, firms in the Islamic framework procure physical capital by using *Ijarah* (leasing) and *Musharaka Mutanaqisa* (equity financing) mode of financing.

$$TC = wL + vK \tag{2}$$

The profit function of a typical equity financed firm will not include explicit and contractually stipulated cost of capital. Let π_T represent total profits for firm 'i'. It can be functionally represented as:

$$\pi_T = pq - wL - vK \tag{3}$$

Here, p is the price of output determined in the market, q is output produced, w is wage per unit of labor employed, L is the number of labor units employed and vK is the rent paid for the use of physical capital. The asset owner who provides the usufruct of assets against rental payments could be the vendor of that asset who manufactures or sells such assets. The owner could also be financial institution or general investors if financing is intermediated through financial institutions like banks and financial markets respectively.

Let us say there are two partners, 'A' and 'B' in a particular project. Then,

$$\pi_A = p_A \pi_T \tag{4}$$

$$\pi_A = p_A(pq - wL - vK) \tag{5}$$

$$\pi_B = p_B \pi_T \tag{6}$$

$$\pi_B = p_B (pq - wL - vK) \tag{7}$$

Here, p_A and p_B are respective profit sharing ratio agreed between A and B. Also, π_T will be equal to:

$$\pi_T = p_A \pi_T + p_B \pi_T \tag{8}$$

Since there are only two partners, $p_A + p_B = 1$. Alternatively, we can also express it by:

$$\pi_A = p_A \pi_T \tag{9}$$

$$\pi_A = \pi_T - p_B \pi_T \tag{10}$$

Hence, it can be seen that non-labor entrepreneurial income for a person or firm will rest on total profits accruing to the firm and that in turn will depend on factors that are commonly faced by all other firms and hence this will ensure equity and distributive justice.

Furthermore, with regards to externalities, we would like to mention another important point. A producer in an Islamic market could still be profit-driven; but, being governed by the Islamic principles, the producer's valuation of economic costs will be modified.

Profit maximization level of output is found by applying the derivative with respect to q and setting it equal to 0:

$$\frac{d\tau}{dq} = \frac{dTR}{dq} - \frac{dTC}{dq} = 0 \quad (11)$$

At the profit-maximizing level of output, it should not be possible to increase profits further by increasing the level of output. Hence, at the profit-maximizing level of output $\frac{d\tau}{dq}=0$. Thus, we get:

$$\frac{dTR}{dq} = \frac{dTC}{dq} \quad (12)$$

Thus, at the profit-maximizing level of output, marginal revenue equals marginal cost.

6 Conclusion

It can be concluded that marginal analysis for commercial undertaking by firms in the Islamic framework is similar. The explicit difference comes in the type of goods produced and the modes of financing used. The more significant and implicit difference comes in moral approach whereby an entrepreneur imbued with the spirit of ethos and philosophy of Islam avoids hoarding, anti-competitive behaviour, price manipulation, cheating, fraud, injustice and social harm in the form of negative externalities. The entrepreneur in the Islamic framework is conscious of the fact that all surplus investable endowments are a trust from Allah. The entrepreneur uses part of the surplus investable endowments in *Zakāt*, *Sadqā* (voluntary charity) and establishing *Waqf* (endowment). Furthermore, for the portion of investable endowments set aside for commercial undertaking, the entrepreneur must also abide by the principles and morals of earning livelihood in the Islamic economics framework.

References

Al-Raysuni, A. (2005). "Imam Al-Shatibi's. Theory of the Higher Objectives and Intents of Islamic Law", Malaysia: The International Institute of Islamic Thought (IIIT).

Alhabshi, S. O. (2014). "The Role of Ethics in Economics and Business.", *Journal of Islamic Economics*, 1(1), 1–15.

Amin, R. M., & Yusof, S. A. (2003). "Allocative Efficiency of Profit Maximization: An Islamic Perspective", *Review of Islamic Economics*, *13*, 5–21.

Andreoni, J. (1990). "Impure Altruism and Donations to Public Goods: A Theory of Warm-Glow Giving. *The Economic Journal*, *100*(401), 464–477.

Andreoni, J. (1989). "Giving with Impure Altruism: Applications to Charity and Ricardian Equivalence. *Journal of Political Economy*, *97*(6), 1447–1458.

Azid, T., Asutay, M., & Burki, U. (2007). "Theory of the Firm, Management and Stakeholders: An Islamic Perspective". *Islamic Economic Studies*, *15*(1), 1–30.

Becker, Gary S. (1976). "The Economic Approach to Human Behavior". Chicago: University of Chicago Press.

Bendjilali, B., & Taher, F. B. (1990). "A Zero Efficiency Loss Monopolist: An Islamic Perspective", *The American Journal of Islamic Social Sciences*, *7*(1), 219–232.

Hasan, Z. (1983). "Theory of Profit: The Islamic Viewpoint". *Journal of King Abdulaziz University: Islamic Economics*, *1*(1), 3–14.

Hasan, Z. (2002). "Maximization Postulates and Their Efficacy for Islamic Economics", *The American Journal of Islamic Social Sciences*, *19*(1), 95–118.

Iannaccone, L. R. (1991). "The Consequences of Religious Market Structure: Adam Smith and the Economics of Religion". *Rationality and society*, *3*(2), 156–177.

Iannaccone, L. R. (1992). "Religious Markets and the Economics of Religion". *Social compass*, *39*(1), 123–131.

Iannaccone, L. R. (1994). "Progress in the Economics of Religion". *Journal of Institutional and Theoretical Economics (JITE)/Zeitschrift für die gesamte Staatswissenschaft*, *150*(4), 737–744.

Iannaccone, L. R. (1995). "Voodoo Economics? Reviewing the Rational Choice Approach to Religion", *Journal for the scientific study of religion*, 76–88.

Iannaccone, L. R., Finke, R., & Stark, R. (1997). "Deregulating Religion: The Economics of Church and State", *Economic Inquiry*, *35*(2), 350–364.

Metwally, M.M. (1997) "Economic Consequences of Applying Islamic Principles in Muslim Societies", *International Journal of Social Sciences*, 24(7, 8, 9): 941–57.

Quoquab, F; Abdullah, N. L. & Ahmad, M. (2015). "Epicureanism & Global Consumerism in Shaping Muslim Buyers' Consumption Pattern: An Islamic Perspective", *International Journal of Innovation & Business Strategy*, 3: 1–12.

Sattar, Z. (1988). "The Ethics of Profits in the Islamic System". *Islamic Quarterly*, 32(2), 69.

Morteza Ezzati

Chapter 24: The Ethics of Consumption in Islam

1 Introduction

Islam or the Religion of Allah is the religion of ethics. As the Prophet says: "Indeed, I have been appointed to complete the noble traits of ethics (انی بعثت لاتمم مکارم الاخلاق). Although some people may see other purposes for religion and consider the nature of religion differently, the Qur'an clearly states the objective and nature of religion in a number of verses as in the following:

لَقَدْ مَنَّ اللَّهُ عَلَى الْمُؤْمِنِينَ إِذْ بَعَثَ فِيهِمْ رَسُولًا مِنْ أَنْفُسِهِمْ يَتْلُو عَلَيْهِمْ آيَاتِهِ وَيُزَكِّيهِمْ وَ يُعَلِّمُهُمُ الْكِتَابَ وَ الْحِكْمَةَ وَ إِنْ كَانُوا مِنْ قَبْلُ لَفِي ضَلَالٍ مُبِينٍ (آل عمران/164)

"Indeed, Allah Has conferred His favor upon the believers when He appointed a Messenger from among them to recite to them His verses and cleanse them and teach them the Book and the Wisdom (behind its verses) even though they were in manifest error before this." (Al-e-Imran, 3: 164).

And elsewhere it emphasizes this:

«هُوَ الَّذِي بَعَثَ فِي الْأُمِّيِّينَ رَسُولًا مِنْهُمْ يَتْلُوا عَلَيْهِمْ آياتِهِ وَ يُزَكِّيهِمْ وَ يُعَلِّمُهُمُ الْكِتابَ وَ الْحِكْمَةَ وَ إِنْ كانُوا مِنْ قَبْلُ لَفِي ضَلالٍ مُبِينٍ» (جمعه/2).

"He is Who appointed among the Ummyion (people of Mecca) a Messenger from among themselves, to recite to them His verses, and cleanse them and teach them the Book and the Wisdom (behind the verses) although they were of before in manifest error" (Al-Jumuah, 2).[1]

Elsewhere in the Qur'an, ethics and morality are commanded by Allah:

إِنَّ اللَّهَ يَأْمُرُ بِالْعَدْلِ وَ الْإِحْسانِ وَ إِيتاءِ ذِي الْقُرْبى وَ يَنْهى عَنِ الْفَحْشاءِ وَ الْمُنْكَرِ وَ الْبَغْيِ يَعِظُكُمْ لَعَلَّكُمْ تَذَكَّرُونَ (نحل/56).

"Indeed, Allah commands justice and Ihsan (beneficence), being generous to near relatives, and warns against indecent, forbidden, and unjust acts. He thus advises you so that perhaps you will take heed (Nahl, 16:56).

1 Other verses of the Qur'an state same purpose of the religion as the prayer of Abraham that states: "Our Lord, please raise up among them an apostle from them who shall recite unto them Thy revelations and teach them the Book and Wisdom and purify them for Thou and Thou are the Mighty, the Wise." (Al-Baqarah, 129). Because this prayer is the prayer of Abraham, it may be first for teaching and then for purification. In other verses such as the verse 164 of Al-Imran, which is the direct word of God, it is purification firstly and then teaching. Of course, the Qur'an is based on ethics and its teachings are the training of the moral issues.

https://doi.org/10.1515/9783110593419-024

And in the Verse 199 of Chapter 7 (Al-'Araf):

خُذِ الْعَفْوَ وَ أْمُرْ بِالْعُرْفِ وَ أَعْرِض عَنِ الجَاهِلِين (اعراف/ 199)

"Adopt forgiveness and enjoin virtue and turn away from the ignorant" (Al-'Araf, 199).

In many other verses too the Qur'an prescribes ethical rules indicating that the essential behavioral framework of Islam revolves around an ethical axis so much so that the prophet related that: "My Lord has appointed me with it (ethics)."

Accordingly, the axis of Islamic teachings is ethics. The objective of the religion is to lead humans to an ethical life. It accomplishes this task through its teachings and their rationalization as well as through motivating incentives that lead to emergence of an ethical human. One dimension of human life is consumption behavior. Much of human effort is focused on satisfying his consumption needs. Islam has focused on this important dimension of human life. If humans adopt the framework of consumption, along with other rules prescribed, proposed by Islam they achieve felicity. Some of Islamic teachings have direct and others indirect influence on consumption. This paper is composed of two parts. In part one, the paper will consider Islamic teachings that directly influence consumption behavior. The second part focuses on analytic explanation of these teachings and the choice of optimal consumption behavior. Accordingly, these teachings are categorized as those that define permissible consumption, those that define the type of consumption, those that define the ethical limits on the amount of consumption and, finally, we consider other teachings that influence indirectly consumption behavior. We will consider, along with this categorization, the indirect influence of other teachings on consumption of individuals who comply with them. In the second part we analyze the influence of ethical teachings within the frameworks of religious (with reference to the Islamic method of motivating ethical behavior) and non-religious on optimal consumption behavior. Finally, the paper summarizes the discussion and concludes.

2 The Ethical Teachings on Consumption

If Ethical teachings related to consumption can be divided into four categories

2.1 Permissibility of Worldly Consumption in Islam

Islam claims to be realistic. Accordingly, the teachings of religion have been presented in full consideration of human characteristics, including innate characteristics and material needs. It is for this reason that it is said that Islam is a complete and comprehensive religion in harmony with human nature. According to Islamic beliefs, Allah, with His Grace, has created the resources necessary to meet the needs of human beings[2] as well as the ways and means of utilizing them (in proportion to his capacity).[3] He has shown humans the appropriate and inappropriate ways of satisfying their needs and has ordained the appropriate ways of doing so. Not only Allah has permitted humans to use the resources He Has gifted to them, He has advised humans to enjoy them fully and not to avoid doing so. With reference to two Verses of the Qur'an we clarify some of the dimensions of this permission:

> "He created for you all that is in the earth... (Baqarah, 2:29).[4]
>
> هُوَ الَّذِي خَلَقَ لَكُمْ مَا فِي الأَرْضِ جَمِيعًا ...

This verse indicates that what is created on the earth is created for all humans. Other verses in the Qur'an expressly state permissibility of the use and enjoyment of all the blessings Allah has created. For example, the following Verse asks rhetorically:

> «قُل مَن حَرَّمَ زينَتَ اللّهِ الَّتي اَخرَجَ لِعِبادِهِ وَ الطَّيبات مِنَ الرِّزقِ ...» (اعراف؛ 32).
>
> Say: 'Who has forbidden the adornment that Allah has brought forth and the good things He has provided for His bondmen?" (Al-'Araf, 7:32).

In such verses, which are numerous in the Qur'an, consumption is permitted, but some of the verses, known as those which express the general principle of permissibility and approval of consumption, there are verses that subject consumption to certain conditions. These conditions express how these resources (provided for all humans by Allah) are to be use, limitations, and other conditions governing their consumption which humans must observe. Consider, for example, the following Verse:

> O humans! Eat of that which is lawful and wholesome in the earth, and do not follow the footsteps of Evil. Lo! He is an open enemy for you (Bagharah, 2:168).
>
> O you who believe! Eat of the good things which We have provided you and give thanks to Allah if it is (indeed) He whom you worship (Al-Baqarah, 2:172).
>
> «يا ايها الذين آمَنوا كُلوا مِن طَيَباتِ ما رَزَقناكُم وَ اشكُرُوا لِلهِ اِن كُنتُم اِيَّاهُ تَعبُدون» (بقره؛ 2: 172)
>
> O, Children of Adam! Wear your adornment at every place of worship, eat and drink, but be not prodigal. Lo! He does not love the prodigal (Al-Araf, 7:31).[5]
>
> «يا بَني آدَم خُذُوا زينَتَكُم عِندَ كُل مَسجِدٍ و كُلوا و اشرَبوا وَ لاتُسرِفوا ...» (اعراف؛ 31)

2 He, it is who created for you all that is in the earth and then directed to the heavens and then fashioned them into seven heavens and while He, of all things, is the Knower (Al-Baqarah, 29).
3 We have created the human from a (sperm) drop, a mixture, testing him; we made him to hear and see. Indeed, We have guided him to the path, he is either grateful or ungrateful (Insan, 2 and 3).
4 Other verses in the Qur'an related to this issue such as Baqarah, 8–87; TA HA, 81; Araf, 31 and etc.
5 Also refer to: Baqarah, 57 and 60; Maedeh, 88; Anam, 142; Araf, 21 and 160; Enfal, 69; Nakhl, 14; Ta Ha, 81; Malek, 15 and etc.

Since Islam is the religion of ethics, most frameworks for consumption are ethical. On this basis, it can be said that in principle consumption is permissible and even recommended that humans benefit from divine grace. This principle makes it possible for the Muslims to use the divine graces in the form of goods and services without any doubt. At the same time, because Islam tends to make it possible for individuals evolve towards a divine goal, it has conditioned consumption and provided supplementary teachings in this regard. These teachings are aspects of human guidance towards development. Anyone who is believer is expected to behave according to these teaching (provided that the means to do so are available).

In general, Islamic teachings that determine the ethical framework of consumption can be divided into three categories:

1. Teachings related to permission to use goods and services.
2. Teachings related to the level of consumption.
3. Other teachings that influence consumption.

Accordingly, consumption is permitted in Islam, but the teachings prescribed by the Lawgiver are ethical aimed at the felicity of humans. If human beings have full faith in what Islam has said, it is expected that they behave according to these teachings, for they encompass both worldly prosperity and, more importantly, the reward and prosperity in the Hereafter. In what follows, we will review these teachings.

2.2 Teachings Related to the Type of Consumption

From the point of view of sacred Islamic law, consumption of goods and services are divided into five categories. The axis of this categorization is ethics. These teachings prohibited consumption of goods and services that negatively influence the ethics of individuals while they permit and approve of consumption of goods and services that positively influence their ethics. These five categories are: obligatory, recommended, permitted, repugnant, and prohibited. Goods and services are evaluated based on their ethical influences. Each of these will be explained briefly.[6]

2.2.1 Goods and Services with Obligatory Consumption (Wajib)

From the religious point of view, consumption of certain goods and services are obligatory. Among the reasons for the obligatory nature of these goods and services provision of the appropriate conditions for the preservation and continuation of

6 The items mentioned in this section serve as a decree on goods that are subject to these five rules. These are a summary of the items contained in the book of the Imam Khomeini titled "Tahrir Al-Wasilah".

life, physical and mental health, some form of the worships that have consumption dimension, preserving the physical and mental health of other people, and so on. These are the foundation of the survival of a healthy body and soul that can provide the beginning of an ethical human life. These goods and services detailed as:
- Since human life is the basis of evolution toward its perfection, including its ethical dimension, movement towards evolution, including his moral development, Islam has made preservation and of life, and the means of its actualization, obligatory. Accordingly, preservation of life is one of the reasons why the consumption of minimum amount of some goods is obligatory. These include minimum amounts of food, clothing, housing, medicine, water, and even goods and services forbidden if their consumption becomes necessary to save life.
- Consumption of goods and services required to maintain physical and mental health is recognized as obligatory in Shari'ah. These include the services of (physical and mental) physicians and prescribed medicines, any preventive medicine, any type of food prescribed by a physician necessary for regaining full health.
- Consumption of goods and services that are necessary for the survival of the relatives and family members is also obligatory including food, clothing, housing, sanitation, and others necessary for their preservation of their life and health.
- Consumption of goods and services that is necessary to preserve the life and health of animals and plants belonging to humans.
- Consumption of goods and services that are necessary to preserve the health and well-being of other human beings, and even animals and plants and it is also essential according to Sharia.
- Performance of some of the obligatory worships can also be in line with the same ethics because worship is also a cleanser and polisher of the human soul to enable its movement toward Islamic teaching and virtuous ethics. These include ritual prayers (Salat), fasting, pilgrimage and so, all of which lead to the purity of spirit.

2.2.2 Recommended (Mustahab) Consumption of Goods and Services

According to Islam, the consumption of some goods and services is considered preferable to non-consumption. These goods and services are recommended for consumption (Mustahab). These types of goods can make it possible for a person to acquire honored ethical characteristics. Not consuming these goods and services does not constitute a transgression but their consumption indicates good ethics or creates the ground for acquiring higher ethical characteristics. These goods and services include:
- Frequent pilgrimage of sacred sites such as Mecca, Masjid al-Nabawi in Medina and the shrine of the Prophet, Al-Aqsa Mosque (Palestine), shrines of other religious leaders. Of course, time and space, economic and social conditions should be considered. These activities lead to the strengthening of the soul and body and prepare people psychologically for undertaking good ethical deeds.

- Consumption of water for Ghusl (full body ablution) and Wudu (partial ablution for ritual daily prayer), or washing hands before eating, and so on for oneself and one's. Physical cleanliness prepares the ground for the purity of the soul for movement toward human perfection.
- Consumption of some goods and services such as toothbrushes, toothpastes, perfumes, brushes, and so on for oneself and one's family, consumption of which indicates positive good ethics of individuals. all of which these are examples of individual positive moral behaviors.
- Consumption of goods and services that help meet the needs of others. Such activities are indication of possession of spirit of other-loving that is willing to sacrifice one's own interests in order to help others and demonstrates a great human ethical value.

2.2.3 Consumption of Permissible (Mubah) Goods and Services

Shari'ah considers consumption of a large number of goods and services which have no particularly harmful effect in and of themselves. These include:

- Variety of foods including meats that are not forbidden, fruits, clothing and housing appropriate to the social condition of the individuals.
- Healthy and appropriate relaxation activities.
- Generally, the consumption of goods and services that do not fall explicitly in the other four categories.[7] It should be noted that obligatory consumption relates to a minimum amount necessary for preservation of life and health. Consuming greater amount of these kinds of goods and services is considered permissible.

2.2.4 Repugnant (Makruh) Consumption of Goods and Services

Repugnant (Makruh) goods and services are those that not consuming them strengthens ethics. These include:

- Meat of draught-animals even though their meats are not considered unclean (such as that of the pig) including the meat of donkey, horse, mule. It is clear that the reason for the repugnance of these meats is due to the fact that they are the means of production and transportation hence destroying them reduces the productive capacity of the society.
- Consumption of certain animal parts (for example, the testicles of sheep and cows).

---

7 Some, like Shahid Thani, do not accept Mubah as a separate decree from the four other decrees (categories). But many jurisprudents including Imam Khomeini have accepted it.

- Poor diet or gluttony are considered repugnant.
- Wearing black and gaudy clothing that leave adverse effects on human spiritual health and enrichment of individual ethics.

2.2.5 Prohibited (Haram) Consumption of Goods and Services

Consumption of some goods and services is forbidden (Haram) by Shari'ah. Consumption of these goods and services have negative impact on physical and spiritual health which are a prerequisite for an individual's movement toward perfection of ethics. These goods and services include:

- Any commodity or service whose consumption causes financial, physical, mental or spiritual damage to an individual or his family has negative influence on his movement toward perfection of ethics.
- Consumption of any kind of goods and services which negatively influences clarity of rational thinking.
- Consumption of goods and services obtained from illegal sources (including their purchase with income from prohibited activities). Such consumption harms the society, strengthens repugnant ethics, and encourages expansion of immorality.
- Consumption of alcoholic beverages, poisons, carrion meat, blood, the meat of unclean animals, anything that has not been slaughtered in the name of the Creator, and socially unacceptable deeds harmful to human dignity or those that encroach on the rights of others.
- Consumption of fraudulent and misleading goods and services such as recreational activities that lead to unethical or immoral behavior.
- Consumption of certain special goods and services, such as the use of gold and silk clothing by men, the use of gold dishes for eating and drinking, use of women's clothing by men (and vice versa for women), which are harmful to the movement toward perfection of ethics.

Based on this brief discussion, if a person has complete faith he complies with these rules. He performs what has been made obligatory (Wajib) and avoids the prohibited (Haram). He performs what has been recommended (Mustahab) to the best of his ability and avoids the repugnant (Makruh). He enjoys consumption of the permissible (Mubah) in his effort to attain the approval of Allah. In this case, the basket of goods he selects are considered an ethical basket. He consumes more of some and less of others, and none of some other goods and services.[8]

---

8 Here we note that the observance of any rule of prohibition or of what Islam recommends has a divine reward. This reward is divine or paradise, or away from hell, or other worldly benefits, and the so on, and a wise person will at present be willing to lose something (such as forbidden goods), which, in turn, should be better in the hands of brought up (For example, divine rewards oretc.).

2.3 Teachings Related to Consumption Level

In Islam, certain teachings have been offered for the level of consumption of goods and services, and Muslims and believers have been asked to adhere to these teachings. If one believes in Allah and His commands, it is expected that these teachings will be followed. These teachings are also referred to as teachings on the ethics of consumption. The most important dimension of these teachings is Qasd – meaning paying attention to what the society considers as reasonable moderation in the amount of consumption. One can consider other principles that govern consumption behavior are explanatory glosses on the principle of moderation. In the what follows, we will explain this basic principle and related teachings.

2.3.1 Teachings Governing Moderation and Balance in Consumption (Qasd)

The rule of moderation in Islam is general and not only for consumption. It is considered an ethical principle that governs all behavior,[9] including consumption.[10] In the verses of the Qur'an and in a number of narrations,[11] the word "Qasd" meaning moderation and balanced is used to indicate "economy" in behavior which is the prescribed ethics for behavior.[12] We mention some of these verses and narrations below:

For further explanation, refer to: Seyyed Mohammad Hossein Tabataba'i; Al-Mizan; following verses 153–7 of Surah Baqara.

This will be done without reducing his satisfaction in general, because if this Muslim man has complete faith, according to his beliefs, what he will gain in return for not consuming some goods is superior to what he will lose. Therefore, when he is given to a person, goods or service that is superior to him, instead of the goods or service available, he must surely increase his satisfaction. According to the framework of rationality, if a person is fully aware, he will prefer superior to lower than for more satisfaction. In this way, a grammatical valuation on the goods will diminish the consumption basket of the submissive consumer of Islam, without sacrificing its satisfaction (but with increasing). Look at Ezzati, Morteza, 2016, Chapter 4.

9 In the good affairs, meditation is not recommended but advancement and overtaking and doing much is recommended. Pay attention to verse 32 of Surah Fate. Of course, in some of the good affairs that are too harmful, the moderation is recommanded.

10 In the Qur'an in 6 verses, the "economy" has been used. In these verses, the economy is to mean the mediation in different affairs. It is also synonymous in the book of the same subject including:
- Foad Efram Al-Bustani; Monjed Al-Talab, the following "economy"
- Azartash, Azarnoosh, Arabic – Farsi contemporary dictionary, under "economy"
- Lewis Maalouf; Al-Mashhad Alabghidi: Under the "Intent"
- Mohammad Hooman; Dictionary of Islamic Economics and the following: "Economy".
- Muhammad Mo'in; Persian Dictionary; the following: "economy" and "economocal".

11 In Qur'an, in the verses: Maede 66; Tawbeh 42; Nahl 9 and 19; Loqman 32; Fater 32, the words with the root "economy" are used that all of them mean "mediation" according to the interpreters and commentators.

12 Refer to mentioned verses in the previous subtitle and the pages 70–255, the volume 4 of "Al-Hayayt".

"Walk modestly and lower your voice; the most hideous of voices is the braying of the donkey" (Loqman, 13:19). «وَ اقصِد في مَشيِك ...» (سوره لقمان؛ 19)

"Those who when they spend are neither wasteful nor miserly, between that is a just stand" (Al-Forqan, 25:67). «والذينَ اذا أنفقوا لَم يُسرِفوا و لَم يَقتُروا و كانَ بَينَ ذالِكَ قَواماً» (فرقان؛ 67)

The Prophet: "مَن اقتصَدَ في مَعيشَتِهِ رَزَقَهُ اللّه وَ مَن بَذَرَ حَرَمَهُ الله" (Al-Hayat, Volume 4, p. 265)

"Allah will provide for whoever is moderate in his living and Will not do so for those who are prodigal."

The Prophet said: "ماعال مَن اقتَصَدَ" (Nahj al-Fisaha, the row 2601).[13] "The person who is moderate (in spending) will not suffer poverty."

Imam Ali (as) advised his son, Imam Hasan (as): "يا بُنَّي اوصيكَ بِتَقوَاللهِ في الغني و الفقر ... و القصد في الغني و الفقر ..." (Al-Hayat, Volume 4, p. 263).[14]

"O my son I advise you to be (constantly) aware of Allah in prosperity and poverty...and moderation in prosperity and poverty."

Based on the verses of the Qur'an and narrations available, moderation is recommended as a general rule of behavior, especially in spending of one's income and in consumption. This rule is a dictate of the religion which must be observed by those who are its followers. There are other religious teachings whose objective is to lead Muslims and Mu'mins (active believers) to choose moderation and balance in their affairs. There are two types of teachings related to immoderate behavior Going beyond acceptable limits and doing less that acceptable minimum.

2.3.2 Teachings Related to the Prohibition of Prodigality (Israf) and Wastefulness (Tabdheer)

One of the main ethical teachings in the field of consumption and economic behaviors is to avoid the prodigality (Israf, اسراف) and "Tabdheer". Etymologically, the root of Israf is "sarafa" meaning overstepping the limit of any action and exceeding the limit considered appropriate.[15] Lavish consumption of goods, wastefulness in spending

13 This Hadith is mentioned in Nahj al-balaqeh by Imam Ali (PBUH).

14 There are various Hadith related to this subject. For more information refer to: Hakimi and others; Al-Hayat, volume 4, pages 70–255; Nahj al-Fasaha, rows 541, 1045, 2181 and 2705 and etc.

15 Some have considered " اسراف" or prodigality using property or charity too much and the etc. Some have also expressed other meanings for it (including: Ahmad Naraghi; 25–623; Mojtaba Bagheri; p. 110, quoted by Ayatollah Montazeri). The validity of these meanings is less likely, because in Qur'anic verses the word "prodigality" is used for acts including consumption the property or charity, and so on. Some of the meanings of prodigality or "اسراف" are as follows: overstepping the limit of any action and doing too much and spending a lot of money on a small scale; and it's about exceeding the usual amount of spending; and saying that "prodigality" or "اسراف" is an act that someone eats something which is forbidden (Haram) or uses the solvent goods more than his needs; and they say that "prodigality" is to

and extravagance in other deeds has been considered by religion. It is forbidden to do more than moderation in the Islamic law, and it is recommended that Muslims and believers avoid it.

The word "Tabdheer," in the present context, means "to dissipate" or "to squander" (تبذیر) or to spend income and wealth carelessly through the careless way. The root of "Tabdheer" is derived from the root "Badhara" ("بذر") meaning to spread seeds. If wealth is consumed excessively and unreasonably, it is considered "squandering". For this reason, Israf (prodigality) and Tabdheer (squandering) have analogous meaning in the context here. However, based on the related verses of the Qur'an, "Israf" is used more for extravagant consumption and "Tabdheer" is used more for wasteful spending.[16] Due to the similarity of the conceptual meaning of the two words, sometimes they are use as synonyms and together.[17] Accordingly, it can be stated that "squander" or "تبذیر" is a kind of "prodigality" or "اسراف" but with a specific meaning of prodigality in the use of wealth and income.[18]

To clarify the issue, we point to several examples of behavior considered as the prodigality in the Qur'an: In one Verse (al-'Araf, 7:31), while Muslims are encouraged to wear pleasant and clean clothing, they are advised not to be extravagant or lavish in doing so in participating in ritual public prayers in mosques. In others (al-'Araf, 7:31; al-An'am, 6:141), over-eating and excessive drinking of permitted drinks are considered prodigality as is also excessive cruelty in permitted retribution for murder (al-'Asra, 17:33), in spending (Forqan, 25:67), and in performing acts that are socially repugnant (al-'Araf, 7:81) and others.

For example, in Verse 141 of Chapter 6 Muslims are advised: "... Eat of the fruits when they ripen and pay what is due (to others) on the harvest day. Lo! Allah does not love the prodigals.

«...كُلوا مِن ثمرهِ إذا آثمر و آتوا حقَّهُ يوم حَصاده و لا تُسرفوا اِنّه لا يحبُّ المسرفين» (انعام؛ 141).

In Verse 33: Chapter 17 while retribution for murder has been permitted, Muslims are warned against exceeding the limit on retaliation prescribed by Allah, for it is considered as Israf (prodigality): "...but do not allow him (the person who has been given the right of retribution against

overstep in quantity and to spend something in your own place beyond the required level (definitions). Also, the prodigal person is someone who oversteps (Islamic vocabulary and terminology).

16 Some experts have considered these two words as the same because of common concepts while it is not correct. Among the cases in which these two synonyms are stated, is the place where the consumption of property has been considered, and has not been used elsewhere and only prodigality is stated. Other differences have also been identified for these two concepts, including excessive use in their own territory and excessive consumption in their non-home use (definitions) (cited by Islamic vocabulary and terminology).

17 Of course, some people have considered "squander" as doing too much in terms of quality and "prodigality" ad doing too much in terms of quantity.

18 Other narratives show this point of view such as the words of Imam Sadeq: "..ان التبذیر من الاسراف ..."; quoted by Mojtaba Baqeri, p. 52.

the person who had murdered a near relative of his) to commit excess in retaliation. Lo! he will be helped (if he does not exceed the prescribed limits)"

«... فَلا يُسرف فِي القتلِ إنَّهُ كانَ مَنصُوراً» (اسراء؛ 33).

"Thus, We recompense those who are prodigal and do not believe in revelations of his Lord. The torment in the life to come will be more severe and longer lasting (TA HA, 20:127).[19]

«وَ كَذالك نَجزي مَن أسرَفَ وَ لَم يُؤمِن بِاياتِ رَبِّهِ وَ لَعَذابُ الاخِرة أشَدُّ و أبقي» (طه؛ 127).

In two verse of the Qur'an, verses 26 and 27 of Chapter 17, the word Tabdheer (Squandering) "تبذير" is mentioned referring to giving financial help to relatives or "Zilghorba", destitudes and poor travelers or "ابن السبيل" meaning spending too much in one specific direction.[20]

According to various verses and narrations[21] relating to this issue, the prohibition of prodigality (اسراف) and squandering (تبذير) is the ethical teaching governing consumption which the believers are required to follow.[22]

It should be stated that the prohibition of "prodigality" (اسراف) and "squandering" (تبذير) imposes limits on consumption that one should not transgress. Question arises what are these limits? Considering that the Qur'an and Sunnah prescribe moderation and balance, this limit can be defined as an acceptable moderate level (Qasd) in behavior. Many narrations from sacred sources indicate that prohibition of prodigality and squandering are complementary to the command of moderation. As indicated in the verses mentioned, compliance with moderation and balance is the principle prescribed behavior but prohibition of prodigality imposes limitation of behavior including consumption. In this context, following narrations are helpful:

It is narrated that al-Imam Ali (as) advised: "فَدَعِ الاسرافَ مقتصداً..." (Al-Hayat, V.4, p. 230): "...therefore, reject prodigality and adopt moderation..." Also, he defined Israf (prodigality) as: "كُلُّ مازادِ عَلَي الاقتصادِ اسراف" (Al-Hayat, V. 4, p. 231): "prodigality is exceeding moderation." Similarly, al-Imam Hasan al-Askari (as) advised: "«... عليكَ بِالاقتصادِ و ايّاكَ و الاسراف" (Al-Hayat, V. 4, p. 230) "Do not be prodigal and adopt moderation."

---

19 Other verses are stated by Qur'an such as Al-Imran, 14; Nesa, 6; Maedeh, 32; Araf, 81; Yunus, 12 and 13; Anbia, 9; Forqan, 67; Shoara, 151; Ya Sin, 19; Zomar, 53; Ghafer, 28,4,43; Zakhraf, 5; Dofan, 21; Zoriat, 34 and etc.

20 In Qur'an, only these two verses have used the root "بذر" for the word of "تبذير": "Give to the near of kin, the needy and the destitute traveler their rights and do not squander" and "for the wasteful are the brothers of satan; and satan is ungrateful to his Lord" (Asra, 26 and 27).

21 Refer to Al-Hayat, V. 4, Pages 50–228.

22 Some in the ethics debates have stated that the use of "اتراف" (means insisting on disobedience in taking blessings) is also an ethical teaching for consumption, while it is a psychological state, and is said to be reticent and prideful of the achievement of wealth. In the Qur'an, the word "Mufkin" has been used for such people.

There are other narrations with similar meanings indicating the principle of moderation and complementarity of prohibition of prodigality and squandering with this principle.

2.3.3 Principle of Prohibition of Avarice (Bukhl: بخل) and Stinginess (Taghteer تقتير)

Taghteer (stinginess) means spending less than the level considered as moderate on consumption of goods and services or in other kinds of behavior.[23] This concept has been synonymous in economic affairs with the word "avarice" (بخل) (especially in consumption and personal matters). Also, the word "Shuh" has been referred to as synonym of "greed and avarice" (بخل), all of which have been criticized in the Qur'an and sacred traditions, and the believers have been called upon to avoid it. Since the principle of moderation is an accepted ethical framework of Islam, behavior that focuses on levels of activities below the moderate level is prohibited. In this context, there are verses in the Qur'an addressed to this prohibition:

--"And those who, when they spend, are neither prodigal nor avaricious; and there is a firm station between the two" (Forqan, 25:67).[24]

«وَالذين إِذا أنفقوا لَم يُسرِفُوا و لَم يَقتُروا و كَانَ بَينَ ذالِكَ قَواما» (فرقان؛ 67).

-- In Verse 36/37: Chapter 4, believers are warned: "...Allah does not love the proud and the boastful and those who are avaricious and enjoin avarice on others...

«...إنَّ الله لا يُحّبُ مختالاً فخوراً آلذين يَبخَلونَ و يأمُرونَ الناسَ بِالبُخل ...»

--"And do not let those who are greedy with what Allah has given them of His Bounty think it is better for them, but rather, it is worse for them. They will be coiled in that which they were greedy on the Day of Resurrection. And to Allah belongs the inheritance of the heavens and the earth. And Allah is Aware of what you do" (Al-Imran, 3:180).

«وَ لا يَحسَبَنَّ الذينَ يَبخَلوُنَ بِما آتاهُمُ اللهُ مِن فَضلهِ هُوَ خَيراً لَهُم بَل هُو شَرٌّ لَهُم سَيُطوَّ قونَ ما بَخِلوا بِه يَومَ القِيامَة ...» (آل عمران؛ 180).

--"...Whosoever is saved from the greed of his own soul, they are the ones who win" (Hashr, 59: 9).[25]

«... وَ مَن يُوقَ شُحَّ نَفسهِ فَأُلئِكَ هُم المُفلِحون» (حشر؛ 9)

23 The word "تقتير" means less than acceptable spending while having wealth, having stinginess, severity on spending money and food stingy on family (Monjed al-Tullab dictionary)

24 In Qur'an, the root of this word is "قتر" used in verses Baqarah, 236; Yunus, 26; Asra, 100; Forqan, 67; Abas, 41 (five times).

25 The words with the root "شح" are mentioned in the Qur'an as follows: Nisa, 128, 5 times; Ahzab, 19, 2 times; Hashr, 9; Taqabon, 16 and all of them mean "stinginess" (بخل).

In this context, few narrations are given as follows:

It is reported from al-Imam Ali (as): "كُن سَمحاً و لا تَكُن مُبذِّراً و كُن مُقَدِّراً و لا تَكُن مُقتِراً" (Nahj alBalaqah, speech 32), "Be easy going but not wasteful; spend in measures and not stingy." Also it is narrated from Imam 'Ali (as): "Avarice is Disgraceful…" ; "البُخلُ عارٌ …" (Nahj alBalaqah, speech 3).

According to narrations and verses, the word Taghteer (stinginess) "تقتير" means spending less than the minimum acceptable level of spending despite possession of wealth by the individuals involved. This is considered a blameworthy ethical characteristic and is prohibited. Similarly, exceeding moderation in spending such as in extravagance (Israf) or wasteful (Tabdheer) is prohibited.

2.3.4 Limit Established by Balance and Moderation (Iqtisad)

The question of how much is the appropriate level of spending has been a serious topic of discussion in economics and ethics. The question of appropriate level of consumption for a Muslim in compliance with the rules prescribed by Islam has been researched and discussed by Muslim scholars and economists resulting in some theories. Generally, based on verses of the Qur'an and sacred traditions, a number of different factors are involved in determining moderation. Nevertheless, it is possible to discuss the most important of these factors as follows:

A. "Prodigality" (اسراف) and "Avarice" (بخل) and (تقتير) "Stinginess"

As mentioned before, "Prodigality" (اسراف) and "Avarice" (بخل) and "Stinginess" (تقتير) are two opposite types of behavior that exceed the prescribed rule of moderation and balance. Verses of the Qur'an and narrations from sacred sources mentioned above address this point. However, in some texts prohibition on prodigality is considered as the governing principle without paying due attention to prescribed compliance with moderation as the fundamental principle and prodigality as well as stinginess as indicators of exceeding the upper and lower limits of moderation.

It is clear that religion has been revealed as guidance to humans how to perfect honored ethical characteristics in their behavior. Allah has prescribed ways and means of acquiring the habit of behaving ethically in the Qur'an. The most important means of doing so is designated as moderation. That is the correct behavior, according to Islam, is moderation in all behavior including consumption. To make clear the boundaries of moderation, Islam has defined and explained behavior that violate the rule of moderation by specifying and explaining such behavior. Since it considers moderation in behavior as ethical, its violation is declared unethical and prohibited. Evidence from the Qur'an and from sacred tradition in support of this conclusion (such as Verse 67: Chapter 25; 36–37:4; 180:3; 9:59; 16:64) makes clear prohibition of avarice and stinginess as behaviors that violate the rule of moderation by exceeding the minimum level of spending, on the one hand, and prodigality as violating upper limit of spending, on the other.

B. Determination of Moderation: Limit of Individual Needs

According to the Qur'an and sacred traditions, Islam has allowed humans to enjoy Divine gifts, but has ordained moderation in their use. An indicator of moderation is human needs based on physical health, number of people under the care of the individual, mental, spiritual and cultural conditions of the individual and his society. These conditions are so crucial that, in exceptional circumstances, may lead to allowing consumption of prohibited commodities and services. It is reported that the Prophet has stated: "إنَّ الله تَعالَي يُنزِلُ المَعُونَة عَلي قَدرِ المَؤنَة وَ يُنزِلُ الصبر عَلي قدرِ البَلاء" (Nahj al-Fasahah, row 776); "Allah Exalted provides assistance according to the person's needs and gives patience according to the strength of adversity." Al-Imam Ali (as) has advised: "فَدَعِ الاسرافَ مُقتَصِداً وَاذكُر في اليومِ غَداً و اَمسِك مِنَ المالِ بِقدرِ ضَرورَتكَ وَ قَدِّم الفَضلَ لِيَومِ حاجَتِك" (Nahj al-Balaqah, letter 21);[26] "Be moderate instead of extravagant, remember today your (needs of) tomorrow, limit your spending to what you need (today) and save the rest for the day of your need."

Given that need is an indicator that defines moderation, the status and social circumstances of individuals becomes a condition defining needs. Islam accepts that humans consume in accordance with their social status and does not consider such consumption as violating the rule of moderation and balance. Because of the importance of social status as a determinant of need, it is considered as a separate criterion in some religious debates and discussions. In fact, however, social status and dignity of a person is the determinant of a specific need of the person commensurate with his social status. Exceeding the limit of consumption defined by social status and dignity of the person is considered extravagant (Israf, rodigality) and not the consumption commensurate with such status and dignity. The Prophet has reported as saying:

> "لِلمُسرِف ثَلاثُ علامات: يأكُلُ ما لَيس لَهُ و يَلبِسُ ما لَيسَ لَهُ و يَشترِي ما لَيسَ لَهُ" (Al-Hayat, V.4, P.23);[27] "The signs of a prodigal person (Musrif) are three: He eats, uses clothing, and consumes what is not his."

26 Refer to detailed narrative in Wasail al-Shia. Also, Imam Sajad has stated in one of the prayers of Sahifeh Sajadiah: "... و نعوذ بك من تناول الاسراف و من فقدان الكفاف ..." that has considered sufficiency as the need extent.

27 For more information about some aspects of this subject refer to Mohammad Taghi Gilak Hakimabadi; Pages: 20–119.

C. Guidance on the Limit of Sufficiency (Kifaf)

Sufficiency limit (حد كفاف) is that amount that meet the needs of a person.[28] Many recommendations have been made regarding the necessity of complying with this limit that, if followed, consumption will achieve balance. Among sacred traditions, it is reported from the Prophet:[29] "Felicity is achieved by a person who has been guided to Islam and who lives within the limits of sufficiency and is content with it;"

"افلح من هدي الي الاسلام و كان عيشه كفافاً و قنع به". (Nahj- al-Fasaha, row 422)

> The Prophet (as) is also reported as saying: "إذا كانَ عِندَكَ ما يَكفيكَ فَلا تَطلُب ما يُطغيكَ" (Nahj- al-Fasaha, row 231); "If you have enough (to meet your needs), do not seek what will lead you to disobedience (of Allah).

> Imam Ali (as) is reported as saying: "ما فَوقَ الكَفافِ اسراف" (Al-Hayat, V.4, p. 231);[30] "What exceeds (the level of) sufficiency is prodigality."

Based on these sacred traditions, it can be claimed that sufficiency is a criterion for determination of ethical level of consumption since spending more than this limit is a movement toward prodigality while spending less is a movement toward stinginess and avarice. Linguistically, "sufficiency, Kifaf" is defined as "whatever is needed, no more and no less." ('Amid Dictionary, intent, sufficiency "كفاف"; Mu'in Dictionary, sufficiency "كفاف").

D. Guidance on Contentment (Ghina'ah)

One of the other serious ethical recommendations about the amount of consumption is contentment defined as the level of consumption which is commensurate with the level of income of the consumer or, in another words, being content with the level of consumption that is sufficient to meet a person's needs. In the sacred tradition, contentment has been advised and is considered so important in economic behavior as to be considered as a highly praised ethical characteristic.[31] In this context, note the following traditions:

---

28 The sufficiency has different meanings. In the word, it is considered enough sustenance (Monjed al-Tullab). In jurisprudential terms – such as Majlesi, Ghazali and Feyz Kashani- it is considered among poverty and wealth. Some see it (as Horr Ameli) as part of the satisfaction of needs that are consistent with change. Some consider it as balanced consumption (Mojtaba Bagheri, pp. 6–32), and they also said that "it is sufficiently livable, that it is sufficient and worthwhile, to demand it, and that day is the daily salary and daily expenses (Ghias al-Loghat), or passing from a day and a power that does not respect and refuse to ask" (Montahi al-Aurb) (Islamic vocabulary and terminology).

29 The words with the root "كفف" (according the word كفاف) are repeated 16 timed in the Qur'an but none of them have the economical concept of the word "sufficiency" or "كفاف" but it is mentioned in the narratives.

30 Also for more information on other Hadith please refer to Hakimi and others; Al-Hayat, V.4, pp. 80–220.

31 Such as Mula Mohsen Feiz Kashani stated in Mahjata al-Beiza: One who wants to reach the queen of contentment deserves to block the way of spending, and it is not possible for him to pay heed to what is possible and who has a large expense (quoted by Mojtaba Baqeri, p. 70).

It is reported from the Prophet: "عَلَيكُم بِالقَناعَةِ فَإنَّ القَناعَةَ مالٌ لايَنفَد" (Nahj- al-Fasaha, row 1980); "Remain content (with whatever you have) because contentment is an asset which will never diminish." The importance of contentment is due to the fact that it creates an internal and emotional reaction in a person that will resist exceeding the limits imposed by the rule of moderation. In a narration from Imam 'Ali (as): "Whatever provides contentment is the limit of sufficiency" which indicates that the level of contentment and the level sufficiency are the same. More explanation of this point will be presented below.

E. Guidance on Asceticism (Al-Zuhd)

Asceticism indicates preference for what is in the Hands of Allah rather than what is held by others[32] (meaning what can be obtained from a worldly life) and is a foundation of ethics which in Islam it is considered a positive ethical characteristic. There is only one mention of Zuhd in the Qur'an referring to "زاهدين" (Hermits).[33] However, the idea of not being preoccupied with desiring worldly goods has been mentioned repeatedly in sacred traditions. For example, It is reported from the Prophet: "إزهَد في الدنيا يُحِبُّكَ اللهُ وَازهَد فيما في أيدي الناس يُحِبُّكَ الناس" (Nahj- al-Fasaha, row 268); "(If you) reject (the goods of) the worldly life, Allah will Love you. (If you) avoid wanting what people have, they will love you." And, Imam 'Ali (as)has said: "...al-Zuhd is wealth..."; ... الزُّهدُ ثروةٌ...»" (Nahj al-Balaqah, aphorism, 4)[34]

Generally, the encouragement to avoid strong attachment to the goods of this life (al-Zuhd) has an ethical dimension. It is motivated by Muslims' belief in acting in ways that attracts the approval of Allah or eternal felicity. It can be argued that encouragement to Zuhd (not being seduced by worldly goods) is encouragement to reduce unnecessary expenditures and increase doing good and beneficent activities and a movement toward balance.

Among meanings which Imam 'Ali (as) has given about Zuhd is the following: "ايها الناس الزَّهادَةُ قَصر الأمَلِ وَ الشُكرُ عِندَ النِعَّم وَ التَّورُّع عِندَ المَحارِمِ فَان عَزَبَ ذالكِ عَنكُم فلا يَغلِبِ الحرامُ صَبَرَكُم و لا تَنسوا عِند النِعَّم شُكرَكُم فَقَد آعذَرَ اللهُ اِليكُم بِحُجَجٍ مُسفِرَةٍ ظاهِرَةٍ و كُتُبٍ بارزَةِ العُذرِ واضحهِ" (Nahj al-Balaqah, speech 80). "O People! Zuhd is constraining desires; gratitude for blessings;

32 It is a lifestyle characterized by abstinence from sensual pleasures, often for the purpose of pursuing spiritual goals. Ascetics may withdraw from the world for their practices or continue to be part of their society, but typically adopt a frugal lifestyle, characterized by the renunciation of material possessions and physical pleasures, and time spent fasting while concentrating on the practice of religion or reflection upon spiritual matters (Monjed al-Tullab; Al-Monjed al-Abjedi/ Azarnoosh Azartash; Arabic-Farsi Dictionary).

33 In Qur'an, the root of this word is stated in Surah Yusuf, 20. In this verse, the asceticism is meant to be despicable and disregarded, which is consistent with the general meaning of asceticism here. Also interpreters and translators of the Qur'an have translated the verse 23 of Surah Hadid with the concept of asceticism.

34 Also refer to other Hadith in Nahj- al-Fasaha, rows 270, 1210, 3121 and etc.

and, self-control to avoid the forbidden. If this overwhelms you, do not allow the forbidden to defeat your patience and do not forget to show gratitude for blessings because Allah Has not left you with any excuses. He Has provided you with clear and strong evidence as well as with prominent, uninhibited and transparent Books." It seems clear, therefore, that in Zuhd, as is explained in this and other sacred traditions, there is the notion of contentment, focus on Allah, non-violation of limits on behavior as prescribed by the Divine, and being satisfied with necessary minimum. All in tandem with guidance on maintaining balance, not being prodigal, being content and being satisfied with minimum necessary within an ethical framework of behavior. Consequently, it can be concluded that the rule on observing moderation and balance is a fundamental ethical principle prescribed for consumers. Guidance on avoiding prodigality, avarice, stinginess, being content, limit of sufficiency, Zuhd and other religious teachings are parameters of determining of what constitutes moderation and balance with which believers are expected to comply.

2.4 Other Ethical Teachings Affecting Consumption Behavior

Religion as the ethics includes a set of other teachings and practical recommendations that fall within the framework of the same five categories including Wajib (Obligatory), 2) Mustahab (Recommended), 3) Mubah (Permitted), 4) Makruh (Repugnant) and 5) Haram (forbidden). Some of these teachings have economic dimensions and some of these teachings have non-economic aspects but affect consumption behavior. Some of the obligatory and recommended duties have ethical influence on economic behavior while their primary objective is nearness and communion with Allah. Some of these will be discussed next.

2.4.1 Ethical Teachings Influencing Consumption Behavior

In this context, a number of religious teachings can be discussed.

2.4.2 Recommendation and Order to Pay Zakat (زكات)

Zakat is essentially an ethical decree to purify the human soul. Giving up a portion of one's wealth in the way of Allah cleanses the soul (from undue attachment to wealth) and strengthens ethics. This is the reason this duty is called Zakat which, in one of its etymological meanings, indicates cleanser of soul. Zakat is not only part of ethically based religions, it is in and of itself, an ethical command that influences consumption behavior since, like an income tax, it reduces the disposable income of the consumer thus affecting the level of consumption. The difference between them is that the charges against income and wealth imposed by religion is a form of worship and communion with the Creator. Believers redeem them in compliance with the commands of the religion whose axis is ethics. Khums (paying 1/5 charge against specific types of incomes) is, like Zakat, another tax-type charge which is also focused on the same objective as Zakat.

2.4.2.1 Zakat (زكات)

Zakat is the spending of some part of the wealth of a person in the way of Allah and the payment of Zakat is legally obligatory.[35] At the beginning of Islam, Zakat was paid on some animals and agricultural products, as well as on gold and silver.[36] Today, payment of Zakat is still being paid by Muslims. The coefficient of this payment is 5% to 10%, depending on income on types of products and assets.[37]

There are various Fiqhi (jurisprudence) views regarding the spectrum of products and assets subject to Zakat. While in the majority School of thought the extent of the spectrum is quite wide that includes any type of income and assets, in Shi'i Fiqh, the spectrum of commodities and assets that are subject to Zakat has changed very little from the days of the Prophet which covered only 9 products and assets. Nevertheless, even in the latter school, there are differences of views as some extend the spectrum of commodities and assets to more than the 9 traditional items. The important point worth emphasizing, however, that these charges are paid with the intention cleansing the soul and of drawing near to Allah but they, nevertheless, influence the disposable income of individuals and thus the amount available for spending on other items. Similarly, Zakat al-Fitr that Muslims pay at the end of the Month of Ramadhan and is a per capita charge on each individual is ethical behavior of helping the poor. Its amount is approximately equivalent to 3 Kilogram of food.[38] Some scholars consider that any transfer payment intended as Sadaqah (voluntary contributions intended to help the less economically able) is a form of Zakat. If accepted, this position expands the spectrum of Zakat (Kia al-Hussaini, 1998).[39]

---

35 In Qur'an, there is used these words with the root "زكو" for 60 times and half of them have the meaning of Zakat as a tax and its payment is recommended such as Baqarah, 43/83/110/177/272; Nisa, 77/162; Anam, 141; Araf, 156; Tubah, 5/11/18/71 and etc.

36 For more information refer to the history of Zakat in Islam by Ejtehadi, Abulqasem, 1363, 40, 309.

37 For information on the quid pro quo, the cases of inclusion and details of these include the treatises of the operation: (i) Rouhollah Mousavi Khomeini; Tahrir al-Wasilah / Seyyed Kazem Sadr; 1375, 99–110.

38 Please refer to Resale Elmieh or Rouhollah Mousavi Khomeini; Tahrir al-Wasilah.

39 Kia al-Hussaini, Seyed Zia al-Din, 1998; in his master's thesis entitled Zakat in the Qur'an and his estimation of the function in Iran, he explains different Qur'anic perspectives on Zakat. One of the views of Allamah Tabatabai expresses the great commentator of the Qur'an that all alms and altruistic assistance to others are considered Zakat.

A noteworthy point is that many verses of the Qur'an emphasize the obligatory nature of Zakat and place it next to the obligatory daily prayers. This indicates the nature of Zakat as an act of worship as it is coupled with the physical and oral act of the 5 daily prayers. The objective of both is the cleansing of the soul which itself revolves around the axis of ethics.

2.4.2.2 Khums (Fifth-One خمس)

Khums is another form of Islamic transfer payment with the same objective as that of Zakat. It appears in one verse of the Qur'an (41:8) only in which it is applied to Ghana'im (wind-fall gains, such as war booty).[40] There is a difference of opinion among Qur'an scholars regarding the interpretation of the word Ghana'im subject to Khums. In the majority school of thought, Ghana'm means underground treasures, war booty and the like windfall gains while in the Shi'I school of thoughts, following the teachings of the Prphetand sacred traditions of the Imams (as) all residual incomes left after the annual expenditure is subject to Khums. These differences notwithstanding, the important point is that Khums too is another Islamic teaching indicating that Islam the axis around which Islam revolves, as related to human behavior, is ethics. Khums too affects disposal income and hence all expenditures.

2.4.2.3 Other Payments in the Way of Allah

In addition to Zakat and Khums, the expiation of sins is also part of the religious payments that are spent on the poor.[41] There are other payments that are usually classified as Sadaqah and fall in the same category, in terms of their objective, as Zakat and Khums. An Islamic state can impose additiona charges as was the case in the earliest Islamic period during the rulers who took charge after the Prophet.[42] These types of payments also have the same effect on income and consumption as Zakat. Basically, a person transfers part of his income to other members of the society. This a general religious ethical behavior.

2.4.3 Prohibition of Certain Incomes

Islam has forbidden some of the ways of earning income that is ethically repugnant. These prohibitions could potentially impact a Muslim's income by limiting the space of choices. On this basis, it can be said that it is one of the moral/ethical teachings that affect the main determinant of consumption, that is, income. In general, the

40 Enfal, 41.

41 For more information refer to Rouhollah Mousavi Khomeini; Tahrir al-Wasilah.

42 Including taxes on public lands.

Shari'ah of Islam, in its primary and secondary sacred sources, prohibits all economic and social activities which prevent the realization of ethical and human values.[43] As a result, earning income from these is also forbidden. Among the forbidden ways to earn income are:

- Earning income from Riba-based activities;
- earning income through hoarding,
- earning income by conducting any type of transaction in which fraud or intentional ambiguity is committed,
- earning income from activities involving gambling and the like,
- earning income from the exchange of goods and services with Haram and harmful effects to society and the individual.[44]

Any income earned from unethical economic activities, such as those mentioned above, is forbidden and cannot be used in consumption. From the point of view of religion, these incomes are, in and of themselves, unethical and so is spending them in consuming goods and services and are destructive to ethics.

2.4.4 The Command to Spend [Infaq (انفاق)] in the Way of Allah

An extremely important Islamic rule governing economic behavior that affects directly the discussion of consumption is Infaq (spending) in the way of Allah. Etymologically, the word Ifaq means digging a hole or underground pathways, in many of its usage it means spending in general.[45] In addition to different meanings, the term "Infaq" "انفاق" has been used with different meanings in the Qur'an and traditions. On the one hand, Infaq means the spending of wealth to the poor and the needy in the way of Allah.[46] On the one hand, it means, in the broad sense, any kind of spending wealth[47] and on the other hand, it is also used (in a negative sense) spending wealth in fighting against the way Allah and (positively) to help the way of Allah.[48] (see also, Dadgar, pp. 7–245). While Infaq means spending any kind of spending in general, in some verses of the Qur'an it is coupled with the words "في سبيل الله" (in the way of Allah (and

---

43 For more information about the discussion refer to Mohammad Baqer Sadr, 1350, 63–358/ Yadullah Dadgar and Najafi, 1379, 9–37.

44 Of course, the subject of Haram income is very large, here only the meaning of what can be effective on Muslim income is given. For a more complete explanation, refer to: Rohullah al-Musawi al-Khamini; "Makasabah Muharramah"; / Mohammad Hussein, Ebrahimi; "Muharramat Makaseb".

45 For more information on some meanings of Infaq, please refer to Mohammad Homan, Islamic economical vocabulary and terms (referring to "Dastoor al-Akhavan") below Infaq. Also Monjed al-Tullab, below "نفق" and Amid Dictionary, below "انفاق").

46 The verses 3, 195, 215, 219, 254, 261, 270 of Baqarah and so on.

47 The verses 36 and 63 of Enfal/ Baqarah 267, Al-Imran 117 and so on.

48 Enfal, 36.

is thus distinguished from other uses of Infaq. Here, we have the latter meaning, that is spending in the way of Allah which has been emphasized in Islam. In a number of cases, the word Infaq is used without qualification but meaning spending in the way of Allah and considered obligatory. For example, spending in support of the family or spending in support of defense of Islam and the like. Among the verses of the Qur'an in this context are the following:

--"O Believers! spend of what We have given you before that Day arrives when there shall be neither trade, nor friendship, nor intercession." (Baqarah, 2:254)

«یا اَیُهَا الذین آمَنوا اَنفِقُوا مِما رَزقناکُم مِن قَبلِ اَن یأتي یَومٌ لا بَیعٌ فیهِ وَ لاخُلَّةٌ وَ لا شَفاعةٌ» (بقره؛ 254).

--"Believe in Allah and His Messenger and spend of that which He has made you successors. Whosoever of you believes and spends shall have a mighty reward" (Hadid, 57:7).

«آمِنوا بِالله وَ رَسوُلِهِ وَ اَنفِقوا مِما جَعَلَکُم مَستَخلَفینَ فِیهِ فَالذینَ آمَنوا مِنکُم و اَنفَقُوا لَهُم اَجرٌ کَبیر» (حدید؛ 7).

--"Say: Whatsoever you expend He will replace it. He is the Best of providers" (Saba, 34:39)

«وَ ما اَنفَقتُم مِن شَيءٍ فَهُوَ یُخلِفُهُ و هو خَیرُ الرازِقین» (سبأ؛ 39).

There are more verses related to this issue but here we limit ourselves to these examples.[49] In a number of noteworthy verses, Infaq is given a very important status as it is coupled with Salat (daily ritual prayers).

According to some views, Infaq means any payment that is spent in the way of Allah, including: Khums, Zakat, atonement, dedication, ransom, Waqf, vow, types of alimony (obligatory and non-obligatory), Qard Hasan, Sadaqah, the so on (Mosavi Isfahani, 1989, p. 449). Accordingly, Infaq is considered as a comprehensive collection of religious spending conditioned on the intention that it is done to achieve nearness to Allah. If we consider this meaning, it can cover all expenditures of a Muslim. But what is known as "Infaq" in its customary understanding is to spend for others for Allah's sake which gives it an ethical of going beyond self-interest. It is possible to classify all that is considered as Infaq as follows:

Expenditure on spouse children, other relatives (first and second degrees), Khums, Zakat (wealth and body), other religious dues, expenditures in defense of religion, expenditures considered payments in the hope of atonements for transgressions, expenditures for sacrifices during the pilgrimage (Hajj), Qardh Hasan, gifts with the intention of achieving nearness to Allah, Sadaqah, and others. It can be understood that any expenditures accepted by religion as expenditures in the way of Allah belongs to the category of Infaq. Some verses of the Qur'an consider that any acceptable expenditure can be considered as Infaq. There are traditions that give precision to the definition of Inafaq:

49 Other verses including Baqarah, 3, 215, 219, 270/ Al Imran, 17/ Nisa, 39/ Enfal, 3/ Haj, 34 and 35/ Qesas, 54/ Sojdeh, 16/ Shora, 38/ Mohammad, 38/ Hadid, 7/ Monafeghon, 10 and etc.

"Whatever you spend and whatever vows you make are known to Allah. And there is no one (can) help the unjust" (Baqarah, 2:270).

«وَ ما اَنفقتُم مِن نَفَقَةٍ اَو نَذَرتُم مِن نَذرٍ فَإِنَّ اللهَ يَعلَمُهُ و ما للظالِمينَ مِن انصارٍ»(بقره؛ 270).

The Prophet is reported to have defined Infaq as:

"دينار اَنفَقتَهُ فِي سَبيلِ اللهِ وَ دينارٌ اَنفَقتَهُ في رَقبَة و دينارٌ تَصَدَّقت بِهِ عَلي مسكينٍ و دينارٌ اَنفَقتَهُ عَلي اَهلِكَ اَعظَمُها اَجراً الذي اَنفقتَه عَلي اَهلِكَ"
(Nahj al-Fasaha, row 1580)

"A Dinar you spent in freeing a slave, a Dinar you spent in helping the destitute, a Dinar you spent on your family."

Of course, there are more verses which consider Infaq as spending in general. And while there are many verses commanding Infaq, there are concurrent command to observe moderation and balance in spending. For example, note the following:

"They ask you what they should spend. Say: the residual" (Baqarah, 2:219)

«يَسئَلونَكَ ماذا يُنفِقون قُلِ العَفو» (بقره؛ 219).

It reported the Prophet:

"كُلوُا و اشرَبوا وَ تُصَدِقوُا وَ البِسوُا في غَيرِ اِسرافٍ و لا مَخيلهٍ (Nahj al-Fasaha, row 2181)"

"Eat, drink, give Sadaqah (to the poor) and wear clothing without being prodigal or arrogance." Verse 67: Chapter 25 praises "Those who when they spend, they are neither prodigal nor stingy (because) stability is between the two" (Forqan, 25:67).

As mentioned, Infaq is to spend one's resources in helping others and forego self-interest. It, therefore, based on the axis of ethics.

2.4.5 Influence of 'Ibadi (activities related to worship rituals) Teachings on Consumption Behavior

Islam has provided specific teachings relating to acts of worship. Some of these are mandatory (Wajib) and others recommended (Mustahab). The axis of acts of worship is to build an ethical personality. Performing these acts, however, involves costs in terms of allocation of time and resources thus leading to reduction of time and resources for consumption of other goods and services. Mandatory activities include daily prayers, fasting of the Month of Ramadhan, Pilgrimage to Mecca, defense of religion (Jihad), enjoining compliance with the rules prescribed by the Creator and discouraging rule violation. Recommended activities include voluntary additional prayers, atonements, voluntary fasting, repeated pilgrimage (mandatory pilgrimage is once only), pilgrimage to sacred sites other than Mecca, renewing contacts with extended family members and any other act of beneficence which has material, non-material, spiritual benefits for others. All of these strengthen ethics but influence the amount of resources available for consumption.

2.5 Influence of Ethical Teachings on Consumption

Compliance with the ethical teachings of Islam that govern consumption impacts greatly personal and social life in the society which we will discuss briefly here. First is the influence of these teachings on the ethics of individuals in that compliance with these teachings strengthens the process of building human ethical personality. Second is the social impact of compliance with these teachings provides support to the poor and the needy which in turn helps economic and cultural development of the society. Third is the impact on individuals' consumption behavior. Compliance of an individual with these teaching means that even if the person has enough financial resources to devote to high levels of consumption beyond his needs, he chooses to consume at a moderate level and use the residual for other purposes. The teachings also induce the stingy to increase their consumption. Fourth, in performing acts of worship individuals use time and resources that reduces their income and hence their consumption. In case of those individuals whose income was at the level of sufficiency, these expenditures may lead to lower level of income. This may induce greater effort at working to supplement their income and consumption. Hence, these teachings affect consumption behavior of many; some reduce their consumption, i.e. those who were consuming more than what was considered as moderate level, and some increase their consumption, that is those who were consuming less that the level minimum level needed to support their lives will now be able to increase their consumption because of the reduction in consumption of the first group will now be allocated to the second. Of course, not spending beyond the moderate level reduces the level of utility for the individual but is compensated by higher level of utility that he gains by his hope in drawing near to Allah and acquire His satisfaction and rewards.[50] Here, we note that compliance with any prohibited or obligatory teachings of Islam receives Divine reward. A rational person would sacrifice the utility he could gain by additional consumption if the utility of what he would gain in return for this sacrifice is higher otherwise it would be contrary to his Fitrah (primordial nature). [For further explanation please refer to: Seyyed Mohammad Hussein Tabataba'i; Al-Mizan; following verses 7–153 of Chapter 2 of the Qur'an. For a believing Muslim, sacrificing some goods and services means that what he expects to gain from this

50 Ezzati, 2016, 149–187. He explains in detail how the decision of a person is to choose the practices of the future reward against world-class deeds.

action is preferred to the disutility of the sacrifice. Hence, the consumption basket of a Muslim organized according to the command of Islam is smaller but provides him with the same or higher level of his total utility (See Ezzati, 2016, 161–185).

3 The Effects of Religious Ethical Teachings on Utility and Optimal Choice of Individuals

In this section we study the influence of the incentive structure which the religion establishes to induce compliance with the teachings of Islam related to ethical behavior.

3.1 Religious Incentive Structure to Induce Ethical Behavior

Consistent with their created nature, humans seek their self-interests and highest possible level of utility. Allah, as the Creator of humans and fully aware of their motives and objectives Has established an incentive structure to guide humans toward ethically good behavior. A believer has faith in the reality of life after death and arranges his living based on his belief in the duality of life Here and in the Hereafter and therefore tries to comply with ethical teachings of Islam. As incentives to promote compliance with ethical teaching Allah has created heaven and hell. In hundreds of verses of the Qur'an, Allah Has emphasized that He created heaven for those who have achieved ethical excellence and hell for those with unethical behavior. Heaven is described as a place in which all that is desirable can be achieved and hell as a place of torture and punishment. There are of course places other than heaven which Allah Has Created and which is even more desirable than heaven. Such places are created for those who go well beyond usual ethical behavior that has attracted the satisfaction and approval of Allah. And, hence, It is named Ridhwan Allah (a kind of Heaven which is earned for achieving the approval and pleasure of Allah) which is reserved, according to Verse 12: Chapter 89, for select people who have behaved extraordinarily in sacrificing their own self-interests in helping others.

In many sacred narrations those whose behavior is compliant with the Way of Allah. In this context, for example, Imam 'Ali (as) has been reported as saying: "Some people worship Allah because they fear hell fire, this the worship of the weak-willed people. Some worship Allah expecting to enter Paradise, this is the worship of the traders. Some worship Allah because they find Him worthy of worship, this is the worship of free people" (Nahj al-Bilaghah, Short Sayings, Number 234). The Creator knows the human being best. Hence, in addition to His gift of creating humans free, His love of humans has provided them with ways and means of of which they need in their movement toward achieving human excellence. Creating humans from the dust of the earth, He gave them the 5 material senses. Through His Spirit, which He blew in the physical body (see 29:15, 72:38), the Creator provided humans with a powerful intellect to empower their creativity and their ability to move toward achieving human excellence. He Created human heart as means of discerning Iman (belief). Using these means humans are empowered to embark on and continue his struggle toward achieving human perfection. Allah, through His perfect knowledge of the being He Created, provided him guidance through His Word in the Qur'an based on these abilities. To summarize: (1) Allah Created humans with a focus on their own self-interest in order that they struggle to achieve their best ends Here and in the Hereafter; (2) through their 5 senses, humans are capable of discerning the pleasures of this world; (3) through their hearts, humans are able to grasp the existence of Allah, the world of the unseen, life after death, accountability of the Day of Judgement, Prophethood, revelations and the like and believe in them; (4) Using their intellect, humans are able to discern good and bad, benefit and harm of actions in this world for themselves thus extrapolate this worldly knowledge to the world of the unseen and the life to come.

Allah has created humans free and placed a high value on their free choice to move toward human perfection. He selected the moto of "No Compulsion in Deen (the way of life that is Islam" (see Verse 256: Chapter 2) as the general methodology of Islam. Consequently, He placed great value on the efforts of those who according to their own free volition chose to comply with His rules prescribed in the Qur'an. Divine rewards and punishments are focused on the life in the world to come to create an incentive that motivate compliance with behavioral rules prescribed by the Deen. Fundamental part of these rules relates to ethics. Since the ways and means of meeting human needs are based on consumption which can lead to the good and positive utility for humans, Allah has provided the knowledge and the incentives that can motivate ethical behavior in consumption. Given the incentive structure provided by Islam, a believing person has a stronger motivation to undertake ethical behavior. Since incentives influence motivation of individuals in acquiring utility, they influence their utility function which in turn influences their decision making that lead to change in behavior. These influences play a role in ethical behavior related to consumption. To illustrate them, we consider the influence of Islam's ethical teachings on allocation of income to personal and worldly consumption in contrast to costs of religious ethical behavior. This analysis relates to the behavior of ordinary people. Different behavior may be observed in case of extraordinary people.

In general, every human activity has some cost either in financial or in terms of time devoted to performing that activity. These coasts are involved even in case of ethical behavior. However, ethical behavior reduces the availability of income or time that can be devoted to worldly consumption. A believer who is familiar with the ethical teachings of Islam will include the costs-rewards of complying with these teachings in his system of preferences. Since individual preferences determine the total utility function, once the individual becomes informed of the ethical teachings governing consumption, his preferences, therefore, his utility function changes. Given his new utility function, the individual will try, based on the strength of his belief, to gain higher utility in the Hereafter, acquire its rewards and avoid its punishments by complying with Islam's ethical teachings. Hence, an important effect of compliance with the ethical teachings of Islam that govern consumption behavior is to change the utility function of the person in which the utility of ethical behavior, like spending his income to help others, increases.

3.2 Voluntary and Compulsory Ethical Behaviors

Ethical behavior is carried out by human beings with knowledge and discretion or with compulsion imposed by social regulations or social institutions. Each of these two types of ethical behavior have their special effect on the utility function of individuals. In the voluntary case, behavior is based on knowledge and motivated by internal forces that lead the person to voluntarily choose to increase his utility. In case of compulsion, personal internal motivations play no part and do not enter the utility function which, as a result, does not change. These kinds of compulsory behaviors create an artificial ethicality and enter the utility function as a constraint on the decision-making process of individuals. If the constraint is removed, it is possible that the ethical behavior will change to become unethical. This is one reason why Allah has sent the Deen (Islam's way of life) to enter the hearts of humans, create internal incentives that motivate stable and sustained ethical behavior. Freedom of choice and religious liberty in tandem with Iman (belief) firmly and deeply rooted in the heart, ethical behaviors become internally institutionalized and sustained to strengthen the society. It is for this reason that the rule of "no compulsion in religion" became a fundamental principle of Islam and explains why the Prophet declared: "I have been appointed to complete that honored characteristics of ethics."

3.3 Effects of Compulsory and Religious Ethical Teachings on the Utility Function

In the case that moral behavior is imposed on individuals by social regulations and institutions, the utility function of the individuals does not change and remains the same as before. If this teaching is a legal and obligatory social norm, only the result affecting the decision is a behavior only a constraint under which the person cannot consume certain products or services even if they have utility. If we assume that an individual is to choose between a personal consumption or spend his income in helping others, if the personal consumption is compulsory, the utility function of the person with respect to the two kinds of expenditures does not change and, on this basis, indifference curves do not change either. As a result, optimal combination does not change for the person remains as before. But if the constraint is binding, the person is forced to optimize under the ethical constraint and, hence, consume within the parameters of the constraint and reduce his utility.

4 Conclusion

Based on the above explanations, Islam as a way of an ethical life that provides felicity in the Hereafter without harming the life Here, has permitted its followers to consume and enjoy the blessings of this life. However, since humans must prepare for the life Hereafter properly, it has provided teachings and guidance for improving human life, just as it has permitted consumption, which, if followed, a person can achieve felicity in the Hereafter without harming his living in this world. This is the comprehensive nature of Islam, in that it focuses on the life in this world and in the world to come.

Some of the teachings that affect the consumption of followers of Islam relate to religious valuation of the types of goods and services available for consumption (that is the five categories of obligatory or Wajib, recommended or Mustahab, permitted or Mubah, repugnant or Makruh, and prohibited or Haram). Some of the teachings are related to the level of consumption of goods and services whose central governing principle is moderation and balance. This teaching and its complementary principles – prohibition of prodigality, squander, stinginess, adoption of contentment, asceticism – affect the consumption of goods and services. There are other teachings in Islam that indirectly affect consumption. Some of these teachings are economic and affect the income of followers of Islam and consequently affect consumption and some are related to acts of ritual worship and indirectly affect the consumption of goods and services.

The teachings presented in Islam for the followers of this religion should be seen as a single set and cannot be considered separately from other teachings. Therefore, it is expected that that those who are perfect followers will comply with all of the teachings. In this case, such a person's consumption behavior falls in a special category. Of course, one cannot assume that all Muslims behave the same. It will all depend on the degree of the strength of their belief and its teachings which then determine the influence of the teachings on their consumption. Therefore, the consumption behavior of an individual falls within the proposed framework of Islam commensurate with the degree of his Iman (Belief).

Since Allah Has Created man and He knows him and his characteristics the best, He has designed His religion and its incentive structure in such a way that motivate humans to behave ethically. It is generally understood that religion enhances the worldly life of humans, it does not harm it. On this basis, religious teachings create an incentive for humans to exercise their free will to behave ethically. Religion has created an incentive structure based on a system of reward and punishment afterlife to motivate ethical behavior. The incentive structure is so designed that believing individuals gain utility by complying with the teachings in their behavior voluntarily. If, on the other hand, compliance is forced (through laws and institutions of state), utility of the behavior declines. The additional utility gained when an individual voluntarily behaves ethically is a superior (to forced compliance) and is a special characteristic of ethical behavior based on deep belief that not only enhance the utility of the individual but increases the welfare of the society

References

Qur'an.
Nahj al-Fasaha, The collection of aphorisms of The Prophet (PBUH), translated and provided by Abolqasem Painadeh, Tehran: Javidan, Third Edition, 1998.
Nahj al-Balaqah, hadiths, letters and sermons of Imam Ali (PBUH), by Seyyed Morteza Razi, translated by Mostafa Zamani, Tehran: Nabavi, 2015.
Sahifeh Sajjadiyeh: The Imam Ali ibn Hussein (PBUH) prayers (Imam Sajjad), translated by Mohammad Mehdi Rezai, Tehran: Jamal.
Ejtahadi, Abulqasem, 1984, investigating financial affairs of Muslims from the beginning to the end of Umayyad period, Tehran, Soroush.
Azartash, Azarnoosh, 2017, Arabic-Persian Dictionary, 18th edition, Tehran, Ney Publication.
Albasati, Foad Afram, 1989, Arabic-Persian Dictionary, translated by Manjed al-Tulab, Mohammad Bandarigi, Tehran, Islami Publication.
Amini, Ebrahim, 1989, the role of ethics in Islamic economics, proceedings of the second assembly of Islamic economic reviews, Mashhad: Islamic Research Foundation of Astan Quds Razavi.
Ansari, Morteza (Sheikh) (1375 AH) Al-Masakbas, second edition, Tabriz: Etelaat Publication.
Bagheri Tudashaki Mojtaba, 1988, the level of consumption from Islamic point of view, Master thesis of Mofid University Economics Department.
Hakimi, Mohammad Reza, and Hakimi, Mohammad, and Hakimi, Ali (1988–1995). Al-Hiahayat, 6 vol., Tehran: Publishing House of Islamic Culture, first and second printing, years 1989–1995.
Yadullah, Dadgar, 1999, Islamic economics and theory; values, recognitions and methods. Tehran, Research Institute of Economics, Tarbiat Modares University.
Dadgar, Yadullah, and Najafi, Seyyed Mohammad Bagher, 2000. Advanced Islamic jurisprudential principles of Islamic economics, Kermanshah: Razi University Press.
Sadr, Seyyed Kazem, 1996. The Economics of Islam, Tehran: Shahid Beheshti University Press.
Sadr, Mohammad Bagher (1971 and 1978). Economics, 2 volumes, translation by Mohammad Kazem Mousavi, (Volume 1) and Abdol Ali Espahbodi (Volume II), Tehran: Bad.
Tabatabaei, Mohammad Hussein; 1984. Al-Mizan. Translated by Seyyed Mohammad Bagher Mousavi Hamedani, Qum: Islamic Printing Office.
Ezzati, Morteza, 2003. The Effect of Religious Belief on Consumer Behavior, Islamic Republic of Iran Journal of Economics, No. 11, Autumn, pp. 11–34.
Ezzati, Morteza, 2005. Estimating the Cost of Religious Costs (Cost in the Way of God) Muslim, Islamic Republic of Iran, No. 18, summer 2005.
Ezzati, Morteza, 2016. Microeconomics 3: An Analysis of Economic Behaviors in the Islamic Framework, Tehran: Samt.
Kia al-Hussaini, Zia al-Din, 1998. Estimate of Zakat payment function, MA thesis of economics at Mofid University (Qum).

Gilak Hakim Abadi, Mohammad Taqi, 1993. A Theory on the Dimensions of Consumption in the Islamic Economic System, Thesis of Master of Science in Economics, Tehran.
Maalouf, Lewis, 007. Al-Mounjd al-Bajdi, translation by Ahmad Sayyah, Tehran: Farhan
Moain, Mohammad, 2009. Farsi Culture, 28th Edition, Tehran: Amir Kabir.
Makaram Shirazi, Naser, 2001. Khums, Qum: Alam Ali Ali ibn Abi Talib (AS) school
Montazeri, Hossein Ali (1410 AD). Khums, Qum: Dar al-Fakr al-Islam.
Montazeri, Hossein Ali (1407 AD). Zakat, Raba'a volumes, Qum: Islamic propaganda office.
M.usavi Isfahani, Jamal al-Din, 1989. Considerations about the Economic Messages of the Qur'an, Tehran: Islamic Culture Publishing Office.
Musavi Rad Lahiji, Hossein, 2000. Zakat, Qum: Imamology Publishing.
Musavi Khomeini, Ruhollah, 1991. Tahrir al-Wasilah, translated by Seyed Mohammad Bagher Mousavi Hamedani, Qum: Dar al-Alam. Moosavi.
Khomeini, Ruhollah, 1993. Makasebe al- Mahroham, second edition, Tehran: Institute of Publishing and Publications of Imam Khomeini Works.
Hooman, Mohammad, 1986. Dictionary of Islamic Expressions, Tehran: Ministry of Planning and Budget.

Mohammad Esma'eil Tavassoli and
Behrouz Mohammadi Monfared

Chapter 25: A Glance at the Ethical Dimensions of Money in Islamic Economic System

1 Introduction

Many of the issues that currently exist in various economic sectors are due to incoherent behavior of society and the governments toward the auspicious phenomenon called money. With the invention of money, human beings were able to circumvent the countless difficulties involved in the barter system of trading and bring about great prosperity through facilitation of transactions. However, usurious capitalists and inept governments have carelessly utilized money ever since to their maximum advantage throughout history.

Due to the fungibility of money, usurious capitalists have taken advantage of the needs of the people and through usurious transactions usurped the properties and assets of people to accumulate wealth thus have enhance enormously the unequal distribution of wealth in the society. In his interpretation of the Qur'an, 'Allameh Tabataba'ei (in *Tafsir Al-Mizan*) has analyzed Riba and its influence on creation of unequal distribution of wealth in the society and provided an explanation as to why the Qur'an has declared it an injustice. He states that the philosophy of prohibition of Riba can be found in the Verse 39 of Chapter 30 the Qur'an.[1]

"وَمَا آتَيْتُمْ مِنْ رِبًا لِيَرْبُوَ فِي أَمْوَالِ النَّاسِ فَلَا يَرْبُو عِنْدَ اللَّهِ وَمَا آتَيْتُمْ مِنْ زَكَاةٍ تُرِيدُونَ وَجْهَ اللَّهِ فَأُولَئِكَ هُمُ الْمُضْعِفُونَ"

> "That which you give in Riba in order that it may increase on (other) people's property will have no increase with Allah; but that which you give in Zakat, seeking Allah's countenance, has manifold increase" (Al-Rum, 30:39)

Allah describes Riba in this Verse as wealth of other people and its growth in the hands of few people the same way that a plant seed absorbs nutrients from the soil and consumes them for its growth, the usurer also annexes people's properties to his wealth, thus reducing the other people properties and expanding his own. The trend continues up until most of the people become poor and deprived while the usurer's growth become highly concentrated. This illuminates the intention of the Verse of the Qur'an (279:2) which in part says: "If you repent then have your principal (that way) you do no injustice and no injustice will be done to you." Hence, Riba is an injustice:

1 Al-Mizan fi Tafsir Al-Qur'an; 1390 LH; Vol. 2; p. 433.

https://doi.org/10.1515/9783110593419-025

فَإِنْ لَمْ تَفْعَلُوا فَأْذَنُوا بِحَرْبٍ مِنَ اللَّهِ وَرَسُولِهِ وَإِنْ تُبْتُمْ فَلَكُمْ رُءُوسُ أَمْوَالِكُمْ لَا تَظْلِمُونَ وَلَا تُظْلَمُونَ (البقره: 279)

> But if you do not do so, then be prepared to face war declared by Allah and His Messenger! If you repent, your principal capital; neither shall you do injustice nor injustice be done to you (Al-Baqara: 279).

Furthermore, number of adverse ethical consequences have been enumerated for Riba in Hadith literature. These include undermining the spirit of cooperation and beneficence while increasing the spirit of greed and covetousness in individuals thereby becoming an instrument of enmity and discord among human beings.

Whenever inept governments faced budgetary deficit, the easiest way out was "printing-new-money" policy. In effect, this policy leads to inflation and undermines the value of money. Continuous reduction in the value of money has adverse economic and social consequences for income and wealth distribution, savings, investment, allocation of resources, economic decision making, government budget, and the balance of payments.

The principal hypothesis of this research is that the main source of such crises is the attitude and anomalous ethical behavior of society and government towards the phenomenon called money. Using historical, explanatory and analytical methods, the research tries to throw light on how governments have created harmful and sustained inflation by disregarding the important and ethical principle of faithfulness to promises. The integrity of money (as standard of value) relies on commitment to promises. Islam has strongly ordained faithfulness to (the terms and conditions) of promises and (contracts). This rule is general and includes all contracts and promises that expect faithfulness (to their terms and conditions). By inference, this rule also covers money, which is, in effect, based on a contract with society. Moreover, the policy of deficit financing by printing money is unjust relative to financing of deficit through imposing additional taxes.

The banks from their inception, worsened wealth inequality through their Riba-based contracts, on the one hand, and through their power to create money, on the other. Unequal distribution of wealth is a clear contradiction of the teachings of Islam. From the point of view of Islam, distribution of wealth must be so designed that it avoids concentration of wealth in the hands of the few and distributed widely among the masses.

In the following discussion, relationship between ethics, economics and Islamic economy are dealt with. Then various ethical dimensions of the relationship between money and Riba, money and government in different monetary systems, as well as money and banks are covered in some detail. It will be demonstrated that most of economic challenges we are facing, have their roots in the unethical behavior of society and government towards the phenomenon of money.

2 Relation Between Ethics and the Economy

The influence and importance of personal ethics, personal characteristics, honesty and trust in general, as well as business ethics in particular, in enhancing the economic efficiency and prevention of Riba-based activities, economic scandals as well as the adverse effects of Riba, bribery, and bureaucratic corruption on human relations as well as on work and personal decision making are undeniable. It is now three decades in which, according to Hausmann, was the period in which the methodology of positivism had waned, Western philosophers and ethicists revived discussions on ethics.[2]

Since "Economics" fundamentally concentrates on study of the behavior of the "economic man", this discipline, as other social sciences, faces a number of challenges. Economic man is an "individual" who interrelates with "other individuals" and is continually in association and interaction with them. The study of the economic behavior of such an individual cannot be solely based on the "principle of independent wants". Wherever the "other" enters the picture, the economic man will face an ethical challenge. Therefore, economic behavior is intermingled with ethical behavior, and thus, economics and ethics become interrelated. Moreover, viewing Economics as an ethical science will perhaps be more fruitful than a discipline that has no commitment to ethical constraints.

According to many economists, contemporary economics suffers from a defect and that is its separation from ethics. Amartya Sen argues that in a discipline, which is essentially a part of humanities, the question of "how to live?" is the most essential inquiry in human progress.[3] As is well known, the father of economics, Adam Smith, was a teacher of the philosophy of ethics. Economics itself was considered a branch of the science of ethics for a long time. It seems that the reason contemporary economists consider their discipline as being separate from ethical values is based on their conception of man and his place in the created order. The viewpoint that developed after the Renaissance, which was based on the centrality of the human being, led to dissolution of the relationship between religion and society as well as between ethics and law and economics.

3 Coupling of Ethics and Economics in The Islamic School of Economics

The Islamic School of Economics has a fundamentally different worldview and anthropology than other schools. It considers the link between morality and the economy inevitable. In this view, Allah is the centerpiece of the universe

2 Haussmann et al., 1993; p. 723.
3 Sen, 2004.

and Center and Axis of the created order. His relationship with the universe and humans is based on His attributes of "Creatorship",[4] "Lordship",[5] "Ownership",[6] and his attribute of being "The Provider".[7] In this perspective, man is the agent/deputy[8] of Allah on the Earth. Nature and all its resources have been entrusted to him as custodian.[9] He is obligated to carry out his economic activities within the framework of divine rules and values. "Purposefulness",[10] "being accountable",[11] "having free choice",[12] "having the potential of living eternally",[13] and "having a dual being" (both material and spiritual) are among fundamental principles of knowledge about humans in Islamic thought. The principle of bi-dimensionality is the most important principle in necessitating the association of ethics and economics. The reason is that, from the point of view of the Qur'an, the primordial being of man in its material dimension is composed of "black clay" and in its spiritual dimension of "the Divine Spirit".[14] Hence, the needs and propensities of man are also bi-dimensional. As a result, his progress requires growth and development in both of these dimensions. Ignoring the spiritual and non-material dimension of human nature, which is one of the foundations of capitalist thought, denigrates the high status of humans. Therefore, Islamic thought rejects the notion of "economic man."[15]

All remarks made for ethical behaviors of human beings also pertain to governments. Observing ethical standards by governments is even more important and more influential than that of individuals. This is because if people do not comply with ethical standards in their voluntary behavior, governments can force them to observe to do so under the threat of punishment and/or by providing encouragement. In conventional secular states, however, if governments themselves do not comply with ethical rules, no other authority exists with the power to force them to do so.

In contrast, in an Islamic system the right to govern and rule belongs to Allah which forms the basis upon which the legitimacy of an Islamic government depends. In such a state, the basis for decision making are Allah and the rules He prescibed.

---

4 e.g. *Al-An'am*: 102; *Al-Ra'd*: 16; *Al-Zomar*: 62; *Qafir*: 62; *Loqman*: 11.
5 e.g. *Al-An'am*: 164; *Al-Sajda*: 5.
6 e.g. *Ale-Imran*: 109 and 129; *Al-Nesa*: 126, 131 and 132.
7 e.g. *Hud*: 6; *Al-Ankabut*: 60; *Saba*: 24; *Yunos*: 31.
8 See *Al-Baqara*: 30.
9 See *Al-Nur*: 33; *Al-Hadid*: 7.
10 See *Al-Mo'menun*: 115 and 116; *Al-A'diat*: 8.
11 See *Al-Taka'sor*: 8; *Nahj Al-Balaqa*: translated by Feyz Al-Islam; Sermon 166.
12 See *Al-Kahf*: 29; *Al-Ra'd*: 11; *Al-Insan*: 3.
13 See *Al-To'ba*: 100; *Al-Nesa'*: 134; *Al-Insan*: 27.
14 See *Al-Sajda*: 7–9; *Al-Hejr*: 28 and 29.
15 Iravani; 1383 SH; p. 91.

Every disagreement or conflict must be settled or resolved by reference to these rules. As Allah says in the Qur'an (10:42, al-Shura):

"وَمَا اخْتَلَفْتُمْ فِيهِ مِنْ شَيْءٍ فَحُكْمُهُ إِلَى اللَّهِ ذَلِكُمُ اللَّهُ رَبِّي عَلَيْهِ تَوَكَّلْتُ وَإِلَيْهِ أُنِيبُ"

> "And in whatsoever you differ, the verdict therein belongs to Allah. Such is my Lord, in Whom I place my trust, and unto Whom I return."

Certainly, such society that believes only in the sovereignty and governance of the Almighty, will only submit to the ruling and reign of God;

"... إِنِ الْحُكْمُ إِلَّا لِلَّهِ ..." (يوسف: 40)

> "... Decision/Judgment belongs Allah only ..." (Yusef, 12:40, in part).

Such belief is founded on the interpretation that the proprietor of the entire universe is the Almighty;

"لِلَّهِ مَا فِي السَّمَاوَاتِ وَمَا فِي الْأَرْضِ ..." (البقره: 284)

> "Whatever is in the heavens and whatever is in the earth belongs to Allah ..." (Al-Baqara, 2: 284, in part).

And the entire course of affairs in the universe and the authority over them is at His disposal;

"... فَاللَّهُ هُوَ الْوَلِيُّ ..." (الشورا: 9)

> "... Allah is the (only) Patron ..." (Al-Shura, 42:9, in part).

And the faithful believer who has such an attitude towards the Almighty, will always consider Him as the only supreme authority:

"... أَنتَ وَلِيِّي فِي الدُّنْيَا وَالْآخِرَةِ" (يوسف: 101)

> "... You are my Patron in this world and the Hereafter ..." (Yusef: 101, in part)

and;

"... مَا لَكُمْ مِنْ دُونِهِ مِنْ وَلِيٍّ ..." (السجده: 4)

> "... You (all) have no Patron other Him ..." (Al-Sajda, 32:4, in part).
>
> The person who realizes that there is no supreme authority and patron other than the Almighty, would submit fully to Him; and in return, the Almighty will not withhold His special caring from him. As is said in the Qur'an (257:2): اللَّهُ وَلِيُّ الَّذِينَ آمَنُوا يُخْرِجُهُمْ مِنَ الظُّلُمَاتِ إِلَى النو
>
> "Allah is the Patron of those who believe. He brings them out of the darkness into Light ..." (Al-Baqara: 257, in part)

and, he has comprehended that the Almighty is the best guardian:

... نِعْمَ الْمَوْلَى وَنِعْمَ النَّصِيرُ (الانفال: 40)

... how splendid such a Protector is, and how spendid is such a Supporter (Al-Anfal: 40, in part).

If man chooses to submit to the authority of the Almighty, he will not be in need of any other lord. The sign of submission to the authority of the Almighty is compliance with His commands in all personal activities and perceiving no other rule than the dictates of Allah in society. Submitting to rules other than those prescribed by Allah is tantamount to rejecting Him:

... وَمَنْ لَمْ يَحْكُمْ بِمَا أَنْزَلَ اللَّهُ فَأُولَئِكَ هُمُ الْكَافِرُونَ (المائده: 44)

... and those who do not judge by what God revealed, are disbelievers (Al-Ma'eda, 5:44, in part).

That is why within religious democratic system, religion acts as the guide and source of legitimacy and the people elect responsible administrators to govern on the basis of Islamic law and jurisprudence. As Imam Khomeini stated:[16] "In Islamic government, the laws of Allah govern and rule; rules prescribed by Islam govern, as ordained by Allah, all individuals and the state."

Since these rules are just and fair, their acceptance and implementation will call forth blessings and prosperity from the heaven and the earth:

وَلَوْ أَنَّ أَهْلَ الْقُرَى آمَنُوا وَاتَّقَوْا لَفَتَحْنَا عَلَيْهِمْ بَرَكَاتٍ مِنَ السَّمَاءِ وَالْأَرْضِ وَلَكِنْ كَذَّبُوا فَأَخَذْنَاهُمْ بِمَا كَانُوا يَكْسِبُونَ (الاعراف: 96)

And if the townsfolk had (only) believed and protected themselves (by complying with the prescribed rules), We would surely have showered blessings[17] from the heaven and the earth on them, but they rejected (them), so We seized them for what they had been acquiring (Al-A'raf, 7:96).

Accordingly, in order to achieve economic goals of development, poverty alleviation, establishing welfare, and implementing justice, the Islamic government must not only observe ethical values, but will enforce such values as well as an important objective.

4 Money, Riba and Ethics

Early human beings were faced with two fundamental difficulties. On the one hand, not all members of the society could provide for all their needs, and on the other, those who could avail themselves of the required provisions were not able to preserve

16 Mousavi Al-Khomeini; 1360 SH; p. 34.

17 Blessing refers to any of the numerous goodnesses/beneficences of life, such as security, comfort, health, resources, offspring, etc.

surplus commodities for a long time. The result of their hard work was always exposed to decay, theft and predation. For example, fishermen who had caught great quantity of fish, the huntsmen who had hunt huge games, or individuals who had gathered large amount of fruits and cereals, could not conserve them for a lifetime. To alleviate this difficulty, the early man began to lend and borrow. The huntsmen lent the excess game meat to those had not succeeded in getting a prey, provided that they would return it later. Consequently, by costless lending and without taking any additional quantity, just on the basis of assurance/promise from the borrower to requite, both parties could achieve their goals. Although this kind of loaning was ideal, but with progresses made in methods of preservation of foodstuff and other supplies from decomposition and external threats, the tendency of individuals towards costless lending was reduced. The situation was further augmented with awareness about dire need of other parties. In the course of time, lenders began to take assurance/promise from the borrower at the time of lending, that he shall return in excess of what he had borrowed. This way Riba came into being in early society and was further expanded with gradual development of economy and trade/commerce.[18] With the commencement of use infinitely durable commodity, such as money, in transactions, no one would extend Qardh Hasan (benevolent loan; loan without interest).[19]

Numerous adverse effects of Riba have been discussed in Hadith literature, paying attention to which can be useful in combating the extremely wicked act of interest taking. A few of these are enumerated below:

1. Expansion of the culture of Riba-based transactions results in obliteration of the spirit of cooperation and beneficence. In reply to a question on the basis of proscription of usury, Imam al-Ridha (as[20]) stated:[21]

   عِلَّةُ تَحْرِيمِ الرِّبَا بِالنَّسِيئَةِ لِعِلَّةِ ذَهَابِ الْمَعْرُوفِ وَ تَلَفِ الْأَمْوَالِ وَ رَغْبَةِ النَّاسِ فِي الرِّبْحِ وَ تَرْكِهِمُ الْقَرْضَ وَ صَنَائِعُ الْمَعْرُوفِ

   "The reason for prohibition of Riba al-Nasiyah is that it obliterates the good, destroys wealth, encourages people to seek returns without work, abandon giving loans without interest, and stop doing good for others"

   It can be deduced from the words of the Eighth Imam (as) that revival of *Qardh Hasan* culture will lead to social solidarity and strong incentive for doing beneficent and desirable deeds. On the other hand, engaging in Riba-based transactions and its financial attractions destroy social solidarity.
2. Engaging in Riba-based activities will enhance the attitude of greed and covetousness. All the Islamic laws and commands are harmoniously in accordance

18 To avoid interest/usury in barter deals, jurisprudence has forbidden taking commodity interest under certain circumstance.

19 Cultural Section; Jame'a Modarressin Howza Elmiya, Qum; 1386 SH; Introduction to Chapter One.

20 Peace Be Upon Him.

21 Al-Hor Al-A'meli; No Date; Vasayel Al-Shia; Vol. 12; p. 425.

and aimed at character development of human beings. This concept has been acknowledged in various verse of the Qur'an and Riwayat of religious leaders (as[22]). Attachment to worldly matters and ignoring ethical values intensifies greed in human beings while felicity and deliverance requires struggle against characteristics such as stinginess, rapaciousness, and covetousness that, through engaging in Riba-based transactions, create societal problems. The Qur'an teaches that charity and *Qardh Hasan are sources of physical and metaphysical felicity of the society:*

فَاتَّقُوا اللَّهَ مَا اسْتَطَعْتُمْ وَاسْمَعُوا وَأَطِيعُوا وَأَنْفِقُوا خَيْرًا لِأَنْفُسِكُمْ وَمَنْ يُوقَ شُحَّ نَفْسِهِ فَأُولَئِكَ هُمُ الْمُفْلِحُونَ (٦١) إِنْ تُقْرِضُوا اللَّهَ قَرْضًا حَسَنًا يُضَاعِفْهُ لَكُمْ وَيَغْفِرْ لَكُمْ وَاللَّهُ شَكُورٌ حَلِيمٌ (٧١) (التغابن: 16 و 17)

Heed Allah (be compliant with the rules Allah has prescribed) as best you can, and listen, and obey, and spend; that is better for your souls. And whoso is saved from his own greed, such are the successful (16). If you lend Allah a Qardh Hasan, He will double it for you and will forgive you, for Allah is Responsive, Clement (17) [Verses 16 and 17: Chapter 64, al-Taghabon].

3. Riba-based transactions are the cause of grudge and enmity. History shows that the debtor always bears a grudge against the creditor and will retaliate at the appropriate time. Individuals who are forced to resort to debt for covering their day-to-day expenses are usually not capable of increasing their income and hence cannot repay principal and interest on the specified times. Therefore, they are forced to receive further loans to pay back their previous debts, and their liabilities will increase continually. Such indebted individuals recognize the creditor who ruthlessly thinks of receiving interest as the only source of their misery. Consequently, where Riba-based transactions are commonplace, grudge and enmity threaten the security of the society.
4. Riba-based transactions lead to diminution of trade and reduction of production; Imam Ali (as) stated:

إِنَّهُ لَو كانَ الرِّبا حَلالاً لَتَرَكَ النّاسُ التِّجاراتِ وَما يَحْتاجونَ إِلَيْهِ فَحَرَّمَ اللّه الرِّبا لِيَفِرَّ النّاسُ مِنَ الْحَرامِ إِلَى الْحَلالِ وَ إِلَى التِّجاراتِ وَ إِلَى الْبَيْعِ وَالشِّراءِ

"If Riba were to be permissible, people would abandon trade and what they need (that would have been needed by people). Allah prohibited Riba so people would move away from prohibited to permissible and to trade and exchange."

22 Peace Be Upon Them.

5 Money, Government and Ethics

In this section, we analyze the ethical dimensions of government behavior in relation to money in various monetary systems. It will be shown that from the time governments undertook the responsibility of printing money, they have, using variety of justifications, broken promises and violated trust, two of the most important ethical values necessary for the stability of human societies: trust and faithfulness to the terms and conditions of contracts and promises. Whenever inept governments faced fiscal deficits, they found printing money as the easiest way to finance their deficits.

5.1 Ethical Dimensions of Full-Alloy Metal-Backed Money System

In this monetary system, all the instrument of exchange in circulation consist of full-alloy money alone or full-alloy money plus receipt/voucher of it. In such cases the volume of money in circulation depends on official price of the commodity from which the bullions or coins are made as well as on the amount of the commodity the country has at its disposal for its use. Though many of the old monetary systems were of this type, such systems no longer exist. Apart from drought and famine which lead to price increases for some commodities, general price increases in this system occurs due to two major reasons: the first relates to the nature of metal money, coinage or otherwise. And, the second relates to circulation of metal money as the formal coinage.

Since full-alloy metal moneys are kind of commodity, notwithstanding their function as "means of exchange," they have inherent value in themselves which fluctuates depending on the demand for and supply of the commodity itself. If, for example, the supply of gold in the country increases, under certain set of circumstances, the price of gold declines and the general level of prices increases, at least in the short-run, according to the law of supply and demand. In Fiqhi terms (jurisprudential nomenclature), this reduction is known as a reduction in "*Maliyyah*" or exchange value, it has no ethical dimension and no compensation rules exists for the reduction in exchange value of this commodity.

5.2 Metal Money as Official Coinage

Circulation of full-metal money soon necessitated changes in order to make economic exchange easier. For a long time after the introduction of full-metal money, large and small bullions were used in exchange transaction which created two problems: exact weight and the purity of the metal contained in the bullions.

To prevent misuse of metal money and to facilitate exchange, it was necessary to mint a mark on a definite quantity of the metal used for trading commodities. As a result, the coins came into being and state offices were established to mint coins.

Nonetheless, this development resulted in another potential cause that gave rise to increase in general price level, or inflation, within the given monetary system, i.e. cheating in the metal alloy of the coins. For instance, when the government was faced with an irredeemable financial crisis, it was not hard for brilliant and creative minds to figure out that the treasury deposits of the state could be substantially raised in a very short time through substitution of a few percentage of copper in place of silver or gold in coins. Replacement of gold and silver of coins with lower-valued metals, which were carried out secretly without changing the marks minted on coins, could miraculously cover the gap between revenues and expenditures of the government and resolve the difficulty of fiscal deficit. The persistent effect of such acts was general increase in prices, which of course occurred slightly later, ultimately revealing the secret of new coinage. In Fiqhi (jurisprudential) terminology, this act is referred as defect in commodity, and if it is accompanied by ignorance of the other party, it is considered as fraud. It is not only forbidden (Haram) from Shari'ah point of view but is also ethically repugnant.

The late Sheikh Tousi, relying on a well-documented report from Mousa Bin Bakr who narrated that in a visit to the Imam Mousa bin Ja'afar (as) he noticed a number of coin Dinars laid before him. The Imam (as) picked one up and broke it in two, looked at them and said:[23]

أَلْقِهِ فِی الْبَالُوعَهِ حَتَّی لَا یُبَاعَ شَیْءٌ فِیهِ غِشٌ

"Throw these coins into a well so as to prevent exchange of a thing in which there Ghashsh (deception, fraud)."

The Messenger of Allah (swt) stated:[24]

مَن غَشَّ مُسلِما في شِراءٍ أو بَيعٍ فليسَ مِنّا

"Anyone who cheats a Muslim in selling or buying, is not of us."

In another narration the Prophet prohibited adding water to the milk being sold:

أن يشاب اللبن بالماء للبيع

Among the Fuqaha of the majority school, Shafi'i is the first to speak, based on these narrations, of inflationary effects and repugnance of minting impure Dirhams on the order of the Muslim ruler. Nawawi quotes him saying:[25] "Minting substandard/defective coins by Muslim leader is repugnant on the basis of a narration from the Prophet saying "anyone who commits Ghashsh (deceit) against us is not of us" and because

23 Al-Hor Al-A'meli; No Date; Vasayel Al-Shia; Vol. 12; p. 29.
24 *ibid.*; Vol. 12; p. 208.
25 Ibn Al-Nawawi; No Date; Vol. 6; Chap. 10.

this act of corrupting the money causes losses to the right holders, increases of prices, destruction of values and other undesirable effects."

The historical examples of cheating in coin alloy, which led to reduction in the value of or general increase in prices, are so numerous that it can be found in every historical period among all nations. An instance of fraudulent policy in the purity of coinage, typically adopted at the time of financial crisis, is narrated in the book titled "The History of Ancient World" by Dyakov writes that "Denarius," the standard silver coin of Roman Empire which was made up of pure silver at the beginning of first century AD, lost about 10 percent of its silver content by the end of that century. By the end of second century AD, it contained only 50 percent silver. Later on, in the year 238 AD when the silver content of Denarius reached 30 percent, rapid reduction of purity led to staggering price increases. Over the next 30 years the silver content of Denarius decreased from 28 percent to 0.02 percent, i.e. it decreased by 1400 times! When the Emperor Diocletian was enthroned, Denarius was practically worthless leading to hyperinflation and economic chaos.[26]

5.3 Ethical Dimensions of Fiat Money System with No Cover Backing

Ever since European countries abandoned the gold standard system and made the circulation of paper money compulsory (i.e. non-inconvertibility of paper money to silver or gold), the limitations that were previously imposed on increasing the volume of money in circulation were lifted, largely enabling the governments to print paper money. Furthermore, with growth and development of the banking system in these countries, the number of payment instruments also increased. This increase in the volume of money brought about a price increase in many countries. It is not very difficult to understand why this happened. Consider the case where the government expenditures increase severely and unexpectedly because of domestic and international crises, and the traditional methods of raising government revenues may be either insufficient or unimplementable. Under these conditions, printing additional amount of paper money would provide the easiest and most workable way out even though it may be associated with irreversible dire consequences. In spite of the fact that the governments are committed to preserve the value of their national currency, the risk of loss of their governing power forces them to be unfaithful to their commitment to preservation of the value of the national money. By printing more currency notes to resolve crises, governments actually violate the central obligation mentioned in monetary law mandating them to preserve the value of their national currency

26 Dyakov; 1353 SH; p. 338.

based on a definite amount of gold.[27] The inevitable and definitive effect of such policies is a general increase in prices, which in fact results in transfer of part of the produce of the society from people to the government interpreted as a "hidden tax". Inflation is in fact a kind of unjust taxation that citizens are forced to pay to preserve the power of the ruling government.

Of course, this act of governments is not new, it has its roots in thousands of years of history. As mentioned earlier, cheating in metal content of coins was a phenomenon experienced repeatedly in different countries when governments faced severe fiscal deficits. The same method with slight changes, mainly due to modification of economic system, has been applied to paper money without any alteration of the nature of the deed.

Revolutions and wars are usually times of financial crises and hard fiscal constraint faced by governments. Under such circumstances, the volume of production, especially consumer and non-military products, declines. Government expenditures, however, increase significantly such that the usual methods of mobilizing revenue (taxes, revenues of government institutions etc.) are not sufficient to meet the financial requirements of the state; hence, emergency measures are generally necessary. From the time when printing of paper money as the legal currency became the responsibilities of the states, independent governments have shown understandable enthusiasm for this type of income generation (printing money). Regardless of the arguments of the proponent of rational finance be, experienced politicians have no doubt that imposition of "forced tax" through inflation is the most effective and politically least risky immediate method of revenue generation. During the American War of Independence (also known as the American Revolution), nearly all the military budget to fight the British was supplied by printing money. During the years 1775 and 1779, the collected taxes of Continental Congress (the Central Government) and the State Governments together did not reach USD 450 million, and the aid received from France, Spain and Holland amounted to USD 8 million. During the French Revolution, massive problems and financial needs forced the revolutionary government to print a large quantity of paper money called "Assignat" which resulted in severe inflation. Similarly, following a lengthy conflict with Napoleon and its heavy costs, printing money by England provided additional resources needed although it led to high inflation.[28]

---

27 For instance, the Monetary and Banking Law of Iran, endorsed in the year 1972, has established "Rial" as the official currency of the country. In Clause B of Article 1, of this law, the definition of "Rial" is presented as "equivalent in value to 0.0108055 gram of pure gold" and in Clause A of Article 2 it states that "the circulating currency of the country can be in form of printed currency notes or minted coins."

28 Qobadi, Raeis Dana; 1368 SH; p. 167.

5.4 Ethical Dimensions of 'Itibari or Constructional Monetary System

'Itibari or constructional[29] affairs[30] are not less than that of real beings. The most obvious example is the language that is used by each and every nation to communicate. May be the first construction and agreement in human society was that which attributed a word or expression (made with sounds) to a connotation. This way the inhabitants of the societies could exchange data and information.[31] The clue to the puzzle of growth, development and excellence of human beings must be looked for in this first validness and social contract that assigns an expression or word (i.e. a name) for every object. Language which is the instrument for exchange of data, has been developing throughout history; it was transformed to written style, and presently exchanges information in electronic form. Almost everyone is aware that computers and information technology are based on binary codes consisting of "on's" and "off's" (or "bits" of "zeros" and "ones"). Human beings have invented computer languages through contract and specific definition of every "bit", thus turning a physical object (i.e. computer) into an effective instrument for exchange of data and information. This invention revolutionized the social life of human beings through massive information and data flow that prepares the ground for entering into the post-industrial era. Additionally, human beings have also utilized many other imperative constructional facts formed through jurisprudence, ordinance or rights/privileges to achieve excellence. An instance of such constructional facts that revolutionized the economic life of human beings is money. Money was initially created from a physical object such as gold or silver, but has been transformed and evolved during the course of history based on the existing requirements and available facilities. Most recently, with the omission of the physical entity and conversion into a kind of data, money

---

29 Constructionism is a philosophical (specifically epistemological) stance in phenomenological sociology in which social realities are seen as the product of socio-historical situated practices rather than objective facts (compare objectivism). Constructionists argue that reality is not wholly external to and independent of how we conceptualize the world: our sign systems (especially language) play a major part in the construction of social reality, which cannot be separated from the sign systems in which it is framed (Oxford Dictionary of Philosophy – Oxford Reference).

30 The term here includes concepts of assumption, contract, and creation of a social phenomenon to meet social needs. John Searle is of the opinion that there exists some institutional affairs which are no doubt factual in nature but do not fit the description of common (material or abstract) objects. Consequently, he recognizes two types of facts, viz. "Brute Facts" or the genetic affairs that everyone is aware of (e.g. existence of Sun and Moon), and "Institutional Facts" such as marriage, promise, money and even verbal expressions, all of which are based on rational credibility intellectual validity. The institutional facts create many realities in the world/universe (Amoli Larijani; 1394 SH; p. 160).

31 See Taba'tabaei, Mohammad Hossein; No Date; *Principles of Philosophy and Realistic Methodology*; Article 6; p. 335.

is stored electronically.[32] These virtual (non-physical) electronic and digital[33] currencies, which are transacted using electronic media, provide the ground for entering into post-industrial mass production phase.

As Tavassoli has shown in his book titled "Analysis of the Nature of Money and Foundations of Monetary Policies in Islamic Economy,"[34] in which, using historical, philosophical and legislative analyses, he demonstrated that it is possible not only to explain the origin of all monetary phenomena of the past but also forecast such phenomena in the future through 'Itibari approach (the approach based on societal agreement and not based on fundamental inherent characteristics of phenomena). According to approach, Tavassoli concludes that "any type of money, including commodity, fiat and electronic, either viewed in terms of value or in terms of its nature, possesses a definite 'Itibari" rank. It is only necessary to analyze the contents and details of such agreement and contract to see how, which assets and with what details society and the state have agreed to define money in various periods.[35] Has this asset (that is the asset which societal agreement calls money) actual (real) physical property? Is it a liability? Is it actual (real) revenue? Does it create real (actual) right? Or are all these characteristics only 'Itibari (granted by societal agreement)? That is has such asset 'Itibari physical property?[36] Is it an 'Itibari liability?[37] Is it an 'Itibari revenue?[38] Does it grant an 'Itibari right?.[39] It is clear that defining a unit of measurement of value unit of value and assigning an amount of value to it are 'Itibari because a social agreement enshrined in the law define these characteristics of money. However, the 'Itibari nature of the medium of exchange character of money requires some analysis and focus. The evidence for this statement is that during the operation of commodity money system, the commodity which was utilized as money and the amount of it that constituted the evaluation standard, were decided and agreed upon (given 'Itibar or validation) by the society. Hence, this money too was 'Itibari to some extent. In such

32 Electronic money (E-money) is the money which exists in banking computer systems and is available for transactions through electronic systems. Its value is equal to that of fiat currency.

33 Bitcoin and E-money are both digital but differ from each other. E-money, e.g. credit cards, debit cards, pay-pal etc. is a mechanism for money transactions for conventional government-issued currencies like US Dollar and Euro, while Bitcoin is a virtual/digital currency operated by a decentralized authority. It is not issued or backed by any banks or governments, nor are individual bitcoins valuable as a commodity. It can be transferred anonymously and therefore, may carry some risks for its users/bearers.

34 Tavassoli, 1394 SH; pp. 78–84.

35 Acknowledging the details of such construction will help in apprehension of its implication in Islamic economy.

36 For the reality and the nature of present-day currencies, the connotation that they are the same as contructional property, must be proved.

37 The bank-generated money may be considered as an example of constructional liability, since it has been produced using minor deposits and the reputation of the bank.

38 Such as the profit made from the construction of stamps.

39 Such as copyright.

system, money at the stage of deciding which commodity should be considered as money and how much of it should constitute the unit of value is an 'Itibari process. When it came to the determination of which commodity should become the medium of exchange, the decision was that the nature of commodities in the money should be minted gold and silver. The exchange value of such medium of exchange and its value as an asset was determined by its supply and demand in the market and not by law.

Based on the analysis of monetary laws of various countries as the only document of validation of money and taking into account the outcomes of the policies as well as the present reality of currencies (which are non-physical abstract objects, independent of gold or any other valuable assets), the principal hypothesis of Tavassoli's research[40] is that "present-day paper/fiat and digital currencies are of various 'Itibari ranks."

For instance, the Monetary and Banking Law of Iran, endorsed in the year 1972, has established "Rial" as the official currency of the country. In Clause B of Article 1, of this law, the definition of "Rial" is presented as "equivalent in value to 0.0108055 gram of pure gold" and in Clause A of Article 2 it states that "the circulating currency of the country can be in form of printed currency notes or minted coins." Analysis of this law reveals that three levels of 'Itibari validation have been implemented.

First level validation: Where the law states "Rial is the official currency of Iran," it assertively validates and nominates an indefinite entity as money.

Second level Validation: Where the law states *"Rial is equivalent in value to 0.0108055 gram of pure gold,"* it considers a definite purchasing power, and validates and delineates the exchange value of the unit of Rial as identical and equivalent to (not the same as) a definite amount of gold or another commodity, which has the same purchasing power and is known to public.

Third Level Validation: Where the law states "the circulating currency of the country can be in form of printed currency notes or minted coins," it validates the currency as a non-physical substance, docketed on papers named banknotes, minted on indicated coins, or stored on digital/electronic chips, and gave it an independent existence and put it in circulation. Later, under the heading of the "Objectives of Monetary Policy," the law commits to preserving the value of Rial based on a benchmark.

The results of analysis indicate that the circulating currency is no more in form of physical coins minted from gold or silver, but a written coin or a digital coin whose value is considered to be equivalent to minted coins has been defined as the medium of exchange. Accordingly, it can be deduced that all forms of the existing currencies are 'Itibari and agreed upon socially, and thus, have been invented through fabrications and contracts. Consequently, all the aspects of present-day currencies,

40 Tavassoli; ibid.

especially their denominational units have been defined based on a specific standards. The governments are obliged to preserve the value of their respective currencies according to their monetary laws. In this manner every facet of money is nothing but a kind of social covenant.

Tavassoli[41] has also analyzed the phenomenon of the money which will be pure 'Itibari money[42] – not yet in widespread use – from the perspective that considers the essence of this money as an asset as 'Itibari (determined by social agreement) and not defined by equivalence with certin amount of pure gold. It is social agreement that defines the exchange value of this money directly. This is achieved by initial assignment and nomination of an indefinite abstract object as the monetary unit (e.g. *Kothar*) and then defining its purchasing power for commodities and services through legislation. Finally, in accordance with the volume of net national product and its pricing based on the new currency unit, as well as the velocity of money circulation, the amount and volume of circulating money is calculated. In this case also, legislation creates assets, and not the inherent value of what would be called money. By extension, the value and the purchasing power of the money is also derived from it 'Itibari definition. At this point, a distinction must be made between purchasing power established through object-oriented description which cannot be altered without changing the law or the act of the ruler and the purchasing power of the money acquired through its scarcity in the market: "The essence of this money is purely 'Itibari". It is a new creation that the law has given it credibility through contract and covenant without established ties to any physical material."

The ethical dimension of money appears in 'Itibar as contract, covenant and promise faithfulness to which appears as one of the most important ethical values of humanity. Now question arises as to the strength of this contract and covenant and how important are they? Can governments easily violate the fidelity to this contract? Is the faithfulness to this contract mandatory? Must all such contracts and covenants verbally and/or officially expressed and written? Answer to all these questions can be deduced from Verse 2: Chapter 5 ("O you who believe, be faithful to contracts",

يَا أَيُّهَا الَّذِينَ آمَنُوا أَوْفُوا بِالْعُقُودِ ... (المائده: 1)

O you who believe! Fulfill any contracts (you may make) ... (Al-Ma'eda: 2, in part)

41 Tavassoli; 1394 SH; p. 92.

42 Manifestation of digital currency called "Bitcoin" is a strong evidence for creation of this kind of money. Nevertheless, the unit value of Bitcoin has been left to be decided through market supply and demand, which can harm its globalization as an international currency, because one of the most important purpose of currencies, in addition to providing an intermediary for transactions, is to offer an evaluation measure as well, which in turn, requires stability of value. As a result, Bitcoin is presently utilized as an asset whose value can increase on a daily. However, Bitcoin experience may lead to inception of national cryptographic digital currencies (cryptocurrencies).

Holy Qur'an sternly emphasizes the significance of remaining faithful to all terms and conditions stipulated in contracts and covenants. The emphasis is so firm that those who violate their commitments are strongly denounced while those who abide by their promises and commitments are praised in a number of verses. agreements have been impressively praised in many Qur'anic verses. The tone of the related verses indicates that the goodness of faithfulness to promises and repugnance of violating them are related to the nature of man.

According to 'Allamah Tabataba'ei,[43] the root and cause of this relates to the fact that neither man nor his societies are without the need for covenants, contracts and promises as well as the necessity of being faithful to their terms and conditions. If we consider the social life of man we note that all amenities we enjoy in this life as well as all the social rights whose achievement give us tranquility are based on social contract and other individual and specific covenants and contracts that are derived from the collective social contract. Hence, neither we nor anyone else could possess anything unless we enter, explicitly or implicitly, into a mutual contract with the society. Once we and others get together to form a society, we have in effect entered into a mutually binding social contract with other citizens even if such is not declared explicitly. Without such an arrangement, society would not form. Even after it forms, we cannot assume that we do not need to be faithful to the social contract because we believe that we have the power and might to do so, or for other reason, we weaken social justice which is pillar of our society and the refuge that protects individuals against the threat of exploitation, slavery and violation of their rights. It is for this reason that the Almighty profoundly insisting upon commitments to remain faithful to promises and covenants as in the following Verse of the Qur'an:

... وَأَوْفُوا بِالْعَهْدِ إِنَّ الْعَهْدَ كَانَ مَسْئُولًا (الإسراء: 34)

... Fulfil your promises; surely (every) promise is accountable (Al-Asra', 17:34; in part)

This honored Verse, as others that praise faithfulness to and chastise the violation of covenants, contracts or promises, relates to mutual agreements between two individuals as well as social contracts or covenants between tribes, groups and nations. Indeed, Islam considers social covenants more important than individual contracts because violations of social contracts lead to destruction of social justice which has more general and its adverse effects on the collectivity far more catastrophic.

In his epistle to Malik Al-Ashtar, Imam 'Ali (as) states:[44]

فَإِنَّهُ لَيْسَ مِنْ فَرائِضِ اللّهِ شَيْءٌ النّاسُ اَشَدُّ عَلَيْهِ اجْتِماعاً، مَعَ تَفَرُّقِ اَهْوائِهِمْ وَ تَشَتُّتِ آرائِهِمْ، مِنْ تَعْظيمِ الْوَفاءِ بِالْعُهُودِ. وَ قَدْ لَزِمَ ذلِكَ الْمُشْرِكُونَ فيما بَيْنَهُمْ دُونَ الْمُسْلمينَ، لِمَا اسْتَوْبَلُوا مِنْ عَواقِبِ الْغَدْرِ

43 Al-Mizan fi Tafsir Al-Qur'an; 1390 LH; Vol. 5; p. 161.
44 Nahj Al-Balaqa; Letter 53.

> "There is no other issue among Allah's ordinances is more important for humanity – despite all their differences--than faithfulness to covenants, something that even the Idolaters respected between themselves, excluding the Muslims because they had experienced the painful consequences of violating covenants." It is also narrated from Imam 'Ali (as): "Allah will not accept deeds unless they are virtuous, neither does he accept any action other than those that are undertaken in faithfulness to terms and conditions of covenants.":[45]

Another anecdote from Imam Ali (PBUH) expresses:

انَّ اللّه تعَالى لا يَقبَلُ الا العمَل الصَّالِحَ، و لا يَقبَلُ اللهُ الا الوفَاء بالشُّروطِ و العُهودِ

> God, the Almighty, will not accept anything except their righteous deeds, and does not consent any conduct other than abiding by commitments and treaties (Qumi; 1416 LH; Safina' Al-Behar; Vol. 2; p. 294).

Prophet Mohammad has been quoted as saying:[46]

وَلاَ دِيْنَ لِمَنْ لاَ عَهْدَ لَهُ

> *"He who is not faithful to his covenants has no religion."*

For this reason, the issue of faithfulness to covenants is inclusive of all humans regardless of their differences. In effect, it is an element of human rights and not a religious right only. It is narrated from the Imam al-Sadiq (as):

ثلاثٌ لَمْ يَجْعَلِ اللّهُ (عَزَّوَجَلَّ) لِأَحَدٍ فِيهِنَّ رُخصَةً اَداءُ الْأَمانَةِ اِلَى الْبَرِّ وَالْفاجِرِ وَالْوَفاءُ بِالْعَهْدِ لِلْبَرِّ وَالْفاجِرِ وَبِرُّ الْوالِدَيْنِ بَرَّيْنِ كانا اَوْ فاجِرَيْنِ

> "There are three issues that Allah (swt) Has not permitted any one to violate: returning a thing placed in his trust to the owner be he virtuous (are in compliance with the rules prescribed by Allah) or evil-doer (rule violators); being faithful to a covenant whether the other party is virtuous or evil doer; and doing good for parents be they virtuous or evil doers."[47])

As apparent from the Qur'anic expression "أَوْفُوا بِالْعُقُودِ" (*fulfil all contracts*), individuals are mandated strictly to abide by contracts/promises. Apparently, this rule is general and includes all promises/contracts. Consequently, it encompasses whatever is conventionally considered as contract or covenant which demands compliance, including money which is also based on social contract and covenant. Islam does not limit the observance of terms and conditions of covenants to any specific contract but has generalized the rule of the necessity of being faithful to any agreement based on which relations are constructed. Based on the above Verse of the Qur'an and other reasoning related to other rules such as the rule of "La dhara wa la dhirar" (rule prohibiting mutual damages); the rule of warranty (Qa'idah al-Dhiman); and the

45 Qumi; 1416 LH; Safina' Al-Behar; Vol. 2; p. 294.
46 Majlesi; Behar Al-Anwar; 1404 LH; Vol. 16; p. 144.
47 Koleini; 1363 SH; Osul-e Ka'fi; Vol. 2; p. 162.

rule of damage (Qa'idah al-Itlaf), the rule necessitating faithfulness to the preservation of the value of money as an instrument of social contract, based on own measure of value, is binding. Islamic government cannot violate the rule other than through "Ahkam Thanawiyyah" ("Secondary Rules," rules that govern decisions of religious law giver to relax one of the "Ahkam Awaliyyah" ("Prior Rules," rules prescribed in the Qur'an) order to protect the Islamic system. Even this exceptional permission is time-bound. It lasts as long as exceptional circumstances which necessitated the relaxation of the Prior Rules have ended. It is important to note, therefore, that "secondary rules" are only valid during the period of serious and existential challenges that arise threatening the Islamic system and which are permitted for only short time periods where the best interests of the system as a whole are involved and last until the urgency that gave rise to implementation of the secondary rules has vanished.[48] Therefore, taking this teaching which indicates the intense concern of the Divine Legislator for preservation of the value of money into account, it follows that the essential objective of monetary policy should be the control of inflation, stability of the general price level and, thereby, preservation of the value of money.

6 Ethical Responsibilities of Islamic Government regarding Irresponsible Monetary Policies

Based on the discussion of the 'Itibari nature of the present form of money and religious teachings in the previous section, it was deduced that the Hukm Awaliyyah (Prior Rule deduced from the Qur'an and narrations from religious leaders) governing money matters requires that the principal objective of monetary policy must be the preservation of the value of the money. In this section, given the responsibilities of an Islamic government as well as the adverse impact of inflation on income and wealth distribution and their injustice in the society, it will be argued, in addition to what was presented above, that Islamic government has the duty of implementing appropriate monetary policy in order to preserve the value of money. Conclusions derived from narrations from religious leaders and scholars indicate that the governing forces of the society are protectors of the lives, property, their personal reputation and dignity and treat them fairly. A few examples follow:

1. The late Sheikh Koleyni narrates Abdullah Bin Mas'oud, who heard the Prophet saying:[49]

---

48 See Tavassoli, Mohammad Esmaeil; 1392 SH; *Principal Objectives of Monetary Policies and the Responsible Authorities (in Islamic Economic System)*; Quarterly Journal of Knowledge of Islamic Economics; No. 6.

49 Koleini; 1363 SH; Kitab Al-Haj; Part 158.

حُرْمَةُ مالِ المسلمِ كحُرْمَةِ دمِهِ

"The sanctity of the possessions of Muslims is the same as the sanctity of their blood (life)."

2. Voram Ibn Abi-Foras narrates Prophet expressing:[50]

ألا كُلُّكُم راعٍ و كُلُّكُم مَسؤولٌ عن رَعِيَّتِهِ فالأميرُ الذي على الناسِ راعٍ و هُو مَسؤولٌ عن رَعِيَّتِهِ

"Beware that each and every one of you is the guardian and caretaker of others and is responsible for all who are in his care. Therefore, the Commander/Ruler is the guardian of the ruled and is responsible for his people who are under his care."

3. In a narration in *Osul-e Ka'fi*,[51] Aba Hamza questions the Imam al-Baqir (as) about the rights due the ruler (the Imam) from his people and the rights of the people over the ruler (the Imam):

قَالَ: سَأَلْتُ أَبَا جَعْفَرٍ عَلَيْهِ السَّلاَمُ مَا حَقُّ اَلْإِمَامِ عَلَى اَلنَّاسِ؟ قَالَ حَقُّهُ عَلَيْهِمْ أَنْ يَسْمَعُوا لَهُ وَ يُطِيعُوا؛ قُلْتُ فَمَا حَقُّهُمْ عَلَيْهِ؟ قَالَ يُقَسِّمُ بَيْنَهُمْ بِالسَّوِيَّةِ وَ يَعْدِلُ فِي اَلرَّعِيَّةِ.

"I asked the Imam: What rights does the Imam (Leader) have over his people over whom he rules?" He: "People must listen and obey" Then, I asked: What are their rights vis-a-vis over their Imam (Leader)?" He answered: "Distribute (wealth) equally/equitably among them and be just to them."

4. Imam Khomeini in his book *Velayat-e Faqih* states:[52]

"The Islamic State is not like any other existing state; for instance, it is not autocratic to allow the head of the government become tyrannical and a dictator to play with people's lives and property and abuse them anyway he wishes. Take the life of anyone and reward anyone he wishes. Give anyone he wishes promises of granting them the nation's properties and possessions. Neither the Messenger nor the Commander of the Faithful Imam 'Ali (as) and other "Khulafa" were not given such authorities (by Allah).

Based on the above, we conclude that the Islamic ruler is the guardian/protector of life, possession, reputation and dignity, or in general protector of the economic, social, cultural, political security of the society. He governs with justice and fairness in compliance with the Divine rules and Shari'ah standards. He does not violate anyone's rights nor reward anyone unjustifiably. He establishes balance nad equilibrium in wealth distribution among the people. Hence, he will not adopt policies that undermine the value of the nation's money that would lead to hyperinflation and maldistribution of income and wealth in favor of the rich at the expense of the poor.

---

50 Voram Collection; No Date; p. 14.
51 Koleini; 1363 SH: Vol. 1; p. 405.
52 Mousavi Al-Khomeini; 1360 SH; p. 52.

7 Money, Banks and Ethics

With the advent of banks in the economy, these institutions utilized, as did the capitalist (who accumulate Riba-based wealth), various Riba-based transactions that led to wealth inequality. Just like governments, banks, employing their enormous power of money creation, use the money of small savers that are deposited with the, to worsen maldistribution of wealth manifold. Two main characteristics of the Western conventional retail banking system: 1) mobilization of fractional reserve resources to create massive amounts of credit money; and, 2) allocation of various kinds of fixed interest rate loan contracts with guaranteed principal. In Islamic economics literature, this is referred to as "Riba-based Banking" whose negative economic and ethical effects were discussed earlier.

The fractional reserve banking and the massive capacity of credit-money creation apparently started with the Stockholm Banco in 1657 under the leadership of Johan Palmstruch (1611–1671), as the bank's general manager. There was, in general, nothing new about this bank as deposit banks existed already in Europe, for example, in Amsterdam and Hamburg. The major differences between Stockholm Banco and these other European banks were two innovations Which were designed and adopted by Johan Palmstruch. First, was the use of the depositors' money to make loans, clearly a violation of trust of depositors. While this brought a lot of business for the bank, it soon created a problem as the bank loaned more money than it had on deposit. To solve this problem, Palmstruch adopted a second innovation by issuing Kredititivseldar (Credit Papers), in effect paper money, the first known European credit money. It was a bank note exchangeable to silver and gold at any time. While successful at first, Palmstruch bank ran into problem again as it loaned more that deposits.

Palmstruch had discovered by experience that not all depositors simultaneously decide to withdraw their money from his bank. Moreover, even the deposits that had been withdrawn by some depositors were replaced by others. Therefore, he did not expect to face any difficulties if he could cautiously lend a portion of the deposits to applicants and keep the rest in his vault. Meanwhile, his bank would earn interests from the borrowers when the principal would be repaid. Although this led to institution of the modern banking system, the story did not end there. Gradually banks realized that they can expand the two sides of their balance sheets without additional deposits or reserves. That is, as soon as they made new loans new deposits were also created. This is the process of money creation. The need for additional reserves is then met ex post. This is the special feature of banks not its Riba-based contracts which provide them with income. They are intermediaries that provide their investors with Riba returns. It is the bank investors and depositors that receive Riba, the bank's income covers its costs of operations. Nonetheless, intermediating Riba-based contracts is itself is considered a sin.

The main power of banks is derived from creation of credit money because they earn all their revenues from interest rates while preserving the property right of the principal loaned for themselves. as well as the principal. Given the high profits banks make from retail banking and their enormous power of creating money, banking mushroomed all over the world, including in Iran, absorbing the income and wealth of the people earned from hard work.[53]

While fractional reserve banking and creation of credit money along with usurious contracts may create economic growth and additional wealth, they create maldistribution of wealth in favor of capitalists and the wealthy. According to research published last year, 48 individuals hold 82% of the world wealth. It is said that wealth begets wealth. This result contradicts the teachings of Islam.[54]

'Allameh Javadi Amoli refers to this type of economy as "Iqtisad Takathuri" (an economy in which wealth concentrates in the hands of a few at the expense of the many) and is considered repugnant according to Islamic teaching.[55] According to him, wealth (in form of capital) serves the same purpose in the economy as does blood in the body. If blood concentrates in a part of the body only, other parts face paralysis. As the Qur'an ordains (Al-Hashr, 59:7), wealth must circulate in the entire economy and not be concentrated in among the rich. In capitalism, the whole wealth is in the hands of a few rich individuals, the rest of the society are left with almost nothing! The failed Eastern Bolshevik socialists had also a similar situation, with the difference that wealth was at the government disposal and the statist. The whole wealth of the former USSR, which spread over a large part of the globe, was in the hand of its central government. Both the Western capitalism and the Eastern Statist system exemplify "Takathuri" systems which the Verse 7 of Chapter 59 of the Qur'an rejects.

Allah has ordained that wealth should not concentrate in the hands of special few. It must circulate in the economy to benefit all. In a stable economic development banking services must reach all. Everyone in the society must have access to loans. All must have access to specialized and technical as well as entrepreneurial knowledge. This is what leads to stable development of the economy which is praiseworthy from

53 The pseudo-money sum in Iran is now over 17 thousand trillion Rials. The central bank, with the release of economic data released in December 2018, announced the liquidity of 17 thousand 645 trillion Rials, which was 15.3 percent compared to the same month last year shows an increase of 22.1%. and interestingly the ratio of Central Bank's money reserves to pseudo-money is less than 10 percent. If no immediate action is taken, the country's economy will enter an irrepressible crisis.

54 The results of the study by Oxfam International reveals that about one percent of the world population, will soon possess over 99 percent of the global wealth. The research indicates that the share of one percent rich population from the global wealth grew from 44 percent in the year 2009 to almost 48 percent in the year 2014. The researchers at Oxfam International predicts that with continuation of the current trend, the share of this one percent rich population will constitute over 50 percent of global wealth by 2015. This forecast is based on the Global Wealth Report by Credit Suisse which analyzes the global wealth distribution from the year 2000 onwards. This report uses the financial and non-financial assets of individuals, mainly consisting of real estate, and after deducting their liabilities, estimates their wealth (Source: Tasnim News Agency).

55 Rajanews; October 14, 2014.

the Shri'ah point of view. Islam encourages establishment of such an economy. The most important characteristic of such an economy is that wealth circulates through it as blood circulates in a healthy body. Therefore, circulation of wealth has to be designed such that it avoids concentration of wealth among special class to allow it to reach the masses in the society.

8 Summary and Conclusions

The experiences that have led us to ethical research in various economic sectors are the results of the lack of consensual certainty in some issues from the theoretical aspects in first place. Secondly the occasionally excruciating consequences as well as policies that were previously quite acceptable, have engulfed our societies into great crises. Therefore, we are forced to analyze the causes of current crises, examine the fairness and justness of the arrangements, and probe the approaches and policies to be adopted. Among the excruciating consequence and crises whose ethical origin is of extreme importance, are the enduring inflation and exceptionally inequitable distribution of income and wealth within the society. The principal hypothesis of this research is that the main source of these crises is the anomalous ethical behavior of society and government towards the phenomenon called money. With the invention of money, human beings were able to circumvent the countless difficulties involved in barter system of trading, and could bring about great prosperity through facilitation of transactions. However, in the course of history, usurious capitalists and stranded governments have immethodically utilized money, in whatever form that it existed, to their maximum advantage. Usurious capitalists have benefitted from the need of people because of the general exchangeability of money. Through usurious lending, they have grasped the properties and assets of peoplé, adding it gradually to their own wealth. This has resulted in exorbitant inequality of wealth, which in turn has provoked anomalous social, ethical and economical effects on the society.

With ascription of the right to print and publish currency notes to the governments, whenever they were impaired by budgetary deficit, notwithstanding their monetary policy, the easiest way out was "printing new money." This in reality manipulated the monetary measures and evaluation criteria. "Printing new money" policy (excessive money supply) leads to hyperinflation and acute devaluation of money. Successive devaluations of money has detrimental economic effects and anomalous consequence on distribution of income, savings, consumption, investment and production, allocation of resources, economic decision-making process, government budget, and international balance of payments. This in fact is nothing but manipulation of the monetary measures and trampling upon important ethical principles of abiding by the promises about money. For the reason that money is founded on the basis of promises and vows, as well as Islam's strict command to redeem the promise/

pledge, whatsoever is conceived as promise or vow and complies with the notion of allegiance and commitment is similarly incorporated. This includes money which is also a kind of social construction. Moreover, financing budgetary deficit through "printing new money" policy to cover the expenditures is inequitable in comparison with taxation. With advent of banks in the economy, these institutions also utilized various extortionate contracts, similar to usurious capitalists, to provoke inequality of wealth. In addition, banks have also aggravated the unequal distribution of wealth within society through colossal capacity of creating credit money, in the same way as the governments, by manipulation of fractional reserve banking. This is despite the fact that such kind of wealth distribution undoubtedly contradicts the teachings of Islam.

Answering the three principal questions, the research tried to point out the roots of the enduring inflation and extremely inequitable distribution of wealth and income. Moreover, their consequent horrifying economic and ethical effects in the society as well as the importance of their ethical origin were also demonstrated. The ethical origin of these crises were attributed to anomalous behavior of the capitalists, the governments, and the banks toward money. According to teachings of Islam, such behaviors and their horrifying consequences are considered against ethical values and are not fair and just.

As a result, everyone must contemplate about what has to be done and what policies must be employed for the circulation of wealth within the entire monetary and financial system of Islamic Economy. The efforts must be directed towards making the governments committed and disciplined, to abolish the possibility of undertaking usurious contracts by the capitalists, and to limit the colossal capacity of banks in creating credit money. Only then it can be expected to avoid accumulation of wealth among certain classes of people and to distribute it amidst the public masses.

References

Holy Qur'an; *translated by* T.B. Irving (Al-Haj Ta'lim Ali); Suhrawardi Research and Publication Center, Tehran-Iran; 2003.

Razi, Al-Sharif Abu Al-Hassan Mohammad; *Nahj Al-Balaqa*; translated by Seyyed Jafar Shahidi; Islamic Evolution Teaching Publications; Tehran; 1374 SH.

Amoli Larijani; Sadeq; *The Knowledge of Principles and Theory of Validation*; Vali-ye Asr Community School; Qum; 1394 SH.

Ibn Al-Nawawi; *Al-Majmou' Sharh Al-Mohazzab*; 10/6; Kitab Al-Zakat; Ba'b Al-Zakat Al-Zahab va Al-Fezze; Dar Al-Fekr; Beirut; No Date.

Iravani, Javad; *Economic Ethics from the Viewpoint of Qur'an and Hadith*; Qur'anic Teachings Journal; Vol. 4; No. 84; Winter 1383; 1383 SH.

Jame'a Modarressin Howza Elmiya, Cultural Section, Qum; *Usury, Historical Background. Usury in Qur'an and Sonnat, Types of Usury, Avoiding Usury*; Boustan Kitab; Qum; 1386 SH.

Tavassoli, Mohammad Esma'eil; *Analysis of the Nature of Money and the Foundations of Monetary Policies in Islamic Economy*; Howza and University Research Institute; Qum; 1394 SH.

Javadi Amoli, Abdollah; *Analysis of Islamic Development Patterns: Interview with Hamshahri Magazine, 1389 SH*; Republished by Rajanews; 1393 SH.

Al-Hor Al-Ameli, Al-Sheikh Mohammad Bin Al-Hassan; *Vasayel Al-Shia Ila Tahsil Masael Al-Sharia*; Dar Ehya Al-torath Al-Arabi; Beirut.

Dyakov, V.; *History of the Ancient World*; translated by Sadeq Ansari, Aliallah Hamedani, Mohammad Baqer Mo'meni; Nashr Andisheh; Tehran; 1353 SH.

Tabataba'ei, Al-Seyyed Mohammad Hossein; *Al-Mizan fi Tafsir Al-Qur'an*; 20 Vols.; Second Edition; Al-A'lami Al-Matbu'at Institute; Beirut; 1394 LH.

Tabataba'ei, Al-Seyyed Mohammad Hossein; *Principles of Philosophy and Realistic Methodology (with Introduction by Morteza Motahhari)*; Islamic Publication Department; Jame'a Modarressin Howza Elmiya; Qum; No Date.

Monetary and Banking Law of Iran (With Amendments); Central Bank of Islamic Republic of Iran; 1351 SH.

Qubadi, Farrokh, and Raeisdana, Fariborz; *Money, Monetary Issues, Inflation and Papyrus*; 1368 SH.

Qumi, Sheikh Abbass; *Safinat Al-Behar*; Islamic Research Foundation; Astan Quds Razavi; Mashhad; 1416 LH.

Koleini, Abu Jafar Mohammad Bin Al-Yaqub; *Al-Kafi; edited/corrected by* Ali Akbar Al-Qaffari; 8 Vols.; Dar Al-Kitab Islamiye; Tehran; 1362 SH.

Majlesi, Mohammad Baqer; *Behar Al-Anwar*; Dar Eh'ya Al-torath Al-Arabi; Beirut.

Veram Collection

Voram Ibn Abi-Foras; *Voram Collection*; Akhundi Publishers; Tehran; No Date.

Mousavi Al-Khomeini, Rouhallah; *Velayat Faqih Hokumat Islami*; Amir Kabir Publications; Tehran; 1360 SH.

Haussmann, D.M. and McPherson, M.S; 1993; *Taking Ethics Seriously: Economics and Contemporary Moral Philosophy*; Journal of Economic Literature; Vol. XXXI; pp. 671–731.

Sen, A.; 1987; *On Ethics and Economics*; Oxford, Blackwell Publishing.

Seyed Kazem Sadr

Chapter 26: Hoarding of Goods, Money and Financial Assets

1 Introduction

Hoarding, warehousing, saving, investment and speculation are practices that share some features in common and are observed in the markets under various conditions. When used as a hedge against inflation, hoarding is considered a rational behavior (Pickhardt and Sardà 2012). Under other conditions, such as when commodities and goods are scarce and markets unstable, hoarding is considered an economically worthless and harmful activity (Welsted 2007). Hoarding will intensify the scarcity of goods under these market conditions and will push up prices (Sadr, 1362/1983). At the same time, hoarding of money will take it out of circulation and inhibits smooth exchange of goods and services (Goldberg, and Karimov 1997). Hoarding of gold and durable assets may be viewed as a saving behavior under normal market conditions and a speculative initiative when financial markets are unstable and volatile.

Maintaining market stability is the goal of all economies. Islam prescribes a set of ethical rules governing behavior of participant to ensure the stability and efficiency of markets (Sadr 2016). It is, therefore, important to identify conditions that lead to emergence of hoarding practices. It is also important to determine the criteria that differentiate between hoarding and the permissible saving and warehousing behavior. This paper attempts to define and explain these concepts analytically and clearly in order to identify distinguishing characteristics of each of these activities. The criteria for their differences will be presented and the market conditions under which these practices harm or improve the welfare of market participants will be presented. The Islamic rules governing market behavior that enhance investment and savings or condemn hoarding and speculation will also be deliberated and their impact on performance of goods as well as financial markets will be illustrated. Heretofore, distinctions between hoarding as exploitation of market conditions and saving behavior in asset portfolio formation have seldom been specified. The paper will also address this deficiency. Next, the motives for withholding money from circulation in the economy and its impact on the market prices will be identified. Islamic rules that motivate market participants and households to spend the excess

Note: I am indebted to the Reverend Seyed Baqir Khosrashahi for his contribution to present the views of the renowned Foqaha on the subject of Ihtikar. I am also thankful to Professor Abbas Mirakhor and Dr. Hasanali Ghanbari for reviewing and commenting on the paper.

https://doi.org/10.1515/9783110593419-026

of their income for the well-being of the community members, rather than to hoard it, will be elaborated first. Moreover, an extensive discourse on Shari'ah rules prohibiting hoarding goods, gold, money and financial assets will be presented. The paper will conclude with recommendations regarding policies that should be implemented by authorities to prevent emergence of conditions that lead to hoarding and speculation practices.

At the outset, it should be mentioned that some economists consider hoarding a rational behavior by households when the economy is suffering from high inflation (Pickhardt and Sardà 2012). They view hoarding as hedging against inflation. Goods are stored by households, not to sell at higher prices, but rather to avoid purchasing them at exorbitant costs in the future. The purpose of this type of advance purchasing is not keeping the goods out of the market in order to sell them at higher prices later. Rather, it is a saving behavior and an intertemporal management of consumption expenditure between the present and the future (Sadr 2016). Some psychologists analyze the same behavior by households as a psychic action in a regular stable market condition. The symptom is collecting and piling up goods and items that have no value to the households; neither at present nor in the future (Welsted 2007). Since this stocking of goods is not done intelligently and rationally, it is not considered hoarding, as will be defined later, by Shari'ah. Hence, the paper will not consider these cases since they do not constitute hoarding per se either from the marketing and/or Islamic perspectives.

Hoarding violates the tenets of ethical system of Islam and, hence, prohibited. As will be observed below, giving and contributing to the wellbeing of the needy is praised and considered an ethical conduct, while, stinginess and hoarding practices are condemned as unethical in Islam. It might therefore be instructive to become familiar with the evolution of ethical school of Islam, prior to an exhaustive discussion of hoarding as an unethical and immoral act.

In the introduction to his book on Islamic ethics, *Perseverance*, the late Seyyed Reza Sadr argues that there are six distinguishable schools of thought in Islam. He identifies them as philosophical, civil law, social, economic and ethical schools. He introduces each briefly, but elaborates in detail on the moral school of Islam (1373/1994). He declares that Islam has put forward a new foundation of ethical edification. Islamic scholars have made valuable efforts to elaborate and refine the subject over the past centuries.

According to S.R.Sadr (1373/1994) the initial foundation of this school of ethics has been laid down by the holy Qur'an. The Messenger has enunciated the moral principles by teaching and training his companions. The Commander of Believers Ali ibn Abitalib (as) writes a treatise on the subject. He is in fact, according to Sadr, the founder of this invaluable school; he delivered all he has learnt from the Messenger to Muslims and to the world. He is the great teacher of morality by his advices and deeds and also is the prime student of the Messenger's school of ethics who announced "I am missioned to complete the ethical virtues" (Bayhaqi 1424 l.h).

One of the sources that has remained memorial from the Imam Ali (as) and is an authentic reference for ethical studies is the letter that he has left as will for his elder son Imam Hasan (as). This letter and others that Imam (as) has written to his followers are reported by Kolaini in his *Ar-Rasael* book[1] and also by Abu Ahmad Hasan ibn Abdullah ibn Saeid Askari in his *Zawajer wa Mawaez* book.[2] The author refers to Asbagh ibn Nabateh.

The first written book on the subject in the second Hijri century belongs to Ismail ibn Mahran Sokuni who was one of the companions of Imam Ali ibn ar-Redza (as). He has titled his book *Attributes of Believers and Depraved* (Sadr, Hasan, P.404, 1375/1996). Other Islamic authors followed suit and compiled many books and treatises. According to S.R.Sadr the best compilation prior to the fifth century is by the renowned scholar Ibn Muskuyeh called *Purity of Self* which is also called *Virtues of Morality*. This book is composed of six treatises. The great Naseeruddin Toosi has benefitted from this work in his invaluable book *Naseri Ethics* (Toosi,1413/1993).

S.R.Sadr laments that over the course of history the authors have inclined to the philosophical school and ethical deliberations have become philosophical in content. He is of the view that the practical aspects of Islamic ethics are significant and should be highlighted. Thus he devotes himself to the applied discourse of Islamic ethics by giving lectures and compiling books. Three volumes of his publications are devoted to this topic, namely the *Perseverance,* 1373/1994). *Envy* 1373/1994), *and Lie* (1373/1994).

2 Praiseworthy Spending versus Morally Reprehensible Stinginess

Humans are repeatedly invited by the holy Qur'an and the noble Prophet to spend their income and wealth in ways that would please the Almighty. He is pleased when humans make charities and help the needy. In about 32 verses of the Qur'an, humans are urged to spend their excess income in activities that pleases the Almighty (Sajjadi and Farid 1378/1999). Holy Qur'an declares that spending as little as an atom's weight of goods will be rewarded by the Lord (99:7).[3] Those who spend benevolently in ease,

---

1 This book is not accessible but Ibn Tawus has referred to the book and reported the letters in his book titled "Kashf ul Mahajjah li Thamarat el Mohajjah". Specifically, the letter to Imam Hasan, known as "will" and also to Mohammad ibn Hanafiah are reported in the latter. Selected parts of Ar-Rasael is compiled by Mirza Abdulla Afandi and a copy of it is available in the Ayatullah Marashi najafi in Qum Iran. Ibn Tawus also reports some of the letters reported in Ar-Rasel in his Al-Lohuf book 91380/2001).

2 Ibn Askari (passed away at 382 Lunar Hijri) is one the great scholars at fourth Lunar Hijri. Fatehi Nejhad has introduced this scholar in the Great Islamic Encyclopedia (pp. 152–154) and has mentioned this work is not acesssbel.

3 The first number indicates that of a Surah and the second the number of the Ayah in the holy Quran.

as well as in hardship, are loved by the Almighty (2:271). The benevolent individual will be rewarded and shall have no fear or grief on the Day of Judgment (2:274). Benevolent giving to please Allah will cancel out some of the evil deeds committed by that individual (2:271). Spending for the sake of Allah is considered as an investment by the holy Qur'an with returns as much as seven hundred times of the original amount of this expenditure: "Those who spend their wealth for Allah's sake may be compared to a grain which sprouts into seven ears with a hundred grains in each ear..." (2:261) (Irving 2003). Benevolent, generous and charitable giving is considered so important and praiseworthy by the Qur'an to constitute an archetypal model for spending. Elements of this model may be described as follows:

1. *What to spend?* Residual of income remaining after livelihood expenses (2:219) and also from what is most preferred.
2. *Who should receive?* Parents, relatives, the poor, the wayfarer, and the orphans (2:215): "Show kindness to both your parents, and with near relatives, orphans, the needy, the neighbor who is related to you as well as the neighbor who is stranger, and your companions by your side and the wayfarer, and anyone else under your control. Allah does not like someone who is conceited, boastful (4:36)" (Irving 2003).
3. *How to give?* Give it openly in public and secretly in private. The latter is preferred to the former (2:271, 2:274).
4. *When to give?* Always; day and night (2:274).
5. *How much to give?* Moderate amount; not too much, not too little. The giver should not cast himself to prediction with his hand, neither be stingy, nor prodigal (2:195): "Those who spend are neither extravagant nor parsimonious and keep between these the just mean (25:3) (Shakir 1993).
6. *What is the Reward?* The Almighty says: "you would not transcend to the position of beneficent unless you spend from what you like most (3:92)."

As much as charity giving is praised in the Quran, stinginess is considered abominable and miserliness held in contempt. In several verses, mean and stingy people are chastised; Almighty reserves humiliating torment for those who are not only tight-fisted themselves, but direct others to be stingy and hide anything that Allah has granted them out of His bounty (4:37). In another verse Almighty warns those who act niggardly and withhold the bounty, which Allah has given them of His grace, from the poor and the needy. They will be charged on Resurrection Day with being so niggardly (3/180). In one chapter of Quran, Allah, in a most alarming language, warns those who accumulate wealth without spending, reckoning that it will be a provision against mishaps. The Almighty adds that such persons shall be hurled into the crushing disaster, a flaming fire (104:2–7). Hence, it is clear that amassing and hoarding wealth without investing in ways prescribed by the Creator is a severe evil act. Evidently, hoarding is a stingy behavior, a refusal to spend in the way of Allah. Consequently, this practice is highly condemned in the holy Qur'an and has been prohibited by the Shari'ah.

3 What is Hoarding

Hoarding means withholding the supply of goods by producers or distributors in order to create an artificial gap between current supply and demand in the market, with intention to derive up prices. If the practice pays off, not only do these producers or distributors continue this practice, but other agents will also follow suit. "Ihtikar," the Arabic word for hoarding, is composed of three components: (1) the act of storing; (2) the good that is stored; (3) expected price increase.

Arab lexicographers are unanimous that "Ihtikar" consists of the first and third elements but differ on the inclusion of the second, the type of the good (Sadr 1362/1981; Madni 2013). Some experts argue that the word refers to food items only.[4] Firuzabadi, a lexicographer himself, however, opines that it includes constraining the supply of both food and non-food commodities to force their prices increase (Al Qamus, vol. 2, p. 13). This difference of opinion in the discourse of literal experts affects the position of the Islamic jurisprudents (Fuqaha) since they depend on such interpretations in their analyses of the practice and issuing their verdict (Fatwa). Their views will be presented later. It will be argued that "Ihtikar", i.e. hoarding, includes both food and non-food commodities and goods.

4 Hoarding versus Monopolizing

Market conditions for emergence of hoarding is different from those of monopolizing production of a good (Sadr 1362/1983; Al Arif 2016). Although severe and harmful for the economy, hoarding is a short-term phenomenon while that of monopoly condition is long run which emerges either through a concessionary grant by the state or a patented right for the use of a specific technology. The monopolist produces a quantity of output that maximizes his profit. The scale of the plant depends on the depth and extent of the market for the product. Since the monopolist has a good estimate of the market demand, he chooses a plant size that would produce maximum profitable output level. Restricting the production of the output to manipulate the market price would not earn him additional profit; it will be a deviation from his optimal equilibrium state. Hoarding activities, on the other hand, are undertaken when commodities and goods are in the distribution phase. If the hoarding period lasts long enough, other firms will enter the market and supply the commodities that are in demand. Consequently, the hoarding practice is not sustainable in the long run.

4 Sihah al loghah, Vol.2,p.635; Ahmed ibn Ali al Qayumi,al mesbah ul Moneer, Vol.1, p.178; Toreihi, Faghruddin, Majmae' al Bahrain, Vol. 3,; Ibn Atheer, An Nehayah, Vol.1, p. 417.

5 Warehousing versus Hoarding

Farm products are produced seasonally while households consume cereals and fruits all through the year. Storing these commodities by brokers when they are harvested and marketing them in all seasons provides utility for the consumers. Usually, only warehousing cost is added to the production cost of these products under normal market conditions. Buyers are more than willing to pay for the inventory cost because the additional utility they obtain from this service is more than that they give up for the additional cost. There are other manufactured goods such as coolers and heaters that are usable at specific season of the year. However, they are produced all throughout the year. Brokers/distributors purchase these goods when they are produced and store them until the season they are in demand. Warehousing, therefore, is a service that creates utility for the consumers. Hoarding, on the other hand, creates disutility for the households; goods are made unavailable when they want them.

In terms of economic criteria, *when the expected market price is higher or equal to the production and storing cost of a unit of the product, it is profitable for store keepers to market the good, provided that the price is higher or equal to the average cost of producing and storing*. Otherwise, the stock keepers could be penalized for their hoarding intentions if they refuse to market the goods. Evidently, if one agent hoards, he or she will have no significant effect on the market. However, if a group of agents do so, particularly when the market is not in equilibrium, either due to external shocks or internal collusion, it will have significant impact on reducing the supply and increasing the price of the hoarded item.

6 Conditions Which Lead to Hoarding

The first and most important condition that induces hoarding practice and manipulation of prices is the non-competitive structure of the markets. In perfect competitive markets neither sellers nor buyers can impact the market price because the share of each one of them in the aggregate market supply is negligible. The hoarding practice is also unlikely in monopolistic markets because it is the seller who sets the market price. The monopolist has no incentive to alter the production and distribution of the goods because it will reduce the expected profit. The condition for hoarding is pervasive in non-competitive, segmented markets where there are few distributors. Any outside shocks or wrong information regarding a decline or a halt in the process of production or import of the product or any required input for production will induce hoarding behavior. When competition is not perfect, market price is not stable and the distribution chains are not efficient. Any impediment to this process may impact the market price. Thus circulation of any unfavorable news concerning the supply of a product may change the market price. Consequently, distributors can easily manipulate the supply of goods and services to influence their demand.

Conditions that instigate hoarding practices maybe generated outside or inside the market. Natural disasters like draught, flood, hurricanes and diseases that damage farm products lead to reduction in their supply. Wars, foreign or domestic, destabilize the economy and endanger the security of the supply of goods and services. These catastrophic events may halt the distribution of commodities and production of inputs. The temporary shortage maybe perceived to be enduring by risk averse consumers who may be induced to buy more goods than they need normally in order to have reserves at home. The inflated demand will eventually raise the market price. In turn, the high prices may tempt the distributors to exploit the situation by curtailing the flow of their products into the market leading to further price increases. Subsequently, hoarding practices continue until new firms enter the market and increase the supply.

Unequal distribution of households' income may exacerbate the impact of hoarding. Only high-income families can afford purchasing goods at high prices. As long as there would be demand for the hoarded goods, the practice continues. The low-income families will suffer most when goods are expensive and scarce. Perception that goods and commodities are in short supply maybe inculcated by the distributers themselves. If few of them control a sizable portion of the market supply, they may collude to withhold the flow of goods or manipulate the market price. Although hoarding is profitable in the short run, the agitated conditions would not last in the long run. Sooner or later, other firms will be informed and enter the market to earn profit. Additional supply of the goods will lower the price to their previous level and eventually hoarding behavior will be eliminated.

7 Type of Goods

Goods that are most likely hoarded are characterized by a type of demand which is price inelastic. When the prices of this kind of goods increase, the quantity purchased does not decrease proportionately. The price increase will subsequently raise the profit of sellers, though it will lower the welfare of the buyers. Food items, medicines and fuels are likely to be hoarded more than luxury goods. The former group is classified as necessary goods, since they are essential for maintaining a decent livelihood. The demand for this category of goods is price inelastic. This feature makes the consumers insensitive to the price changes. If the suppliers succeed to make the consumers believe that goods are in short supply, buyers react more vigorously to the rise in their prices compared to that of luxury items. Similarly, expected price rise in the future, leads to increase demand. Consumers purchase more food and other needed items.

8 Government Intervention

Sometimes government intervention may itself lead to instability in the market. Setting a ceiling for the market price or a quota for the amount of the good to be purchased may create excess demand and create black market for the necessary goods. The price ceiling is usually lower than the prevailing market price. It makes suppliers unwilling to offer their stock at the lower set price. The intervention will further widen the gap between the total supply and demand and hence results in formation of black markets for the necessary goods. Therefore, government's market stabilization policies, rationing and price controls, should be carried out prudently. Intervention measures should be taken only when shortage of necessary goods and price hikes are results of deliberate actions of stock keepers.

9 Kanz, Speculation and Investment

Hoarding practices do not take place only in the goods market; they may appear as well in the financial markets. If the structure of the latter markets is not competitive and their performance is not stable, they become prone to speculative activities. Dealers will be tempted to withhold financial securities for some time to raise their prices later. This practice has precedence at the rise of Islam in Arabia when some businessmen used to withhold gold and silver coins which were the medium of exchange in that economy. Storing those coins, called Dinar and Dirham, constrained smooth circulation of money in the nascent Islamic economy and depreciated the value of other assets and tradable goods. This practice, called Kanz, was vehemently condemned and prohibited by the holy Quran (9:34). The dealers who engaged in this practice were warned that their action was tantamount to declaring war against the Almighty (9:35).

At the time, gold and silver were the most popular and tradable assets not only in Arabia but also in Rome and Persia, the ultimate trade centers for Arab merchants. Dinar and Dirham were the currencies of Rome and Persia, respectively. Keeping the currency out of circulation would harm trade activities and lead to inflation in the Arabian economy.

When coins were not at hand, gold and silver bullions were used, instead, in market transactions (Sadr 2016). Quranic prohibition of Kanz encompasses not only the coins but gold and silver assets in general which were the most liquid assets at the time. It may be inferred that withholding any tradable or financial asset out of market exchange is prohibited. This conclusion, to be explored further, has profound implication for speculation in securities in the financial markets. Based on the Kanz prohibition rule, no individual or group of agents is permitted to withhold financial assets in order to sell them later at higher prices. Circulation of false information regarding future price changes or returns to securities is also prohibited according to the rule which bans deceptive practices (Sadr 2016). Compliance with this rule provides security for market transactions and stability to the prices.

The renowned exegete Mohammad Hosain Tabatabaei presents an extensive interpretation about the Qur'anic verse on Kanz (9:34) referred to above. It is preceded by another verse (9:33) which condemns the behavior of non-Muslim religious authorities, at the time, who spent people's wealth in futile activities. The practice created no economic values and did not benefit the community. Thus, it did not please Allah,. In the subsequent verse, the holy Quran warns that those who hoard their gold and silver wealth and do not invest it in the way of Allah, i.e. in the economy, will be punished severely. Their foreheads and flanks will be burned by the hell's fire, made of those riches.

Unfortunately, the practice of accumulating wealth in the form of gold and silver bullions with conspicuous consumption habits continued after the holy Prophet. This life style was criticized vehemently by the Prophet's famous companion Abuzar Ghaffari (Tabatabaei 1347/1968) who, in particular, criticized the conduct and lavish lifestyle of Mo'awieh, being financed by the public treasury. He was then the governor of province of Sham (the territory that included modern day Syria, Lebanon, Jordan and Palestine).

Tabatabaei, unlike other exegetes, argues that the rule of prohibiting Kanz (unproductive accumulation of wealth) is general and is not applicable exclusively to non-Muslims. Muslims, too, must not keep their riches out of market circulation. Further, he declares that the rule is not confined to gold and silver coins and assets, but encompasses all wealth and goods that have economic values and are exchanged in the markets.

The reported Quranic verses further state that wealth must be spent in the way of Allah. The question is whether the latter implies the required canonically mandatory spending like Zakat or goes beyond that to extend to the recommended spending as well. Tabatabaei considered that the review of Abuzar's debates with Mo'awiah, as well as a Prophet's traditions, narrated by Ka'bul Ahbar, indicates that, the verse implies giving more than the prescribed spending (Tabatabaei 1347/1968). People are not only prohibited from hoarding their wealth and commanded to allow it to circulate in the economy, but should also use the wealth to provide for their own needs as well as that of the poor and needy households. They should not be niggardly in spending on themselves and others. Tabatabaei further suggests that the prohibition on hoarding covers not only food items but all commodities, services and financial assets that are in demand in the markets (Tabatabaei 1347/1968).

It is clear that the rule prohibiting Kanz governs all assets including financial assets. It remains to clarify how speculation in these assets is different from investment activity in the financial market. Investment in both goods and financial markets refers to the allocation of capital and other inputs to production of goods and services or to commercial activities in order to create new products that markets value or to enhance the production or marketing value of an existing product. Value-creating activities are praised highly in Islam and all competent entrepreneurs are incentivized to undertake investment projects (Sadr 2016; Mirakhor & Askari 2010). Marketing of new shares requires promotion and advertising efforts. At times, portfolio of shares, including the new and old shares, may be composed and be offered like new products. Financial products and derivatives, which represent ownership rights to real investment projects or the benefits from operating plants, are financial investment. A speculative activity differs from an investment as the former entails creation of no real value either in the production or marketing of assets; it is simply an attempt to increase the price of assets by hoarding or collusion. To differentiate between the two, the same criteria that identified the difference between hoarding and warehousing can be applied here too. *If the market share price of a unit of investment in a project is higher than the production and marketing cost of that unit, the share should be offered for sale. If it is held off the market to create artificial scarcity of the shares, the behavior is speculative in nature.*

10 Prohibition of Hoarding in Islamic Jurisprudence

To review the opinion of Fuqaha (Islamic Jurisprudents) on hoarding, the spectrum of this practice and its impact on the market can be divided into four successive phases and the verdicts about this practice for each phase is reported (Sadr 1362/1983).

The First Phase: In this phase hoarding is not perceptible in the market and rules governing hoarding are followed by the market participants.

The Second Phase: In this phase, hoarding is perceptible in the market but generates no disorder or instability in the market.

The Third Phase: In this phase, hoarding practices are not only perceptible but create shortages of supply. Consumers are burdened and have to bear additional transaction costs of collecting information, finding suppliers and endure other inconveniences for procuring what they need.

The Fourth Phase: In this phase, hoarding is widespread and pervasive, goods become scarce and prices unstable. Consumers become vulnerable to instability and can hardly obtain commodities and goods they need.

10.1 The First Phase

The first phase is akin to orderly and stable market performance. Inventories are kept corresponding to saving motive. This activity has no harmful effect on the supply or the price of the good or commodity being stocked. Individual market participants and groups comply with rules governing market behavior; they abstain from activities that may hurt other participants' business or public interests. Overall, no misconduct or harmful activity is performed by the agents.

This is the state in which Islamic rules governing exchange are operative fully leading to a steady state economy. It is noteworthy that many of ethical codes of conduct are prescribed as rules of behavior in Islam. Prohibition of wasting goods, prodigality and lavishness, doing harm to others, cheating and fraud are some examples of these rules (Sadr 2016). Here, few more directives from the holy Prophet of Islam and the true Imams from his progeny, i.e., the Grand Leaders of the early Muslim communities, will be offered by referring to some of their traditions, advice and recommendations.

On one occasion, Imam Abul Hasan directed farm producers to market their produce soon after the harvest and purchase their sustenance on a day-to-day basis from the market (Kolaini, Forue' Kafi, Vol.6, p. 166). This directive has the effect of protecting farmers from the temptation of hoarding their output. On another occasion, Imam Sadiq (as) quotes the Prophet that the trader who travels from one town to another to bring in the goods that are in demand in the market is praiseworthy, but the hoarder who does otherwise is cursed (Kolaini, ibid, p. 165). Imam Baqir (as) also quotes the Prophet that if a trader stocks and stores food products for 40 days with the intention to sell them at higher price and then spends the proceeds for charity, the reward would not equate the sin of hoarding he has committed (Wasa'el ash-Shi'ah, vol.12, p. 314).

The Prophet narrates that once Jebra'il glanced over the hell and found a desert full of fire. He asked for whom was this fire prepared? For three groups was the answer: Those who commit hoarding, those who drink liquor and those who set up houses of ill-repute (Wasa'el asShi'ah, ibid, p. 314). Once food prices rose excessively in the city of Medinah. Imam Sadiq (as) inquired of the food reserves in his home. He learned that there is enough for a number of months. The Imam (as) ordered his stock of food to be sold in the market. To his surprise, the home care taker complained that food items are scarce in the city and the family would suffer having no reserves in the coming months. Imam reaffirmed his order and commented that, like the rest of the community members, family needs will be purchased daily. Imam instructed later that bread be prepared half with wheat and half with barley, despite having access to the best quality wheat. He stated, then, that he wished to be witnessed by the Almighty that he is among the best of managers of home economics (Kolaini, Kafi, vol.5, p. 166).

The conduct of the Prophet and the Imams from his progeny (as) on various occasions and conduct of their own lives as well as the advice and directives that they offer to their companions constitute the moral norms and ethical conducts for both businessmen and others to be followed. Compliance with these rules would obviate any motivation for misbehavior or malpractice (such as hoarding or speculation) by the members of the community.

10.2 The Second Phase

Some hoarding incidence occurs in the market but has no harmful impact on the market aggregate supply and price. Households have access to supply chains and procure what they need easily. Keeping inventories is a saving initiative or a warehousing activity. A companion of Imam Sadiq (as) requests that the Imam instruct him about hoarding. Imam explains that it is when you buy a product that is not abundant in the market and store it to benefit from its price increase. However, if the item is available and accessible in the market, it may be stored if it is beneficial to do so (Al-Horr Al-Ameli, Wasa'el ash-Shiah, vol.12, p. 315). On another occasion the Imam (as) is asked about storing edible oil in excess of the immediate need. He replies that its storage is permissible if it is available in the market (ibid).

The above instructions succinctly demonstrate the difference between warehousing and hoarding. The former creates utility for consumers and the latter does otherwise. Saving is praiseworthy while hoarding is condemned. In this context, Fuqaha express the opinion that stocking of goods as inventories is permissible when they are being supplied by other agents in the market. Shaykh Tousi considers hoarding, i.e., store keeping, as permissible (in his book: An-Nihayah, p.374) "if others are selling the good at the market price". He further states in another book (Al-Mabsut, p. 195) that the practice is not even disliked. 'Allamah Al-Helli also approves the practice if it is for personal use or if others are supplying the good (At-Tazkerah, vol. 1, p. 585). The verdict of the author of "Kanzul 'Irfan" is similar (vol.2, p. 43). There seems to be consensus among Fuqaha on permissibility of this activity when alternative suppliers are present on the market. In conclusion, storing goods in this second phase with its market condition is, in fact, saving or inventory keeping and is permissible. It is not "undesirable" from the Shari'ah stand point. The criteria that were proposed before to differentiate these two behaviors seem compatible with the Shari'ah.

10.3 The Third Phase

In this phase hoarding is widely practiced. Goods are inventoried only to create a shortage and increase prices. However, goods are still available in the market, though at higher prices. While the economy is not yet facing a crisis, this phase is the focus of all jurisprudents that treat hoarding activities as utterly prohibited at this stage. Traditions reported from the Imams (as) prohibit hoarding under this market condition. Imam Sadiq(as) narrates that once during the life time of the Prophet a food item became scarce. Citizens approached the Prophet asking him to force the sole supplier of that item to dishoard his stock and offer them for sale. The Prophet, after praising the Almighty, ordered the supplier to do so (Al-Horr Al-Ameli, Wasa'el., Vol.12, p. 316).

Complying with the Prophet's order is an obligation for the believers. Had the seller refused to follow the command, his hoarding would have been considered sinful. In the words of Imam Ali (as), the Prophet not only stated the rule that hoarding is forbidden, he mandated further that all the hoarded products to be removed from the inventories and be offered for sale (Ibid, p. 317). Prophet's intervention in the market clearly demonstrates prohibition of hoarding under market conditions characterizing this phase.

In an inquiry about the legitimacy of hoarding food stuff, Imam Sadiq (as) responded that if a food item is adequately available and its storage does not cause a shortage in the market nor does it create inconvenience for consumers, it is not harmful; otherwise it is forbidden (Ibid, p. 313). On another occasion, a companion reports that Imam Sadiq (as) asked me about my business. "A wheat seller", I replied, and added that "I encounter both boom and bust market conditions. When I find the wheat supply is diminishing, I store them as my inventory". "What do market participants call your practice?" the Imam asked him again. "Hoarding", I uttered. "Are there other wheat sellers in the market?" the Imam inquired next. I declared that "I offer only one per thousand of the aggregate market supply". "Then your inventory keeping is all right," the Imam (as) remarked (Ibid, p. 316). The Imam (as) additionally stated that a businessman at the time of the Prophet used to purchase all the food products that were imported to the Medinah market. Once, the Prophet warned him of hoarding that merchandise: "Abstain from this practice" the Prophet told him. This confirms further the prohibition of this practice in Islam under conditions that characterize the third phase.

Another indication for unlawfulness of hoarding is the unanimous agreement among the Fuqaha that the stock of the goods that are hoarded must be released for sale. Evidently, if this action was not legitimate, Shari'ah scholars would not issue a verdict that businessmen are to release their hoarded stock for sale. It is however worth remembering that the ownership rights of the stock keeper are considered sacred; the proceeds of the sale of his released stock are his own. In case he refuses to abide with the rule, the government is authorized to auction the stock and pay him the proceeds.

10.4 The Fourth Phase

This phase refers to market conditions under which commodities are scarce and unattainable in the market. No one has easy access to them; they are taken out of market and are hoarded by distributors. The community faces a crisis; the economy becomes unstable and vulnerable to collapse. All Fuqaha have condemned and prohibited hoarding under such conditions, labeling it as a great sin. The government is authorized to intervene in the market and force the hoarded stock of goods to be offered for sale voluntarily by the hoarder or sell it itself otherwise on behalf of the hoarder. Many Fuqaha have declared hoarding a prohibited act both in this and in the previous phase, the third phase.[5] They all have judged that hoarding in this fourth phase of the economy is illegal and Haram; there is consensus among Fuqaha concerning elimination of hoarding in this last phase.

There are other rules in Islam that have much broader scope than that of hoarding. They include prohibition of doing harm to the neighbors or the community, rejection of any activity that will destabilize the economy and constrain orderly functioning of the economy as well as activities that generate no economic value, such as gambling, bribery and fraud (Sadr 2016). They prohibit and ban hoarding practices as well. These latter rules encompass unlawfulness of keeping stocks under conditions prevailing in the fourth phase of the economy. While the Fuqaha have debated the applicability of the rule prohibiting hoarding to the phase three, legitimacy of application of the rule prohibiting to the phase four is a matter of consensus among them.

11 Goods that are Subject to Hoarding

There are traditions that apply explicitly the hoarding prohibition to the following commodities: wheat, barley, dates, raisin, olive oil, cooking oil, and salt. Question arises whether these specific items are only examples illustrating the application of the rule prohibiting hoarding or are they the only set of goods subjected to the rule while the hoarding of other commodities and goods is permissible? At first glance, the narrations may imply that the practice is restricted to the set of commodities mentioned. In this context, one narration explicitly affirms this limitation and some eminent Fuqaha such as Tousi (in An-Nahaye), Ansari (in Al-Makaseb), and Bahrani (in Al-Hada'iq) have taken the same position. However, some other Fuqaha have argued that the specified commodities have been in intensive demand at the time of the Prophet and the Imams (as). Hence, they are only examples and the rule on prohibition of hoarding is general and comprehensive covering all goods needed by people. The stated traditions, therefore, do not imply that hoarding of goods other than those named is permissible. What supports this judgment is the fact that Fuqaha have repeatedly ruled out those goods that are needed by people and are essential for maintaining a decent living standard. They cannot be made inaccessible by hoarding. This verdict implies that goods, inputs or assets that are critical for consumption, production or commercial activities cannot be hoarded. Interestingly, when Imam Ali ibn Abi Talib (as) was the temporal ruler of the entire Islamic State and appointed Malik Ashtar to be the governor of the Egypt, wrote him a letter containing a number of decrees

5 Among them are Shaikh Morteza Ansari in his "Makasib, vol. 4, p. 364", Helli in "Qawaid, vol., p. 11", Ibn Idris in "Saraer, vol. 2, p. 238" and M.J. Musavi in "Meftah Al-karamah, vol. 8, p. 186" books. Shahid Thani in "Loma'h, vol. 1, p. 331", Yusuf Bahraini in "Hadiq An-Nazerah, vol. 18, p. 61", Noori in "Mostadrak, vol. 2, p. 468" and Khomaini in "Al-Baie', vol. 3, p. 414" books.

to be followed and implemented (Sadr 2016). In this letter there is a decree in which the Imam (as) emphasizes that market price should be equitable to both buyers and sellers. If ever they were manipulated by hoarding practices, the governor must intervene to prevent the practice. The Imam (as) does not limit prohibition of hoarding to a few commodities only, rather all goods and commodities that are demanded by the people are covered (Nahjul-Balaghah, Letter 52). The mandate praises the commercial services that merchants provide and instructs Malik, the governor, to facilitate and support their services: "...then, I advise you to be good to the traders and manufacturers, whether residents or those who travel for the purpose of production and exchange, for they are the source of utility and means of welfare and comfort for the people. They travel near and far, on land and the seas, on mountains and deserts, and where few people choose to live and where others do not dare to go. They are peaceful and avoid conflicts. Encourage them with your presence among them and show concern for their affairs, whether they live where you are or in other locations around it."

The Imam, however, warns his appointed governor, Malik, that: "Despite this, know, however, that among them are those who misbehave badly. They practice hoarding for profits, setting their own prices as they wish. This is a way to harming public interest and a failure on the part of rulers. Therefore, put a stop to this hoarding practice, because the Messenger prohibited it so that exchange would become uncomplicated and easy, based on justice, which would not do injustice to either the buyer or the seller. Therefore, punishthe hoarders who choose to ignore your order, without overdoing it, and make an example of them for others."

Therefore, it can be concluded reasonably that prohibition of hoarding is not confined to specific goods listed in some traditions. Rather it encompasses all goods, inputs and materials that are in demand in the market. This conclusion has important implications for the financial markets. As noted above, prohibition of hoarding is not restricted to food items; it encompasses all things of value that are in demand in either the goods or financial markets. Accordingly, no financial asset could be held out of market circulation in order to force its price up and gain from this speculative activity. The rule prohibiting hoarding as well as that of Kanz precludes absolutely all speculative activities related to financial products. In this context, Imam Musa Sadr stated, in a sermon on the conclusion of Month of Ramadhan, that not only a true Muslim rejects hoarding goods and wealth, but abstains from hoarding his knowledge and expertise, position and opportunities, contribution to the community and helping others (Lisan ul Haal, 21, November 1971).

12 Government Price Setting

Does Shari'ah authorize the state to set the prices of hoarded commodities and goods? Most of the Fuqaha reject government intervention in the market through price setting. A tradition that was reported above from the Prophet states that when he learned that a trader was hoarding, ordered him to make his hoarded stock available for public sale in the market. However, he did not dictate a price for the product (al-Kafi, vol. 5, p. 164). Based on this tradition of the Prophet and others reported from the great Imams (as) who followed him, Fuqaha do not consider that Shari'ah grants price-setting authority to states. The only exception is under market conditions like those of Phase four as explained above, when the economy is out of equilibrium due to outbreak of a war or a natural disaster, and markets have become dysfunctional. If goods are sold at exorbitant prices, price setting is permissible (Khoei, Misbah al-Fuqaha, no date). Indeed, in many jurisprudential discourses, hoarding and price-setting activities are debated jointly and considered prohibited.

13 Conclusions

Hoarding is a short-run market imperfection phenomenon when some necessary goods and commodities are stocked and made scarce in the market to force their prices to rise. It is different from monopoly condition which is a long-run market imperfection. Hoarding is also distinguishable from warehousing which is a valuable marketing practice. The latter makes the goods available at the time they are in demand whereas the former makes them unavailable and creates disutility for the consumers. Saving is also differentiable from hoarding. The former is practiced when a portion of households' income or wealth is deposited in a financial institution to be pooled with savings of others and be invested in profitable ventures later. Although necessary goods are most often the subject of hoarding, the practice is not limited to them. Shari'ah prohibits withdrawal from the market of any commodity, good and asset, real or financial, that are exchanged in the market.

Market conditions that are prone to induce hoarding were described as when the supply of goods is severely constrained in the market and consumers have to bear considerable transaction costs to find them. Hoarding of goods are absolutely prohibited at this stage. Under these and more severe conditions where markets are unstable and out of equilibrium, governments are permitted to intervene to prevent hoarding practices. Under normal market conditions where goods are available in the market, state intervention is considered neither beneficial nor permissible. Rather, governments should always supervise market performance to make sure that no impediment constrains competition. They should also procure buffer stocks to make up for any shortage, if it occurs. Furthermore, they should contribute to the fast and easy circulation of information in all markets to ensure prevalence of competitive and stable conditions. Economic criteria to identify hoarding from warehousing in the goods and commodity markets, and also investment from speculation in the financial markets, were formulated in the paper and could be applied by the local and the central governments to preclude hoarding practices and to stabilize market performance.

References

Al-Ameli, Zeinuddin bin Ali. *Masalik al Afham*,53, Qum: Muassahtul Maarif al-Islamiah,1371/1992.

Ansari, Murtaza. *Kitab al-Makasib*, 4, Qum:Majma' al-Fikr al-Islami, 1419 lunar /1998.

Al Arif, M. Nur Rianto. "Monopoly and Ikhtikar in Islamic Economics", *Shirka Journal of Economics and Business*, 1, no.3, 2016.

Bahrani, Yusuf.*Hadaeq an-Nadzerah*, 18, Qum: Jameatul Mudarresin Houzah Ilmiah Qum, 1363/1984.

Bayhaqi, Ahmad ibn Hosain, *As Sonan al Kobra,* Vol 10.P 323, Beirut, Dar Kotob al elmiah, 1424 (lunar hijri)/2003.

Fatehi Nejhad,Enayatullah, Abu Ahmad Askari, *The Great Islamic Encyclopedia,* Tehran, Center for The Great Islamic Encyclopedia 1367/1987.

Fayruzabadi, Muhammad ibn Yaqub. *Al-Qamus al-Mohit*, 2, Beirut: Darul Kotob el-Ilmiah, M.A. Baydzun, no date.

Goldberg, Linda S. and Il'dar Karimov "Black-Markets for Currency, Hoarding Activity and Policy Reforms", *Journal of International Economics* vol. 42 3/4 (May1997): 349–370.

Helli, Najmuddin Ja'far ibn Hasan. *Shari'al Islam fi Masael el-Halal wal Haram*, Tehran: Ismaeelian, 1408 lunar/1988.

Helli, Hasan ibn yusuf. *Al-Qawaed al-Ahkam fi Ma'refat el Halal wa al-Haram*, 2, Qum: Muassah an-Nashr al-Islami, 1371/1992.

Al-Hurr el-Ameli, Muhammad ibn al-Hasan. *Wasael sh Shiah,* 12, Qum: Muassahtul Ahlul bait li-Ihya at Torath, no date.

Ibn Atheer, Mubarak ibn Mohammad. *An Nahayah fi Ghareeb el- Hadith wal-A'thar*, Qum: Muassah Ismaeelian, 1367/1988.

Ibn Idris, Muhammad ibn Ahmad. *Kitab us Saraer*, 2, Qum: Muassah an-Nashr al-Islami, 1390/2011.

Irving, T.B. *The Qur'an: Text, translation and commentary*, 2nd ed., Tehran: Research and Publication Center, 2003.

Ibn Tawus, Ali ibn Musa ibn Ja'far Ibn, *Kashf ul Mahajah li Thamarat el Mohajjah,* Najaf, Manshurat al matbaah al Haydariah,1370/1950.

Ibn Tawus, Ali ibn Musa ibn Ja'far, *Al Lohuf Ala Qatla al Tofuf.* No place, Osveh, No date.

Jouhari, Ismaeel ibn Hama'd. *As Siha'h*,2, Beirut: Dar ul Ilm lil Malaeen,1404 lunar /1984.

Kolaini, Muhammad ibn yaqub. *Foru' Kafi*, 6, edited by Ali Akbar Ghaffari,Tehran: Dar ul Kotob el-Islamiah,1365/1986.

Madni, Abdul Hai, "The Hoarding in Islamic Marketing", *IOSR Journal Of Humanities And Social Science*, 17, Issue 2, 2013.

Mirakhor, Abbas and Hossein Askari. *Islam and the Path to Human and Economic Development*, New York: Palgrave-Macmillan, 2010.

Musawi Ameli, Muhammad Jawad. *Miftah al Karamah*, 8, Beirut: Darut Turath, no date.

Musawi al Khoei, Seyed Abul Qasim. *Mesbah ul Fiqahah*, 5, Reiterated by Towheedi, M.A., óQum: davari, 1377/1998.

An-Najafi, Muhammad hasan. *Jawaher ul Kalam*, 22, Tehran:1393/2014.

An-Naraqi, Mulla Ahmad. *Mustand ush Shiah*, 14, Qum: Muassah Ahlul bait li-Ihya at Torath, 1415 lunar/1994.

Pickhardt, Michael and Jordi Sardà. *Cash, Hoarding and the Underground* Münster, Center of Applied Economic Research, 2012.
Al-Qayyumi, Ahmad ibn Mhammad ibn Ali. *Al-Misbahul Monir*,1, Al-Maktabatul Asriah, 1418 lunar/ 1997.
Qur'an, Translated by Shakir, M.H., Qum Iran: Ansariyan Publications, 1372/1993.
Sadr, Seyed Kazem. *The Economic System of the Early Islamic Period,* New York: Palgrave-Macmillan, 2016.
Sadr, Seyed Kazem. *Ihtikar: An Economic and Jurisprudential Analysis*, Qum Iran: 22 Bahman Publisher, 1362/1983.
Sadr, Hasan, *Ta'sees as Shiaah li Olum al Islam,* Beyrut, A'lami, 1375/1996.
Sadr, Seyyed Reza, *Perseverance*, edited by Seyed Baqir Khosroshahi, Qum, Bustan Ketab Institute, 1373/1994.
Sadr, Seyyed Reza, *Envy*, edited by Seyed Baqir Khosroshahi, Qum, Bustan Ketab Institute, 1373/1994.
Sadr, Seyyed Reza, *Lie*, edited by Seyed Baqir Khosroshahi, Qum, Bustan Ketab Institute, 1373/1994.
Sadr, Seyed Musa. *Fasting Ethics*, Tehran: Imam Musa Sadr Institute of Research and Cultural Studies, 1387/2009.
Sadr, Seyed Musa." *The blessings and Obligation of Al-Fitr Feast.*" Beirut: Lisan ul- Haal newspaper, (21 November) 1971.
Sajjadi, M.S. and M. Farid Tonkaboni. *Ethics from the Quran and Etrat Perspective*, Tehran: Daftar Nashr Farhang Islami, 1378/1999.
Tabatabaei, Mohammad Hosain. *Al- Mizan Fi Tafseer Al- Quran*, 18, Translated by M.B. Musavi, Tehran: Mohammadi Publication House, 1347/1968.
At-Tusi, Muhammad ibn al-Hasan. *Al-Mabsu,t* 2, Tehran: Al-Maktabatul Murtazawiah, no date.
At Toraihi, Fakhroddin. *Majmaul Bahrain*, 3. Tehran: Maktabatul Murtazavi, 1375/1996.
Welsted, Alison C. "Compulsive hoarding and the theory of value: an economic model of excessive accumulation," A Thesis Submitted in Partial Fulfilment of the Requirements for the Degree Of Doctor Of Philosophy. The University of British Columbia, 2007.

Majid Reza'ei Davani

Chapter 27: Ethics and Economy of Islamic Government

1 Introduction

With the establishment of the Islamic administration in Medina, the concepts of Islamic Economy attained a more significant status. In the early years following *Mab'ath* (literary meaning resurgence, it refers to the first revelation) of Prophet Mohammad, many important economic commands including *Infaq*,[1] non-extravagance (*Israf*) and fairness in transactions,[2] *Mavasat* (sympathy and assistance to the needy),[3] common ownership of land,[4] necessity of expertise in economic planning,[5] *Tat'fif* (short-weighing) were addressed to the faithful. However, establishment of the Prophet's administration and its dominance resulted in governmental laws, revenue resources and their responsibilities that were either ordered from the Almighty or emplaced by the Holy Prophet. The concepts that were debated during the ten-year period of the Holy Prophet's administration include:

1. The status of *Anfal* (spoils of war and booties) and the necessity of contributing Khums from them as the share of the Almighty and the Holy Prophet;
2. Necessity of paying *Zakat* (welfare tax) for definite purposes;
3. The legal condition of annexed territories to the Islamic Government including the conquered, compromised and other territories;
4. *Fai* (booty from enemy obtained without fighting);
5. *Jizyah* (compensations from non-Muslims);
6. Share of the Government revenue from allocated territories;
7. Distributing the surplus property among the public and supplying the deprived and needy;
8. Allocation of financial resources such as mines and land to people for reclamation;
9. Determining regulations for using sources of wealth such as water and minerals.

In the time after the administration of the Holy Prophet and during the expansion of the realm of Islam into other territories, the Islamic government added additional practices. After the Holy Qur'an and the Holy Prophet's conduct, the correspondences by Imam Ali to various governors are considered the most important documents

1 *Al-Mozam'mel*: 20.
2 *Al-A'raf*: 29–30.
3 *Al-Ma'arej*: 24 and 25.
4 *Al-A'raf*: 10; *Ibrahim*: 32.
5 Yusof: 55.

https://doi.org/10.1515/9783110593419-027

related to public finance. In the epistle by Imam Ali to Malik Al-Ashtar Nakha'ei, the fundamental mission of a religious government have been discussed in detail. They include: domestic and foreign security, tax collection, development of the country, and attending to the livelihood of the people. Undoubtedly, this is one of the most significant documents of the early Islamic Era.[6] This epistle covers the following topics:

1. The relations between government and people;
2. The status of administrative and decision-making systems;
3. The military, judiciary system, and government authorities;
4. Concepts of taxation and public treasury, archivists and collectors;
5. The markets and the government supervision over them;
6. The deprived and their essential requirements;
7. Security concepts and the in-charge officers; and,
8. The foreign relations.

Several valuable points that are mentioned in this epistle are still counted as the practical guidelines for the Muslim scholars.

With the increased revenue of overnment and both the diversity and vastness of the newly annexed territories, there grew a need for compilation and editing of rules and regulations for the financial administrative system. Compiled jurisprudential books of the first centuries of the Islamic Era include special sections on *Zakat*, *Khums*, *Kharaj* (tribute), *Qana'em* (booties), *Anfal*, *Moqufat* (endowments), *Jizyah* (compensations from non-Muslims), *Fai* (booty from enemy obtained without fighting), and land rulings. Important monographs have been dedicated to special topics such as *Kitab Al-Kharaj* (Book of Tributes) by Qazi Abu Yusof in the Second Century AH during the reign of Caliph Haroon Abbassi; *Kitab Al-Kharaj* (Book of Tributes) by Yah'ya Bin Adam in second century AH; Kitab Al-Amval (Book of Assets) by Abu-Obaid in second and third centuries AH. Many more volumes have been authored by Islamic scholars and there are several original writings on Hadith, jurisprudence and regulation of financial resources of Islamic Government.[7] A number of topics on public finance are also addressed in books on leadership (*Imamat*) and governance as well as their prevailing responsibilities and obligations. They include *Kitab Al-Ahkam Al-Soltaniye* written by Abu Ya'la Al-Farra Hanbali and *Al-Ahkam Al-Soltaniye va Al-Velayat Al-Diniye* authored by Abu Al-Hassan Al-Maverdi Shafe'ei. Both authors are considered great scholars of the Fifth Century AH. Their monographs are outstanding sources, covering governance, leadership qualities of governors and their responsibilities in *Jihad*, judiciary, leadership (*Imamat*) and guidance (*Vilayat*) in prayers and Haj. They also address the responsibilities of governors on the topics of *Zakat*, *Qana'em*,*Kharaj*, *Jizyah*, *Mavat* (abandoned) lands, water and pastures, mines and

6 Al-Razi Al-Sharif Abu Al-Hassan Mohammad; *Nahj Al-Balaqa*; research by Sobhi Al-Saleh; Letter 53.

7 Modarresi Tabataba'ei, Hossein; *Land in Islamic Jurisprudence*; Vol. 2; pp. 271–286.

governmental administrations. The administrative division called *Al-Hisbah* (state inspectorate) Department commanded by the governors performed the duties of monitoring and inspecting various undertakings in order to enhance the markets and trading in accordance with the public interest. Some of the responsibilities of governments have been addressed in the books on *Al-Hisbah*, the most important of which is Ma'alem Al-Qorba fi Ahkam Al-Hisbah by Mohammad Bin Mohammad Bin Ahmad Al-Qurashi also known as Ibn Al-Okhva, a scholar from Seventh and Eighth centuries AH. Inspection of various industries including those related to food, hygiene, manufacturing, decoration, clothing and coinage has been listed among the duties of the civil authorities. Contemporary writings on the Islamic State and the Islamic Economic System also touch on these subjects.

It must be noted that the distinction of judicial-jurisprudential affairs from ethics has not been clearly indicated in writings and Hadith of First Century AH. In later periods, authors began to draw a distinction between ethics and judicial-jurisprudential affairs. Looking at all periods, this essay will attempt to explain the ethics of Islamic finance under six headings: 1. ethics of assuming power, 2. objectives, 3. appointing government authorities, 4. decision-making, 5. collecting revenues, and 6. allocating Bait Al-Mal.

2 Fundamental Concepts (Ethics, Legitimacy of Assuming Power and Its Objectives)

1. Since society cannot attain consistency without a government and there is a constant need for management and regulation, the activities of society are realized through state/governmental institutions. With the exception of the Khawarej (dissidents), most Muslims agree on the necessity of a leader (i.e. Imam in Shia sect). Resolving disagreements, avoiding chaos, establishing cooperation and harmony in society, and protecting society from harm and foreign aggression all require a systemizing authority which addresses essential public demands. Governance of the state/governmental institution and its supremacy will result in orchestration of society. Taking into account the numerous social commands of Islam, the social life of Muslims is not possible without a government. In absence of an Islamic government, the possibility of observing many religious commands becomes nil, and religion cannot be acknowledged in an accurate and comprehensive manner. Therefore, presence of the Islamic Government is necessary for exercising Islam and its economy.
2. The Islamic state must be accountable to both the people and to the Almighty and, therefore, is responsible for steering society towards the objectives and obligations demanded by the religion. This results in a distinction between the fundaments of legitimacies and authorities of a religious government than that

of a secular government. While both secular and religious governments aim to satisfy the fleeting material interests of their constituents, religious governments must also attend to the spiritual needs of both individuals and society at large.. It strengthens the social spirit in human beings and binds them to their past and future as well as to that of society. It synchronizes the interests of an individual with the interests of others and prevents conflicts.

3. The principal objective of the state is the advancement of human beings in both individual and social scopes. Shaping of commendable individuals for the position of divine ruler and leader and formation of Utopia constitute the main objective in the mission of prophets.[8] The Holy Qur'an has been revealed for the guidance and enlightenment of the people and their deliverance from darkness. This task has been undertaken by the Almighty who leads mankind out of darkness towards edification.[9] Prophets have been chosen by the Almighty to continue this path, which is manifested in spiritual allegiance.[10]
4. The objective of appointing messengers as well as revealing the book and the balance (measuring criteria) by the Almighty has mentioned in Holy Qur'an as resurgence of people to equity and justice:

لَقَدْ أَرْسَلْنَا رُسُلَنَا بِالْبَيِّنَاتِ وَأَنْزَلْنَا مَعَهُمُ الْكِتَابَ وَالْمِيزَانَ لِيَقُومَ النَّاسُ بِالْقِسْطِ وَأَنْزَلْنَا الْحَدِيدَ فِيهِ بَأْسٌ شَدِيدٌ وَمَنَافِعُ لِلنَّاسِ وَلِيَعْلَمَ اللَّهُ مَنْ يَنْصُرُهُ وَرُسُلَهُ بِالْغَيْبِ إِنَّ اللَّهَ قَوِيٌّ عَزِيزٌ (الحديد: 25)

We certainly have sent our messengers with clear explanations, and sent the Book and the balance down along with them, so that men may conduct themselves with equity. We have sent iron down laden with grim violence as well as (other) benefits for mankind, so that God may know who supports Him and His messengers even though (He is) unseen. God is Strong, Mighty. (Al-Hadid: 25)

Scopes of social justice include economical, judicial, administrative etc.

5. Puissance, such as wealth, is an advantage in Islam. However, there are ethical ways of achieving it, and gaining it through repression, collusion, coercion and deception is not approved. Spiritual leaders have employed the most virtuous methods to gain power, although their personal characters remarkably surpassed that of others. Cooperation of the public is an indispensable entity in establishing Islamic Government, without which even the Holy Prophet, who had thorough righteousness and divine legitimacy, did not form a government. His Holiness's advice to Imam Ali was also the same; therefore, despite having objections to the mode of electing the Caliph, Imam Ali did not seek caliphate until people appealed to him. Similar to the Holy Prophet who established government with the allegiance of people, an Imam must also wait for public support. That is the

8 *Ibrahim*: 1.
9 *Al-Baqara*: 257.
10 *Velayat-e Faqih: Velayat, Fiqahat va Idalat*; pp. 100–102.

reason for the Holy Prophet to advise Imam as "if you do not have any supporter, stay at home; an Imam has to be like *Ka'aba;* people approach the *Ka'aba*; an Imam does not approach people to request them."[11] Imam Ali states:[12]

أَمَا وَ الَّذِى فَلَقَ الْحَبَّةَ وَ بَرَأَ النَّسَمَةَ لَوْ لَا حُضُورُ الْحَاضِرِ وَ قِيَامُ الْحُجَّةِ بِوُجُودِ النَّاصِرِ وَ مَا أَخَذَ اللَّهُ عَلَى الْعُلَمَاءِ أَلَّا يُقَارُّوا عَلَى كِظَّةِ ظَالِمٍ وَ لَا سَغَبِ مَظْلُومٍ لَأَلْقَيْتُ حَبْلَهَا عَلَى غَارِبِهَا

"Behold, by Him who split the grain (to grow) and created living beings, if people had not approached me, and supporters had not exhausted the argument, and if there had been no pledge of the Almighty with the learned to the effect that they should not acquiesce in the gluttony of the oppressor and the hunger of the oppressed, I would have cast the bridle of Caliphate camel on its own shoulders."

The ruler has responsibilities and obligations for administrating the religious society and his moral and spiritual competence legitimizes his holding of power.

6. Advancement of cultural, ethical, methodical and cognitive qualities are among the principal objectives of the Islamic Government. The most important part of it, however, is augmentation of religious perception and greater utilization of Islamic teachings. The Almighty considers teaching and purification among the main aims of sending prophets.[13] The Holy Prophet advised Ma'adh Bin Jabal before his mission to Yemen:[14] "Teach them the Book of God and rectify their conduct with your decent ethics." Imam Ali has enumerated the rights of people over the ruler as benevolence of the ruler towards the public, complete defrayal of their share from the *Bait Al-Mal*, educating and training them, and alleviating ignorance.[15] The Almighty considers praying, paying of Zakat, and "enjoining the good/right and forbidding the evil/wrong"[16] as the characteristics of the faithful at the time of their domination over the earth.[17]
7. Implementing *Hudud* of God (punishments which under Islamic *Sharia* are mandated and fixed) and reviving the traditions of the Holy Prophet are among the chief intentions of Islamic Government. Imam Ali does not consider acceptance of rulership as an indication of power hunger and acquiring worldly wealth. His Holiness looked at it as restitution of righteousness and spirituality, rectification of the world, protection of the oppressed, and restoration of discontinued *Hudud*.[18]

---

11 *Behar Al-Anvar*; Vol. 93; p. 15 and Vol. 29; p. 419.

12 *Nahj Al-Balaqa*; Sermon 3; p. 50.

13 *Al-e Imran*: 164.

14 Al-Harrani, Abu Mohammad Al-Hassan Bin Ali Bin Al-Hossain Bin Sho'ba; *Tohf Al-Oqul An Al-e Al-Rasul*; p. 25.

15 *Nahj Al-Balaqa*; Sermon 34; p. 79.

16 *Amr bi al-Maruf wa'l-Nahy an al-Munkar.*

17 *Al-Haj*: 41.

18 *Nahj Al-Balaqa*; Sermon 131; p. 189.

3 Ethics and the Economic Obligations of Islamic Government

The Government has certain duties, some of which are manifested with ethics. The ethical obligations of the Government include.

3.1 Economic Justice

Justice is the most ethical obligation of the Government towards society. Imam Ali was once asked about the value of justice and generosity. He replied:[19] "Justice puts every matter in its place and generosity deviates it from its path; Justice is the universal law, but generosity and parsimony are exceptional instances; consequently, justice is superior."

Undoubtedly, one of the most important aims in establishment of government is to provide for economic justice, which cannot be realized in the absence of an administration. Societies that expected justice from the market operations could never perceive it. Expectation of justice without effective functioning of a government is a misapprehension.[20]

Realization of economic justice depends on several issues. Divergence from economic justice depends upon discrimination in utilization of public facilities and natural resources, expansion of poverty, exaggerated prices, and widening of class differences and other issues. Therefore, many methods have been contemplated in Islamic school of thought for realization of economic justice.

3.2 Economic Security

Supporting home ownership and labor, as well as protecting people's assets against contravention and theft are perceptible indications of economic security. For working in an Islamic environment, people must be assured that they can utilize the remainder peacefully and no one may assail their properties if they gain wealth legally, and pay their taxes and social dues. There is no definite limit to the wealth of individuals, and if the Government wants to attain social balance, it must do so through levying appropriate legal taxes and not by arbitrary confiscation.

In a safe and secure society, the offenders of laws are punished and abiding by law is urged. If anyone's rights are violated, he must be compensated. In the epistle to Malik Al-Ashtar, Imam Ali quotes the Holy Prophet as having been heard many times:[21]

19 *Nahj Al-Balaqa*; Hekmat 429.
20 Namazi, Hossein; *Economic Systems*; pp. 104–112.
21 *Nahj Al-Balaqa*; Letter 53; p. 439.

لَنْ تُقَدَّسَ أُمَّةٌ لَايُؤْخَذُ لِلضَّعِيفِ فِيهَا حَقُّهُ مِنَ الْقَوِيِّ غَيْرَ مُتَتَعْتِعٍ

> "A society where the rights of the poor is not reclaimed without stammer from the rich, is not sacred/blessed."

Security of roads for transportation of commodities, security in money market and deterrence of counterfeit banknotes and forged coinage, and bogus/fake documents are among the essential concerns of any society. Ibn Khaldun reiterates:[22]

> "If the ruler is sympathetic, people will work extensively for the prosperity of their society; but if the properties of people are aggressed, their motivation is devastated, the markets will recede, the prosperity of cities will reduce, the economic activists will abandon the region, cities will be ruined, and this will propagate to the Government."

3.3 Public Welfare and Economic Development

Benefitting from greater divine endowments, providing welfare and comfort, and producing higher economic growth and development can stand among other objectives of Government decision- and policy-makings. Early in its history, the Islamic society improved the livelihood of its members day-after-day. Whatever amount was added to Bait Al-Mal, was divided among the members of society. Basically, governments cannot survive without high revenue, ample investments and actualization of public welfare. Possession of sufficient defensive power to disappoint enemies of invasion of the country, earning great tax revenues to distribute among the needy and achieve economic justice, expansion of infrastructural facilities, research, science and technology are all considered as the objectives of establishing a government. However, they cannot be achieved without economic development, improved public welfare and increased public income.

4 Ethics and Appointment of Islamic Government Authorities

Among the ethical issues addressed in Islam is the morality of selecting good leaders and administrators. An individual appointed to any position must have both appropriate expertise and moral character. An ineligible and impious administrator will not invite people to devoutness. The following criteria must be kept in mind in selecting government authorities.

22 Ibn Khaldun, Abd Al-Rahman; *Introduction*; pp. 286–287.

1. In view of the religion, rulership of a society requires knowledgableness, capableness, piousness and justness/fairness. Loss of justice and piety will cause the dispossession of the status of rulership. Durability of the conditions is an irremissible principle.[23]
2. Government executives must be selected from among experienced individuals of noble families who are famous for their munificent morality, generosity/cordiality and providence.[24]
3. Judges must be chosen from the finest people who are not prone to obstinacy and error, and aspire righteousness and trueness, so as to perpetuate justice.[25]
4. Advisers should possess bravery, sublimity, piety and austerity, lest they dissuade authorities from attempting to help people.[26]
5. The ministers and consultants of the ruler must be reputable, and have not helped the oppressors. The best of them speaks the truth (although it might be bitter), is honest, pious, and far from cajolery.[27]
6. Military commanders must be compassionate to religion, country and the regime. They must be chaste, tolerant, charitable, powerful in executing their duties, and away from frailty. They should treat soldiers equitably, provide them with their needs, and alleviate their financial difficulties.[28]
7. In collecting taxes, government authorities must observe virtuousness and honesty. They must not charge people excessively, and must be lenient during hardships. They should not take public assets for their personal use. Tax revenues should be entrusted to benevolent fiduciaries who always consider the Almighty and fear the afterlife consequences of their deeds, hence never transgress/commit sins.[29]
8. The bureaucratic system of the state must employ eligible, wise, intelligent, capable and trustworthy individuals.[30]
9. Individuals who betray public properties, are ignorant, jealous, miserly, cruel or bribable must not be appointed in administrative berths.[31]
10. Overseers ought to be appointed to monitor administrators and report their performance to the ruler. This will enable the ruler to acknowledge the errors and drawbacks of the system, and rectify them.[32]

---

23 *Nahj Al-Balaqa*; pp. 247, 248 and 189; *Al-Hayat*; Vol. 2; p. 267.
24 *Nahj Al-Balaqa*; p. 435.
25 *Nahj Al-Balaqa* pp. 434 and 435.
26 *Nahj Al-Balaqa* p. 430.
27 *i Nahj Al-Balaqa*.
28 *i Nahj Al-Balaqa*. pp. 432 and 433.
29 *Nahj Al-Balaqa* pp. 380–383 and 436.
30 *Nahj Al-Balaqa*. p. 437.
31 *ibid*. pp. 430, 189, 462, 412 and 366; Al-Reyshahri, Mohammad; *Movasa'a Al-Imam Ali-ibn-Abitaleb fi Al-Kitab va Al-Sona' va Al-Tarikh*; Vol. 4; pp. 135–137.
32 *Movasa'a Al-Imam Ali-ibn-Abitaleb fi Al-Kitab va Al-Sona' va Al-Tarikh*; Vol. 4; p. 139.

11. Government authorities must avoid totalitarianism and treat people fairly. People must be able to approach them effortlessly. Various affairs must be conveyed to the public. Authorities should act as serving and caring fathers to the public, consider the concerns and difficulties of the society as their own, and try to resolve them.[33]

5 Ethics and the Decision-Making Criteria of Islamic Government

Taking into account the above-mentioned criteria for selecting government authorities, if all the criteria are observed, the religious faith and belief is strengthened. The chief administrators of the society themselves will abide by religious regulations and confines. Under such circumstances the decision-makings will be carried out on the bases of following criteria, which have been extracted from religious documents.

1. **Principle of Public Expediency**: Government decision-making is based on recognition of public expediency. National and public interests form the foundations of the determinations.
2. **Principle of Unworldliness**: The decision-making process of the Government must lead to enhancement of spiritual affairs and must not contradict them.
3. **Principle of Public Compassion**: The relation between the Government and its people is that of serving and not hectoring. The ruler must act as a kind patron and his administrators are representatives/attorneys of the public who should act for the reasonable and conventional interests of the people. Government/public assets must be utilized for the welfare and comfort of the society.
4. **Principle of Trust**: The public and the private sectors are not competitors, but the environment must be such that they trust and help each other so as to assure public interests.
5. **Principle of Saving and Optimal Utilization of Resources**: Using public assets must be with extreme cautious so as to avoid squander and profligacy. Public resources must be utilized in quantities that just satisfy the requirements. Imam Ali advises his administrators:[34]

أدِقُّوا أقْلَامَكُمْ- وَ قَارِبُوا بَيْنَ سُطُورِكُمْ- وَ احْذِفُوا عَنِّي فُضُولَكُمْ وَ اقْصِدُوا قَصْدَ الْمَعَانِي- وَ إِيَّاكُمْ وَ الْإِكْثَارَ- فَإِنَّ أَمْوَالَ الْمُسْلِمِينَ لَا تَحْتَمِلُ الْإِضْرَارَ

"Reduce the line spacing in your letters, confine to necessary subjects, and avoid oversize writing which wastes paper; because the properties of Muslims cannot tolerate losses."

33 *Nahj Al-Balaqa*; Letter 53; pp. 439–442.
34 *Vasayel Al-Shia*; Vol. 12; p. 299.

He commands his secretary Obaidollah Bin Abi Rafe’ to write calligraphically:[35]

أَلِقْ دَوَاتَکَ وَ أَطِلْ جِلْفَةَ قَلَمِکَ وَ فَرِّجْ بَیْنَ السُّطُورِ وَ قَرْمِطْ بَیْنَ الْحُرُوفِ فَإِنَّ ذَلِکَ أَجْدَرُ بِصَبَاحَةِ الْخَطِّ

“Put cotton fibers in the inkpot, take a long writing quill pen, space the lines appropriately, and write the alphabets closely; these will make your inscription look attractive.”

Thus, in addition to the importance of writing letters in a manner to be readable by others, there is an insistence on proper utilization of public properties (Bait Al-Mal).

6. **Principle of Transparency in Decision-making and Legislation**: Excepting the security issues where the public interest demands secrecy, all that the Government intends to domust be notified to the public accurately and openly, so as to determine the responsibilities of every individual. Regulations should be legislated such that to prevent committing offences. People must not be forced to violate the law. And the law has to be precise enough to allow swift understanding, else it would lead to a kind of profligacy.

6 Ethics and Revenue Collection by Islamic Government

6.1 Ethical Objectives of *Zakat*

The intentions underlying *Zakat* in the Islamic System can be acknowledged either from the reiterations in religious literature or the blessings that accompany this command. The following are excerpts of the said literature, some being solely ethical in scope.

a. **Supplying the needs of the poor**: Existence of the poor, the desperate and the insolvent as well as other requirements of the society constitute the basic foundations for the statute of *Zakat*. The Almighty has anticipated that such requirements be supplied through the surplus income of the rich. The amount of *Zakat* has been determined so as to satisfy the needs of the society. Imam Reza remarked: “The intentions behind *Zakat* has been providing the livelihood of the needy and conserving the affluence of the rich.” Another Hadith from Imam Sadeq states: “*Zakat* has been designed for trialing the rich and helping the poor.” He further expressed: “God, the Almighty and the Merciful, has considered a share of the properties of the rich for the poor to satisfy their needs. If this share were not

35 *Nahj Al-Balaqa*; Hekmat 315; p. 530.

sufficient, He would have undoubtedly increased it. The impoverishment of the needy, is due to betrayal of the rich in not contributing their *Zakat*."[36]

b. **Conservation and Consecration of Property**: Numerous anecdotes/apothegms (*Ravayat*) assert that defrayal of *Zakat* results in protection of property from deterioration or diminution. In a way, *Zakat* is considered as an insurance for the property. Holy Prophet stated: "Conserve your property with *Zakat*." Imam Sadeq reiterated: "No property on land or in oceans is destructed, unless due to non-payment of *Zakat*; therefore, conserve your property with *Zakat*." Imam Reza disclosed: "When Zakat is not paid, the livestock perish."[37] The appearance of these anecdotes/apothegms (*Ravayat*) indicate that conservation of property through the defrayal of *Zakat* has unworldly causes not revealed to human beings.

   In addition to conserving property, *Zakat* causes the growth of assets as well. Holy Prophet expressed: "If you desire God to increase your assets, pay the conceived*Zakat*." Imam Baqer stated: "*Zakat* raises the livelihood." Imam Sadeq told Mafzal: "Convey to the companions to pay *Zakat* to the needy, and I guarantee the return of what they relinquish."[38] The reason for blessing of the assets by paying Zakat is also unworldly, and the Almighty blesses the livelihood of individuals. By defrayal of Zakat and supplying the needs of the deprived, their purchasing power increases. This leads to enhanced consumption, which in turn, will result in production boom and economic growth. The fruits of such boom and growth are greater income for the owners of capital.[39]

c. **Social Balance**: Among the important objectives of Islamic taxation (including Zakat) is social balance and reducing the income gap between different social classes.[40]

d. **Purification and Edification of Soul**: The Almighty intends to purify the body and soul of the faithful through payment of Zakat, and to relieve him from the obscure dependence and lure to the world, even for a moment. Holy Qur'an states:[41]

   خُذْ مِنْ أَمْوَالِهِمْ صَدَقَةً تُطَهِّرُهُمْ وَتُزَكِّيهِمْ بِهَا وَصَلِّ عَلَيْهِمْ إِنَّ صَلَاتَكَ سَكَنٌ لَهُمْ وَاللَّهُ سَمِيعٌ عَلِيمٌ

   Accept alms out of their property; you would cleanse them and purify them by means of it. Pray for them; your will surely mean relief for them; and God is Alert, Aware.

   In addition to its worldly impacts, Zakat strengthens the spirit of faith and saves the faithful from worldly impurities and lures. Those who do not pay Zakat deprive themselves from perfection, sow the seeds of stinginess and greed in their selves, and prepare the ground for pride and arrogance against the commands of the Almighty.

---

36 *Vasayel Al-Shia*; Vol. 6; pp. 4–6; B 1; *Min Abvab Ma' Tojeb Fihe Al-Zakat*; H. 6, 7 and 9.
37 *Vasayel Al-Shia*; Vol. 6; p. 6.
38 *Mizan Al-Hekmat*; Chapter 1578.
39 *Principles of Islamic Economy*; p. 355.
40 *Eqtesadona*; pp. 676–680.
41 *Al-Toba*; 103.

6.2 Ethical Utilization of *Zakat*

In accordance with the following noble verse in Holy Qur'an, Zakat can be allocated for eight different purposes, most of which are ethical in nature.:[42]

إِنَّمَا الصَّدَقَاتُ لِلْفُقَرَاءِ وَالْمَسَاكِينِ وَالْعَامِلِينَ عَلَيْهَا وَالْمُؤَلَّفَةِ قُلُوبُهُمْ وَفِي الرِّقَابِ وَالْغَارِمِينَ وَفِي سَبِيلِ اللَّهِ وَابْنِ السَّبِيلِ فَرِيضَةً مِنَ اللَّهِ وَاللَّهُ عَلِيمٌ حَكِيمٌ

Alms are (meant)only for the poor, the needy, the officials working at (collecting and distributing) it, those (possible converts) whose hearts are being reconciled (to truth), for freeing (ransoming of) captives and debtors, and in (striving along) God's sake/cause, and for the wayfarer, as a duty imposed by God. God is Aware, Wise.

1. **The Poor and the Underprivileged**: are those who do not have enough annual income to cover the expenses of an appropriate livelihood for themselves and their dependents. Therefore, if an individual has a job that sustains the livelihood of him and his dependents according to his social status, he is not considered among the poor or the underprivileged.[43] Those who practically do not work, in spite of availability of suitable jobs for them, are not poor. However, those who do not find the appropriate opportunity despite delirious job hunting can avail of Zakat. In addition, during the training for a job, the individual can benefit from Zakat.[44]
2. **Those Whose Hearts Are Being Reconciled**: are the pagans (*Kafir*) who appeased for joining *Jihad* or converting to Islam, as well as the punic Muslims; they get a share of Zakat for greater reconciliation with Islamic faith.
3. **Liberating the Slaves**: is another predicted utilization of Zakat for slaves who are unable to pay the dues for liberating themselves, or those who are suffering, or even the slaves who are not at hardship.[45] This kind of allocation is obsolete today unless its meaning is expanded to encompass modern day subordination and despotism. Using Zakat for alleviation of cruelty can also be considered as "for God's sake/cause" discussed hereunder.
4. **Debtors**: are those who cannot pay back their liabilities, in spite of having enough money to cover their annual living expenses. Such debts must not have felonious or sinfulorigins. That is, the amount/assets they owe should not have been spent for immorality or misdemeanor, or in a squandered manner. The liability might have arisen due to debt, installment purchase, guaranteeing of destroyed assets, alimony (*Mahriye*) etc.
5. **Sake of God**: There is a difference in interpreting "God's Sake/Cause." Sunni Muslims generally attribute it to *Jihad* for God's Sake, while Shia consider it for all

42 *Al-Toba*; 60.
43 *Tahrir Al-Vasileh*; Vol. 1; p. 334.
44 *Tahrir-Al-Vasileh*; Vol. 1; p. 334.
45 *Tahrir-Al-Vasileh*; Vol. 1. p. 337.

kinds of public charity including the construction of bridges, schools, mosques and roads, repulsing sedition and corruption from Islamic territory, and whatever helps in maintaining *Sharia*. All types of benefaction that serve the general public are conceived as "for God's Sake/Cause." Nonetheless, *Jihad* for the cause of God is one the most important instances as mentioned in the writings of many Shia scholars, but is not the sole option. It includes all the measures demanded for the interest of Islam and Muslims, whether *Jihad* and defense, or civil, economic, educational and cultural matters. "God's Sake/Cause" refers to whatever acts in society that satisfies God.

Nevertheless, in the phrases of some jurisprudents "public expediency" is restricted to spiritual affairs, e.g. Jihad, Haj, constructing mosques and religious centers, publishing religious texts/books, constructing seminaries, confronting cultural invasion etc. Thus, civil constructions are not included. Still other jurisprudents, e.g. Sahib Jawaher, are of the opinion that "God's Sake/Cause" encompasses all benevolences and any minor benefaction for the public.Accordingly, all kinds of expenditures from Zakat, including helping the poor and the underprivileged, liberating of slaves etc., are possible. But the interpretation for "general public interests" has greater support among scholars.[46]

6. **Wayfarers:** are those travelers who have stayed put in their journeys due to penuriousness and cannot move any further. Spending Zakat for wayfarers is in fact a kind of insurance which is paid from Bait Al-Mal to those stranded. The purpose of the journey should not be sinful, otherwise no assistance is provided.

6.3 Method of *Zakat* Collection in Islamic Jurisprudence

a. Criteria for Zakat Collectors:

Certain characteristics for Zakat collecting officers are mentioned in anecdotes/apothegms (*Ravayat*) which have been considered in various jurisprudential writings. In addition to general characteristics such as wisdom, maturity and believing in Islam, other criteria including faith, justice, discretion, not being a descendant of Prophet, and awareness about different issues in collecting Zakat, which have been cited in jurisprudential literature.

It is stated in anecdotes/apothegms (*Ravayat*) that Imam Ali issued many orders to the officials in-charge of Zakat collection and advised them about various delicate issues. For example, Letter 25 of Nahj Al-Balaqa states:[47]

---

46 *Tahrir Al-Vasileh*; Vol. 1; p. 338; *Kitab Al-Zakat*; Vol. 3; pp. 108–127.

47 *Nahj Al-Balaqa*; translated by Seyyed Jafar Shahidi; p. 287.

> "When you dispatch the properties of Muslims with someone, make sure that he is a faithful believer who delivers it entirely to the Islamic Ruler, and allows him (the Ruler) so that it may be distributed equitably among the entitled individuals; do not choose anyone except you are sure about his fairness and honesty, so he would not behave maliciously or cause damage; (the officer) must neither harass them nor exhaust them during the transit. Send us immediately whatever has been collected to allow timely distribution among the needy, as God has commanded. Advise the trustworthy person who is bringing it to us, not to separate a she-camel from its young; not to milk the she-camel too much to starve its young; not to ride the she-camel harshly to exhaust her; to establish justice between the camels; to leave the exhausted camel to rest and recover. Tell him to stop at water ponds and do not divert them from oases (where the camel graze and rest) towards dug-well in deserts; to leave them on their own to quench their thirst and hunger, and reach us fleshy and plump by the will of God, not exhausted and lean. Only then we can distribute them in accordance with the Book of God and the tradition of Holy Prophet. This will increase your reward before God much more and brings you nearer to salvation/redemption; if God wills."

On the basis of the above-mentioned letter and Letter 26 of Nahj Al-Balaqa, as well as other recommendations of religious leaders, the Zakat collecting officials must have the following characteristics:
1. Must be trustworthy of their honesty, be faithful and god-fearing (devout), abstain from sins, be reliable and just, and avoid cheating.
2. Must be caring of Muslims' assets. Should always be thoughtful about safeguarding Bait Al-Mal, protect the collected Zakat, and deliver it secured and intact to the treasury. Must be tolerant and precise, and act with no coercion. Must observe benevolence and fairness. If Zakat consists of livestock, must not endanger the safety of the animal and provide them with sufficient fodder, water and rest period, and prevent them from losing weight or ailment on way to Government headquarters.

The first criterion points to spiritual obligation and trustworthiness of the official. While the second is indicative of his wisdom in conserving Bait Al-Mal, expertise in transfer of assets to the government treasury, and prevention of its wastage or damage. Of course, possession of these characters is not limited to Zakat officials, but anyone who deals with Bait Al-Mal must be trustworthy and committed. The officials must have an appropriate knowledge about preserving Bait Al-Mal, else they would act either like a thief who has a torch, or a visually impaired person who falls in a deep well. Both will damage Bait Al-Mal.

b. Attitude of Officials towards Zakat Payers:

The manner and attitude of officials in encountering public is an important and sensitive issue. Perhaps appropriate conduct of an official will result in collection of greater amount of Zakat with people handing over the requested amounts satisfactorily. On the contrary, harsh and impolite behaviorby the official leads to non-cooperation of public and reduced amount of Zakat. Imam Ali has many excellent pieces of advice for Zakat and *Kharaj* (tribute) officials. The initial part of Letter 25 of Nahj Al-Balaqa is reproduced hereunder for the purpose of guidance of the Zakat collecting officials:

> "Do not give up fearing of God who is unique. Do not frighten any Muslim! Do not approach them in case they do not invite you! Do not tax them more than what is actually due from them to God! When you reach a tribe, to assess a tax on them, then stay only at their watering-place (a well or water-hole) and do not enter their houses. Then go to them maintaining your dignity and prestige and when you are in their midst, wish them peace and blessings of God and do not hesitate to respect them. Tell them that the Islamic Rulerhas sent you to collect from them their dues to God. Ask them whether they possess enough to pay the dues of God that you may gather them and pass them on to the Ruler. If somebody answered you negatively, then do not worry him and accept his plea. If someone answered positively, then go with him,without frightening him or making him nervous; do not behave with them with undue harshness. Then accept the gold or silver which he offers. If he has livestock (cows, sheep and camels) then do not enter the herd without his permission because most of it belongs to him. If you have to enter the herd then do not enter like the one who has conquered and has takenthe possession of cattle, or as if you want to hurt them. Do not frighten the cattle so as to make them disperse. Do not treat the owner harshly for taking the dues to God. Then divide the herd into two parts and allow the owner to select the one for himself. If he selects one part for keeping himself, then do not object to it. Again divide the part which he has left for the share of Zakat to be selected into two parts, and once again allow him to select the lot which he wants to retain for himself. Never object to his selection. Continue in this way until you arrive at the lot which constitutes the share of God (Zakat) then take possession of it. Even if, in spite of all these precautions, he thinks the division was unfair and unjust, then mix the whole lot and go through the process once again. Remember not to accept old and diseased camels or such that their limbs are damaged."[48]

A number of fundamental principles lie in the context of the letter:

1. Public servants should treat the public with kindness. No entry is allowed into the property of others without their permission.
2. It warns that Zakat is a kind of worship, and that it is God's share of people's property. One of the conditions of defraying Zakat is that the person intends to get closer to God; thus paying Zakat is considered worship.[49]
3. The precept of trusting the people is one of the most important ethical commands which should govern the relationship between the Government and the public. The officials must have confidence in the deeds and the words of the people. Islam rests its arguments on the basis of righteousness and truthfulness of people. Officials must behave so as to induce a sense of assurance among people that their words are accepted People must feel that Zakat is a form of worship and its non-payment is a loss of faith. Only then will people tell the truth about their wealth and pay their dues accordingly, just as many present day believers pay their Zakat and Khums voluntarily. Nonetheless, some wealthy people will intend

48 *Nahj Al-Balaqa*; translated by Seyyed Jafar Shahidi; pp. 278–287.
49 Tahrir Al-Vasileh; Vol. 1; p. 341.

to bypass Zakat payment by abusing the Government's trust. Thus the Government is bound to protect the Bait Al-Mal and precisely monitor the situation to prevent manipulation. In addition, it should be made clear that if a person is obliged to pay Zakat and refrains from contributing, the Government can claim it forcefully. This is also mentioned in jurisprudential writings that the Islamic Ruler can wage a war on those who refuse to pay their Zakat dues, in order to force them to obey the command of God.[50] The initial intention of Islam is that people pay their Zakat voluntarily, so that they also benefit from the spiritual reward of that deed. For the method of dividing the property between the owner and the Government, the conditions of the possessor must be taken into account to satisfy him. But the share of the Government cannot be given from the defective portion of the commodity or the unhealthy livestock, mainly because the right of God and the deprived has to be retained likewise.

6.4 Mandates/Obligations of the Muslim Ruler about *Kharaj* (Tribute/Land Revenues)

Islamic Leader (Imam) or Ruler can remit the tributes of some territories, either fully or partly, based on the interests of the public, because receiving tribute or territorial tax must be of benefit to the country. If payment of tribute puts people out of agricultural occupation, and make them work in unproductive businesses, then the country is weakened in food production, and would be forced to import agricultural commodities. Thus, establishing tributes would damage the economy of the Islamic country. After appointing Malik Al-Ashtar as the Governor of Egypt, Imam Ali writes to him:[51]

> "And for collection of Kharaj (tribute/land revenues), you must always keep in view the welfare of the taxpayers which is of greater importance than the taxes themselves; and nothing will be organized if their livelihood in not coordinated; because people are the targets of all Government expenditures, and the State really lives upon the revenues collected from the tax-payers; therefore, more importance should be attached to the fertility of land than to the collection of taxes, because actual taxable capacity of people rests upon the fertility of the land; the ruler, who does not pay attention to the prosperity of his subjects and fertility of the land but concentrates only on collection of revenues, lays waste the land and consequently ruins the State and brings destruction to the creatures of God; his rule cannot last for long. If the tax-payers complain to you of the heavy taxes, of any accidental calamity, of the vagaries of the rain falls, of the recession of the means of irrigation, of floods or destruction of their crops on account of excessive rainfall, and if their complaints are true, then reduce their taxes accordingly; decrease in State revenue due to such reasons should not depress you, because they can enhance their livelihood, save more and return it to the State in the shape of the prosperity of its cities and improvement of the

50 *Jawaher Al-Kalam*; Vol. 15; p. 13.

51 *Nahj Al-Balaqa*; translated by Seyyed Jafar Shahidi; Letter 53; pp. 333 and 334.

> country at large. At the same time you will be in a position to command and secure their love, respect and praises along with the revenues...."

Therefore, the Islamic Ruler must conceive justice, humanitarian and Islamic ethics in collecting *Kharaj* (tribute/land revenue). While Imam Ali had strictly ordered his governors to collect the defined tributes/land revenues from people, he had also instructed them to:[52]

> "Treat the people (tax-payers) with equity and justice and think about their wishes with patience and kindness, because you are the treasurer of the subjects, representative of the people and the officer on behalf of higher authority. Do not forceanybody to forsake his requirements and to do without his necessities (so that he may pay the taxes). In collection of taxes and revenues do not sell their winter and summer clothing, their slaves or such of their livestock as are of service to them.Do not resort to whipping, do not touch their property...."

In assessing *Kharaj* (tribute/land revenues) and method of collecting it, the prevailing circumstances over the farmers and producers must always be born in mind. Imam Ali ordered Malik to restrain from concentrating mainly on collection of land revenues and taxes, but keep in view the main objective of tax collection in his decision-making process i.e. prosperity of the State and welfare of the people (the taxpayers). When the conditions of agricultural production is not desirable, and drought, pests, tainted seeds have hindered the output of land, and people are experiencing hardship, the amount of taxes must be reduced. This will allow faster recovery, amelioration of the livelihood of people, and booming of economy and must continue till the circumstances for payment of taxes are restored.[53] Therefore, the method of collecting *Kharaj* (tribute/land revenues) must not hinder economic growth, diminish production incentives, and investment of capital. Appropriate concessions must be provided at the time of recession to allow people gain strength and have greater propensity for payment of it in the following years.[54] The amount of *Kharaj* must be in accordance with the financial ability of the tax-payer. No harsh or cruel act must be used and people should not be forced to sell their belongings and properties for paying their dues.[55] The Government, under special circumstances, can abstain from collecting Kharaj and relieve the problems of producers by exempting them from paying taxes.

---

52 *Nahj Al-Balaqa*; translated by Seyyed Jafar Shahidi Letter 51; p. 324; also see *Darasat fi Velayat-e Al-Faqih va Feqh Al-Dolat Al-Islamiyeh*; Vol. 3; pp. 501 and 502 and *Vasayel Al-Shia*; Vol. 11; p. 85.

53 *Nahj Al-Balaqa*; Letter 53; p. 436.

54 *The Government and Economic Policies*; p. 370.

55 *Bait Al-Mal*; p. 408.

6.5 *Jizyah* (Compensations from Non-Muslims)

The specific tax collected from non-Muslim (People of the Book i.e. monotheists consisting of Jews, Christians and Zoroastrians) residing in Islamic territories is called *Jizyah*. The Islamic State receives this kind of tax as a compensation for protecting the lives and properties of non-Muslims, instead of the usual Islamic taxes such as *Zakat*, *Khums*, *Kharaj* and any other dues that are collected from Muslims. By accepting the rule of Islam and availing of support by the Islamic Government, "People of the Book" who comprise Jews, Christians and Zoroastrians must pay their share of the expenditures that the Government bears for social and security purposes. Therefore, they pay *Jizyah* in place of *Zakat* and *Kharaj*.[56]

Jizyah can be calculated as a per capita annual tax for each adult *Dhimmi* (non-Muslimsliving in an Islamic State with legal protection) man, or can be in the form of land tax. Thus, during the times of peace, the land remains in the ownership of non-Muslims and they hand over a part of their produce as compensation (*Jizyah*).[57] Women, children, the insane and the poor are exempted from *Jizyah*.[58]

"People of the Book" are not required to pay *Zakat* and other Islamic taxes, and if they convert to Islam, they will be exempted from *Jizyah*, but are obligated to pay *Zakat*. Through defrayal of *Jizyah*, "People of the Book" also become exempted from participating in wars with enemies, and the Government takes up the responsibility of protecting their lives and belongings. In Early Islamic Era, if "People of the Book" volunteered for participation in wars, or in case the State could not protect them under the prevailing circumstance, their *Jizyah* was paid back to them. In the treaty between Holy Prophet and the citizens of Najran, it is stated:[59]

> "... the properties of the citizens of Najran and surrounding areas, their lives, their religion and their houses of worship, their residing and non-residing relatives and kin, and whatever they own, whether small or large, are under the protection of God and his messenger Prophet Mohammad ... They will not be sent to fight the enemies of Islam, and are not obliged to pay one-tenth of their assets as compensation."

Historical scripts show that when Heraclius, the Emperor of Byzantine, was readying for battle against Muslims, and the news of his preparation for campaign and the Battle of Yarmouk spread, Muslims returned all the sums collected from Jizyah and *Kharaj* and told their subjects that they were unable to protect and defend them, so they returned the enormous sums to Christians. The people replied:[60] "Your rule

56 *Darasat fi Velayat-e Al-Faqih va Feqh Al-Dolat Al-Islamiyeh*; Vol. 3; p. 373.
57 *Darasat fi Velayat-e Al-Faqih va Feqh Al-Dolat Al-Islamiyeh*; pp. 363 and 433–437.
58 *Darasat fi Velayat-e Al-Faqih va Feqh Al-Dolat Al-Islamiyeh*; pp. 419 and 424.
59 Hamidullah, Mohammad; *Letters and Political Treaties of Prophet Mohammad and the Documents of Early Islamic Era*; Translated by Hosseini; p. 229.
60 *Fotouh Al-Baldan*; p. 187; *Kitab Al-Kharaj*; p. 139.

and fairness is more important to us than the conditions we were living under previously; may God give you rule over us again and make you victorious over the Romans."

7 Ethical Principles Governing Allocation of Bait Al-Malin Islamic States

Certain rationales must be observed while allocating public properties, in order to conform to Islamic objectives. They include.

7.1 Viewing Public Properties (Bait Al-Mal) as Trusts

Public properties are entrusted to the Islamic Ruler. They belong to the Almighty and must be utilized for the benefit of the people. The Ruler is obliged to preserve them in the best possible way and utilize them for those who deserve it. Therefore, the Ruler is a trustee/custodian and improper expenditure is considered as defalcation, or the least, it requires guaranteed compensation. Imam Ali replied Abdollah Bin Zam'a, one of his companions, when he asked for a property:[61]

> إِنَّ هَذَا اَلْمَالَ لَيْسَ لِي وَ لاَ لَكَ وَ إِنَّمَا هُوَ فَيْءٌلِلْمُسْلِمِينَوَ جَلْبُ أَسْيَافِهِمْ فَإِنْ شَرِكْتَهُمْ فِي حَرْبِهِمْ كَانَ لَكَ مِثْلُ حَظِّهِمْ وَ إِلاَّ فَجَنَاةُ أَيْدِيهِمْ لاَ تَكُونُ لِغَيْرِ أَفْوَاهِهِمْ

> "This property neither belongs to me nor to you, but is Fai of Muslims and the result of their bravery in war; if you have participated in Jihad along with them, you will get an equal share as theirs, and if you have not, then the remunerations cannot be allotted to you."

At the time of request by Aqil, Imam stated: "Many a times Aqil requested me to give him some wheat from public storehouse, and thought that I would trade my faith; I heated a piece of iron and neared it to his body so that he should realize the punishment of God." Such an act indicates that Imam Ali considered inappropriate distribution of Bait Al-Mal as a cruelty to the public and punishable by hellfire. He further adds: "If the seven heavens and whatever exists below it are given to me, I would never ever agree to take away a barley-husk from an ant who carries it."[62] When his holiness was being blamed for equal division of Bait Al-Mal among people, he stated:[63]

61 *Nahj Al-Balaqa*; Sermons 232 and 353.
62 *Nahj Al-Balaqa;* Sermons 224; p. 346.
63 *Nahj Al-Balaqa.*; Sermons 126; p. 183.

لَوْ كَانَ اَلْمَالُ لِي لَسَوَّيْتُ بَيْنَهُمْ فَكَيْفَ وَ إِنَّمَا اَلْمَالُ مَالُ اَللَّهِ

> "If what I am to distribute was my own personal property, then also I would have distributed it equally among people; leave apart Bait Al-Mal which belongs to the Almighty."

Imam Ali calls the collectors of *Kharaj* as the treasurers and trustees of the peasants and representatives and ambassadors of the nation and state. He advises them to "treat people with justice and fairness; consider people's demands and be tolerant; satisfy their needs patiently."[64]

فَأَنْصِفُوا اَلنَّاسَ مِنْ أَنْفُسِكُمْ وَ اِصْبِرُوا لِحَوَائِجِهِمْ فَإِنَّكُمْ خُزَّانُ اَلرَّعِيَّةِ وَ وُكَلاَءُ اَلْأُمَّةِ

> "Treat the people (tax-payers) with equity and justice and think about their requests with patience and kindness, because you are the treasurer of the subjects, representative of the people, and the officer on behalf of higher authority."

7.2 Public Utilization of Bait Al-Mal

Bait Al-Mal must be allocated to each and every member of society, and all people are equal in utilizing it. In Early Islamic Era, after using Bait Al-Mal for definite purposes, the remaining amount was distributed equally among the people. The policy of the Holy Prophet was to distribute it equally among Muslims, not differentiating between early Muslims and new converts. This method continued even after the Holy Prophet, until the reign of the Second Caliph who changed the system and discriminated Muslims based on their precedence in converting and intimacy to the Holy Prophet. Imam Ali revived equal distribution of Bait Al-Mal and insisted on it. An Arab woman and a newly liberated woman went to Imam Ali to receive their share of Bait Al-Mal; his Holiness gave each of them a few dirhams and a quintal of wheat. The Arab woman objected: "Do I have to get equal to a non-Arab?" His Holiness replied: "I searched the Book of God and didn't find any mention about the difference between the offsprings of Ismail and Isaac."[65]

In early days of his rule, Imam Ali described the method of the Holy Prophet in distributing Bait Al-Mal for the people. He announced that it belonged to all Muslims and no one had any preeminence or advantage over the others. Then he ordered his treasurer Obaidollah Bin Abi Arfa' to give three dinars to each of Muhajirin (Emigrants), Ansar (Helpers) and others, and as a result a liberated slave and a Quraish Arab received equally. A number of the elite dissented and waged war on him.[66]

---

64 *Nahj Al-Balaqa.*; Letter 51; p. 425.

65 *Al-Sonan Al-Kobra*; Vol. 6; p. 349.

66 *Explanation of Nahj Al-Balaqa*; Vol. 7; pp. 37 and 38.

7.3 Distribution of Bait Al-Mal at its Collectorate

Bait Al-Mal must primarily be utilized for the benefit of the region from which it was collected, and its excess can be transferred to the Central Government. This will lead to a positive view about the utilization of Bait Al-Mal on part of the public, assuring them about appropriate disbursement of the collected taxes and duties from their territory. In a letter to Qutham Bin Abbas, the Governor of Mecca, Imam Ali writes:[67]

وَ أُنظُرْ إِلَى مَا اِجْتَمَعَ عِنْدَكَ مِنْ مَالِ اَللَّهِ فَاصْرِفْهُ إِلَى مَنْ قِبَلَكَ مِنْ ذَوِي اَلْعِيَالِ وَ اَلْمَجَاعَةِ مُصِيباً بِهِ مَوَاضِعَ اَلْفَاقَةِ وَ اَلْخَلاَّتِ وَ مَا فَضَلَ عَنْ ذَلِكَ فَاحْمِلْهُ إِلَيْنَا لِنَقْسِمَهُ فِيمَنْ قِبَلَنَا

> "Look carefully after the properties of God which have been accumulated in Public Treasury. Spend its money on the poor people of your territory; and send to us (the centre) the surplus amount left over after such expenditure, for distribution among the poor throughout the State."

The Holy Prophet used to distribute the Zakat collected from bedouins and city-dwellers among themselves, respectively.[68]

The Prophet Mohammad commanded Mo'adh Bin Jabal and other Zakat collectors to receive Zakat from the rich and distribute it among the poor in the same territory.[69] The important point is that whatever Bait Al-Mal is expended within the territory, must be contributed through the Zakat on the revenues of the people. Other revenues from *Fai* (booty from enemy obtained without fighting) and *Anfal* (spoils of war and booties), which are originally utilized to cover the expenses of administrating the State and other general demands, are to be thought of in accordance with the public interests. Although regional growth and development and delivering basic requirements and priorities of the territory are also considered as public interests, but they come next to those of the overall Islamic State. For example, if there are abundant streams or other water resources in a region, supplying water to various parts of that region have priority, although water is considered as *Anfal* and belongs to the Islamic State. Allocation of public properties in any region is subject to "Principle of Public Expediency." Under certain conditions, however, public interest might dictate that the properties and assets collected in one region of the Islamic State be transferred to some other parts, in order to protect the sovereignty and alleviate poverty.[70]

---

67 *Nahj Al-Balaqa*; Letter 67; pp. 457 and 458.

68 *Vasayel Al-Shia*; Vol. 6; pp. 184–197.

69 *Al-Sonan Al-Kobra*; Vol. 7; pp. 8 and 9.

70 See *Scientific Perspectives of Expenses and Revenues in Islamic States*; pp. 165–167.

7.4 Priority of the Poor and Equity/Parity of Allotments

Impartiality is the rule in all decision-makings about allocation of Bait Al-Mal. Distribution of public facilities must provide for and should guarantee impartiality.

Alleviation of the ominous shadow of poverty is one the most important strategies in establishment of economic justice. Poverty is so devastating for the individuals and the society that Holy Prophet considers it as equivalent to atheism:[71]

كادَ الْفَقْرُ أَنْ يَكُونَ كُفْراً

Supplying the needs of the poor includes all the citizens of a country and is not limited to Muslims. While passing Kufa, Imam Ali saw a beggar who asked for help. His Holiness asked who he was, to which the companions replied: "He is a non-Muslim." He said: "You benefitted from his services until he grew old, weak and needy; now you do not sustain him! Provide him from Bait Al-Mal."[72]

In his treasured epistle to Malik Al-Ashtar, Imam Ali describes the important duties of the Islamic Ruler towards the poor and alleviation of poverty and sorrow from the miserable. He explains that the Almighty would not excuse the ruler for incapability in satisfying the needs of the poor from the Bait Al-Mal. His Holiness enumerates seven different social classes: 1. soldiers and army personnel; 2. administrators; 3. judges; 4. government officials; 5. *Jizyah*- and *Kharaj*-payers; businessmen, 6. manufacturers and traders; and, 7. the deprived. He recommends the following for the deprived:[73]

> "Fear the Almighty about the conditions of lower and deprived class of the society, the crippled, the needy, the entangled, and the destitute, who have no support, no resources and no opportunities. Among them some come out begging and some (who maintain self-respect) do not beg, but their conditions speak of their distress, poverty, destitution and wants. For the sake of God, protect them and their rights, and fix a share for them from Bait Al-Mal and also reserve a share in kind of crops etc. from government granaries in cities where food-grains are stored as are cultivated on State-owned land, because the share of those living far away from any particular city is equal to the share of those living nearby, and you are made responsible for guarding the rights of the poor people and for looking after their welfare. Take care that the conceit of your position and vanity of wealth may not deceive you to lose sight of such a grave and important responsibility. Yours is such an important post that you cannot claim immunity from the responsibility of even minor errors of commission or omission with an excuse that you were engrossed in the major problems of the State which you have solved diligently.Do not be arrogant and vain against them. Remember that you have to take particular care of those who cannot reach you, whose poverty-stricken and disease-ridden sight maybe hateful to you, and whom society treats with disgust, detestation and contempt. Appoint a respectable, honest and pious person – a person who fears God and who can treat them honorably, order him to find out everything about them and to submit a report to you.Then treat these poor people in such a way that on the Day of

71 *Behar Al-Anwar*; Vol. 72; p. 30.

72 *Vasayel Al-Shia*; Vol. 11; p. 49.

73 *Nahj Al-Balaqa*; Letter 53; pp. 438 and 439.

> Judgment you can plead your case successfully before the Almighty because of all classes of your subjects this class deserves more of your attention, sympathy and fair-deal.Though every one of these poor persons deserves your sympathy, yet you should pay more attention to young orphans and old cripples. They neither have any support nor canthey conveniently come out begging. Remember that the fulfillment of this obligation and duty is considered as a tiresome burden by most of the rulers butto those who desire to achieve His Blessings and to enter into His Realm, even this work seems light and congenial."

7.5 Non-Stocking

Among the methods that the Holy Prophet used in allocating from the Bait Al-Mal was non-stocking of the funds and swiftness in their consumption for delivering the essential supplies.[74]

The Prophet Mohammad was profoundly worried whenever he could not distribute Bait Al-Mal properties before dusk.[75] A Hadith has been quoted from Holy Prophet who said: "If I possess gold as much as Mount Uhud, I would be pleased to distribute it within three days and have nothing left except a little to cover my debts."[76]

During the time of Prophet Mohammad a number of essential requirements existed which were to be supplied. Moreover, the livelihood level of his companions was so low that he always tried to improve it through allocation of Bait Al-Mal. His Holiness used to alleviate their accumulated difficulties, especially because many of his companions were from the poor and the liberated slaves, or had lost all their belongings during emigration from Mecca. Moreover, the authorities of Persian and Roman Empires accumulated a large volume of riches in their treasuries to supply the needs of their courts. Instead of improving the income level of the public or expending for enhancing social welfare, they consumed the treasury for their lavish lifestyles. The same procedures were followed during the reigns of Umayyad and Abbasid caliphates who allocated large amounts for their revelry and debauchery. The annual revenue, in fact, is to cover the annual expenses of the State, and need not be saved for the subsequent years. Of course, if financing the State requires saving for emergency circumstances like wars, earthquakes etc., the Government must maintain a part of its revenue as contingency allowance, which is not against the policies of Holy Prophet. And at times of shortages of funds, His Holiness used to borrow money to provide for the essential requirements. Thus there is no harm if the Government decides to save a portion of the revenue to cover the contingency costs of the following year without borrowing. Nonetheless, the essential expenditures of the present year have

74 *Sonan Abi Davoud*; Vol. 2; pp. 151 and 152; H. 2953.
75 *Al-Sonan Al-Korba*; Vol. 6; p. 357.
76 *Kitab Al-Amval*; p. 262.

precedence over those of the following year, and the Government must prioritize its expenses to allow proper decision-making.

Imam Ali also followed the same policies. At times, he distributed the excess Bait Al-Mal four times a year and always stated: "I am not a treasurer for the public assets but have the duty of dividing it among the public."[77] Salem Mojaddadi recalls: "I witnessed that some goods were brought to His Holiness at dusk; he commanded to distribute it. The Companions said: 'it's late and would do the needful the following day.' His Holiness asked: 'do you guarantee to be alive till the next day?' And ordered them to distribute it immediately, with no hesitation."[78] "After completion of the work, he cleared the place and prayed there."[79]

7.6 Non-Extravagance and Opulence In Providing the Expenses of Government Authorities

Government authorities or regional administrators have personal needs such as accommodation and transport. Today, it is customary to provide housing, conveyance etc. for Government officials from Bait Al-Mal to facilitate their activities. Utilization of public properties must be within the framework of regulations, and the officers should not be free to spend at their wish. In olden days when servants were hired for housekeeping, their wage was also considered as essential expenses of the officers. A Hadith from Prophet Mohammad is quoted saying:[80]

ألا من ولي لنا شيئاً وَ لَمْ تَكُنْ لَهُ امرأةٌ فليتزوّج امرأةً و مَنْ لَمْ يَكُنْ لَهُ مَسْكَنٌ فَلْيَتَّخِذْ مَسْكَناً وَ مَنْ لَمْ يَكُنْ لَهُ مَرْكَبٌ فَلْيَتَّخِذْ مَرْكَباً وَ مَنْ لَمْ يَكُنْ لَهُ خادِمٌ فَلْيَتَّخِذْ خادِماً فَمَنْ اتَّخَذَ سِوي ذلِكَ كَنْزاً و ابِلا جاءَ يَوْمَ القِيامَة غالا سارِقاً

> "Anyone who accepts an administrative position and is not married, can receive from Bait Al-Mal an allowance to cover the costs of wedding; if one does not have a house, can be availed of one; if one does not have a steed, can get one; and if one does not have a servant, can hire one; however, if he takes more gold or camel from Bait Al-Mal than required, the Almighty will punish him as a tyrant or thief on the Judgment Day."

In another Hadith quoted, Holy Prophet had appointed a man at some administrative job in another territory. When the period of job was over, and the man was returning to his homeland, he took some of the items at his disposal, saying that they were gifted to him. Prophet Mohammad stated: "Why do the authorities think that they have been given gifts? Could they get those items, had they remained at home? Swear

77 *Kitab Al-Amval*; p. 284.
78 *Behar Al-Anwar*; Vol. 40; p. 321.
79 *Behar Al-Anwar*. p. 333; Ibn Abi Al-Hadid; *Explanation of Nahj Al-Balaqa*; Vol. 2; p. 199.
80 *Kidat Al-Amval*; p. 279.

to God that such people will be resurrected on the Judgment Day with those things (camels, cows, sheep) hanging round their necks and tolling.[81]

The Government officials cannot take more than their share from Bait Al-Mal. The Holy Prophet used to content himself with very little amounts. Imam Ali tried to revive the Holy Prophet's method. Devotion of the Imam and his furious letter to Othman Bin Hanif are widely apprehended.[82] Not only did he not use public properties, but he contributed a large part of his personal belongings for distribution among the needy. The case of borrowing of a necklace from the treasury by Imam's daughter and rebuking of Ali Bin Abi Rafe', the secretary and treasurer of Bait Al-Mal, and the case of his dealing with Aqil are just some instances.[83] One of the companions named Antare' approached Imam Ali at Khurnaq. Imam was dressed in a worn cotton costume shivering from cold. Antare' asked: "O Leader of the faithful, the Almighty has reserved a share of these properties for you and your family. Why do you put yourselves in hardship?" Imam replied: "I would not take anything from your property; this is the costume I was wearing when I left Madina and don't have anything else."[84] While entering Kufa, Imam ordered to transfer his belongings and furniture from Madina and told the people of Kufa: "If at the time of exiting Kufa I have anything other than these furniture, my steed and my servant, I would be a tyrant.[85] He covered his expenses from his gardens in Madina, and while he fed people with bread and meat, he himself ate stale bread soaked in oil.[86]

Whatever the case may be, the expenses of authorities must be contented to supply of essential requirements, and this important attitude must be established in using Bait Al-Mal. It is not acceptable to the public that government officials be provided extravagant lifestyle at the expense of Bait Al-Mal and tax revenues.

7.7 Equal Opportunity

The natural riches at the disposal of the leader (Imam), the government, and the public sector have been constituted for the purpose of general public and everyone has a share in it.

The government must provide equal opportunity for everyone to work and benefit from the available resources. Holy Qur'an states:[87]

81 *Kidat Al-Amval.*

82 See Rezaei, Majid; *Piousness and Contentment; Compendium on Imam Ali*; Vol. 7; pp. 181–184.

83 *Behar Al-Anwar*; Vol. 40; pp. 337, 338 and 347; *Nahj Al-Balaqa*; Sermon 224; p. 346.

84 *Kitab Al-Amval*; p. 284; *Kashf Al-Qamme fi Ma'refat Al-A'ema*; Translated by Al-Manaqeb; Vol. 1; p. 230.

85 *Explanation of Nahj Al-Balaqa*; Vol. 2; p. 200.

86 *Explanation of Nahj Al-Balaqa*; Vol. 2; p. 200.

87 *Al-Rahman*: 10.

وَالْأَرْضَ وَضَعَهَا لِلْأَنَامِ

And the earth, He has laid it out for humanity.

Exploitation of these riches must be with the permission of the government and in accordance with its economic policies, which are based on principles of economic justice. Prophet Mohammad and Imam Ali divided Bait Al-Mal properties equally among the public and this was objected by materialists/unbelievers.[88]

Since the conditions for reclamation of land and its proprietorship could not lead to centralization/integration, Holy Prophet publicly announced that anyone who reclaimed an abandoned piece of land, would become its titleholder. He also legalized equal exploitation of water, fuel and pasture resources for all people.[89]

7.8 Safeguarding the Rights of Laborers and Farmers

One of the last instructions of Holy Prophet to Imam Ali before his demise was to announce on the rostrum that anyone who reduced the wage of a laborer, has reserved his place in the Hell. His Holiness advised the Imam lest farmers beoppressed in his presence, or be taxed more than that ordained on their land.[90]

7.9 Monitoring Markets

The Government is responsible for supervising over the markets and preventing vicious acts which thwart apprehension of fair prices (e.g. hoarding, mongering (تَلَقّی رُکبان), usury, monopolizing etc.).

Establishment of economic justice in markets is based on apprehension of fair prices, and any function which causes deviation from natural pricing must be abolished. Prophet Mohammad commanded hoarders to exhibit their goods and avoid hiving.[91]

Imam Ali also prohibited hoarding. In his epistle to Malik Al-Ashtar, besides praising traders and businessmen, he advises: “Many of them are stingy misers, intensely self-centered and selfish. They suffer from the obsession of grasping and accumulating wealth. They often hoard their goods to get more profit out of them by creating scarcity and by indulging in black-marketing. Such a condition is extremely injurious to the public on one hand, and disgraceful to the ruler on the other. You

88 *Nahj Al-Balaqa*; Sermons 126, 224 and 232; *Vasayel Al-Shia*; Vol. 11; p. 81 and Vol. 18; p. 521.

89 *Vasayel Al-Shia*; Vol. 17; pp. 326–328; Al-Nouri, Mirza Hossein; *Mostadrak Al-Vasayel va Mostanbat al-Masa'el*; Vol. 17; p. 114; *Al-Sonan Al-Kobra*; Vol. 6; pp. 142 and 143.

90 *Al-Hayat*; Vol. 2; p. 495.

91 *Al-Hayat*; Vol. 2; p. 494.

must put a stop to all such practices because the Holy Prophet has explicitly prohibited them. Remember that trade should go on between the buyers and sellers according to correct measures and weights. It should be based on such reasonable terms that neither the consumers nor the suppliers face any losses. But even with all the sympathetic treatments accorded to them and with all the facilities provided to them, if the traders and industrialists carry on hoarding and black-marketing, then you must punish them according to the intensity of their crime."[92]

Usury is an issue which is against justice, and according to Holy Qur'an is a kind of injustice/oppression:[93]

فَإِنْ لَمْ تَفْعَلُوا فَأْذَنُوا بِحَرْبٍ مِنَ اللَّهِ وَرَسُولِهِ وَإِنْ تُبْتُمْ فَلَكُمْ رُءُوسُ أَمْوَالِكُمْ لَا تَظْلِمُونَ وَلَا تُظْلَمُونَ

> If you do no not do so, then be prepared to face war declared by God and His messenger! If you repent, you may retain your principal; neither shall you make (the debtor) suffer loss, nor shall you be made to suffer loss.

Usury is one of the Great/Major Sins, which interrupts rational social relationships and must be abolished from Islamic markets. Mongering (تَلَقّی رُکبان), i.e. purchase of goods from foreign traders at lower prices in suburbs of the cities, has been prohibited by Holy Prophet and other religious leaders.[94] Moreover, any act that causes deviation of transactions from their natural path must be monitored and banned by the government; e.g.the *Bai'Al-Mudhtar*(sale deal where the seller is under some sort of duress to sell the commodity); sale of commodities from suburban manufacturers by city traders; cheating in deals; and trading low-quality commodities especially food and hygienic stuffs. In religious scripts, *Muhtasib* is a Government officer who inspects market affairs and is responsible for preventing the improper acts such as extortion and iniquity, helping the state keep flows of supply and demand unobstructed. The Islamic markets were totally under supervision during the times of Prophet Mohammad and Imam Ali and the offenders were held accountable for their deeds.[95]

References

Holy Qur'an; *translated by* T.B. Irving (Al-Haj Ta'lim Ali); Suhrawardi Research and Publication Center, Tehran-Iran; 2003.

92 *Nahj Al-Balaqa*; Letter 53; p. 438.

93 *Al-Baqara*: 279.

94 *Vasayel Al-Shia*; Vol. 12; p. 326.

95 See *Eqtesadona*; pp. 649–652; Nazarpour, Mohammad Taqi; *Markets*; pp. 512–525; Malik, Mohammad Reza; *Obligations and Responsibilities of Islamic Government in Economy*; pp. 51–53; Al-Qurashi, Mohammad Bin Mohammad Bin Ahmad; *Ma'alem Al-Qurbat fi Ahkam Al-Hasaba*; pp. 222–242.

Ibn Abi Al-Hadid; *Explanation of Nahj Al-Balaqa; researched by* Mohammad Abolfazal Ibrahim; 20 Vol.; Second Edition; Cairo, Dar Al-Ihya Al-Kotob Al-Arabiya; 1385 LH. Qom Manshurat Maktaba; Ayatollah Al-Uzma Al-Marashi Al-Najafi; 1404 LH.
Ibn Khaldoun, Abdol Rahman; *Introduction*; Dar Al-Ihya Al-Torath Al-Arabi.
Abu Davoud, Soleiman Bin Al-Ash'ath Al-Sajestani; ***Sonan Abi Davoud***; 2 Vol.; First Edition; Beirut; Dar Al-Janan; 1409 LH.
Abu Obaid, Al-Qasem Bin Salam; *Kitab Al-Amval*; First Edition; Beirut; Dar Al-Kitab Al-Elmiya; 1406 LH.
Abu Yousof, Yaqub Bin Ibrahim; *Kitab Al-Kharaj*; Beirut; Dar Al-Ma'refa; 1399 LH.
Bilazari, Abu Al-Hassan Ahmad Bin Yahya; *Fotouh Al-Baldan*; Beirut; Dar Al-Kitab Al-Elmiya; 1398 LH.
Beihaqi, Ahmad Bin Al-Hossein; *Al-Sonan Al-Kobra*; 10 Vol.; Beirut; Dar Al-Ma'refa; No Date.
Javadi Amoli, Abdollah; *Velayat Faqih: Leadership, Jurisprudence and Justice*; Qom; Asra' Publishing Center; 1378 LH.
Hor Al-Ameli, Al-Sheikh Mohammad Bin Al-Hassan; *Vasayel Al-Shia*; 20 Vols.; *edited/corrected by* Abdol Rahim Al-Rabani Al-Shirazi; Maktabe Al-Islamiye; 1403 LH.
Harrani, Abu Mohammad Al-Hassan Bin Ali Bin Al-Hossein Bin Sho'ba; *Tohf Ul-Oqul An Al-ul-Rasul*; *edited/corrected by* Ali Akbar Al-Qaffari; Second Edition; Qum; Islamic Publication Institute; 1363 SH.
Hosseini, Seyyed Reza; *Optimal Consumption Pattern within the Framework of Islamic Income Allocation Model*; Islamic Economy; No. 34; Summer 1388 SH.
Hakimi, Mohammad Reza, Al-Hakimi, Mohammad, Al-Hakimi; *Al-Hayat*; 6 Vols.; First Edition; Islamic Culture Publication Office-Tehran; 1406 LH.
Hamidullah, Mohammad; *Letters and Political Treaties of Prophet Mohammad and the Documents of Early Islamic Era*; *Translated by* Hosseini; Tehran; Soroush; 1374 SH.
Department for Collaboration of Howza and University; *Principles of Islamic Economy*; Tehran; Samt; 1371 SH.
Rezaei, Majid; *Piousness and Contentment; Compendium on Imam Ali*; Vol. 7; edited by Ali Akbar Rashad; Tehran; Publication Center of Islamic Culture and Thought Research Institute; 1380 SH.
Rashid Reza, Seyyed Mohammad; *Tafsir Al-Minar*; Dar-ul-Ma'rafa Al-Taba'a va Al-Nashr; Second Edition; Beirut; No Date.
Razi, Al-Sharif Abu Al-Hassan Mohammad; *Nahj Al-Balaqa*; translated by Seyyed Jafar Shahidi; Islamic Evolution Teaching Publications; Tehran; 1374 SH.
Razi, Al-Sharif Abu Al-Hassan Mohammad; *Nahj Al-Balaqa*; researched by Sobhi Al-Saleh; Qum; Markaz Al-Bahouth Al-Islamiya; 1395 LH.
Reyshahri, Mohammad; *Movasa'a Al-Imam Ali-ibn-Abitaleb fi Al-Kitab va Al-Sona' va Al-Tarikh*; 12 Vol.; First Edition; Qum; Dar Al-Hadith; 1421 LH.
Reyshahri, Mohammad; *Mizan Al-Hikmat*; Qum; Markaz Al-Nashr Maktab Al-E'lam Al-Islami; 1362 SH.
Sadr, Al-Seyyed Mohammad Baqer; *Eqtesadona*; First Edition; Maktab Al-E'lam Al-Islami; 1417 LH.
Tabataba'ei, Al-Seyyed Mohammad Hossein; *Al-Mizan fi Tafsir Al-Qur'an*; 20 Vols.; Second Edition; Al-A'lami Al-Matbu'at Institute; Beirut; 1394 LH.
Tabarsi, Abu Ali, Al-Fazl Bin Hassan; *Majma' Ul-Bayan*; 5 Vol. (10 Sections); Islami-ye Publishers; 1380 LH.
Al-Farra, Abu Ya'la Mohammad Bin Al-Hossein; *Al-Ahkam Al-Soltaniye va Al-Velayat Al-Diniye*; *corrected/edited by* Mohammad Hamed Al-Foqa; Second Edition; Qum;Markaz Al-Nashr Maktab Al-E'lam Al-Islami; 1406 LH.
Al-Qurashi, Mohammad Bin Mohammad Bin Ahmad (Ibn Al-Okhvat); *Ma'alem Al-Qurbat fi Ahkam Al-Hasaba*; corrected/edited by Ruben Levi; Cambridge; Dar Al-Fonoun; 1937 AD.
Katani, Abdul-Hai; *Nizam Al-Hokoumat Al-Nabaviya Al-Mosamma Al-Taratib Al-Edariya*; 2 Vol. Beirut; Dar Al-Ehya Al-Torath Al-Arabi; No Date.

Gilac Hakimabadi, Mohammad Taqi; *The Government and Its Economic Policies;Compendium on Imam Ali*; Vol. 7; edited by Ali Akbar Rashad; Tehran; Publication Center of Islamic Culture and Thought Research Institute; 1380 SH.

Malik, Mohammad Reza; *Obligations and Responsibilities of Islamic Government in Economy*; Islamic Economy Technical Quarterly; Vol. 3; No. 12; winter 1382 SH.

Maverdi, Abol-Hassan; Ali Bin Mohammad; *Al-Ahkam Al-Soltaniya*; Qum; Markaz Al-Nashr Maktab Al-E'lam Al-Islami; Second Edition; 1406 LH.

Majlesi, Mohammad Baqer; *Behar Al-Anwar*; 110 Vol. Tehran; Al-Maktabat Al-Islamiya; 1375 SH.

Mahmoudi, Mohammad Baqer; *Nahj Al-Sa'adat fi Mostadrak Nahj Al-Balaqa*; 8 Vol., First Edition; Al-Najaf Al-Ashraf; Al-Mat'aba Al-Ne'man; 1378 LH.

Moddaresi Tabataba'ei; Hossein; *Land in Islamic Jurisprudence*; 2 Vol. Tehran; Islamic Culture Publication Office; 1362 SH.

Makarem Shirazi; Naser; *Anwar Al-Fiqahat; Kitab Al-Tejarat; Al-Makaseb Al-Mahramat*; Qum; Hadaf Publishers; 1415 LH.

Montazeri, Hossein Ali; *Kitab Al-Zakat*; 4 Vol.; First Edition; Vol. 1 and 2; Qum; Markaz Al-Nashr; Maktab Al-E'lam Al-Islami; 1404 and 1406 LH and Vol. 3 and 4; Tafakkor Publications; 1411 LH.

Montazeri, Hossein Ali; *Darasat fi Velayat Al-Faqih and Fiqh Al-Dolat Al-Islamiya*; 4 Vol.; First Edition;Vol. 1 and 2; Qum; Markaz Al-Alami L-Al-Derasat Al-Islami; 1408 LH and Vol. 3 and 4; Tafakkor Publications; 1411 LH.

Mousavi Al-Khomeini, Al-Seyyed Ruhollah (Imam); *Tahrir Al-Vasile'*; 2 Vol.; Al-Najaf Al-Ashraf; Mat'ab Al-Adab.

Najafi, Mohammad Hassan; *Jawahir Al-Kalam fi Sharh Shara'e Al-Islam*; 43 Vols.; Dar Al-Kitab Islamiye; Tehran; 1365 SH.

Nazarpour, Mohammad Taqi; *Markets; Compendium on Imam Ali*; Vol. 7; edited by Ali Akbar Rashad; Tehran; Publication Center of Islamic Culture and Thought Research Institute; 1380 SH.

Nazari, Hassan Aqa, and Mohammad Taqi Gilac Hakimabadi; *Scientific Perspectives of Expenses and Revenues in Islamic States*; First Edition; Qum; Howza and University Research Institute; and Tehran; Economic Affairs Institute; 1382 SH.

Namazi, Hossein; *Economic Systems*; First Edition; Tehran; Inteshar Publications Co.; 1382 SH.

Nouri, Mirza Hassan; *Mostadrak Al-Vasayel Va Mostanbat Al-Masa'el*; 18 Vol.; First Edition; Al Al-Bayt (PBUT) L-Ehya Al-Itrath Institute; Qum; 1408 LH.

Ali Reza Lashkari

Chapter 28: Principles of Defining Public Domain in Islam in Contrast to Neoclassical and Communitarian Viewpoints

1 Introduction

Perhaps the most basic and the most expected application of the state/government in the social life of human beings is to provide order and security in the light of law enforcement. However, it has gradually become clear that the endorsed laws have a tremendous influence on governing structures, type of government interactions, people's mode of life, and lastly distribution of resources among individuals. These in turn severely affect how the desired goals of a society are achieved.

Philosophical considerations about the best way to organize and arrange social, economic and political institutions are among the important and pioneering issues in determining the status/position of government in an economic system. Consequently, political philosophers have always sought to establish the fundamental principles which allow to define a particular form of state/government that shows how people in a proper/good state can avail of their rights. Within this framework, various issues including the quality of human life, selecting the mode of governance by the people, as well as the distinguishing features of the good and bad governments can be debated (Miller, 2003, p. 15).

Accordingly, in order to identify the realm/extent of state/government intervention, the political philosophy of each system must be scrutinized, which addresses the fundamental queries about society, government, statesmanship, social life, individual rights and the mutual responsibilities of individual and society towards each other. Therefore, such concerns as public affairs, public domain, or public interest must be analyzed with respect to private affairs and personal interests.

Since the foundations of the state/government relies on public affairs, and the broader the realm of public affairs, the wider the extent of the state authority, the means of circumspection and intellection about economy and state/government intervention includes distinguishing between private and public affairs. Consequently, we are faced with a set of concerns about the main attribute that qualifies human functions and interactions as public affairs. Human motivations, essence of his interests and their mode of realization constitute the most important issues in this field. Recognizing the various stance towards these matters can help clearly distinguish the methods of reasoning from the fundamental approaches. In fact, such approaches are formed in response to the concept of beneficence/goodness and the relationship between personal good and social good.

https://doi.org/10.1515/9783110593419-028

2 Concept of "Goodness" in Western Ethical/Moral Schools

In accordance with the modern Western attitude, the post-medieval theories in the field of ethics/morality have a different approach than the Aristotelian thought. Aristotle's virtuous approach speaks of "what kind of human I must become" and "what to do" to achieve the desirable supremacy. Therefore, there exists a connection between the present status of every individual and what one can and should become. Ethical norms are the factors that bring about the transfer of human beings in the course of achieving the goal of supremacy and ultimate perfection.

Unlike Aristotelian theory, in modern moral philosophy, where the concept of human nature has been revolutionized/evolved, virtue has been obliterated from human life, and "Virtue Ethics" is wiped out of moral philosophy. In the new moral/ethical theories, the emphasis has been on the act/deed itself, rather than the cause. Accordingly the questions of "what should I do" and "how to distinguish between good and evil/bad," have replaced the "what to do" question. If an ultimate perfection is also sought, it is not considered as a virtue of human self, but is looked upon as an outcome of the acts, such as profit and advantage. The moral philosophers have accordingly addressed human acts in two different branches of philosophical studies, viz. normative ethics and meta-ethics (Frankena, 1997, p. 5).

In the normative ethics, two basic themes are discussed. The first involves examining moral propositions, such as "truthfulness is good" and "oppression is bad/evil." The second theme covers the criteria and measures for judging the goodness or badness/evilness of an act from the point of view of ethics/morality. This later theme can be of interest in the current article, for it relates the motives of the subject.

Theories about the criteria of judgment in the acts/deeds of the subject are categorized into two broad categories of deontological theories and teleological theories.

2.1 Deontology

Deontologists believe that the characteristics of act by itself can lead to the correctness or wrongness of that act, regardless of its consequences and the amount of beneficence/goodness that entail it. The morality of the acts thus depends on their intrinsic nature and their compliance with a single general rule/principle. In view of a deontologist, an act such as "abiding by a promise" is justified (according to religious beliefs), and thus it has been commanded/ordered. The mere existence of these features suffices for distinguishing that the act of "abiding by a promise" is correct/ethical, although there is no goodness or benefit in doing it.

Immanuel Kant, who was one of the greatest deontological theorists, believed that in addition to the effects and phenomena, human self also possesses practical wisdom, which is the source of morality/ethics. From the point of view of Kant, ethics is the same as the obligation to observe the general law. In addition, moral laws are independent of human intentions, sentiments and circumstances. Nonetheless, ethical principle and absolute intention acceptable to Kant is as follows: "Act as though your maxim should serve simultaneously as a universal law (for all rational beings)" (Kant, 2002, p. 56).

2.2 Consequentialism

The consequentialist or teleological school considers the result or outcome of the act as the criterion for evaluating the validity and invalidity as well as distinguishing good from evil. From the perspective of a consequentialist, the only effective feature in considering the correctness or wrongness of an act is the benefit or the good that results from carrying it out. Therefore, the nature of an act by itself does not have any role in its validity and goodness, or invalidity and evilness. Any action that has good consequences is considered good and valid, and any action that has adverse consequences is bad and invalid. Accordingly, the set of good deeds can even be ranked, while the set of evil deeds can be judge.

But the question about how to define the measures and criteria for the goodness or the evilness of the outcomes and consequences of acts remains to be answered. Also, the desirable ethical/moral consequences are the source of disagreement with the consequentialists. Based on their view about which outcome is good and which one is bad, teleologists are divided into two major factions.

2.2.1 Egoism/Egoists

From the point of view of egoists, the individual not only seeks to obtain the most good, benefit or expedience, but his unique duty is to provide the highest possible conquering over the evil for himself (Frankena, 1997, p. 20).

2.2.2 Utilitarianism/Utilitarianists

This faction is the most prominent and most popular viewpoint among consequentialists, and James Stuart Mill, one of the greatest philosophers of this school, has presented its most effective interpretation/application. His interpretation has significantly influenced the neoclassical economics.

In this school, the criterion for evaluating/assessing the correctness and validity of an act is defined on the basis of its effects on the general good, as well as its overall benefit. Since correctness and righteousness are defined as the greatest good of the society, the evaluation of acts is also based on the same principle. In view of utilitarianists, the benefit of the individual or some members of the society, is not the criterion for assessing the validity and correctness of an act. But the overall benefit and goodness of the act is considered as the criterion for its evaluation/assessment. Therefore, contrary to the egoistic approach that conceives the greatest benefit of the subject individuals as the criterion for evaluation, utilitarianism regards the maximum beneficence of the whole society as the criterion for ethical/moral judgment of the acts (Frankena, 1997, p. 20).

In view of utilitarianists, expediency is identified/recognized in terms of benefit, and no expediency is placed higher than the "benefit" in rank. Therefore, all the *a priori* rules, such as justice, which can place the benefit in particular contexts, are identified in an *a posteriori* manner which depend on benefit. In John Stuart Mill's view, the sense of justice is not independent and a standard *per se*. He is of the opinion that the justice, which is based on benefit, constitutes the most imperative and most dedicated part of ethics/morality. According to him, justice is a term applied to the levels of ethical/moral rules that are intimately linked to the main traits of human wellbeing. As a result, justice is the same as the rights that guarantee the social benefits of human beings (Mill, 2009, p. 78–79).

3 Impact of Neoclassical Utilitarianism on the Definition of "Public Affair/Domain"

In the neoclassical notion where good is defined on the basis of personal benefit, and every person is free to pursue his or her own interest, public affair acquires its meaning as an extrapolation of private affair. It is thus defined in conjunction with private affair. As long as securing private benefit can be achieved without state/government intervention, the domain and affair fall within the private realm. And public affairs have no implications under such circumstances. The public affairs are basically applicable where obtaining private benefit is not possible without state/government intervention. In fact, state/government intervention is justified within the context/framework of retrieval of utility, which is itself based on personal interest. In this approach, the public affair cannot be extended beyond personal interest and may not be accepted without considering personal goals.

One of the basic concepts used by neoclassical economists for defining private affairs is the concept of exchange and its implications in maximizing the benefits of individuals. Individuals pursue and maximize their interests through the mechanism of exchange.

To distinguish between private and public affairs, neoclassical economists emphasize/focus on which affairs are transferred through market exchange and pricing system, and which affairs fall outside this circle. Affairs that are not included in this system, but are influenced by private concerns are considered public. Within the market exchange and pricing system, all the transaction and exchange impacts and benefits (or losses) are confined to the parties of the transaction. Consequently, the market system can be effective in maximizing the benefits of individuals. As long as this kind of transaction/exchange is dealt with, it is placed within the private domain.

But if all the benefits and impacts of the exchange are not confined to the parties and extend beyond them, the market system does not expose all the impacts in the exchange, and thus the market fails to provide the required efficiency. The benefits and losses that are not covered by the market during such exchanges constitute the external impacts which fall within the public domain and require state/government supervision/intervention.

It can be noted that the main distinguishing feature of this interpretation is the definition and recognition of public affairs in reference to the concept of personal benefit. It can only be meaningful where the personal benefit cannot be pursued expediently. In the other words, public affairs cannot extend beyond personal benefit or beyond such affairs that are in response to unsatisfied/unattainable human needs in connection with personal prejudice and objective. Therefore, activities are organized in juxtaposition of gaining benefits through market and non-market instruments even in the public domain. Either the personal interests are compatible with one another, as in the case of public goods, where the pursuit of a public interest is conceivable, or such compatibility is not possible in any ways, and personal interests are in conflict with the interests of others. The latter situation reflects a sort of external impact.

In viewpoint of neoclassical economics, where the interests of some individuals have an impact on the interests of others, the problem of incompatibility of costs or private and social benefits arises. As a result, economic efficiency is not established and markets fail. There are two usual strategies for restoring efficiency in such economies. One solution is to change the status of social costs or benefits into private costs or benefits. This strategy attempts to eliminate the effects of individuals on the benefits or costs of others.

Accordingly, the conditions must be transformed in such a way that interdependence of individuals, and hence the effect of economic behavior of individuals on each other, is eliminated. As Collins and Jones wrote: In order to reduce externality effects, the state/government can either subsidize the polluting factory to use pollution-reduction technologies, or subsidize people around the factory to move to another location (Cullis and Jones, 2009, p. 45).

In the second solution, the status of private costs or benefits changes to that social costs or benefits. Layard and Walters followed the same strategy and believe For stimulating private behavior in order to achieve a state of equilibrium, the private costs must be equaled to social costs through taxation (Layard and Walters, 1978, p. 195).

Therefore, in order to reduce the status of inefficient production Q2 to efficient production Q1, the state/government will charge a tax equivalent to P1P2.

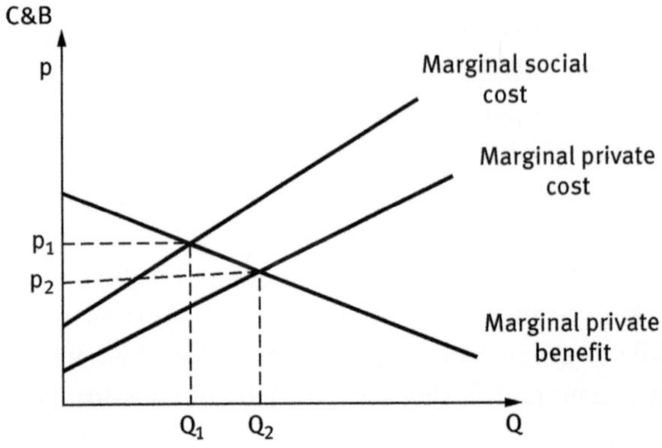

Figure 28.1: Taxation of Private Cost to Increase Socilal Benefit.

Of course, when externalities in production are positive, the subsidy instrument can be used to equalize private benefit with social benefits. In such cases, the state/government pays subsidies for those commodities (or services) which have positive externalities to increase their status of production from Q1 to Q2.

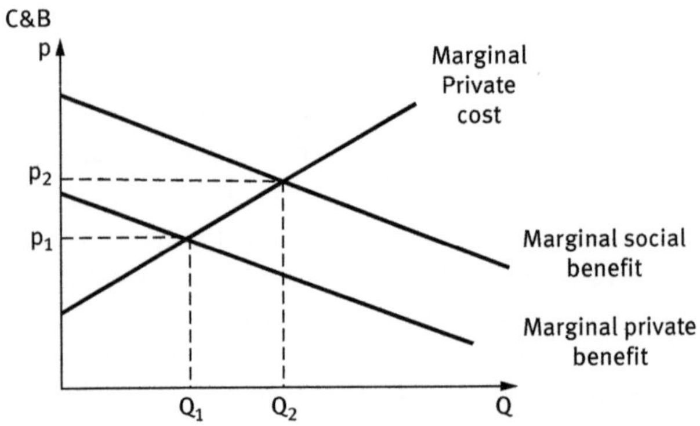

Figure 28.2: Social Versus Private Optimum.

In both the above cases, the state/government decisions are based either on non-market solutions, e.g. relocation and transfer of parties involved, or market solutions, e.g. taxation or subsidization to provide for efficiency. The measures are based on individual behaviors so as to maximize private benefits. By targeting specific economic benefits and measures (such as efficiency, productivity, and profitability), the state/government does not seek to protect general public interests. In fact, the state/government must necessarily support the interests of those who are struggling to increase their capital and profits. As a result, the role of state/government will be confined to protecting the production and exchange structures in order to increase and improve the said measures.

4 Attempts to Maintain the Expanse of Public Domain

In another viewpoint, the public affair is defined and interpreted based on social life, and not private benefit. This interpretation is in accordance with the more traditional concept supported by Aristotle wherein the description of public interest and expediency were more prominent. In the more traditional sense, public affair inferred existence, inwardness and purpose, which were unexplainable in terms of individual personal benefit and private preferential arrangements (Arendt, 1958, p. 9).

Aristotle believed that public life in the "polis" was essential to flourishing of supreme social nature of human beings. Thus, the "polis" provided a plan for perfect harmony of man and nature, and progress was founded on human nature. As a result, it performed based on the claim of observing the perfect harmony of human life. The "republic" meant establishment of mutual commitments and friendly ties between people in areas beyond family affiliation or friendship, and led to flourishing of the social dimensions of human beings.

Accordingly, the difference between the private and the public domains was also established on the same foundations. While provision of basic necessities was the most important concern of human beings in the private domain, they were considered equal citizens in the public domain and sought to determine and provide public and community benefits. As a result, the domain of human social life was completely distinct from economic and private domains. This kind of separation provided the opportunity as well as the possibility of transcending human virtues and perfections within the public domain, i.e. where the "polis" had an active presence.

4.1 Protesting the Change of Private Domain in New Era

A number of intellectuals believe that the former concept of public domain of the West, and consequently the concept of state/government, have been invaded by the criteria and standards of the private domain. This has resulted in conversion of the public domain into an arena for managing the livelihood provisions and production affairs, thus obliterating the boundary between the two domains (d'Entreves, 2016).

Thus, with the prevalence of the former doctrine, the state/government has been transformed into an efficient instrument of production and profit making. It constitutes an administrative system for the society in which politics, consultancy and practice do not provide the options for pursuing the expediency and benefit of the public. The state/government relies on a concept of power within its hierarchical system whose core and principal axis is utilitarianism. Such colossal change in the definition of the private domain has connected/linked the state/government as well as the public domain to certain benefits and expediencies which can no longer be considered as public. The consequences of this new attitude are crucial in determining the performance of the markets.

In the opinion of the first doctrine, the only concrete social reality is the individual and his preferences (individualism). The public affairs that are not based on the reality, are metaphysical concept, and perhaps, analogical. But some intellectuals who consider a more traditional notion of public affairs, believe that social institutions have their own reality. Institutions are not established in response to the needs of individuals (although they often address such needs). They encompass private players and explicitly introduce their fundamental social relations as the basis of their existence as individuals. This view hypothesizes a social authority that supersedes the definition of personal objectives and distances from neoclassical individualism.

4.2 Domination of Market System in the society, the Most Important Consequence of Dependence of the Public Domain on the criteria of the Private Domain

The neoclassical model, which involves profiteering and expediency incentives, has the ability to create a specific entity called the market to control the entire economy through trade and barter. When this happens, the effects over the organization of the whole society will be remarkable and very significant. Under such circumstances, the economic system will no longer be integrated and governed by social relations, but supersedes the latter. As a result, many important social values and concepts acquire their status within the framework of market operations.

Because of the effects of prevalence of market regulations over all social values and structures, some Western political philosophers, including Arendt, believe that the public domain must be protected from the threats of the private domain. In other words, the public domain must not allow the private domain to define and control it. Accordingly, Arendt considers the term "public affair" to include two distinct but closely interrelated phenomena. (Arendt, 1958, p. 50–52). First dimension encompasses what Arendt calls "public manifestation/appearance," i.e. everything that appears in public can be seen and heard by everybody and has the widest possible publicity. Depending on the amount that human personality is considered as a social construct, public manifestation/appearance can be seen as an attempt to create or strengthen the link between the individuals and the entire society, which has special significance in preserving their identities (thus an aspect of public affair relates individuals with the entire society).

From the point of view of Arendt, different types of mass communication fall within public domain as long as they provide the opportunity for the individuals to appear.

As put forth by Arendt, the second dimension of the public affairs, however, defines it as the universe. Arendt considers the universe to be a human construct. This universe encompasses all the things that define our tangible common life. It bonds us together and, in addition, serves all our needs. Therefore, public affairs have an external existence for doing so. According to Arendt, since our sense of reality depends on public realm, the existence of such realities is necessary and imperative. Human beings imagine, experience and create the reality of their personal and social lives in a way that they have already believed. We have in common with those who live with us, but also with those who were here before and with those who will come after us. But such a common world can survive the coming and going of the generation only to the extent that is appears in public (Arendt, 1958, p. 55). According to Arendt, with the rise of the "social" in the age of modernity, and the narrowing or elimination of the public sphere, the common world also is eliminated. In the "social", focus is on the private world and pursuing private economic interests.

This view, however, contradicts neoclassical economic thinking in which our mental reality does not rely on our bond with a larger whole, and thus it forms independently. The external world comprises a set of opportunities whose priorities have been previously defined by the available instruments. The opportunities are followed in accordance with preferential and well-defined arrangements. In classical economic thinking, this mental reality has precedence over both social life and politics.

Therefore, if the concepts of the public domain encompass human universe and precede the preferential arrangements of individuals, they will bear a significant fundamental function for the individual. This function of public domain has been completely ignored in the classical perspective.

5 "Social Good" in Communitarian Viewpoint and Public Domain

Although the origin and intellectual foundations of communitarianism is different from liberalism, but both criticize individualism and the lack of sufficient attention toward society in shaping the choices and attitudes of individuals. Michael Sandel, Charles Taylor, Alasdair Macintyre and Michael Walzer are the most prominent theorists of communitarian approach.

About the inadequacy/insufficiency of Kant's individualism, Sandel opines that the "ethical individual" of Kant, who is the reference for moral judgments in ethical cases and principles of justice, provides an image based on the premise that the identity of individual is distinct from his destinations, objectives and knowledge. According to Sandal, individual identity is not ontologically independent of his objectives, destinations and desires. These objectives and destinations are part of the identity of individuals and are not in their possession to be pushed aside and separate them from their selves (Sandel, 1982, p. 166).

Therefore, the disagreement between communitarians and individualists arises about whether the individual can determine his own good and destination independent of the reference community? In view of communitarians, formation of an individual's perception about goodness, happiness, or expediency and, in general, effective values in individual decision-making, are influenced by the society in which he lives. In spite of the belief in individual's choice, the communitarians also acknowledge the influence of society on the process of choosing. Thus, goodness and expediency resulting from such a process can be termed "Social Good." And the purpose of social good is to discern individual's beneficence within the framework of social relationships, influenced by the beliefs and commitments that exist in society. Such discernment is, however, not inherent.

In Sandel's view, Justice which is related with the fair distribution of valuable things in the society, ends where the consent about "what is good" and "what makes our lives better" is agreed upon. Therefore, part of the debate on justice concerns the recognition of things that are valuable and must be fairly distributed. Justice is founded on discernment through collective conception/wisdom about good and valuable things. According to Sandel, recognition of valuable affairs that are obtained through collective conception/wisdom, is the same as social good and is ranked higher that the arrangement of individual preferences.

Similarly, Sandel emphasizes the concern over growing ethical/moral contentions in politics and the consequent promotion of collective/collaborative morale. He believes that the development of the sense of solidarity and mutual responsibility, which are necessary for a just society, must be apprehended in the political domain.

> A more robust public engagement with our moral disagreements could provide a stronger, not a weaker, basis for mutual respect. Rather than avoid the moral and religious convictions that our fellow citizens bring to public life, we should attend to them more directly – sometimes by challenging and contesting them, sometimes by listening to and learning from them. There is no guarantee that public deliberation about hard moral questions will lead in any given situation to agreement – or even to appreciation for the moral and religious views of others. It's always possible that learning more about a moral or religious doctrine will lead us to like it less. But we cannot know until we try.
>
> A politics of moral engagement is not only a more inspiring ideal than a politics of avoidance. It is also a more promising basis for a just society. (Sandel, 2009; p. 268).

Sandel is fearful that the field of evaluation and judgment about affairs as well as that of defining good and valuable things be left to the markets. He is of the opinion that if the markets are not to change the norms that govern the social institutions, their ethical/moral limits/boundaries must be publicly debated.

The important point is that despite Sandel emphasis on social good, he reduces it to encompass the domain of individual interest. In other words, although the society and mass/collective teachings are important in ranking individual preferences, yet it is still the preferences of an individual that is significant. And the expediencies and mass/collective interests that are returned to the society, however, do not materialize.

As a result, it should be clearly mentioned in debates whether the expediency as an objective and destination is relevant to the individuals or the society. All individualists, either consequentialist or utilitarianist, and communitarians take into account the individual expediency.

6 Public/Social Good in Islamic System

In Islamic philosophy, the word "good" has a different meaning than that in Western philosophy. In Islamic terminology, this term is closely connected/tied to the connotation of "expediency" and is recognized as the latter.

In order to get acquainted with the status of the concept of "expediency" in the Islamic system as well as its impact on the state/government responsibilities/obligations, it is necessary to examine its connotation in various fields of Islamic sciences and achieve a coherent understanding about it. Accordingly, the concept of expediency in two branches viz. ethics of political philosophy and Islamic political jurisprudence is reviewed in the following.

6.1 Consequentialism in Islam

As stated earlier, the ethical schools of thought are divided into two categories of teleology and deontology. Initially, the proximity of the moral system of Islam with these perspectives must be analyzed to find out its compatibility with the either of the two.

The analysis of the views of Muslim philosophers illustrates the greater compatibility of the moral school of Islam with consequentialism (i.e. teleological). On the consequentiality of human actions, Mesbah Yazdi writes:

> "Man has an objective in all his actions, and in turn, this objective sometimes becomes a prelude to something else, which subsequently is the forerunner in achieving a third objective, so forth. However, there is one final purpose and destination for our actions, which will be realized, although imperceptibly, putatively/circumstantially and semi-consciously; we call this the "ultimate objective." (Mesbah Yazdi, 1391 SH, 29).

A number of Qur'anic verses and anecdotes/apothegms (*Ravayat*) proclaim that the good/benevolent deeds of man are the cause of happiness/felicity and salvation of mankind, and point to the concept of consequentialism. Some verses of Holy

Qur'an categorize human actions under such titles as trade, and buying and selling (Al-Saf: 10).[1]

In the moral system of Islam, there is a destination that is the cause of the goodness of any task, the ethical/moral desirability of every act, and the value of any deed. That is nothing but the happiness/felicity of the subject/doer of the deed. Achieving a prosperous/felicitous life is the outcome of human endeavor, and the ethical/moral guidelines determine the direction and trend that lead human beings to happiness/felicity (Shirvani, 1382 SH.).

As a result, the outcomes/consequences of the acts from the viewpoint of Islam are bonded with human happiness/felicity, and any act that leads to the happiness/felicity of human beings is considered congenial and desirable.

6.2 Essence/Quiddity of Destination/Consequence and Expediency in Islamic Ethical/Moral System

As stated, the objective of all human acts in Islam is attaining happiness/felicity. Since human acts can bring about happiness/felicity for mankind, they acquire a specific quality and capability, referred to as "expediency." It should be noted that in the same way as the utilitarian ethical system, where acquisition of pleasure and desirability constitutes the ultimate objective of human acts, acquisition of happiness/felicity is formally recognized as the ultimate goal of human beings in view of Muslim ethical philosophers. Of course, the quest for happiness/felicity in Islamic viewpoint is the same as the quest for pleasure, but as it will be discussed in the following paragraphs, the concept of hedonism has fundamental differences in the ethical/moral system of Islam and the West.

Similar to the quest for pleasure, the quest for happiness/felicity is an innate tendency of human beings. The reason for innateness of these tendencies is that man has been created in a way to be formatively and involuntarily attracted towards happiness/felicity as well as pleasure, and tends to escape from suffering/woe. This means such affairs cannot be intrinsically included in the realm of ethics/morality.

---

1 يَا أَيُّهَا الَّذِينَ آمَنُوا هَلْ أَدُلُّكُمْ عَلَى تِجَارَةٍ تُنْجِيكُمْ مِنْ عَذَابٍ أَلِيمٍ (الصف: 10)

O you who believe! Shall I lead you to a bargain that will save you from painful torment?

and also, Al-Toba': 111

إِنَّ اللَّهَ اشْتَرَى مِنَ الْمُؤْمِنِينَ أَنْفُسَهُمْ وَأَمْوَالَهُمْ بِأَنَّ لَهُمُ الْجَنَّةَ يُقَاتِلُونَ فِي سَبِيلِ اللَّهِ فَيَقْتُلُونَ وَيُقْتَلُونَ وَعْدًا عَلَيْهِ حَقًّا فِي التَّوْرَاةِ وَالْإِنْجِيلِ وَالْقُرْآنِ وَمَنْ أَوْفَى بِعَهْدِهِ مِنَ اللَّهِ فَاسْتَبْشِرُوا بِبَيْعِكُمُ الَّذِي بَايَعْتُمْ بِهِ وَذَلِكَ هُوَ الْفَوْزُ الْعَظِيمُ (التوبه: 111

Surely God has bought up their persons and their property from the believers, so they may have the Garden (instead). They fight for God's sake; they kill and are killed as a rightful promise from Him (to be found) in the Old Testament, the Gospel and the Qur'an; and who is more Trustworthy with His word than God? So rejoice in your bargain which you have reached with Him; that will be the supreme Achievement.

Therefore, individuals may not be admired or blamed for questing/seeking pleasure or escaping from suffering/woe (Mesbah Yazdi, 1391 SH, 31).

6.3 Relationship between Pleasure and Felicity

The existence of the human tendency towards pleasure is not denied in Holy Qur'an, but a part of its teachings as well as its instructive/training method is dictated on the basis of this innate desire of human beings. Use of the terms such as happiness/felicity ("*Sa'adah*" or "سعادت"), deliverance/salvation ("*Falah*" or "فلاح"), emancipation/redemption ("*Fowz*" or "فوز") and the like in Holy Qur'an connotes intrinsic quest of human beings for prosperity. Therefore, they must act in accordance with religious orders to achieve their desires (Mesbah Yazdi, 1391 SH, 52).

In the opinion of Avicenna, pleasure is fundamentally associated with human perfection, and encompasses four elements viz. "apprehension/cognition," "attainment/achievement and conscience," "excellence/perfection" and "goodness." Since these four elements are dubious and multi-faceted, pleasure is also considered as a multi-faceted affair. The important point is that affairs which bring about greater pleasure and happiness/felicity, are considered more exceptional/perfect. This is because each of the faculties of human self has its own specific perfection/excellence, and achieving their respective perfection/excellence leads to happiness/felicity (Avicenna, 1364 SH, 109).

As a result, a faculty whose perfection/excellence is more superior, more permanent, more durable or more realizable/achievable, or is in the most perfect and supreme condition in terms of essence and perception, will necessarily have a higher and more superior level of pleasure and happiness/felicity.

However, the highest faculty in man is "the faculty of intellect and conception," and therefore, the highest perfection/excellence for man is intellectual. As a result, the pleasure of achieving such perfection must constitute the highest pleasure for mankind. The outcome of such an attitude is that pleasure-seeking will be intermingled with perfection/seeking and human happiness/felicity will be achieved through attaining the highest perfections.

Happiness/felicity is a pleasure that does not prevent more important pleasures, or does not bring about greater suffering/woe, while misery/infelicity is a suffering that does not prevent greater sufferings/woes, or does not prelude a more important pleasure (Motahhari, 1366 SH, 60–62).

6.4 Egoistic Consequentialism

At this point, the question is "what is the source for human pursuit of happiness (and pleasure-seeking/hedonism)?" The answer on the basis of the Islamic teachings is that pursuit of happiness and pleasure in man originates from narcissism (self-love). Narcissism is the most inclusive instinct in man, i.e. man loves pleasure and happiness, and hates pain and misery/wrath. Self-love appears as a motive that pushes man towards work and effort. In the debate on "ultimate cause" in philosophy, it is also argued that human beings always pursue a destination and purpose in their voluntary behaviors. But the destination of any deed depends on its doer/subject, and hence, any good deed will lead to perfection and happiness of its doer/subject. Even a deed such as kindness to another individual is actually aimed at the perfection and advantage of the benefactor. Because the benefactor is saddened by seeing the helplessness of another individual, and helps the stranded individuals to relieve his own grief (Tabataba'ei, 1362 SH, 183).

Consequentialism in Islamic ethical/moral system is thus considered to be egoistic. The sacred Qur'anic verses indicate that the ultimate destination and basic desirability of the human deeds are emancipation/redemption ("*Fowz*" or "فوز") and deliverance/salvation ("*Falah*" or "فلاح") of the doer/subject. Holy Qur'an calls on human beings to perform good deeds in order to be salved and redeemed. No one has ever been asked to do anything for deliverance and redemption of others. In only few cases where individuals have been asked to attempt guiding and directing others, such deeds are aimed at achieving happiness/felicity for themselves((Shirvani, *op. cit)*.

As a result, the ethical/moral system of Islam seems to be consequential; i.e. ethical/moral deeds in Islam have a goal and purpose (destination). Moreover, it is egoistic in essence; i.e. the goal and purpose of the deed is related to its doer/subject (ibid).

6.5 Nature of Public Expediency in Political and Economic Philosophy of Islam

Considering ethical/moral and faith system of Islam to be compatible with egoistic consequentialism might lead to the conclusion that the political and economic system of Islam is compliant and concordant with the views of individualists. However, judging this case should not be solely based on egoism, and analysis of different aspects of human life and society, and even the universe, from the viewpoint of Islam must also be taken into consideration. One of the most influential topics on the orientation of ethical schools about egoism and their characters/qualities, as well as their relation to society, lies in their definition of human beings, expediency, happiness/felicity and pleasure. Egoism does not necessarily mean sacrificing the expediency/interests of the society and others for the benefit of individuals. Depending on the attitude/view towards human beings and the world, the conflict between individual and collective/social benefits can be minimized. One can claim that the egoism of a Muslim individual is associated with his responsibleness/accountability towards others, and his happiness is only achieved through altruism. Therefore, the expediency and the destiny of the individual is linked to the expediency and destiny of the society, and there is no incoherence/separation between the two. In other words, it is not enough to agree only on the basis of egoism, but it is also important to consider its status. The difference on this viewpoint distinguishes Islamic stand from that of individualism and communitarianism.

6.5.1 Difference between Islamic and Utilitarian Viewpoints about Expediency

One of the differences between Islamic and utilitarian views about expediency is manifested in the attitude of the religious individuals towards the universe. The difference originates from the belief of Muslims in the afterlife and the next world, and its role in determining the destination of the ethical/moral deed. In the utilitarianist perspective, pleasure (even if spiritual) is formed on the basis of sensual faculties/human senses, as well as individual knowledge and recognition. Thus, the only source for recognition of pleasure and expediency is the individual himself. However, pleasure is the same as individual happiness/felicity in Islam, and all forms of happiness are not necessarily acknowledged/understood by human sensual faculties. In some cases, these pleasures are presented/delivered to man by the Almighty Creator of the universe.

In fact, for a person who believes in the afterlife, the pleasures and happiness are not confined to those of this world, and principally, he pursues the pleasures of the next world. His mind dictates that in order to attain those pleasures, even if they are not presently understandable to him, he must heed the authentic countersigns/words that have been delivered on the topic. Accordingly, espousing the divine prophets becomes rationally obligatory.

For the reasons stated above, and in order to achieve perfection and happiness of the individual, self-love and narcissism are contingent on altruism. This perception of the destination and expediency of the individual is precisely the opposite of that of the liberal ethical system, in which altruism is contingent on narcissism/self-love. In the liberal system, in spite of the superiority of qualitative pleasures over quantitative ones, altruism is rational and justified only when it results in increased satisfaction. In the Islamic system, however, narcissism is coalesced with altruism. A Muslim considers other individuals as part of his own existence, and endeavoring for others cause is of such high value to him that he counts others as his own self. As a result, altruism will become harmonized with narcissism and the conflict between the individual and the society will be eliminated. This view is, however, perceptibly different than that of collectivists who believe in overall deprivation of individual authorities in lieu of the society. The individual has the authority/freedom to be indifferent to others, but this means losing one's happiness/felicity and even exposing the society to destruction and collapse.

As evident from previous discussions, the question is not only why the individual pursues happiness in his behaviors, but what kind of individual behavior results in the happiness or the misery of the society as a whole. It can be acknowledged that the answer to the latter question requires circumventing the scope of discussions about the mode and quality of narcissism, and concentrating on the horizons of human life and the fate of the society. It actually requires to discuss the essence/quiddity of the expediency and happiness of the society, thus putting public expediency against individual expediency as the turning point in the moral philosophy, politics and economy.

The difference in attitudes will bear many important effects on the domain of state/government administration and authority, as well as its orientations and policies. For instance, an attitude that considers public expediency to be nothing more than compatibility of all private expediencies, cannot ultimately surpass the negative concept/impression of freedom. On the other hand, those who consider the expediency of individuals as a sole function of public expediency, can at most achieve the positive concept/impression of freedom. While in many cases, they easily ignore the individual expediency under the pretext of public expediency. These views are in fact considered to occupy the two ends of the same spectrum, and as a result, public expediency is converted into a criterion for arbitration of the organization of these two domains.

6.6 Concept of Public Affair in Islam

In analyzing the concept of public affair in the Islamic system, we are confronted with various questions like: "Are the nature and scope of public affair, defined on the basis of the definition of the scope of private domain in the same way as the neo-classical school?;" "Is there a need to initially define the concept of private affair?;" and, "Isn't there a need for the state/government intervention as long as the motives/incentives for encouraging individuals to indulge in economic activities exist in the private domain?;" and, "Is there a need for the private sector to actively engage in production, distribution and other economic affairs?"

Such tenets have a direct effect on the extent of the Islamic state/government authority and the domain of economic freedom. On this basis, and in accordance with the teachings of Islam, it can be concluded that economic freedom is an accepted principle, as far as it does not threaten other values and public expediency.

6.6.1 Public Expediency and Its Relationship with Identities of Human Beings and Society

In order to explain the public domain and the role of the state/government in the economy, the Islamic school, like every other political and economic system, must answer the following question about public expediency:

"What is the nature of the public expediency and what role does it play in achieving human objectives in life?"

When the expediency and the interest of the individual in society are considered, it is inevitable to examine the public expediency in the political philosophy of Islam.

Moreover, the nature/existence of human beings before and after the inception of society must also be analyzed.

6.6.1.1 Human Beings Prior to Inception of Society

The points to ponder in the pre-societal stage are the internal orientation and motivation, as well as the requirements, benefits and destinations in response to which human society has been formed. Several core opinions exist in this regard:

A) Man is compelled to opt for social life, i.e. social living for human beings is not a choice but a compulsion. This view which occupied one end of the spectrum is consistent with the Hegelian collectivist approaches, e.g. communism. Society as a non-experienceable entity supersedes and governs individuals. Society is authentic and human beings are considered to be naturally-civic.

B) Human nature does not require social life, i.e. human beings are not considered to be naturally-civic. Man opts for social life voluntarily and according to rational calculations/deliberation. Theorists supporting the authenticity of benefit/profit, subscribe to the second viewpoint. They consider human being as a creature who seeks happiness and satisfaction and employs any means to satisfy his desires. Earning pleasure and escaping sorrow/woe exists in human nature, and therefore, presence of the state/government is necessary for the society.

   In this perspective, social life is thought to be choosing an activity to earn maximum profits and to use the available chances and opportunities. The motive and incentive of man in making the choice does not arise from human nature and instinct. Rather, his rationality prescribes such a path for him. As a result, intrinsic and natural forces, such as perfectionism/idealism, have no role in choosing such a path.

C) Social life and civilness/civilizedness are in accordance with the requirements of human nature. That meanserefore if human nature is considered without other factors and incentives, the nature and instincts of man demand social life and civilness/civilizedness.

In Tabataba'ei's view, humans are social on the basis of their nature, instinct and internal orientation, and naturally seek to interact with others. Allameh believes that man has a natural tendency to interact, and to realize what exists in his nature, he must indulge in social life. Nonetheless, this does not mean compulsion and lack of authority in his social life. Rather, it means that human beings are obligated to follow this path in order to fulfill their intrinsic requirement.

On natural civilizedness of human beings, Martyr Motahari writes: “It is true to say that human talents and probable virtues/perfections will not proliferate except in the light of social life. Moreover, such talents and demands are emplaced within the inner nature of human beings at the time of creation, and drive human beings towards social life. In addition, the requirements of human life are not provided except through civilization. This orientation is not in conflict with the relative independence of individual wisdom and volition as well as his discrimination. Needs and talents are concealed and exist latently in human beings and do not emerge except in the light of social life. However, human beings have voluntarily and rationally opted for social life (Motahhari, 1383, 120–121).

As a result and with the assumption that only social life can guarantee human perfection and satisfy his perfection-seeking nature, many of the virtuous attributes ensure human excellence/supremacy, such as dedication/sacrifice and self-abnegation,[2] can be realized within the society. Social life is the inevitable way to be chosen and pursued. The motivation of man in choosing this path is different from what neoclassical economists believe. The need for the realization of the talents and evolution of human beings fundamentally distinguishes between these two attitudes.

6.6.1.2 Human Beings after the Inception of Society

Having accepted that social life of human beings is a prelude to achieving perfection, it is possible to follow the concept of public expediency on the basis of the perception of the individual and the society.

As stated earlier, individual motivations for achieving the greatest self-satisfaction in the neoclassical theory constitute the incentives for economic activity of the individual and happiness/felicity of the individual is also defined on that basis. Prevalence of the self-balancing/self-regulating phenomenon also guarantees collective/social happiness/felicity. Failure of the said phenomenon is an exception to the general classical circumstances, and requires intervention by the state/government.

But if the self-balance/self-regulation of conflicting motives is not approved by the Islamic system, and if free activity based on individual interest and selfishness is not conceived as the path to collective/social happiness/felicity, public expediency will therefore not be defined in parallel with individual expediency and in accordance to individualistic viewpoints. Consequently, another solution for providing expediency must be thought of.

6.6.1.3 Philosophical Approach towards Individual and Society Among Muslim Intellectuals

The subject of individual or social authenticity is one of the fundamental issues which has been debated independently and specifically by philosophers in the recent centuries. It has been referred by the pioneering intellectuals, although under varying titles

2 Ale-Emran: 92
(لَنْ تَنَالُوا الْبِرَّ حَتَّى تُنْفِقُوا مِمَّا تُحِبُّونَ وَمَا تُنْفِقُوا مِنْ شَيْءٍ فَإِنَّ اللَّهَ بِهِ عَلِيمٌ (آل عمران: 92
You will never attain virtue until you spend (benevolently) something you are fond of; while God is Aware of anything you may spend.

such as the “natural civilizedness of human beings” or “importance of the state/government and society.” For this reason, the opinions of the past intellectuals have to be received from the context of their overall stances. However, with accentuation of the concept of “individual” in the Western thought, and the necessity of adopting relevant principles within the political systems, the subject has recently been pursued more explicitly and more boldly/strongly. Taking into account that the necessity of establishing Islamic system within the political realm has been addressed by the Muslim scholars only in recent times, the subject of individual or social authenticity has also been debated with considerable delay. A review of the thoughts and opinions of contemporary Muslim intellectuals in general, and that of Shiite scholars in particular, reveals that there is no difference about the acceptance of the authenticity of individual. All the Muslim intellectuals render the individual as an independent identity/entity other than the society. But interestingly, most of these thinkers acknowledge an independent identity for the society than that of the individual as well.

The reason for such arguments as provided by Muslim scholars are the sacred verses of Holy Qur’an which define an ineluctable fate and death for nations/societies, similar to those of individuals.

قُلْ لَا أَمْلِكُ لِنَفْسِي ضَرًّا وَلَا نَفْعًا إِلَّا مَا شَاءَ اللَّهُ لِكُلِّ أُمَّةٍ أَجَلٌ إِذَا جَاءَ أَجَلُهُمْ فَلَا يَسْتَأْخِرُونَ سَاعَةً وَلَا يَسْتَقْدِمُونَ (يونس: 49)

> Say: “I control no harm nor any advantage by myself except concerning whatever God may wish.” Each nation has a deadline; whenever their deadline comes, they will not postpone it for an hour nor will they advance it. (Yunes: 49)[3]

It is believed that the meaning of “fate” (or “deadline”) used in case of nations is not the same as that for individuals, because in other instances, the term used is “*Every soul will be tasting death.*”[4]

---

3 And Al-A’raf: 39
(وَقَالَتْ أُولَاهُمْ لِأُخْرَاهُمْ فَمَا كَانَ لَكُمْ عَلَيْنَا مِنْ فَضْلٍ فَذُوقُوا الْعَذَابَ بِمَا كُنْتُمْ تَكْسِبُونَ (الأعراف: 39)
The first of them will tell the last: “What advantage have you over us? Taste torment because of what you have earned!”

4 Ale-Emran: 185
كُلُّ نَفْسٍ ذَائِقَةُ الْمَوْتِ وَإِنَّمَا تُوَفَّوْنَ أُجُورَكُمْ يَوْمَ الْقِيَامَةِ فَمَنْ زُحْزِحَ عَنِ النَّارِ وَأُدْخِلَ الْجَنَّةَ فَقَدْ فَازَ وَمَا الْحَيَاةُ الدُّنْيَا إِلَّا مَتَاعُ الْغُرُورِ (آل عمران: 185)
Every soul will be tasting death; you will merely be repaid your earnings on Resurrection Day. Anyone who is snatched from the Fire and shown into the Garden will have triumphed. What does worldly life mean except the enjoyment of illusion?
Al-Anbia’: 35
كُلُّ نَفْسٍ ذَائِقَةُ الْمَوْتِ وَنَبْلُوكُمْ بِالشَّرِّ وَالْخَيْرِ فِتْنَةً وَإِلَيْنَا تُرْجَعُونَ (الانبياء: 35)
Every soul shall taste death. We will test you (all) with something bad and something good as a trial; then to Us will you be returned!
Al-Ankabut: 57
كُلُّ نَفْسٍ ذَائِقَةُ الْمَوْتِ ثُمَّ إِلَيْنَا تُرْجَعُونَ (العنكبوت 57)
Every soul must taste of death, then to Us you shall be brought back

The term "Ummah" means community/society and refers to a mass of people (Sadr, Mohammad Baqer, 1381 SH, 62).

Recognition of collective identity in Islam means that the existence of a society is interpreted as a realm of public interest, which although not interconnected with individual interests, but does not necessarily stops to pursue the private interests. These benefits do not spontaneously generate and maximize under the light of individual activities. In fact, the authenticity of the individual as well as his motives and interests do not determine everything, including the domain and mode of the state/government activity. Not everything is overshadowed by individual motivations and interests. In this manner the society acquires an identity that affects the individual identity, and consequently the type of influence it has on the individuals will be of great significance in attaining their objectives and destinations. For this reason, the requirements of society are placed higher than the requirements of individual authenticity by the Muslim scholars. In addition to the ontological point of view, this approach greatly influences the cognitive and the legal values so that in case of conflicts between the rights of the society and the rights of individuals, the former supersedes.

Some Muslim intellectuals in the field of social sciences are of the opinion that there is no need to believe in the true existence of society in Islamic studies to prove the sociological principles on ground of psychology. The main concern of the social thinkers is to acknowledge and analyze the impacts of various phenomena on volitions and actions of individuals after the inception the society. Therefore, it will suffice to accept that after the association of individuals and inception of society new phenomena will occur which did not previously exist under non-societal circumstances (Bostan, 1390 SH).

Accordingly, the new issue will be to determine the best social structure that serves to achieve the destinations. In fact, the collective identity itself is produced on the basis of the type of governing relationships within the society, and in turn, it influences the individual identities as well. As a result, the question to be answered regarding the said issue would be how the relationships among the individuals on the one hand, and between the individual and the state/government on the other, must be regulated so that the collective identity be in line with individual evolution/perfection.

All that obtained from such relationships and in accordance with the desirable destination of Islamic system constitute social expediency. The persistent existence of this expediency results in a positive impact on the performance of individuals to achieve perfection/supremacy.

Taking into account the importance of such a process in formation of collective identity and ultimately the individual identity, negligence in regulating relationships of different segments of the society in absence of self-regulation and self-balance cannot be permitted under any circumstances.

Thus the next issue would be how to identify and safeguard social expediency and what would be the role and responsibilities of the Islamic ruler in this regard. It can be expected that the concept of public domain in the political and economic system of Islam will be clarified by answering these questions. Accordingly, all the issues concerning the public domain fall into the decision-making realm of the Islamic ruler.

In fact, not only the protection of the rights of individuals, but also expediency of the collective identity depend on the existence of a just and righteous state/government. From the jurisprudential point of view, the establishment of an Islamic state/government is necessary for this purpose.

In the political philosophy of Islam, the private sector is of utmost importance for recognition of individual identity and the need to respect individual rights. This way the Islamic economic system distances itself from the socialism. But because of the recognition of collective identity and interests, this system believes in the necessity of the state/government for providing such expediency. Accordingly, the scope of the state/government presence/intervention will be broader than that depicted in neoclassical or communitarian theories. In addition, the market mechanism which is based on the incentives for individual benefit-seeking and its related efficiency, does not constitute the framework for decision- and policy-makings of the state/government. Rather, the efficiency must be defined in terms of the concepts and motives of the Muslim individual and the economic system of Islam, and should make the ground for state/government policy-making.

It should be noted that the adopted foundations at this stage are of utmost importance for the definition of the private sector and the state within the political and economic systems. Therefore, affairs such as education, health and hygiene which fall within the domain of public interest are classified under the scope of the Islamic State's responsibilities.

7 Summary of Expediencies and Responsibilities of the State/Government in Different Schools

The scopes of state/government activity and its intervention in the economy of society within the framework of different economic systems are defined on the basis of their respective ethical and philosophical viewpoints. On the one hand, the extent of the prospect of life and the definition of incentives/motives, and on the other the existential attributes of human life, are among the important foundations in delineating the mode of interaction between individuals as well as defining the status of state/government. The prerequisite for recognition of collective identity as an objective and independent phenomenon is acknowledgment of the independence of collective good and expediency from the expediency of individuals. As a result, the destinations of individual as well as state/government activities within the society will not be limited to individual expediency. But the expediency of the entire society is also taken into account in evaluation of the activities. Since such expediency is related to the fate/destiny of all the members of society, it will be positioned at a level higher than the individual expediency and is of greater value than that. Therefore, care must be taken to protect and prevent obliteration of such expediency. Establishment of Islamic state under the supervision of an impartial/just ruler constitute a circumspection to maintain such expediency.

While acknowledging the fundamental significance of individual expediency and the necessity of respecting it, the Islamic ruler acquires the status of an authority who is responsible for protecting and safeguarding the "public expediency" and guarantees achieving happiness/felicity of the society. This attribute of Islamic state/government distinguishes it from liberal, socialist, and even communitarian states/governments.

With implementation of Islamic principles, not only the public domain emerges from the shadow of private sector and market, but it acquires such an importance that will prevail over the private domain. The concept of market and its status within the framework of Islamic economy and society will also be defined on the same ground. This approach allows entry into the market relations and interactions of the individuals who have been influenced by Islamic teachings. Such individuals are not indifferent towards social/collective expediency. In the Islamic perspective, despite that the market is an institution with an extensive and important scope in the economic system, it can perform as an instrument for the realization of social expediency. However, it does not constitute the focal point of the economic system and does not define the values, ethical system and social expediency. As a result, the expected performance in view of neoclassical economists does not provide a fundamental measure for evaluating economic activities of the Islamic state/government, especially regarding decision- and policy-makings. This attitude towards the society and collective expediency altogether separates/demarcates the public domain in the Islamic system from that defined in neoclassical economics.

It can be seen that the attitude towards individual, society, and their expediencies have a fundamental impact on the economic system and the scope of state/government intervention. Table 28.1 depicts the attitude of different schools towards expediency and good/benefaction. It also indicates their relation with distributive approach, as one of the most controversial duties/responsibilities of the state/government, the type of state/government, and the difference between the Islamic approach with the rival schools.

Table 28.1: Difference of Islamic School with Other Schools Regarding Individual and Public Expediencies and the Stance/Status of the State/Government.

School Expediency	Liberalism (Utilitarianism)	Liberalism (Teleological)	Communitarians	Islam
Individual	Consequence of the Act (Worldly Scope)			
		Motive of the Act (Worldly Scope)		
Social			Consequence of the Act (Worldly Scope)	
Individual and Collective				Consequence of the Act (Both Worldly and Unworldly Scopes)
State/Government Intervention and Distributive Approach	Minimal and without Distributive Approach	Possesses State/ Governmental Distributive Approach	Based on Societal Values, Possesses state/Governmental Distributive Approach	Government Intervention Only on the Basis of Collective Expediency (Considering Individual Expediency)

References

Holy Qur'an; *translated by* T.B. Irving (Al-Haj Ta'lim Ali); Suhrawardi Research and Publication Center, Tehran-Iran; 2003.

Al-Tabataba'ei, Mohammad Hossein; *Nahayat Al-Hekma'*; Qum; Islamic Publication Institute; 1362 SH.

Arendt, Hannah; *The Human Condition, 2nd Ed.*; Chicago: University of Chicago Press; 1958.

Bostan; Hossein; Qami be suye elme dini (*A Step Towards Religious Sciences*); Research Institute of Howze and University; 1390 SH.

Cullis, John; and Jones, Philip; *Public Finance and Public Choice: Analytical Perspectives, 3rd Ed.*; Oxford; New York: Oxford University Press; 531 p.; 2009.

d'Entreves, Maurizio Passerin; 2016, *Hannah Arendt* in Zalta, Edward N.; The Stanford Encyclopedia of Philosophy; 2016; Retrieved 15 April 2017.

Frankena, William K.1973, *Ethics*. Prentice-Hall. 2nd Ed: 1973.

Ibn Sina, 1364 SH. *Al-Mabdá wa Al-Ma'ad (The Origin and the Day of Judgment)*; corrected by Abdollah Noorani; Tehran; McGill Institute of Islamic Studies in collaboration with Tehran University [in Persian].

Kant, Immanuel, 2002, *Groundwork for the Metaphysics of Morals*; edited and translated by Allen W. Wood; Yale University Press; New Haven and London.

Layard, P.R.G.; and Walters, A. A.; *Microeconomic Theory*; New York: McGraw Hill; 1978.
Mesbah Yazdi, Mohammad Taqi; *Akhlaq dar eslam (Ethics in Islam)*; Vol.1; researched and written by Mohammad Hossein Eskandari; Qum: The Imam Khomeini Educational Research Institute [in Persian]; 1391 SH.
Mill, John Stuart; *Utilitarianism*: From the 1879 Edition; The Floating Press; 2009.
Miller, David; *Political Philosophy: A Very Short Introduction*; New York, Oxford University Press; 2003.
Motahari, Morteza; *Philosophical Articles (Maqalate Falsafi)*; Tehran: Hekmat Publishers [in Persian]; 1365 SH.
Motahari, Morteza; *Bist Goftar (Twenty Speeches)*; A collection of 10 essays by Motahari; Tehran: Sadra Publishers; 1383 SH.
Sandel, Michael J.; Justice: *What's the Right Thing to Do?*; London: Allen Lane; 320 pp.; 2009.
Shirvani, Ali; *Egoism in Islam*; Pegahe Hawzeh; vol. 110; pp. 26–29, [in Persian]; 1382 SH.

List of Figures

https://doi.org/10.1515/9783110593419-029

List of Tables

https://doi.org/10.1515/9783110593419-030

Contributing Authors' Short Bios

Mostafa Kazemi Najaf Abadi is Assistant Professor at the Departmet of Economics, Hawzah and University Research Institute, at Qum, Iran. He also is the manager of the Department of Economics in the Arabic section of the Al-Mustafa Al-Alamia University. He is a member of the Board of Directors of the Islamic Economic Association. He received his Ph.D. from the Allameh Tabataba'i University. He studies Methodology of Jurisprudence (*usul*), Islamic Philosophy and Theology. The focus of his thesis was waqf of money and design of a waqf fund. His book, titled "Non-Bank Financial Intermediaries" was published by the Al-Mustafa Al-Alamia University in 2018. His Research interest is Charity in Islamic Economics. He Teaches Islamic banking, Islamic Microeconomics, Islamic Macroeconomics and Econometrics.

Hafiz Saeed Ahmed is a trained Islamic scholar who specializes in Hadith studies. He received an M.Phil degree in Hadith and its Sciences from the International Islamic University Islamabad (IIUI), Pakistan, and Shahadatul Aalmiyah from the renowned Jamia Darul uloom Karachi, Pakistan. He is currently a Ph.D. student of Islamic Sciences at the HITEC University in Taxila, Pakistan, where his research focuses on the comparative study of the principles of *Ahnaaf* and *Muhadditheen* regarding the legislative role of Sunnah (Prophet's Traditions).

Salman Ahmed serves as Assistant Professor of Financial Economics at SZABIST Karachi and heads Finance Faculty Cluster. He holds Ph.D. Economics from National University of Malaysia. He also did Masters in Economics from Institute of Business Administration, Karachi. He has published several papers in SSCI, ESCI and Scopus indexed journals as well as chapters in books published by Web of Science publishers. He has presented in international conferences in Turkey, Malaysia, Brunei, Indonesia and Pakistan. He is recipient of 2 Emerald Highly Commended Paper Awards in 2018. He is Editorial Advisory Board Member of Emerald IJIMEFM (Indexed in SSCI). He has worked as Research Consultant for Banker's Academy, USA, USIP, USA, Edbiz Consulting, UK, CBER, IBA and Trainer for JusliVentures, Malaysia and Coca Cola Pakistan. In his corporate career, he had worked for Meezan Bank, ABN AMRO Bank, Citi Bank and Reuters.

Mohamad Akram is currently the Executive Director of International Shari'ah Research Academy for Islamic Finance (ISRA) and Professor at International Centre for Education in Islamic Finance (INCEIF). Prior to joining ISRA he was an Assistant Professor at the Kulliyah of Islamic Revealed Knowledge and Human Sciences, International Islamic University, Malaysia (IIUM). In the period 2002–2004, he was a Visiting Assistant Professor at the University of Sharjah, Sharjah, United Arab Emirates. At present, he is the Member of Bank Negara Malaysia Shari'ah Advisory Council, Chairman of Shari'ah Board of Employees Provident Fund Malaysia (EPF), Member of Shariah Supervisory Council of Labuan Financial Services Authority (FSA), Member of Board of Trustees of Malaysian Islamic Economic Development Foundation (YaPEIM), Member of Shariah Advisory Board ZI Shariah Advisory, Member of Shariah Board DDCAP, London, Member of Shariah Advisor of Dar Al Takaful, Dubai, Member of Shariah Advisory Board, Eco Islamic Bank, Republic of Kyrgyzstan, Member of Shariah Advisory Council International Islamic Financial Market (IIFM), Bahrain, Member of Shariah Advisor of National Takaful Company PSC, Watania, Abu Dhabi, Member Financial Regulation Advisory Council of Experts (FRACE), Central Bank of Nigeria, Member of The Panel of Recognized International Market Experts in Finance ("P.R.I.M.E. Finance") and other Boards locally and internationally. Prof. Akram holds a B.A. Honours degree in Islamic Jurisprudence and Legislation from the University of Jordan, Amman, Jordan and a Ph.D. in Principles of Islamic Jurisprudence (Usul al-Fiqh) from the University of Edinburgh, Scotland, United Kingdom. He has presented many papers related to Islamic Banking and Finance and other

https://doi.org/10.1515/9783110593419-031

Fiqh topics at national and International level and has conducted many training sessions particularly on Islamic Banking and Finance for different sectors since 1999. He is a registered Shariah Advisor for Islamic Securities with the Securities Commission of Malaysia and has acted as Shariah advisor in the issuance of several sukuks. In addition, he is also prolific author of academic works specifically in the areas of Islamic Banking and Finance. He is the recipient of Zaki Badawi Award for Excellence in Shariah Advisory and Research. Recipient of the Most Outstanding Individual Contribution to Islamic Finance during KLIFF 2016 organised by CERT. Winner of the 2017/1439H Malaysian Islamic Personality Award conferred by The Government of Malaysia on the occasion of the birthday of the Prophet Muhammad (peace be upon him).

Bilal Sajid Channa, hailing from Ratodero, Sindh, Pakistan, is currently a student at the Institute of Business Administration, Karachi, pursing his Bachelor's in Business Administration. He has been part of the US State Department sponsored KL-YES program (2014–2015) having spent an academic year in the US. He has worked with Sasui Women's Welfare Association with issues related to debt slavery. He holds a deep interest in Philosophy and Political Science and is a student of Economics.

Majid Rezaei Davani is Assistant Professor of Economics at Mofid University, Qum Iran. He is the author of books and refereed Journal articles in the field of Islamic Economics and public sector. He is a member of Shariah Board at Securities and Exchange Organization (SEO) and Central Bank of the Islamic Republic of Iran(CBI).

Mohammad Ali Farahani Fard, Collaborative researcher, has been a member at Qom high institute for Feqh and Islamic sciences. He is the co-author of books and author of refereed Journal articles on Islamic Economics and philosophy of Islamic economics. He is Collaborative researcher at Research institute For Islamic culture and thought at present. He received his Ph.D. from Qom Seminary school (4th Grade Hawzah, Qom).

Saeed Farahani Fard, Associate Professor, has been faculty member at several universities and research institute in Iran such as Qom University, University for economic sciences in Tehran (now Kharazmi), Research institute For Islamic culture and thought for more than 20 years. He also has served as vice-president and Vice-Chancellor for Education at University for economic sciences Tehran. He is also member of scientific Committee in Research institute of Hawzah and university, Research institute For Islamic culture and thought, and Al-Mustafa international university. He is a Vice Chancellor for Research and Technology at Qom university at present. He is the author of books and refereed Journal articles on Islamic Economics and Banking, environment and Natural Resource Economics. He is chief editor of Eghtesad-E-Moghavemati Research journal and a member of editorial board of national journals. He received his Ph.D. from Tarbiat Modarres University Tehran Iran.

Omar Clark Fisher is co-founder of multiple Islamic financial services businesses since 1992: BM Leasing (USA-1992), First Takaful USA (USA-1997), Takaful Taawuni with Bank Al Jazira (Saudi Arabia-2000), Unicorn Investment Bank (Bahrain-2004), and T'Azur a regional Takaful company (Bahrain-2007). More recently, Dr. Omar is co-founder of Khidr Solutions (UAE-2011) and IW Technologies (UAE-2017) as startups for advisory on strategy and business development to Takaful Operators plus FinTech and blockchain advice for financial intelligence education to serve our Youth. Prior to 1992, Dr. Omar served as Investment Guarantee Officer at Overseas Private Corporation, Wash. D.C. and as management consultant at A.D. Little Inc. Cambridge, USA. Dr. Omar holds a B.A. from Yale University, MEd. From Trinity College University of Dublin, MSM from A.D. Little School of Management (now HULT International Business School) and Ph.D. from International Islamic University of Malaysia and Camden University of Del. USA.

Seyyed Reza Hosseini is Assistant Professor and the Head of the Social Science Department at the Research Institute of Hawzah and University, Qum, Iran. He also has served at research institute, Dar-ul-hadith in, Qum, Iran during the 1997–2005 period. He has been a member of the Economic curriculum program at the Ministry of Higher Education at the Al-Mostafa International University in Iran. He is the author of books and refereed journal articles on Islamic Economics, social security and economic development. He is a member of editorial board of the Biquarterly Journal of Iran's Economic Essays. He received his Ph.D. from the Research Institute of Hawzah and University and He has completed advance Islamic studies in Jurisprudence, Methodology of Jurisprudence(usul), Islamic Philosophy and Theology; at Hawzeh, Qum, Iran.

Zamir Iqbal is currently serving as the Vice President, Finance and CFO of the Islamic Development Bank. Prior to joining the Islamic Development Bank, he served as Head of the World Bank Global Islamic Finance Development Center in Istanbul. He has more than 25 years of experience of capital markets, asset management, risk management, and financial sector at the World Bank. Islamic finance has been his research focus and he has co-authored several articles and books on Islamic finance on the topics of banking risk, financial inclusion, economic development, financial stability, and risk-sharing. He played an instrumental role in the publication of World Bank and IsDB's first Global Report on Islamic Finance. He earned his Ph.D. in international finance from the George Washington University and served as Professional faculty at Carey Business School of Johns Hopkins University.

Abdul Khaleq Karimi is a graduate of Islamic economics from the Imam Khomeini Educational and Research Institute, and Quranic Science and Hadith from the Al-Mustafa International University, and also has completed Undergraduate levels of Qum Seminary studies. He is the author of journal articles on Islamic Economics, Economic Development, Islamic Banking, and Islamic business ethics. He is a researcher at the Al-Mustafa University and at the Presidential Research Center of the Islamic Republic of Iran and a member of the Islamic Economics Association of the Qum Seminary. His master's thesis titled "Islamic Banking Indices", selected at Sheikh Tusi Festival in 2011–2012. He is writing his Ph.D. thesis.

Seyed Zia Al-Din Kiaalhoseini is Assistant Professor at the Department of Economics at Mofid University, Qum, Iran, and the Dean of the Faculty of Economics. He has also studied in Hawzah (Islamic Seminary of Qum) for more than 20 years. His main areas of interest include Islamic economics, monetary economics, and microeconomics. He has presented and published articles in relevant academic journals. He has also been involved in several research projects about Islamic fiscal issues.

Ali Reza Lashkari is Assistant Professor at the Research Institute of Hawzah and University(RIHU), Qum Iran. He has published books titled: The orientation of Islamic taxes, Trade and Inequality in the Context of Globalization and Foundations of Social Justice in Islam. Some articles that he has published in research journals include "Rights, Justice, and Society", "Individual and Public Good from the Perspective of Islam and Competing Schools". Also he has taught "public sector" at the Mofid University and is teaching Macroeconomics and Islamic economic system at the Qum University. He received his Ph.D. from the Research Institute of Hawzah and University (RIHU) in Iran.

Abbas Mirakhor is the First Holder of the Chair of Islamic Finance at the International Center for Education in Islamic Finance (INCEIF) and Former Executive Director and Dean of the Executive Board at the International Monetary Fund (IMF). He is the author of An Introduction to Islamic Finance, Risk Sharing in Finance, and The Stability of Islamic Finance, among others.

Behrouz Muhammadi Munfared is Assistant Professor at the Tehran University. He also has served at the Islamic Science and Culture Research Center during 2010–2017 period. He is the author of books and refereed journal articles on Philosophy of Religion, Moral Philosophy and other rational sciences. Some of his books are Justification of the Ethical Belife, Strategy of the Ethics of Awaiting and Religious Ethics. He received his Ph.D. in the field of ethics from the Qum University. He also has the highest levels of education in the Qum Seminary.

Majid Habibian Naghibi is Assistant Professor of Economics at Allameh Tabataba'i University (Tehran, Iran), and Professor of Jurisprudence at the Islamic Seminary (Qum, Iran), and also a member of Fiqhi board of the Islamic Capital Market (Securities and Stock Organization). He has been studying and teaching Islamic courses in the seminary, in addition to teaching Islamic economics at various levels (undergraduate, graduate and doctorate) at the university. He also teaches jurisprudence at higher levels of the seminary.His research field are Islamic Economics, development and planning, Islamic money market and Islamic capital market. He is the author of published books titled "Al Qard Al Hassan and Economic Development Strategies", "Benefit Securities: Fiqhi and Economic Analysis" and "A Review of Value-Added Tax from the Perspective of the Islamic Shari'a". His research and extention activities are: Administrating Economic Researches Center; managing research planning of some institutes and universities, and acting as the vice-president of Tarbiat Modares Higher Education Institute of the Seminary.

Seyyed Hossein Nasr is a world renown scholar on Islam and is currently a University Professor at George Washington University, Washington, D.C., USA. He has published over fifty books and hundreds of articles in numerous languages and translations. He graduated from Massachusetts Institute of Technology with an undergraduate degree in Physics and Mathematics. He went on to Harvard University where he studied Geology and Geophysics, and then completed a Ph.D. in the History of Science and Philosophy.

Mohammad Javad Nourahmadi graduated from the Allameh Tabataba'i University of Iran in 2011 in the monetary Economics. He is Assistant Professor at the Theoretical Economics Department in Faculty of Economics at Allameh Tabataba'i University from 2011 to now. His research fields of interest are Religious Economics, Economic Justice Theories, Economic Systems and Behavioral Economics. He teaches Microeconomics, Econometrics, Economic systems and History of Economic Thoughts. His most important books are: Ownership, Justice and Growth in the Process of Development of Economic Thoughts, Imam Sadiq University (AS). Press. Religious Economics: From the Viewpoint of Muslim and Christian Economic Scholars, Imam Sadiq University (AS). Press.

Pooya Pirmaleki is Assistant Professor at the Imam Sadiq University, Tehran Iran. He received his Ph.D. from the Kharazmi University. He conducted a scoping review followed by a systematic review in the field of "Management and Religion" in his Ph.D. theses. His Ph.D. proposal has been selected as one of the finalists for the Management, Spirituality and Religion (MSR) 2016 Most Promising Dissertation awards. Pooya's Ph.D. dissertation was reviewed and determined to be of the highest quality, both in rigor and relevance to research needs as identified by MSR community.

Junaid Qadir is currently an Associate Professor in the Information Technology University (ITU) of Punjab, Pakistan, where he is the director of the IHSAN Research Lab. His research focuses on diverse topics such as Islamic social science, ethics and technology, applied machine learning, computer systems and networking, and information and communication technology for human development (ICTD).

Seyyed Mohammad Kazem Rajaee is Assistant Professor at the Department of Economics, Imam Khomeini Institute of Education and Research in Qum (Iran). He has served as the Presidential advisor in the ninth government and he also has been a member of the scientific council of the Presidential Strategic Review Center (2010–2013). He is the head of the research center of Applied Social- Economic of Qadr since 2008, (with more than 60 applied research project). He Studies Jurisprudence, Methodology of Jurisprudence (usul) In Hawzeh in Qum. The focus of his thesis was on Islamic market, Justice and Islamic Microeconomics. He has published many books and articles on these topics. He teaches Islamic jurisprudence and principles, Justice, Islamic market and Islamic Microeconomics.

Amana Raquib is currently serving as an Assistant Professor of Religion and Philosophy at the Department of Social Sciences and Liberal Arts, Institute of Business Administration (IBA). She completed her Ph.D. from the University of Queensland, Brisbane, Australia. She is the author of book titled Islamic Ethics of Technology: an objectives approach. Her research interests lie in the areas of philosophy of technology, philosophy of science, Islamic theology, Islamic ethics, Islamic critical and evaluation of postmodern techno-culture in context of Islamic principles, more specifically consumerism and its philosophical and existential underpinnings. She is recently working in the area of Entrepreneurship from an Islamic perspective. Recent article in this regard is Entrepreneurship as an Agent for Social-Ethical Reform: An Islamic Perspective published in the journal, Islam and Civilizational Renewal. She is currently working on a funded project studying Quranic reflection (tadabbur) and its effects on spiritual struggle, consumption (hedonism), gratitude and environmental consciousness.

Mohammad Reza Yousefi Shaykh Robat is Associate Professor of Economics at the Department of Economics at Mofid University (Qum, Iran). He has participated in international seminars and conferences. He is also a member of the Islamic Economics Association of Iran, and one of the founders of the Association of Islamic Economics in Hawzah (Islamic Seminary). He is the author of several books and has published articles in Islamic Economics and Monetary Economics in refereed Journals. He is a member of editorial board of some national economic journals.

Seyed Kazem Sadr is Professor and a research fellow at the Shahid Beheshti University, Tehran Iran where he has taught more than 30 years. He also has served at the International Center for Education in Islamic Finance in Kuala Lumpur, Malaysia during the 2013–2016 period. He has been a member of the Islamic Banking drafting committee at the Finance Ministry, a member of the Economic curriculum program at the Ministry of Higher Education and also consultant at the Agricultural Bank, all in Iran. He is the author of books and refereed Journal articles on Islamic Economics and Banking, Agricultural and Natural Resource Economics. He is a member of editorial board of national and international journals. He received his Ph.D. from the Ohio State University.

Abulfazl Pasebani Someeh received his Ph.D. from the Mofid University and in his thesis criticized G. Akerlof's theory and Analyzed the issue of fair wages. He is now an Assistant Professor and a faculty member of Mofid University in Qum and Tehran (Iran) for over 15 years. He is a member of the Islamic Economics Association of Iran. He is the author of Several Fundamental Articles about Justice, inequality and institutions. He is a member of the editorial board of the Quarterly Journal of Islamic Economics & Banking and the referee for several academic journals.

Seif I. Tag el-Din is an IsDB-prize Laurette in Islamic economics with Ph.D. economics (Edinburgh University; M.Sc. statistics (Univ. of Glasgow), BSc. Statistics (Univ. of Khartoum). Currently he is professor of economics at Imam Mohamed bin Saud University of Riyadh. He took leading part in the establishment of the UK-based MIHE (Markfield institute of Higher Education) during the period 2001–2010 through development and delivery of MA modules in Islamic economics, banking and finance. He published a wide range of research papers and articles in Islamic economics and finance since early 1980s as well as offered consultancy services on Islamic finance to notable financial institutions including the Saudi National Commercial Bank (1992–1999), London Deutch Bank 2008–2009 and the Saudi Monetary Agency 2017. Tag el-Din is the innovator of the so-called Istisnaa-Hedged Musharakah.

Mohammad Esmaeil Tavassoli has been a researcher at the Center for Economic Studies at the University of Mofid, Qum, from 2000 to 2007. and is at present Assistant Professor, Faculty of Economics, Allameh Tabataba'i University, Tehran, Iran, He is author of many books inclding 1. feasibility study of Zakat implementation in Iran, 2. Analysis of the nature of money and the foundations of applying monetary policy in Islamic economics, 3. A glance at: Zakat in Islam and some of its current issues (From the spiritual, Jurisprudence and economic point of view), and numerous articles in the fields of money and its issues in the Islamic economics, Islamic banking and Islamic finance, and is a member of the Islamic Economic Society of Iran. He obtained his Ph.D. in Economics (Islamic Economics) from the Research Institute of Hawzeh and University, Iran, Qum.

Mojtaba Bagheri Toudeshki is a faculty member at the Mofid University, Qum Iran. He is the author of journal articles on Islamic economics (poverty, consumption etc.), and money and banking. He received his Ph.D. from the Mofid University and teaches economics, public finance, public finance in Islam, jurisprudence diciplines, energy and resources economics, money and banking economics at the Mofid University.

Mohammad Javad Tavakoli is Assistant Professor at the Imam Khomeini Education and Research Institute, Qum (Iran. He is also the Editor in Chief of the *Journal of Marifat-e Egtesad-e Islami*, an academic semi-annual journal on Islamic economics. He is the author of books and refereed journal articles on Islamic economics and banking, and philosophy of economics. He received his Ph.D. from the Imam Khomeini Education and Research Institute.

Index

https://doi.org/10.1515/9783110593419-032